Contract Law for Paralegals
Traditional and E-Contracts

Kathleen Mercer Reed
The University of Toledo,
Director of Paralegal Studies

Henry R. Cheeseman
University of Southern California,
Marshall School of Business

Upper Saddle River, New Jersey
Columbus, Ohio

Library of Congress Cataloging-in-Publication Data
Reed, Kathleen Mercer.
  Contract law for paralegals : traditional and e-contracts / Kathleen Mercer Reed, Henry R. Cheeseman.
    p. cm.
  Includes bibliographical references and index.
  ISBN-13: 978-0-13-235819-4 (pbk.)
  ISBN-10: 0-13-235819-0 (pbk.)
  1. Contracts—United States. 2. Legal assistants—United States—Handbooks, manuals, etc.
    I. Cheeseman, Henry R. II. Title.
  KF801.Z9R44 2009
  346.7302—dc22

                                                                        2008034378

Editor in Chief: Vernon Anthony
Acquisitions Editor: Gary Bauer
Development Editor: Linda Cupp
Editorial Assistant: Megan Heintz
Production Coordination: Thistle Hill Publishing Services, LLC
Project Manager: Christina Taylor
Senior Operations Supervisor: Pat Tonneman
Art Director: Diane Ernsberger
Cover Designer: Jason Moore
Cover art/image/photo[s]: Purestock X
Director of Marketing: David Gesell
Marketing Manager: Leigh Ann Sims
Marketing Assistant: Les Roberts

Photo credits: Chapter-opening photo courtesy of Getty Images, Inc. All individual photos for Paralegal Perspective features were provided by the photo subjects.

This book was set in 11/13 Goudy by S4Carlisle and was printed and bound by Edwards Brothers. The cover was printed by Phoenix Color Corp.

Pearson Education Ltd., London
Pearson Education Singapore Pte. Ltd.
Pearson Education Canada, Inc.
Pearson Education—Japan

Pearson Education Australia Pty. Limited
Pearson Education North Asia Ltd., Hong Kong
Pearson Educación de Mexico, S.A. de C.V.
Pearson Education Malaysia Pte. Ltd.

Prentice Hall
is an imprint of

www.pearsonhighered.com

10 9 8 7 6 5 4 3 2 1
ISBN-13: 978-0-13-235819-4
ISBN-10: 0-13-235819-0

PREFACE

■ ABOUT THE AUTHORS

 **KATHLEEN MERCER REED** is the chair of the Department of Undergraduate Legal Specialties and the director of paralegal studies at the University of Toledo. The award-winning paralegal programs within her department hold prestigious American Bar Association approval and were named a "Program of Excellence" by the Ohio Board of Regents.

Professor Reed is a graduate of the University of Toledo, holding a bachelor's of science in interdisciplinary studies and an associate degree in legal assisting. She received her juris doctor (J.D.) from the University of Toledo College of Law and is a member of the State Bar of Ohio. She is a member of the Ohio State Bar Association, the Toledo Bar Association, and admitted to practice before the U.S. Supreme Court. She is the past president of the Paralegal Association of Northwest Ohio and the past chair of the Ohio State Bar Association's Paralegal Committee.

Professor Reed's legal experience includes employment with Hallett & Hallett Law Offices of Wauseon, Ohio; with the Honorable Richard L. Speer, U.S. bankruptcy judge in Toledo, Ohio; and with the law firm of Nathan & Roberts of Toledo, Ohio. She has been on the faculty at UT since 1987, teaching in such areas as legal ethics, litigation, torts, and civil procedure. Professor Reed arranges and supervises over 60 internship placements every year. She was instrumental in developing one of the first paralegal courses in the country to be offered online, through distance education.

Professor Reed has written numerous articles on paralegal issues, and she has authored four paralegal textbooks in addition to this textbook for Prentice Hall. She is also the author of a genealogy research book now in its third edition.

During her tenure at UT, Professor Reed has established two paralegal scholarship funds and arranged for the McQuade Endowment, a contribution that established and maintains the McQuade Courtroom in the Paralegal Studies Program. This high-tech courtroom is an integral part of teaching paralegals to use the technology important to today's practice of law.

She is married to Thomas Reed. Their canine companion is Casey Reed. The three spend weekends at their cottage on Lake Gage in northeast Indiana.

 **HENRY R. CHEESEMAN** is clinical professor of business law and director of the legal studies program at the Marshall School of Business of the University of Southern California (USC), Los Angeles, California.

Professor Cheeseman earned a bachelor's degree in finance from Marquette University, a master's degree in both business administration and in tax from the University of Southern California, a juris doctor (J.D.) degree from the University of California at Los Angeles (UCLA) School of Law, a master of business administration with emphasis on law and economics from the University of Chicago, and a master of laws (LL.M.) degree from Boston University.

Professor Cheeseman earned the "Golden Apple" Teaching Award on many occasions by being voted the best professor at the Marshall School of Business of the University of Southern California. He has been named a Faculty Fellow at the Center for Excellence in Teaching at USC by the dean of the Marshall School of Business; USC's Torch and Tassel Chapter of the Mortar Board has named Professor Cheeseman Faculty of the Month of USC.

Professor Cheeseman writes leading business law and legal environment textbooks that are published by Prentice Hall. These include *Business Law; Legal, E-Commerce, Ethical and International Environments; Contemporary Business and Online Commerce; The Legal Environment of Business and Online Commerce; Essentials of Contemporary Business Law;* and *Introduction to Law: Its Dynamic Nature.*

Professor Cheeseman is an avid traveller and amateur photographer.

■ TO STUDENTS

Before I became an attorney, I graduated from the University of Toledo's Paralegal Studies Program and worked for many years as a paralegal. As a result, I may be unique from other textbook authors because I have valuable firsthand insight into what interests paralegal students and what students most want to know about a course.

As a former paralegal, I know what students must know for future employment. As an educator, I place my students in internships and know what the attorney/employer looks for in an employee.

So when Prentice Hall approached me about coauthoring this contract law textbook with renowned author Henry Cheeseman, I jumped at the chance to bring my singular knowledge and background to the table. Of course, this contract law textbook has all of the important theoretical information on contracts: the background, the elements, how breach occurs, defenses, common law, the UCC, and so on. The text is especially current with information about e-contracts, incredibly important today because we purchase so many items online.

But what I'm most excited about is bringing to this textbook the "face" of successful paralegals and making the textbook relevant to the paralegal profession. To that end, one of the features of the textbook, the "Paralegal Perspective," presents guest articles written by some of the country's most successful working paralegals.

Not surprisingly, you'll notice that some of the paralegals participating in this feature work in contract law. Most of them, however, work in other areas of the law. Including their stories in this contract law textbook will both interest and benefit you.

Students frequently ask, "How is this subject relevant to what I'll do as a paralegal?" For instance, perhaps you have already decided that you only want to work in personal injury litigation. You might ask, "So why should I take a course in estate and probate law?" I explain to students that many areas of the law overlap, and a paralegal doesn't have the luxury of operating in a vacuum. If one of the parties to personal injury litigation dies as a result of his or her injuries, paralegals should know something about estate and probate because they will be filing papers and working with their attorney in the probate court!

Similarly, a paralegal doesn't have to be a "contract law paralegal" to understand and work on contract law matters. For example, estate and probate paralegals might review contracts to determine if any part of the contract is valid after a party's death. Corporate paralegals draft and review contracts related to goods and services. Real estate paralegals draft numerous contracts for closings. And almost every area of law requires a client contract when the client engages the services of the law firm. The list goes on and on. You will see that contract law can be an exciting and rewarding career specialization.

I hope you enjoy this textbook. I know it will make a difference to your future career as a professional paralegal.

Kathleen Mercer Reed

■ ABOUT THE BOOK

For students to receive the most benefit from their college learning experience, the textbook they use in a course must have an in-depth coverage of the subject and inspire critical thinking while keeping interest in the material high. *Contract Law for Paralegals: Traditional and E-Contracts* accomplishes this by combining the ethical, practical, and professional topics relating to contract law with the most contemporary cases and substantive material.

The goals of a contract law course should be to provide students with a strong foundation in the *essential principles* of contracts and to ensure their *familiarity with* and *recognition of* issues that arise in the area of contracts. In other words, the point of a contract law course is not to make a contract law paralegal out of every student. Instead, students finishing a contract law course should have a well-rounded approach to contracts that will transition to their working as a paralegal in many different areas of law.

To accomplish all of this, this contract law textbook has all of the in-depth coverage on traditional contracts you would expect from a college-level textbook. Part of the coverage that sets this textbook apart from the rest is that it is also up to date with information about *E-contracts*, which are incredibly important today when we purchase so many items online. "Old school" texts have all technology matters segmented into a separate chapter, as if it's some specialty issue that belongs in a miscellaneous category. In real life, it's not that way, and the organization and approach of this textbook—with E-contract and technology matters located throughout each chapter—acknowledges that.

Within this in-depth coverage of contract law, this textbook provides numerous ways for students to improve their critical thinking skills. Although important in every academic area of study, critical thinking is especially important for those working in the legal profession. For instance, it does the legal professional no good to memorize the elements of a good and valid contract. The legal professional—in your case, the *paralegal*—must know how to *apply* those elements to the client's unique situation. Many of the special features talked about here are designed to help the student learn this *application* of law to fact.

However, what makes this textbook *really* different from the rest—and why we know it will keep your interest in the material high—relates to the basic premise of this textbook. *Every paralegal, not just the "contract law" paralegal, works with contracts and must understand contract law.*[1]

For example, estate and probate paralegals review contracts to determine if any part of the contract is valid after one of the parties' death. Corporate paralegals draft and review contracts related to goods and services. Real estate paralegals draft contracts for closings. The list goes on and on.

So this textbook offers paralegal students the opportunity to study the depth and breadth of contract law while, at the same time, challenging them to develop

---

[1]Recent surveys support this premise. For instance, see the National Association of Legal Assistants' (NALA's) 2008 Utilization and Compensation Survey at http://www.nala.org/Survey_Table.htm. Information on the many areas of law in which paralegals are employed can be found on pages 12–14 in Section 2 of this report.

high-level critical thinking skills through a textbook containing paralegal practice tips, robust exercises, critical thinking exercises, skill-building exercises, examples, charts, and other innovative features.

■ CHAPTER STRUCTURE

Each chapter of this textbook has in-depth contract law coverage and provides numerous ways for students to improve their critical thinking skills. Chapters contain the substantive law relating to contracts—common law, case law, the UCC, statutory law, and the *Restatement*—and interesting features to help the student understand the substantive law.

Every chapter opens with a **Case Scenario**. This hypothetical case gives students a real-world situation to consider as they read that particular chapter. As a reinforcement, each chapter then ends by revisiting that Case Scenario and asking questions about possible outcomes relating to the hypothetical. Students are given information on a real case involving the same or similar facts, and they are also given a case citation so they can locate and read the real-life case. The Case Scenario feature gives students a frame of reference as they read the chapter, and it provides for an end-of-chapter review of the material as well.

The **Chapter Objectives** feature encourages students to watch for particular concepts in the chapter. The feature also reinforces the learning outcomes for that chapter.

Key Terms in each chapter are boldface when first introduced and then defined in the margin.

Contract law **Cases** are highlighted throughout each chapter. These are sometimes **Landmark Cases,** and sometimes just real cases that illustrate and explain concepts covered in the chapter. Although these cases are presented in a shorter format than the actual case opinion, the case citation is always given so students can locate and read the case in its entirety. Case citations are also presented in the proper "Blue Book" format for consistency with the techniques paralegal students have learned in their legal research course.

Relevant **Laws** are provided in boxes accompanying chapter discussions. As students are reading along, the law referenced in the discussion is located right there. This cuts down on shuffling back and forth between text and appendix or outside resources. These boxes may include references to specific state law, the Uniform Commercial Code, Web sites with information, or other places where students can find additional information.

■ SPECIAL FEATURES

All of the special features of this textbook relate to the basic premise of this textbook: Every paralegal—not just the "contract law" paralegal—works with contracts and must understand contract law.

Paralegal Perspective

One of the most interesting special features of this textbook is the "Paralegal Perspective." This feature introduces students to the "face" of paralegals working in many different areas of the law. Through articles written by those paralegals themselves, they explain how and why they work with contracts, even if they are not employed as a "contract law paralegal." Students will enjoy getting to know these successful paralegals from all across the country.

Career Front

The "Career Front" special feature contains sample job descriptions for paralegal jobs in many different areas of the law. This is a further expansion on the premise that paralegals working in almost every area of the law work with contracts. For instance, the job description for a paralegal working in alternative dispute resolution shows that the paralegal works to create mediation agreements and settlement agreements. Not only will paralegal students see how and why they might work with contracts in their future employment, they will also begin to pinpoint the area of law in which they might like to work when they graduate.

Marketplace

The "Marketplace" feature contains real job advertisements for paralegals gathered from classified advertisements, Web sites, and other sources from all across the country. Many of the job advertisements were for jobs seeking a "contract law" paralegal. But the majority of the job advertisements in this special feature were for jobs in *other* areas of the law. This is yet another expansion of the premise that paralegals working in almost every area of the law work with contracts. The point for students is that, no matter what area of law they have selected for their future career, they *will* be working with contracts. Although for obvious reasons the actual name and address of the employer is not listed, the "Marketplace" feature illustrates to students the many diverse job opportunities they can expect upon graduation.

The Ethical Paralegal

Ethics and appropriate ethical conduct is a cornerstone of the practice of law and the legal profession. "The Ethical Paralegal" feature introduces the student to ethics situations and cases involving paralegals. This feature enforces for the student the important concept that "ethics" is not just something contained in an ethics course.

Paralegal Portfolio Exercise

The "Paralegal Portfolio Exercises" contained in this textbook accomplish several important goals for paralegal students. One is to inspire students to create various legal documents while in school so they know how to create them for their first day on the job. Equally as important is teaching students to use the "Portfolio" feature as a tool that will help them get the job in the first place. For students not familiar with a portfolio, the following paragraphs describe its purposes and features.

An employment portfolio is a collection of samples of a prospective employee's *best* work. Traditionally, the portfolio is arranged in an attractive binder or file folder. However, new technology and techniques are being applied to portfolios so they can also be maintained on the Web through companies such as Epsilen (an academic version of the social networks like Facebook and MySpace).

The point is that a portfolio represents the prospective employee's (in your case, the *paralegal's*) best organization, writing, and critical thinking skills. The portfolio presents the paralegal's abilities in a much stronger, more positive way than if paralegals tried to describe to the employer the work they are capable of doing. By using a portfolio, paralegals have concrete evidence of their abilities and talents. The portfolio builds confidence in the candidate's skills, knowledge, and abilities in the prospective employer's mind. The portfolio can be an important tool to help students get their first job as a paralegal.

Finally, many paralegal programs actually require students to maintain a portfolio throughout their studies, with the completed portfolio reviewed and graded in a capstone course. This "Portfolio" feature will provide tools for students to complete such required portfolio assignments.

■ END-OF-CHAPTER MATERIAL

End-of-chapter materials are always important in every textbook for a student's review of the chapter materials. But in a great textbook, the end-of-chapter materials also set the stage for what students will see and learn in the next chapter.

Each chapter in this textbook concludes with **Internet Exercises and Case Questions**. In addition to increasing students' knowledge of contract law, the Internet Exercises will help students increase their knowledge of locating and understanding case law.

The **Chapter Summary** in this textbook is different from the usual narrative style of summarizing a chapter into one or two paragraphs. Instead, the "Chapter Summary" here reiterates all of the key points of the chapter. Although not a substitute for *reading* the chapter, the "Chapter Summary" is a reinforcement feature that students will find helpful when studying for exams.

Terms and Concepts is a compilation of all of the "Key Terms" defined in the margin throughout that chapter. This is another important reinforcement feature for the student.

The **Case Scenario Revisited** follows up on the "Case Scenario" from the beginning of the chapter. Students will have already considered a hypothetical case as they read the particular chapter. The "Case Scenario Revisited" feature asks questions about possible outcomes relating to the hypothetical case. Students are given information on a real case involving the same or similar facts, and they are also given a case citation so they can locate and read the real-life case. This feature provides students with another type of end-of-chapter review of the material.

A number of **Critical Legal Thinking Cases** follows. These are real-life cases, carefully selected to expand on what students have just learned and to help students apply legal theory to practical application. Although these cases are presented in a short paragraph summary, the case citation is always given so students can locate and read the case in its entirety. Case citations are presented in the proper "Blue Book" format for consistency with the techniques paralegal students have learned in their legal research course. The questions at the end of each of these "Critical Legal Thinking Cases" are presented in a way to encourage the kind of critical thinking the paralegal needs on the job. Rather than asking the student a specific question about the case, these questions are designed to help the student learn the application of law to fact.

The **Ethics Cases** feature highlights real-life cases involving various ethical values and moral principles relating to the area of contract law. These cases are presented not just to illustrate *legal* ethics, but rather, the ethical values that form a background for a practice in contract law. These cases are presented in a short paragraph summary, but the case citation is always given so students can locate and read the case in its entirety. Case citations are presented in the proper "Blue Book" format for consistency with the techniques paralegal students have learned in their legal research course.

The **Briefing the Case Writing Assignment** presents another reinforcement tool for students. The feature has the added benefit of teaching students to locate and understand real-life cases and to summarize quickly the key points of a case, much like students will need to do for an attorney when employed as a paralegal.

Each chapter concludes with a **Practice Tip**. These tips inform students of resources, methods, and techniques involved in today's practice of law. The goal of this feature is to give students the tools they need to prepare them for their first day on the job.

ADDITIONAL TEXTBOOK FEATURES

Because case law is so important to today's study of contemporary contract law, the many important court cases provided through the textbook are easy to locate through a **Case Listing**.

A **Glossary** is provided at the end of the textbook to assist the student with quickly locating terminology important to contract law.

Appendixes at the end of the textbook provide students with important information relating to features, terms, and concepts in contract law. Appendix A includes critical legal thinking techniques for case briefing. Appendix B contains the cases relating to the "Briefing the Case Writing Assignment." Even if the instructor does not assign these case briefing exercises, these contemporary cases are important reading. Appendix C contains sample contracts in areas such as employment, credit card, and software, as well as a checklist for contract reviews and a number of sample contracts. Appendix D contains selected portions of the Uniform Commercial Code.

AN INTEGRATED SUPPLEMENTS PACKAGE

Student supplements emphasize concept review and retention, skill building, and other practical applications designed to prepare students for their first day on the job. Instructor supplements make life a bit simpler for professors by providing them with sample assignments, suggested exam questions, and supporting materials that encourage the students' critical thinking.

Companion Website   The companion website features an online study guide that students can use to review key concepts, find helpful links to online resources, and prepare for tests and quizzes. Go to **www.prenhall.com/reed**.

Instructor Resources   All instructor supplements are available for download from the Instructor Resource Center. To access instructor materials online, instructors need to request an instructor access code. Go to **www.pearsonhighered .com/irc**, where you can register for an instructor access code. Within 48 hours of registering you will receive a confirming e-mail including an instructor access code. Once you have received your code, locate your text in the online catalog and click on the Instructor Resources button on the left side of the catalog product page. Select a supplement and a login page will appear. Once you have logged in, you can access instructor material for all Prentice Hall textbooks.

Instructor's Manual   A comprehensive outline of the text by chapter. Also included are terms with definitions, chapter objectives, a key questions checklist, and sample syllabi.

Test Item File   A bank of questions specially designed to aid in the preparation of tests. Each question includes a corresponding difficulty level, enabling the easy creation of tailor-made testing material.

TestGen   Test management software containing all the material from the Test Item File. This user-friendly software allows instructors to view, edit, and add test questions with a few clicks of the mouse.

PowerPoints   A ready-to-use PowerPoint slideshow, designed for classroom presentation. Use "as-is," or edit content to fit your individual class needs.

courseconnect™

CourseConnect Online Contract Law Course Looking for robust online course content to reinforce and enhance your student learning? We have the solution: CourseConnect! CourseConnect courses contain customizable modules of content mapped to major learning outcomes. Each learning object contains interactive tutorials, rich media, discussion questions, MP3 downloadable lectures, assessments, and interactive activities that address different learning styles. CourseConnect Courses follow a consistent 21-step instructional design process, yet each course is developed individually by instructional designers and instructors who have taught the course online. Test questions, created by assessment professionals, were developed at all levels of Bloom's Taxonomy. When you buy a CourseConnect course, you purchase a complete package that provides you with detailed documentation you can use for your accreditation reviews. CourseConnect courses can be delivered in any commercial platform such as **WebCT, BlackBoard, Angel,** or **eCollege** platforms. For more information, contact your representative or call 800-635-1579.

■ ACKNOWLEDGMENTS

Special thanks to the reviewers of this text:

Elaine S. Lerner,
Kaplan University

Brian McCully,
Fresno City College

Kent D. Kauffman,
Ivy Tech Community College–
 Ft. Wayne

Buzz Wheeler,
Highline Community College.

Heidi Getchell-Bastien,
Northern Essex Community College

In addition, the author wishes to acknowledge the invaluable assistance of the following:

Dawn Knisel for her amazing cite-checking work of every case in this textbook. This feature will show paralegal students the proper "Blue Book" format for this important legal writing technique.

Cheryl Skolmowski for her help and support on many aspects of the textbook.

Kelly Mercer Vogelsong for her assistance.

The National Association of Legal Assistants and the National Association of Paralegal Associations.

Paralegals from across the country who participated in the "Paralegal Perspective" feature. This feature puts a "face" on the practicing paralegal and gives paralegal students an understanding of why contract law is so important.

My longtime friend Karen Brenner Wasil for her insight into what happens when a contract lands on a paralegal's desk for review.

Attorney John Gustafson, my bankruptcy court colleague, for his insight into that area of practice and how it affects contracts.

And, most of all, thanks to my best friends Tom and Casey.

BRIEF CONTENTS

PART I
TRADITIONAL AND E-COMMERCE CONTRACTS   1

CHAPTER 1   NATURE OF TRADITIONAL AND E-CONTRACTS   3

CHAPTER 2   AGREEMENT   33

CHAPTER 3   CONSIDERATION AND EQUITY   67

CHAPTER 4   CAPACITY AND LEGALITY   91

CHAPTER 5   GENUINENESS OF ASSENT   127

CHAPTER 6   WRITING, FORMALITY, AND E-COMMERCE
SIGNATURE LAW   153

CHAPTER 7   THIRD-PARTY RIGHTS AND DISCHARGE   175

CHAPTER 8   REMEDIES FOR BREACH OF TRADITIONAL AND
E-CONTRACTS   205

CHAPTER 9   E-CONTRACTS AND INTERNET LAW   245

PART II
DOMESTIC AND INTERNATIONAL SALES AND
LEASE CONTRACTS   285

CHAPTER 10   FORMATION OF SALES AND LEASE
CONTRACTS   287

CHAPTER 11   PERFORMANCE OF SALES AND LEASE
CONTRACTS   313

CHAPTER 12   REMEDIES FOR BREACH OF SALES AND
LEASE CONTRACTS   337

CHAPTER 13   SALES AND LEASE WARRANTIES   367

PART III
CONTRACT RELATIONSHIPS AND SPECIAL FORMS   389

CHAPTER 14   RELATIONSHIP OF TORT LAW TO
CONTRACT LAW   391

CHAPTER 15   SPECIAL FORMS OF CONTRACTS   427

LIST OF CASES REPORTED 453

APPENDIX A   CRITICAL LEGAL THINKING TECHNIQUES FOR CASE BRIEFING   461

APPENDIX B   CASES FOR "BRIEFING THE CASE WRITING ASSIGNMENTS"   467

APPENDIX C   SAMPLE CONTRACTS   483

APPENDIX D   UNIFORM COMMERCIAL CODE (UCC)   530

GLOSSARY   532

INDEX   544

CONTENTS

PART I
TRADITIONAL AND E-COMMERCE CONTRACTS   1

CHAPTER 1
Nature of Traditional and E-Contracts   3

Case Scenario   3
Chapter Objectives   3
Chapter Introduction   4
Contract Overview   4
    Definition of a Contract   4
    Parties to a Contract   5
    Elements of a Contract   5
    Defenses to the Enforcement of a Contract   6
    Form Contracts   7
Sources of Contract Law   8
    The Common Law of Contracts   8
    The Uniform Commercial Code (UCC)   8
    The Restatement of the Law of
        Contracts   9
    Objective Theory of Contracts   10
Classifications of Contracts   16
    Bilateral and Unilateral Contracts   16
    Incomplete or Partial Performance   16
    Express and Implied-in-Fact Contracts   18
    Quasi-Contracts (Implied-in-Law
        Contracts)   22
    Formal and Informal Contracts   24
    Valid, Void, Voidable, and Unenforceable
        Contracts   26
    Executed and Executory Contracts   26
Internet Exercises and Case Questions   28
Chapter 1 Summary   28
Terms and Concepts   29
Case Scenario Revisited   30
Critical Legal Thinking Case   30
Ethics Cases   31
Briefing the Case Writing Assignment   31
Practice Tip   31

CHAPTER 2
Agreement   33

Case Scenario   33
Chapter Objectives   33
Chapter Introduction   34
Agreement   34
    Offer   34
Acceptance   51
    Who Can Accept an Offer?   51
    Unequivocal Acceptance   51
    Silence as Acceptance   53
    Time of Acceptance   54
    Mode of Acceptance   55
Internet Exercises and Case Questions   60
Chapter 2 Summary   61
Terms and Concepts   62
Case Scenario Revisited   63
Critical Legal Thinking Cases   63
Ethics Cases   64
Briefing the Case Writing Assignment   65
Practice Tip   65

CHAPTER 3
Consideration and Equity   67

Case Scenario   67
Chapter Objectives   67
Chapter Introduction   67
Consideration   68
    Requirements of Consideration   68
    Gift Promises   70
Contracts Lacking Consideration   75
    Illegal Consideration   75
    Illusory Promises   76
    Moral Obligation   76
    Preexisting Duty   76
    Past Consideration   77
    Output Contract   80
    Requirement Contract   80
    Best-Efforts Contract   80
Settlement of Claims   80

Equity   81
   Promissory Estoppel   82
   Equitable Remedies   83
Internet Exercises and Case Questions   83
Chapter 3 Summary   84
Terms and Concepts   85
Case Scenario Revisited   85
Critical Legal Thinking Cases   86
Ethics Cases   87
Briefing the Case Writing Assignment   89
Practice Tip   89

CHAPTER 4
Capacity and Legality   91

Case Scenario   91
Chapter Objectives   91
Chapter Introduction   91
Minors   92
   The Infancy Doctrine   93
   Disaffirmance   93
   Minor's Duty of Restoration and Restitution   93
   Misrepresentation of Age   94
   Ratification   95
   Parents' Liability for Their Children's Contracts   97
   Necessaries of Life   97
Mentally Incompetent Persons   100
   Adjudged Insane   100
   Insane But Not Adjudged Insane   101
Intoxicated Persons   103
Legality   105
   Contracts Contrary to Statutes   105
   Usury Laws   106
   Sabbath Laws   106
   Contracts to Commit Crimes   106
   Contracts Contrary to Public Policy   106
   Gambling Statutes   108
   Effect of Illegality   108
Special Business Contracts   110
   Contracts in Restraint of Trade   110
   Licensing Statutes   110
   Exculpatory Clauses   112
Unconscionable Contracts   115
   Elements of Unconscionability   116
Internet Exercises and Case Questions   118
Chapter 4 Summary   118
Terms and Concepts   121
Case Scenario Revisited   122
Critical Legal Thinking Cases   122

Ethics Cases   123
Briefing the Case Writing Assignment   124
Practice Tip   124
Paralegal Portfolio Exercise   125

CHAPTER 5
Genuineness of Assent   127

Case Scenario   127
Chapter Objectives   127
Chapter Introduction   127
Mistake   128
   Unilateral Mistake   128
   Mutual Mistake   130
Fraud   132
   Fraud in the Inception   132
   Fraud in the Inducement   132
   Fraud by Concealment   134
   Silence as Misrepresentation   134
   Misrepresentation of Law   137
   Innocent Misrepresentation   138
Undue Influence   140
Duress   142
   Economic Duress   143
Internet Exercises and Case Questions   144
Chapter 5 Summary   144
Terms and Concepts   145
Case Scenario Revisited   146
Critical Legal Thinking Cases   146
Ethics Cases   148
Briefing the Case Writing Assignment   149
Practice Tip   150
Paralegal Portfolio Exercise   150

CHAPTER 6
Writing, Formality, and E-Commerce Signature Law   153

Case Scenario   153
Chapter Objectives   153
Chapter Introduction   153
Statute of Frauds   154
   Writing Requirement   154
   Contracts That Must Be in Writing   154
   Promissory Estoppel   161
Formality of the Writing   162
   Required Signature   162
   Integration of Several Writings   163
   Interpreting Contract Words and Terms   164
   Merger, or Integration, Clause   165

Parol Evidence Rule   165
   Exceptions to the Parol Evidence Rule   *166*
Internet Exercises and Case Questions   167
Chapter 6 Summary   167
Terms and Concepts   169
Case Scenario Revisited   169
Critical Legal Thinking Cases   169
Ethics Cases   172
Briefing the Case Writing Assignment   172
Practice Tips   173
Paralegal Portfolio Exercise   173

CHAPTER 7

Third-Party Rights and Discharge   175

Case Scenario   *175*
Chapter Objectives   *175*
Chapter Introduction   175
Assignment of Rights   176
   Form of Assignment   *176*
   Rights That Can and Cannot Be Assigned   *177*
   Effect of an Assignment of Rights   *178*
   Notice of Assignment   *179*
   Anti-Assignment and Approval Clauses   *179*
Delegation of Duties   181
   Duties That Can and Cannot Be Delegated   *182*
   Effect of Delegation of Duties   *182*
   Anti-Delegation Clause   *183*
   Assignment and Delegation   *183*
Third-Party Beneficiaries   183
   Intended Beneficiaries   *183*
   Incidental Beneficiaries   *186*
Covenants and Conditions   187
   Covenants   *187*
   Conditions of Performance   *188*
Discharge of Performance   190
   Discharge by Agreement   *190*
   Discharge by Impossibility   *192*
   Force Majeure Clauses   *194*
   Commercial Impracticability   *194*
   Discharge by Operation of Law   *194*
Internet Exercises and Case Questions   196
Chapter 7 Summary   196
Terms and Concepts   198
Case Scenario Revisited   199
Critical Legal Thinking Cases   200
Ethics Cases   201
Briefing the Case Writing Assignment   202
Practice Tip   202

CHAPTER 8

Remedies for Breach of Traditional and E-Contracts   205

Case Scenario   *205*
Chapter Objectives   *205*
Chapter Introduction   206
Performance and Breach   206
   Complete Performance   *207*
   Substantial Performance: Minor Breach   *207*
   Inferior Performance: Material Breach   *207*
   Anticipatory Breach   *208*
Monetary Damages   212
   Compensatory Damages   *212*
   Sale of Goods   *213*
   Construction Contracts   *213*
   Employment Contracts   *213*
   Mitigation of Damages   *214*
   Consequential Damages   *216*
   Nominal Damages   *222*
   Enforcement of Remedies   *222*
Rescission and Restitution   224
Equitable Remedies   227
   Specific Performance   *227*
   Reformation   *231*
   Quasi-Contract   *231*
   Injunction   *231*
Torts Associated with Contracts   232
   Intentional Interference with Contractual Relations   *233*
   Breach of the Implied Covenant of Good Faith and Fair Dealing   *235*
Internet Exercises and Case Questions   237
Chapter 8 Summary   237
Terms and Concepts   239
Case Scenario Revisited   240
Critical Legal Thinking Cases   240
Ethics Cases   242
Briefing the Case Writing Assignment   243
Practice Tip   243

CHAPTER 9

E-Contracts and Internet Law   245

Case Scenario   *245*
Chapter Objectives   *245*
Chapter Introduction   245
The Internet and the World Wide Web   246
   The Internet   *246*
   The World Wide Web   *247*
   E-Mail   *249*

Domain Names   250
E-Contracts   256
Software and E-Licensing   257
   Licensing of Informational Rights   259
   Exclusive License   259
   Licensing Agreement   261
   Licensing Information Technology Rights   262
Breach of License Agreements   266
   Adequate Assurance of Performance   267
   Licensee's Refusal of Defective Tender   267
   Licensee's Revocation of Acceptance   267
Remedies for Breach   268
   Cancellation   268
   Licensor's Damages   268
   Licensor's Right to Cure   269
   Licensee's Damages   269
   Licensee Can Obtain Specific Performance   270
   Liquidation of Damages   270
Limitation of Remedies   270
Online Privacy   272
Cyber Crimes   273
   State Criminal Laws   275
Internet Exercises and Case Questions   277
Chapter 9 Summary   277
Terms and Concepts   278
Case Scenario Revisited   279
Critical Thinking Cases   279
Ethics Cases   282
Briefing the Case Writing Assignment   283
Practice Tip   283

PART II
DOMESTIC AND INTERNATIONAL SALES AND LEASE CONTRACTS   285

CHAPTER 10
Formation of Sales and Lease Contracts   287
Case Scenario   287
Chapter Objectives   287
Chapter Introduction   287
Uniform Commercial Code (UCC)   288
Article 2 (Sales)   289
   What Is a Sale?   289
   What Are Goods?   290
   Goods Versus Services   290
   Who Is a Merchant?   292

Article 2A (Leases)   292
   Definition of a Lease   293
   Finance Lease   293
Formation of Sales and Lease Contracts: Offer   294
   Open Terms   294
   Consideration   296
Formation of Sales and Lease Contracts: Acceptance   296
   Methods of Acceptance   296
   Accommodation Shipment   296
UCC Statute of Frauds   298
   Exceptions to the Statute of Frauds   298
   When Written Modification Is Required   299
   Parol Evidence   300
Internet Exercises and Case Questions   304
Chapter 10 Summary   304
Terms and Concepts   306
Case Scenario Revisited   307
Critical Legal Thinking Cases   307
Ethics Cases   309
Briefing the Case Writing Assignment   310
Practice Tip   310

CHAPTER 11
Performance of Sales and Lease Contracts   313
Case Scenario   313
Chapter Objectives   313
Chapter Introduction   313
Identification and Passage of Title   314
   Identification of Goods   314
   Passage of Title   315
   Shipment and Destination Contracts   315
   Delivery of Goods Without Moving Them   315
Risk of Loss: No Breach of Sales Contract   315
   Carrier Cases: Movement of Goods   316
   Noncarrier Cases: No Movement of Goods   317
   Goods in the Possession of a Bailee   317
Risk of Loss: Conditional Sales   319
   Sale on Approval   319
   Sale or Return   319
   Consignment   319
Risk of Loss: Breach of Sales Contract   321
   Seller in Breach   321
   Buyer in Breach   322
Risk of Loss: Lease Contracts   322

Sales by Nonowners   323

    Void Title and Lease: Stolen Goods   323

    Voidable Title: Sales or Lease of Goods to Good Faith Purchasers for Value   324

    Entrustment Rule   324

Internet Exercises and Case Questions   329

Chapter 11 Summary   329

Terms and Concepts   331

Case Scenario Revisited   332

Critical Legal Thinking Cases   332

Ethics Cases   334

Briefing the Case Writing Assignment   335

Practice Tip   335

CHAPTER 12

Remedies for Breach of Sales and Lease Contracts   337

Case Scenario   337

Chapter Objectives   337

Chapter Introduction   337

Seller's and Lessor's Performance   338

    Place of Delivery   338

Buyer's and Lessee's Performance   343

    Right of Inspection   343

    Payment   344

    Acceptance   344

    Revocation of Acceptance   345

Seller's and Lessor's Remedies   345

    Right to Withhold Delivery   345

    Right to Stop Delivery of Goods in Transit   346

    Right to Reclaim Goods   346

    Right to Dispose of Goods   346

    Right to Recover the Purchase Price or Rent   347

    Right to Recover Damages for Breach of Contract   347

    Right to Cancel a Contract   348

Buyer's and Lessee's Remedies   349

    Right to Reject Nonconforming Goods or Improperly Tendered Goods   349

    Right to Recover Goods from an Insolvent Seller or Lessor   350

    Right to Obtain Specific Performance   350

    Right to Cover   350

    Right to Replevy Goods   351

    Right to Cancel a Contract   351

    Right to Recover Damages for Nondelivery or Repudiation   351

    Right to Recover Damages for Accepted Nonconforming Goods   352

Additional Performance Issues   353

    Assurance of Performance   353

    Anticipatory Repudiation   354

    Statute of Limitations   354

    Agreements Affecting Remedies   354

Internet Exercises and Case Questions   355

Chapter 12 Summary   355

Terms and Concepts   360

Case Scenario Revisited   360

Critical Legal Thinking Cases   361

Ethics Cases   363

Briefing the Case Writing Assignment   364

Practice Tip   364

Paralegal Portfolio Exercise   364

CHAPTER 13

Sales and Lease Warranties   367

Case Scenario   367

Chapter Objectives   367

Chapter Introduction   367

Express Warranty   368

    Basis of the Bargain   369

    Statements of Opinion   369

    Damages Recoverable for Breach of Warranty   371

Implied Warranties   372

    Implied Warranty of Merchantability   372

    Implied Warranty of Fitness for Human Consumption   374

    Implied Warranty of Fitness for a Particular Purpose   375

Warranty Disclaimer   378

    Conspicuous Display of Disclaimer   379

Special Warranties of Title and Possession   380

    Warranty of Good Title   381

    Warranty of No Security Interests   381

    Warranty of No Infringements   381

    Warranty of No Interference   381

Internet Exercises and Case Questions   382

Chapter 13 Summary   382

Terms and Concepts   384

Case Scenario Revisited   385

Critical Legal Thinking Cases   385

Ethics Cases   386

Briefing the Case Writing Assignment   387

Practice Tip   387

PART III
CONTRACT RELATIONSHIPS AND SPECIAL FORMS 389

CHAPTER 14

Relationship of Tort Law to Contract Law 391

Case Scenario 391
Chapter Objectives 391
Chapter Introduction 391
Product Liability 392
Negligence and Fault 392
  Negligence 392
  Misrepresentation 394
Strict Liability 394
  Liability Without Fault 395
  All in the Chain of Distribution Are Liable 395
  Parties Who Can Recover for Strict Liability 395
  Damages Recoverable for Strict Liability 397
Defective Product 398
  Defect in Manufacture 398
  Defect in Design 401
  Crashworthiness Doctrine 404
  Failure to Warn 405
  Defect in Packaging 410
  Failure to Provide Adequate Instructions 412
  Punitive Damages 413
Defenses To Product Liability 415
  Generally Known Dangers 415
  Government Contractor Defense 415
  Assumption of the Risk 415
  Misuse of the Product 416
  Correction of a Product Defect 416
  Supervening Event 416
  Statute of Limitations and Statute of Repose 418
  Contributory Negligence and Comparative Fault 418
Internet Exercises and Case Questions 419
Chapter 14 Summary 419
Terms and Concepts 421

Case Scenario Revisited 421
Critical Legal Thinking Cases 421
Ethics Cases 423
Briefing the Case Writing Assignment 423
Practice Tip 423
Paralegal Portfolio Exercise 424

CHAPTER 15

Special Forms of Contracts 427

Case Scenario 427
Chapter Objectives 427
Chapter Introduction 427
Negotiable Instruments 427
  Functions of Negotiable Instruments 428
  Types of Negotiable Instruments 428
  Draft 428
  Checks 429
  Promissory Notes 430
  Certificates of Deposit 430
Agency Contracts 434
  Agency Formation 434
  Persons Who Can Initiate an Agency Relationship 434
  Principal–Agent Relationship 435
  Employer–Employee Relationship 435
  Contract Liability to Third Parties 435
  Agent's Misrepresentation 438
  Agency Termination 440
Labor Contracts 441
  Labor Law 442
  Collective Bargaining 444
  Effect of Bankruptcy on Labor Contracts 444
Internet Exercises and Case Questions 445
Chapter 15 Summary 446
Terms and Concepts 448
Case Scenario Revisited 449
Critical Legal Thinking Cases 449
Ethics Cases 450
Briefing the Case Writing Assignment 451
Practice Tip 451

LIST OF CASES REPORTED 453

Appendix A

Critical Legal Thinking Techniques for Case Briefing   461

Key Terms   461

Briefing a Case   461

Elements of a Case Brief   461

Case for Briefing   463

Brief of Case A.1   466

Appendix B

Cases for "Briefing the Case Writing Assignments"   467

Appendix C

Sample Contracts   483

How the Contract "Arrives"   483

Contract Review is Necessary   483

Timing for Contract Completion   484

Checklists for Contract Reviews   484

Appendix D

Uniform Commercial Code (UCC)   530

Articles of the Uniform Commercial Code (UCC)   530

Uniform Commercial Code (UCC) Locator   530

Articles of the Uniform Commercial Code (UCC)   530

GLOSSARY   532

INDEX   544

FEATURES

CAREER FRONT

Job Description: Alternative Dispute Resolution (ADR) Paralegal 8

Job Description: Bankruptcy Paralegal 12

Job Description: Collections Paralegal 39

Job Description: Business Franchise Paralegal 69

Job Description: Contract Administration Paralegal 92

Job Description: Securities/Municipal Bonds Paralegal 137

Job Description: Construction Law Paralegal 165

Job Description: Personal Injury/Medical Malpractice/Product Liability Paralegal 180

Job Description: Business Formation Paralegal 211

Job Description: Business Franchise Paralegal 255

Job Description: Criminal Law Paralegal 300

Job Description: Labor/Employment 323

Job Description: Trust Paralegal 353

Job Description: Employee Benefits Paralegal 371

Job Description: Corporate Contracts Paralegal 400

Job Description: Municipal Paralegal 439

CONTEMPORARY ISSUE

The Evolution of the Modern Law of Contracts 6

Arbitration and Contract Law 7

Option Contracts 50

Software Contracts 59

When Is Consideration Inadequate? 74

Special Business Contracts 80

Special Types of Minors' Contracts 99

Covenant Not to Compete 115

What Constitutes a Signature? 163

Commercial Impracticability 195

Jurisdiction in Contemporary Contract Law Cases 223

Must a Wedding Ring Be Returned if the Engagement Is Broken Off? 226

Hard Dealing for the Hard Rock Cafe 228

The Meaning of a Handshake 233

UCC "Firm Offer" Rule 295

UCC Permits Additional Terms 297

"Battle of the Forms" 298

UCC Written Confirmation Rule 299

Contemporary Issue: Shipping Terms 316

Effect of Bankruptcy on Executory Contracts and Unexpired Leases 318

Insuring Against Loss of Goods 322

Bulk Sales Law Dumped 328

Lost Volume Seller 348

Restatement of Torts Definition of Strict Liability Restatement (Second) of Torts 396

Formal Requirements for a Negotiable Instrument 432

Chapter 11 Debtor Can Reject Collective Bargaining Agreement 445

E-COMMERCE & INFORMATION TECHNOLOGY

Ready for Love? Not Before You've Been NDA'd 18

Contracting by Fax and E-Mail 35

Online Auctions 42

Computer Shrinkwrap Licenses and Contracts Enforceable 53

Breach of an Internet Contract 211

The Uniform Electronic Transactions Act (UETA) 258

Software and Information Access Contracts 261

Unfair and Deceptive Acts over the Internet 302

ENTREPRENEUR AND THE LAW

Owner of *Scrabble* Spelled "L-O-S-E-R" 19

ETHICS SPOTLIGHT

Scrabble Owner Held Liable on an
Implied-in-Fact Contract   21

"A Contract Is a Contract Is a Contract"   38

Equity Saves Contracting Party   81

An Unlicensed Contractor Gets Dunked   111

Unconscionable Contract   116

Proving Fraud   133

Undue Influence   141

Economic Duress   143

Statute of Frauds   155

An Oral Contract Is Not Worth the Paper It's
Written On   160

Promissory Estoppel   161

Successive Assignments of the Same
Right   181

Satisfaction Clause: "I Don't Like It"   191

Interference with a Contract   243

A Chicken Farmer Gets Plucked   301

Corn Farmers Get Shucked   327

Good Faith and Reasonableness   343

Unconscionable Contract   355

Design Defect in Pool Equipment   405

General Motors Liable for Design Defect   417

INTERNATIONAL LAW

The United Nations Convention on Contracts for
the International Sale of Goods   27

China Adopts New Contracts Law   60

Signatures in Foreign Countries   166

Letters of Credit in International Trade   303

International Trade Terms   328

Negotiable Instruments Payable in Foreign
Currency   433

INTERNET & TECHNOLOGY

Uniform Computer Information Transactions Act
(UCITA)   9

E-Commerce   15

Nondisclosure Agreements   000

Free Speech and the Internet   247

Domain Name Anticybersquatting Act   251

Armani Outmaneuvered for Domain
Name   254

Domain Names Sold for Millions   254

E-Contracts Writing Requirement   256

E-Signatures   256

Click-Wrap Licenses   260

Counteroffers Ineffectual Against
Electronic Agents   261

Consumers Saved from Electronic Errors   267

Electronic Self-Help   269

Counterfeit Access Device and Computer Fraud
and Abuse Act   273

Electronic Funds Transfer Act   274

Cyber Identity Fraud   274

Information Infrastructure Protection Act
(IIP Act)   275

Computer Hacker Found Guilty
of Cyber Crime   275

Warranty Disclaimers in Software Licenses   379

LANDMARK LAW

The Uniform Commercial Code (UCC)   289

Magnuson-Moss Warranty Act Protects
Consumers   380

Federal Labor Union Statutes   442

MARKETPLACE

Job Announcement: Contract Specialist Paralegal
Position   17

Job Announcement: Corporate Real Estate
Paralegal   46

Job Announcement: Transactional Paralegal   79

Civil Rights Paralegal Needed   100

Job Announcement: Securities Litigation
Paralegal   131

Job Announcement: Lease Administration
Paralegal   157

Job Announcement: Medical Malpractice
Paralegal   185

Job Announcement: Corporate
Paralegal Hire   232

Job Announcement: Corporate Securities Paralegal   260

Job Announcement: Labor Litigation Paralegal   295

Job Announcement: Commercial Litigation Paralegal   318

Job Announcement: Business Law Paralegal   349

Job Announcement: Litigation Paralegal   378

Job Announcement: Construction Litigation Paralegal   412

Job Announcement: Vendor Contracts Paralegal   434

PARALEGAL PERSPECTIVES

Amy L. Evard, Corporate Paralegal   4

Rhonda Gray, Regulatory Services Paralegal   10

Linda Ledford, Contracts Paralegal   24

Allison Alger, Business Legal Assistant   34

Natalie H. Holman, Litigation Paralegal   43

Sara Hall, Health Care Paralegal   50

Rebecca Cain, Discovery Management Paralegal   68

Susan M. Bartel, Real Estate Paralegal   73

Robert Lee Dickens, Contracts Manager   75

Angel Dietzel, Privacy and Data Security Specialist   92

Brandy Spurgin, Civil Rights Legal Assistant   99

Toni D. Mers, Trusts and Estate Paralegal   103

Teresa J. Turner, Real Estate and Land Use Law Paralegal   128

Patty Ketcher, Probate and Estate Planning Paralegal   132

Denise Schmidt, Litigation Paralegal   140

Kim A. Spitzmiller, Intellectual Property Paralegal   161

Stephanie Runion, Family and Domestic Law Paralegal   164

Della Wallace, Environmental Litigation Paralegal   176

Heather Fauber, Commercial Law Paralegal   181

Karen Billieu, Probate and Estate Planning Paralegal   206

Amy Gabbard, Corporate Real Estate Transactions Paralegal   222

Raeann Bromark, Project Paralegal   246

Cynthia A. Laquinta, Corporate Litigation Paralegal   257

Cathy D. Canny, Senior Litigation Paralegal   288

Fern Burnett, Corporate Paralegal   292

Lori Rickard, Advertising and Marketing Paralegal   314

Andrea Powell, Risk Manager   321

Cathy Lynn Davis, Civil Litigation Paralegal   338

Karen Wasil, Chief Compliance Officer   351

Stephannie Keefe Gamill, City/Municipal Paralegal   368

Andrea Z. Zwegat, Intellectual Property Paralegal   378

Jennifer Wallace, Commercial Litigation Paralegal   392

Ron J. Taylor, Corporate Paralegal   398

Tracy A. Williams, Paralegal and Trustee Assistant   433

Kristen A. Leeb, Corporate Paralegal   439

THE ETHICAL PARALEGAL

Integrity   25

Confidentiality   47

Competence   79

Fees   95

Making Legal Services Available   134

Communication with Clients   159

Unauthorized Practice of Law   183

Conflict of Interest   214

Reporting Misconduct   263

Avoid the Appearance of Impropriety   297

Working to Improve the Legal System   317

Candor and Honesty   344

Advertising and Solicitation   382

Billing Practices   416

Disruptive Courtroom Tactics   432

Traditional and E–Commerce Contracts

PART **ONE**

Chapter 1   Nature of Traditional and E-Contracts

Chapter 2   Agreement

Chapter 3   Consideration and Equity

Chapter 4   Capacity and Legality

Chapter 5   Genuineness of Assent

Chapter 6   Writing, Formality, and E-Commerce Signature Law

Chapter 7   Third-Party Rights and Discharge

Chapter 8   Remedies for Breach of Traditional and E-Contracts

Chapter 9   E-Contracts and Internet Law

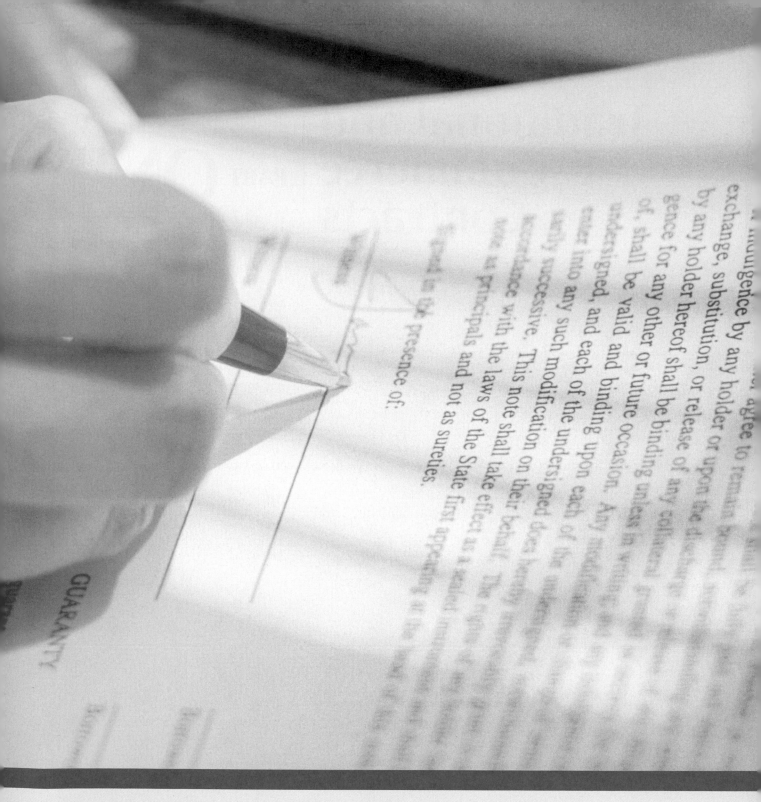

The movement of the progressive societies has hitherto been a movement from status to contract.

—*Sir Henry Maine*
Ancient Law, Chapter 5

Nature of Traditional and E-Contracts

CASE SCENARIO

Casey and Tom have lived together for six years but never married. During their time together, Tom earned a substantial income and bought a house worth over $1 million. Casey gave up a high-paying job and moved in with Tom (he didn't want her to work). After an argument, Tom broke up with Casey and told her she had to leave his house. Even though they had split, Tom continued to support Casey for another year. Then, after he began seeing another woman, he refused to provide Casey with any future support. Casey has hired the law firm where you work as a paralegal to represent her in an action against Tom.

CHAPTER OBJECTIVES

After studying this chapter, you should be able to:

1. Define *contract*.

2. List the elements necessary to form a valid contract.

3. Distinguish between bilateral and unilateral contracts.

4. Describe and distinguish between express and implied-in-fact contracts.

5. Describe and distinguish among valid, void, voidable, and unenforceable contracts.

■ CHAPTER INTRODUCTION

Contracts are the basis of many of our daily activities. They provide the means for individuals and businesses to sell and otherwise transfer property, services, and other rights. The purchase of goods, such as books and automobiles, is based on sales contracts; the hiring of employees is based on service contracts; the lease of an apartment is based on a rental contract; the sale of goods and services over the Internet is based on electronic contracts. The list is almost endless. Without enforceable contracts, commerce would collapse.

Contracts are voluntarily entered into by parties. The terms of a contract become *private law* between the parties. One court has stated, "The contract between parties is the law between them and the courts are obliged to give legal effect to such contracts according to the true interests of the parties."[1]

Nevertheless, most contracts are performed without the aid of the court system. This is usually because the parties feel a moral duty to perform as promised. Although some contracts, such as illegal contracts, are not enforceable, most are **legally enforceable**.[2] This means that if a party fails to perform a contract, the other party may call on the courts to enforce the contract.

This chapter introduces you to the study of traditional and Internet contract law. Such topics as the definition of *contract*, requirements for forming a contract, sources of contract law, and the various classifications of contracts are discussed.

legally enforceable contract
If one party fails to perform as promised, the other party can use the court system to enforce the contract and recover damages or other remedy.

■ CONTRACT OVERVIEW

Definition of a Contract

A *contract* is an agreement that is enforceable by a court of law or equity. A simple and widely recognized definition of *contract* is provided by the *Restatement (Second)*

PARALEGAL PERSPECTIVE

Amy L. Evard is a graduate of Saint Mary-of-the-Woods College's Paralegal Studies Program. She works as a corporate paralegal for the law firm of Barnes & Thornburg LLP in Elkhart, Indiana.
I work in a law firm that represents business clients in various areas of the law. A part of my job involves assisting the clients with business transactions (under the supervision of an attorney) from the initial drafting and due diligence stages through closing.

During the initial stages of a business transaction in which we represent the buyer, I am responsible for reviewing and organizing documents that the seller produces. One type of document that a buyer may request is a contract between the seller and customers/vendors. I review and summarize the terms and conditions of the contract for the attorney's review.

In a case in which we represent the seller, I draft documents for review by the attorney. Such documents may include purchase agreements, deeds, lease agreements, and consents of the officers/shareholders approving the transaction.

The attorneys rely on me to organize and maintain the documents that are prepared and received throughout the course of a business transaction, and to prepare draft versions of many forms of transactional documents for their review. I provide efficiency and organizational advantages to the attorney while providing economic efficiencies for the client.

---

[1]*Rebstock v. Birthright Oil & Gas Co.*, 406 So. 2d 636 (La. App. 1981).
[2]*Restatement (Second) of Contracts*, Section 1.

of Contracts: "A contract is a promise or a set of promises for the breach of which the law gives a remedy or the performance of which the law in some way recognizes a duty."[3]

Parties to a Contract

Every contract involves at least two parties. The **offeror** is the party who makes an offer to enter into a contract. The **offeree** is the party to whom the offer is made (see Exhibit 1.1). In making an offer, the offeror promises to do—or to refrain from doing—something. The offeree then has the power to create a contract by accepting the offeror's offer. A contract is created if the offer is accepted. No contract is created if the offer is not accepted.

offeror
The party who makes an offer to enter into a contract. The party who makes an offer.

offeree
The party to whom an offer to enter into a contract is made. The party to whom an offer has been made.

Exhibit 1.1 Parties to a Contract

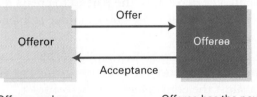

Offeror makes an offer to the offeree.

Offeree has the power to accept the offer and create a contract.

Elements of a Contract

For a contract to be enforceable, the following four basic requirements must be met:

1. **Agreement.** To have an enforceable contract, there must be an agreement between the parties. This requires an *offer* by the offeror and an *acceptance* of the offer by the offeree. There must be mutual assent by the parties.
2. **Consideration.** The promise must be supported by a bargained-for consideration that is legally sufficient.

   Example: Gift promises and moral obligations are not considered supported by valid consideration.
3. **Contractual capacity.** The parties to a contract must have the ability to enter into a contract. This ability is referred to as "capacity."

   Example: Certain parties, such as persons adjudged insane, do not have contractual capacity.
4. **Lawful object.** The object of the contract must be lawful.

   Example: Contracts to accomplish illegal objects or contracts that are against public policy are void.

agreement
The manifestation by two or more persons of the substance of a contract.

consideration
Something of legal value given in exchange for a promise.

contractual capacity
The legal qualification or competency to understand the nature and effects of one's acts so as to enter into a contract.

lawful object
Where the focus or purpose of the contract is legal.

[3]*Restatement (Second) of Contracts*, Section 1. The *Restatement* is a summary of judge-made doctrines and input from law professors, practicing attorneys and judges. It is important to remember that the *Restatement* is not the law. However, the *Restatement* is held in very high regard as an authority on the topic of contract law.

Concept Summary

Elements of a Contract

1. Agreement
2. Consideration
3. Contractual capacity
4. Lawful object

Defenses to the Enforcement of a Contract

Even if all of the elements to a contract are present—at least on its face—there may still be some *defenses* that could be raised to the enforcement of the contract. The following are two of those defenses:

genuineness of assent
The requirement that a party's assent to a contract be genuine.

writing and form
Certain contracts must be in writing or in a particular form in order to be enforceable.

1. **Genuineness of assent.** The consent of the parties to create a contract must be genuine. If the consent is obtained by duress, undue influence, or fraud, there is no real consent.
2. **Writing and form.** The law requires that certain contracts be in writing or in a certain form. Failure of these contracts to be in writing or to be in proper form may be raised against the enforcement of the contract.

CONTEMPORARY Issue

common law
Developed by judges who issued their opinions when deciding a case. The principles announced in these cases became precedent for later judges deciding similar cases.

classical law of contracts
Objective rules of forming contracts which give certainty and predictability in their enforcement.

THE EVOLUTION OF THE MODERN LAW OF CONTRACTS

The use of contracts originally developed in ancient times. The common law of contracts developed in England around the fifteenth century. American contract law evolved from the English **common law**.[4]

At first, the United States adopted a casual approach to the law of contracts. The central theme of this theory was *freedom of contract*. The parties (such as consumers, shopkeepers, farmers, and traders) generally dealt with one another face to face, had equal knowledge and bargaining power, and had the opportunity to inspect the goods prior to sale. Contract terms were openly negotiated. There was little, if any, government regulation of the right to contract. This "pure," or **classical**, **law of contracts** produced objective rules, which, in turn, produced certainty and predictability in the enforcement of contracts. It made sense until the Industrial Revolution.

The Industrial Revolution changed many of the underlying assumptions of pure contract law. For example, as large corporations developed and gained control of crucial resources, the traditional balance of parties' bargaining power shifted: Large corporations now had the most power. The chain of distribution for goods also changed because (1) buyers did not have to deal face to face with sellers and (2) there was not always an opportunity to inspect the goods prior to sale.

---

[4]Note that, in the legal profession, the term "common law" is sometimes used interchangeably with the terms "case law" or "precedent."

Form Contracts

Eventually, sellers began using *form contracts* that offered their goods to buyers on a take-it-or-leave-it basis.[5] The majority of contracts in the United States today are form contracts.

Example: Automobile contracts, mortgage contracts, sales contracts for consumer goods, and such are examples of form contracts.

Both federal and state governments have enacted statutes intended to protect consumers, debtors, and others from unfair contracts. In addition, the courts have developed certain common law legal theories that allow some oppressive or otherwise unjust contracts to be avoided. Today, under this modern law of

CONTEMPORARY Issue

ARBITRATION AND CONTRACT LAW

The use of the court system to resolve business and other disputes can take years and cost thousands, if not millions, of dollars in legal fees and expenses. In commercial litigation, the normal business operations of the parties are often disrupted. To avoid or lessen these problems, businesses are increasingly turning to methods of **alternative dispute resolution (ADR)** and other aids to resolve disputes. One of the most common forms of ADR is **arbitration**. Other forms of ADR are mediation, conciliation, mini-trial, fact finding, and using a judicial referee. Arbitration clauses are frequently found in contracts. These clauses essentially require disputes to be resolved in a private forum rather than a court. Arbitration clauses can be found everywhere these days; from cell-phone contracts to video-rental contracts.

In arbitration, the parties choose an impartial third party to hear and decide the dispute. This neutral party is called the *arbitrator*. Arbitrators are usually members of the American Arbitration Association (AAA) or another arbitration association. Labor union agreements, franchise agreements, leases, and other commercial contracts often contain arbitration clauses that require disputes arising out of the contract to be submitted to arbitration. If there is no arbitration clause, the parties can enter into a submission agreement whereby they agree to submit a dispute to arbitration after the dispute arises.

Evidence and testimony are presented to the arbitrator at a hearing held for this purpose. Less formal evidentiary rules are usually applied in arbitration hearings than at court. After the hearing, the arbitrator reaches a decision and enters an award. The parties often agree in advance to be bound by the arbitrator's decision and award. If the parties have not so agreed, the arbitrator's award can be appealed to the court. The court gives great deference to the arbitrator's decision.

Congress enacted the Federal Arbitration Act to promote the arbitration of disputes. About half of the states have adopted the Uniform Arbitration Act. This act promotes the arbitration of disputes at the state level. Many federal and state courts have instituted programs to refer legal disputes—which include contract disputes—to arbitration or another form of ADR.

Arbitration clauses might immediately seem as though they exist to favor companies. However, for the individual, arbitration clauses can provide a resolution that is faster and cheaper than going to court.

alternative dispute resolution (ADR)
Methods of resolving disputes other than litigation.

arbitration
A form of ADR in which the parties choose an impartial third party to hear and decide the dispute. A nonjudicial method of dispute resolution whereby a neutral third party decides the case.

---

[5]Sometimes a "form contract" is referred to as an "adhesion contract." An adhesion contract is a contract that is offered on a "take-it-or-leave-it" basis. In other words, the terms of an adhesion contract are not negotiable.

CAREER FRONT

contracts, there is substantial government regulation of the right to contract. This has been further expanded by the use of the Internet and e-commerce.

■ SOURCES OF CONTRACT LAW

There are several sources of contract law in the United States, including the *common law of contracts*, the *Uniform Commercial Code*, and the *Restatement (Second) of Contracts*. The following paragraphs explain these sources in more detail.

The Common Law of Contracts

common law of contracts
Contract law developed primarily by state courts.

A major source of contract law is the **common law of contracts**, which developed from early court decisions that became precedent for later decisions. There is a limited federal common law of contracts that applies to contracts made by the federal government. The larger and more prevalent body of common law has been developed from state court decisions. Thus, although the general principles remain the same throughout the country, there is some variation from state to state.

The Uniform Commercial Code (UCC)

Uniform Commercial Code (UCC)
Comprehensive statutory scheme that includes laws that cover aspects of commercial transactions.

Another major source of contract law is the **Uniform Commercial Code (UCC)**. The UCC, first drafted by the National Conference of Commissioners on Uniform

State Laws in 1952, has been amended several times. Its goal is to create a uniform system of commercial law among the fifty states. The provisions of the UCC normally take precedence over the common law of contracts (the provisions of the UCC are discussed in other chapters in this book).

The UCC is divided into nine main articles. Remember that the UCC applies only to the sale and lease of goods—not other types of contracts.

Every state has adopted at least part of the UCC. In the area of contract law, these are two of the major provisions of the UCC:

- **Article 2 (Sales).** This article prescribes a set of uniform rules for the creation and enforcement of contracts for the sale of goods. These contracts are often referred to as **sales contracts**.

  Example: The sale of equipment is a sales contract subject to Article 2 of the UCC.

- **Article 2A (Leases).** This article prescribes a set of uniform rules for the creation and enforcement of contracts for the lease of goods. These contracts are referred to as **lease contracts**.

  Example: The lease of an automobile is a lease subject to Article 2A of the UCC.

The Restatement of the Law of Contracts

In 1932, the American Law Institute completed the **Restatement of the Law of Contracts**. The *Restatement* is a compilation of contract law principles as agreed on by the drafters. The *Restatement*, which is currently in its second edition, is cited in this book as *Restatement (Second) of Contracts*. Note that the *Restatement* is not law. However, lawyers and judges often refer to it for guidance in contract disputes because of its stature.

Article 2 (Sales)
The second article of the Uniform Commercial Code which prescribes the rules for the creation and enforcement of contracts for the sale of goods.

sales contracts
Refers to the sale of goods under Article 2 of the UCC.

Article 2A (Leases)
Article of the UCC that governs lease of goods.

lease contracts
Contracts for the exclusive real or personal property for a specified period.

Restatement of the Law of Contracts
A compilation of model contract law principles drafted by legal scholars. The *Restatement* is not law.

 # INTERNET & TECHNOLOGY

Uniform Computer Information Transactions Act (UCITA)

The National Conference of Commissioners on Uniform State Laws (a group of lawyers, judges, and legal scholars) drafted the **Uniform Computer Information Transactions Act (UCITA)**. The UCITA establishes uniform legal rules for the formation and enforcement of electronic contracts and licenses. The UCITA addresses most of the legal issues that are encountered while conducting e-commerce over the Internet.

The UCITA is a model act that does not become law until a state legislature adopts it as a statute for the state. Although most states have not adopted the UCITA, the UCITA has served as a model for states that have enacted their own statutes that govern e-commerce. Because of the need for uniformity of e-commerce rules, states are attempting to adopt uniform laws to govern the creation and enforcement of cyberspace contracts and licenses.

Uniform Computer Information Transactions Act (UCITA)
A model act that provides uniform and comprehensive rules for contracts involving computer information transactions and software and information licenses.

PARALEGAL PERSPECTIVE

Rhonda Gray is a graduate of the Legal Studies Program at Wilmington College in New Castle, Delaware. She works as a regulatory services paralegal for XL Insurance America, Regulatory Services Group.
During my previous career as a property and casualty insurance underwriter, above anything else, I enjoyed work pertaining to contracts: developing policies for new programs, comparing competitor policies, and interpreting policy language. Consequently, it was a natural choice to pursue a second career as an insurance paralegal.

Because policies are contracts of adhesion, insurance products are highly regulated on both federal and state levels. I typically research several statutes and regulatory bulletins a day to determine how they might impact our duties to policyholders, policy provisions, and rating methodologies.

My past experience as an underwriter in conjunction with paralegal training has served me well. However, to remain a useful resource to my employer, continuing education in commercial insurance, contract law, and computer skills is a must.

I enjoy my work and the support I provide for XL America's Regulatory Services Group immensely. The challenges of deadlines, compiling meaningful information to solve our business needs, and juggling several projects at a time keep me interested, engaged, and continually striving for excellence.

Objective Theory of Contracts

objective theory of contracts
A theory that says that the intent to contract is judged by the reasonable person standard and not by the subjective intent of the parties.

reasonable person standard
The standard by which the court decides if the parties intended to create a contract. A "reasonable person" is a fictitious person of ordinary prudence.

The **objective theory of contracts** holds that the intent to enter into an express or implied-in-fact contract is judged by the **reasonable person standard**. Would a hypothetical reasonable person conclude that the parties intended to create a contract after considering (1) the words and conduct of the parties and (2) the surrounding circumstances? For example, no valid contract results from offers that are made in jest, anger, or undue excitement.

Under the objective theory of contracts, the subjective intent of a party to enter into a contract is irrelevant. The following two cases illustrate the application of the objective theory of contracts.

CASE 1.1 OBJECTIVE THEORY OF CONTRACTS

City of Everett v. Mitchell, 631 P.2d 366 (Wash. 1981).

> *"The objective manifestation theory of contracts lays stress on the outward manifestation of assent made by each party to the other. The subjective intention of the parties is irrelevant."*

> Judge Dolliver, *Supreme Court of Washington*

Facts

Al and Rosemary Mitchell owned a small secondhand store. The Mitchells attended Alexander's Auction, where they frequently shopped to obtain merchandise for their business. While at the auction, they purchased a used safe for $50. They were told by the auctioneer that the inside compartment of the safe was locked and that no key could be found to unlock it. The safe was part of the Sumstad estate. Several days after the auction, the Mitchells took the safe to a locksmith to have the locked compartment opened. When the locksmith opened the compartment, he found $32,207 in cash. The locksmith called the City of Everett Police, who impounded the money. The City of Everett commenced an interpleader action against the Sumstad estate and the Mitchells. The trial court entered summary judgment in favor of the Sumstad estate. The court of appeals affirmed. The Mitchells appealed.

Issue

Was a contract formed between the seller and the buyer of the safe?

Language of the Court

The objective manifestation theory of contracts stresses the outward manifestation of assent made by each party to the other. The subjective intention of the parties is irrelevant. A contract is an obligation attached by the mere force of law to certain acts of the parties, usually words, which ordinarily accompany and represent a known intent. If, however, it were proved by twenty bishops that either party, when he used the words intended something else than the usual meaning which the law imposes on them, he would still be held.

The Mitchells were aware of the rule of the auction that all sales were final. Furthermore, the auctioneer made no statement reserving rights to any contents of the safe to the estate. Under these circumstances, we hold reasonable persons would conclude that the auctioneer manifested an objective intent to sell the safe and its contents and that the parties mutually assented to enter into that sale of the safe and the contents of the locked compartment.

Decision

The state supreme court held that under the objective theory of contracts, a contract was formed between the seller and the buyer of the safe. The court reversed the appellate court's grant of summary judgment to the Sumstad estate and remanded the case to the trial court for entry of judgment in favor of the Mitchells.

Law & Ethics Questions

1. Does the objective theory of contracts work? Is it easy to define a "reasonable person"?

2. **Ethics** Did the seller of the safe act ethically in alleging that no contract had been made with the Mitchells?

3. What do you think would be the economic consequences to business if the courts recognized a subjective theory of contracts?

Web Exercises

1. **Web** Visit the website of the Supreme Court of Washington at www.courts .wa.gov.

2. **Web** Use www.google.com and find an article about the objective theory of contracts.

CAREER FRONT

Job Description: Bankruptcy Paralegal

The bankruptcy paralegal may work for a debtor law firm, a creditor law firm, or a bankruptcy trustee law firm. The bankruptcy paralegal can be involved with contracts in bankruptcy in the following ways:

Responsibilities in a Debtor Law Firm

- Participate in first client interview with attorney.
- Prepare client representation agreement.
- Meet with client to obtain background information for filing petition, schedules, and statement of financial affairs.
- Obtain debt information; draft list of debts and debtor contracts.
- Obtain asset information and prepare list of assets.
- Order asset appraisals.
- Draft petitions, schedules, and statement of financial affairs.
- Assist in preparing of disclosure statement and plan of reorganization in Chapter 11 cases.
- Draft debtor's monthly operating reports in Chapter 11 cases.
- Assist in preference action litigation.

Responsibilities for Creditor Law Firm

- Review debtor schedules and statement of affairs. Obtain all necessary data from client to draft proofs of claim.
- Draft notice of appearance and motion for admission *pro hac vice* for attorneys not admitted to the bar in the state of the court proceeding.
- Draft motions for avoidance of liens and reaffirmation agreements; arrange for execution of same.
- Draft complaints as Code allows.

Responsibilities for Trustee Law Firm

- Conduct Uniform Commercial (UCC) searches and real property searches to determine status of liens on property and/or equipment.
- Arrange for appraisals of real and personal property, including those under land contract.
- Draft complaints and motions for relief from stay with supporting affidavits in adversary proceedings.
- Attend Section 341 meeting(s).
- Attend plan confirmation hearing.
- Maintain log to track discharge and status of bankruptcy.
- Draft request for information on real estate owned by debtor; analyze and summarize contracts for sale of property; prepare lien priority exhibits for use in trial.

Source: Excerpted by permission from the National Association of Legal Assistants (www.nala.org) and the National Federation of Paralegal Associations, Inc. (www.paralegals.org).

CASE 1.2   OBJECTIVE THEORY OF CONTRACTS

Welles v. Academy of Motion Picture Arts & Sci., No. CV 03-05314 DDP (JTLx), 2004 U.S.
Dist. LEXIS 5756, at *1 (C.D. Cal. Mar. 4, 2004).

> *"Courts presume that a contract, deliberately entered into, expresses the true
> intent and meaning of the parties. A court will not set aside contractual obligations
> because one party misunderstood, or failed to read, the contract."*

> Judge Pregerson,

> *United States District Court for the Central District of California*

Facts

Orson Welles won an Academy Award Oscar from the Academy of Motion Picture Arts and Sciences for the Best Original Screenplay for the 1941 film *Citizen Kane*. After Orson Welles died, the right of ownership to the original Oscar passed to his wife, and when she died it passed to her daughter, Beatrice Welles (Welles). In 1988, Welles requested a duplicate Oscar from the Academy, stating that her father had lost the original Oscar many years ago. The Academy provided her with a duplicate Oscar, and she signed the following Receipt and Addendum.

Receipt

I hereby acknowledge receipt from you of replica No. 2527 [duplicate Oscar] of your copyrighted statuette, commonly known as the "Oscar", as an award for Orson Welles, Original Screenply—"Citizen Kane". I acknowledge that my receipt of said replica does not entitle me to any right whatsoever in your copyright, trademark and service mark of said statuette and that only the physical replica itself shall belong to me. In consideration of your delivering said replica to me, I agree to comply with your rules and regulations respecting its use and not to sell or otherwise dispose of it, nor permit it to be sold or disposed of by operation of law, without first offering to sell it to you for the sum of $1.00. You shall have thirty days after any such offer is made to you within which to accept it. This agreement shall be binding not only on me, but also on my heirs, legatees, executors, administrators, estate, successors and assigns. My legatees and heirs shall have the right to acquire said replica, if it becomes part of my estate, subject to this agreement.

Addendum

Any member of the Academy who has heretofore received any Academy trophy shall be bound by the forgoing receipt and agreement with the same force and effect as though he or she had executed and delivered the same in consideration of receiving such trophy.

In 1994, Welles discovered and obtained possession of the orignal Oscar. Welles decided that she wanted to sell the original Oscar through public auction at Christie, Manson & Woods International (Christie's). The Academy objected, and Christie's withdrew the original Oscar from auction pending the resolution of the dispute between Welles and the Academy. Welles sued the Academy for a judicial declaration that she was the rightful owner of the original Oscar and had the right to sell it. The Academy defended that the Receipt and Addendum prevented her from selling the original Oscar. Welles argued that the language of the Addendum "Any member of the Academy ..." did not apply to her because she was not a member of the Academy. The Academy responded that it intended that the language should apply to Welles and asked the court to reform the Receipt and Addendum to apply to Welles and to order that the Academy had a right of first refusal to purchase the original Oscar for $1.00.

Issue

Does the Receipt and Addendum prohibit Welles from selling the original Oscar?

Language of the Court

A written contract, once executed, carries with it a legal presumption that it correctly expresses the intention of the parties. Where one party claims that a contract was entered into pursuant to a unilateral mistake, in order to be granted reformation, that party must prove that the other party knew of or suspected the mistake at the time the contract was executed. The Academy asserts that it committed a unilateral mistake by using the form Receipt that contained the Addendum concerning "members" in its agreement with Welles, a nonmember. The burden is on the Academy to show that Welles knew or suspected the Academy's mistake—namely, that the Academy intended that the Addendum apply to her.

In order for a court to reform a contract, there must be a mutual intention of the parties for the reformed contract to express. Welles states in her declaration that she "did not and would not under any circumstances agree to give the Academy a right of first refusal for $1.00 on the original statuette awarded to my father." The Academy asserts that it intended to preclude Welles from selling any Oscar. Thus, the court finds that there was no meeting of the minds, and no mutual intention of the parties on which a reformed contract would be based. The intention of the parties must be derived from the language of the contract if possible. The Academy does not dispute that the plain langauge of the Addendum does not apply to Welles. Instead, the Academy argues that because Welles was unique—the replacement Oscar given to her was the first one given to a nonmember who was not the original recipient of the award—the Academy erred and sent Welles a form that did not apply to her. Courts presume that a contract, deliberately entered into, expresses the true intent and meaning of the parties. A court will not set aside contractual obligations because one party misunderstood, or failed to read, the contract. Here, the Academy failed to ensure that the Addendum applied to Welles. The Academy drafted the document, and the court will not set aside the contract because the Academy failed to review its own form. Per the Receipt's terms, the Addendum does not apply to Welles's original Oscar which she received from her father's estate.

Decision

The U.S. district court applied the objective theory of contracts and decided that the Academy's subjective belief that the Addendum applied to Welles did not change the express language of the contract. The district court granted Welles's motion for summary judgment, holding that the Academy did not have a right of first refusal in Welles's original Oscar. The district court held that Welles had unrestricted property rights in the original Oscar, which she could dispose of as she saw fit.

Law & Ethics Questions

1. What does the objective theory of contracts provide? Explain.

2. Do you think the Academy had the subjective intent to provide in the contract that it had the right of first refusal if Welles tried to sell the original Oscar? Does this matter in contract interpretation?

3. **Ethics** Was it ethical for the Academy to try to get out from under the terms of a contract that it drafted?

Web Exercises

1. **Web** Visit the website of the U.S. District Court for the Central District of California at www.cacd.uscourts.gov.

2. **Web** Use www.google.com and find and read a short bibliography of Orson Welles.

3. **Web** Visit the website of the Academy of Motion Picture Arts and Sciences at www.oscars.org.

4. **Web** Use www.google.com and find a movie clip of *Citizen Kane*.

INTERNET & TECHNOLOGY

E-Commerce

As we entered the twenty-first century, a new economic shift brought the United States and the rest of the world into the Information Age. Computer technology and the use of the Internet increased dramatically. A new form of commerce—**electronic commerce**, or **e-commerce**—is flourishing. All sorts of goods and services are now sold over the Internet. You can purchase automobiles and children's toys, participate in auctions, purchase airline tickets, make hotel reservations, and purchase other goods and services over the Internet.

Much of the new cyberspace economy is based on electronic contracts and the licensing of computer information. E-commerce created problems for forming contracts over the Internet, enforcing e-commerce contracts, and providing consumer protection. In many situations, traditional contract rules apply to e-contracts. Many states have adopted rules that specifically regulate e-commerce transactions. The federal government has also enacted several laws that regulate e-contracts. Contract rules that apply to e-commerce are discussed in this and in the following chapters.

e-commerce
The sale of goods and services by computer over the Internet.

■ CLASSIFICATIONS OF CONTRACTS

There are several types of contracts. Each differs somewhat in formation, enforcement, performance, and discharge. The different types of contracts are discussed in the following paragraphs.

Bilateral and Unilateral Contracts

bilateral contract
A contract entered into by way of exchange of promises of the parties; a "promise for a promise."

unilateral contract
A contract in which the offeror's offer can be accepted only by the performance of an act by the offeree; a "promise for an act."

Contracts are either *bilateral* or *unilateral*, depending on what the offeree must do to accept the offeror's offer. A contract is **bilateral** if the offeror's promise is answered with the offeree's promise of acceptance. In other words, a bilateral contract is a "promise for a promise." This exchange of promises creates an enforceable contract. No act of performance is necessary to create a bilateral contract.

A contract is **unilateral** if the offeror's offer can be accepted only by the performance of an act by the offeree. There is no contract until the offeree performs the requested act. An offer to create a unilateral contract cannot be accepted by a promise to perform. It is a "promise for an act."

The language of the offeror's promise must be carefully scrutinized to determine whether it is an offer to create a bilateral or a unilateral contract. If there is any ambiguity as to which it is, it is presumed to be a bilateral contract.

Example: Suppose Mary Douglas, the owner of the Chic Dress Shop, says to Peter Jones, a painter, "If you promise to paint my store by July 1, I will pay you $3,000." Peter promises to do so. A bilateral contract was created at the moment Peter promised to paint the dress shop (a promise for a promise). If Peter fails to paint the store, he can be sued for whatever damages result from his breach of contract. Similarly, Peter can sue Mary if she refuses to pay him after he has performed as promised.

Example: However, if Mary had said, "If you paint my shop by July 1, I will pay you $3,000," the offer would have created a unilateral contract. The offer can be accepted only by the painter's performance of the requested act. If Peter does not paint the shop by July 1, there has been no acceptance, and the painter cannot be sued for damages.

Incomplete or Partial Performance

Problems can arise if the offeror in a unilateral contract attempts to revoke an offer after the offeree has begun performance. Generally, an offer to create a unilateral contract can be revoked by the offeror any time prior to the offeree's performance of the requested act. However, the offer cannot be revoked if the offeree has begun or has substantially completed performance.

Example: Suppose Alan Matthews tells Sherry Levine that he will pay her $5,000 if she finishes the Boston Marathon. Alan cannot revoke the offer once Sherry starts running the marathon.

MARKETPLACE

Contract Specialist Paralegal Position Job Announcement

Fortune 200 company has immediate full-time openings for a paralegal to provide assistance in our expanding Contract Review Center. Openings are available both for experienced and entry-level candidates.

The suitable candidate must have at least an associate degree in paralegal studies (from an American Bar Association approved program). However, preference will be given to those holding a bachelor's degree and a post-baccalaureate certificate in paralegal studies from an American Bar Association approved program. Preference is also given to those having prior contract experience.

Responsibilities of this position include the following:

1. Day-to-day processing of builder contracts and other contractual agreements;
2. Build and maintain relationships with internal and external customers;
3. Manage lease process;
4. Facilitate communications across all functions;
5. Manage/Facilitate daily contract process
    a. Review and modify
    b. Record to contract log
    c. Track metric on contracts
    d. Scan for electronic filing
    e. Send to the customer
    f. Follow-up for executed copies
6. Assist in contract negotiation, writing contract addendums and protecting the company's legal rights under contract;
7. Assist in monitoring and managing general liability claims and legal matters;
8. Assist in monitoring construction defect and other litigation;
9. Communicate effectively with parent company;
10. Understand customers' requirements, resolve issues, and build good relationships internally and externally;
11. Be an active part of the team working to reduce/limit risk exposure;
12. Participate in continuous improvement activities.

Specialists must have excellent PC skills, verbal and written communication skills, and be detail oriented in a very fast-paced, analytical document preparation center. We offer a professional working environment, competitive pay, and a comprehensive benefits package for the motivated self-starter.

For consideration, please forward your resume and salary expectations to:

nondisclosure agreement
A contract not to reveal any facts or information on a particular matter.

 E-Commerce & Information Technology

Ready for Love? Not Before You've Been NDA'd

You're out on a date and your partner whispers sweet nothings in your ear. What's a guy or girl to do? Quick, whip out a **nondisclosure agreement**—or NDA as they are called—and have the other side sign it before responding. That is what many entrepreneurs and techies are doing, having their boyfriends, girlfriends, family members, friends, and others sign NDAs before revealing anything about what they are doing.

NDAs have been around for a long time, and traditionally have been used among lawyers, investment bankers, and others involved in secret takeovers and other large corporate deals. NDAs swear the signatory to secrecy about confidential ideas, trade secrets, and other nonpublic information revealed by the party proffering the NDA. But today many entrepreneurs, particularly those in high-tech industries, are handing out NDAs as fast as business cards. An NDA serves a purpose in that it protects a person who has a great idea (or so he or she thinks) and wants to share it with a potential partner, investor, lawyer, or investment banker, but wants an assurance that the recipient of the information will not steal or reveal the information to anyone else.

NDAs are enforceable contracts, so if someone violates it the disclosing party can sue the breaching party for damages. Bill Gates of Microsoft has plumbers and other persons who work on his house sign NDAs. Sabeer Bhatia, the founder of Hotmail, collected more then 400 NDAs in two years before selling his company to Microsoft for $400 million.

Although it may not be hard to get some people to sign NDAs, others balk. Some friends and relatives refuse to sign NDAs thrust on them because they present an aura of distrust. And it is particularly insulting to sign an NDA and then to hear a harebrained idea from the disclosing party. Industry bigwigs—venture capitalists, securities analysts, and successful technology companies—routinely refuse to sign NDAs because they see too many similar ideas and do not want their tongues tied by any single one. NDAs will continue to increase in use, however. So the next time you are at a party and you ask someone what they do, don't be surprised if you are NDA'd!

Express and Implied-in-Fact Contracts

An *actual contract* (as distinguished from a quasi-contract, discussed later in this chapter) may be either *express* or *implied-in-fact*.

express contract
An agreement that is expressed in written or oral words.

Express contracts are stated in oral or written words. Examples of such contracts include an oral agreement to purchase a neighbor's bicycle and a written agreement to buy an automobile from a dealership.

implied-in-fact contract
A contract where agreement between parties has been inferred because of their conduct.

Implied-in-fact contracts are implied from the *conduct of the parties*. This supports the important concept in contract law that not all contracts need to be in writing. Implied-in-fact contracts leave more room for questions. The following elements must be established to create an implied-in-fact contract:

1. The plaintiff provided property or services to the defendant.
2. The plaintiff expected to be paid by the defendant for the property or services and did not provide the property or services gratuitously.
3. The defendant was given an opportunity to reject the property or services provided by the plaintiff but failed to do so.

Entrepreneur and the Law

> ## OWNER OF *SCRABBLE* SPELLED "L–O–S–E–R"
>
> Implied-in-fact contracts are implied from the conduct of the parties. Consider the following case.
>
> Selchow & Richter (S&R) owns the trademark to the famous board game *Scrabble*. Mark Landsberg wrote a book on strategy for winning at *Scrabble* and contacted S&R to request permission to use the *Scrabble* trademark. In response, S&R requested a copy of Landsberg's manuscript, which he provided. After prolonged negotiations between the parties regarding the possibility of S&R's publication of the manuscript broke off, S&R brought out its own *Scrabble* strategy book. No express contract was ever entered into between Landsberg and S&R. Landsberg sued S&R and its subsidiary, Scrabble Crossword Game Players, Inc., for damages for breach of an implied contract.
>
> Was there an implied-in-fact contract between the parties?
>
> The district court and appellate court held that an implied-in-fact contract had been formed between the parties and that the contract was breached by the defendants. The court noted that the law allows for recovery for the breach of an implied-in-fact contract when the recipient of a valuable idea accepts and uses the information without paying for it even though he knows that compensation is expected. Here, the court found (1) that Landsberg's disclosure of his manuscript was confidential and for the limited purpose of obtaining approval for the use of the *Scrabble* mark, and (2) given Landsberg's express intention to exploit his manuscript commercially, the defendant's use of any portion of it was conditioned on payment. Landsberg was awarded $440,300 damages. (Learn more about the *Scrabble* case in the Ethics Spotlight on page 21.)

In the following case, the court had to decide whether the plaintiffs could sue a defendant for breach of an implied-in-fact contract.

CASE 1.3 IMPLIED-IN-FACT CONTRACT

Wrench LLC v. Taco Bell Corp., 256 F.3d 446 (6th Cir. 2001).

"The district court found that appellants produced sufficient evidence to create a genuine issue of material fact regarding whether an implied-in-fact contract existed between the parties."

Judge Graham,

United States Court of Appeals for the Sixth Circuit

Facts

Thomas Rinks and Joseph Shields created the "Psycho Chihuahua" cartoon character, which they promote, market, and license through their company, Wrench LLC. The Psycho Chihuahua is a clever, feisty, cartoon character dog with an attitude; a self-confident, edgy, cool dog who knows what he wants and will not back down. Rinks and Shields attended a licensing trade show in New York City, where they were approached by two Taco Bell employees, Rudy Pollak, a vice president, and Ed Alfaro, a creative services manager. Taco Bell owns and operates a nationwide chain of fast-food Mexican restaurants. Pollak and Alfaro expressed interest in the Psycho Chihuahua character for Taco Bell advertisements because they thought his character would appeal to Taco Bell's core consumers, men ages 18 to 24. Pollak and Alfaro obtained some Psycho Chihuahua materials to take back with them to Taco Bell's headquarters.

Later, Alfaro contacted Rinks and asked him to create art boards combining Psycho Chihuahua with the Taco Bell name and image. Rinks and Shields prepared art boards and sent them to Alfaro, along with Psycho Chihuahua T-shirts, hats, and stickers. Alfaro showed these materials to Taco Bell's vice president of brand management as well as to Taco Bell's outside advertising agency. Alfaro tested the Psycho Chihuahua marketing concept with focus groups. Rinks suggested to Alfaro that instead of using the cartoon version of Psycho Chihuahua in its advertisements, Taco Bell should use a live Chihuahua dog manipulated by computer graphic imaging that had the personality of Psycho Chihuahua and a love for Taco Bell food. Rinks and Shields gave a formal presentation of this concept to Taco Bell's marketing department. One idea presented by Rinks and Shields was a commercial in which a male Chihuahua dog passed by a female Chihuahua dog in order to get to Taco Bell food. Taco Bell did not enter into an express contract with Wrench LLC, Rinks, or Shields.

Just after Rinks and Shields's presentation, Taco Bell hired a new outside advertising agency, Chiat/Day. Taco Bell gave Chiat/Day materials received from Rinks and Shields regarding the Psycho Chihuahua. Three months later, Chiat/Day proposed using a Chihuahua in Taco Bell commercials. One commercial had a male Chihuahua passing up a female Chihuahua to get to a person seated on a bench eating Taco Bell food. Chiat/Day says that it conceived these ideas by itself. In July 1997, Taco Bell aired its first Chihuahua commercial in the United States, and it became an instant success and the basis of its advertising. Taco Bell paid nothing to Wrench LLC or to Rinks and Shields. Plaintiffs Wrench LLC, Rinks, and Shields sued defendant Taco Bell to recover damages for breach of an implied-in-fact contract. On this issue, the district court agreed with the plaintiffs. The decision was appealed.

Issue

Do the plaintiffs, Wrench LLC, Rinks, and Shields, state a cause of action for the breach of an implied-in-fact contract?

Language of the Court

The district court found that appellants produced sufficient evidence to create a genuine issue of material fact regarding whether an implied-in-fact contract existed between the parties. On appeal, Taco Bell argues that this conclusion was erroneous, and asserts that the record contains no evidence of an enforceable contract. We agree with the district court's finding that appellants presented sufficient evidence to survive summary judgment on the question of whether an implied-in-fact contract existed under Michigan law.

Decision

The U.S. Court of Appeals held that the plaintiffs had stated a proper cause of action against defendant Taco Bell for breach of an implied-in-fact contract. The Court of Appeals remanded the case for trial.

Law & Ethics Questions

1. What does the doctrine of implied-in-fact contract provide? Explain.

2. **Ethics** Did Taco Bell act ethically in this case? Did Chiat/Day act ethically in this case?

3. Do you think there was an implied-in-fact contract in this case? If so, what damages should be awarded to the plaintiffs?

4. Several terms were used in this case that the paralegal student needs to know to fully understand this case. Look up the terms "summary judgment," "material fact," and "punitive damages" in a legal dictionary or thesaurus.

Web Exercises

1. **Web** Visit the website of the U.S. Court of Appeals for the Sixth Circuit at www.ca6.uscourts.gov.

2. **Web** Visit the website of Taco Bell Corporation at www.tacobell.com. Can you find any reference to the "Psycho Chihuahua" commercial?

3. **Web** Use www.google.com and find an article that discusses the "Psycho Chihuahua" advertising campaign used by Taco Bell.

ETHICS SPOTLIGHT

SCRABBLE OWNER HELD LIABLE ON AN IMPLIED-IN-FACT CONTRACT

"Finding that S & R had denied the existence of the contract in bad faith and without probable cause, the district court impose[d] punitive damages on S & R. This factual finding was not clearly erroneous. Indeed defendants have offered no evidence to suggest that they acted in good faith. We therefore affirm the initial $100,000 punitive damage award."

Judge Goodwin

Implied-in-fact contracts are implied from the conduct of the parties. Consider the following case. Selchow & Richter Company (S&R) owns the trademark to the famous board game *Scrabble*. Mark Landsberg wrote a book on strategy for winning at *Scrabble* and contacted S&R to request permission to use the *Scrabble* trademark. In response, S&R requested a copy of Landsberg's manuscript, which he provided. After prolonged negotiations between the parties regarding the possibility of S&R's publication of the manuscript broke off, S&R brought out its own *Scrabble* strategy book. No express contract was ever entered into between Landsberg and S&R. Landsberg sued S&R for damages for breach of an implied contract.

Was there an implied-in-fact contract between the parties? The U.S. District Court and the U.S. Court of Appeals held that an implied-in-fact contract had been formed between the parties and that the contract was breached by the defendants. The U.S. Court of Appeals noted, "California law allows for recovery for the breach of an implied-in-fact contract when the recipient of a valuable idea accepts the information knowing that compensation is expected, and subsequently uses the idea without paying for it."

Here, the court found (1) that Landsberg's disclosure of his manuscript was confidential and for the limited purpose of obtaining approval for the use of the *Scrabble* mark, and (2) given Landsberg's express intention to exploit his manuscript commercially, the defendant's use of any portion of it was conditioned on payment. Landsberg was awarded the profits that S&R made on the sale of the book plus $100,000 punitive damages, bringing the total award to $440,300. The U.S. Court of Appeals stated, "Finding that S & R had denied the existence of the contract in bad faith and without probable cause, the district court impose[d] punitive damages on S & R. This factual finding was not clearly erroneous. Indeed defendants have offered no evidence to suggest that they acted in good faith. We therefore affirm the initial $100,000 punitive damage award." *Landsberg v. Selchow & Richter Co.*, 802 F.2d 1193 (9th Cir. 1986).

Law & Ethics Questions

1. Does the implied-in-fact doctrine provide any useful protections? Explain.
2. **Ethics** Did Selchow & Richter act ethically in this case?
3. **Ethics** Will the doctrine of implied-in-fact contract encourage more ethical behavior?
4. **Ethics** Was the award of punitive damages justified in this case? Why or why not?

Web Exercises

1. **Web** Visit the website of the U.S. Court of Appeals for the Ninth Circuit at www.ca9.uscourts.gov.
2. **Web** Go to the website www.scrabble.com. This is the official worldwide web page for *Scrabble*.
3. **Web** Use www.google.com and find an article that discusses strategy for playing *Scrabble*.

Quasi-Contracts (Implied-in-Law Contracts)

quasi-contract
An obligation created by the law to avoid injust erichment in the absence of an agreement between the parties.

The equitable doctrine of **quasi-contract**, also called **implied-in-law contract**, allows a court to award monetary damages to a plaintiff for providing work or services to a defendant even though no actual contract existed between the parties. Recovery is generally based on the reasonable value of the services received by the defendant.[6]

The doctrine is intended to prevent *unjust enrichment* and *unjust detriment*. It does not apply where there is an enforceable contract between the parties. A quasi-contract is imposed where (1) one person confers a benefit on another who retains the benefit and (2) it would be unjust not to require that person to pay for the benefit received.

Example: Heather is driving her automobile when she is involved in a serious automobile accident in which she is knocked unconscious. She is rushed to Metropolitan Hospital, where the doctors and other staff perform the necessary medical procedures to save her life. Heather comes out of her coma, and after recovering she is released from the hospital. Subsequently, Metropolitan Hospital sends Heather a bill for its services. The charges are reasonable. Under the doctrine of quasi-contract, Heather is responsible for any charges that are not covered by her insurance coverage.

In the following case, the court found a quasi-contract.

---

[6]Monetary awards can be recovered when seeking quasi-contractual remedies. These can be available when no contract is found to exist, but there has been unjust enrichment to one of the parties to the dispute. One type of quasi-contractual remedy used is *Quantum Meruit*, where the value of the services are calculated.

CASE 1.4 QUASI-CONTRACT

Powell v. Thompson-Powell, No. 04-12-0027, 2006 Del. LEXIS 10, *1 (C.P. Kent Jan. 18, 2006).

"A contract implied in law permits recovery of that amount by which the defendant has benefited at the expense of the plaintiff in order to preclude unjust enrichment."

Judge Trader, *Court of Common Pleas of Delaware*

Facts

Samuel E. Powell Jr. and Susan Thompson-Powell, husband and wife, borrowed $37,700 from Delaware Farm Credit and gave a mortgage to Delaware Farm Credit that pledged two pieces of real property as collateral for the loan. The first piece of property was 2.7 acres of land owned as martial property, and the other piece of property was owned by Susan, which she had inherited. Eight years later, Samuel Jr. and Susan defaulted on the mortgage. Samuel Jr. went to his father, Samuel E. Powell Sr., and orally agreed that if his father would pay the mortgage and the back taxes, he would pay his father back. Samuel Sr. paid off the mortgage and the back taxes owed on the properties. Susan was not a party to this agreement.

Two years later, Samuel Jr. and Susan were divorced. The divorce court ordered that the 2.7 acres of marital real property be sold and the sale proceeds divided 50 percent to each party. When the property was sold, Samuel Jr. paid Samuel Sr. half of the monies he had previously borrowed from his father. Samuel Sr. sued Susan to recover the other half of the money. Susan defended, alleging that she was not a party to the contract between Samuel Jr. and Samuel Sr. and therefore was not bound by it. Samuel Sr. argued that Susan was liable to him for half of the money based on the doctrine of quasi-contract.

Issue

Is Susan liable for half the money borrowed by Samuel Jr. from Samuel Sr. under the doctrine of quasi-contract?

Language of the Court

The primary issue in this case is whether the plaintiff can recover from Susan Thompson-Powell on the theory of contract implied in law. A contract implied in law permits recovery of that amount by which the defendant has benefited at the expense of the plaintiff in order to preclude unjust enrichment. To claim restitution, the plaintiff must show that the defendant was unjustly enriched and secured a benefit that it would be unconscionable to allow her to retain.

The essential elements of a quasi-contract are a benefit conferred upon the defendant by the plaintiff, appreciation or realization of the benefit by the defendant, and acceptance and retention by the defendant of such benefit under such circumstances that it would be inequitable to retain without paying the value thereof.

In the case before me the plaintiff paid the mortgage of the son and daughter-in-law at a time when the bank was about to foreclose on the mortgage. If the property had been sold at a foreclosure sale, neither Samuel E. Powell Jr. nor Susan Thompson-Powell would have received any benefit from the sale of the marital property. Additionally, payment of the mortgage protected Susan Thompson-Powell's inherited property. Thus, because of the plaintiff's acts in preserving the real estate from foreclosure Susan Thompson-Powell received a substantial benefit at the plaintiff's expense. Since the retention of the benefit in this case is unjust, she must repay her share of the money advanced by the plaintiff.

Decision

The court held that Samuel E. Powell Sr. was entitled to recover from Susan Thompson-Powell half of the money advanced for her benefit.

Law & Ethics Questions

1. What does the doctrine of quasi-contract provide? Explain.

2. **Ethics** Was it ethical for Susan Thompson-Powell to not pay back half of the money borrowed from Samuel E. Powell Sr.?

3. **Ethics** What is the doctrine of quasi-contract designed to prevent? Explain.

Web Exercises

1. **Web** For the complete opinion of this case, go to www.google.com.

2. **Web** Visit the website of the Court of Common Pleas of Delaware at www.courts.delaware.gov.

3. **Web** Use www.google.com and find an article that discusses the doctrine of quasi-contract.

PARALEGAL PERSPECTIVE

Linda Ledford is a 1993 graduate of the University of Toledo's associate degree Paralegal Studies Program. She is currently completing her bachelor of science in paralegal studies at UT. Linda also works as a contracts paralegal in the Office of the General Counsel at the University of Toledo in Toledo, Ohio.

I work as a contracts paralegal with my alma mater, under the supervision of the vice president and general counsel. It is my responsibility to review a majority of the incoming and outgoing contracts, whether academic, service, or purchasing.

As a state entity, the university has a strict set of regulations that govern its ability to contract with other parties. I make sure the contracts comply with these statutory regulations, as well as UT's policies and procedures. After my initial review, I provide to the general counsel an overall perspective of the contract, outlining issues to be addressed. And, if necessary, I also offer alternative terms or the reasoning that prohibits acceptance of certain terms.

Another aspect of my position is drafting contract templates to be used by the various departments on campus. I may also participate in the negotiations of an agreement or provide clarification to our vendors. In my capacity, I am fortunate to work with people in all aspects of the university and be a part of the level of customer service that maintains a good working relationship with our myriad of customers.

Formal and Informal Contracts

formal contract
A contract that requires a special form or method of creation.

Contracts may be classified as either *formal* or *informal*. **Formal contracts** are contracts that require a special form or method of creation. The *Restatement (Second) of Contracts* identifies the following types of formal contracts:[7]

- **Negotiable instruments.** Negotiable instruments, which include checks, drafts, notes, and certificates of deposit, are special forms of contracts

---

[7]*Restatement (Second) of Contracts*, Section 6.

recognized by the UCC. They require a special form and language for their creation and must meet certain requirements for transfer.

- *Letters of credit.* A letter of credit is an agreement by the issuer of the letter to pay a sum of money upon the receipt of an invoice and other documents. **Letters of credit** are governed by the UCC.
- *Recognizances.* In a recognizance, a party acknowledges in court that he or she will pay a specified sum of money if a certain event occurs. A **bail bond** is an example of a recognizance.
- *Contracts under seal.* This type of contract is one to which a seal (usually a wax seal) is attached. Although no state currently requires contracts to be under seal, a few states provide that no consideration is necessary if a contract is made under seal.

All contracts that do not qualify as formal contracts are called **informal contracts (or simple contracts)**. The term is a misnomer. Valid informal contracts (e.g., leases, sales contracts, service contracts) are fully enforceable and may be sued upon if breached. They are called informal contracts only because no special form or method is required for their creation.

 # THE ETHICAL PARALEGAL

Integrity

Fear of discipline (or losing one's job) is an inadequate and, at best, only partial motivation for paralegals to conduct themselves as legal professionals with integrity. More likely is that the paralegal's *basic integrity* is what will influence that paralegal's professional behavior.

However, because legal professionals are held to such high standards of moral and ethical conduct, all states have adopted rules to encourage a legal professional's ethical behavior where basic integrity might be lacking. The majority of states have adopted their rules from the American Bar Association's Model Rules of Professional Conduct.[8] ABA Model Rule 8.1 states that legal professionals should be persons of integrity.

The paralegal should be aware that violations of ethics rules can lead to serious sanctions. If an attorney violates an ethical rule, sanctions range from disbarment for extremely unethical activities to a warning for minor infractions. **Paralegals must always be aware that under the doctrine of *respondeat superior*, their actions are imputed to the supervising attorney.** In other words, if the paralegal does something unethical, the attorney will receive the punishment for that paralegal's unethical behavior.

Although most of ethics rules pertain exclusively to attorneys, the paralegal can also personally face serious penalties for unethical conduct. These penalties range from criminal and civil penalties to contempt of court charges, fines, and even a jail sentence. Ethics violations are normally investigated and prosecuted by the state bar association, the state disciplinary council, or the local bar association's grievance committees.

So ethical paralegals should always conduct themselves with integrity—a broad concept that includes morality, ethics, etiquette, and professional values and attitudes.

negotiable instrument
Commercial paper that must meet these requirements: (1) be in writing, (2) be signed by the maker or drawer, (3) be an unconditional promise or order to pay, (4) state a fixed amount of money, (5) not require any undertaking in addition to the payment of money, (6) be payable on demand or at a definite time, and (7) be payable to order or to bearer. A special form of contract that satisfies the requirement established by Article 3 of the UCC. Also called commercial paper.

letter of credit
A written instrument addressed by one person to another requesting the latter to give credit to the person in whose favor it is drawn.

bail bond
A three-party contract that involves the state, the accused, and a surety under which the surety guarantees the state that the accused will appear in court as the case proceeds.

informal contract
A contract that is not formal. Valid informal contracts are fully enforceable and may be sued upon if breached.

---

[8]Copies of the ABA Model Rules of Professional Conduct are available from Service Center, American Bar Association, 321 North Clark Street, Chicago, IL 60610, 1-800-285-2221. The Model Rules can also be viewed online at http://www.abanet.org/cpr/mrpc/mrpc_toc.html.

Valid, Void, Voidable, and Unenforceable Contracts

Contract law places contracts in the following categories:

valid contract
A contract that meets all of the essential elements to establish a contract; a contract that is enforceable by at least one of the parties.

1. *Valid contract.* A **valid contract** meets all the essential elements to establish a contract. In other words, it must (1) consist of an agreement between the parties, (2) be supported by legally sufficient consideration, (3) be between parties with contractual capacity, and (4) accomplish a lawful object. A valid contract is enforceable by at least one of the parties.

void contract
A contract that has no legal effect; a nullity.

2. *Void contract.* A **void contract** has no legal effect. It is as if no contract had ever been created.

    Example: A contract to commit a crime is void. If a contract is void, neither party is obligated to perform, and neither party can enforce the contract.

voidable contract
A contract where one or both parties have the option to avoid their contractual obligations. If a contract is avoided, both parties are released from their contractual obligations.

3. *Voidable contract.* A **voidable contract** is one where at least one party has the *option* to avoid his or her contractual obligations. If the contract is avoided, both parties are released from their obligations under the contract. If the party with the option chooses to ratify the contract, both parties must fully perform their obligations.

    Example: With certain exceptions, contracts may be voided by minors, insane persons, intoxicated persons, persons acting under duress or undue influence or fraud, and in cases involving a mutual mistake.

unenforceable contract
A contract where the essential elements to create a valid contract are met, but there is some legal defense to the enforcement of the contract.

4. *Unenforceable contract.* With an **unenforceable contract**, there is some legal defense to the enforcement of the contract.

    Example: If a contract is required to be in writing under the Statute of Frauds but is not, the contract is unenforceable. The parties may voluntarily perform a contract that is unenforceable.

Executed and Executory Contracts

A completed contract—that is, one that has been fully performed on both sides—is called an **executed contract**. A contract that has not been performed by both sides is called an **executory contract**. Contracts that have been fully performed by one side but not by the other are classified as executory contracts.

executed contract
A contract that has been fully performed on both sides; a completed contract.

Example: Suppose Elizabeth Andrews signs a contract to purchase a new Jaguar automobile from Ace Motors. She has not yet paid for the car, and Ace Motors has not yet delivered it. This is an executory contract. Assume the car was paid for, but Ace Motors has not yet delivered the car. Here, the contract is executed by Elizabeth but is executory as to Ace Motors. This is an executory contract. Assume that Ace Motors now delivers the car to Elizabeth. The contract has been fully performed by both parties. It is an executed contract.

executory contract
A contract that has not yet been fully completed or performed.

Concept Summary

Classifications of Contracts

FORMATION

1. *Bilateral contract.* A promise for a promise.
2. *Unilateral contract.* A promise for an act.
3. *Express contract.* A contract expressed in oral or written words.
4. *Implied-in-fact contract.* A contract inferred from the conduct of the parties.
5. *Quasi-contract.* A contract implied by law to prevent unjust enrichment.
6. *Formal contract.* A contract that requires a special form or method of creation.
7. *Informal contract.* A contract that requires no special form or method of creation.

(continued)

ENFORCEABILITY

1. **Valid contract.** A contract that meets all the essential elements of establishing a contract.
2. **Void contract.** No contract exists.
3. **Voidable contract.** A contract for which a party has the option of voiding or enforcing the contract.
4. **Unenforceable contract.** A contract that cannot be enforced because of a legal defense.

PERFORMANCE

1. **Executed contract.** A contract that is fully performed on both sides.
2. **Executory contract.** A contract that is not fully performed by one or both parties.

INTERNATIONAL LAW

The United Nations Convention on Contracts for the International Sale of Goods

The **United Nations Convention on Contracts for the International Sale of Goods** (**CISG**) came into effect on January 1, 1988, climaxing more than 50 years of negotiations. The CISG is the work of many countries and several international organizations. There are now approximately 70 signature countries to the CISG. In adopting the CISG, the UN stated the following in its preamble:

PREAMBLE

The State Parties to this Convention,

Considering that the development of international trade on the basis of equality and mutual benefit is an important element in promoting friendly relations among States,

Being of the opinion that the adoption of uniform rules which govern contracts for the international sale of goods and take into account the different social, economic and legal systems would contribute to the removal of legal barriers in international trade and promote the development of international trade,

Have agreed as follows:

[The text of the CISG followed the Preamble]

The CISG provides legal rules that govern the formation, performance, and enforcement of international contracts entered into between international businesses. Many of its provisions are remarkably similar to those of the U.S. UCC, for example. It incorporates rules from all the major legal systems. It has, accordingly, received widespread support from developed, developing, and communist countries.

The CISG applies to contracts for the international sale of goods. That is, the buyer and seller must have their places of business in different countries. In addition, either (1) both of the nations must be parties to the convention or (2) the contract must specify that the CISG controls. The contracting parties may agree to exclude (i.e., opt out of) or modify its application.

Web Exercise

1. **Web** To view the CISG, go to www.uncitral.org/pdf/english/texts/sales/cisg/CISG.pdf.
2. **Web** Use www.google.com and find out whether the United States has adopted the CISG.

United Nations Convention on Contracts for the International Sale of Goods (CISG)
Seventy countries and several international organizations created this law which governs contracts for the international sale of goods.

INTERNET EXERCISES AND CASE QUESTIONS

Working the Web Internet Exercises

1. Go to www.findlaw.com and review the extensive material on contracts. Determine the statute of limitations on written contracts in your jurisdiction.
2. Review www.perkinscoie.com as an example of one law firm's website. Examine the materials collected there on contract law by using the search feature for "contracts." How many different kinds can you find?
3. For international sales contracts, compare the CISG and the UCC by visiting the website www.cisg.law.pace.edu, which contains the entire text of the CISG and related information.
4. What is the rule regarding contractual capacity of minors in your jurisdiction? Use www.findlaw.com again to locate the statute. Hint: Using FindLaw, narrow your search by selecting your state first. Then enter your search terms.

CHAPTER 1 SUMMARY

CONTRACT OVERVIEW, p. 4

Definition of Contract

A contract is "a promise or a set of promises for the breach of which the law gives a remedy or the performance of which the law in some way recognizes a duty."

Parties to a Contract

1. *Offeror.* The party who makes an offer to enter into a contract is the offeror.
2. *Offeree.* The party to whom the offer is made is the offeree.

Elements of a Contract

1. Agreement
2. Consideration
3. Contractual capacity
4. Lawful object

Defenses to the Enforcement of a Contract

1. Genuineness of assent
2. Writing and form

Forms Contracts

SOURCES OF CONTRACT LAW, p. 8

Sources of Contract Law

1. Common law of contracts (law)
2. Uniform Commercial Code (law)
3. *Restatement (Second) of Contracts* (advisory only, not law)

Theories of Contract Law

1. *Classical law of contracts.* According to this theory, parties were free to negotiate contract terms without government interference.
2. *Modern law of contracts.* According to this theory, parties may negotiate contract terms subject to government regulations.

CLASSIFICATIONS OF CONTRACTS, p. 16

Formation

1. *Bilateral contract.* This is a promise for a promise.
2. *Unilateral contract.* This is a promise for an act.
3. *Express contract.* This is a contract expressed in oral or written words.
4. *Implied-in-fact contract.* This is a contract implied from the conduct of the parties.
5. *Quasi-contract.* This is a contract implied by law to prevent unjust enrichment and unjust detriment.
6. *Formal contract.* This is a contract that requires a special form or method for creation.
7. *Informal contract.* This is a contract that requires no special form or method for creation.

Enforceability

1. *Valid contract.* A valid contract meets all the essential elements to establish a contract.
2. *Void contract.* No contract exists.
3. *Voidable contract.* A voidable contract is one where one or both parties have the option of avoiding or enforcing the contract.
4. *Unenforceable contract.* An unenforceable contract is a contract that cannot be enforced because of a legal defense.

Performance

1. *Executed contract.* A contract that is fully performed on both sides is called an executed contract.
2. *Executory contract.* A contract that is not fully performed by one or both parties is called an executory contract.

TERMS AND CONCEPTS

Agreement 5
Alternative dispute resolution (ADR) 7
Arbitration 7
Article 2 (Sales) 9
Article 2A (Leases) 9
Bail bond 25
Bilateral contract 29
Classical law of contracts 6
Common law 6
Common law of contracts 6
Consideration 5
Contractual capacity 5
Electronic commerce (e-commerce) 15
Executed contract 26
Executory contract 26
Express contract 29
Formal contract 29

Genuineness of assent 6

Informal contract (simple contract) 25

Implied-in-fact contract 29

Lawful object 5

Lease contract 9

Legally enforceable 4

Letter of credit 25

Negotiable instrument 24

Nondisclosure agreement (NDA) 18

Objective theory of contracts 10

Offeree 28

Offeror 28

Quasi-contract (implied-in-law contract) 29

Reasonable person standard 10

Restatement of the Law of Contracts 9

Sales contract 9

The United Nations Convention on Contracts for the International Sale of Goods (CISG) 27

Unenforceable contract 27

Uniform Commercial Code (UCC) 8

Uniform Computer Information Transactions Act (UCITA) 9

Unilateral contract 16

Valid contract 26

Void contract 26

Voidable contract 26

Writing and form 6

CASE SCENARIO REVISITED

Let's go back to the Case Scenario at the beginning of the chapter. What would be the focus of your law firm's representation of Casey against Tom? Now that you understand more about implied-in-fact contracts, do you think an implied-in-fact contract could result from the conduct of unmarried persons who live together? To help you with your answer, take a look at the case of *Marvin v. Marvin*, 557 P.2d 106 (Cal. 1976).

CRITICAL LEGAL THINKING CASE

Critical Legal Thinking Case 1.1 *Bilateral or Unilateral Contract* G. S. Adams Jr., vice president of the Washington Bank & Trust Co., met with Bruce Bickham. An agreement was reached whereby Bickham agreed to do his personal and corporate banking business with the bank and the bank agreed to loan Bickham money at 7½ percent interest per annum. Bickham would have 10 years to repay the loans. For the next two years the bank made several loans to Bickham at 7½ percent interest. Adams then resigned from the bank. The bank notified Bickham that general economic changes made it necessary to charge a higher rate of interest on both outstanding and new loans. Bickham sued the bank for breach of contract. Was the contract a bilateral or a unilateral contract? Does Bickham win? *Bickham v. Washington Bank & Trust Co.*, 515 So. 2d 457 (La. App. 1987).

ETHICS CASES

Ethics Case 1.1   The Lewiston Lodge of Elks sponsored a golf tournament at the Fairlawn Country Club in Poland, Maine. For promotional purposes, Marcel Motors, an automobile dealership, agreed to give any golfer who shot a hole-in-one a new Dodge automobile. Fliers advertising the tournament were posted in the Elks Club and sent to potential participants. On the day of the tournament, the new Dodge automobile was parked near the clubhouse with one of the posters conspicuously displayed on the vehicle. Alphee Chenard Jr., who had seen the promotional literature regarding the hole-in-one offer, registered for the tournament and paid the requisite entrance fee. While playing the 13th hole of the golf course, in the presence of the other members of his foursome, Chenard shot a hole-in-one. When Marcel Motors refused to tender the automobile, Chenard sued for breach of contract. Was the contract a bilateral or a unilateral contract? Does Chenard win? Was it ethical for Marcel Motors to refuse to give the automobile to Chenard? *Chenard v. Marcel Motors*, 387 A.2d 596 (Me. 1978).

Ethics Case 1.2   Loren Vranich, a doctor practicing under the corporate name Family Health Care, P.C., entered into a written employment contract to hire Dennis Winkel. The contract provided for an annual salary, insurance benefits, and other employment benefits. Another doctor, Dr. Quan, also practiced with Dr. Vranich. About nine months later, when Dr. Quan left the practice, Vranich and Winkel entered into an oral modification of their written contract whereby Winkel was to receive a higher salary and a profit-sharing bonus. During the next year, Winkel received the increased salary. However, a disagreement arose, and Winkel sued to recover the profit-sharing bonus. Under Montana law, a written contract can be altered only in writing or by an executed oral agreement. Dr. Vranich argued that the contract could not be enforced because it was not in writing. Does Winkel receive the profit-sharing bonus? Did Dr. Vranich act ethically in raising the defense that the contract was not in writing? *Winkel v. Family Health Care, P.C.*, 668 P.2d 208 (Mont. 1983).

BRIEFING THE CASE WRITING ASSIGNMENT

Read Case A.1 in Appendix A (*Mark Realty, Inc. v. Rogness*). This case is excerpted from the appellate court's opinion. Review and brief the case. After briefing the case, you should be able to answer the following questions:

1. Who is the plaintiff? Who is the defendant?
2. Why did it make a difference if the court found the contract to be unilateral or bilateral? Who would win in each situation?
3. Which party did the appellate court find in favor of? What evidence did the court cite in reaching its conclusion?
4. How might owners of property protect themselves from paying a broker's commission if the owners sold the property themselves?

PRACTICE TIP

All contracts begin by setting out the date and the names of the parties contracting, using a format such as this:

AGREEMENT dated the _____ day of _____, 20_____, between _____ and _____.

"When I use a word," Humpty Dumpty said, in rather a scornful tone, "it means just what I choose it to mean—neither more nor less."

"The question is," said Alice, "whether you can make words mean so many different things."

"The question is," said Humpty Dumpty, "which is to be master—that's all."

—Lewis Carroll
Alice's Adventures in Wonderland (1865)

Agreement

CASE SCENARIO

The law firm where you work as a paralegal is representing Cheryl and Jim, husband and wife. One Friday night after work, Cheryl and Jim were drinking margaritas with their friend Nicholas.[1] Jim made a written offer to sell Nicholas 600 acres of hunting property that the couple owns for $5,000. Nicholas appeared to take the offer seriously and offered $5 to bind the deal. The next day, Nicholas pressured Jim and Cheryl to close on the hunting property. Because the property is actually worth $500,000, Jim and Cheryl refused to perform the contract.

---

[1] The specific issue of voluntary intoxication as it relates to capacity to contract is discussed in Chapter 4. For now, focus on the broader issue of this being a serious offer.

CHAPTER OBJECTIVES

After studying this chapter, you should be able to:

1. Define *offer* and *acceptance*.
2. Identify the terms that can be implied in a contract.
3. Understand *special offers* like auctions and advertisements.
4. Define *counteroffer* and describe the effects of counteroffers.
5. Describe how offers are terminated.
6. Describe auctions.
7. Understand how an offer can be accepted, including *acceptance by silence*.

■ CHAPTER INTRODUCTION

Contracts are voluntary agreements between the parties; that is, one party makes an offer that is accepted by the other party. Without *mutual assent*, there is no contract. Assent may be expressly evidenced by the oral or written words of the parties or implied from the conduct of the parties. This chapter discusses offer and acceptance.

PARALEGAL PERSPECTIVE

Allison Alger graduated in 2004 with her bachelor's degree in paralegal from Lewis-Clark State College in Lewiston, Idaho. She works in Lewiston as a legal assistant for the firm of Aherin, Rice & Anegon.

I work in a law firm with three attorneys who all do very different work, such as personal injury, medical malpractice, workers' compensation, family law, criminal work, and probates. Primarily, I work with cases involving business matters (corporations, LLCs, etc.), estate planning, probates, property matters, divorces, legal malpractice, and personal injury.

My responsibilities include drafting numerous legal documents for the attorneys' review such as on business and property matters, preparing and witnessing wills and other documents for estate planning, preparing agreements in divorce matters, and researching the breach of duty or contracts in legal malpractice cases. A substantial portion of my work is done independently under the guidelines set forth to me by each attorney.

It is vital for me to have a clear understanding of contract law in order to perform my work. I believe that this understanding comes from applying the valuable knowledge that I gained in the classroom to each of the cases that I am presented with in the workplace.

■ AGREEMENT

agreement
The manifestation by two or more persons of the substance of a contract.

Agreement is the manifestation by two or more persons of the substance of a contract. It requires an *offer* and an *acceptance*. The process of reaching an agreement usually proceeds as follows. Prior to entering into a contract, the parties may engage in preliminary negotiations about price, time of performance, and such. At some point during these negotiations, one party makes an offer. The person who makes the offer is called the **offeror**, and the person to whom the offer is made is called the **offeree**. The offer sets forth the terms under which the offeree is willing to enter into the contract. The offeree has the power to create an agreement by accepting the offer.

offeror
The party who makes an offer to enter into a contract. The party who makes an offer.

offeree
The party to whom an offer to enter into a contract is made. The party to whom an offer has been made.

Offer

Section 24 of the *Restatement (Second) of Contracts*[2] defines an **offer** as "the manifestation of willingness to enter into a bargain, so made as to justify another person in understanding that his assent to that bargain is invited and will conclude it." The following three elements are required for an offer to be effective:

offer
The manifestation of willingness to enter into a bargain, so made as to justify another person in understanding that his assent to that bargain is invited and will conclude it. [Section 24 of *Restatement (Second) of Contracts*]

1. The offeror must *objectively intend* to be bound by the offer.
2. The terms of the offer must be definite or reasonably *certain*.
3. The offer must be *communicated* to the offeree.

   Exhibit 2.1 shows the making of an offer.

_____

[2]Again, remember that the *Restatement* is not "law." The *Restatement* is a summary of judge-made doctrines and input from law professors, practicing attorneys, and judges. However, even though the *Restatement* is not law, it is held in very high regard as an authority on the topic of contract law and is followed by many courts.

Exhibit 2.1 Offer

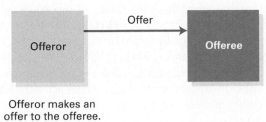

Offeror makes an
offer to the offeree.

Objective Intent

The intent to enter into a contract is determined using the **objective theory of contracts**—that is, whether a reasonable person viewing the circumstances would conclude that the parties intended to be legally bound. Subjective intent is irrelevant. Therefore, no valid contract results from preliminary negotiations, offers that are an expression of opinion, or offers made in jest, anger, or undue excitement.

Preliminary Negotiations: For example, a question such as "Are you interested in selling your building for $2 million?" is not an offer. It is an invitation to make an offer or an invitation to negotiate. The statement "I will buy your building for $2 million" is a valid offer, however, because it indicates the offeror's present intent to contract.

Offers That Are Made in Jest, Anger, or Undue Excitement: For example, suppose the owner of Company A has lunch with the owner of Company B. In the course of their conversation, Company A's owner exclaims in frustration, "For $2 I'd sell the whole computer division!" An offer such as that cannot result in a valid contract.

Offers That Are an Expression of an Opinion: A lawyer who tells her client that she thinks the lawsuit will result in an award of $100,000 cannot be sued for the difference if the trial jury awards only $50,000. The lawyer's statement is not an enforceable promise.

objective theory of contracts
A theory that says that the intent to contract is judged by the reasonable person standard and not by the subjective intent of the parties.

 # E-Commerce & Information Technology

Contracting by Fax and E-Mail

Throughout history, contract law has struggled to keep pace with inventions that change the way that we communicate and form contracts with each other. The latest technological challenges to come down the pike are the fax machine and e-mail, both of which have become indispensable means of business communication. Although faxes and e-mails have revolutionized communications by enabling the instantaneous exchange of written documents between people in distant corners of the world, they have also caused a variety of problems. For example, amid the flurry of faxes and e-mails that are sent back and forth during the contractual negotiations, it is sometimes difficult to tell exactly when the haggling ended and an agreement was reached.

There are several problems that the courts must address concerning faxes and e-mails as contracts. First, the courts must examine them to determine if an agreement was reached and, if so, the terms of the agreement. Courts examine faxes and e-mails the same way they examine other documents in determining whether a meeting of the minds was reached. Therefore, it is important for businesses to retain copies of faxes and e-mails so they can substantiate the contracts they have entered into. Second, to reinforce a written contract against a party, his

(continued)

or her signature must appear in writing. Most court decisions that have addressed the issue have recognized the enforceability of signatures sent by fax. Otherwise, the rules regarding oral contracts apply to faxes. The enforceability of "signatures" sent by e-mail is not yet totally settled by the courts.

As faxes and e-mails are used increasingly to communicate everything from orders for concert tickets to multimillion-dollar orders for equipment, judges and juries will be called on to read through stacks of faxes and e-mails to decide if disputing parties ever really reached an agreement and, if so, what they really agreed on.

Definiteness of Terms

The terms of an offer must be clear enough for the offeree to be able to decide whether to accept or reject the terms of the offer. If the terms are indefinite, the courts cannot enforce the contract or determine an appropriate remedy for its breach.

To be considered definite, an offer (and contract) generally must contain the following terms: (1) identification of the parties, (2) identification of the subject matter and quantity, (3) consideration to be paid, and (4) time of performance. Complex contracts usually state additional terms.

Implied Terms

The common law of contracts required an exact specification of contract terms. If one essential term was omitted, the courts would hold that no contract had been made. This rule was inflexible.

The modern law of contracts is more lenient. The *Restatement (Second) of Contracts* merely requires that the terms of the offer be "reasonably certain."[3] Accordingly, the court can supply a missing term if a reasonable term can be implied.[4] The definition of *reasonable* depends on the circumstances. Terms that are supplied in this way are called **implied terms**.

implied term
A term in a contract that can reasonably be supplied by the courts.

Generally, time of performance can be implied. Price can be implied if there is a market or source from which to determine the price of the item or service—for example, the "blue book" for an automobile price, the New York Stock Exchange for a stock price. The parties or subject matter of the contract usually cannot be implied if an item or a service is unique or personal, such as the construction of a house or the performance of a professional sports contract.

In the following case, the court applied the adage "A contract is a contract is a contract."

CASE 2.1 CONTRACT

Marder v. Lopez, 450 F.3d 445 (9th Cir. 2006).

"Though in hindsight the agreement appears to be unfair to Marder—she only received $2,300 in exchange for a release of all claims relating to a movie that grossed over $150 million."

Judge Pregerson, *United States Court of Appeals for the Ninth Circuit*

---

[3] *Restatement (Second) of Contracts*, Section 204.
[4] Section 87(2) of the *Restatement (Second) of Contracts* states that an offer which the offeror should reasonably expect to induce action or forbearance of a substantial character on the part of the offeree before acceptance and which does induce such action or forbearance is binding as an option contract to the extent necessary to avoid injustice.

Facts

The movie *Flashdance* tells a story of a woman construction worker who performs at night as an exotic dancer. She performs an innovative form of dancing that includes a chair dance. Her goal is to obtain formal dance training at a university. The movie is based on the life of Maureen Marder, a nightclub dancer. Paramount Pictures Corporation used information from Marder to create the screenplay for the movie. Paramount paid Marder $2,300 and Marder signed a General Release that provides that Marder "releases and discharges Paramount Pictures Corporation . . . of and from each and every claim, demand, debt, liability, cost and expense of any kind or character which have risen or are based in whole or in part on any matters occurring at any time prior to the date of this Release." Marder also released Paramount from claims "arising out of or in any way connected with either directly or indirectly, any and all arrangements . . . in connection with the preparation of screenplay material and the production, filming and exploitation of . . . *Flashdance*."

Paramount released the movie *Flashdance*, which grossed over $150 million in domestic box office and is still shown on television and distributed through DVD rentals. Subsequently, Sony Music Entertainment paid Paramount for release of copyright and produced a music video for the Jennifer Lopez song "I'm Glad." The video featured Lopez's performance as a dancer and singer. Marder believed that the video contains recreations of many well-known scenes from *Flashdance*.

Marder brought a lawsuit in U.S. district court against Paramount, Sony, and Lopez. Marder sought a declaration that she had rights as a co-author of *Flashdance* and a co-owner with Paramount of the copyright to *Flashdance*. She sued Sony and Lopez for allegedly violating her copyright in *Flashdance*. The district court dismissed Marder's claims against Paramount, Sony, and Lopez. Marder appealed.

Issue

Was the General Release signed by Marder an enforceable contract?

Language of the Court

The Release's language is exceptionally broad and we hold that it is fatal to each of Marder's claims against Paramount. Such a release of "each and every claim" covers all claims within the scope of the language. Accordingly, the law imputes to Marder an intention corresponding to the reasonable meaning of her words and acts. Here, Marder released a broad array of claims relating to any assistance she provided during the creation of a Hollywood movie. Thus, the only reasonable interpretation of the Release is that it encompasses the various copyright claims she asserts in the instant suit.

Though in hindsight the agreement appears to be unfair to Marder—she only received $2,300 in exchange for a release of all claims relating to a movie that grossed over $150 million—there is simply no evidence that her consent was obtained by fraud, deception, misrepresentation, duress, or undue influence.

We also affirm the district court's dismissal of claims against Sony and Lopez. As we held above, under the terms of the Release, Marder cannot sue Paramount to assert a co-ownership in Flashdance. It is therefore impossible for her to establish a prima facie case of copyright infringement against Sony and Lopez.

Decision

The U.S. Court of Appeals held that the General Release signed by Marder was an enforceable contract. The court of appeals affirmed the judgment of the district court that dismissed Marder's complaint against Paramount, Sony, and Lopez.

Law & Ethics Questions

1. What does the adage "A contract is a contract is a contract" mean? Was it applied in this case?

2. **Ethics** Why did Marder bring this lawsuit? Did she act ethically in bringing this lawsuit? Why or why not?

3. **Ethics** Do you think Paramount should have paid Marder more money after the movie *Flashdance* became a success?

Web Exercises

1. **Web** Visit the website of the U.S. Court of Appeals for the Ninth Circuit at www.ca9.uscourts.gov.

2. **Web** Use www.google.com and find a video clip from the movie *Flashdance*.

3. **Web** Visit the website of Jennifer Lopez at www.jenniferlopez.com.

4. **Web** Use www.google.com and find a video clip of Jennifer Lopez's music video where she dances and sings the song "I'm Glad."

ETHICS SPOTLIGHT

"A CONTRACT IS A CONTRACT IS A CONTRACT"

"The disputed agreement transferred plaintiff's copyright in the Mighty Morphin Power Rangers' logo with as much specificity as the law requires."

Judge Kozinski

Mighty Morphin Power Rangers was a phenomenal success as a television series. The Power Rangers battled to save the universe from all sorts of diabolical plots and bad guys. They were also featured in a profitable line of toys and garments bearing the Power Rangers' logo. The Power Rangers' name and logo are known to millions of children and their parents worldwide. The claim of ownership of the logo for the Power Rangers ended up in a battle in a courtroom.

David Dees is a designer who works as d.b.a. David Dees Illustration. Saban Entertainment, Inc. (Saban), which owns the copyright and trademark to Power Rangers figures and the name "Power Ranger," hired Dees as an independent contractor to design a logo for the Power Rangers. The contract signed by the parties was titled "Work-for-Hire/Independent Contractor Agreement." The contract was drafted by Saban with the help of its attorneys; Dees signed the agreement without the representation of legal counsel.

Dees designed the logo currently used for the Power Rangers and was paid $250 to transfer his copyright ownership in the logo. Subsequently, Dees sued Saban to recover damages for copyright and trademark infringement. Saban defended, arguing that Dees was bound by the agreement he had signed.

The trial court agreed with Saban, finding that the "Work-for-Hire/Independent Contractor Agreement" was an enforceable contract between the parties and that Dees had transferred his ownership interests in the logo to Saban. Dees appealed. The court of appeals affirmed the judgment for Saban, stating, "The disputed agreement transferred plaintiff's copyright in the Mighty Morphin Power Rangers' logo with as much specificity as the law requires." The court found that a contract is a contract is a contract, at least in this case. Dees's appeal to the U.S. Supreme Court was denied. *Dees v. Saban Entm't, Inc.*, 131 F.3d 146 (9th Cir. 1997).

Law & Ethics Questions

1. Should a contract be enforced as written, even if it is later discovered that one party benefited substantially more than the other party to the contract?
2. **Ethics** Did Dees act ethically by suing for more money?

Web Exercises

1. **Web** Visit the U.S. Court of Appeals for the Ninth Circuit at www.ca9.uscourts.gov.
2. **Web** Use www.google.com and find a video clip of the Mighty Morphin Power Rangers.

Communication

An offer cannot be accepted if it is not communicated to the offeree by the offeror or a representative or an agent of the offeror.

Example: Suppose Mr. Jones, the CEO of Ace Corporation, wants to sell a manufacturing division to Baker Corporation. He puts the offer in writing, but he does not send it. Assume that Mr. Griswald, the CEO of Baker Corporation, visits Mr. Jones and sees the written offer lying on Jones's desk. Griswald tells his CEO about the offer. Because Mr. Jones never communicated the offer to the CEO of Baker Corporation, there is no offer to be accepted.

CAREER FRONT

Job Description: Collections Paralegal

A collections paralegal can be involved with contracts in the following ways:

Preliminary Investigation

- Obtain all documentation from the client concerning the account, including information about the debtor, invoices, contracts, promissory notes, payments, and related correspondence.
- Investigate public records for information about debtor's financial status, including real estate records and prior judgments.
- Draft demand letter to debtor.

Commencement of Formal Action

- Draft complaint and prepare exhibits (such as a copy of the contract) in support of complaint.
- Monitor date for response to complaint and, if appropriate, draft motion for default judgment for attorney review.
- Assist attorney at hearing for initial claim for plaintiff.

(continued)

- Draft documents for examination of debtor for attorney review; assist attorney with examination.
- Draft sworn denial if collection is sued on a sworn account.
- Draft journal entry, default or otherwise.
- Obtain certified copy of judgment transcript.

Post-Judgment Activities

- Abstract the judgment, obtain a writ of execution, and request that the sheriff attempt to collect what is owed on the writ of execution.
- Arrange for indemnity bond from sheriff.
- Draft notice of lien on real property.
- Prepare bid and attend sheriff's sale of real property.
- Track redemption period and, if appropriate, prepare documents to redeem real property.
- Arrange for posting or publication of notice of sale.
- Maintain communication with sheriff about levy on personal property.
- Negotiate agreement for payment arrangements for attorney/client approval.
- Draft promissory note reflecting payment agreement.
- Correspond with client informing status of collection.
- Maintain judgment account worksheet to record payments, collection costs, and court costs.
- When debt is collected, draft satisfaction of judgment to release judgment.
- Draft release of judgment or release of lien.
- If or when appropriate, file request for dismissal form.

Source: Excerpted by permission from the National Association of Legal Assistants (www.nala.org) and the National Federation of Paralegal Associations, Inc. (www.paralegals.org).

Special Offers

In several special situations there is a question of whether an offer has been made. *Advertisements*, *rewards*, and *auctions* are examples of such situations. These special offers are discussed in the following paragraphs.

advertisement
A general advertisement is an invitation to make an offer. A specific advertisement is an offer.

Advertisements   **Advertisements** for the sale of goods, even at specific prices, generally are treated as *invitations to make an offer*.

Example: Catalogs, price lists, quotation sheets, offering circulars, and other sales materials are viewed in the same way. This rule is intended to protect advertiser/sellers from the unwarranted breach of contract suits for nonperformance that would otherwise arise if the seller ran out of the advertised goods.

There is one exception to this rule: An advertisement is considered an offer if it is so definite or specific that it is apparent that the advertiser has the present intent to bind himself or herself to the terms of the advertisement.

Example: An automobile dealer's advertisement to sell a "previously owned maroon 2004 Lexus 330 SUV, serial no. 3210674, $30,000" is an offer. Because the advertisement identifies the exact automobile for sale, the first person to accept the offer owns the automobile.

Consider the two examples just cited in light of the case *Mesaros v. United States*. In that case, the court had to decide whether an advertisement was a solicitation of an offer or an offer.

CASE 2.2   INVITATION TO MAKE AN OFFER

Mesaros v. United States, 845 F.2d 1576 (Fed. Cir. 1988).

> "It is well established that materials such as those mailed to prospective customers
> by the Mint are no more than advertisements or invitations to deal."
>
> Judge Skelton, *United States Court of Appeals for the Federal Circuit*

Facts

The U.S. Congress directed the secretary of the treasury to mint and sell a stated number of specially minted commemorative coins to raise funds to restore and renovate the Statue of Liberty. The U.S. Mint mailed advertising materials to persons, including Mary and Anthony C. Mesaros, husband and wife, that described the various types of coins that were to be issued. Payment could be made by check, money order, or credit card. The materials included an order form. Directly above the space provided on this form for the customer's signature was the following: "YES, Please accept my order for the U.S. Liberty Coins I have indicated." Mary Mesaros forwarded to the mint a credit-card order of $1,675 for certain coins, including the $5 gold coin. All credit-card orders were forwarded by the Mint to Mellon Bank in Pittsburgh, Pennsylvania, for verification, which took a period of time. Meanwhile, cash orders were filled immediately, and orders by check were filled as the checks cleared. The issuance of 500,000 gold coins was exhausted before Mesaros's credit-card order could be filled. The Mint sent a letter to the Mesaroses, notifying them of this fact. The gold coin increased in value by 200 percent within the first few months of 1986. Mary and Anthony C. Mesaros filed a class action lawsuit against the United States, seeking in the alternative either damages for breach of contract or a decree of mandamus ordering the Mint to deliver the gold coins to the plaintiffs. The district court held for the Mint. The Mesaroses appealed.

Issue

Was the U.S. Mint's advertisement a solicitation of an offer or an offer?

Language of the Court

The plaintiffs contend that the materials sent to them by the Mint, including the order form, constituted an offer that upon acceptance by the plaintiffs created a binding contract between them and the government whereby the government was bound and obligated to deliver the coins ordered by them. The great weight of authority is against the plaintiffs. It is well established that materials such as those mailed to prospective customers by the Mint are no more than advertisements or invitations to deal. They are mere notices and solicitations for offers that create no power of acceptance in the recipient.

A basic rule of contracts holds that whether an offer has been made depends on the objective reasonableness of the alleged offeree's belief that the advertisement or solicitation was intended as an offer. Generally, it is considered unreasonable for a person to believe that advertisements and solicitations are offers that bind the advertiser. Otherwise, the advertiser could be bound by an excessive number of contracts requiring delivery of goods far in excess of amounts available. That is particularly true in the instant case where the gold coins were limited to 500,000 by the act of Congress.

We conclude that a thorough reading, construction, and interpretation of the materials sent to the plaintiffs by the Mint makes clear that the contention of the plaintiffs that they reasonably believed the materials were intended as an offer is unreasonable as a matter of law. This is especially true in view of the words "YES, Please accept my order..." that were printed on the credit-card form, which showed that the credit-card order was an offer from the plaintiffs to the Mint to buy the coins, which offer might or might not be accepted by the Mint. Accordingly, the Mint materials were intended solely as solicitations of offers from customers that were subject to acceptance by the Mint before the Mint would be bound by a contract.

Decision

The court of appeals held that the advertising materials sent out by the U.S. Mint were a solicitation to make an offer and not an offer. Therefore, the Mint wins.

Law & Ethics Questions

1. Should an advertisement be treated as an offer instead of as an invitation to make an offer? Why or why not?

2. **Ethics** Do you think the Mesaroses acted ethically by suing the Mint?

3. Would it cause any problems for businesses if advertisements were considered offers? Explain.

Web Exercises

1. **Web** Visit the website of the U.S. Court of Appeals for the Federal Circuit at www.fedcir.gov.

2. **Web** Visit the website of the U.S. Mint at www.usmint.gov.

3. **Web** Use www.google.com and find an article that discusses U.S. Liberty Coins and their value today.

 # E-Commerce & Information Technology

Online Auctions

Auctions have been used traditionally to sell horses, antiques, paintings, and other such one-of-a-kind items. A bidder usually had to be physically present at the auction to bid, although some auctions allow telephone bids from prequalified callers. Because of these restrictions, auctions occupied a small portion of the U.S. economy. But no more, thanks to the advent of the Internet.

Led by the giant online auction house eBay, online auctions have exploded on the Internet. eBay started as a small online auction house that made a market in such consumer collectibles as Pez dispensers, Beanie Babies, and such. After seeing how successful this mode of business was for these items, eBay expanded into a full-service online auctioneer. By the year 2000, eBay was offering several million items each day for sale over the Internet. The millions of eBay's cybershoppers are loyal, spending an average of 130 minutes per month at the eBay auction site.

eBay does not own the items it sells. Instead, sellers list the items they want to auction on the eBay site, and buyers bid for the items. The purchase contract is between the cyberseller and the cyberbuyer. One of the problems with Internet auctions is that many sellers do not take credit cards, so payment must be made

(continued)

by check or cash. Thus, many transactions take days, if not weeks, to complete. eBay takes a 6 percent commission on items sold by its online auction house. In the beginning of online auctions, most of the goods sold were goods that were customarily sold at flea markets, antique stores, and classified advertisements. Today, many businesses have started using eBay auctions to sell their excess inventory or to sell mainstream consumer and business goods. Business sales through online auctions now exceed nonbusiness sales.

eBay is now receiving stiff competition from many other online auctioneers. The giant e-commerce leader Amazon.com conducts online auctions, and many small online auction houses specialize in selling jewelry, baseball cards, horses, and other items. eBay itself began offering localized auctions in individual cities for such large items as cars and furniture. Even traditional auction houses such as Sotheby's, which auctions pricey items like paintings, jewelry, and antiques, have begun selling through online auctions. As proven by the success of eBay and other online auctioneers, consumers and businesses have embraced the dynamic pricing and fluid give-and-take of Internet auctions. Auctions, which have been around for most of history, are again giving fixed-priced selling, which has only been around for about 100 years, a run for its money.

Rewards   An offer to pay a **reward** (e.g., for the return of lost property or the capture of a criminal) is an offer to form a unilateral contract. To be entitled to collect the reward, the offeree must (1) have knowledge of the reward offer prior to completing the requested act and (2) perform the requested act.

reward
To collect a reward, the offeree must (1) have knowledge of the reward offer prior to completing the requested act and (2) perform the requested act.

Example: John Anderson accidentally leaves a briefcase containing $500,000 in negotiable bonds on a subway train. He places newspaper ads stating, "$5,000 reward for return of briefcase left on a train in Manhattan on January 10, 2010, at approximately 10 A.M. Call 212-555-6789." Helen Smith, who is unaware of the offer, finds the briefcase. She reads the luggage tag containing Anderson's name, address, and telephone number, and she returns the briefcase to him. She is not entitled to the reward money because she did not know about it when she performed the requested act.

PARALEGAL PERSPECTIVE

Natalie H. Holman is a litigation paralegal with the law firm of Randall, Blake & Cox, PLLC, in Lewiston, Idaho. She is a graduate of Lewis-Clark State College with an associate of applied science (AAS) and bachelor of applied science (BAS) degrees in paralegal studies.

As a litigation paralegal, the attorneys in my firm depend on me to evaluate, prepare, and assist them with their complex case files. Many of these cases include disputes arising from real estate contracts, such as construction contracts, purchase and sale agreements, and leases.

After the attorney holds the initial conference with the client to determine his/her/their dispute, it is my responsibility to review the information provided by the client, organize the case file, carefully outline the elements of the case that are in dispute, inform the supervising attorney of my findings, and begin drafting the initial pleadings to commence a lawsuit.

When bringing a real estate dispute before the court, the contract is always the most important element of a plaintiff's case. It is my duty to understand and prepare the attorney for the variety of different ways the contract can be applied to the facts of a particular case. Without understanding the different elements of a contract, this interpretation would be difficult to convey to the supervising attorney.

My work as a litigation paralegal is demanding but rewarding when the client and attorneys are pleased with my hard work and the outcome of a case.

auction with reserve
Unless expressly stated otherwise, an auction is an auction with reserve; that is, the seller retains the right to refuse the highest bid and withdraw the goods from sale.

auction without reserve
An auction in which the seller expressly gives up his or her right to withdraw the goods from sale and must accept the highest bid.

Auctions   At an auction, the seller offers goods for sale through an auctioneer. Unless otherwise expressly stated, an auction is considered an **auction with reserve**—that is, it is an invitation to make an offer. The seller retains the right to refuse the highest bid and withdraw the goods from sale. A contract is formed only when the auctioneer strikes the gavel down or indicates acceptance by some other means. The bidder may withdraw his or her bid prior to that time.

If an auction is expressly announced to be an **auction without reserve**, the participants reverse the roles: The seller is the offeror, and the bidders are the offerees. The seller must accept the highest bid and cannot withdraw the goods from sale. A seller who sets a minimum bid has to sell the item only if the highest bid is equal to or greater than the minimum bid.

In the following case, the court addressed the issue of an auction.

CASE 2.3   AUCTION

Lim v. The.TV Corp. Int'l, 121 Cal. Rptr. 2d 323 (Ct. App. 2002).

> *"Defendant put the name "Golf.tv" up for public auction, and plaintiff bid on that name and no other. That was an offer and acceptance, and formed a contract."*

Judge Epstein, *Court of Appeals of California*

Facts

The island nation of Tuvalu was awarded the top-level domain name "tv." Thus, Tuvalu controlled who could use domain names with the suffix "tv" on the Internet. For example, if a person named Jones acquired the suffix tv, her domain name on the Internet would be "jones.tv." Tuvalu hired The.TV Corporation International, a California corporation doing business under the name dotTV, to sell Internet names bearing the top-level domain name "tv." In April 2000, dotTV posted the name "golf.tv" for sale on its website, to be sold to the highest bidder. Je Ho Lim, a resident of South Korea, submitted the highest bid of $1,010 and authorized dotTV to charge his credit card for the amount of the bid. DotTV sent the following e-mail to Lim confirming the sale:

> DotTV—The New Frontier on the Internet
> E-Mail Invoice for Domain Registration
> NAME: Je Ho Lim
> Congratulations!
> You have won the auction for the following domain name:
> DOMAIN NAME: --golf
> SUBSCRIPTION LENGTH: 2 years, starts from activation date
> Amount (US$): $1,010 (first year registration fee)
> Please remember that the annual registration fee increases by 5% annually.
> You have the guaranteed right to renew the registration indefinitely.
> DotTV expects to charge your card and activate the registered domain name by May 15, 2000.
> See ya on the new frontier of the Internet!
> Lou Kerner CEO, dotTV Corporation www.TV

Shortly thereafter, dotTV sent another e-mail to Lim that stated, "We have decided to release you from your bid" and that Lim should disregard the prior e-mail because of "an e-mail error that occurred." Later, dotTV publicly offered the domain name "golf.tv" with a beginning bid of $1 million. DotTV claimed that its original e-mail to Lim concerned a different domain name, "--golf," instead of "golf." Lim countered that characters such as two dashes ("--") are not recognized on the Internet and therefore the name "--golf" is an invalid domain name. When dotTV refused to transfer the domain name "golf.tv" to Lim, Lim sued dotTV for breach of contract. The trial court dismissed Lim's case against dotTV. Lim appealed.

Issue

Did Lim properly state a cause of action for breach of contract against dotTV?

Language of the Court

Defendant put the name "Golf.tv" up for public auction, and plaintiff bid on that name and no other. That was an offer and acceptance, and it formed a contract. The distinction between "Golf.tv" and "--Golf.tv" comes from the acceptance e-mail sent by defendant. Certainly the hyphens preceding the name "golf" could not defeat the existence of an already formed contract. Defendant was accepting plaintiff's bid; it plainly was not making a counteroffer, particularly because, according to the pleading, the name "--Golf" did not "compute"; it did not qualify as a domain name. The e-mail must be read as an acknowledgment of plaintiff's winning bid and acceptance of the contract.

Decision

The court of appeals held that plaintiff Lim had properly pleaded a cause of action against defendant dotTV for breach of contract and reinstated Lim's case against dotTV.

Law & Ethics Questions

1. Explain the difference between an auction with reserve and an auction without reserve. Which is presumed if there is no other statement to the contrary?

2. **Ethics** Did dotTV act ethically in this case? Why do you think that dotTV reneged on its e-mail confirmation to Lim?

3. Are Internet domain names valuable? How do you register an Internet domain name?

Web Exercises

1. **Web** Visit the website of the Court of Appeal of California, Second Appellate District at www.courtinfo.ca.gov/courts/courtsofappeal.

2. **Web** Visit the website of dotTV at www.tv.

3. **Web** Think up an Internet domain name you would like to have. Go to the Network Solutions website at www.networksolutions.com to see if that name is available.

Concept Summary

Types of Auctions

Type	Offer
Auction with reserve	No. It is an invitation to make an offer. Because the bidder is the offeror, the seller (the offeree) may refuse to sell the goods. An auction is with reserve unless otherwise stated.
Auction without reserve	Yes. The seller is the offeror and must sell the goods to the highest bidder (the offeree). An auction is without reserve only if it is stipulated as such.

MARKETPLACE

Corporate Real Estate Paralegal Job Announcement

National corporation seeks an experienced corporate real estate paralegal to work in its legal department. The paralegal will assist with preparing purchase agreements and other real estate transaction paperwork.

Pay to $60k. Must have at least 3 years of experience as a corporate paralegal with a large law firm or corporate legal department. Experience handling commercial real estate transactions strongly preferred. Bachelor's and/or paralegal certificate strongly preferred.

Please e-mail your resume to:

Termination of Offers

An offer may be terminated by the actions of the parties or by operation of laws. The termination of offers is discussed in the following paragraphs.

Revocation of an Offer by the Offeror   Under the common law, an offeror may revoke (i.e., withdraw) an offer any time prior to its acceptance by the offeree. Generally, an offer can be so revoked even if the offeror promised to keep the offer open for a longer time. The revocation may be communicated to the offeree by the offeror or by a third party and made by (1) the offeror's express statement (e.g., "I hereby withdraw my offer") or (2) an act of the offeror that is inconsistent with the offer (e.g., selling the goods to another party). Most states provide that a revocation is not effective until it is actually received by the offeree or the offeree's agent.

Offers made to the public may be revoked by communicating the revocation by the same means used to make the offer.

Example: If a reward offer for a lost watch was published in two local newspapers each week for four weeks, notice of revocation must be published in the same newspapers for the same length of time. The revocation is effective against all offerees, even those who saw the reward offer but not the notice of revocation.

THE ETHICAL PARALEGAL

Confidentiality

If an attorney is to be able to represent a client adequately, the attorney must know all of the facts relating to the client's case. However, without the attorney's guarantee of confidentiality, the client would never disclose all of those facts to the attorney. As a result, ABA Model Rule 1.6 requires that the legal professional owes the client a duty of confidentiality.[5]

One area in which the ethical paralegal should be on guard is protecting the client's confidentiality when technology is used in the law office. If an e-mail or a fax on case strategy was inadvertently sent by the paralegal to opposing counsel instead of co-counsel, a client's case would be seriously compromised. Although this example brings up questions regarding opposing counsel's duty regarding receipt of privileged and confidential information, it still remains that the client's confidentiality would have been breached, and it would have been the paralegal who did so.

Rejection of an Offer by the Offeree   An offer is terminated if the offeree **rejects** it. Any subsequent attempt by the offeree to accept the offer is ineffective and is construed as a new offer that the original offeror (now the offeree) is free to accept or reject. A rejection may be evidenced by the offeree's express words (oral or written) or conduct. Generally, a rejection is not effective until it is actually received by the offeror.

rejection
Nonacceptance or withdrawal of the offer prior to its acceptance.

Example: Harriet Jackson, sales manager of IBM Corporation, offers to sell 1,000 computers to Ted Green, purchasing manager of General Motors Corporation, for $250,000. The offer is made on August 1. Green telephones Jackson to say that he is not interested. This rejection terminates the offer. If Green later decides that he wants to purchase the computers, an entirely new contract must be formed.

Counteroffer by the Offeree   A **counteroffer by the offeree** simultaneously terminates the offeror's offer and creates a new offer.

counteroffer
A response by an offeree that contains terms and conditions different from or in addition to those of the offer. A counteroffer terminates an offer.

Example: Suppose that Fei Jia says to Harold Brown, "I will sell you my house for $700,000." Brown says, "I think $700,000 is too high; I will pay you $600,000." Brown has made a counteroffer. The original offer is terminated, and the counteroffer is a new offer that Jia is free to accept or reject.

In the following case, the court found that a counteroffer had been made.

CASE 2.4   COUNTEROFFER

McLaughlin v. Heikkila, 697 N.W.2d 231 (Minn. Ct. App. 2005).

> "A written offer does not evidence a completed contract
> and a written acceptance is required."
>
> Judge Dietzen, *Court of Appeals of Minnesota*

---

[5] Copies of the ABA Model Rules of Professional Conduct are available from Service Center, American Bar Association, 321 North Clark Street, Chicago, IL 60610, 1-800-285-2221. The Model Rules can also be viewed online at http://www.abanet.org/cpr/mrpc/mrpc_toc.html.

Facts

Wilbert Heikkila listed eight parcels of real property for sale. David McLaughlin submitted written offers to purchase three of the parcels. Three printed purchase agreements were prepared and submitted to Heikkila with three earnest-money checks from McLaughlin. Writing on the purchase agreements, Heikkila changed the price of one parcel from $145,000 to $150,000, the price of another parcel from $32,000 to $45,000, and the price of the third parcel from $175,000 to $179,000. Heikkila also changed the closing dates on all three of the properties, added a reservation of mineral rights to all three, and signed the purchase agreements.

McLaughlin did not sign the purchase agreements to accept the changes before Heikkila withdrew his offer to sell. McLaughlin sued to compel specific performance of the purchase agreements under the terms of the agreements before Heikkila withdrew his offer. The district court granted Heikkila's motion to dismiss McLaughlin's claim. McLaughlin appealed.

Issue

Did a contract to convey real property exist between Heikkila and McLaughlin?

Language of the Court

A written offer does not evidence a completed contract and a written acceptance is required. Minnesota has followed the "mirror image rule" in analyzing acceptance of offers. Under that rule, an acceptance must be coextensive with the offer and may not introduce additional terms or conditions. The district court correctly concluded that Heikkila's alterations of the purchase agreements constituted a rejection and counteroffer. Heikkila withdrew the counteroffer before McLaughlin provided a written acceptance, as he was entitled to do. Only a written acceptance by McLaughlin of the written terms proposed by Heikkila on the purchase agreements would have created a binding contract for the sale of land. Without a written acceptance and delivery to the other party to the agreement, no contract was formed.

Decision

The court of appeals held that because McLaughlin did not sign or otherwise accept in writing Heikkila's counteroffers, there was no contract for the sale of land between the parties. The court of appeals affirmed the district court's grant of summary judgment in favor of Heikkila.

Law & Ethics Questions

1. What is a counteroffer? When a counteroffer is made, what happens to the prior offer?

2. The term "mirror image" is used in this case. Look up that term in a legal dictionary or thesaurus.

3. **Ethics** Did McLaughlin have much of a chance to win this lawsuit?

4. **Ethics** Did Heikkila act ethically in withdrawing his offers in this case?

Web Exercises

1. **Web** Visit the website of the Court of Appeals of Minnesota at www.courts
.state.mn.us.

2. **Web** Use www.google.com and find an article that discusses counteroffers.

Concept Summary

Termination of an Offer by Action of the Parties

Action	Description
Revocation	The offeror *revokes* (withdraws) the offer any time prior to its acceptance by the offeree.
Rejection	The offeree rejects the offer by his or her words or conduct.
Counteroffer	A counteroffer by the offeree creates a new offer and terminates the offeror's offer.

Destruction of the Subject Matter   An offer terminates if the subject matter of the offer is destroyed through no fault of either party prior to the offer's acceptance. For example, if a fire destroys an office building that has been listed for sale, the offer automatically terminates.

Death or Incompetency of the Offeror or Offeree   The death or incompetency of either the offeror or the offeree terminates an offer. Notice of the other party's death or incompetence is not a requirement.

Example: Suppose that on June 1, Shari Hunter offers to sell her house to Damian Coe for $100,000, provided he decides on or before June 15. Hunter dies on June 7, before Coe has made up his mind. Because there is no contract prior to her death, the offer automatically terminates on June 7.

Supervening Illegality   If the object of an offer is made illegal prior to the acceptance of the offer, the offer terminates. This situation, which usually occurs when a statute is enacted or a court case is announced that makes the object of the offer illegal, is called a **supervening illegality**.

Example: Suppose City Bank offers to loan ABC Corporation $5 million at an 18 percent interest rate. Prior to ABC's acceptance of the offer, the state legislature enacts a statute that sets a usury interest rate of 12 percent. City Bank's offer to ABC Corporation is automatically terminated when the usury statute becomes effective.

Lapse of Time   An offer expires at the **lapse of time** of an offer. An offer may state that it is effective only until a certain date. Unless otherwise stated, the time period begins to run when the offer is actually received by the offeree and terminates when the stated time period expires.

Example: Statements such as "This offer is good for 10 days" or "This offer must be accepted by January 1, 2002" are examples of such notices.

If no time is stated in the offer, the offer terminates after a "reasonable time" dictated by the circumstances. A reasonable time to accept an offer to purchase stock traded on a national stock exchange may be a few moments, but a reasonable time to accept an offer to purchase a house may be a few days. Unless otherwise stated, an offer made face to face or during a telephone call usually expires when the conversation ends.

supervening illegality
The enactment of a statute, regulation, or court decision that makes the object of an offer illegal. This action terminates the offer.

lapse of time
An offer terminates when a stated time period expires. If no time is stated, an offer terminates after a reasonable time.

PARALEGAL PERSPECTIVE

Sara Hall is a graduate of the University of Tennessee at Chattanooga's Legal Studies Program. She currently works in the health care sales industry in Tennessee.

Before entering into the health care sales industry, I worked as an in-house paralegal for a local utility. As an in-house paralegal, contracts were a part of my daily routine. Our clients were not clients in the traditional sense of the word. The clients were the other divisions in the utility. Those divisions relied on our legal expertise to assist them in the closing of contracts and other agreements for services provided by outside vendors.

As an in-house paralegal, it was my job to first review the request for purchase (RFP) documents that were sent out prior to selecting a vendor for the needed service. Next, I would review the response to the RFP to ensure that all legal obligations had been met by the chosen vendor. Lastly, I would use those documents to draft the contract to be reviewed by my supervising attorney. It was very important for me to complete all of those tasks in a timely and accurate manner in order to best assist my attorney and the company.

Even though my career has transitioned into health care sales, contracts are still important in my daily routine. In order to close deals, I have to first review the drafted contract and negotiate its terms to best meet the needs of the clients as well as the needs of my company. Contracts are a part of nearly every industry and are significant in nearly all aspects of daily life. My understanding of the legalities surrounding contracts has greatly assisted me in my success today.

Concept Summary

Termination of an Offer by Operation of Law

Action	Description
Destruction of the subject matter	The subject matter of the offer is destroyed prior to acceptance through no fault of either party.
Death or incompetency	Prior to acceptance of the offer, either the offeror or the offeree dies or becomes incompetent.
Supervening illegality	Prior to the acceptance of an offer, the object of the offer is made illegal by statute, regulation, court decision, or other law.
Lapse of time	An offer terminates upon the expiration of a stated time in the offer. If no time is stated, the offer terminates after a "reasonable time."

CONTEMPORARY Issue

OPTION CONTRACTS

An offeree can prevent the offeror from revoking his or her offer by paying the offeror compensation to keep the offer open for an agreed-upon period of time. This payment is called an option contract. In other words, the offeror agrees not to sell the property to anyone but the offeree during the option period. The death or incompetency of either party does not terminate an option contract unless the contract is for the performance of a personal service.

Example: Anne Mason offers to sell a piece of real estate to Harold Greenberg for $1 million. Greenberg wants time to make a decision, so he pays Mason $20,000 to keep her offer open to him for six months. At any time during the option period, Greenberg may exercise his option and pay Mason the $1 million purchase price. If Greenberg lets the option expire, however, Mason may keep the $20,000 and sell the property to someone else.

■ ACCEPTANCE

Acceptance is "a manifestation of assent by the offeree to the terms of the offer in a manner invited or required by the offer as measured by the objective theory of contracts."[6] Recall that generally (1) unilateral contracts can be accepted only by the offeree's performance of the required act and (2) a bilateral contract can be accepted by an offeree who promises to perform (or, where permitted, by performance of) the requested act.

acceptance
Acquiescence (acceptance of guilt).

Who Can Accept an Offer?

Only the offeree has the legal power to accept an offer and create a contract. Third persons usually do not have the power to accept an offer. If an offer is made individually to two or more persons, each has the power to accept the offer. Once one of the offerees accepts the offer, it terminates as to the other offerees. An offer that is made to two or more persons jointly must be accepted jointly.

Exhibit 2.2 illustrates the acceptance of an offer.

Exhibit 2.2 Acceptance

Offeree accepts the
offeror's offer and
creates a contract.

Unequivocal Acceptance

The offeree's acceptance must be unequivocal. For an acceptance to exist, the offeree must accept the terms as stated in the offer. This is called the **mirror image rule**. Generally, a "grumbling acceptance" is a legal acceptance.

Example: A response such as "Okay, I'll take the car, but I sure wish you would make me a better deal" creates an enforceable contract.

An acceptance is equivocal if certain conditions are added to the acceptance.

Example: If the offeree responds, "I accept, but only if you repaint the car red." There is no acceptance in this case.

In the following case, the court had to decide whether there had been an acceptance of an offer.

unequivocal acceptance
Where acceptance of the contract is definite and absolute.

mirror image rule
States that for an acceptance to exist, the offeree must accept the terms as stated in the offer.

moral obligation
A duty that rests on moral considerations alone and is not imposed or enforced by positive law; a duty binding in conscience but not in law.

CASE 2.5   ACCEPTANCE

Montgomery v. English, 902 So. 2d 836 (Fla. Dist. Ct. App. 2005).

"Florida employs the "mirror image rule" with respect to contracts. Under this rule, in order for a contract to be formed, an acceptance of an offer must be absolute, unconditional, and identical with the terms of the offer."

Judge Palmer, *Court of Appeal of Florida*

---

[6] *Restatement (Second) of Contracts*, Section 50(1).

Facts

Norma English made an offer to purchase a house from Michael and Lourie Montgomery. English included in her offer a request to purchase several items of the Montgomerys' personal property. After the Montgomerys received English's offer, they made several changes to the document, including (1) deleting certain items from the personal property section of the offer, (2) deleting a provision regarding latent defects, (3) deleting a provision regarding building inspections, and (4) adding a specific "AS IS" rider. The Montogomerys signed the counteroffer and delivered it to English. English initialed some, but not all, of the Montgomerys' changes. When the Montgomerys refused to sell the house to English, English sued for specific performance of the contract. The trial court held in favor of English and ordered specific performance. The Montgomerys appealed.

Issue

Was an enforceable contract made between English and the Montgomerys?

Language of the Court

The Montgomerys argue that the trial court erred in denying their motion for summary judgment because the record demonstrated that there had been no meeting of the minds between the parties as to the essential terms of the contract. We agree. Florida employs the "mirror image rule" with respect to contracts. Under this rule, in order for a contract to be formed, an acceptance of an offer must be absolute, unconditional, and identical with the terms of the offer. Applying the mirror image rule to these undisputed facts we hold that, as a matter of law, the parties failed to reach an agreement on the terms of the contract and, therefore, no enforceable contract was created.

Decision

The court of appeal held that no contract had been created between the parties. The court of appeal reversed the trial court's order of specific performance and remanded the case to the trial court with instructions to enter summary judgment in favor of the Montgomerys.

Law & Ethics Questions

1. What does the mirror image rule provide? Explain.
2. **Ethics** Did the Montgomerys act ethically when they backed out of selling the house?
3. **Ethics** Did English act ethically by trying to force the sale of the house to her?

Web Exercises

1. **Web** Visit the website of the Court of Appeal of Florida, Fifth District, at www.5dca.org.
2. **Web** Use www.google.com and find an article that discusses the mirror image rule.

E-Commerce & Information Technology

Computer Shrinkwrap Licenses and Contracts Enforceable

Although around for centuries, sales of goods through the mail reached new heights with the sale of computer hardware and software through the Internet. One only has to pick up the telephone or log onto the computer to order thousands of dollars of computer hardware and software. Computer hardware usually arrives via mail or overnight carrier (United Parcel Service) within a few days, whereas software can arrive the same way or downloaded from your computer. Also in the box, or on the computer, is the contract, either a license agreement in the case of most software or a sales contract in the case of most computer equipment. These licenses or contracts contain the terms upon which the licensor or seller is willing to license or sell the goods to the user. The user usually has some stated period of time, often 30 days, to accept or reject the goods based on the license or contract terms. One issue has been presented to the courts by these types of licenses and sales: Are the terms of the previously unseen license or sales contract valid and enforceable? This issue was addressed by the court in the following two cases.

In *ProCD, Incorporated v. Ziedenberg*, ProCD had spent over $10 million to develop a database of names called SelectPhone. ProCD sells this database to both commercial and consumer users who are licensed to use the information in seeking customers. Matthew Zeidenberg purchased a version of SelectPhone for $150 but then offered it for sale over the Internet at a lower price than ProCD charged. ProCD sued Ziedenberg for violating its license agreement, which prohibited the resale of the data. Ziedenberg countered that the license agreement did not apply because it was included in the software box and that he had not had the opportunity to read it before buying the software. The trial court sided with Ziedenberg and held that the "shrinkwrap license"—so-called because retail software packages are covered in plastic or cellophane—was not enforceable; ProCD appealed.

The court of appeals had to address an issue of first impression: Are licenses and contracts inside software boxes and computer equipment boxes enforceable against the purchaser? The court answered yes. The court noted that modern commercial transactions would be hindered if such contracts and licenses were not recognized as enforceable. The court found that with the "accept-or-return" nature of these agreements, the purchaser or licensee could read and accept the terms of the offer or could return the goods. Therefore, potential licensees or purchasers had adequate protection against contracts they did not want to accept; they could return the goods and not accept them. The court of appeals held that Ziedenberg was bound by the license received in the box from ProCD. [*ProCD, Inc. v. Ziedenberg*, 86 F.3d 1447 (1996).]

Silence as Acceptance

Silence usually is not considered acceptance, even if the offeror states that it is. This rule is intended to protect offerees from being legally bound to offers because they failed to respond. Nevertheless, silence *does* constitute acceptance in the following situations:

1. The offeree has indicated that silence means assent.

   Example: "If you do not hear from me by Friday, ship the order."

2. The offeree signed an agreement indicating continuing acceptance of delivery until further notification.

Example: Book-of-the-month and CD-of-the-month club memberships are examples of such acceptances.

3. Prior dealings between the parties indicate that silence means acceptance.

Example: A fish wholesaler who delivers 30 pounds of fish to a restaurant each Friday for several years and is paid for the fish can continue the deliveries with expectation of payment until notified otherwise by the restaurant.

4. The offeree takes the benefit of goods or services provided by the offeror even though he or she (a) has an opportunity to reject the goods or services but fails to do so and (b) knows the offeror expects to be compensated.

Example: A homeowner who stands idly by and watches a painter she has not hired mistakenly paint her house owes the painter for the work.

Time of Acceptance

Under the common law of contracts, acceptance of a bilateral contract occurs when the offeree *dispatches* the acceptance by an authorized means of communication. This rule is called the **acceptance-upon-dispatch rule** or, more commonly, the **mailbox rule**.

Mailbox Rule

With a bilateral contract, it is important to know when a contract is accepted. Contemporary contract law has created numerous places that acceptance might happen: by telephone, fax, telegram, and e-mail, for instance. But before these contemporary forms of methods of acceptance were used, acceptance of a contract was normally done through the postal service. As a result, the mailbox rule came into being.

Under the mailbox rule, an acceptance is effective when it is dispatched—or put into the mailbox—even if it is lost in transmission. If an offeree first dispatches a rejection and then sends an acceptance, the mailbox rule does not apply to the acceptance.[7]

The problem of lost acceptances can be minimized by expressly altering the mailbox rule. The offeror can do this by stating in the offer that acceptance is effective only upon actual receipt of the acceptance. In the following case, the court enforced the mailbox rule.

CASE 2.6 *MAILBOX RULE*

Soldau v. Organon, Inc., 860 F.2d 355 (1988).

Background and Facts

John Soldau was discharged by his employer, Organon, Inc. (Organon). He received a letter from Organon offering to pay him double the normal severance pay in exchange for a release by Soldau of all claims against Organon regarding the discharge. Soldau signed and dated the release and deposited it in a mailbox outside of a post office. When he returned home, he had received a check from Organon for the increased severance pay. Soldau returned to the post office, persuaded a postal employee to open the mailbox, and retrieved the release. He cashed the

acceptance-upon-dispatch rule
A rule that states that an acceptance is effective when it is dispatched, even if it is lost in transmission.

---
[7]*Restatement (Second) of Contracts*, Section 40.

severance paycheck and brought this action against Organon, alleging a violation of the federal Age Discrimination in Employment Act. The district court granted summary judgment for Organon. Soldau appealed.

Issue

Did Soldau accept the release contract?

In the Language of the Court

Per Curiam The district court was clearly correct under California law. Under federal as well as California law, Soldau's acceptance was effective when it was mailed. The so-called "mailbox" or "effective when mailed" rule was adopted and followed as federal common law by the Supreme Court prior to Erie R.R. Co. v. Tomkins, 304 U.S. 64 (1938).

We could not change the rule, and there is no reason to believe the Supreme Court would be inclined to do so. It is almost universally accepted in the common law world. It is enshrined in the Restatement (Second) of Contracts, Section 63(a), and endorsed by the major contract treatises. Commentators are also virtually unanimous in approving the "effective when mailed" rule, pointing to the long history of the rule; its importance in creating certainty for contracting parties; and its essential soundness, on balance, as a means of allocating the risk during the period between the making of the offer and the communication of the acceptance or rejection to the offeror.

Decision and Remedy

The court of appeals applied the "mailbox rule" and found that the acceptance was effective when Soldau first deposited it in the mailbox outside the post office. His later retrieval of the release did not undo his acceptance.

Case Questions

1. **Critical Legal Thinking** Should the mailbox rule be changed to place the risk of loss of lost letters on the sender? Or is the present rule the best rule?

2. **Ethics** Did Soldau act ethically in this case?

3. **Business Application** How can businesses that make offers protect themselves from the risk of loss associated with the mailbox rule?

Mode of Acceptance

The acceptance must be **properly dispatched**. The acceptance must be properly addressed, packaged in an appropriate envelope or container, and have prepaid postage or delivery charges. Under common law, if an acceptance is not properly dispatched, it is not effective until it is actually received by the offeror.

Generally, an offeree must accept an offer by an *authorized* means of communication. The offer can stipulate that acceptance must be by a specified means of communication (e.g., registered mail, telegram). Such stipulation is called **express authorization**. If the offeree uses an unauthorized means of communication to transmit the acceptance, the acceptance is not effective, even if it is received by the offeror within the allowed time period, because the means of communication was a condition of acceptance.

proper dispatch
The acceptance must be sent in a way that is properly addressed, packaged, and postage applied.

express authorization
A stipulation in the offer that says the acceptance must be by a specified means of communication.

Most offers do not expressly specify the means of communication required for acceptance. The common law recognizes certain implied means of communication. **Implied authorization** may be inferred from what is customary in similar transactions, usage of trade, or prior dealings between the parties. Section 30 of the *Restatement (Second) of Contracts* permits implied authorization "by any medium reasonable in the circumstances."

The following case brings up many of the elements of offer and acceptance.

CASE 2.7 COUNTEROFFER

Ellefson v. Megadeth, Inc., No. 04 Civ. 5395 (NRB), 2005 U.S. Dist. LEXIS 545, at *1 (S.D.N.Y. Jan. 12, 2005).

"The issue presented by this motion is reminiscent of a first year law school contracts exam. We begin with the fundamental tenet: to have a valid contract, there must be both an offer and an acceptance."

Judge Buchwald, *United States District Court for the Southern District of New York*

Facts

David Mustaine and David Ellefson are original members of the heavy metal rock band Megadeth. The band was initially formed in 1983, with Mustaine as the lead guitarist, lead vocalist, and lead songwriter. Ellefson was the band's bassist. In 1990, the parties formed a corporation, Megadeth, Inc., with Mustaine owning 80 percent of the corporation and Ellefson 20 percent. Approximately 13 years later, Ellefson sued Mustaine and Megadeth, Inc., alleging that the defendants (collectively Mustaine) had defrauded Ellefson out of his share of the corporation's profits.

In October 2003, Ellefson and Mustaine entered into negotiations to settle the case. Both parties were represented by attorneys. Mustaine sent a proposed Settlement and General Release to Ellefson whereby Mustaine would purchase Ellefson's interest in the corporation and various licensing and recording agreements. The settlement offer was received by Ellefson on April 16, 2004.

Negotiations over the proposed settlement continued uneventfully for the next four weeks. Mustaine imposed a 5 o'clock deadline on Friday, May 14, 2004, for completion of the settlement. On May 13, Mustaine e-mailed Ellefson that the offer to Ellefson terminated as of 5 P.M. PST on Friday, May 14. The following day, Friday, May 14, the attorneys for both sides traded e-mails proposing changes to the offer. At 4:45 P.M., minutes prior to the expiration of Mustaine's offer, Mustaine e-mailed Ellefson an execution (read-only) copy of the settlement agreement, reiterated the 5 o'clock deadline, and stated that he reserved the right to make further changes to Exhibits A and B the following week. Ellefson signed a copy of the settlement agreement and faxed the signature page to Mustaine. Mustaine alleges that Ellefson's faxed signature page was received before the 5 o'clock deadline. Ellefson alleges that his fax was not sent by the 5 o'clock deadline.

On Thursday, May 20, 2004, Mustaine sent Ellefson fully executed copies of the settlement agreement by regular mail. On May 24, Ellefson e-mailed Mustaine that he was withdrawing from the negotiations and was withdrawing all proposals.

Mustaine responded that there was a signed settlement agreement in place which Ellefson had faxed on May 15, 2004.

On June 2, 2004, Ellefson received the finalized settlement agreement that had been sent by Mustaine by regular mail on May 20, 2004.

Mustaine argues that there was an enforceable settlement agreement between the parties. Ellefson argues that there was not an enforceable settlement agreement between the parties.

Issue

Was an enforceable settlement agreement reached between the parties?

Language of the Court

The issue presented by this motion is reminiscent of a first year law school contracts exam. We begin with the fundamental tenet: to have a valid contract, there must be both an offer and an acceptance. These critical elements insure that there has been mutual assent by the parties to be bound by the terms of the contract. One party makes an offer to enter into a mutual obligation, and the other party can either accept or reject this offer. However, once the offer has been accepted, the parties have formed a contract and are bound by the terms of that agreement, even if later events make them regret their decisions. In the case at hand, the issue is whether the exchange between Ellefson and Mustaine fulfilled the requirements of offer and acceptance.

Contracts are often formed after receipt of a defective acceptance. This is because an acceptance that does not unequivocally comply with the terms of original offer is considered a counteroffer. Any new terms or modified terms in the defective acceptance are treated as new terms of the counteroffer, which the original offeror may then choose to accept or reject. A late acceptance is a form of defective acceptance, and therefore is considered a counteroffer which the original offeror can decide to either accept or reject. Therefore, in order for a contract to exist after receipt of a late acceptance, the original offeror must accept the offeree's counteroffer.

It is undisputed that Mustaine conditioned his offer to Ellefson on the requirement that it be accepted by Ellefson by 5 P.M. PST on Friday, May 14. Further, there is no evidence to support Mustaine's claim that Ellefson's fax was sent within that deadline; accordingly, Ellefson did not comply with the terms of the offer and no contract was formed upon its receipt. Because Ellefson's acceptance did not fully comply with the terms of the original offer, it was not a valid acceptance and thus is viewed as a counteroffer.

Ellefson asserts that his faxed signature page cannot reasonably be construed as a counteroffer since it was utterly silent as to the terms of the Agreement. We find Ellefson's arguments unpersuasive. Regardless of Ellefson's subjective intent, it is the objective significance of his actions that controls. By faxing a signed signature page to an undisputed, execution version of the Agreement, Ellefson signaled his willingness to be bound by its terms, rather than, as he now claims, a desire to continue negotiations. Upon receipt of this fax, Mustaine could reasonably infer that Ellefson offered to bind himself to the terms of the Agreement (sent to him just minutes earlier) if Mustaine was willing to accept his counteroffer. The fact that the signature page did not contain all of the terms is immaterial, as the terms of the contract are not disputed and were contained in the underlying Agreement. Once Mustaine received the fax, Mustaine was free either to accept or reject Ellefson's counteroffer. While Mustaine could accept or reject Ellefson's counteroffer, Mustaine had to manifest his consent to be bound by the counteroffer. Without such evidence of mutual assent, no contract had been formed.

We do concur with Mustaine's alternative contention that the mailing of the completed contract on May 20, 2004, constituted an acceptance of Ellefson's counteroffer. This act established Mustaine's unequivocal intention to accept Ellefson's counteroffer and be bound by the terms of the Agreement. Under the mailbox rule, Mustaine's acceptance is considered complete upon mailing. Therefore, Mustaine accepted Ellefson's counteroffer prior to Ellefson's May 24 withdrawal of that offer, and an enforceable contract was formed on May 20, 2004.

Ellefson argues that the Court should reject Mustaine's acceptance because the use of regular U.S. mail was an unreasonable method of acceptance in light of the parties' previous conduct. Prior communications between parties had been almost exclusively by fax or e-mail. Therefore, "it was patently unreasonable for Mustaine to mail a purported acceptance by 'snail mail' without even advising Ellefson that it was mailed." [Ellefson's Memorandum]

Under California law, any reasonable and usual mode of communication may be used to accept an offer unless a specific mode is prescribed. Therefore, in the absence of any specific restriction, defendants' acceptance by mail is reasonable. Having examined all the surrounding circumstances, we find no impediment to Mustaine's acceptance by regular mail. First, the original offer and Ellefson's counteroffer contained no restrictions on the mode of acceptance. Second, the use of fax and e-mail to negotiate the Agreement does not preclude Mustaine from using mail to accept Ellefson's counteroffer by sending a fully-executed hard copy of the Agreement, and Ellefson offers no relevant authority to challenge this proposition.

Mustaine's last offer to Ellefson stated that Mustaine reserved the right to make "further changes pending our finalizing Exhibits A and B and the full execution of the agreement early next week." Ellefson's counteroffer signaled his willingness to comply with these terms, including completion by Mustaine the following week. Therefore Mustaine's mailing of the fully-executed contract the following Thursday was consistent with these terms, and reasonable under the circumstances. We therefore find that an enforceable contract was formed on May 20, 2004, prior to Ellefson's attempted withdrawal.

Decision

The U.S. district court held that an enforceable settlement agreement had been entered into by the parties. The U.S. district court granted Mustaine's motion to enforce the settlement agreement against Ellefson.

Law & Ethics Questions

1. What is an offer? What is an acceptance?

2. What does the mailbox rule provide? Explain.

3. Do you think the proper mode of acceptance was used in this case?

4. **Ethics** Was it ethical for Ellefson to try to revoke his acceptance of the settlement agreement?

5. **Ethics** Did Mustaine act ethically in this case?

Web Exercises

1. **Web** Visit the website of the U.S. District Court for the Southern District of New York at www.nysd.uscourts.gov.

2. **Web** Visit the website of Megadeth at www.megadeth.com.

3. **Web** Use www.google.com and find a video clip of the band Megadeth.

CONTEMPORARY Issue

SOFTWARE CONTRACTS

It is possible that opening a package—such as a package of software—can constitute acceptance of an agreement. The following is a sample of terminology accompanying such software:

SINGLE PC LICENSE AGREEMENT AND LIMITED WARRANTY
READ THIS LICENSE CAREFULLY BEFORE USING THIS PACKAGE. BY USING THIS PACKAGE, YOU ARE AGREEING TO THE TERMS AND CONDITIONS OF THIS LICENSE. IF YOU DO NOT AGREE, DO NOT USE THE PACKAGE. PROMPTLY RETURN THE UNUSED PACKAGE AND ALL ACCOMPANYING ITEMS TO THE PLACE YOU OBTAINED THEM FOR A FULL REFUND OF ANY SUMS YOU HAVE PAID FOR THE SOFTWARE.

Note that to be effective this sort of language must normally be set in all capital letters. The purpose of the all-caps statement is to put the customer on notice that opening the package constitutes agreement with the software contract.

Concept Summary

Offer and Acceptance

Communication by Offeror	Effective When
Offer	Received by offeree
Revocation of offer	Received by offeree
Communication by Offeree	**Effective When**
Rejection of offer	Received by offeror
Counteroffer	Received by offeror
Acceptance of offer	Sent by offeree
Acceptance after previous rejection of offer	Received by offeror

**Unified Contract Law
(UCL)**
A new business and commercial contract law enacted by China.

INTERNATIONAL LAW

China Adopts New Contracts Law

After 15 years of negotiations, China officially joined the ranks of the World Trade Organization (WTO) in late 2001. In preparation for this, the National People's Congress of China took many steps to ensure success, including modernizing the country's legal system. Just two years earlier China dramatically overhauled its contract laws by enacting the **Unified Contract Law (UCL)**. This new set of laws effectively wiped out or drastically changed many business and commercial contract laws that had been the standard for many years.

The UCL was designed to provide users with a consistent and easy-to-understand set of statues that more closely resembled international business contracting principles. This was a necessary step to ensure that China was accepted into the WTO and to help the country move closer to the global economic powerhouse it is now becoming.

According to the UCL, the new guidelines exist to "protect contracting parties' legal rights, maintain social economic order, and improve the construction of socialist modernization." The general provisions of the UCL also require that a contract "not interrupt social-economic order or harm public interests" and the contracting parties be "honest and trustworthy, and respect societal ethics."

The UCL covers all the parts of contract law that should be familiar to Western businesses, including the definition of a contract, acceptance, consideration, performance, breach of contract, and remedies. Even so, many aspects of the UCL differ from U.S. contract law, and anyone doing business in China or with a Chinese company should study it carefully.

Web Exercises

1. **Web** To learn more about Chinese law, visit the Library of Congress guide to China at www.loc.gov/law/guide/china.html.
2. **Web** To learn more about doing business in China, visit the U.S.-China Business Council's website at www.uschina.org.

INTERNET EXERCISES AND CASE QUESTIONS

Working the Web Internet Exercises

1. Visit cori.missouri.edu. Use this site to aid in drafting specific types of contracts and/or clauses. Test your ability by visiting the site and searching for employment agreements that have noncompetition clauses.
2. To review the basic elements of a contract, visit www.freeadvice.com/law/518us.htm.
3. For some tips on entering into contracts, see www.jamesmartinpa.com/50tips_revisited.htm.

CHAPTER 2 SUMMARY

AGREEMENT, p. 34

Offer

1. *Offer.* An offer is a manifestation by one party of a willingness to enter into a contract.
2. *Offeror.* The offeror is the party who makes an offer.
3. *Offeree.* The offeree is the party to whom an offer is made. This party has the power to create an agreement by accepting the terms of the offer.

OFFER, p. 34

Requirements of an Offer

1. *Objective intent.* The intent to enter into a contract is determined by the *objective theory of contract*—that is, whether a reasonable person viewing the circumstances would conclude that the parties intended to be legally bound.
2. *Definite terms.* The terms of an offer must be definite so that the agreement between the parties can be determined. Reasonable terms (e.g., price, time for performance) may be *implied*.
3. *Communication.* The offer must be communicated to the offeree by the offeror.

Special Offer Situations

1. *Advertisement.*
   a. *General rule.* Generally, an advertisement is an invitation to make an offer.
   b. *Exception.* An advertisement is an offer if it is so definite and specific as to show the advertiser's intent to be bound to the terms of the advertisement.
2. *Reward.* A reward is an offer to create a unilateral contract.
3. *Auction:*
   a. *Action with reserve.* An action with reserve is an invitation to make an offer. The seller retains the right to refuse the highest bid and withdraw the goods from sale.
   b. *Auction without reserve.* An auction without reserve is an offer. The seller must accept the highest bid (above the minimum bid). This type of auction must be stipulated.

TERMINATIONS OF OFFERS, p. 46

Termination of an Offer by Action of the Parties

1. *Revocation.* The offeror may *revoke* (withdraw) an offer any time prior to its acceptance by the offeree.
2. *Rejection.* An offer is terminated if the offeree rejects the offer by his or her words or conduct.
3. *Counteroffer.* A counteroffer by the offeree terminates the offeror's offer (and creates a new offer).

Termination of an Offer by Operation of Law

1. *Destruction of the subject matter.* An offer terminates if the subject matter of the offer is destroyed prior to acceptance through no fault of either party.

2. ***Death or incompetency.*** The death or incompetency of either the offeror or the offeree prior to acceptance terminates the offer.
3. ***Supervening illegality.*** If prior to the acceptance of an offer the object of the offer is made illegal by statute, regulation, court decision, or other law, the offer terminates.
4. ***Lapse of time.*** An offer terminates upon the expiration of a stated time in the offer. If no time is stated, the offer terminates after a "reasonable time."

Option Contract

If an offeree pays the offeror compensation to keep an offer open for an agreed on period of time, an *option contract* is created. The offeror cannot sell the property to anyone else during the option period.

ACCEPTANCE, p. 51

Acceptance

Acceptance is manifestation of assent by the offeree to the terms of the offer. Acceptance of the offer by the offeree creates a contract.

Rules for Acceptance

1. ***Mirror image rule.*** Under the common law of contracts, an offeree must accept the terms offered by the offeror to create a contract. Any change in terms by the offeree constitutes a counteroffer, not an acceptance.
2. ***Acceptance-upon-dispatch rule.*** Unless otherwise provided in the offer, acceptance is effective when it is dispatched by the offeree. This rule is often called the *mailbox rule*.
3. ***Proper dispatch rule.*** An acceptance must be properly addressed, packaged, and have prepaid postage or delivery charges to be effective when dispatched. Generally, improperly dispatched acceptances are not effective until actually received by the offeror.
4. ***Mode of acceptance.*** Acceptance must be by the express means of communication stipulated in the offer, or, if no means is stipulated, then by reasonable means in the circumstances.

TERMS AND CONCEPTS

Acceptance   51

Acceptance-upon-dispatch rule (mailbox rule)   54

Advertisements   40

Agreement   34

Auction with reserve   44

Auction without reserve   44

Counteroffer   47

Express authorization   55

Implied authorization   56

Implied terms   36

Lapse of time   49

Mirror image rule   51

Moral obligation   51

Objective theory of contracts   35

Offer   34

Offeree   34

Offeror   34

Properly dispatched   55

Rejection of an offer by the offeree   47

Rewards   43

Supervening illegality   49

Unequivocal acceptance   51

Unified Contract Law (UCL)   60

CASE SCENARIO REVISITED

Remember the case scenario at the beginning of the chapter involving Jim and Cheryl's hunting property? Because Jim actually wrote out an agreement for sale of the property, can he argue that his offer was made in jest? Could Nicholas have *really* taken the offer seriously, because he certainly knew the difference between the amount Jim offered the property for and what the property was really worth? What you have learned in this chapter will help you answer these questions. You can also review the case of *Lucy v. Zehmer*, 84 S.E.2d 516 (Va. 1954).

CRITICAL LEGAL THINKING CASES

Critical Legal Thinking Case 2.1 *Terms of a Contract* Ben Hunt and others operated a farm under the name S.B.H. Farms. Hunt went to McIlory Bank & Trust and requested a loan to build hog houses, buy livestock, and expand farming operations. The bank agreed to loan S.B.H. Farms $175,000, for which short-term promissory notes were signed by Hunt and the other owners of S.B.H. Farms. At that time, oral discussions were held with the bank officer regarding long-term financing of S.B.H.'s farming operations; no dollar amount, interest rate, or repayment terms were discussed. When the owners of S.B.H. Farms defaulted on the promissory notes, the bank filed for foreclosure on the farm and other collateral. S.B.H. Farms counterclaimed for $750,000 damages, alleging that the bank breached its oral contract to provide long-term financing. Was there an oral contract for long-term financing? *Hunt v. McIlory Bank & Trust*, 616 S.W.2d 759 (Ark. Ct. App. 1981).

Critical Legal Thinking Case 2.2 *Implied Terms* MacDonald Group, Ltd. (MacDonald), is the managing general partner of "Fresno Fashion Square," a regional shopping mall in Fresno, California. The mall has several major anchor tenants and numerous smaller stores and shops, including Edmond's of Fresno, a jeweler. Edmond's signed a lease with MacDonald that provided that "there shall not be more than two jewelry stores" located in the mall. Nine years later, MacDonald sent Edmond's notice that it intended to expand the mall and lease space to other jewelers.

The lease was silent as to the coverage of additional mall space. Edmond's sued MacDonald, arguing that the lease applied to mall additions. Who wins? *Edmond's of Fresno v. MacDonald Group, Ltd.*, 217 Cal. Rptr. 375 (Ct. App. 1985).

Critical Legal Thinking Case 2.3 *Counteroffer* Glende Motor Company (Glende), an automobile dealership that sold new cars, leased premises from certain landlords. One day, fire destroyed part of the leased premises, and Glende restored the leasehold premises. The landlords received payment of insurance proceeds for the fire. Glende sued the landlords to recover the insurance proceeds. Ten days before the trial was to begin, the defendants jointly served on Glende a document titled "Offer to Compromise Before Trial," which was a settlement offer of $190,000. Glende agreed to the amount of the settlement but made it contingent on the execution of a new lease. The next day, the defendants notified Glende that they were revoking the settlement offer. Glende thereafter tried to accept the original settlement offer. Has there been a settlement of the lawsuit? *Glende Motor Co. v. Superior Court*, 205 Cal. Rptr. 682 (Ct. App. 1984).

Critical Legal Thinking Case 2.4 *Acceptance* Peter Andrus owned an apartment building that he had insured under a fire insurance policy sold by J. C. Durick Insurance (Durick). Two months prior to the expiration of the policy, Durick notified Andrus that the building should be insured for $48,000 (or 80 percent of the building's value), as required by the insurance company. Andrus replied that (1) he wanted insurance to match the amount of the outstanding mortgage on the building (i.e., $24,000) and (2) if Durick could not sell this insurance, he would go elsewhere. Durick sent a new insurance policy in the face amount of $48,000 with the notation that the policy was automatically accepted unless Andrus notified him to the contrary. Andrus did not reply. However, he did not pay the premiums on the policy. Durick sued Andrus to recover these premiums. Who wins? *J.C. Durick Ins. v. Andrus*, 424 A.2d 249 (Vt. 1980).

Critical Legal Thinking Case 2.5 *Mailbox Rule* William Jenkins and Nathalie Monk owned a building in Sacramento, California. They leased the building to Tuneup Masters for five years. The lease provided that Tuneup Masters could extend the lease for an additional five years if it gave written notice of its intention to do so by certified or registered mail at least six months prior to the expiration of the term of the lease.

Three days before the expiration of the lease, Larry Selditz, vice president of Tuneup Masters, prepared a letter exercising the option, prepared and sealed an envelope with the letter in it, prepared U.S. Postal Service Form 3800, affixed the certified mail sticker on the envelope, and had his secretary deliver the envelope to the Postal Service annex located on the ground floor of the office building. Postal personnel occupied the annex only between the hours of 9 and 10 A.M. At the end of each day, between 5 and 5:15 P.M., a postal employee picked up outgoing mail. The letter to the landlords was lost in the mail. The landlords thereafter refused to renew the lease and brought an unlawful detainer action against Tuneup Masters. Was the notice renewing the option effective? *Jenkins v. Tuneup Masters*, 235 Cal. Rptr. 214 (Ct. App. 1987).

ETHICS CASES

Ethics Case 2.1 Howard R. Wright hired John W. Cerdes to construct a home for him at a price of $43,150. The contract was silent regarding the time of completion. Construction was not completed after nine months. At that time, Wright obtained an injunction ordering Cerdes to stop work. Wright hired other contractors to complete the building. Cerdes sued Wright for breach of contract, claiming he was due the contract price. How long should Cerdes have had to complete the house? Was it ethical for Wright to hire other contractors to complete the building? See *Cerdes v. Wright*, 408 So. 2d 926 (La. App. 1981) to help you with your answers.

Ethics Case 2.2 Rudy Turilli operated the "Jesse James Museum" in Stanton, Missouri. He contends the man who was shot, killed, and buried as the notorious desperado Jesse James in 1882 was an impostor and that Jesse James lived for many years thereafter under the alias J. Frank Dalton and last lived with Turilli at his museum until the 1950s. Turilli appeared before a nationwide television audience and stated that he would pay $10,000 to anyone who could prove his statements were wrong. After hearing this offer, Stella James, a relative of Jesse James, produced affidavits of persons related to and acquainted with the Jesse James family, constituting evidence that Jesse James was killed, as alleged in song and legend, on April 3, 1882. When Turilli refused to pay the reward, James sued for breach of contract. Was it ethical for Turilli to refuse to pay? In a breach of contract suit, who wins? See *James v. Turilli*, 473 S.W.2d 757 (Mo. Ct. App. 1971) to help you with your answer.

BRIEFING THE CASE WRITING ASSIGNMENT

Read Case A.2 in Appendix A (*Traco, Inc. v. Arrow Glass Co., Inc.*). This case is excerpted from the appellate court opinion. Review and brief the case. After briefing the case, you should be able to answer the following questions:
1. Who was the plaintiff? Who was the defendant?
2. Was there an express agreement between the parties?
3. What does the doctrine of promissory estoppel provide? Explain.
4. Did the court apply the doctrine of promissory estoppel in this case?

PRACTICE TIP

Once the date and the parties to the contract are set out (see the Practice Tip in Chapter 1), the next step in drafting the contract is to follow with an introduction as to what the parties would like to contract. The form for this introduction is as follows:

WITNESSETH:

WHEREAS, _____ and _____ wish to _____, all on the terms set forth;

The word "WHEREAS" is a formal term used in most contracts. The purpose of using this term is to mark a set of recitals and/or indicating that background information is about to be given.

Many bar associations and legal experts recommend using "plain English" language in the contract. Those same groups sometimes argue that recitals don't serve any real purpose. For more on this topic, read an article on the subject on the American Bar Association's website: www.abanet.org/buslaw/blt/2003-03-04/adams.html.

The law has outgrown its primitive stage of formalism when the precise word was the sovereign talisman, and every slip was fatal. It takes a broader view today. A promise may be lacking, and yet the whole writing may be "instinct with an obligation," imperfectly expressed.

—*Justice Cardozo*
Wood v. Duff Gordon, 222 N.Y.88, 91 (1917)

Consideration and Equity | CHAPTER 3

CASE SCENARIO

Jan and Dean were married 10 years ago.[1] At the time of their marriage, Dean was the president of a successful advertising agency, and Jan owned a gym. Several months after their marriage, Jan became ill and was unable to work. She asked Dean to devote full time to the gym. If he would agree, they would operate the business together, share equally in the ownership of its assets, and divide any profits equally. Dean agreed and terminated his advertising agency business. Ten years later, Jan divorced Dean and denied him any rights to the gym. The law firm where you work as a paralegal represents Dean.

■ CHAPTER INTRODUCTION

To be enforceable, a contract must be supported by "consideration," which is broadly defined as something of legal value. It can consist of money, property, the provision of services, the forbearance of a right, or anything else of value. Most contracts that are not supported by consideration are not enforceable. The parties may voluntarily perform a contract that is lacking in consideration. This chapter discusses consideration, promises that lack consideration, and promises that are enforceable without consideration.

---

[1]Remember that domestic relations law may override any contract law principles in such a real scenario, at least in certain states. In Massachusetts, for example, this would be an alimony issue for Dean, and his lawyer most likely wouldn't pursue an action based on regular contract law. In fact, if Dean's attorney didn't make it a central issue in the divorce, he would probably be guilty of malpractice.

CHAPTER OBJECTIVES

After studying this chapter, you should be able to:

1. Define *consideration*.
2. Identify when there is *inadequacy* of consideration.
3. Analyze whether contracts are *lacking* in consideration.
4. Explain the doctrines of *preexisting duty* and *past consideration*.
5. Apply the doctrine of *promissory estoppels*.

The doctrine of equity is also discussed in this chapter. Equity is a branch of law based on fairness, justice, and honesty. Equity is imposed when there is no adequate remedy available at law. Equitable remedies are sometimes applied in contract cases, especially specific performance, rescission, and injunction.

PARALEGAL PERSPECTIVE

Rebecca Cain is a graduate of the University of Toledo's Paralegal Studies Program. She works in the Discovery Management Unit for Nationwide Mutual Insurance Company, Office of Chief Legal Officer, at Nationwide's world headquarters in Columbus, Ohio.

I work in a corporate litigation environment where my job involves different aspects of the discovery process such as gathering voluminous amounts of documents, electronic document searches, and dealing with e-discovery issues.

Throughout the discovery process I may be required to gather hundreds of thousands of documents for a production request. After gathering these documents, I may be required to review them for determination as to whether or not they are responsive to the litigation at hand. During the review process, contracts and other documents collected for discovery are flagged as "responsive" or "nonresponsive." These documents are then reviewed by legal counsel to decide whether or not they will be produced in court.

By working with electronic services, such as CaseVault, the process of reviewing documents online is now easier and faster. This enables legal counsel to review the exact same documents I have already reviewed, no matter where they are physically located, to determine which documents must be produced for discovery purposes.

Today I use all of my paralegal skills: written and verbal communication skills, analytical decision making, organizational skills, time management, computer skills, and much more! I thoroughly enjoy my job in the Discovery Management Unit and find it very rewarding, knowing I am making the jobs of the attorneys I work for much easier.

■ CONSIDERATION

consideration
Something of legal value given in exchange for a promise.

Consideration must be given before a contract can exist. **Consideration** is defined as something of legal value given in exchange for a promise. Consideration can come in many forms. The most common types consist of either a tangible payment (e.g., money, property) or the performance of an act (e.g., providing legal services). Less usual forms of consideration include the forbearance of a legal right (e.g., accepting an out-of-court settlement in exchange for dropping a lawsuit) and noneconomic forms of consideration (e.g., refraining from "drinking, using tobacco, swearing, or playing cards or billiards for money"[2] for a specified time period).

Written contracts are presumed to be supported by consideration. This rebuttable presumption, however, may be overcome by sufficient evidence. A few states provide that contracts made under seal cannot be challenged for lack of consideration.

Requirements of Consideration

Consideration consists of two elements: (1) Something of legal value must be given (e.g., either a legal benefit must be received or legal detriment must be

[2]*Hamer v. Sidwa*, 27 N.E. 256 (N.Y. 1891).

suffered) and (2) there must be a bargained-for exchange. Each of these is discussed in the paragraphs that follow.

1. *Legal value*—Under the modern law of contracts, a contract is considered supported by **legal value** if (1) the promisee suffers a *legal detriment* or (2) the promisor receives a *legal benefit*.

   Example: Suppose the Dallas Cowboys contract with a tailor to have him make uniforms for the team. The tailor completes the uniforms, but the team manager thinks the color is wrong and refuses to allow the team to wear them. The tailor has suffered a legal detriment (time spent making the uniforms). Under the modern rule of contracts, there is sufficiency of consideration and the contract is enforceable.

2. *Bargained-for exchange*—To be enforceable, a contract must arise from a **bargained-for exchange**. In most business contracts, the parties engage in such exchanges. The commercial setting in which business contracts are formed leads to this conclusion.

legal value
Where the promisee suffers a legal detriment or the promisor receives a legal benefit.

bargained-for exchange
Exchange that parties engage in that leads to an enforceable contract.

CAREER FRONT

Business Franchise Paralegal

- Draft franchise agreement and related agreements/contracts.
- Draft Federal Trade Commission (FTC) disclosure statements and franchise offering circulars.
- Compile information for inclusion in FTC disclosure statements and franchise offering circulars.
- File offering circulars, annual reports, and amendments in registration states.
- File notices of intent to sell franchises/business opportunities or exemption notices in registration states.
- Communicate with state regulators about registration/disclosure requirements.
- Review and file advertising/promotional materials with registration states.
- Administer disclosure process of prospective franchisees.
- Draft franchise documents for execution.
- Communicate with client or franchisee about execution of documents.
- Communicate with client or franchisee about compliance with franchise agreement.
- Draft default notices to franchisees.
- Monitor franchisee compliance with terms of franchise and other agreements.
- Write policies for disclosure and franchising processes.
- Monitor activities of franchise salespeople.
- Prepare earnings claims information to give to franchisees.
- Review requests for transfer of franchise and prepare documents for execution.
- Draft documents for repurchasing franchise business.
- Draft documents for terminating franchise agreement.
- Maintain repository and/or database of franchise activity.
- Review and draft documents for franchisee financing.

Source: Excerpted by permission from the National Association of Legal Assistants (www.nala.org) and the National Federation of Paralegal Associations, Inc. (www.paralegals.org).

Concept Summary

Consideration

Type of Consideration	Description of Element
Legal value	Where:
	(1) the promisee suffers a *legal detriment* or
	(2) the promisor receives a *legal benefit*.
Bargained-for-exchange	Exchange that the parties actively engage in and that leads to an enforceable contract.

Gift Promises

gift promise
An unenforceable promise because it lacks consideration.

Gift promises, also called gratuitous promises, are unenforceable because they lack consideration. To change a gift promise into an enforceable promise, the promisee must offer to do something in exchange—that is, consideration—for the promise. A completed gift promise cannot be rescinded for lack of consideration.

Example: Suppose Mrs. Colby promised to give her son $10,000 and then rescinded the promise. The son would have no recourse because it was a gift promise that lacked consideration. If, however, Mrs. Colby promised her son $10,000 for getting an "A" in his business law course and the son performed as required, the contract would be enforceable.

Example: On May 1, Mr. Smith promises to give his granddaughter $10,000 on June 1. If on June 1 Mr. Smith actually gives the $10,000 to his granddaughter, it is a completed gift promise. Mr. Smith cannot thereafter recover the money from his granddaughter, even if the original promise lacked consideration.

Case 3.1 involves an uncompleted gift promise. Case 3.2 involves completed gifts.

CASE 3.1   GIFT PROMISE

Alden v. Presley, 637 S.W.2d 862 (Tenn. 1982).

> *"The court of appeals concurred in the finding that there was no gift for failure to deliver."*
>
> Judge Fones, *Supreme Court of Tennessee*

Facts

Elvis Presley, a singer of great renown and a man of substantial wealth, became engaged to Ginger Alden. He was generous with the Alden family, paying for landscaping the lawn, installing a swimming pool, and making other gifts. When his fiancée's mother, Jo Laverne Alden, sought to divorce her husband, Presley promised to pay off the remaining mortgage indebtedness on the Alden home, which Mrs. Alden was to receive in the divorce settlement. On August 16, 1977, Presley died suddenly, leaving the mortgage unpaid. When the legal representative of Presley's estate refused to pay the $39,587 mortgage, Mrs. Alden brought an action to enforce Presley's promise. The trial court denied recovery. Mrs. Alden appealed.

Issue

Was Presley's promise to pay the mortgage enforceable?

Language of the Court

In the instant case, the trial court held decedent did make a promise unsupported by consideration to plaintiff, that no gift was consummated for failure of delivery, that plaintiff suffered no detriment as she "wound up much better after her association with Elvis A. Presley than if he had never made any promise to Jo Laverne Alden." The court of appeals concurred in the finding that there was no gift for failure to deliver, holding that delivery is not complete unless complete dominion and control of the gift is surrendered by the donor and acquired by the donee.

Decision

The Supreme Court of Tennessee held that Presley's promise was a gratuitous executory promise that was not supported by consideration. As such, it was unenforceable against Presley's estate. The court dismissed the case and assessed costs against the plaintiff.

Law & Ethics Questions

1. Should gratuitous promises be enforced? Why or why not?
2. **Ethics** Was it unethical for the representative of Presley's estate to refuse to complete the gift? Did he have any other choice?
3. Does it make a difference if a gift promise is executed or executory? Explain.

Web Exercises

1. **Web** Visit the Supreme Court of Tennessee at www.tsc.state.tn.us/geninfo/bio/supreme/biosc.htm.
2. **Web** Use www.google.com and find a brief biography of Elvis Presley.
3. **Web** Visit the website of Graceland, the home of Elvis Presley, at www.elvis.com/graceland.
4. **Web** Go to www.elvis.com to see a video clip of Elvis Presley singing a song.

CASE 3.2 GIFT

Cooper v. Smith, 800 N.E.2d 372 (Ohio Ct. App. 2003).

> "Many gifts are made for reasons that sour with the passage of time. Unfortunately, gift law does not allow a donor to recover/revoke a gift simply because his or her reasons for giving it have soured."

> Judge Harsha, *Court of Appeals of Ohio*

Facts

In May 2001, Lester Cooper suffered serious injuries that caused him to be hospitalized for an extended period of time. While he was hospitalized, Julie Smith, whom Cooper had met the year before, and Janet Smith, Julie's mother, made numerous trips to visit him. Although Julie was married to another man at the time, a romantic relationship developed between Cooper and Julie. While in the hospital, Cooper proposed marriage to Julie, and she accepted. Julie obtained a divorce from her husband in October 2001. Cooper ultimately received a $180,000 settlement for his injuries.

After being released from the hospital, Cooper moved into Janet's house and lived with Janet and Julie. Over the next couple of months, Cooper purchased a number of items for Julie, including a diamond engagement ring, a car, a computer, a tanning bed, and horses. On Julie's request, Cooper paid off Janet's car. Cooper also paid for various improvements to Janet's house, such as having a new furnace installed and having wood flooring laid in the kitchen. By December 2001, the settlement money had run out, and Julie had not yet married Cooper. In the summer of 2002, Julie and Cooper had a disagreement, and Cooper moved out of the house. Julie returned the engagement ring to Cooper. Cooper sued Julie and Janet to recover the gifts or the value of the gifts he gave them. The magistrate who heard the case dismissed Cooper's case, and the trial court affirmed the dismissed of the case. Cooper appealed.

Issue

Can Cooper recover the gifts or the value of the gifts he gave to Julie and Janet Smith?

Language of the Court

Unless the parties have agreed otherwise, the donor is entitled to recover the engagement ring (or its value) if the marriage does not occur, regardless of who ended the engagement. While we are willing to imply a condition concerning the engagement ring, we are unwilling to do so for other gifts given during the engagement period. Unlike the engagement ring, the other gifts have no symbolic meaning. Rather, they are merely "tokens of love and affection" which the donor bore for the donee. Many gifts are made for reasons that sour with the passage of time. Unfortunately, gift law does not allow a donor to recover/revoke a gift simply because his or her reasons for giving it have soured.

Generally, a completed gift is absolute and irrevocable. If we were to imply a condition on gifts given during the engagement period, then every gift the donor gave, no matter how small or insignificant, would be recoverable. We believe the best approach is to treat gifts exchanged during the engagement period (excluding the engagement ring) as absolute and irrevocable gifts unless the donor has expressed intent that the gift be conditioned on the subsequent marriage. Cooper offered no evidence establishing that he gave the gifts on the express condition that they be returned to him if the engagement ended. Thus, the gifts are irrevocable gifts and Cooper is not entitled to their return.

Decision

The court of appeals held that the gifts made by Cooper to Julie (other than the engagement ring) and to Janet were irrevocable gifts that he could not recover simply because his engagement to Julie ended. The court of appeals affirmed the judgment of the trial court, allowing Julie and Janet Smith to keep these gifts.

Law & Ethics Questions

1. Should the return of an engagement ring and other gifts made during the engagement period be treated differently when the engagement is broken off? Explain.

2. **Ethics** Did Julie and Janet Smith act ethically in keeping the gifts Cooper had given them? Did Cooper act ethically in trying to get the gifts back?

3. Does the no-fault rule regarding the return of engagement rings on the termination of an engagement save court expenses? Explain.

Web Exercises

1. **Web** Visit the website of the Court of Appeals of Ohio and find the Fourth District at: www.sconet.state.oh.us.

2. **Web** Use www.google.com and find an article about gifts and contracts.

PARALEGAL PERSPECTIVE

Susan M. Bartel is a 1997 graduate of the Bachelor's Degree Paralegal Studies Program at David N. Myers University in Cleveland, Ohio. She also holds an associate degree in paralegal studies from Cuyahoga Community College in Parma, Ohio. Susan also received her master of science degree in urban studies from Cleveland State University in Cleveland. Susan is employed by the Roman Catholic Diocese of Cleveland in its Real Estate and Legal Services Department.

The paralegal profession has been a very positive career choice for me, giving me the opportunity to assist attorneys in many areas of law, including loan acquisition and refinancing, construction contracts, real estate transactions, leases, tax matters, probate, and corporate law.

All areas of law require comprehensively drafted contracts. It is critically important that all of the necessary provisions are set forth in the contract in a concise and clear manner so that the parties are aware of the terms and conditions of the contract. The contract should set forth not only present conditions but also future considerations such as termination or dissolution of the contract. Under the supervision of an attorney, the paralegal provides a vital resource in reviewing the contract to see that the document contains the necessary information for a particular matter and also includes all of the elements of a legal and binding contract.

The use of paralegals in drafting contracts for review by attorneys, or in reviewing contracts that attorneys have previously drafted, is an effective way for the law firm or legal department and the client to save money and time.

CONTEMPORARY Issue

WHEN IS CONSIDERATION INADEQUATE?

"Plaintiff expressly testified that 'other good and valuable consideration' meant the love and affection plaintiff and James Paul DeLaney had for one another. In Illinois, love and affection do not constitute legal consideration."

Judge Lorenz

adequate consideration
A value of the bargain that is equal to or reasonably proportioned to the value of that for which it is given.

The courts usually do not inquire into **adequate consideration**. Generally, parties are free to agree on the consideration they are willing to pay or receive under a contract. This rule is based on the court's reluctance to inquire into the motives of a party for entering into a contract or to save a party from a "bad deal."

Some states recognize an exception to the general rule that the courts will not examine the sufficiency of consideration. These states permit a party to escape from a contract if the inadequacy of consideration "shocks the conscience of the court." This standard, which is applied on a case-by-case basis, considers the value of the item or service contracted for, the amount of consideration paid, the relationship of the parties, and other facts and circumstances of the case.

Consider this situation: Mr. and Mrs. James Paul DeLaney were married in January 1953. A few years later, they acquired a painting, allegedly the work of Peter Paul Rubens, titled *Hunting of the Calydonian Boar*. In 1966, the DeLaneys moved into an apartment building and became friends with Mr. and Mrs. Nicholas T. O'Neill. Mr. DeLaney and Mr. O'Neill became close friends. On August 18, 1970, Mr. DeLaney purportedly sold the Rubens painting to Mr. O'Neill for $10 and "other good and valuable consideration." A written contract embodying the terms of the agreement was prepared and signed by Mr. DeLaney and Mr. O'Neill. Mrs. DeLaney was not informed of the sale. At the time of the sale, Mr. DeLaney told Mr. O'Neill that the painting was worth at least $100,000. The painting, however, remained with DeLaney and was in storage at the time of this lawsuit. In 1974, Mrs. DeLaney instituted a divorce action against Mr. DeLaney. At that time she learned of the purported sale of the painting to O'Neill. In the divorce action, Mrs. DeLaney claimed an interest in the painting as marital property. Mr. O'Neill instituted this action seeking a declaratory judgment regarding title to the painting.

The trial court held in favor of Mrs. DeLaney and voided the sales contract between Mr. DeLaney and Mr. O'Neill. The appellate court affirmed. The courts held that the consideration paid by Mr. O'Neill for the painting "shocked the conscience of the court" and thereby rendered the transfer void. The appellate court stated,

> Plaintiff expressly testified that "other good and valuable consideration" meant the love and affection plaintiff and James Paul DeLaney had for one another. In Illinois, love and affection do not constitute legal consideration. Thus, the only remaining valid consideration for the transaction was the tender of $10. A purchase price of $10 for such a valuable work of art is so grossly inadequate consideration as to shock the conscience of this court, as it did the trial court's. To find $10 valid consideration for this painting would be to reduce the requirement of consideration to a mere formality. This we will not do.

Critics of this case argue that the parties should be free to contract based on what they feel is adequate consideration in the circumstances. Proponents of this case argue that courts should be allowed to examine the adequacy of consideration underlying a contract to prevent unfair contracts. *O'Neill v. DeLaney*, 415 N.E.2d 1260 (Ill. App. Ct. 1980).

(continued)

Law & Ethics Questions

1. What does the doctrine of inadequacy of consideration provide? Explain.
2. **Ethics** Was it ethical for O'Neill to pay so little for the painting?
3. **Ethics** Did Mrs. DeLaney have a good lawful cause of action against O'Neill?

Web Exercises

1. **Web** Visit the website of the Appellate Court of Illinois, First District, at www.state.il.us/court/appellatecourt.
2. **Web** Use www.google.com and see if you can find a photo of Peter Paul Rubens's *Hunting of the Calydonian Boar*. Can you find the value of this painting?

■ CONTRACTS LACKING CONSIDERATION

Some contracts seem as though they are supported by consideration even though they are not. The following types of contracts fall into this category.

Illegal Consideration

A contract cannot be supported by a promise to refrain from doing an illegal act because that is **illegal consideration**. Contracts based on illegal consideration are void.

illegal consideration
A promise to refrain from doing an illegal act. Such a promise will not support a contract.

Example: A statement such as "I will burn your house down unless you agree to pay me $10,000" cannot become an enforceable contract. Even if the threatened party agrees to make the payment, the contract is unenforceable and void because it is supported by illegal consideration (arson is unlawful).

PARALEGAL PERSPECTIVE

Robert Lee Dickens is the contracts manager for the University of Texas at San Antonio. He received a Master of Arts in legal studies from Texas State University in San Marcos, Texas, in May 2006. Robert also holds certifications in the contracting and purchasing fields from the state of Texas and the National Institute for Government Purchasing. His article "Finding Common Ground in the World of Electronic Contracts: The Consistency of Legal Reasoning in Clickwrap Cases" was published in the Summer 2007 issue of the Marquette Intellectual Property Law Review.

In my current position, my responsibilities include negotiating, drafting, and finalizing the terms, conditions, and scope of work requirements for the university's vendor service agreements. A primary aspect of this responsibility involves educating the associated university departments ("Users") about the basic concepts of contract law.

It is possible, for example, that a User may receive a "Memorandum of Understanding" or a "Letter of Intent" from a potential contractor. It is important for this User to understand that regardless of what the document is called, signing such a document could still result in an enforceable contract. This understanding, of course, requires a general knowledge of the elements of an enforceable contract. The User must be cognizant that if all the elements of a contract are present, then it is an enforceable Agreement.

It is equally important that the User understands the concept of mutuality of assent. The User may be unaware that an enforceable contract requires mutuality of assent, and that mutual assent requires the presence of clear and definite terms. On a service agreement, the most important of these terms is arguably the service itself. A User, however, may request an answer as to whether the terms of an agreement are acceptable without ever defining the intent of the services. The problem with this approach is that the intent of the parties, or the scope of services, is what

(continued)

actually drives the Agreement and the associated terms and conditions. It is easy to get this concept turned around, but doing so is a critical mistake. It would be impossible, for example, to know whether a software contract required a "mutual confidentiality" clause without knowing whether there will be an interchange of data between the parties. To facilitate the completion of this software agreement, the contract drafter must somehow obtain this information from the User. Although the User may not need to be familiar with the phrase "mutual assent," it is imperative that the User understands the need to establish unambiguous terms, as well as the requirements to do so.

An accomplished contracts professional must always keep in mind that it is the User that will be administering the agreement. The professional must therefore ensure not only that the intent of the parties is defined in an accurate and understandable manner, but also that the User understands the terms of the agreement that has been drafted on his or her behalf. This understanding can only occur if someone takes the time to educate the User properly on the pertinent aspects of the Agreement. For this reason, it is imperative for the contracts professional to have much more than just a general knowledge of contract law.

Illusory Promises

illusory promise
A contract into which both parties enter, but one or both of the parties can choose not to perform their contractual obligations. Thus the contract lacks consideration.

If parties enter into a contract but one or both of the parties can choose not to perform their contractual obligations, the contract lacks consideration. Such promises, which are known as **illusory promises** (or **illusory contracts**), are unenforceable.

Example: A contract that provides that one of the parties has to perform only if he or she chooses to do so is an illusory contract.

Moral Obligation

moral obligation
A duty that rests on moral considerations alone and is not imposed or enforced by positive law; a duty binding in conscience but not in law.

Promises made out of a sense of **moral obligation** or honor are generally unenforceable on the grounds that they lack consideration. In other words, moral consideration is not treated as legal consideration. Contracts based on love and affection and deathbed promises are examples of such promises. A minority of states hold that moral obligations are enforceable.

Preexisting Duty

preexisting duty
A promise lacks consideration if a person promises to perform an act or do something he or she is already under an obligation to do.

A promise lacks consideration if a person promises to perform an act or do something he or she is already under an obligation to do. This is called a **preexisting duty**. The promise is unenforceable because no new consideration has been given.

Example: Many states have adopted statutes that prohibit police officers from accepting rewards for apprehending criminals.

In the private sector, the preexisting duty rule often arises when one of the parties to an existing contract seeks to change the terms of the contract during the course of its performance. Such midstream changes are unenforceable: The parties have a preexisting duty to perform according to the original terms of the contract.

Unforeseen Difficulties

Sometimes a party to a contract runs into substantial *unforeseen difficulties* while performing his or her contractual duties. If the parties modify their contract to accommodate these unforeseen difficulties, the modification will be enforced even though it is not supported by new consideration.

Example: Suppose a landowner enters into a contract with a contractor who agrees to excavate the hole for the foundation of a major office building. When the excavation is partially completed, toxic wastes are unexpectedly found at the site. Removal of toxic wastes is highly regulated by law and would substantially increase the cost of the excavation. If the landowner agrees to pay the contractor increased compensation to remove the toxic wastes, this modification of the contract is enforceable even though it is unsupported by new consideration.

Past Consideration

In a business setting, problems of **past consideration** often arise when a party to a contract promises to pay additional compensation for work done in the past.

Example: Felipe Chavez, who has worked for the Acme Corporation for 30 years, is retiring. The president of Acme says, "Because you were such a loyal employee, Acme will pay you a bonus of $25,000." The corporation refuses to pay the $25,000. Unfortunately for Mr. Chavez, the contract is unenforceable because it is based on past consideration.

In the following case, the court had to decide whether there was consideration.

past consideration
A prior act or performance. Past consideration (e.g., prior acts) will not support a new contract. New consideration must be given.

CASE 3.3   CONSIDERATION

In re Wirth, 789 N.Y.S.2d 69 (App. Div. 2005).

> "*The Pledge Agreement further stated: 'I acknowledge that Drexel's promise to use the amount pledged by me shall constitute full and adequate consideration for this pledge.'*"
>
> Judge Schmidt, *Supreme Court of New York, Appellate Division*

Facts

Raymond P. Wirth signed a Pledge Agreement that stated that in consideration of his interest in education, and "intending to be legally bound," he irrevocably pledged and promised to pay Drexel University the sum of $150,000. The Pledge Agreement provided that an endowed scholarship would be created in Wirth's name. Wirth died two months after signing the pledge but before any money had been paid to Drexel. When the estate of Wirth refused to honor the pledge, Drexel sued the estate to collect the $150,000. The estate alleged that the pledge was unenforceable because of lack of consideration. The surrogate court denied Drexel's motion for summary judgment and dismissed Drexel's claim against the estate. Drexel appealed.

Issue

Was the Pledge Agreement supported by consideration and therefore enforceable against the estate of Wirth?

Language of the Court

Pursuant to Pennsylvania's Uniform Written Obligations Act: "A written release or promise, hereafter made and signed by the person releasing or promising, shall not be invalid or unenforceable for lack of consideration, if the writing also contains an additional express statement, in any form or language, that the signer intends to be legally bound." Pursuant to this statute, the Pledge Agreement does not fail for lack of consideration, as the decedent expressly stated his intent to be legally bound by the pledge.

Moreover, even if we were to determine that the decedent, as promisor, anticipated consideration in return for his promise, there was no failure of consideration. The Pledge Agreement, which also was executed by representatives of Drexel, provided that the pledged sum "shall be used by" Drexel to create an endowed scholarship fund in the decedent's name, per the terms of the attached Letter of Understanding. The Pledge Agreement further stated: "I acknowledge that Drexel's promise to use the amount pledged by me shall constitute full and adequate consideration for this pledge."

In our view, pursuant to the terms of the Pledge Agreement, Drexel provided sufficient consideration by expressly accepting the terms of the Pledge Agreement and by promising to establish the scholarship fund in the decedent's name. The fact that the decedent died before the initial gift was transferred into a special account set up by Drexel and therefore the scholarship fund was not yet implemented, did not negate the sufficiency of the promise as consideration to set up the fund.

Decision

The appellate court held that the Pledge Agreement was supported by consideration and was therefore enforceable against the estate of Wirth. The appellate court reversed the decision of the surrogate court and granted Drexel's motion for summary judgment against the estate of Wirth.

Law & Ethics Questions

1. What is consideration? What happens if there is lack of consideration supporting a promise? Explain.

2. **Ethics** Was it ethical for the estate of Wirth to try to back out of the pledge agreement made by Wirth before he died?

3. What special statute did Pennsylvania enact that solves the issue of lack of consideration in many contracts? Explain.

Web Exercises

1. **Web** Visit the website of the Supreme Court of New York, Appellate Division, Second Department, at www.courts.state.ny.us/courts/ad2.

2. **Web** Visit the website of Drexel University at www.drexel.edu and Drexel Online at www.drexel.com.

3. **Web** Use www.google.com and find an article that discusses a pledge or gift to your college or university.

Concept Summary

Promises Lacking Consideration

Type of Consideration	Description of Promise
Illegal consideration	Promise to refrain from doing an illegal act.
Illusory promise	Promise in which one or both parties can choose not to perform their obligation.
Moral obligation	Promise made out of a sense of moral obligation, honor, love, or affection. Some states enforce these types of contracts.
Preexisting duty	Promise based on the preexisting duty of the promisee to perform. The promise is enforceable if (1) the parties rescind the contract and enter into a new contract or (2) there are unforeseen difficulties.
Past consideration	Promise based on the past performance of the promisee.

THE ETHICAL PARALEGAL

Competence

An attorney has a double duty to represent a client competently. The common law of torts controls where an attorney has committed professional negligence. ABA Model Rule 1.1 requires that the attorney have legal knowledge, skill, thoroughness and preparation so as to be competent in representing a client.[3]

The ethical paralegal must share the attorney's requirement of competence by engaging in education and training. As a paralegal student, you are engaging in that education and training right now. However, to maintain your competence, you will need to attend continuing legal education seminars and keep up with the case law in your area throughout your professional career.

MARKETPLACE

Transactional Paralegal Job Announcement

Large law firm has an immediate need for a transactional paralegal in its Equipment & Financing Dept. Work includes document preparation, filing documents/UCCs, contract preparation and review, and document distribution. High-profile position with direct contact w/clients and opposing counsel.

Requirements: 4 yr. degree/paralegal certification, 2+ years exp. as corporate transactional paralegal. Some overtime and travel required.

Forward resume to:

---

[3]Copies of the ABA Model Rules of Professional Conduct are available from Service Center, American Bar Association, 321 North Clark Street, Chicago, IL 60610, 1-800-285-2221. The Model Rules can also be viewed online at http://www.abanet.org/cpr/mrpc/mrpc_toc.html.

CONTEMPORARY Issue

SPECIAL BUSINESS CONTRACTS

Generally, the courts tolerate a greater degree of uncertainty in business contracts than in personal contracts, under the premise that sophisticated parties know how to protect themselves when negotiating contracts. The law imposes an obligation of good faith on the performance of the parties to requirements and output contracts.

The following are special types of business contracts that specifically allow a greater degree of uncertainty concerning consideration:

Output Contract

In an **output contract**, the seller agrees to sell all of its production to a single buyer. Output contracts serve the legitimate business purposes of (1) assuring the seller of a purchaser for all its output and (2) assuring the buyer of a source of supply for the goods it needs.

Example: Organic Foods Inc. operates farms that produce organically grown grains and vegetables. Whole Food Markets is a grocery store chain that sells organically grown foods. Whole Food Markets contracts with Organic Foods Inc. to purchase all of the organic foods grown by Organic Foods, Inc. this year. This is an example of an output contract: Organic Foods Inc. must sell all of its output to Whole Foods Market.

Requirements Contract

A **requirements contract** is one in which a buyer contracts to purchase all of the requirements for an item from one seller. Such contracts serve the legitimate business purposes of (1) assuring the buyer of a uniform source of supply and (2) providing the seller with reduced selling costs.

Example: The Firestone Tire Company manufactures tires used on automobiles. Ford Motor Company manufactures automobiles on which it must place tires before the automobiles can be sold. Ford Motor Company enters into a contract with Firestone Tire Company to purchase all of the tires it will need this year from Firestone Tire Company. This is an example of a requirements contract: Ford Motor Company has agreed to purchase all of the tires it will need from Firestone Tire Company.

Best-Efforts Contract

A **best-efforts contract** contains a clause that requires one or both of the parties to use their *best efforts* to achieve the objective of the contract. The courts generally have held that the imposition of the best-efforts duty provides sufficient consideration to make a contract enforceable.

Example: Real estate listing contracts often require a real estate broker to use his or her best efforts to find a buyer for the listed real estate. Contracts often require underwriters to use their best efforts to sell securities on behalf of their corporate clients.

---

output contract
A contract in which one party agrees to sell his or her entire output and the other agrees to buy it.

requirement contract
A contract in which the purchaser agrees to buy all of its needs of specified material from a particular supplier, and the latter agrees to fill all of the purchaser's needs during the period of the contract.

best-efforts contract
A contract clause that requires one or both of the parties to use their best efforts to achieve the objective of the contract.

■ SETTLEMENT OF CLAIMS

The law promotes the voluntary settlement of disputed claims. Settlement saves judicial resources and serves the interests of the parties entering into the settlement.

In some situations, one of the parties to a contract believes he or she did not receive what he or she was due. This party may attempt to reach a compromise with the other party (e.g., by paying less consideration than was provided for in the contract). The compromise agreement is called an **accord**. If the accord is performed, it is called a **satisfaction**. This type of settlement is called an **accord and satisfaction** or a compromise. If the accord is not satisfied, the other party can sue to enforce either the accord or the original contract.

Example: Suppose that a contract stipulated the cost of a computer system to keep track of inventory, accounts receivable, and so on, is $100,000. After it is installed, the computer system does not perform as promised. To settle the dispute, the parties agree that $70,000 is to be paid as full and final payment for the computer. This accord is enforceable even though no new consideration is given because reasonable persons would disagree on the worth of the computer system that was actually installed.

accord
An agreement whereby the parties agree to accept something different in satisfaction of the original contract.

satisfaction
The performance of an accord.

accord and satisfaction
The settlement of a contract dispute.

■ EQUITY

Reviewing common law, you may remember that two separate courts developed in England: the courts of law and the Chancery Courts (or courts of equity). The equity courts developed a set of maxims based on fairness, equality, moral rights, and natural law that were applied in settling disputes. **Equity** was resorted to when (1) an award of money damages "at law" would not be the proper remedy or (2) fairness required the application of equitable principles. Today, in most U.S. states, the courts of law and equity have been merged into one court. In an action "in equity," the judge decides the equitable issue; there is no right to a jury trial in an equitable action. The doctrine of equity is sometimes applied in contract cases.

equity
A doctrine that permits judges to make decisions based on fairness, equality, moral rights, and natural law.

ETHICS SPOTLIGHT

EQUITY SAVES CONTRACTING PARTY

"[T]here is only minimal delay in giving notice, the harm to the lessor is slight, and the hardship to the lessee is severe."

Judge Abbe

The courts usually interpret a valid contract as a solemn promise to perform. This view of the sanctity of a contract can cause an ethical conflict. Consider the following case.

A landlord leased a motel he owned to lessees for a 10-year period. The lessees had an option to extend the lease for an additional 10 years. To do so, they had to give written notice to the landlord three months before the first 10-year lease expired. The lease provided for forfeiture of all furniture, fixtures, and equipment installed by the lessees, free of any liens, upon termination of the lease.

For almost 10 years the lessees devoted most of their assets and a great deal of their energy building up the business. During this time, they transformed a disheveled, unrated motel into a AAA three-star operation. With the landlord's knowledge, the lessees made extensive long-term improvements that greatly increased the value of both the property and the business. The landlord knew that the lessees had obtained long-term financing for the improvements that would extend well beyond the first 10-year term of the lease. The landlord also knew that the only source of income the lessees had to pay for these improvements was the income generated from the motel business. The lessees told the landlord orally in a conversation that they intended to extend the lease.

The lessees had instructed their accountant to exercise the option on time. Despite reminders from the lessees, the accountant failed to give the written notice within three months of the expiration of the lease. As soon as they discovered the mistake, the lessees personally delivered written notice of renewal of the option to the landlord, 13 days too late. The landlord rejected it as late and instituted a lawsuit for unlawful detainer to evict the lessees.

The trial and appellate courts held in favor of the lessees. They rejected the landlord's argument for the strict adherence to the deadline for giving written notice of renewal of the lease. Instead, the courts granted **equitable relief** and permitted the late renewal notice. The court reasoned that "there is only minimal delay in giving notice, the harm to the lessor is slight, and the hardship to the lessee is severe." *Romasanta v. Mitton*, 234 Cal. Rptr. 729 (Ct. App. 1987).

equitable relief
The kind of relief sought in a court with equity powers (e.g., injunction, specific performance of a contract).

Law & Ethics Questions

1. **Ethics** Did the landlord act ethically in this case?
2. **Ethics** Should the court have applied equity and saved the lessees from their mistake? Or should they have been held to the terms of the lease?

Web Exercises

1. **Web** Visit the Court of Appeal of California, Second Appellate District, at www.courtinfo.ca.gov/courts/courtsofappeal.
2. **Web** Use www.google.com and find an article that discusses the application of equity to contract disputes.

Promissory Estoppel

promissory estoppel
An equitable doctrine that prevents the withdrawal of a promise by a promisor if it will adversely affect a promisee who has adjusted his or her position in justifiable reliance on the promise. An equitable doctrine that permits enforcement of oral contracts that should have been in writing. It is applied to avoid injustice.

The courts have developed the doctrine of **promissory estoppel** or (**detrimental reliance**) to avoid injustice. This doctrine is a broad policy-based doctrine. It is used to provide a remedy to a person who has relied on another person's promise, but that person withdraws his or her promise and is not subject to a breach of contract action because one of the two elements discussed in this chapter (i.e., agreement or consideration) is lacking. The doctrine of promissory estoppel *estops* (prevents) the promisor from revoking his or her promise. Therefore, the person who has detrimentally relied on the promise for performance may sue the promisor for performance or other remedy the court feels is fair to award in the circumstances.

For the doctrine of promissory estoppel to be applied, the following elements must be shown:

1. The promisor made a promise.
2. The promisor should have reasonably expected to induce the promisee to reply on the promise.
3. The promisee actually relied on the promise and engaged in an action or forbearance of a right of a definite and substantial nature.
4. Injustice would be caused if the promise were not enforced.

Example: XYZ Construction Company, a general contractor, requests bids from subcontractors for work to be done on a hospital building that XYZ plans to submit a bid to build. Bert Plumbing Company submits the lowest bid for the plumbing work, and XYZ incorporates Bert's low bid in its own bid for the general contract. In this example, the doctrine of promissory estoppel prevents Bert from withdrawing its bid. If XYZ is awarded the contract to build the hospital, it could enforce Bert's promise to perform.

Equitable Remedies

Courts today can award both legal and equitable remedies, so plaintiffs may request both types of relief in the same case. Three types of economic compensation, or **remedies at law**, can be awarded to a plaintiff. These forms of economic compensation are land (real property), items of value (personal property), and money. If a party wants a remedy other than economic compensation, or if the court concludes that a remedy at law is not appropriate or adequate, the court may award an equitable remedy.

Remedies in equity are based on settled rules of fairness, justice, and honesty. The main remedies in equity are specific performance, rescission, and injunction.

Specific Performance

The equitable remedy of **specific performance** may be used when the contract involves something unique and money damages are not appropriate. In this case, the court would order the party or parties to perform exactly what was promised in the contract.

Example: A contract for the sale of a painting might be appropriate for specific performance because the subject of the contract (the painting) is so unique that money damages will not enable a buyer to obtain a substantially identical substitute in the marketplace.

Rescission

A court may find that the only equitable remedy is to undo a contract. The remedy of **rescission** terminates the contract and returns the parties to the positions they occupied prior to the contract.

Example: A customer might want to rescind, or cancel, an agreement to purchase a high-definition television because the seller misrepresented its quality. The court might order a rescission of the agreement if no money has yet changed hands. If the customer has already paid for the television, the rescission would also involve **restitution**, returning to each party any money or other items of value (the television) that had been exchanged.

Injunction

Although rare in a contractual dispute, an **injunction** may be ordered by the court to direct the defendant to carry out—or refrain from carrying out—the contract. Persons who violate an injunction are typically held in contempt of court and punished with a jail sentence or fine.

equitable remedies
A remedy based upon settled rules of fairness, justice, and honesty.

remedies at law
Economic compensation in the form of real property, personal property, and money.

specific performance
A remedy that orders the breaching party to perform the acts promised in the contract; usually awarded in cases where the subject matter is unique, such as in contracts involving land, heirlooms, and paintings. Judgment of the court ordering a licensor to specifically perform the license by making the contracted-for unique information available to the licensee. A decree of the court that orders a seller or lessor to perform his or her obligations under the contract; usually occurs when the goods in question are unique, such as art or antiques.

rescission
An action to rescind (undo) the contract. Rescission is available if there has been a material breach of contract, fraud, duress, undue influence, or mistake.

restitution
Returning of goods or property received from the other party to rescind a contract; if the actual goods or property is not available, a cash equivalent must be made.

injunction
A court order that prohibits a person from doing a certain act.

INTERNET EXERCISES AND CASE QUESTIONS

Working the Web Internet Exercises

1. For a simplified explanation of the concept of consideration, see www .lectlaw.com/def/c098.jtm and visit the encyclopedia section. Type in "consideration."
2. Check out the summary of consideration available at www.law.cornell.edu.

CHAPTER 3 SUMMARY

CONSIDERATION, p. 68

Consideration

Consideration involves a thing of value being given in exchange for a promise. It may be tangible or intangible property, performance of a service, forbearance of a legal right, or another thing of value.

Requirements of Consideration

1. *Legal value.* Something of legal value must be given as consideration. Either (a) the promisee suffers a *legal detriment* or (b) the promisor receives a *legal benefit*.
2. *Bargained-for-exchange.* A contract must arise from a bargained-for-exchange. *Gift promises* (or *gratuitous promises*) are unenforceable because they lack consideration.

Special Contracts

1. *Requirements contracts.* Contracts in which the buyer agrees to purchase all the requirements for an item from a single seller are enforceable if the parties act in good faith.
2. *Output contracts.* Contracts in which the seller agrees to sell all its production to a single buyer are enforceable if the parties act in good faith.
3. *Best-efforts contracts.* Contracts that require a party to use its best efforts to accomplish the objective of the contract are enforceable.

CONTRACTS LACKING CONSIDERATION, p. 75

The following contracts are unenforceable because they lack consideration:

1. *Illegal consideration.* Promise to refrain from doing an illegal act.
2. *Illusory promise.* If one or both parties to a contract can choose not to perform their contractual duties.
3. *Moral obligation.* Promise made out of a sense of moral obligation, honor, love, or affection.
4. *Preexisting duty.* Promise to perform an act or do something that a person is already under an obligation to do.
5. *Past consideration.* Promise based on a party's past consideration.

EQUITY, p. 81

1. *Remedy in equity.* A remedy allowed by courts in situations where remedies at law are not appropriate.
2. *Remedies.* Remedies in equity are based on settled rules of fairness, justice, and honesty.
3. *Equitable remedies.*
   a. *Specific performance.* An equitable remedy requiring exactly the performance that was specified in a contract.
   b. *Rescission.* An equitable remedy where a contract is terminated and the parties are returned to the positions they occupied before the contract was made.
   c. *Injunction.* A court decree ordering a person to do or refrain from doing a certain act or activity.

PROMISSORY ESTOPPEL, p. 82

Promissory estoppel is a policy-based equitable doctrine that prevents a promisor from revoking his or her promise even though the promise lacks consideration. The requirements are:

1. The promisor made a promise.
2. The promisor should have reasonably expected to induce the promisee to rely on the promise.
3. The promisee actually relied on the promise and engaged in an action or forbearance of a right of a definite and substantial nature.
4. Injustice would be caused if the promise were not enforced.

TERMS AND CONCEPTS

Accord   81

Accord and satisfaction (compromise)   81

Adequacy of consideration   74

Bargained-for exchange   69

Best-efforts contract   80

Consideration   68

Equitable relief   82

Equitable remedies   83

Equity   81

Gift promises (gratuitous promises)   70

Illegal consideration   75

Illusory promises (illusory contracts)   76

Injunction   83

Legal value   69

Moral obligation   76

Output contract   80

Past consideration   77

Preexisting duty   76

Promissory estoppel (detrimental reliance)   82

Remedies at law   83

Requirements contract   80

Rescission   83

Restitution   83

Satisfaction   81

Specific performance   83

CASE SCENARIO REVISITED

What you have learned about enforceability will help you understand Dean's rights to the gym in this chapter's case scenario. Did consideration exist in Jan and Dean's agreement? Take a look at *Penley v. Penley*, 332 S.E.2d 51 (N.C. 1985), to aid you in your answer.

CRITICAL LEGAL THINKING CASES

Critical Legal Thinking Case 3.1 *Forbearance to Sue* When John W. Frasier died, he left a will that devised certain of his community and separate property to his wife, Lena, and their three children. These devises were more valuable to Lena than just her interest in the community property that she would otherwise have received without the will. The devises to her, however, were conditioned on the filing of a waiver by Lena of her interest in the community property, and if she failed to file the waiver, she would then receive only her interest in the community property and nothing more. Lena hired her brother, D. L. Carter, an attorney, to represent her. Carter failed to file the waiver on Lena's behalf, thus preventing her from taking under the will. Instead, she received her interest in the community property, which was $19,358 less than she would have received under the will. Carter sent Lena the following letter:

> This is to advise and confirm our agreement—that in the event the J. W. Frasier estate case now on appeal is not terminated so that you will receive settlement equal to your share of the estate as you would have done if your waiver had been filed in the estate in proper time, I will make up any balance to you in payments as suits my convenience and will pay interest on your loss at 6 percent.

The appeal was decided against Lena. When she tried to enforce the contract against Carter, he alleged that the contract was not enforceable because it was not supported by valid consideration. Who wins? *Frasier v. Carter*, 432 P.2d 32 (Idaho 1968).

Critical Legal Thinking Case 3.2 *Past Consideration* A. J. Whitmire and R. Lee Whitmire were brothers. R. Lee Whitmire married Lillie Mae Whitmire. For four years, A. J. performed various services for his brother and sister-in-law. During this time, R. Lee and Lillie Mae purchased some land. Fifteen years later, in the presence of Lillie Mae, R. Lee told A. J., "When we're gone, this land is yours." At that time, A. J. had not done any work for R. Lee or Lillie Mae for 16 years, and none was expected or provided in the future. Thirty years later, after both R. Lee and Lillie Mae had died, A. J. filed a claim with the estate of Lillie Mae seeking specific performance of the earlier promise to give him the land. Does A. J. get the property? *Whitmire v. Watkins*, 267 S.E.2d 6 (Ga. 1980).

Critical Legal Thinking Case 3.3 *Preexisting Duty* Robert Chuckrow Construction Company (Chuckrow) was employed as the general contractor to build a Kinney shoe store. Chuckrow employed Ralph Gough to perform the carpentry work on the store. The contract with Gough stipulated that he was to provide all labor, materials, tools, equipment, scaffolding, and other items necessary to complete the carpentry work. Gough's employees erected 38 trusses at the job site. The next day, 32 of the trusses fell off the building. The reason for the trusses having fallen was unexplained, and evidence showed it was not due to Chuckrow's fault or a deficiency in the building plans. Chuckrow told Gough that he would pay him to reerect the trusses and continue work. When the job was complete, Chuckrow paid Gough the original contract price but refused to pay him for the additional cost of reerecting the trusses. Gough sued Chuckrow for this expense. Can Gough recover? *Robert Chuckrow Constr. Co. v. Gough*, 159 S.E.2d 469 (Ga. Ct. App. 1968).

Critical Legal Thinking Case 3.4 *Promissory Estoppel* Nalley's, Inc. (Nalley's) was a major food distributor with its home office in the state of Washington. Jacob Aronowicz and Samuel Duncan approached Nalley's about the possibility of their company manufacturing a line of sliced meat products to be distributed by Nalley's. When Nalley's showed considerable interest, Aronowicz and Duncan incorporated as Major Food Products, Inc. (Major). Meetings to discuss the proposal continued at length with Charles Gardiner, a vice president and general manager of Nalley's Los Angeles division. Gardiner delivered a letter to Major, agreeing to become the exclusive Los Angeles and Orange Country distributor for Major's products, but he stated in the letter "that should we determine your product line is not representative or is not compatible with our operation we are free to terminate our agreement within 30 days." Nalley's was to distribute the full production of products produced by Major.

Based on Gardiner's assurances, Major leased a plant, modified the plant to its specifications, purchased and installed equipment, signed contracts to obtain meat to be processed, and hired personnel. Both Aronowicz and Duncan resigned from their positions at other meat-processing companies to devote full time to the project. Financing was completed when Aronowicz and Duncan used their personal fortunes to purchase the stock of Major. Gardiner and other representatives of Nalley's visited Major's plant and expressed satisfaction with the premises. Major obtained the necessary government approvals regarding health standards and immediately achieved full production. Because Nalley's was to pick up the finished products at Major's plant, Nalley's drivers visited Major's plant to acquaint themselves with its operations.

Gardiner sent the final proposal regarding the Nalley's and Major relationship to Nalley's home office for final approval. One week later, Nalley's home office in Washington made a decision not to distribute Major's products. Nalley's refused to give any reason to Major for its decision. No final agreement was ever executed between the parties. Immediate efforts by Major to secure other distribution for its products proved unsuccessful. Further, because Major owned no trucks itself and had no sales organization, it could not distribute the products itself. In less than six months, Major had failed, and Aronowicz's and Duncan's stock in Major was worthless. Major, Aronowicz, and Duncan sued Nalley's for damages under the doctrine of promissory estoppel. Do they win? *Aronowicz v. Nalley's, Inc.*, 106 Cal. Rptr. 424 (Ct. App. 1972).

ETHICS CASES

Ethics Case 3.1   Kortney Dempsey took a cruise on a ship operated by Norwegian Cruise Line (Norwegian). In general, suits for personal injuries arising out of maritime torts are subject to a three-year statute of limitations. However, Congress permits this period to be reduced to one year by contract. The Norwegian passenger ticket limited the period to one year. Evidence showed that the cruise line ticket contained the notation "Important Notice" in a bright red box in the bottom-right corner of each of the first four pages of the ticket. The information in the box stated that certain pages of the ticket contain information that "affect[s] important legal rights." In addition, at the top of page 6 of the ticket, where the terms and conditions begin, it is stated in bold letters: "Passengers are advised to read the terms and conditions of the Passenger Ticket Contract set forth below." The clause at issue, which appears on page 8, clearly provides that suits must be brought within one year of injury. More than one year after Dempsey had taken the cruise (but within three years), she filed suit against Norwegian, seeking damages for an alleged injury suffered while on the cruise. Dempsey asserted that the one-year limitations period had not been reasonably communicated to her. Did Dempsey act ethically in suing when she did? Did Norwegian act ethically in reducing the limitations period to one year? Who wins the lawsuit? *Dempsey v. Norwegian Cruise Line*, 972 F.2d 998 (9th Cir. 1992).

Ethics Case 3.2 Genaro Munoz owned property that he leased to Goodwest Rubber Corporation (Goodwest) for five years. The lease granted Goodwest the option to buy the property at a fair market value. Goodwest sought to exercise the option to purchase the property and tendered $80,000 to Munoz. When Munoz rejected this offer, Goodwest filed suit, seeking specific performance of the option agreement. The court was presented with a single issue for review: Was a price designation of "fair market value" definite enough to support an action for specific performance? Do you think Munoz acted ethically in refusing to honor the option? Who wins? *Goodwest Rubber Corp. v. Munoz*, 216 Cal. Rptr. 604 (Ct. App. 1985).

Ethics Case 3.3 Ocean Dunes of Hutchinson Island Development Corporation (Ocean Dunes) was a developer of condominium units. Prior to the construction, Albert and Helen Colangelo entered into a purchase agreement to buy one of the units and paid a deposit to Ocean Dunes. A provision in the purchase agreement provided the following:

> *If Developer shall default in the performance of its obligations pursuant to this agreement, Purchaser's only remedy shall be to terminate this agreement, whereupon the Deposit shall be refunded to Purchaser and all rights and obligations thereunder shall thereupon become null and void.*

The purchase agreement provided that if the buyer defaulted, the developer could retain the buyer's deposit or sue the buyer for damages and any other legal or equitable remedy. When Ocean Dunes refused to sell the unit to the Colangelos, they sued, seeking a decree of specific performance to require Ocean Dunes to sell them the unit. Ocean Dunes alleged that the provision just quoted prevented the plaintiffs from seeking any legal or equitable remedy. Was the defendant's duty under the contract illusory? Was it ethical for Ocean Dunes to place the provision at issue in the contract? *Ocean Dunes of Hutchinson Island Dev. Corp. v. Colangelo*, 463 So. 2d 437 (Fla. Dist. Ct. App. 1985).

Ethics Case 3.4 Red Owl Stores, Inc., a Minnesota corporation with its home office at Hopkins, Minnesota, owns and operates grocery supermarkets and grants franchises to franchisees to also operate such stores. Joseph Hoffman, who operated a bakery with his wife in Wautoma, Wisconsin, was interested in obtaining a Red Owl franchise to operate a grocery store in Wisconsin. Hoffman contacted a representative of Red Owl and had numerous conversations regarding this proposal. Ten months later, Mr. Lukowitz became Red Owl's representative for the territory comprising upper Michigan and most of Wisconsin. Hoffman mentioned to Lukowitz that he had the capital to invest, and Lukowitz assured him that would be sufficient to open a Red Owl franchise.

To gain experience in the grocery store business, and on the advice of Lukowitz and other Red Owl representatives, Hoffman bought a small grocery store in Wautoma. After three months of operating this store, a Red Owl representative came in and took inventory, checked operations, and found the store was operating at a profit. Lukowitz advised Hoffman to sell the store to his manager and assured Hoffman that Red Owl would find a larger store for him elsewhere. Although Hoffman was reluctant to sell at that time because it meant losing the summer tourist business, he sold on the assurance he would be operating a Red Owl store at a new location by the fall. Again, Lukowitz assured Hoffman that the capital he had was sufficient to open a Red Owl franchise.

Red Owl had selected a site in Chilton, Wisconsin, for the proposed store. On Red Owl's insistence, Hoffman obtained an option to purchase the site. Hoffman and his wife rented a house in Chilton. Hoffman met with Lukowitz, who assured him, "Everything is ready to go. Get your money together and we are set." Lukowitz told Hoffman he must sell his bakery business and building in Wautoma, which was the only "hitch" in the entire plan. Hoffman sold his bakery building but retained the equipment to be used in the proposed Red Owl store. During the next two months, Red Owl prepared various financial projections for the proposed site. Hoffman met with Lukowitz and the credit manager for Red Owl, who demanded that Hoffman have more capital to invest in the store. Hoffman contacted his father-in-law, who agreed to provide the additional money. A week later Red Owl sent Hoffman a telegram demanding that he have more capital to invest. When Hoffman could not raise the additional money, the transaction fell through. Hoffman did not purchase the store site in Chilton and forfeited the option payment. The parties had never entered into a final agreement regarding the franchise.

Hoffman sued Red Owl under the doctrine of promissory estoppel, seeking damages for the money lost on the option payment on the Chilton property and the lease payments on the house in Chilton. Did the representatives of Red Owl Stores, Inc. act ethically in this case? Should the equitable doctrine of promissory estoppel apply in this case? *Hoffman v. Red Owl Stores, Inc.*, 133 N.W.2d 267 (Wis. 1965).

BRIEFING THE CASE WRITING ASSIGNMENT

Read Case A.3 in Appendix A (*Congregation Kadimah Toras-Moshe v. DeLeo*). This case is excerpted from the court of appeals opinion. Review and brief the case. After briefing the case, you should be able to answer the following questions:

1. What was the plaintiff suing for? Explain.
2. What was the defendant estate's defense?
3. How did the court decide this case?

PRACTICE TIP

Once the date and the parties to the contract are set out (see the Practice Tip in Chapter 1), and the introduction as to what the parties would like to contract is written (see the Practice Tip in Chapter 2), the next step in drafting the contract is to follow with a recital describing the transaction. The form for this introduction is as follows:

NOW THEREFORE, _____ and _____ agree as follows:

1. _____
   _____
2. _____
   _____
3. _____
   _____

An unconscionable contract is one which no man in his senses, not under delusion, would make, on the one hand, and which no fair and honest man would accept on the other.

—*Hume v. United States*

132 U.S. 406 (1889).

Capacity and Legality | CHAPTER 4

CASE SCENARIO

The law firm where you work as a paralegal represents Michael, an auto sales dealer. James, a minor, entered into a contract to purchase a 2008 Hummer from Michael. James paid $5,000 in cash and agreed to pay $1,000 per week until the full purchase price of $50,000 was paid. Five weeks later, a connecting rod on the vehicle's engine broke. James took the car to a garage, where it was repaired at a cost of $4,000. James refused to pay for the repairs and told Michael he was "getting out" of the contract to purchase the Hummer.

■ CHAPTER INTRODUCTION

Generally, the law presumes that the parties to a contract have the requisite **contractual capacity** to enter into the contract. Certain persons do not have this capacity, however, including minors, insane persons, and intoxicated persons. The common law of contracts and many state statutes protect persons who lack contractual capacity from having contracts enforced against them. The party asserting incapacity or his or her guardian, conservator, or other legal representative bears the burden of proof.

An essential element for the formation of a contract is that the object of the contract be lawful. A contract to perform an illegal act is called an **illegal contract** and is void. That is, it cannot be enforced by either party to the contract. The term "illegal contract" is a misnomer, however, because no contract exists if the object of the contract is illegal. In addition, courts hold that **unconscionable contracts**

contractual capacity
The legal qualification or competency to understand the nature and effects of one's acts so as to enter into a contract.

illegal contract
A contract to perform an illegal act.

unconscionable contracts
A contract so oppressive or unfair that it would be unjust for the court to enforce it.

CHAPTER OBJECTIVES

After studying this chapter, you should be able to:

1. Define and describe the infancy doctrine.

2. Define *legal insanity* and *intoxication* and explain how they affect contractual capacity.

3. Identify illegal contracts that are contrary to statutes and those that violate public policy.

4. Describe covenants not to compete and exculpatory clauses and identify when they are lawful.

5. Define *unconscionable contracts* and determine when these contracts are unlawful.

are unenforceable. An unconscionable contract is one that is so oppressive or manifestly unfair, it would be unjust to enforce it.

Capacity to contract and the lawfulness of contracts are discussed in this chapter.

PARALEGAL PERSPECTIVE

Angel Dietzel is a graduate of Athens Technical College's Paralegal Studies Program, Athens, Georgia. She works as a privacy and data security specialist for McKesson Technology Solutions in Atlanta, Georgia.

As a privacy and data security specialist, my focus is on various components of privacy and security compliance programs. These programs are supervised by the chief privacy and data security officer.

The responsibilities associated with my job are varied. They include assessing and evaluating compliance initiatives, performing audits and evaluations, performing legal research, updating policies and procedures, and performing specific contractual audit reviews. The everyday realm of responsibilities associated with organizing and maintaining files and databases is ever present.

The variety of programs and responsibilities assigned to me makes my job interesting and challenging. I'm an integral part of the team. As such, there is always opportunity to learn more and grow. The only limitation I have is self-imposed.

I find this to be an exciting yet complex industry in which flexibility and adaptability are valued traits.

CAREER FRONT

Job Description: Contract Administration Paralegal

A contract administration paralegal works with contracts in numerous ways, such as the following:

- Works with internal business groups representing outside vendor services to determine need for and scope of potential contract.
- Negotiates contract terms with outside vendor.
- If vendor does not provide contract, drafts contract for outside services.
- Reviews vendor contract for accuracy of scope, provisions, and cost. Revises and/or amends vendor contract as necessary to obtain adequate protection for company.
- Maintains database and/or central repository of all existing contracts with outside vendors.
- Creates contract clause manual for boilerplate contract language.
- Develops standard services contracts for routine services.

Source: Excerpted by permission from the National Association of Legal Assistants (www.nala.org) and the National Federation of Paralegal Associations, Inc. (www.paralegals.org).

■ MINORS

minor
A person who has not reached the age of majority.

Minors do not always have the maturity, experience, or sophistication needed to enter into contracts with adults. Common law defines minors as females younger than 18 years and males younger than 21 years. In addition, many states have enacted statutes that specify the *age of majority*. The most prevalent age of majority is 18 for both males and females. Any age below the statutory age of majority is called the *period of minority*.

The Infancy Doctrine

To protect minors, the law recognizes the **infancy doctrine**, which gives minors the right to *disaffirm* (or *cancel*) most contracts they have entered into with adults. This right is based on public policy that reasons minors should be protected from the unscrupulous behavior of adults. In most states, the infancy doctrine is an objective standard. If a person's age is below the age of majority, the court will not inquire into his or her knowledge, experience, or sophistication. Generally, contracts for the necessaries of life, which we discuss later in this chapter, are exempted from the scope of this doctrine.

Under the infancy doctrine, a minor has the option of choosing whether to enforce a contract (i.e., the contract is *voidable* by a minor). The adult party is bound to the minor's decision. If both parties to a contract are minors, both parties have the right to disaffirm the contract.

If performance of the contract favors the minor, the minor will probably enforce the contract. Otherwise, he or she will probably disaffirm the contract. A minor may not affirm one part of a contract and disaffirm another part.

infancy doctrine
A doctrine that allows minors to disaffirm (cancel) most contracts they have entered into with adults.

Disaffirmance

A minor can expressly **disaffirm** a contract orally, in writing, or through his or her conduct. No special formalities are required. The contract may be disaffirmed at any time prior to the person's reaching the age of majority plus a "reasonable time." The designation of a reasonable time is determined on a case-by-case basis.

disaffirmance
The act of a minor to rescind a contract under the infancy doctrine. Disaffirmance may be done orally, in writing, or by the minor's conduct.

Minor's Duty of Restoration and Restitution

If a minor's contract is executory and neither party has performed, the minor can simply disaffirm the contract: There is nothing to recover because neither party has given the other party anything of value. If the parties have exchanged consideration and partially or fully performed the contract by the time the minor disaffirms the contract, however, the issue becomes one of what consideration or restitution must be made. The following rules apply:

- *Competent party's duty of restitution*—If the minor has transferred consideration—money, property, or other valuables—to the competent party before disaffirming the contract, that party must place the minor in status quo. That is, the minor must be restored to the same position he or she was in before the minor entered into the contract. This restoration is usually done by returning the consideration to the minor. If the consideration has been sold or has depreciated in value, the competent party must pay the minor the cash equivalent. This action is called the competent party's **duty of restitution**.
- *Minor's duty of restoration*—Generally, a minor is obligated only to return the goods or property he or she has received from the adult in the condition it is in at the time of disaffirmance (subject to several exceptions, discussed later in this chapter), even if the item has been consumed, lost, or destroyed or has depreciated in value by the time of disaffirmance. This rule is called the minor's **duty of restoration**. It is based on the rationale that if a minor

duty of restitution
Where, upon disaffirmance, the competent party returns the consideration of the contract back to the minor.

duty of restoration
Where, upon disaffirmance, the minor returns the goods or property back to the competent party.

had to place the adult in status quo upon disaffirmance of a contract, there would be an incentive for an adult to deal with a minor.

Example: When Sherry is 17 years old (a minor) she enters into a contract to purchase an automobile costing $10,000 from Bruce, a competent adult. Bruce, who believes Sherry is an adult and does not ask for verification of her age, delivers ownership of the automobile to Sherry after he receives her payment of $10,000. Subsequently, before Sherry reaches the age of 18 (the age of majority) she is involved in an automobile accident not caused by her own negligence. The automobile sustains $7,000 worth of damage in the accident (and is now only worth $3,000). Sherry can disaffirm the contract, return the damaged automobile to Bruce, and recover $10,000 from Bruce. In this result, Sherry recovers her entire $10,000 purchase price from Bruce, and Bruce only has a damaged automobile worth $3,000.

Example: When Sherry is 17 years old (a minor) she enters into a contract to purchase an automobile costing $10,000 from Bruce, a competent adult. Bruce, who believes Sherry is an adult and does not ask for verification of her age, delivers ownership of the automobile to Sherry after he receives her payment of $10,000. Subsequently, before Sherry reaches the age of 18 (the age of majority) she is involved in an automobile accident caused by her own recklessness. The accident happened because Sherry was driving 70 miles per hour in a 45 mph traffic zone. The automobile sustains $7,000 worth of damage in the accident (and is now only worth $3,000). Sherry can disaffirm the contract and return the damaged automobile to Bruce, but she can only recover $3,000 from Bruce. In this result, Bruce is made whole (he keeps $7,000 of Sherry's money and has a damaged automobile worth $3,000). Sherry has $3,000.

On occasion, minors might misrepresent their age to adults when entering into contracts. Most state laws provide that minors who misrepresent their age must place the adult in status quo if they disaffirm the contract.

Example: When Sherry is 17 years old (a minor) she enters into a contract to purchase an automobile that costs $10,000 from Bruce, a competent adult. Bruce, who has doubts that Sherry is an adult, asks Sherry for verification of her age. Sherry produces a driver's license that shows she is 19 years old. Bruce delivers ownership of the automobile to Sherry after he receives her payment of $10,000. Subsequently, before Sherry reaches the age of 18 (the age of majority) she is involved in an automobile accident caused by another driver's negligence. Sherry is not at fault. The automobile sustains $7,000 worth of damage in the accident (and is now only worth $3,000). Sherry can disaffirm the contract and return the damaged automobile to Bruce, but she can only recover $3,000 from Bruce. This is because she lied about her age. In this result, Bruce is made whole (he keeps $7,000 of Sherry's money and has a damaged automobile worth $3,000).

A few states have enacted statutes that require the minor to make restitution of the reasonable value of the item when disaffirming any contract.

Misrepresentation of Age

On occasion, minors might misrepresent their age to adults when entering into contracts. Under the common law, such a minor would still have the right to disaffirm the contract. Most states, however, have changed this rule in recognition of its unfairness to adults. The revised rule provides that minors who misrepresent their age must place the adult in status quo if they disaffirm the contract. In other words, a minor who has misrepresented his or her age when entering into a contract owes the duties of restoration and restitution when disaffirming it.

Example: Sherry McNamara, a minor, misrepresents that she is an adult and enters into a contract to purchase an automobile costing $20,000 from Bruce Ruffino, a competent adult. Ruffino delivers the automobile after he receives payment in full. The automobile later sustains $7,000 worth of damage in an accident that is not McNamara's fault. To disaffirm the contract, McNamara must return the damaged automobile plus $13,000 to Ruffino.

THE ETHICAL PARALEGAL

Fees

An attorney cannot divide fees with nonattorneys. ABA Model Rule 5.4 specifically prohibits fee splitting with nonattorneys.[1] So, for example, the ethical paralegal cannot have a contract with the attorney that would give the paralegal a percentage of the attorney's fees for case referrals.[2]

This does not mean the paralegal can never recieve a bonus or salary increase. But it does mean that such a bonus or salary increase cannot be based on the outcome of a case, the profits of the firm, or a percentage of a particular legal fee.

Ratification

If a minor does not disaffirm a contract either during the period of minority or within a reasonable time after reaching the age of majority, the contract is considered ratified (accepted). Hence, the minor (who is now an adult) is bound by the contract; the right to disaffirm the contract is lost. Note that any attempt by a minor to ratify a contract while still a minor can be disaffirmed just as the original contract can be disaffirmed.

The **ratification**, which relates back to the inception of the contract, can be by express oral or written words or implied from the minor's conduct (e.g., after reaching the age of majority, the minor remains silent regarding the contract).

Example: When June is 17 years old (a minor) she enters into a contract and purchases a used automobile from Ken, a sane adult, for $10,000. June pays Ken $10,000 and Ken signs over the ownership of the automobile to June. When June reaches the age of 18 (the age of majority) she has not yet disaffirmed the contract. If June waits one month after reaching the age of majority and has not yet disaffirmed the contract, then she will be considered to have ratified the contract. She cannot thereafter disaffirm the contract.

Case 4.1 presents the issue of whether a minor had ratified a contract when he reached the age of majority.

ratification
The act of a minor after the minor has reached the age of majority by which he or she accepts a contract entered into when he or she was a minor. When a principal accepts an agent's unauthorized contract. The acceptance by a corporation of an unauthorized act of a corporate officer or agent.

---

[1]Copies of the ABA Model Rules of Professional Conduct are available from Service Center, American Bar Association, 321 North Clark Street, Chicago, IL 60610, 1-800-285-2221. The Model Rules can also be viewed online at http://www.abanet.org/cpr/mrpc/mrpc_toc.html.
[2]*Plumlee v. Paddock*, S.W.2d 757 (Tex. 1992).

CASE 4.1 MINOR'S CONTRACT

Jones v. Flight Sport Aviation, Inc., 623 P.2d 370 (Colo. 1981).

> *"A minor may disaffirm a contract made during his minority within a reasonable time after attaining his majority or he may, after becoming of legal age, by acts recognizing the contract, ratify it."*

> Judge Erickson, *Supreme Court of Colorado*

Facts

William Michael Jones, a 17-year-old minor, signed a contract with Free Flight Sport Aviation, Inc. (Free Flight) for the use of recreational skydiving facilities. A covenant not to sue and an exculpatory clause exempting Free Flight from liability were included in the contract. One month later, Jones attained the age of majority (18 years of age). Ten months later, while on a Free Flight skydiving operation, the airplane crashed shortly after takeoff from Littleton Airport. Jones suffered severe personal injuries. Jones filed suit against Free Flight, alleging negligence and willful and wanton misconduct. The trial court granted summary judgment in favor of Free Flight. The Colorado court of appeals affirmed. Jones appealed.

Issue

Did Jones ratify the contract?

Language of the Court

As a matter of public policy, the courts have protected minors from improvident and imprudent contractual commitments by declaring that the contract of a minor is voidable at the election of the minor after he attains his majority. A minor may disaffirm a contract made during his minority within a reasonable time after attaining his majority or he may, after becoming of legal age, by acts recognizing the contract, ratify it.

Affirmance is not merely a matter of intent. It may be determined by the actions of a minor who accepts the benefits of a contract after reaching the age of majority, or who is silent or acquiesces in the contract for a considerable length of time. We conclude that the trial court properly determined that Jones ratified the contract, as a matter of law, by accepting the benefits of the contract when he used Free Flight's facilities on October 19, 1974.

Decision

The Supreme Court of Colorado held that Jones had ratified his contract with Free Flight by continuing, for 10 months after reaching the age of majority, to perform under the contract. Therefore, the covenant not to sue and the exculpatory clause exempting Free Flight from liability to Jones were enforceable. The court affirmed the decision of the trial court and court of appeals in favor of Free Flight.

Law & Ethics Questions

1. Should a person be allowed to disaffirm his or her minor's contract after reaching the age of majority? What is a reasonable length of time after reaching the age of majority to permit disaffirmance?

2. Ethics Did Jones act ethically by suing Free Flight Sport Aviation in this case?

3. Should the covenant not to sue have been enforced here even though Jones was an adult?

Web Exercises

1. Web Visit the website of the Supreme Court of Colorado at www.coloradosupremecourt.com.

2. Web Use www.google.com and find a video clip of someone skydiving.

Parents' Liability for Their Children's Contracts

Generally, parents owe a legal duty to provide food, clothing, shelter, and other necessaries of life for their minor children. Parents are liable for their children's contracts for necessaries of life if they have not adequately provided such items.

The parental duty of support terminates if a minor becomes emancipated. **Emancipation** occurs when a minor voluntarily leaves home and lives apart from his or her parents. The courts consider factors such as getting married, setting up a separate household, or joining the military service in determining whether a minor is emancipated. Each situation is examined on its merits.

emancipation
When a minor voluntarily leaves home and lives apart from his or her parents.

Necessaries of Life

Minors are obligated to pay for the **necessaries of life** that they contract for. Otherwise, many adults would refuse to sell these items to them. There is no standard definition of what is a *necessary of life*, but items such as food, clothing, shelter, and medical services are generally understood to fit this category.

necessaries of life
A minor must pay the reasonable value of food, clothing, shelter, medical care, and other items considered necessary to the maintenance of life.

Example: Goods and services such as automobiles, tools of trade, education, and vocational training have also been found to be necessaries of life in some situations. The minor's age, lifestyle, and status in life influence what is considered necessary. For example, necessaries for a married minor are greater than those for an unmarried minor.

The seller's recovery is based on the equitable doctrine of quasi-contract rather than on the contract itself. Under this theory, the minor is obligated only to pay the reasonable value of the goods or services received. Reasonable value is determined on a case-by-case basis.

In Case 4.2, the court found a minor liable for necessaries of life.

CASE 4.2 NECESSARIES OF LIFE

Yale Diagnostic Radiology v. Estate of Fountain, 838 A.2d 179 (Conn. 2004).

"The rule that a minor's contracts are voidable, however, is not absolute. An exception to this rule, eponymously known as the doctrine of necessaries, is that a minor may not avoid a contract for goods or services necessary for his health and sustenance."

Judge Borden, *Supreme Court of Connecticut*

Facts

Harun Fountain, a minor, was shot in the back of the head at point-blank range by a playmate. Fountain required extensive lifesaving medical services from a variety of medical service providers, including Yale Diagnostic Radiology. The expense of the services rendered by Yale to Fountain totaled $17,694. Yale billed Vernetta Turner-Tucker (Tucker), Fountain's mother, for the services. Tucker, however, declared bankruptcy and had Yale's claim against her discharged in bankruptcy. Tucker, on behalf of Fountain, sued the boy who shot Fountain and recovered damages in a settlement agreement. These funds were placed in an estate on Fountain's behalf under the supervision of the probate court.

Yale filed a motion with the probate court for payment of the $17,694 from the estate. The probate court denied the motion. Yale appealed to the trial court, which held in favor of Yale. The trial court held that minors were liable for their necessaries. Fountain's estate appealed.

Issue

Is Fountain's estate liable to Yale under the doctrine of necessaries?

Language of the Court

Connecticut has long recognized the common-law rule that a minor child's contracts are voidable. The rule that a minor's contracts are voidable, however, is not absolute. An exception to this rule, eponymously known as the doctrine of necessaries, is that a minor may not avoid a contract for goods or services necessary for his health and sustenance.

Thus, when a medical service provider renders necessary medical care to an injured minor, two contracts arise: the primary contract between the provider and the minor's parents; and an implied in law contract between the provider and the minor himself. The primary contract between the provider and the parents is based on the parents' duty to pay for their children's necessary expenses, under both common law and statute. The primacy of this contract means that the provider of necessaries must make all reasonable efforts to collect from the parents before resorting to the secondary, implied in law contract with the minor.

The secondary implied in law contract between the medical services provider and the minor arises from equitable considerations, including the law's disfavor of unjust enrichment. Therefore, where necessary medical services are rendered to a minor whose parents do not pay for them, equity and justice demand that a secondary implied in law contract arise between the medical services provider and the minor who has received the benefits of those services. These principles compel the conclusion that, in the circumstances of the present case, the estate of Fountain is liable to plaintiff Yale under the common-law doctrine of necessaries, for the services rendered by Yale to Fountain.

Decision

The Supreme Court of Connecticut held that under the doctrine of necessaries, Fountain's estate is liable to Yale for the expense of the services rendered to Fountain. The court affirmed the judgment of the trial court in favor of Yale.

Law & Ethics Questions

1. What is the doctrine of necessaries? Explain.

2. What is a parent's legal responsibility for medical services and other necessaries provided to his or her child?

3. **Ethics** Was it ethical for Fountain's mother not to pay Yale for the medical service rendered to her child? Was it ethical for her to avoid this bill by declaring bankruptcy?

4. Ethics Should Yale have just written off this debt and not pursued Fountain's estate for payment? Why or why not?

Web Exercises

1. Web Visit the website of the Supreme Court of Connecticut at www.jud.state.ct.us.

2. Web Use www.google.com and find an article that discusses minors' contracts.

CONTEMPORARY Issue

SPECIAL TYPES OF MINORS' CONTRACTS

The infancy doctrine of the common law of contracts allows minors to disaffirm many contracts they have entered into with adults. Based on public policy, many states have enacted statutes that make certain specified contracts enforceable against minors—that is, minors cannot assert the infancy doctrine against enforcement for these contracts. These usually include contracts for the following:

- Medical, surgical, and pregnancy care
- Psychological counseling
- Health insurance
- Life insurance
- The performance of duties relating to stock and bond transfers, bank accounts, and the like
- Educational loan agreements
- Contracts to support children
- Contracts to enlist in the military
- Artistic, sports, and entertainment contracts that have been entered into with the approval of the court (many of these statutes require that a certain portion of the wages and fees earned by the minor be put in trust until the minor reaches the age of majority)

PARALEGAL PERSPECTIVE

Brandy Spurgin is a graduate of the University of Tennessee at Chattanooga's Legal Assistant Studies Program. Brandy works full time as a legal assistant for a civil rights attorney in Chattanooga, Tennessee, while she attends law school at Nashville School of Law, with a projected graduation date of 2011.

Contracts are invaluable tools in every business that allow everyone the opportunity to take control of the conditions under which they do business and conduct transactions. As such, contracts are important in all businesses but are especially important in every field of law.

There are some contracts that at first glance one might overlook but nevertheless *are* contracts. For example, in criminal law, the prosecution must make plea bargains with the defense. In personal injury law, the attorneys must examine insurance policies, which are contracts. These may not be the first contracts that come to mind when the subject of contracts is addressed. However, this sort of contract is just as important to the parties involved as any others.

In civil rights law, I deal with countless contract issues arising from our own contracts for representation, insurance policies, employment contracts, and criminal pleas. The subject of contracts is a requirement in some form for every field of law and cannot be avoided.

I draft and revise attorney-client contracts, draft and review settlement agreements, and review employment contracts regularly. This portion of my job is immensely important to my performance as well as the quality of service to our clients.

■ MENTALLY INCOMPETENT PERSONS

Mental incapacity may arise because of mental illness, brain damage, mental retardation, senility, and the like. The law protects people suffering from substantial mental incapacity from enforcement of contracts against them because such persons may not understand the consequences of their actions in entering into a contract.

To be relieved of his or her duties under a contract, the law requires a person to have been legally insane at the time of entering into the contract. This state is called **legal insanity**. Most states use the *objective cognitive "understanding" test* to determine legal insanity. Under this test, the person's mental incapacity must render that person incapable of understanding or comprehending the nature of the transaction. Mere weakness of intellect, slight psychological or emotional problems, or delusions does not constitute legal insanity.

The law has developed two standards concerning contracts of mentally incompetent persons: (1) adjudged insane and (2) insane but not adjudged insane.

legal insanity
A state of contractual incapacity as determined by law.

Adjudged Insane

In certain cases, a relative, a loved one, or another interested party may institute a legal action to have someone declared legally (i.e., adjudged) insane. If after hearing the evidence at a formal judicial or administrative hearing the person is **adjudged insane**, the court makes that person a ward of the court and appoints a guardian to act on that person's behalf. Any contract entered into by a person who has been adjudged insane is *void*. That is, no contract exists. The court-appointed guardian is the only one who has the legal authority to enter into contracts on behalf of the person.

adjudged insane
A person who has been adjudged insane by a proper court or administrative agency. A contract entered into by such a person is void.

Example: Ted, Heather, and Jed are the three surviving relatives of their grandmother, Mabel. For years Mabel has exhibited substantial mental impairment such that she is incapable of understanding or comprehending the nature of her transactions. The three grandchildren bring a proceeding in family court asking the court to adjudge Mabel insane. After a hearing in which evidence is introduced, the judge decides that Mabel is permanently insane and issues a judgment saying so. Mabel has now been adjudged insane. The court appoints Heather as guardian. Subsequently, Mabel enters into a contract with Sidell's Siding Company to put new siding on her house. This is a void contract. Only Heather can enter into such a contract on behalf of Mabel.

Insane But Not Adjudged Insane

If no formal ruling has been made—that is, if a person is **insane but not adjudged insane**—any contracts entered into by a person who suffers from a mental impairment that makes him or her legally insane are voidable by the insane person. Unless the other party does not have contractual capacity, he or she does not have the option to void the contract.

Example: Ted, Heather, and Jed are the three surviving relatives of their grandmother, Mabel. For years Mabel has exhibited substantial mental impariment such that she is incapable of understanding or comprehending the nature of her transactions. The three grandchildren have never brought a legal proceeding to have Mabel legally declared insane. Mabel enters into a contract with Sidell's Siding Company to put new siding on her house. This is a voidable contract that is only voidable by Mabel. Sidell's Siding Company cannot avoid the contract; only Mabel can.

Some people have alternating periods of sanity and insanity. Any contracts made by such persons during a lucid interval are enforceable. Contracts made while the person was not legally sane can be disaffirmed.

A person who has dealt with an insane person must place that insane person in status quo if the contract is either void or voided by the insane person. Most states hold that a party who did not know he or she was dealing with an insane person must be placed in status quo upon avoidance of the contract. Insane persons are liable in *quasi-contract* to pay the reasonable value for the necessaries of life they receive.

In Case 4.3, the court had to decide whether mental incapacity relieved a person from a contract.

insane but not adjudged insane
A person who is insane but has not been adjudged insane by a court or administrative agency. A contract entered into by such person is generally voidable. Some states hold that such a contract is void.

CASE 4.3 MENTAL CAPACITY

Campbell v. Carr, 603 S.E.2d 625 (S.C. Ct. App. 2004).

"*This inadequate consideration combined with Carr's weakness of mind, due to her schizophrenia and depression, makes it inequitable to order specific performance.*"

Judge Anderson, *Court of Appeals of South Carolina*

Facts

Martha M. Carr suffered from schizophrenia and depression. Schizophrenia is a psychotic disorder characterized by disturbances in perception, inferential thinking, delusions, hallucinations, and grossly disorganized behavior. Depression is characterized by altered moods and a diminished ability to think or concentrate. Carr was taking two prescription drugs for her mental diseases: Haldol and Cogentin.

Carr, a resident of New York, inherited from her mother a 108-acre tract of unimproved land in South Carolina. Carr contacted Raymond C. and Betty Campbell (Campbell), who had leased the property for 30 years, about selling the property to them. Carr asked Campbell how much the property was worth, and Campbell told Carr that the tax assessor's agricultural assessed value of the property was $54,000. Carr and Campbell entered into a written contract for $54,000, which averaged $500 an acre. Campbell paid Carr earnest money. Carr subsequently missed the closing day for the sale of the property, returned the earnest money, and refused to sell the property to Campbell. Campbell sued Carr to obtain a court judgment ordering Carr to specifically perform the contract and sell the property to Campbell. At trial, evidence and expert witness testimony placed the value of the property at $162,000, or $1,500 an acre. Testimony showed that Campbell knew the value of the property exceeded $54,000. The court agreed with Campbell and ordered Carr to specifically perform the contract. Carr appealed.

Issue

Did Carr, because of her mental diseases of schizophrenia and depression, lack the mental capacity to enter into the contract with Campbell?

Language of the Court

An action for specific performance is one in equity. Specific performance should be granted only if there is no adequate remedy at law and specific enforcement of the contract is equitable between the parties. Equity will not decree specific performance unless the contract is fair, just, and equitable.

The consideration stated in the contract between Carr and the Campbells was inadequate. The $54,000 sales price in the contract was significantly below the appraised value of $162,000, the Collateral I.D. report's expected sell value of $129,625 to $145,180, and the Richmond County Tax Assessor's fair market value of $103,700. This inadequate consideration combined with Carr's weakness of mind, due to her schizophrenia and depression, makes it inequitable to order specific performance. The Campbells, as the prospective purchasers, had greater knowledge of the real estate value of the land, having leased the land for 30 years for personal hunting and farming purposes, compared with Carr, who lived in New York, had not visited the property since she was a child, and had no knowledge of the fair market value of the property. Additionally, Carr suffers from mental illness.

Decision

The court of appeals held that Carr's mental diseases of schizophrenia and depression affected her ability to make an informed decision regarding the sale of the property. The court of appeals reversed the trial court's decision ordering specific performance.

Law & Ethics Questions

1. What does the doctrine of incapacity to contract provide? Explain.
2. **Ethics** Did the Campbells act ethically in this case?
3. **Ethics** Was it ethical for Carr to withdraw from the contract? Did she have sufficient reason to withdraw from the contract?

Web Exercises

1. **Web** Visit the website of the Court of Appeals of South Carolina at www.judicial.state.sc.us/appeals.
2. **Web** Use www.google.com and find an article that discusses schizophrenia.

Concept Summary

Disaffirmance of Contracts Based on Legal Insanity

Type of Legal Insanity	Disaffirmance Rule
Adjudged insane	Contract is void. Neither party can enforce the contract.
Insane but not adjudged insane	Contract is voidable by the insane person; the competent party cannot void the contract.

PARALEGAL PERSPECTIVE

Toni D. Mers is a trusts and estates paralegal at the law firm of Mc-Culloch, Felger, Fite & Gutmann Co., L.P.A., in Piqua, Ohio. She received an associate of applied business in legal assisting at Edison Community College in Piqua.

As a trusts and estates paralegal, I manage files (under the supervision of an attorney) pertaining to trusts, estates, guardianships, and powers of attorney.

How are contracts involved in my job? One of my responsibilities is to research and track assets. Almost all assets owned by an individual, an estate, or a trust are held subject to contract terms in documents such as deeds (contracts in form of warranties found in warranty deeds), leases, notes, trust agreements, life insurance policies, certificates of deposit, and brokerage accounts.

When reviewing contracts prepared by others, it is important to note the following: (1) proper execution, (2) contract details, (3) contract duration, and (4) applicable provisions. You must determine what portion, if any, of the contract is effective after death.

When preparing contracts, important issues include fiduciary capacity, clarity, and conciseness. For example, a trustee or attorney in fact (under durable power of attorney) may have very broad contracting authority; an executor or administrator may not. It is also critical to focus on stating only the necessary terms, with clarity and precision.

Being able to interpret and prepare contracts is essential to nearly every paralegal specialty. There is no substitute for analytically reviewing existing or proposed contracts by applying the fundamentals of contract law learned through higher education. To avoid becoming lackadaisical when reviewing and preparing contracts, it is also beneficial to refresh your skills through seminars or additional education.

◼ INTOXICATED PERSONS

Most states provide that contracts entered into by certain **intoxicated persons** are voidable by those persons. The intoxication may occur because of alcohol or drugs. The contract is not voidable by the other party if that party had contractual capacity.

Under the majority rule, the contract is voidable only if the person was so intoxicated when the contract was entered into that he or she was incapable of understanding or comprehending the nature of the transaction. In most states, this rule holds even if the intoxication was self-induced. Some states allow the person to disaffirm the contract only if the person was forced to become intoxicated or did so unknowingly.

The amount of alcohol or drugs necessary to be consumed for a person to be considered legally intoxicated to disaffirm contracts varies from case to case. The factors that are considered include the user's physical characteristics and his or her ability to "hold" intoxicants.

intoxicated person
A person who is under contractual incapacity because of ingestion of alcohol or drugs to the point of incompetence.

A person who disaffirms a contract based on intoxication generally must be returned to the status quo. In turn, the intoxicated person generally must return the consideration received under the contract to the other party and make restitution that returns the other party to status quo. After becoming sober, an intoxicated person can ratify the contracts he or she entered into while intoxicated. Intoxicated persons are liable in *quasi-contract* to pay the reasonable value for necessaries they receive.

In Case 4.4, the court found that a person was not bound to a contact she entered while intoxicated.

CASE 4.4 INTOXICATION

Smith v. Williamson, 429 So. 2d 598 (Ala. Civ. App. 1982).

"The record further shows that Williamson had consumed a pint of 100-proof vodka and that she remained in an agitated state over the sale of her home."

Judge Bradley, *Court of Civil Appeals of Alabama*

Facts

Carolyn Ann Williamson entered into a contract to sell her house to Mr. and Mrs. Matthews at a time when her house was threatened with foreclosure. Evidence showed that Williamson was an alcoholic. Having read about the threatened foreclosure in the newspaper, attorney Virgil M. Smith appeared at Williamson's home to discuss the matter with her. Williamson told Smith that she expected to receive $17,000 from the sale but had actually received $1,700. On the following day, after drinking a pint of 100-proof vodka, Williamson and her son went to Smith's office, where Smith prepared a lawsuit to have the sale of the house set aside based on Williamson's lack of capacity due to alcoholism. At that time, Smith loaned Williamson $500 and took back a note and mortgage on her house to secure repayment of this amount and his attorney fees. Evidence showed that Smith did not allow Williamson's son to read the mortgage. The sale to Mr. and Mrs. Matthews was set aside. Subsequently, Smith began foreclosure proceedings on Williamson's house to recover attorney's fees and advances. Williamson filed this lawsuit to enjoin the foreclosure. The trial court held that Smith's mortgage was void and permanently enjoined him from foreclosing on Williamson's house. Smith appealed.

Issue

Was Williamson's alcoholism a sufficient mental incapacity to void the mortgage?

Language of the Court

In essence, Smith takes the position that while Williamson had been drinking on the morning that she executed the mortgage to him, the transaction was still valid because she had sufficient capacity to understand the nature of the act, and it was free from fraud and undue influence. To accept Smith's position would require us to ignore certain subtle ironies arising from the facts of this appeal and the nature of the fiduciary relationship between attorney and client.

The record indicates that Williamson executed the note and mortgage on her home to Smith the following morning. The record further shows that Williamson had consumed a pint of 100-proof vodka and that she remained in an agitated state over the sale of her home. To hold that Williamson was incapable of understanding the nature of the transaction with the Matthewses and then to hold that she was able to comprehend the nature of her dealings with Smith would be to reach illogical results, especially in light of the facts presented at trial.

Decision

The court of appeals held that Williamson was not bound to the contract and mortgage with attorney Smith because she was mentally incompetent by reason of intoxication at the time she signed the documents. The court of appeals affirmed the trial court's decision that had held Smith's mortgage void and permanently enjoined him from foreclosing on Williamson's property.

Law & Ethics Questions

1. Should the law protect persons who voluntarily become intoxicated from their contracts?

2. **Ethics** Do you think that attorney Smith acted ethically in this case?

3. Do you think many business deals are entered into after the parties have been drinking? Should these deals be allowed to be voided?

Web Exercises

1. **Web** Visit the Court of Civil Appeals of Alabama at www.judicial.state.al.us.

2. **Web** Use www.google.com and find a case in which someone has be let out of his or her contract because of intoxication.

■ LEGALITY

One requirement to have an enforceable contract is that the object of the contract must be lawful. Most contracts that individuals and businesses enter into are **lawful contracts** that are enforceable. These include contracts for the sale of goods, services, real property, and intangible rights; the lease of goods; property leases; licenses; and other contracts.

lawful contracts
To be an enforceable contract, the object of the contract must be lawful.

Some contracts have illegal objects. Contracts with an illegal object are *void* and therefore unenforceable. They are called illegal contracts. The following paragraphs discuss various illegal contracts.

Contracts Contrary to Statutes

Both federal and state legislatures have enacted statutes that prohibit certain types of conduct.

Example: Penal codes make certain activities crimes; antitrust statutes prohibit certain types of agreements between competitors, and so on. Contracts to perform activities prohibited by statute are illegal contracts.

Usury Laws

State **usury laws** set an upper limit on the annual interest rate that can be charged on certain types of loans. The limits vary from state to state. Lenders who charge a higher rate than the state limit are guilty of usury. These laws are intended to protect unsophisticated borrowers from loan sharks and others who charge exorbitant rates of interest.

Most states provide criminal and civil penalties for making usurious loans. Some states require lenders to remit the difference between the interest rate charged on the loan and the usury rate to the borrower. Other states prohibit lenders from collecting any interest on the loan. Still other states provide that a usurious loan is a void contract, permitting the borrower not to have to pay the interest or the principal of the loan to the lender.

Most usury laws exempt certain types of lenders and loan transactions involving legitimate business transactions from the reach of the law. These exemptions often include loans made by banks and other financial institutions, loans above a certain dollar amount, and loans made to corporations and other businesses.

Sabbath Laws

Certain states have enacted laws—called **Sabbath laws, Sunday laws**, or **blue laws**—that prohibit or limit the carrying on of certain secular activities on Sundays. Except for contracts for the necessaries of life, charitable donations, and such, these laws generally prohibit or invalidate executory contracts entered into on Sundays. Many states do not actively enforce these laws. In some states, they have even been found to be unconstitutional.

Contracts to Commit Crimes

As mentioned previously, contracts to commit criminal acts are void. If the object of a contract becomes illegal after the contract is entered into because the government has enacted a statute that makes it unlawful, the parties are discharged from the contract. The contract is not an illegal contract unless the parties agree to go forward and complete it.

Contracts Contrary to Public Policy

Certain contracts are illegal because they are **contrary to public policy**. Such contracts are void. Although *public policy* eludes a precise definition, the courts have held contracts to be contrary to public policy if they have a negative impact on society or interfere with the public's safety and welfare.

Immoral contracts—that is, contracts whose objective is the commission of an act considered immoral by society—may be found to be against public policy.

Example: A contract based on sexual favors has been held to be an immoral contract and void as against public policy. Judges are not free to define morality based on their individual views. Instead, they must look to the practices and beliefs of society when defining immoral conduct.

Case 4.5 raises the issue of whether a contract violated public policy and was therefore illegal.

CASE 4.5 ILLEGAL CONTRACT

Flood v. Fiduciary & Guar. Life Ins. Co., 394 So. 2d 1311 (La. App. 1981).

> *"Louisiana follows the majority rule that holds, as a matter of public policy, that a beneficiary named in a life insurance policy is not entitled to the proceeds of the insurance if the beneficiary feloniously kills the insured."*
>
> Judge Lear, *Court of Appeals of Louisiana*

Facts

Ellen and Richard Alvin Flood, a married couple, lived in a mobile home in Louisiana. Richard worked as a maintenance man, and Ellen was employed at an insurance agency. Evidence at trial showed that Ellen was unhappy with her marriage. Ellen took out a life insurance policy on the life of her husband and named herself as beneficiary. The policy was issued by Fidelity & Guaranty Life Insurance Company (Fidelity). Seven years after the marriage, Richard became unexpectedly ill. He was taken to the hospital, where his condition improved. After a visit at the hospital from his wife, however, Richard died. Ellen was criminally charged with the murder of her husband by poisoning. Evidence showed that six medicine bottles at the couple's home, including Tylenol and paregoric bottles, contained arsenic. The court found that Ellen had fed Richard ice cubes laced with arsenic at the hospital. Ellen was tried and convicted of the murder of her husband. Ellen, as beneficiary of Richard's life insurance policy, requested Fidelity to pay her the benefits. Fidelity refused to pay the benefits and returned all premiums paid on the policy. This suit followed. The district court held in favor of Ellen Flood and awarded her the benefits of the life insurance policy. Fidelity appealed.

Issue

Was the life insurance policy an illegal contract that is void?

Language of the Court

Louisiana follows the majority rule that holds, as a matter of public policy, that a beneficiary named in a life insurance policy is not entitled to the proceeds of the insurance if the beneficiary feloniously kills the insured.

The genesis of this litigation is the escalating criminal action of Ellen Flood, bent on taking the life of her lawful husband. Our courts have previously adjudicated (1) the issue of the cause of death of Richard Flood, (2) the culprit in that death, and (3) the motives for the death. Under the peculiar circumstances of the case, it was unreasonable of the trial court not to consider and to assign great weight to the mountain of evidence tending to prove Mrs. Flood's scheme to defraud both the insurer, Fidelity, and the insured, Mr. Flood. It is clear to us that the entirety of the transaction here reviewed is tainted with the intendment of Ellen Flood to contravene the prohibitory law.

Life insurance policies are procured because life is, indeed, precarious and uncertain. Our law does not and cannot sanction any scheme that has as its purpose the certain infliction of death for, inter alia, financial gain through receipt of the proceeds of life insurance. To sanction this policy in any way would surely shackle the spirit, letter, and life of our laws.

Decision

The court of appeals held that the life insurance policy Ellen had taken out on the life of her husband was void based on public policy, and that Ellen could not recover the life insurance proceeds from the death of her husband, whom she had killed. The court of appeals reversed the decision of the district court.

Law & Ethics Questions

1. Should Ellen Flood have been allowed to retain the insurance proceeds in this case?

2. **Ethics** Did Ellen Flood act unethically in this case? Did she act illegally?

3. What would be the economic consequences if persons could recover insurance proceeds for losses caused by their illegal activities (e.g., murder, arson)?

Web Exercises

1. **Web** Visit the website of the Court of Appeals of Louisiana, First Circuit, at www.la-fcca.org.

2. **Web** Use www.google.com and find an article or case that discusses murder to recover life insurance proceeds.

Gambling Statutes

gambling statutes
Statutes that make certain forms of gambling illegal.

All states either prohibit or regulate gambling, wagering, lotteries, and games of chance via **gambling statutes**. States provide various criminal and civil penalties for illegal gambling. There is a distinction between lawful risk-shifting contracts and gambling contracts.

Example: If property insurance is purchased on one's own car and the car is destroyed in an accident, the insurance company must pay the claim. This agreement is a lawful risk-shifting contract because the purchaser had an "insurable interest" in the car. Insurance purchased on a neighbor's car would be considered to be gambling, however. The purchaser does not have an insurable interest in the car and is betting only on its destruction.

There are many exceptions to wagering laws.

Example: Many states have enacted statutes that permit games of chance under a certain dollar amount, bingo games, lotteries conducted by religious and charitable organizations, and the like. Many states also permit and regulate horse racing, harness racing, dog racing, and state-operated lotteries.

Effect of Illegality

Because illegal contracts are void, the parties cannot sue for nonperformance. Further, if an illegal contract is executed, the court generally leaves the parties where it finds them.

Certain situations are exempt from the general rule of the effect of finding an illegal contract. If an exception applies, the innocent party may use the court system to sue for damages or to recover consideration paid under the illegal contract. The following persons can assert an exception:

1. Innocent persons who were justifiably ignorant of the law or fact that made the contract illegal.

Example: A person who purchases insurance from an unlicensed insurance company may recover insurance benefits from the unlicensed company.

2. Persons who were induced to enter into an illegal contract by fraud, duress, or undue influence.

   Example: A shop owner who pays $5,000 "protection money" to a mobster so his store will not be burned down by the mobster can recover the $5,000.

3. Persons who entered into an illegal contract and withdraw before the illegal act is performed.

   Example: If the president of New Toy Corporation pays $10,000 to an employee of Old Toy Corporation to steal a trade secret from his employer but reconsiders and tells the employee not to do it before he has done it, the New Toy Corporation may recover the $10,000.

4. Persons who were less at fault than the other party for entering into the illegal contract. At common law, parties to an illegal contract were considered **in pari delicto** (in equal fault). Some states have changed this rule and permit the less-at-fault party to recover restitution of the consideration they paid under an illegal contract from the more-at-fault party.

   In Case 4.6, the court had to decide the lawfulness of a contract.

in pari delicto
In equal fault; equally culpable or criminal.

CASE 4.6   ILLEGAL CONTRACT

Ryno v. Tyra, 752 S.W.2d 148 (Tex. App. 1988).

"*The trial court could not have compelled Ryno to honor his wager by delivering the BMW to Tyra. However, Ryno did deliver the BMW to Tyra, and the facts incident to that delivery are sufficient to establish a transfer by gift of the BMW from Ryno to Tyra.*"

Judge Farris, *Court of Appeals of Texas*

Facts

R. D. Ryno Jr. owned Bavarian Motors, an automobile dealership in Fort Worth, Texas. One day, Lee Tyra discussed purchasing a BMW M-1 from Ryno for $125,000. Ryno then suggested a double-or-nothing coin flip, to which Tyra agreed. If the seller Ryno won the coin flip, Tyra would have to pay $250,000 for the car; if the buyer Tyra won the coin flip, he would get the car for free. When Tyra won the coin flip, Ryno said, "It's yours," and handed Tyra the keys and title to the car. Tyra drove away in the car. This suit ensued as to the ownership of the car. The trial court held in favor of Tyra. Ryno appealed.

Issue

Was there an illegal contract? Who owns the car?

Language of the Court

Ryno complains that the trial court erred in granting Tyra judgment because the judgment enforces a gambling contract. We find there was sufficient evidence to sustain the jury finding that Ryno intended to transfer to Tyra his ownership interest in the BMW at the time he delivered the documents, keys, and possession of the automobile to Tyra. We agree with appellant Ryno that his wager with Tyra was unenforceable. The trial court could not have compelled Ryno to honor his wager by delivering the BMW to Tyra. However, Ryno did deliver the BMW to Tyra, and the facts incident to that delivery are sufficient to establish a transfer by gift of the BMW from Ryno to Tyra.

Decision

Tyra, the patron at the car dealership who won the coin toss, owns the car. The court of appeals found that because gambling was involved, this was an illegal contract. However, the court decided to leave the parties where it found them—that is, with Tyra in possession of the car. The court of appeals affirmed the trial court's judgment in favor of Tyra.

Law & Ethics Questions

1. Should the court have lent its resources to help Ryno recover the car?

2. **Ethics** Did Ryno act ethically in this case?

3. What is the moral of this story if you ever win anything in an illegal gambling contract?

Web Exercises

1. **Web** Visit the website of the Court of Appeals of Texas, Second District, at www.2ndcoa.courts.state.tx.us.

2. **Web** Use www.google.com and find an article about illegal gambling contracts.

■ SPECIAL BUSINESS CONTRACTS

The issue of the lawfulness of contracts applies to several special business contracts. These include contracts that restrain trade, contracts to provide services that require a government license, exculpatory clauses, and covenants not to compete. These contracts are discussed in the following paragraphs.

Contracts in Restraint of Trade

contracts in restraint of trade
An economic policy of competition in the U.S.; contracts restraining trade are illegal.

The general economic policy of the United States favors competition. At common law, **contracts in restraint of trade**—that is, contracts that unreasonably restrain trade—are held to be unlawful.

Example: It would be an illegal restraint of trade if all the bakers in a neighborhood agreed to fix the prices of the bread they sold. The bakers' contract would be void.

Licensing Statutes

licensing statute
Statute that requires a person or business to obtain a license from the government prior to engaging in a specified occupation or activity.

All states have **licensing statutes** that require members of certain professions and occupations to be licensed by the state in which they practice. Lawyers, doctors, real estate agents, insurance agents, certified public accountants, teachers, contractors, hairdressers, and such, are among them. In most instances, a license is granted to a person who demonstrates that he or she has the proper schooling, experience, and moral character required by the relevant statute. Sometimes, a written examination is also required.

Problems arise if an unlicensed person tries to collect payment for services provided to another under a contract. Some statutes expressly provide that unlicensed persons cannot enforce contracts to provide these services. If the statute is silent on the point, enforcement depends on whether it is a *regulatory statute* or a *revenue-raising statute*.

Regulatory Statutes

Licensing statutes enacted to protect the public are called **regulatory statutes**. Generally, unlicensed persons cannot recover payment for services that a regulatory statute requires a licensed person to provide.

regulatory statute
A licensing statute enacted to protect the public.

Example: State law stipulates that legal services can be provided only by lawyers who have graduated from law school and passed the appropriate bar exam. Nevertheless, suppose Marie Sweiger, a first-year law student, agrees to draft a will for Randy McCabe for a $150 fee. Because Sweiger is not licensed to provide legal services, she has violated a regulatory statute. She cannot enforce the contract and recover payment from McCabe.

Revenue-Raising Statutes

Licensing statutes enacted to raise money for the government are called **revenue-raising statutes**. A person who provides services pursuant to a contract without the appropriate license required by such a statute can enforce the contract and recover payment for services rendered.

revenue-raising statute
A licensing statute with the primary purpose of raising revenue for the government.

Example: Suppose a state licensing statute requires licensed attorneys to pay an annual $200 license fee without requiring continuing education or other new qualifications. A licensed attorney who forgets to pay the fee can enforce contracts and recover payment for the legal services he or she renders. The statute merely gathers revenue; protection of the public is not a factor.

ETHICS SPOTLIGHT

AN UNLICENSED CONTRACTOR GETS DUNKED

"The obvious statutory intent is to discourage persons who have failed to comply with the licensing law from offering or providing their unlicensed services for pay."

Justice Eagleson

Hydrotech Systems, Ltd. (Hydrotech) was a New York corporation that manufactured and installed patented equipment to simulate ocean waves. Oasis Waterpark (Oasis) was a California corporation that owned and operated a water-oriented amusement park in Palm Springs, California. Wessman Construction Company, Inc. (Wessman) was Oasis's general contractor at the park.

Wessman contracted with Hydrotech to design and construct a 29,000-square-foot "surfing pool" at the park, using Hydrotech's wave equipment. The total contract price was $850,000. Hydrotech was aware of a California law that requires a contractor to have a California contractor's license to provide construction services in California. The statute stipulates that an unlicensed contractor cannot sue in a California court to recover compensation for work requiring a California contractor's license (California Business and Professional Code Section 7031).

Because it was concerned with the licensing problem, Hydrotech wished only to sell and deliver the equipment and to avoid involvement in the design and construction of the pool. However, Oasis insisted that Hydrotech's unique expertise in design and construction was essential. Oasis induced Hydrotech to provide these services by promising to pay Hydrotech even if the law provided otherwise.

Relying on these promises, Hydrotech furnished equipment and services in full compliance with the contract. Hydrotech had been paid $740,000 during the course of the contract. When it billed Oasis for the remaining $110,000, Oasis refused to pay. Hydrotech sued Oasis and Wessman for damages in California court for breach of contract and fraud. The defendants moved the court to dismiss the action because Hydrotech did not possess a California contractor's license, as required by law.

The California Supreme Court agreed with the defendants and ordered Hydrotech's complaint dismissed. The court found that Hydrotech had violated the licensing statute. The court stated, "The obvious statutory intent is to discourage persons who have failed to comply with the licensing law from offering or providing their unlicensed services for pay. Because of the strength and clarity of this policy, it is well settled that Section 7031 applies despite injustice to the unlicensed contractor." *Hydrotech Sys. Ltd. v. Oasis Waterpark*, 803 P.2d 370 (Cal. 1991).

Law & Ethics Questions

1. **Ethics** Did Oasis act unethically by not paying Hydrotech? Explain.
2. **Ethics** Did Hydrotech act unethically by providing services in California without the proper license? Explain.

Web Exercises

1. **Web** Visit the website of the Supreme Court of California at www.courtinfo.ca.gov/ courts/supreme.

Exculpatory Clauses

exculpatory clause
A contractual provision that relieves one (or both) of the parties to the contract from tort liability for ordinary negligence.

An **exculpatory clause** is a contractual provision that relieves one (or both) of the parties of a contract from tort liability. An exculpatory clause can relieve a party of liability for ordinary negligence. It cannot be used in a situation involving willful conduct, intentional torts, fraud, recklessness, or gross negligence.

Example: Exculpatory clauses are often found in leases, sales contracts, ticket stubs to sporting events, parking lot tickets, service contracts, and the like. Such clauses do not have to be reciprocal (i.e., one party may be relieved of tort liability, whereas the other party is not).

Generally, the courts do not favor exculpatory clauses unless both parties have equal bargaining power. The courts are willing to permit competent parties of equal bargaining power to establish which of them bears the risk. The court considers the precise contract language in addition to other considerations when making its determination.

Example: Jim Jackson voluntarily enrolled in a parachute jump course and signed a contract containing an exculpatory clause that relieved the parachute center of liability. After receiving proper instruction, he jumped from an airplane. Unfortunately, Jim was injured when he could not steer his parachute toward the target area. He sued the parachute center for damages, but the court enforced the exculpatory clause, reasoning that parachute jumping did not involve an essential service and there was no decisive advantage in bargaining power between the parties.

Exculpatory clauses that either affect the public interest or result from superior bargaining power are usually found to be void as against public policy. Although the outcome varies with the circumstances of the case, the greater the degree to which the party serves the general public, the greater the chance the exculpatory clause will be struck down as illegal. The courts consider such factors as the type of activity involved; the relative bargaining power, knowledge, experience, and sophistication of the parties; and other relevant factors.

In Case 4.7, the court had to decide the legality of an exculpatory clause.

CASE 4.7 EXCULPATORY CLAUSE

Zivich v. Mentor Soccer Club, Inc., 696 N.E.2d 201 (Ohio 1998).

> *"Yet the threat of liability strongly deters many individuals from volunteering for nonprofit organizations."*
>
> Judge Sweeney, *Supreme Court of Ohio*

Facts

Pamela Zivich registered her 7-year-old son Bryan to play soccer with the Mentor Soccer Club, Inc. (Club). The club is a nonprofit organization composed primarily of volunteers in the Mentor, Ohio, area who provide children the opportunity to learn and play soccer. The club's registration form, which Mrs. Zivich signed, contained the following language:

> *Recognizing the possibility of physical injury associated with soccer and for the Mentor Soccer Club, and the USYSA [United States Youth Soccer Association] accepting the registrant for its soccer programs and activities, I hereby release, discharge and/or otherwise indemnify the Mentor Soccer Club and the USYSA, its affiliated organizations and sponsors, their employees, and associated personnel, including the owners of the fields and facilities utilized by the Soccer Club, against any claim by or on behalf of the registrant as a result of the registrant's participation in the Soccer Club.*

Bryan attended soccer practice with his father, Philip Zivich. During practice, the team participated in an intrasquad scrimmage. After the scrimmage, Bryan jumped onto the soccer goal and was swinging back and forth on it, but the goal was not anchored down. It tipped backward, and Bryan fell. The goal came down on his chest, breaking three of his ribs and his collarbone and severely bruising his lungs. Bryan's parents sued the club for negligence to recover damages for injuries suffered by Bryan and the loss of consortium for themselves. The club moved for summary judgment, asserting that the exculpatory agreement signed by Bryan's mother barred the claims. The trial court agreed and granted the club's summary judgment motion. The court of appeals affirmed. The plaintiffs appealed to the Supreme Court of Ohio.

Issue

Did the exculpatory agreement signed by Mrs. Zivich on behalf of her son release the club from liability for the child's claims and the parents' claims?

Language of the Court

It cannot be disputed that volunteers in community recreational activities serve an important function. Organized recreational activities offer children the opportunity to learn valuable life skills. It is here that many children learn how to work as a team and how to operate within an organizational structure. Children also are given the chance to exercise and develop coordination skills. Due in great part to the assistance of volunteers, nonprofit organizations are able to offer these activities at minimal cost. Clearly, without the work of its volunteers, these nonprofit organizations could not exist, and scores of children would be without the benefit and enjoyment of organized sports.

Yet the threat of liability strongly deters many individuals from volunteering for nonprofit organizations. Therefore, faced with the very real threat of a lawsuit, and the potential for substantial damage awards, nonprofit organizations and their volunteers could very well decide that the risks are not worth the effort. Hence, invalidation of exculpatory agreements would reduce the number of activities made possible through the uncompensated services of volunteers and their sponsoring organizations.

Therefore, we conclude that although Bryan, like many children before him, gave up his right to sue for the negligent acts of others, the public as a whole received the benefit of these exculpatory agreements. Because of this agreement, the Club was able to offer affordable recreation and to continue to do so without the risks and overwhelming costs of litigation. Bryan's parents agreed to shoulder the risk. Public policy does not forbid such an agreement. In fact, public policy supports it.

Decision

The Supreme Court of Ohio held that a parent's signature on an exculpatory agreement on behalf of his or her child releases the other party from liability to the child, the parent who signed the agreement, and the other parent. The Supreme Court affirmed the decisions of the trial court and court of appeals in favor of Mentor Soccer Club.

Law & Ethics Questions

1. Do exculpatory agreements serve any valid purpose? Should exculpatory agreements be enforceable?

2. **Ethics** Was it ethical for Mrs. Zivich to sign the exculpatory agreement and then bring this lawsuit?

3. What would have been the consequences if the court had found the exculpatory agreement to be invalid in this case?

Web Exercises

1. **Web** Visit the website of the Supreme Court of Ohio at www.sconet.state.oh.us.

2. **Web** Use www.google.com and find an example of an exculpatory clause.

CONTEMPORARY Issue

COVENANT NOT TO COMPETE

Entrepreneurs and others often buy and sell businesses. The sale of a business includes its "goodwill," or reputation. To protect this goodwill after the sale, the seller often enters into an agreement with the buyer not to engage in a similar business or occupation within a specified geographic area for a specified period of time following the sale. This agreement is called a **covenant not to compete**, or a **noncompete clause**.

Covenants not to compete that are *ancillary* to a legitimate sale of a business or employment contract are lawful if they are reasonable in three aspects: (1) the line of business protected, (2) the geographic area protected, and (3) the duration of the restriction. A covenant found to be unreasonable is not enforceable as written. The reasonableness of covenants not to compete is examined on a case-by-case basis. If a covenant not to compete is unreasonable, the courts may either refuse to enforce it or change it so it is reasonable. Usually, the courts choose the first option.

Example: Suppose Stacy Rogers is a certified public accountant (CPA) with a lucrative practice in San Diego, California. Her business includes a substantial amount of goodwill. When she sells her practice, she agrees not to open another accounting practice in the state of California for a 20-year period. This covenant not to compete is reasonable in the line of business protected but is unreasonable in geographic scope and duration. It will not be enforced by the courts as written. The covenant not to compete would be reasonable and enforceable if it prohibited Ms. Rogers only from practicing as a CPA in the city of San Diego for three years.

Employment contracts often contain noncompete clauses that prohibit an employee from competing with his or her employer for a certain time period after leaving the employment. These covenants not to compete are also judged using the reasonableness standard.

covenant not to compete
An agreement where a party agrees not to engage in a similar business or occupation within a specified geographic area for a specified period of time following a sale.

■ UNCONSCIONABLE CONTRACTS

The general rule of freedom of contract holds that if (1) the object of a contract is lawful and (2) the other elements for the formation of a contract are met, the courts will enforce a contract according to its terms. Although it is generally presumed that parties are capable of protecting their own interests when contracting, it is a fact of life that dominant parties sometimes take advantage of weaker parties. As a result, some otherwise lawful contracts are so oppressive or manifestly unfair that they are unjust. To prevent the enforcement of such contracts, the courts developed the equitable **doctrine of unconscionability**, which is based on public policy. A contract found to be unconscionable under this doctrine is called an unconscionable contract, or a **contract of adhesion**.

The courts are given substantial discretion in determining whether a contract or contract clause is unconscionable. There is no single definition of *unconscionability*. The doctrine may not be used merely to save a contracting party from a bad bargain.

doctrine of unconscionability
Where an otherwise lawful contract will not be enforced because it is so oppressive or manifestly unfair that it is unjust.

Elements of Unconscionability

The following elements must be shown to prove that a contract or clause in a contract is unconscionable:

1. The parties possessed severely unequal bargaining power.
2. The dominant party unreasonably used its unequal bargaining power to obtain oppressive or manifestly unfair contract terms.
3. The adhering party had no reasonable alternative.

Unconscionable contracts are sometimes found where there is a consumer contract that takes advantage of uneducated, poor, or elderly people who have been persuaded to enter into an unfair contract. This often involves door-to-door sales and sales over the telephone.

Example: Suppose a door-to-door salesperson sells a poor family a freezer full of meat and other foods for $3,000, with monthly payments for 60 months at 20 percent interest. If the actual cost of the freezer and the food is $1,000, this contract could be found to be unconscionable.

The unequal bargaining power of the elderly is a very contemporary, real-life issue important to contract law. The Model Rules of Professional Conduct of the American Bar Association give guidance when lawyers and paralegals have clients—including the elderly—with diminished capacity.[3] The area of elder law is a fast-growing area of law for paralegals, and an understanding of the relationship of contract law to elder law is important.

If the court finds that a contract or contract clause is unconscionable, it may (1) refuse to enforce the contract, (2) refuse to enforce the unconscionable clause but enforce the remainder of the contract, or (3) limit the applicability of any unconscionable clause so as to avoid any unconscionable result. The appropriate remedy depends on the facts and circumstances of each case. Note that because unconscionability is a matter of law, the judge may opt to decide the case without a jury trial.

ETHICS SPOTLIGHT

UNCONSCIONABLE CONTRACT

"Considering the terms of the arbitration clause in the light of the commercial context in which it operates and the legitimate needs of the parties at the time it was entered into, we have little difficulty concluding that its terms are so extreme as to appear unconscionable according to the mores and business practices of the time and place."

Judge Kline

Sometimes contracts favor one party over another party. This imbalance often occurs when the strongest party drafts the contract and presents it to the other party on a take-it-or-leave-it basis. Mere unbalanced contracts are not necessarily illegal, but those that overreach and are too lopsided can be found to be unenforceable under the equitable doctrine of unconscionability. Consider the following case.

Supercuts, Inc., a Delaware corporation, conducts a national hair care franchise business. David E. Lipson was the president of Supercuts. For just over one year, Supercuts employed William N. Stirlen as its vice president and chief financial officer. Stirlen signed

---

[3]Model Rule 1.14 of the American Bar Association Model Rules of Professional Conduct.

an employment agreement prepared by Supercuts. The contract provided for Stirlen to receive an annual salary of $150,000, stock options, a bonus plan, a supplemental retirement plan, and a $10,000 signing bonus. The contract was an at-will employment contract, meaning Stirlen could be terminated without cause at any time.

After beginning work, Stirlen informed Lipson and other corporate officers of various problems and "accounting irregularities" he feared might be in violation of state and federal statutes. Stirlen also expressed concern that the company's decline in profits "was being hidden in the books and from public shareholders." Stirlen provided senior managers with accounting statements outlining the accounting irregularities. After Stirlen brought these issues to Supercuts's outside auditors, Lipson allegedly reprimanded Stirlen and accused him of being a "troublemaker." Lipson also told him that if Stirlen did not reverse his position on these issues, he would no longer be considered a "member of the team." When Stirlen did not comply, Lipson suspended Stirlen from his job; Stirlen was fired the following month.

Stirlen sued Supercuts and Lipson for breach of contract, wrongful termination in violation of public policy, and intentional misrepresentation. The defendants made a motion to the court alleging that the arbitration clause in Stirlen's employment contract required the dispute to be arbitrated. Stirlen countered that the arbitration clause, and other clauses in Supercuts' contract, were unconscionable and therefore unenforceable. The challenged clauses provided that (1) Stirlen would have to submit to final and binding arbitration all disputes concerning the contract, but Supercuts could go to court on most matters if it sued Stirlen, (2) any damages that could be awarded Stirlen could not exceed the actual damages for breach of contract, and (3) any salary or benefits payable to Stirlen would cease pending the outcome of any action between the parties.

Stirlen argued that the employment contract was so one-sided as to be "unconscionable." The court of appeals held that a contract is unconscionable if it "does not fall within the reasonable expectations of the weaker party" or if the contact is "unduly oppressive." Supercuts's attorneys argued that Stirlen was a sophisticated business executive who knew what he was doing when he signed Supercuts's contract.

After weighing all the evidence, the court found that Supercuts's contract was an unconscionable contract—a contract of adhesion—that was unenforceable. The court found Supercuts's contract to be unconscionable in the following ways: Supercuts reserved the right to sue in court but denied this right to Stirlen; Supercuts limited the damages that Stirlen could recover from them in violation of the law; and state law provided that a party could not require another party to waive the ability to sue for fraud, which Supercuts required Stirlen to do. The court also held that Stirlen could proceed with his lawsuit against Supercuts to recover damages. The court concluded, "Considering the terms of the arbitration clause in the light of the commercial context in which it operates and the legitimate needs of the parties at the time it was entered into, we have little difficulty concluding that its terms are so extreme as to appear unconscionable according to the mores and business practices of the time and place." *Stirlen v. Supercuts, Inc.,* 60 Cal. Rptr. 2d 138 (Ct. App. 1997).

Law & Ethics Questions

1. What does the doctrine of unconsiconability provide? Explain.
2. **Ethics** Is the doctrine of unconscionability based on ethics principles? Explain.
3. **Ethics** Did Supercuts act ethically in drafting its employment contract? Should it have been more "fair"?
4. **Ethics** Did Stirlen act ethically by refusing to be a "team member"?

Web Exercises

1. **Web** Visit the website of the Court of Appeal of California, First Appellate District, at www.courtinfo.ca.gov/courts/courtsofappeal.
2. Visit the website of Supercuts at www.supercuts.com. Can you find this corporation's Code of Ethics?

INTERNET EXERCISES AND CASE QUESTIONS

Working the Web Internet Exercises

1. This chapter discussed capacity in relation to a minor. Locate the statute for your state that deals with when a minor has reached "majority" for purposes of entering into a contract.
2. Review the laws of your jurisdiction regarding minors and purchases of alcohol and tobacco, purchases of motor vehicles, and renting of an apartment.
3. Find the website for your state that explains the requisite level of intoxication for a driving-while-impaired traffic citation. Would that minimum amount be sufficient to provide a lack-of-capacity defense to a contract claim?
4. Find your state statutes relating to usury. What is the maximum allowable interest rate?
5. An extensive overview of contract law can be found at Contracts home page (by Craig Smith, Santa Barbara College of Law), www.west.net/~smith/contracts.htm. Review the "Policing the Bargain" page. Note that *capacity* is listed with other problem areas.

CHAPTER 4 SUMMARY

MINORS, p. 92

Minors

1. *Infancy doctrine.* Minors under the age of majority may *disaffirm* (cancel) most contracts they have entered into with adults. Such a contract is *voidable* by the minor but not by the adult.
2. *Disaffirmance.* Disaffirmance must occur before or within a reasonable time after the minor reaches the age of majority.
3. *Competent party's duty of restitution.* If a minor disaffirms a contract, the adult must place the minor in status quo by returning the value of the consideration that the minor paid.
4. *Minor's duty upon disaffirmance:*
   a. *Minor's duty of restoration.* Generally, upon disaffirmance of a contract, a minor owes a duty to return the consideration to the adult in whatever condition it is in at the time of disaffirmance.
   b. *Minor's duty of restitution.* A minor's duty is to place the adult in status quo by returning the value of the consideration paid by the adult at the time of contracting if the minor (1) misrepresented his or her age or (2) intentionally or with gross negligence caused the loss to the adult's property.
5. *Ratification.* If a minor does not disaffirm a contract during the period of minority or within a reasonable time after reaching the age of majority, the contract is *ratified* (accepted).
6. *Necessaries of life.* Minors are obligated to pay the reasonable value for the necessaries of life (e.g., food, clothing, shelter).

7. *Special contracts.* Many states have enacted statutes that make minors liable on certain types of contracts, such as for medical care, health and life insurance, educational loan agreements, and the like.
8. *Emancipation.* Emancipation occurs when a minor voluntarily leaves home and lives apart from his or her parents. The parents' duty to support the minor terminates upon emancipation.

MENTALLY INCOMPETENT PERSONS, p. 100

Mentally Incompetent Persons

1. *Adjudged insane.* Contracts by persons who have been adjudged insane are *void*. That is, such a contract cannot be enforced by either the sane or insane party.
2. *Insane but not adjudged insane.* Contracts by persons who are insane but have not been adjudged insane are *voidable* by the insane person but not by the competent party to the contract.
3. *Duty of restitution.* A person who has dealt with an insane person must place the insane person in status quo by returning the value of the consideration paid by the insane person at the time of contracting. Most states place the same duty on insane persons when they void a contract.
4. *Necessaries of life.* Insane persons are obligated to pay the reasonable value for the necessaries of life.

INTOXICATED PERSONS, p. 103

Intoxicated Persons

1. *Intoxicated persons.* Contracts by intoxicated persons are *voidable* by the intoxicated person but not by the competent party to the contract.
2. *Duty of restitution.* Both parties owe a duty to place the other party in status quo by returning the value of the consideration paid by the other party at the time of contracting.
3. *Necessaries of life.* Intoxicated persons are obliged to pay the reasonable value for the necessaries of life.

LEGALITY, p. 105

Contracts Contrary to Statutes

Contracts that violate statutes are illegal, void, and unenforceable.

1. *Usury laws.* These set the upper limit on the annual interest rate that can be charged on certain types of loans by certain lenders.
2. *Gambling statutes.* These make certain types of gambling illegal.
3. *Sabbath laws.* These prohibit or limit the carrying on of certain secular activities on Sundays. They are also called *Sunday laws* or *blue laws*.
4. *Criminal statutes.* Contracts to commit crimes are illegal.

5. *Licensing statutes:*
   a. *Regulatory statutes.* These are licensing statutes enacted to protect the public. Unlicensed persons cannot recover payment for providing services that a licensed person is required to provide.
   b. *Revenue-raising statutes.* These are licensing statutes enacted to raise money for the government. Unlicensed persons can enforce contracts and recover for rendering services.

Contracts Contrary to Public Policy

Contracts that violate public policy are illegal, void, and unenforceable.

1. **Immoral contracts.** A contract whose objective is the commission of an act considered immoral by society is illegal.

Effect of Illegality

1. **General rule.** An illegal contract is *void*. Therefore, the parties cannot sue for nonperformance. If the contract has been executed, the court will *leave the parties where it finds them.*

SPECIAL BUSINESS CONTRACTS, p. 110

Special Business Contracts

1. **Contracts in restraint of trade.** Contracts that unreasonably restrain trade are illegal contracts.
2. **Exculpatory clauses.** Contract clauses that relieve one or both of the parties to the contract from tort liability for ordinary negligence are called exculpatory clauses. Exculpatory clauses that affect public interests, result from superior bargaining power, or attempt to relieve one of liability for intentional torts, fraud, recklessness, or gross negligence are illegal. Reasonable exculpatory clauses between parties of equal bargaining power are legal.
3. **Covenants not to compete.** These are contracts that provide that a seller of a business or an employee will not engage in a similar business or occupation within a specified geographic area for a specified time following the sale of the business or termination of employment. Also called *noncompete clauses.* They are illegal if they are *unreasonable* in the line of business, geographic area, or time. Reasonable noncompete clauses are legal and enforceable.

UNCONSCIONABLE CONTRACTS, p. 115

Unconscionable Contracts

Contracts that are oppressively unfair or unjust are called *unconscionable contracts,* or *contracts of adhesion.*

1. **Elements of unconscionable contracts:**
   a. The parties possessed severely unequal bargaining power.
   b. The dominant party unreasonably used its power to obtain oppressive or manifestly unfair contract terms.
   c. The adhering party had no reasonable alternative.

2. *Remedies for unconscionability.* Where a contract or contract clause is found to be unconscionable, the court may do one of the following:
   a. Refuse to enforce the contract.
   b. Refuse to enforce the unconscionable clause but enforce the remainder of the contract.
   c. Limit the applicability of any unconscionable clause so as to avoid any unconscionable result.

TERMS AND CONCEPTS

Adjudged insane   100

Contract in restraint of trade   110

Contractual capacity   91

Contracts contrary to public policy   106

Covenant not to compete (noncompete clause)   115

Disaffirmance   93

Doctrine of unconscionability   115

Duty of restitution   93

Duty of restoration   93

Emancipation   97

Exculpatory clause   112

Gambling statute   108

Illegal contract   91

Immoral contract   106

Infancy doctrine   93

In pari delicto   109

Insane, but not adjudged insane   101

Intoxicated persons   103

Lawful contract   105

Legal insanity   100

Licensing statute   110

Minor   92

Necessaries of life   97

Ratification   95

Regulatory statute   111

Revenue-raising statute   111

Sabbath laws (Sunday law, blue law)   106

Unconscionable contract (contract of adhesion)   91

Usury law   106

CASE SCENARIO REVISITED

Let's go back to the case scenario involving the minor, James, and his purchase of a Hummer. Knowing what you know now, do you believe James can disaffirm the contract? How much, if anything, would James have to reimburse Michael? Can Michael refuse to pick up the car and make James fulfill the contract? The case of *Halbman v. Lemke*, 298 N.W.2d 562 (Wis. 1980), should help you answer these questions.

CRITICAL LEGAL THINKING CASES

Critical Legal Thinking Case 4.1 *Ratification*   Charles Edwards Smith, a minor, purchased an automobile from Bobby Floars Toyota (Toyota). Smith executed a security agreement to finance part of the balance due on the purchase price, agreeing to pay off the balance in 30 monthly installments. Smith turned 18, which was the age of majority in his state. Smith made 10 monthly payments after turning 18. He then decided to disaffirm the contract and stopped making the payments. Smith claims that he may disaffirm the contract entered into when he was a minor. Toyota argues that Smith has ratified the contract since attaining the age of majority. Who is correct? *Bobby Floars Toyota, Inc. v. Smith*, 269 S.E.2d 320 (N.C. Ct. App. 1980).

Critical Legal Thinking Case 4.2 *Adjudged Insane*   Manzelle Johnson, who had been adjudicated insane, executed a quitclaim and warranty deed conveying real estate she owned to her guardian, Obbie Neal. Neal subsequently conveyed the real estate to James R. Beavers by warranty deed. Charles L. Weatherly, Johnson's subsequent guardian, brought this action, seeking a decree of the court that title to the real estate be restored to Johnson because of her inability to contract. Should Johnson be allowed to void the contract? *Beavers v. Weatherly*, 299 S.E.2d 730 (Ga. 1983).

Critical Legal Thinking Case 4.3 *Intoxication*   Betty Galloway, an alcoholic, signed a settlement agreement upon her divorce from her husband, Henry Galloway. Henry, in Betty's absence in court, stated that she had lucid intervals from her alcoholism, had been sober for two months, and was lucid when she signed the settlement agreement. Betty moved to vacate the settlement agreement after she had retained present legal counsel. Four months later Betty was declared incompetent to handle her person and her affairs, and a guardian and conservator was appointed. Betty, through her guardian, sued to have the settlement agreement voided. Who wins? *Galloway v. Galloway*, 281 N.W.2d 804(N.D. 1979).

Critical Legal Thinking Case 4.4 *Licensing Statute*   The state of Hawaii requires a person who wants to practice architecture to meet certain educational requirements and to pass a written examination before that person is granted a license to practice. After receiving the license, an architect must pay an annual license fee of $15. Ben Lee Wilson satisfied the initial requirements and was granted an architecture license. Four years later Wilson failed to renew his license by paying the required annual fee. Wilson contracted with Kealakekua Ranch, Ltd., and Gentry Hawaii (defendants) to provide architectural services for the Kealakekua Ranch Center project. Wilson provided $33,994 of architectural services to the defendants. The defendants refused to pay this fee because Wilson did not have an architectural license. Wilson sued to collect his fees. Who wins? *Wilson v. Kealakekua Ranch, Ltd.*, 551 P.2d 525 (Haw. 1976).

Critical Legal Thinking Case 4.5 *Covenant Not to Compete* Gerry Morris owned a silk screening and lettering shop in Tucson, Arizona. Morris entered into a contract to sell the business to Alfred and Connie Gann. The contract contained the following covenant not to compete: "Seller agrees not to enter into silk screening or lettering shop business within Tucson and a 100-mile radius of Tucson, for a period of ten (10) years from the date of this agreement and will not compete in any manner whatsoever with buyers, and seller further agrees that he will refer all business contracts to buyers." Morris opened a silk screening and lettering business in competition with the Ganns and in violation of the noncompetition clause. The Ganns brought this action against Morris for breach of contract and to enforce the convenant not to compete. Is the convenant not to compete valid and enforceable in this case? *Gann v. Morris*, 596 P.2d 43 (Ariz. Ct. App. 1979).

Critical Legal Thinking Case 4.6 *Exculpatory Clause* Grady Perkins owned the Raleigh Institute of Cosmetology (Institute), and Ray Monk and Rovetta Allen were employed as instructors there. The school trained students to do hair styling and coloring, cosmetology, and other beauty services. The students received practical training by providing services to members of the public under the supervision of the instructors. Francis I. Alston went to the institute to have her hair colored and styled by a student who was under the supervision of Monk and Allen. Before receiving any services, Alston signed a written release form that released the institute and its employees from liability for their negligence. While coloring Alston's hair, the student negligently used a chemical that caused Alston's hair to fall out. Alston sued the institute, Perkins, Monk, and Allen for damages. The defendants asserted that the release form signed by Alston barred her suit. Is the exculpatory clause valid? *Alston v. Monk*, 373 S.E.2d 463 (N.C. Ct. App. 1988).

Critical Legal Thinking Case 4.7 *Exculpatory Clause* Wilbur Spaulding owned and operated the Jacksonville racetrack at the Morgan Country Fairgrounds, where automobile races were held. Lawrence P. Koch was a flagman at the raceway. One day when Koch arrived at the pit shack at the raceway, he was handed a clipboard on which was a track release and waiver of liability form that released the racetrack from liability for negligence. Koch signed the form and took up his position as flagman. During the first race, the last car on the track lost control and slid off the end of the track, striking Koch. Koch suffered a broken leg and other injuries and was unable to work for 14 months. Koch sued Spaulding for damages for negligence. Spaulding asserted that the release form signed by Koch barred his suit. Is the exculpatory clause valid against Koch? *Koch v. Spaulding*, 529 N.E.2d 19 (Ill. App. Ct. 1988).

ETHICS CASES

Ethics Case 4.1 Joe Plumlee owned and operated an ambulance company. He alleged that the law firm of Paddock, Loveless & Roach agreed to pay him an up-front fee and a percentage of the law firm's fees generated from personal injury case referrals. When the law firm did not pay Plumlee, he sued to recover damages for breach of contract. Texas law prohibits lawyers from sharing fees with laypersons (Tex. Penal Code Section 38.12; Supreme Court of Texas). A disciplinary rule also forbids such activity (State Bar Rules Art. X, Section 9). The law firm asserted that the contract could not be enforced because it would be an illegal contract. Who wins? Did Plumlee act ethically in this case? If the contract existed, did the lawyers act ethically? *Plumlee v. Paddock*, 832 S.W.2d 757 (Tex. App. 1992).

Ethics Case 4.2   Richard Zientara was a friend of Chester and Bernice Kaszuba. All three were residents of Indiana. Bernice, who was employed in an Illinois tavern where Illinois state lottery tickets were sold, had previously obtained lottery tickets for Zientara because Indiana did not have a state lottery. One day, Zientara requested that Kaszuba purchase an Illinois lottery ticket for him. He gave Kaszuba the money for the ticket and the numbers 6–15–16–23–24–37. Kaszuba purchased the ticket, but when it turned out to be the winning combination worth $1,696,800, she refused to give the ticket to Zientara and unsuccessfully tried to collect the money. Zientara filed suit against Kaszuba in Indiana, claiming the ticket and proceeds thereof. Was the contract legal? Did the Kaszubas act ethically in this case? *Kaszuba v. Zientara*, 506 N.E.2d 1 (Ind. 1987).

BRIEFING THE CASE WRITING ASSIGNMENT

Read Case A.4 in Appendix A (*Carnival Leisure Industries, Ltd. v. Aubin*). This case is excerpted from the court of appeals opinion. Review and brief the case. After briefing the case, you should be able to answer the following questions:
1. What were the plaintiff's contentions on appeal?
2. What law was applied by the court in this case: Bahamian law or Texas law? Why was that law applied?
3. What is the consequence of finding an illegal contract? Apply this rule to the facts of this case.
4. Did Aubin act ethically in avoiding an obligation that he knowingly made? Do you think he would have given back the money if he had won at gambling?

PRACTICE TIP

After the date and the parties to the contract are set out (see the Practice Tip in Chapter 1), and the introduction as to what the parties would like to contract is written (see the Practice Tip in Chapter 2), and the recital (see the Practice Tip in Chapter 3), the final step in drafting the contract is to end with the signature section. The form for this introduction is as follows:

IN WITNESS WHEREOF _____ and _____ have executed this Agreement.

_____

_____

PARALEGAL PORTFOLIO EXERCISE

Now that you have learned the basic contact form (from the Practice Tips located in Chapters 1 through 4), you should be able to be able to draft a simple contract. This will be especially important when you are employed as a paralegal and asked to draft a contract for your attorney's review.

Using the fact situation that follows, draft a simple contract:

A client at the law firm where you work as a paralegal, Sarah Smith, would like to enter into an agreement with Kelly Henry. Sarah would like to sell to Kelly a one-carat square diamond ring that Sarah no longer wears. The diamond does have a slight flaw in it, which Sarah has pointed out to Kelly. But Sarah wants to make sure the agreement reflects the flaw, so there is no chance Kelly will later ask for her money back. Sarah and Kelly have settled on a price of $800 for the ring. They want to close the deal on August 5, 2008.

"Freedom of contract
begins where equality of
bargaining power begins."
—*Oliver Wendell Holmes Jr.,*
June 4, 1928

Genuineness of Assent | CHAPTER 5

CASE SCENARIO

The law firm where you work as a paralegal represents the estate of Philip Moore. Mr. Moore had six children, all who had frequent contact with him and helped with his needs prior to 2006. In 2006, his eldest son, Gary, advised his siblings that he would begin managing their father's business affairs. In March 2007, after much urging by Gary, Mr. Moore deeded his 80-acre farm in Nebraska to Gary for $23,500. Investigation has shown that at the time of the sale, the reasonable fair market value of the farm was between $145,000 and $160,000. At the time Mr. Moore signed over the real estate, his health had deteriorated. He was, for the most part, an invalid, relying on Gary for all of his personal needs, transportation, banking, and other business matters. Additionally, Mr. Moore was born in France and could not read or write English.

◼ CHAPTER INTRODUCTION

Voluntary *assent* by the parties is necessary to create an enforceable contract. Assent is determined by the relevant facts surrounding the negotiation and formation of the contract. Assent may be manifested in any manner sufficient to show agreement, including express words or conduct of the parties.

A contract may not be enforced if the assent of one or both of the parties to the contract was not genuine or real. **Genuine assent** may be missing because a party entered into a contract based on mistake, fraudulent misrepresentation, duress, or undue influence. Problems concerning **genuineness of assent** are discussed in this chapter.

genuine assent
Where agreement (or assent) to the contract by both parties is genuine and real.

genuineness of assent
The requirement that a party's assent to a contract be genuine.

CHAPTER OBJECTIVES

After studying this chapter, you should be able to:

1. Explain *genuineness of assent.*
2. Explain how *mutual mistake of fact* excuses performance.
3. Describe *intentional misrepresentation* (fraud).
4. Describe *duress.*
5. Define *undue influence.*

PARALEGAL PERSPECTIVE

Teresa J. Turner is a transactional paralegal with the law firm Spink Butler, LLP, in Boise, Idaho, specializing in real estate and land use law. She graduated summa cum laude from Boise State University with a certificate of paralegal studies and a bachelor of applied science in legal studies.

Having worked in the legal field for over 20 years in Colorado and Idaho, I've been involved with contracts in every area of my career in real estate transactions (e.g., real estate purchase agreements), business transactions (e.g., corporate merger agreements), land use (e.g., development agreements), business entities (e.g., shareholder agreements), securities (e.g., stock purchase agreements), probate (e.g., executory contracts involving the decedent), estate planning (e.g., trusts and beneficiary agreements), bankruptcy (e.g., secured loan agreements), and torts (e.g., insurance policies). I've never encountered an area of law in which contracts are not involved, from a single-page letter of intent to buy property to a complex business merger agreement hundreds of pages long, and everything in between.

Reviewing, analyzing, and drafting contracts are a routine and almost daily task in my current position as a real estate paralegal. My attorneys rely on me for drafts or thorough legal analyses of contracts involving our clients, making the attorneys much more productive and efficient in their practices. One of the more interesting contracts I drafted recently was an agreement to release future interests in property on the occurrence of certain events, and the agreement was placed into escrow with specific written instructions to the escrowee (yet another contract) for disposition of this executory agreement.

Working with contracts in all areas of law is always interesting and challenging, and I'm frequently encountering new or unique contractual provisions. Transactions of every nature are made or broken within the "four corners" of a contract.

■ MISTAKE

mistake
An unintentional act, omission, or error arising from ignorance, surprise, imposition, or misplaced confidence (mutual mistake).

rescission
An action to rescind (undo) the contract. Rescission is available if there has been a material breach of contract, fraud, duress, undue influence, or mistake.

unilateral mistake
When only one party is mistaken about a material fact regarding the subject matter of the contract.

A **mistake** occurs where one or both of the parties have an erroneous belief about the subject matter, value, or some other aspect of a contract. Mistakes may be either *unilateral* or *mutual*. The law permits **rescission** of some contracts made in mistake.

Unilateral Mistake

Unilateral mistakes occur when only one party is mistaken about a material fact regarding the subject matter of the contract. In the three following types of situations, a contract may not be enforced because of such a mistake:

1. One party makes a unilateral mistake of fact and the other party knew (or should have known) a mistake was made.[1]
2. A unilateral mistake occurs because of a clerical or mathematical error that is not the result of gross negligence.
3. The mistake is so serious that enforcing the contract would be unconscionable.[2]

In most cases, however, the mistaken party is not permitted to rescind the contract. The contract is enforced on its terms.

---

[1]In instances where unilateral mistake can rescind a contract, some courts hold that the nonmistaken party has to not only *know* the other party has made a mistake but that the nonmistaken party also has to have been under some duty to correct the other party.
[2]*Restatement (Second) of Contracts*, Section 153.

Example: Suppose Trent Anderson wants to purchase a car from the showroom floor. He looks at several models. Although he decides to purchase a car with a sunroof, he does not tell the salesperson about this preference. The model named in the contract he signs does not have this feature, although he believes it does. Anderson's unilateral mistake does not relieve him of his contractual obligation to purchase the car.

In Case 5.1, the court had to decide whether to allow a party out of a contract because of the party's unilateral mistake.

CASE 5.1   UNILATERAL MISTAKE

Wells Fargo Credit Corp. v. Martin, 650 So. 2d 531 (Fla. Dist. Ct. App. 1992).

> *"We accept the trial court's conclusion that the amount of the sale was grossly inadequate. This inadequacy, however, occurred due to an avoidable, unilateral mistake by an agent of Wells Fargo."*

> Judge Altenbernd, *Court of Appeal of Florida*

Facts

Wells Fargo Credit Corporation (Wells Fargo) obtained a judgment of foreclosure on a house owned by Mr. and Mrs. Clevenger. The total indebtedness stated in the judgment was $207,141. The foreclosure sale was scheduled for 11 A.M. on July 12, 1991, at the west front door of the Hillsborough County Courthouse.

Wells Fargo was represented by a paralegal, who had attended more than 1,000 similar sales. Wells Fargo's handwritten instruction sheet informed the paralegal to make one bid at $115,000, the tax-appraised value of the property. Because the first "1" in the number was close to the "$," the paralegal misread the bid instruction as $15,000 and opened the bidding at that amount.

Harley Martin, who was attending his first judicial sale, bid $20,000. The county clerk gave ample time for another bid and then announced, "$20,000 going once, $20,000 going twice, sold to Harley Martin." The paralegal shouted, "Stop! I'm sorry, I made a mistake!" The certificate of sale was issued to Martin. Wells Fargo filed suit to set aside the judicial sale based on its unilateral mistake. The trial court held for Martin. Wells Fargo appealed.

Issue

Does Wells Fargo's unilateral mistake constitute grounds for setting aside the judicial sale?

Language of the Court

We accept the trial court's conclusion that the amount of the sale was grossly inadequate. This inadequacy, however, occurred due to an avoidable, unilateral mistake by an agent of Wells Fargo. As between Wells Fargo and a good faith purchaser at the judicial sale, the trial court had the discretion to place the risk of this mistake upon Wells Fargo.

Thus, we affirm the trial court's orders denying relief to Wells Fargo. We are certain that this result seems harsh to Wells Fargo. Nevertheless, Mr. Martin's bid was accepted when the clerk announced "sold." Without ruling that a unilateral mistake by the complaining party could never justify relief, we hold that the trial court had the discretion under these facts to make Wells Fargo suffer the loss.

Decision

The appellate court held that Wells Fargo's unilateral mistake did not entitle it to relief from the judicial sale.

Law & Ethics Questions

1. Not all jurisdictions would have decided as harshly as the court did in this case. Although the court's opinion in *Wells Fargo* is indeed a trend, it is still not the approach the majority of the courts would have taken.

2. Should contracts be allowed to be rescinded because of unilateral mistakes? Why or why not?

3. **Ethics** Did Wells Fargo act ethically in trying to set aside the judicial sale?

4. Do you think mistakes such as that made by Wells Fargo happen very often in business?

Web Exercises

1. **Web** Visit the website of the District Court of Appeal of Florida, Second District, at www.2dca.org.

2. **Web** Visit the website of Wells Fargo Financial at www.wellsfargofinancial.com.

3. **Web** Use www.google.com and find an article or case that involves a unilateral mistake.

Mutual Mistake

mutual mistake
A mistake common to both contracting parties, where each is laboring under the same misconception as to a past or existing material fact.

Either party may rescind a contract if there has been a **mutual mistake of a past or existing material fact.**[3] A *material fact* is one that is important to the subject matter of a contract. An ambiguity in a contract may constitute a mutual mistake of a material fact. An ambiguity occurs when a word or term in the contract is susceptible to more than one logical interpretation. If there has been a mutual mistake, the contract may be rescinded on the ground that no contract has been formed because there has been no "meeting of the minds" between the parties.

In the celebrated case *Raffles v. Wichelhaus*,[4] which has become better known as the case of the good ship *Peerless*, the parties agreed on a sale of cotton that was to be delivered from Bombay by the ship. There were two ships named *Peerless*, however, and each party, in agreeing to the sale, was referring to a different ship. Because the sailing time of the two ships was materially different, neither party was willing to agree to shipment by the other *Peerless*. The court ruled there was no binding contract because each party had a different ship in mind when the contract was entered into.

The courts must distinguish between *mutual mistakes of fact* and *mutual mistakes of value*. A **mutual mistake of value** exists if both parties know the object of

[3] *Restatement (Second) of Contracts*, Section 152.
[4] *Raffles v. Wichelhaus*, 159 Eng. Rep. 375 (Ex. 1864).

MARKETPLACE

Job Announcement: Securities Litigation Paralegal

Responsibilities

Working under the supervision of attorneys, the securities litigation paralegal assists with document collection, review, and production in connection with internal investigations, regulatory investigations, and civil actions. Specific responsibilities:

- Supports attorneys in the collection of documents, including contracts with vendors and suppliers, in connection with internal investigations, regulatory investigations and civil actions, including traveling to client offices and other locations throughout the United States and abroad.
- Analyzes and reviews documents for responsiveness, legal privileges, and personal privacy issues.
- Organizes documents for secondary and final review by attorneys.
- Supports attorneys in preparation of privilege logs and production of documents to regulatory agencies and civil litigants.
- Performs other related duties as assigned.

Experience/Education

- Bachelor's degree and paralegal certificate from an ABA-approved program required.
- Strong organizational skills.
- Exhibits an aptitude for understanding complex issues and procedures.
- Proficiency with MS 2007 Excel/Word and Windows environment.
- Competency in using web-based tools.
- Detail oriented, punctual, cooperative.
- Excellent interpersonal and communication skills.
- Commitment to firm's core values and commitment to firm's client service standards.
- Ability to travel to domestic and international locations required.

The company offers a friendly work environment, competitive salary, and excellent benefits. Relocation assistance will be provided. Please visit our website for more information about the firm.

Send resumes by e-mail to:

---

the contract but are mistaken as to its value. Here, the contract remains enforceable by either party because the identity of the subject matter of the contract is not at issue. If the rule were different, almost all contracts could later be rescinded by the party who got the "worst" of the deal.

Example: Suppose Helen Pitts cleans her attic and finds a painting of a tomato soup can. She has no use for the painting, so she offers to sell it to Qian Huang for $100. Qian, who likes the painting, accepts the offer and pays Helen $100. It is later discovered that the painting is worth $1 million because it was painted by Andy Warhol. Neither party knew this at the time of contracting. It is a mistake of value. Helen cannot recover the painting.

PARALEGAL PERSPECTIVE

Patty Kechter is a graduate of the paralegal program at Lewis-Clark State College in Lewiston, Idaho. She is employed as a paralegal at the law firm of Randall, Blake & Cox, PLLC, in Lewiston for an attorney who specializes in real estate law, corporate law, probate law, and estate planning.

I work for an attorney who specializes in real estate law, corporate law, probate law, and estate planning. Each of these areas involves contracts of some sort.

In the real estate area, I draft contracts for real estate purchases and sales that involve not only real estate, but equipment purchases and accounts receivables. It is very important that these contracts spell out completely what both sides of the transaction want to accomplish.

The corporate law practice involves contracts regarding purchase and sale of businesses and also stock sales and transfers. Again, it is very important that every detail is completely understood and in writing.

We use contracts at times in estates for agreements between heirs and devisees. These agreements help make the estate process proceed smoothly.

My attorney depends on me to draft these documents for his review. It is really important that a paralegal understands the client's wants and needs because, most times, the paralegal is the client's first contact. Clients rely on the paralegal to draft documents that meet their needs and include all aspects of the transaction.

■ FRAUD

fraudulent misrepresentation (fraud)
Where one person to a contract intentionally induces (or causes) another person to rely and act on an assertion not in accord with the facts.

A misrepresentation occurs when an assertion is made that is not in accord with the facts.[5] An intentional misrepresentation occurs when one person consciously decides to induce another person to rely and act on a misrepresentation. International misrepresentation is commonly referred to as **fraudulent misrepresentation,** or **fraud.** When fraudulent misrepresentation is used to induce another to enter into a contract, the innocent party's assent to the contract is not genuine, and the contract is voidable by the innocent party.[6] The innocent party can either rescind the contract and obtain restitution or enforce the contract and sue for contract damages.

Fraud in the Inception

fraud in the inception
Occurs if a person is deceived as to the nature of his or her act and does not know what he or she is signing. A real defense against the enforcement of a negotiable instrument; a person has been deceived into signing a negotiable instrument thinking that it is something else.

Fraud in the inception, or **fraud in the factum,** occurs if a person is deceived as to the nature of his or her act and does not know what he or she is signing. Contracts involving fraud in the inception are void rather than just voidable.

Example: Suppose Heather brings her professor a grade card to sign. The professor signs the front of the grade card. On the back, however, are contract terms that transfer all of the professor's property to Heather. Here, there is fraud in the inception. The contract is void.

Fraud in the Inducement

fraud in the inducement
Occurs when the party knows what he or she is signing, but has been fraudulently induced to enter into the contract. A personal defense against the enforcement of a negotiable instrument; a wrongdoer makes a false statement to another person to lead that person to enter into a contract with the wrongdoer.

A great many fraud cases concern **fraud in the inducement.** Here, the innocent party knows what he or she is signing but has been fraudulently induced to enter into the contract. Such contracts are voidable by the innocent party.

---

[5]*Restatement (Second) of Contracts,* Section 159.
[6]*Restatement (Second) of Contracts,* Sections 163 and 164.

ETHICS SPOTLIGHT

PROVING FRAUD

To prove fraud, the following elements must be shown:

1. The wrongdoer made a false representation of material fact.
2. The wrongdoer intended to deceive the innocent party.
3. The innocent party justifiably relied on the misrepresentation.
4. The innocent party was injured.

Each of these elements is discussed in the following paragraphs.

MATERIAL MISREPRESENTATION OF FACT

A misrepresentation may occur by words (oral or written) or by the conduct of a party. To be actionable as fraud, the misrepresentation must be of a past or existing *material fact*. This means the misrepresentation must have been a significant factor in inducing the innocent party to enter into the contract. It does not have to have been the sole factor. Statements of opinion or predictions about the future generally do not form the basis for fraud.

INTENT TO DECEIVE

To prove fraud, the person making the misrepresentation must have either had knowledge that the representation was false or made it without sufficient knowledge of the truth. This is called **scienter** ("guilty mind"). The misrepresentation must have been made with the intent to deceive the innocent party. Intent can be inferred from the circumstances.

scienter
Guilty knowledge; intent to deceive or manipulate.

RELIANCE ON THE MISREPRESENTATION

A misrepresentation is not actionable unless the innocent party to whom the misrepresentation was directed acted on it. Further, an innocent party who acts in reliance on the misrepresentation must justify his or her reliance. Justifiable reliance is generally found unless the innocent party knew the misrepresentation was false or was so extravagant as to be obviously false.

Example: Reliance on a statement such as "This diamond ring is worth $10,000, but I'll sell it to you for $100" would not be justified.

INJURY TO THE INNOCENT PARTY

To recover damages, the innocent party must prove the fraud caused economic injury. The measure of damages is the difference between the value of the property as represented and the actual value of the property. This measure of damages gives the innocent party the "benefit of the bargain." In the alternative, the buyer can rescind the contract and recover the purchase price.

Individuals must be on guard in their commercial and personal dealings not to be taken by fraud. Basically, if it sounds "too good to be true," it is a signal that the situation might be fraudulent. Although the law permits a victim of fraud to rescind the contract and recover damages from the wrongdoer, often the wrongdoer cannot be found or the money has been spent.

There are various types of fraud. Some of the most common ones are discussed in this chapter.

Example: Suppose Lyle Green tells Candice Young he is forming a partnership to invest in drilling for oil and invites her to invest in this venture. In reality, though, Green intends to use whatever money he receives for his personal expenses, and he absconds with Young's $30,000 investment. Here, there has been fraud in the inducement. Young can rescind the contract and recover the money from Green, if he can be found.

THE ETHICAL PARALEGAL

pro bono
For the good; work or services performed free of charge.

Making Legal Services Available

Surveys show that a high percentage of Americans cannot afford a lawyer. The ethical paralegal should be concerned that all people have access to legal representation, regardless of their ability to pay. ABA Model Rules 1.5 and 6.1 both deal with this important issue.[7]

To fill this need, many bar organizations have established **pro bono** programs where attorneys volunteer to represent clients at no charge. Paralegals can play an important role in pro bono activities. Even if the paralegal's law firm doesn't handle pro bono cases, the paralegal might volunteer for pro bono projects sponsored by the local bar association or paralegal association. However, the ethical paralegal should be cautious and take into consideration any possible conflicts of interest (as set out in the Ethical Paralegal feature in Chapter 8).

Fraud by Concealment

fraud by concealment
Occurs when one party takes specific action to conceal a material fact from another party.

Fraud by concealment occurs when one party takes specific action to conceal a material fact from another party.[8]

Example: Suppose ABC Blouses, Inc. contracted to buy a used sewing machine from Wear-Well Shirts, Inc. ABC asked to see any past repair invoices on the machine. Wear-Well indicated no repairs were made to sewing machine. Relying on the knowledge that the machine was in good condition and never had to be repaired, ABC bought the machine. If ABC later should discover a significant repair record has been concealed, it can sue Wear-Well for fraud in concealing the past repairs.

Silence as Misrepresentation

Generally, neither party to a contract owes a duty to disclose all the facts to the other party. Ordinarily, such silence is not a misrepresentation unless (1) nondisclosure would cause bodily injury or death, (2) there is a fiduciary relationship (i.e., a relationship of trust and confidence) between the contracting parties, or (3) federal and state statutes require disclosure. The *Restatement (Second) of Contracts* specifies a broader duty of disclosure: Nondisclosure is a misrepresentation if it would constitute a failure to act in "good faith."[9]

In Case 5.2, the court found fraud and awarded punitive damages.

CASE 5.2 FRAUD

Krysa v. Payne, 176 S.W.3d 150 (Mo. Ct. App. 2005).

"Punitive damages differ from compensatory damages in that compensatory damages are intended to redress the concrete loss that the plaintiff has suffered by reason of the

---

[7]Copies of the ABA Model Rules of Professional Conduct are available from Service Center, American Bar Association, 321 North Clark Street, Chicago, IL 60610, 1-800-285-2221. The Model Rules can also be viewed online at http://www.abanet.org/cpr/mrpc/mrpc_toc.html.

[8]*Restatement (Second) of Contracts*, Section 160.

[9]*Restatement (Second) of Contracts*, Section 161.

defendant's wrongful conduct, while the well-established purpose of punitive damages is to inflict punishment and to serve as an example and a deterrent to similar conduct."

Judge Ellis, *Court of Appeals of Missouri*

Facts

Frank and Shelly Krysa were shopping for a truck to pull their 18-foot trailer. During the course of their search they visited Payne's Car Company, a used car dealership owned by Emmett Payne. Kemp Crane, a salesman, showed the Krysas around the car lot. The Krysas saw an F-350 truck that they were interested in purchasing. Crane told the Krysas the truck would tow their trailer, the truck would make it to 400,000 miles, and it was "a one-owner trade-in." The Krysas took the truck for a test drive and decided to purchase the truck. The Krysas, who had to borrow some of the money from Mrs. Krysa's mother, paid for the truck and took possession.

Later that day, the Krysas noticed that the power locks did not work on the truck. A few days later, the truck took three hours to start. The heater was not working. Mr. Krysa tried to fix some problems and noticed the radiator was smashed up, the radiator cap did not have a seal, and the thermostat was missing. Mr. Krysa noticed broken glass on the floor underneath the front seats and realized the driver's side window had been replaced. Shortly thereafter, Mr. Krysa attempted to tow his trailer, but within a few miles he had his foot to the floor trying to get the truck to pull the trailer. A large amount of smoke was pouring out of the back of the truck. Mr. Krysa also noticed the truck was consuming a lot of oil. Mr. Krysa obtained a CARFAX report for the truck, which showed the truck had 13 prior owners. Evidence proved that the truck was actually two halves of different trucks that had been welded together. An automobile expert told the Krysas not to drive the truck because it was unsafe.

Mr. Krysa went back to the dealership to return the truck and get his money back. Payne told Krysa he would credit the purchase price of the truck toward the purchase of one of the other vehicles on the lot, but he would not give Krysa his money back. Krysa could not find another vehicle on Payne's used car lot that would suit his needs. The Krysas sued Payne for fraudulent nondisclosure and fraudulent misrepresentation, and they sought to recover compensatory and punitive damages. The jury returned a verdict for the Krysas and awarded them $18,449 in compensatory damages and $500,000 in punitive damages. Payne appealed the award of punitive damages.

Issue

Did Payne engage in fraudulent nondisclosure, fraudulent misrepresentation, and reckless disregard for the safety of the Krysas and the public to support the award of $500,000 in punitive damages?

Language of the Court

Punitive damages differ from compensatory damages in that compensatory damages are intended to redress the concrete loss that the plaintiff has suffered by reason of the defendant's wrongful conduct, while the well-established purpose of punitive damages is to inflict punishment and to serve as an example and a deterrent to similar conduct. While the damage actually sustained by the Krysas was relatively small and was economic in nature, the record clearly supports a finding that Payne acted indifferently to or in reckless disregard of the safety of the Krysas in selling them a vehicle that he knew or should have known was not safe to drive and that the potential harm to the Krysas was much greater than the harm that was actually incurred.

The evidence also supported a finding that the harm sustained by Krysas was the result of intentional malice, trickery, or deceit, and was not merely an accident. Payne had a significant amount of work done to the vehicle to make it appear to be in good shape. This included, among numerous other repairs, straightening both the bed and cab of the truck. Payne's salesman, Crane, lied to the Krysas on several occasions about the condition of the truck, its origin, and its capabilities. This evidence, in addition to other evidence previously described, sufficiently established that Payne affirmatively misrepresented the condition of the F-350 to the Krysas in an attempt to trick them into buying the vehicle.

In sum, while the harm actually sustained by the Krysas in this case was economic as opposed to physical, Payne's conduct did pose a significant risk to the physical welfare of Respondents and evinced an indifference to or reckless disregard of the health or safety of the Krysas and the general public as well. Furthermore, the conduct was consistent with Payne's regular business practices and was not an isolated incident, involved acts of intentional trickery and deceit, and targeted victims that were financially vulnerable. Thus, in society's eyes, viewing the totality of the circumstances, Payne's conduct can only be seen as exhibiting a very high degree of reprehensibility.

Payne contends that the ratio between the actual damages awarded, $ 18,449.53, and the punitive award, $ 500,000, is grossly excessive, in that the ratio of punitive to actual damages is approximately 27:1. The initial problem with Payne's argument is that it fails to consider the evidence of the potential harm that could have been sustained by the Krysas. In this case, given the relatively small amount of actual damages awarded, the egregious nature of Payne's acts, Payne's open refusal to alter his behavior, and the magnitude of the potential harm that could have been sustained had the structural problems with the truck not been discovered by the Krysas's expert, the ratio of the punitive to actual damages does not, in and of itself, offend due process.

Decision

The court of appeals found that Payne's fraudulent concealment, fraudulent misrepresentation, and reckless disregard for the safety of the Krysas and the public justified the award of $500,000 of punitive damages to the Krysas.

Law & Ethics Questions

1. What is fraudulent concealment? What is fraudulent misrepresentation?

2. What are punitive damages? Why are they awarded?

3. **Ethics** Did Payne, the used car dealer, act ethically in this case?

4. **Ethics** Do you have any apprehension about purchasing a car from a used car dealership? Why or why not?

Web Exercises

1. **Web** For the complete opinion of this case, go to www.google.com.

2. **Web** Visit the website of the Court of Appeals of Missouri, Western District, at www.courts.mo.gov.

3. **Web** Use www.google.com and find an article or case about a fraudulent transaction.

CAREER FRONT

Securities/Municipal Bonds Paralegal Job Description

A securities/municipal bonds paralegal works with contracts in the following ways:

- Draft registration statement and prospectus.
- Coordinate filing of registration statement and exhibits.
- Draft questionnaires for officers, directors, and principal shareholders.
- Draft promissory notes.
- Draft underwriting agreements.
- Draft trust indentures.
- Draft bond purchase agreements.
- Draft NASDAQ and National Market System listing applications.
- Draft and file documents for renewing or withdrawing the registration of broker/dealers with salespersons.
- Research and obtain information concerning filings with NASD and SEC.
- Draft lease agreement, loan agreement, agreement of sale, facilities financing agreement, ordinance, or contracts.
- Draft letter of transmittal and other tender offer documents.
- Draft confidential offering memorandum.
- Draft security agreements, including deeds, guaranties, mortgages.
- Draft summaries of documents to use in preparing preliminary official statements and official statements.
- Coordinate accuracy of statements with underwriter.
- Finalize basic documents and distribute for execution.
- Draft necessary resolutions authorizing the issuance of bonds.
- Send bond forms to printer.
- Obtain Committee on Uniform Securities Identification Procedures (CUSIP) number for offerings.
- Proof first gallery of bonds and check manufacturing schedule, coupon amounts, and CUSIP numbers.
- Check bonds at time of closing and read bond numbered 1. Draft closing documents for issuer, including authorizing resolutions, authentication order to trustee, incumbency certificate, nonarbitrage certificates, and CUSIP numbers.
- Draft resolutions and officers' certificates for corporate approval and execution.
- Draft tax election and arrange for filing.
- Draft recording certificate.
- Draft financing statements.
- Obtain certificates from state agencies (e.g., good standing of company).
- Attend closing; check all certificates and opinions, security agreements, insurance policies, and legal descriptions.
- Compile closing transcript, prepare index, and organize closing binders.
- Draft regulation of public companies.
- Prepare drafts of proxy material and statements.
- Draft annual report to shareholders.

Excerpted by permission from the National Association of Legal Assistants (www.nala.org) and the National Federation of Paralegal Associations, Inc. (www.paralegals.org).

Misrepresentation of Law

Usually, a **misrepresentation of law** is not actionable as fraud. The innocent party cannot generally rescind the contract because each party to a contract is assumed to know the law that applies to the transaction, either through his or

misrepresentation of law
When a party to a contract misstates the law related to that contract—whether innocently or intentionally.

her own investigation or by hiring a lawyer. There is one major exception to this rule: The misrepresentation will be allowed as grounds for rescission of the contract if one party to the contract is a professional who should know what the law is and intentionally misrepresents the law to a less sophisticated contracting party.[10]

Innocent Misrepresentation

innocent misrepresentation
Occurs when a person makes a statement of fact that he or she honestly and reasonably believes to be true, even though it is not. Occurs when an agent makes an untrue statement that he or she honestly and reasonably believes to be true.

An **innocent misrepresentation** occurs when a person makes a statement of fact that he or she honestly and reasonably believes to be true even though it is not. Innocent misrepresentation is not fraud. If an innocent misrepresentation has been made, the aggrieved party may rescind the contract but may not sue for damages. Innocent misrepresentation often is treated as a mutual mistake.

In Case 5.3, the court allowed a contract to be rescinded because of fraud.

CASE 5.3   FRAUD

Wilson v. Western Nat'l Life Ins. Co., 1 Cal. Rptr. 2d (Ct. App. 1991).

"*A material misrepresentation or concealment entitles the injured party to rescission.*"

Judge Stone, *Court of Appeals of California*

Facts

Daniel and Doris Wilson were husband and wife. One day Daniel fainted from a narcotics overdose and was rushed, unconscious, to the hospital. Doris accompanied him. Daniel responded to medication used to counteract a narcotics overdose and recovered. The emergency room physician noted that Daniel had probably suffered from a heroin overdose and had multiple puncture sites on his arms. Two months later an agent for Western National Life Insurance Company (Western) met with the Wilsons in their home for the purpose of taking their application for life insurance. The agent asked questions and recorded the Wilsons' responses on a written application form. Daniel answered the following questions:

	Yes	No
13. In the past 10 years, have you been treated or joined an organization for alcoholism or drug addiction? If "Yes," explain on the reverse side.		X
17. In the past 5 years, have you consulted or been treated or examined by any physician or practitioner?		X

---

[10]*Restatement (Second) of Contracts*, Section 170.

Both of the Wilsons signed the application form and paid the agent the first month's premium. Under insurance law and the application form, the life insurance policy took effect immediately. Daniel Wilson died from a drug overdose two days later. Western rescinded the policy and rejected Doris Wilson's claim to recover the policy's $50,000 death benefit for Daniel's death, alleging failure to disclose Daniel's heroin overdose incident. Doris sued to recover the death benefits. The trial court granted summary judgment for Western. Doris appealed.

Issue

Was there a concealment of a material fact that justified Western's rescission of the life insurance policy?

Language of the Court

Plaintiff asserts the court erroneously granted summary judgment because Western failed to prove she or decedent made a misrepresentation in the application. We disagree. In her deposition, plaintiff testified neither she nor decedent told the agent about decedent's fainting spell or his hospital treatment two months earlier. Thus, there is no question but that they omitted medical information. Knowledge of the true facts by plaintiff and decedent is beyond dispute.

Plaintiff further argues the misrepresentation, if one occurred, was not material. Plaintiff's argument must fail. The trial court properly found the omissions to be material and the evidence supporting its materiality uncontradicted. The trial court had before it evidence from Western that the application would not have been accepted, and decedent would not have been found to be insurable, had he disclosed on the application the episode when he became unconscious from a narcotics overdose.

A material misrepresentation or concealment entitles the injured party to rescission. Concealment, whether intentional or unintentional, entitles the injured party to rescind insurance. Western properly rescinded the insurance contract and its obligation to provide coverage terminated as of the date of application.

Decision

The appellate court held there was concealment by the Wilsons that warranted rescission of the life insurance policy by Western.

Law & Ethics Questions

1. Should a contract be allowed to be rescinded because of an *innocent* misrepresentation? Why or why not?

2. **Ethics** Do you think the concealment in this case was intentional or innocent?

3. Do you think there is very much insurance fraud in the United States? Explain.

Web Exercises

1. **Web** Visit the website of the Court of Appeal of California at www.courtinfo .ca.gov/courts/courtsofappeal.

2. **Web** Use www.google.com and find an article or case about insurance fraud.

PARALEGAL PERSPECTIVE

Denise Schmidt is employed as a litigation paralegal with the law firm of Bahret & Associates Co., L.P.A., in Holland, Ohio. The law firm primarily handles defense civil litigation.

My main duties are concentrated in discovery. Most of our cases revolve around insurance coverage, so I spend a lot of my time assisting the attorney in reviewing and interpreting different insurance contracts or policies. Not only do I have to review the policy applicable to our own client (the defendant), but I must also obtain and review any other policies or contracts that may provide coverage on the alleged claims. I also review these contracts for indemnification language and the possibility of potential claims or additional defenses.

I have also had case assignments in which the incident at issue involves real estate contracts. For example, I've worked on several cases involving a slip and fall at a restaurant resulting from unnatural accumulations of ice and snow. In those cases, not only do I review the insurance contracts, but I may have to review the applicable lease contracts, land contracts, or purchase agreements. I'm looking to the contracts and other documents to determine who owns the property, who owns the restaurant, and who is responsible for removal of the ice and snow.

If a lawsuit settles, I assist in the drafting of, or reviewing of, the settlement agreement and/or release. It is very important to make sure any claims that are being asserted against our client are fully discharged and that no future claims can be made that would stem from the incident in question.

Concept Summary

Types of Misrepresentation

Type of Misrepresentation	Legal Consequences: Innocent Party May	
	Sue for Damages	Rescind Contract
Fraud in the inception	Yes	Yes
Fraud in the inducement	Yes	Yes
Fraud by concealment	Yes	Yes
Silence as misrepresentation	Yes	Yes
Misrepresentation of law	Usually no	Usually no
Innocent misrepresentation	No	Yes

■ UNDUE INFLUENCE

undue influence
Taking advantage of a person's weakness, infirmity, age, or distress in order to change that person's actions or decisions.

The courts may permit the rescission of a contract based on the equitable doctrine of **undue influence.** Undue influence occurs when one person (the dominant party) takes advantage of another person's mental, emotional, or physical weakness and unduly persuades that person (the servient party) to enter into a contract. The persuasion by the wrongdoer must overcome the free will of the innocent party. A contract entered into because of undue influence is voidable by the innocent party.[11] Wills are often challenged as having been made under undue influence.

---

[11]*Restatement (Second) of Contracts*, Section 176.

The following elements must be shown to prove undue influence:

1. A fiduciary or confidential relationship must have existed between the parties.
2. The dominant party must have unduly used his or her influence to persuade the servient party to enter into a contract.

If there is a confidential relationship between persons—such as a lawyer and a client, a doctor and a patient, a psychiatrist and a patient—any contract made by the servient party that benefits the dominant party is presumed to be entered into under undue influence. This rebuttable presumption can be overcome through proper evidence.

Example: Mr. Johnson, 70 years old, has a stroke and is partially paralyzed. He is required to use a wheelchair, and he needs constant nursing care. Prior to his stroke, Mr. Johnson had executed a will, leaving his property upon his death equally to his four grandchildren. Edward, a licensed nurse, is hired to care daily for Mr. Johnson, and Mr. Johnson relies on Edward's care. Edward works for Mr. Johnson for two years before Mr. Johnson passes away. It is discovered that Mr. Johnson had executed a new will three months before he died, leaving all of his property to Edward. If it is shown that Edward has used his dominant and fiduciary position to influence Mr. Johnson unduly to change his will, then the will is invalid. If no undue influence is shown, the second will is valid, and Edward will receive the property left to him by Mr. Johnson in the will.

ETHICS SPOTLIGHT

UNDUE INFLUENCE

"Any species of coercion, whether physical, mental, or moral, which subverts the sound judgment and genuine desire of the individual, is enough to constitute undue influence."

Judge Bownes

Religions obviously have an influence on their members. People who practice religions often donate money and property to their place of worship and religious causes. Most religious giving (and church asking) is legitimate. Sometimes there are charges of illegal and unethical conduct, however. Sometimes the charge is undue influence. Consider the following case.

Elizabeth Dayton Dovydenas was born in 1952. As an heir to the Dayton-Hudson department store chain fortune, she was worth approximately $19 million. She married Jonas Dovydenas. When Elizabeth was interested in finding a church to attend, the couple's housekeeper suggested her church, The Bible Speaks (TBS). Elizabeth and Jonas went to a TBS service, liked what they saw, and left a $500 check in the collection plate.

After this, pastors from TBS contacted them and set up a tea with Carl Stevens, the founder of TBS. Stevens had been a fundamentalist preacher for 26 years. At the first meeting, Stevens asked Elizabeth for money for a counseling center, and she gave him a check for $2,000. Elizabeth became a devout member of TBS. Eventually, Elizabeth met with Stevens alone every day after Bible classes and attended other functions with him. She abandoned her prior friends and saw little of her family.

One day in the fall of 1984, as she was driving with Stevens, Elizabeth heard a voice telling her to give $1 million to TBS. Elizabeth gave $1 million of Dayton-Hudson stock to TBS. Elizabeth was led to believe that large gifts by her to TBS could affect events on earth. She was also told she had to obey Stevens because he was the highest authority on earth.

In March 1985, Elizabeth told Stevens that she heard God tell her to give $5 million to TBS in June. Elizabeth had planned a trip to Florida on April 18. Before she left, she was told that a TBS pastor had been detained in Romania and that "they're probably pulling his fingernails out right now." Elizabeth went to Florida but called Stevens on April 21 and told him she wanted to give the $5 million right away so the pastor would be released. Stevens did not tell her the pastor had already been released. Elizabeth was cautioned against telling anyone that she had worked a miracle. The gift of $5 million of Dayton-Hudson stock was completed on May 13.

After her relatives tricked Elizabeth away from Stevens, Elizabeth was deprogrammed from her "cult" experience. Elizabeth then sued to rescind her $1-million and $5-million gifts to TBS, alleging that Stevens and TBS had engaged in undue influence. The U.S. District Court agreed and ordered that both gifts be rescinded. On appeal, the U.S. Court of Appeals stated,

> Undue influence, while sometimes susceptible of proof by direct testimony, may be exercised by indirect and secret ways, which are disclosed only in their result. Because undue influence is often practiced in "veiled and secret ways," its existence may be inferred from such factors as disproportionate gifts made under unusual circumstances, the age and health of the donor, and the existence of a confidential relationship. Two other factors are also important. One, attempts by the recipient to isolate the donor from her former friends and relatives can be considered in determining undue influence. Two, a court can also consider that the donor acted without independent and disinterested advice. Any species of coercion, whether physical, mental, or moral, which subverts the sound judgment and genuine desire of the individual, is enough to constitute undue influence.

The U.S. Court of Appeals reversed as to the $1-million gift, finding no undue influence at the time this gift was made. The U.S. Court of Appeals affirmed that the $5-million gift had been made based on undue influence and must be rescinded. *Dovydenas v. The Bible Speaks*, 869 F.2d 628 (1st Cir. 1989).

Law & Ethics Questions

1. What is undue influence? Is it hard to prove? Explain.
2. **Ethics** Did Stevens and the other members of TBS act ethically in this case?
3. Should the plaintiff have been saved from her folly? Why or why not?

Web Exercises

1. **Web** Visit the website of the Court of Appeal of California at www.ca1.uscourts.gov.
2. **Web** Use www.google.com and find an article that discusses the history of the Dayton-Hudson Corporation.
3. **Web** Use www.google.com. Find an article that discusses what further happened in this story after this case was decided.

■ DURESS

duress
Occurs where one party threatens to do a wrongful act unless the other party enters into a contract.

Duress occurs when one party threatens to do some wrongful act unless the other party enters into a contract. If a party to a contract has been forced into making the contract, the assent is not voluntary. Such a contract is not enforceable against the innocent party.

Example: If someone threatens to harm another person unless that person signs a contract, this is *physical duress*. This contract cannot be enforced against the duressed party.

The threat to commit physical harm or extortion unless someone enters into a contract constitutes duress. So does a threat to bring (or not drop) a criminal lawsuit. Such threats are duress even if the criminal lawsuit is well founded.[12] A threat to bring (or not drop) a civil lawsuit, however, does not constitute duress unless such a suit is frivolous or brought in bad faith.

---

[12]*Restatement (Second) of Contracts*, Section 177.

Economic Duress

The courts have recognized another type of duress called *economic duress*, which usually occurs when one party to a contract refuses to perform his or her contractual duties unless the other party pays an increased price, enters into a second contract with the threatening party, or the like. The duressed party must prove he or she had no alternative but to acquiesce to the other party's threat.

ETHICS SPOTLIGHT

ECONOMIC DURESS

"I have a check for you, and you just take it or leave it: this is all you get. If you don't take this, you have got to sue me."

General Contractor to Subcontractor

Economic duress is also called **business compulsion**, **business duress**, and **economic coercion**. The appropriateness of these terms becomes apparent when the facts of the following case are examined.

Ashton Development, Inc. (Ashton) hired Bob Britton, Inc. (Britton), a general contractor, to build a development for it. Britton signed a contract with a subcontractor, Rich & Whillock, Inc. (R&W), to provide grading and excavation work at the project. R&W proceeded with the excavation work and rock removal, which included blasting. After completing all the required work and receiving $109,363 in payments to date, R&W submitted a final bill to Britton for $72,286.

Britton refused to pay this amount. R&W told Britton it would go "broke" if payment was not received. One month later, Britton presented R&W with an agreement whereby Britton would pay $25,000 upon the signing of the agreement and another $25,000 one month later. When R&W complained of the financial bind it was in, Britton stated, "I have a check for you, and you just take it or leave it: this is all you get. If you don't take this, you have got to sue me." After claiming it was "blackmail," R&W accepted the $25,000 check. Britton did not pay the other $25,000 until one month later.

After receiving payment, R&W sued Britton for breach of contract. The trial and appellate courts held in favor of R&W, finding that Britton's tactics amounted to economic duress. In applying the doctrine of economic duress to the case, the court stated, "The underlying concern of the economic duress doctrine is the enforcement in the marketplace of certain minimal standards of business ethics." The court found that Britton had acted in bad faith when it refused to pay R&W's final billing and offered instead to pay a compromise amount of $50,000. At the time of its bad faith breach and settlement offer, Britton knew that R&W was a new company, overextended to creditors and subcontractors, and faced with imminent bankruptcy if not paid its final billing. Under these circumstances, the court found that the settlement agreement was unenforceable. The court ordered Britton to pay the balance due on the contract to R&W. *Rich & Whillock, Inc. v. Ashton Dev., Inc.*, 204 Cal. Rptr. 86 (Ct. App. 1984).

economic duress
Occurs when one party to a contract refuses to perform his or her contractual duties unless the other party pays an increased price, enters into a second contract with the threatening party, or undertakes a similar action.

Law & Ethics Questions

1. What is economic duress? What distinguishes it from just plain hard business tactics?
2. **Ethics** Did Britton act ethically in this case?

Web Exercises

1. **Web** Visit the website of the Court of Appeal of California at www.courtinfo.ca.gov/courts/courtsofappeal.

Working the Web Internet Exercises

1. For a practical Q & A on contract basics, see public.findlaw.com/library/contracts-law.html.
2. For an interesting case involving genuineness of assent, go to www.legalwa.org and search for *Barnes v. Treece*, 549 P.2d 1152 (Wash. Ct. App. 1976).

CHAPTER 5 SUMMARY

MISTAKE, p. 128

Unilateral Mistakes

Unilateral mistakes occur when only one party is mistaken about a material fact regarding the subject matter of a contract. The legal consequences are as follows:

1. *General rule.* The mistaken party is not permitted to rescind the contract.
2. *Exceptions.* The mistaken party can rescind the contract if:
   a. The other party knew or should have known of the mistake and took advantage of it.
   b. The mistake occurred because of a clerical or mathematical error that was not the result of gross negligence.
   c. The mistake is so serious that enforcing the contract would be unconscionable.

Mutual Mistakes

1. *Mutual mistake of fact.* If both parties are mistaken about the essence or object of a contract, either party may rescind the contract.
2. *Mutual mistake of value.* If both parties know the object of a contract but are mistaken as to its value, neither party may rescind the contract.

FRAUD, p. 132

Elements of Fraud

Fraudulent misrepresentation. Fraudulent misrepresentation occurs when a person intentionally makes an assertion that is not in accord with the facts. Also called *fraud.*

1. *Elements of fraud:*
   a. The wrongdoer made a false representation of material fact.
   b. The wrongdoer intended to deceive the innocent party.
   c. The innocent party justifiably relied on the misrepresentation.
   d. The innocent party was injured.
2. *Legal consequence if fraudulent misrepresentation is found.* The innocent party may:
   a. Rescind the contract and obtain restitution, or
   b. Enforce the contract and sue for damages

Types of Fraud

Common types of fraud:

1. *Fraud in the inception.* With this type of fraud, an innocent person is deceived as to the nature of his or her act. Also called *fraud in the factum.*

2. *Fraud in the inducement.* With this type of fraud, the wrongdoer fraudulently induces another party to enter into a contract.
3. *Fraud by concealment.* With this type of fraud, the wrongdoer takes specific action to conceal a material fact from the other party.
4. *Silence as misrepresentation.* With this type of fraud, the wrongdoer remains silent when he or she is under a legal obligation to disclose a material fact.
5. *Misrepresentation of law.* A professional who should know what the law is may intentionally misrepresent the law to a less sophisticated party.

Innocent Misrepresentation

When a person unintentionally makes an assertion that is not in accord with the facts, the innocent party may rescind the contract but cannot recover damages. Innocent misrepresentation is not fraud.

UNDUE INFLUENCE, p. 140

Undue Influence

Undue influence occurs when one person takes advantage of another person's mental, emotional, or physical weakness and unduly persuades that person to enter into a contract. A contract entered into under undue influence cannot be enforced.

1. *Elements of undue influence:*
   a. A fiduciary or confidential relationship existed between the dominant and servient parties.
   b. The dominant party unduly used his or her influence to persuade the servient party to enter into a contract.
2. *Presumption.* If there is a confidential relationship between persons, any contract by the servient party that benefits the dominant party is presumed to have been entered into under undue influence. This position is a *rebuttable presumption.*

DURESS, p. 142

Duress

Duress occurs when one party threatens to do some wrongful act unless the other party enters into a contract. A contract entered into under duress cannot be enforced. Types of duress:

1. Physical duress
2. Extortion

TERMS AND CONCEPTS

Duress   142
Economic duress (business compulsion, business duress)   143
Fraud by concealment   134
Fraud in the inception   132
Fraud in the inducement   132
Fraudulent misrepresentation (fraud)   132
Genuine assent   127
Genuineness of assent   127
Innocent misrepresentation   138

Misrepresentation of law   137

Mistake   128

Mutual mistake   130

Pro bono   134

Rescission   128

Scienter   133

Undue influence   140

Unilateral mistake   128

CASE SCENARIO REVISITED

Remember the case at the beginning of this chapter? If Mr. Moore's other children brought an action to cancel the deed transferring the farm to Gary, what would be the basis for that action? Review the case of *Schaneman v. Schaneman*, 291 N.W.2d 412 (Neb. 1980) to help you with your answer.

CRITICAL LEGAL THINKING CASES

Critical Legal Thinking Case 5.1 *Unilateral Mistake*   Mrs. Chaney left a house in Annapolis, Maryland. The representative of her estate listed the property for sale with a real estate broker, stating the property was approximately 15,650 square feet. Drs. Steele and Faust made an offer of $300,000 for the property, which was accepted by the estate. A contract for the sale of the property was signed by all the parties. When a subsequent survey (done before the deed was transferred) showed the property had an area of 22,047 square feet, the estate requested that the buyers pay more money for the property. When the estate refused to transfer the property to the buyers, they sued for specific performance. Can the estate rescind the contract? *Steele v. Goettee*, 542 A.2d 847 (Md. 1988).

Critical Legal Thinking Case 5.2 *Unilateral Mistake*   The County of Contra Costa, California, held a tax sale in which it offered for sale a vacant piece of property located in the city of El Cerrito. Richard J. Schultz, a carpenter, saw the notice of the pending tax sale and was interested in purchasing the lot to build a house. Prior to attending the tax sale, Schultz visited and measured the parcel, examined the neighborhood and found the houses there to be "very nice," and had a title search done that turned up no liens or judgments against the property. Schultz did not, however, check with the city zoning department regarding the zoning of the property.

Schultz attended the tax sale and, after spirited bidding, won with a bid of $9,100 and received a deed to the property. Within one week of the purchase, Schultz discovered that the city's zoning laws prevented building a residence on the lot. In essence, the lot was worthless. Schultz sued to rescind the contract. Can the contract be rescinded? *Schultz v. County of Contra Costa, Cal.*, 203 Cal. Rptr. 760 (Ct. App. 1984).

Critical Legal Thinking Case 5.3 *Mutual Mistake*   Ron Boskett, a part-time coin dealer, purchased a dime purportedly minted in 1916 at the Denver Mint; he paid nearly $450. The fact that the "D" on the coin signified Denver mintage made the coin rare and valuable. Boskett sold the coin to Beachcomber Coins, Inc.

(Beachcomber), a retail coin dealer, for $500. A principal of Beachcomber examined the coin for 15 to 45 minutes prior to its purchase. Soon thereafter, Beachcomber received an offer of $700 for the coin, subject to certification of its genuineness by the American Numismatic Society. When this organization labeled the coin counterfeit, Beachcomber sued Boskett to rescind the purchase of the coin. Can Beachcomber rescind the contract? *Beachcomber Coins, Inc. v. Boskett*, 400 A.2d 78 (N.J. Sup. Ct. App. Div. 1979).

Critical Legal Thinking Case 5.4 *Fraud* Robert McClure owned a vehicle salvage and rebuilding business. He listed the business for sale and had a brochure printed that described the business and stated the business grossed $581,117 and netted $142,727 the prior year. Fred H. Campbell saw the brochure and inquired about buying the business. Campbell hired a CPA to review McClure's business records and tax returns, but the CPA could not reconcile them with the income claimed for the business in the brochure. When Campbell asked McClure about the discrepancy, McClure stated that the business records did—and tax returns did not—accurately reflect the cash flow or profits of the business because it was such a high-cash operation with much of the cash not being reported to the Internal Revenue Service on tax returns. McClure signed a warranty that stated the true income of the business was as represented in the brochure.

Campbell bought the business based on these representations. However, the business, although operated in substantially the same manner as when owned by McClure, failed to yield a net income similar to that warranted by McClure. Evidence showed that McClure's representations were substantially overstated. Campbell sued McClure for damages for fraud. Who wins? *Campbell v. McClure*, 227 Cal. Rptr. 450 (Ct. App. 1986).

Critical Legal Thinking Case 5.5 *Fraud* James L. "Skip" Deupree, a developer, was building a development of townhouses called Point South in Destin, Florida. All the townhouses in the development were to have individual boat slips. Sam and Louise Butner, husband and wife, bought one of the townhouses. The sales contract between Deupree and the Butners provided that a boat slip would be built and was included in the price of the townhouse. The contract stated that permission from the Florida Department of Natural Resources (DNR) had to be obtained to build the boat slips. It is undisputed that a boat slip adds substantially to the value of a property and the Butners relied on the fact that the townhouse would have a boat slip.

Prior to the sale of the townhouse to the Butners, the DNR had informed Deupree it objected to the plan to build the boat slips and that permission to build them would probably not be forthcoming. Deupree did not tell the Butners this information but instead stated there would be "no problem" in getting permission from the state to build the boat slips. The Butners purchased the townhouse. When the DNR would not approve the building of the boat slips for the Butners' townhouse, they sued for damages for fraud. Who wins? *Deupree v. Butner*, 522 So. 2d 242 (Ala. 1988).

Critical Legal Thinking Case 5.6 *Innocent Misrepresentation* W. F. Yost, who owned the Red Barn Barbecue Restaurant (Red Barn), listed it for sale. Richard and Evelyn Ramano of Rieve Enterprises, Inc. (Rieve), were interested in buying the restaurant. After visiting and conducting a visual inspection of the premises, Rieve entered into a contract to purchase the assets and equipment of Red Barn, as well as the five-year lease of, and option to buy, the land and the building. Prior to the sale, the restaurant had been cited for certain health violations that Yost had corrected. In the contract of sale, Yost warranted that "the premises will pass all inspections" to conduct the business.

Rieve took possession immediately after the sale and operated the restaurant. After two weeks, when the Board of Health conducted a routine inspection, it cited 52 health code violations and thereupon closed the restaurant. Rieve sued to rescind the purchase agreement. Evidence established that Yost's misrepresentations were innocently made. Can Rieve rescind the contract? *Yost v. Rieve Enter., Inc.*, 461 So. 2d 178 (Fla. Dist. Ct. App. 1984).

Critical Legal Thinking Case 5.7 Duress   Judith and Donald Eckstein were married and had two daughters. Years later, Judith left the marital abode in the parties' jointly owned Volkswagen van with only the clothes on her back. She did not take the children, who were 6 and 8 years old at the time. She had no funds, and the husband promptly closed the couple's bank account. The wife was unemployed. Shortly after she left, the husband discovered her whereabouts and the location of the van and seized and secreted the van. The husband refused the wife's request to visit or communicate with her children and refused to give her clothing. He told her she could see the children and take her clothes only if she signed a separation agreement prepared by his lawyer. The wife contacted Legal Aid but was advised she did not qualify for assistance.

The wife was directed to go to her husband's lawyer's office. A copy of a separation agreement was given to her to read. The separation agreement provided that the wife (1) give custody of the children to her husband, (2) deed her interest in their jointly owned house to the husband, (3) assign her interest in a jointly owned new Chevrolet van to her husband, and (4) waive alimony, support, maintenance, court costs, attorneys' fees, and any right to inheritance in her husband's estate. By the agreement, she was to receive $1,100 cash, her clothes, the Volkswagen van, and any furniture she desired. The wife testified that her husband told her over an interoffice phone in the lawyer's office that if she did not sign the separation agreement, he would get her for desertion, she would never see her children again, and she would get nothing—neither her clothes nor the van—unless she signed the agreement. The wife signed the separation agreement. Immediately thereafter, her clothes were surrendered to her, and she was given $1,100 cash and the keys to the Volkswagen van. The husband filed for divorce. The wife filed an answer seeking to rescind the separation agreement. Can she rescind the separation agreement? *Eckstein v. Eckstein*, 379 A.2d 757 (Md. Ct. Spec. App. 1978).

ETHICS CASES

Ethics Case 5.1   The First Baptist Church of Moultrie, Georgia, invited bids for the construction of a music, education, and recreation building. The bids were to be accompanied by a bid bond of 5 percent of the bid amount. Barber Contracting Company (Barber Contracting) submitted a bid in the amount of $1,860,000. A bid bond in the amount of 5 percent of the bid—$93,000—was issued by The American Insurance Company. The bids were opened by the church, and Barber Contracting's was the lowest bid.

On the next day, Albert W. Barber, the president of Barber Contracting, informed the church that his company's bid was in error and should have been $143,120 higher. The error was caused in totaling the material costs on Barber Contracting's estimate worksheets. The church had not been provided these worksheets. Barber Contracting sent a letter to the church, stating it was withdrawing its bid. The next day, the church sent a construction contract to Barber Contracting, containing the original bid amount. When Barber Contracting refused to sign the contract and refused to do the work for the original contract price, the church signed a contract with the second-lowest bidder, H & H Construction and Supply Company, Inc., to complete the work for $1,919,272. The church sued Barber Contracting and the American Insurance Company, seeking to recover the amount of the bid bond. Who wins? Did Barber act ethically in trying to get out of the contract? Did the church act ethically in trying to enforce Barber's bid? *First Baptist Church of Moultrie v. Barber Contracting Co.*, 377 S.E.2d 717 (Ga. Ct. App. 1989).

Ethics Case 5.2   Lockheed Missiles & Space Company, Inc. (Lockheed) sent out a request to potential subcontractors, seeking bids for the manufacture of 124 ballast cans for the Trident II nuclear submarines it was building for the U.S. Navy. In February 1989, Lockheed received eight bids, including one from Sulzer Bingham Pumps, Inc. (Sulzer). Sulzer was the lowest bidder, at $6,544,055. The next lowest bid was $10,176,670, and the bids ranged up to $17,766,327. Lockheed itself estimated the job would cost at least $8.5 million. Lockheed's employees were shocked by Sulzer's bid and thought it was surprisingly low.

Lockheed then inspected Sulzer's Portland facility to evaluate Sulzer's technical capabilities. The inspection revealed that Sulzer would have to make many modifications to its existing facility in order to complete the contract.

Lockheed did not reveal its findings to Sulzer. In addition, it never notified Sulzer that its bid was significantly lower than the next lowest bid and lower than Lockheed's own estimate of the cost of the job as well. Finally, Sulzer was never told that Lockheed suspected the contract could not be completed at the bid price.

Lockheed accepted Sulzer's bid, and Sulzer started work. Nine months later, Sulzer revised its estimate of the cost of the job and asked Lockheed for an additional $2,110,000 in compensation. When Lockheed rejected this request, Sulzer sued Lockheed, asking the court to either increase the price of the contract to $8,645,000 or, alternatively, to rescind its bid. Did Lockheed act ethically in this case by not notifying Sulzer of the suspected mistake? Did Sulzer act ethically by trying to get out of the contract because of its own economic misjudgments? Legally, who wins? *Sulzer Bingham Pumps, Inc. v. Lockheed Missiles & Space Co.*, 947 F.2d 1362 (9th Cir. 1991).

BRIEFING THE CASE WRITING ASSIGNMENT

Read Case A.5 in the Case Appendix (*Continental Airlines, Inc. v. McDonnell Douglas Corp.*). This case is excerpted from the appellate court opinion. Review and brief the case. After briefing the case, you should be able to answer the following questions:

1. When did the action commence? When was the decision of the appellate court rendered?
2. Were the statements made by McDonnell Douglas opinions (i.e., puffing) or statements of fact?
3. Were the statements made by McDonnell Douglas material? What evidence supports your conclusion?
4. Did Continental rely on the statements of McDonnell Douglas? What evidence supports your conclusion?
5. Do false representations made recklessly and without regard to the truth constitute fraud?
6. What damages were awarded to Continental?

After working with the Practice Tips in Chapters 1 through 4, and then completing the Portfolio Exercise in Chapter 4, you have mastered the basic structure of a simple contract. However, sometimes contracts come in the form of a letter. Here is a basic structure for a letter contract:

Date: _____, 20_____

_____

_____

_____

Dear _____:

This letter will confirm our agreement as follows:

1. _____

_____

2. _____

_____

Sincerely yours,

_____

_____

_____

Being able to draft a simple letter contract for your attorney's review will be especially important when you are employed as a paralegal. Using the same facts from the Paralegal Portfolio Exercise in Chapter 4, create a letter contract for Sarah and Kelly.

A verbal contract isn't worth the paper it's written on.

—*Samuel Goldwyn*

Writing, Formality, and E-Commerce Signature Law

CHAPTER 6

CASE SCENARIO

The law firm where you work as a paralegal represents Bell Enterprises, a company in the business of selling gold and silver. A long-time customer of the company, Gary McGraw, placed an order for 300 ounces of silver for $10,000. The company immediately ordered and paid for the silver. Once the silver arrived at Bell Enterprises, the company contacted McGraw about payment. He told the company to continue to hold it in its vault, and he would be in to pick it up soon. Meanwhile, the price of silver fell substantially. When McGraw refused to pick up and pay for the silver, the company sold it for $4,000, thereby incurring a loss of $6,000.

■ CHAPTER INTRODUCTION

Certain types of contracts must be in writing. In addition, other issues regarding the form of a contract may arise, such as the form of signature that is required on a written contract, whether a contract can be created by the integration of several documents, whether any previous oral or written agreements between the parties can be given effect, and how contract language should be interpreted. Issues regarding the writing and formality of contracts are discussed in this chapter.

CHAPTER OBJECTIVES

After studying this chapter, you should be able to:

1. List the contracts that must be in writing under the *Statute of Frauds*.

2. Explain the effect of *noncompliance* with the Statute of Frauds.

3. Describe how the Statute of Frauds is applicable to the *sale of goods*.

4. Apply the *Parol Evidence Rule*.

■ STATUTE OF FRAUDS

In 1677, the English Parliament enacted a statute called "An Act for the Prevention of Frauds and Perjuries." This act required that certain types of contracts had to be in writing and signed by the party against whom enforcement was sought. Today, every U.S. state has enacted a **Statute of Frauds** that requires certain types of contracts to be in *writing*. This statute is intended to ensure that the terms of important contracts are not forgotten, misunderstood, or fabricated.

statute of frauds
State statute that requires certain types of contracts to be in writing.

Writing Requirement

Although the statutes vary slightly from state to state, most states require the following types of contracts to be in writing.[1]

- Contracts involving interests in land
- Contracts that by their own terms cannot possibly be performed within one year
- Collateral contracts in which a person promises to answer for the debt or duty of another
- Promises made in consideration of marriage
- Contracts for the sale of goods for more than $500
- Real estate agents' contracts
- Agents' contracts where the underlying contract must be in writing
- Promises to write a will
- Contracts to pay debts barred by the statute of limitations or discharged in bankruptcy
- Contracts to pay compensation for services rendered in negotiating the purchase of a business
- Finder's fee contracts

Contracts That Must Be in Writing

Generally, an *executory contract* that is not in writing even though the Statute of Frauds requires it to be is unenforceable by either party. The Statute of Frauds is usually raised by one party as a defense to the enforcement of the contract by the other party.

If an oral contract that should have been in writing under the Statute of Frauds is already executed, neither party can seek to rescind the contract on the ground of noncompliance with the Statute of Frauds. That is, the contract may be voluntarily performed by the parties.

Generally, contracts listed in the Statute of Frauds must be in writing to be enforceable. There are several equity exceptions to this rule. The contracts that must be in writing pursuant to the Statute of Frauds and the exceptions to this rule are discussed in the following paragraphs.

Contracts Involving Interests in Land

Under the Statute of Frauds, any contract that transfers an ownership interest in **real property** must be in writing to be enforceable. Real property includes the land itself, buildings, trees, soil, minerals, timber, plants, crops, fixtures, and things permanently affixed to the land or buildings. Certain items of personal property that are permanently affixed to the real property are fixtures that become part of the real property.

real property
The land itself as well as buildings, trees, soil, minerals, timber, plants, crops, and other things permanently affixed to the land.

---

[1]*Restatement (Second) of Contracts*, Section 110.

Example: Built-in cabinets in a house are *fixtures* that become part of the real property.

Other contracts that transfer an ownership interest in land must be in writing under the Statute of Frauds. These interests include the following:

- *Mortgages*—Borrowers often give a lender an interest in real property as security for the repayment of a loan. This action must be done through the use of a written **mortgage** or **deed of trust.**

  Example: Suppose ABC Corporation purchases a factory and borrows part of the purchase price from City Bank. City Bank requires that the factory be used as collateral for the loan and takes a mortgage on the factory. Here, the mortgage must be in writing to be enforceable.

- *Leases*—A **lease** is the transfer of the right to use real property for a specified period of time. Most Statutes of Frauds require leases for a term over one year to be in writing.
- *Life estates*—On some occasions, a person is given a **life estate** in real property. In other words, the person has an interest in the land for the person's lifetime, and the interest will be transferred to another party on that person's death. A life estate is an ownership interest that must be in writing under the Statute of Frauds.
- *Easements*—An **easement** is a given or required right to use another person's land without owning or leasing it. Easements may be either express or implied. Express easements must be in writing to be enforceable; implied easements need not be written.

mortgage
An interest in real property given to a lender as security for the repayment of a loan.

deed of trust
An instrument that gives the creditor a security interest in the debtor's property that is pledged as collateral.

lease
A contract for the exclusive possession of lands or tenements for a determinate period; a contract by which the lessor grants the lessee the exclusive right to possess and use personal property of the lessor for a specified period.

life estate
An interest in the land for a person's lifetime; upon that person's death, the interest will be transferred to another party.

easement
A right to use someone else's land without owning or leasing it. A given or required right to make limited use of someone else's land without owning or leasing it.

ETHICS SPOTLIGHT

STATUTE OF FRAUDS

Bronco Wine Company (Bronco) crushed grapes and sold them for use in bulk wines. It purchased the grapes it needed from various grape growers. In 1981, Bronco entered into an oral contract with Allied Grape Growers (Allied), a cooperative corporation of many grape growers, to purchase 850 tons of Carnelian grapes for delivery in 1982. Allied had originally contracted to sell these grapes to United Vintners but received special permission to sell the grapes to Bronco instead.

The 1982 grape crop was the largest to date in California history, and there was a glut of foreign wines on the market. Thus, the price of grapes and wines decreased substantially. Bronco accepted and paid for one shipment of Carnelian grapes from Allied but refused to accept the rest. By the time Bronco started to reject the highly perishable goods, it was too late for Allied to resell the grapes to United Vintners or others.

Allied sued for breach of contract, and Bronco alleged the Statute of Frauds as its defense. In essence, Bronco argued that it did not have to perform because the contract was not in writing.

The appellate court applied the doctrine of promissory estoppel and prohibited Bronco from raising the Statute of Frauds against enforcement of its oral promise to buy the grapes from Allied. The court stated, "In California, the doctrine of estoppel is proven where one party suffers an unconscionable injury if the Statute of Frauds is asserted to prevent enforcement of oral contracts. There is substantial evidence that Allied's loss was unconscionable given these facts. The Statute of Frauds should not be used in this instance to defeat the oral agreement reached by the parties in this case." The appellate court affirmed the trial court's verdict awarding damages to Allied. *Allied Grape Growers v. Bronco Wine Company*, 203 Cal. App.3d 432 (1988).

1. Is it ever ethical to raise the Statute of Frauds against the enforcement of an oral contract?
2. Should courts apply the equitable doctrine of estoppel to save contracting parties from the Statute of Frauds?

Part Performance Exception

If an oral contract for the sale of land or transfer of another interest in real property has been partially performed, it may not be possible to return the parties to their status quo. To solve this problem, the courts have developed the equitable doctrine of **part performance**. This doctrine allows the court to order such an oral contract to be specifically performed if performance is necessary to avoid injustice. For this performance exception to apply, most courts require that the purchaser either pay part of the purchase price and take possession of the property or make valuable improvements on the land.

Case 6.1 involves the doctrine of part performance.

part performance
An equitable doctrine that allows the court to order an oral contract for the sale of land or transfer of another interest in real property to be specifically performed if it has been partially performed and performance is necessary to avoid injustice.

CASE 6.1 PART PERFORMANCE

Sutton v. Warner, 15 Cal. Rptr. 2d 632 (Ct. App. 1993).

"The doctrine of part performance by the purchaser is a well-recognized exception to the Statute of Frauds as applied to contracts for the sale of real property."

Judge Kline, P. J., *Court of Appeal of California*

Facts

Arlene and Donald Warner inherited a third interest in a home at 101 Molimo Street in San Francisco. The Warners bought out the other heirs and obtained a $170,000 loan on the property. Donald Warner and Kenneth Sutton were friends. Donald Warner proposed that Sutton and his wife purchase the residence. His proposal included a $15,000 down payment toward the purchase price of $185,000. The Suttons were to pay all the mortgage payments and real estate taxes on the property for five years, and at any time during the five-year period they could purchase the house. All this was agreed to orally. The Suttons paid the down payment and cash payments equal to the monthly mortgage to the Warners. The Suttons paid the annual property taxes on the house. The Suttons also made improvements to the property. Four and a half years later, the Warners reneged on the sales/option agreement. At that time, the house had risen in value to between $250,000 and $320,000. The Suttons sued for specific performance of the sales agreement. The Warners defended, alleging that the oral promise to sell real estate had to be in writing under the Statute of Frauds and was therefore unenforceable. The trial court applied the equitable doctrine of part performance and ordered specific performance. The Warners appealed.

Issue

Does the equitable doctrine of part performance make this oral contract for the sale of real property enforceable even though the statute of frauds may apply?

Language of the Court

The doctrine of part performance by the purchaser is a well-recognized exception to the Statute of Frauds as applied to contracts for the sale of real property. The question here, then, is whether the continued possession of the property by the Suttons and their other actions are sufficiently related to the option contract to constitute part performance. The trial court responded in the affirmative. After entering the oral agreement, the Suttons

*made a $15,000 down payment and increased their monthly payments to the Warners
from the original monthly rental payment to payments in the precise amount of the vari-
able mortgage payments due under the $170,000 loan. They reimbursed the Warners for
property taxes in the sum of $800 every six months.*

*Although it was disputed whether the dollar value of improvements made by the Sut-
tons in reliance upon the oral agreement constituted "substantial" improvements, it is
undisputed that many of the improvements—such as painting the interior of the house and
the installation of a toilet and entry lamp—were done by the Suttons' own labor. The trial
court found that these actions were unequivocally related to the purchase agreement.*

*The actions taken by the Suttons in reliance upon the oral agreement, when consid-
ered together with the Warners' admission that there was an oral agreement of some
duration, satisfy both elements of the part performance doctrine.*

Decision

The court of appeal held that the doctrine of part performance applied and that
the Statute of Frauds did not prevent the enforcement of the oral contract to sell
real estate. The court of appeal affirmed the judgment of the trial court that
ordered specific performance to the Suttons.

Law & Ethics Questions

1. What purposes are served by the Statute of Frauds? Explain.

2. **Ethics** Did the Warners act ethically in this case? Did the Statute of Frauds
   give them a justifiable reason not to go through with the deal?

3. Should important business contracts be put in writing? Why or why not?

Web Exercises

1. **Web** Visit the website of the Court of Appeal of California at www
   .courtinfo.ca.gov/courts/courtsofappeal.

2. **Web** Use www.google.com and find an article about the Statute of Frauds.

3. *Contemporary Issue* The Internet and e-mail are increasingly affecting the
   writing feature of the Statute of Frauds. Does an e-mail satisfy the writing
   and signature requirements? For more on this important contemporary issue,
   find and review the case *Shattuck v. Klotzbach*, 14 Mass. L. Rep. 360 (Super.
   Ct. 2001).

MARKETPLACE

Lease Administration Paralegal Job Announcement

Central Ohio corporation is in need of a lease administrator with paralegal certification. Must have experience in retail lease administration, including managing
direct reports, excellent understanding of retail lease language, administering
contracts, ability to meet tight deadlines and manage multiple assignments.

Excellent compensation package. Interested candidates should submit resume to:

One-Year Rule

one-year rule
An executory contract that cannot be performed by its own terms within one year of its formation must be in writing.

According to the Statute of Frauds, an executory contract that cannot be performed by its own terms within one year of its formation must be in writing.[2] This **one-year rule** is intended to prevent disputes about contract terms that may otherwise occur toward the end of a long-term contract. If the performance of the contract is possible within the one-year period, the contract may be oral. The extension of an oral contract might cause the contract to violate the Statute of Frauds.

Example: Suppose the owner of a Burger King franchise hires Eugene Daly as a manager for 6 months. This contract may be oral. Assume that after 3 months, the owner and manager agree to extend the contract for an additional 11 months. At the time of the extension, the contract would be for 14 months (the 3 left on the contract plus 11 added by the extension). The modification would have to be in writing because it exceeds the one-year rule.

Guaranty Contract

guaranty contract
The contract between the guarantor and the original creditor.

original (primary) contract
In a guaranty situation, this is the first contract between the debtor and the creditor.

guarantor
The person who agrees to pay the debt if the primary debtor does not. The third person who agrees to be liable in a guaranty arrangement.

A **guaranty contract** occurs when one person agrees to answer for the debts or duties of another person. Guaranty contracts are required to be in writing under the Statute of Frauds.[3]

In a guaranty situation, there are at least three parties and two contracts (see Exhibit 6.1). The *first contract*, which is known as the **original,** or **primary, contract,** is between the debtor and the creditor. It does not have to be in writing (unless another provision of the Statute of Frauds requires it to be). The *second contract,* called the guaranty contract, is between the person who agrees to pay the debt if the primary debtor does not (i.e., the **guarantor**) and the original creditor. The guarantor's liability is secondary because it does not arise unless the party primarily liable fails to perform.

Example: Wei Wang, a recent college graduate, offers to purchase a new automobile on credit from a Mercedes-Benz automobile dealership. Because Wei, a student, does not have a credit history, the dealer will agree to sell the car to her only if there is a guarantor. Wei's father signs the guaranty contract. He becomes responsible for any payments his daughter fails to make.

main purpose or leading object exception
If the main purpose of a transaction and an oral collateral contract is to provide pecuniary benefit to the guarantor, the collateral contract does not have to be in writing to be enforced.

The "Main Purpose" Exception If the main purpose of a transaction and an oral collateral contract is to provide pecuniary (i.e., financial) benefit to the guarantor, the collateral contract is treated like an original contract and does not have to be in writing to be enforced.[4] This exception is called the **main purpose,** or **leading object, exception** to the Statute of Frauds. This exception is intended to ensure that the primary benefactor of the original contract (i.e., the guarantor) is answerable for the debt or duty.

Example: Suppose Ethel Brand is president and sole shareholder of Brand Computer Corporation, Inc. Assume that (1) the corporation borrows $100,000 from City Bank for working capital, and (2) Ethel orally guarantees to repay the loan if the corporation fails to pay it. City Bank can enforce the oral guaranty contract against Ethel if the corporation does not meet its obligation because the main purpose of the loan was to benefit her as the sole shareholder of the corporation.

[2]*Restatement (Second) of Contracts*, Section 130.
[3]*Restatement (Second) of Contracts*, Section 112.
[4]*Restatement (Second) of Contracts*, Section 116.

Exhibit 6.1 Guaranty Contract

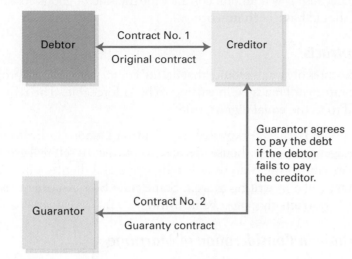

THE ETHICAL PARALEGAL

Communication with Clients

ABA Model Rule 1.4 requires that the attorney communicate with clients so as to keep them reasonably informed about the case and thus able to make informed decisions regarding the representation.[5] Although a nonattorney is prohibited from giving legal advice (see this feature in Chapter 7 for a discussion of the unauthorized practice of law), the ethical paralegal can help keep clients advised of the status of their case.

Many times the paralegal is the client's main contact with the law office. The paralegal can assist in returning clients' phone calls promptly and in sending the client regular written reports on how the case is proceeding. Again, although the paralegal should be careful never to give legal advice, the ethical paralegal can still serve as a conduit between the attorney and the client.

Contracts for the Sale of Goods

Section 201 of the Uniform Commercial Code (UCC) is the basic Statute of Frauds provision for sales contracts. It requires that contracts for the sale of goods costing *$500 or more* be in writing to be enforceable.[6] If the contract price of an original sales contract is below $500, it does not have to be in writing under the **UCC Statute of Frauds**, but if a modification of the contract increases the sales price to $500 or more, the **modification** has to be in writing to be enforceable.[7]

Example: Echo enters into an oral contract to sell James her used car for $10,000, with the delivery date to be May 1. When May 1 comes and James tenders $10,000

Section 201 of the Uniform Commercial Code (UCC)
A rule sometimes referred to as "the Statute of Frauds"; requiring that contracts for the sale of goods costing $500 or more be in writing.

UCC Statute of Frauds
A rule that requires all contracts for the sale of goods costing $500 or more and lease contracts involving payments of $1,000 or more to be in writing.

modification
An alteration that does not change the general purpose and effect of that which is modified (modification of the agreement).

---

[5]Copies of the ABA Model Rules of Professional Conduct are available from Service Center, American Bar Association, 321 North Clark Street, Chicago, IL 60610, 1-800-285-2221. The Model Rules can also be viewed online at http://www.abanet.org/cpr/mrpc/mrpc_toc.html.

[6]UCC Section 2-201(1).

[7]UCC Section 2-209(3).

to Echo, Echo refuses to sell her car to James. The contract will not be enforced against Echo because it was an oral contract for the sale of goods costing $500 or more, and it should have been in writing.

Agents' Contracts

equal dignity rule
A rule that says that agents' contracts to sell property covered by the Statute of Frauds must be in writing to be enforceable.

Many state Statutes of Frauds require that *agents' contracts* to sell real property covered by the Statute of Frauds be in writing to be enforceable. The requirement is often referred to as the **equal dignity rule**.

Example: Suppose Barney Berkowitz hires Cynthia Lamont, a licensed Century 21 real estate agent, to sell his house. Because a contract to sell real estate must be in writing, pursuant to the Statute of Frauds, the equal dignity rule requires the agents' contract to be in writing as well. Some state Statutes of Frauds expressly list the agents' contracts that must be in writing.

Promises Made in Consideration of Marriage

prenuptial agreement
A contract entered into by parties prior to their marriage that defines their ownership rights in each other's property; it must be in writing.

Under the Statute of Frauds, a unilateral promise to pay money or property in consideration for a promise to marry must be in writing. For example, a **prenuptial agreement**, which is a contract entered into by parties prior to marriage that defines their ownership rights in each other's property, must be in writing.

ETHICS SPOTLIGHT

AN ORAL CONTRACT IS NOT WORTH THE PAPER IT'S WRITTEN ON

The Statute of Frauds, which requires certain contracts to be in writing before they are enforceable, is designed to prevent fraud. Entrepreneurs and other businesspersons should know the requirements of the state's Statute of Frauds: otherwise, they may find themselves with an unenforceable oral contract. Consider the following case.

Whitman Heffernan Rhein & Co., Inc. (Whitman) is a company that provides financial advice to firms planning mergers and acquisitions. The Griffin Company (Griffin) was negotiating to purchase Resorts International, Inc. from Donald Trump. Whitman alleged that it entered into an oral contract to provide the Griffin Company with financial and investment advice in connection with the negotiation of the purchase of Resorts International. Once Griffin completed the acquisition of Resorts International from Trump, Whitman requested payment for its services from Griffin. When Griffin did not pay, Whitman sued Griffin to recover payment.

Griffin asserted the New York Statute of Frauds in defense, arguing that Whitman's alleged contract to provide services in negotiating the purchase of a business had to be in writing to be enforceable, and because Whitman's complaint alleged that it was an oral contract, it was not enforceable. The New York court agreed with Griffin and held that the alleged contract was oral and therefore barred by the Statute of Frauds. The court stated,

New York General Obligation Law § 5-701(a)(10) provides that an agreement is void, unless evidenced by a writing signed by the party to be charged, if the agreement is a contract to pay compensation for services rendered in negotiating the purchase of a business. The term "negotiating" includes assisting in the consummation of the transaction.

The moral of story: Get it in writing! *Whitman Heffernan Rhein & Co. v. Griffin Co.,* 557 N.Y.S.2d 342 (App. Div. 1990).

Law & Ethics Questions

1. What is the purpose of the Statute of Frauds? Explain.
2. Was the legal claim clear in this case?
3. **Ethics** Does applying the Statute of Frauds ever cause an unfair result? Explain.

Web Exercises

1. **Web** Visit the website of the Supreme Court of New York, Appellate Division, First Department, at www.courts.state.ny.us/courts/ad1.
2. **Web** Use www.google.com and find an article that discusses your state's Statute of Frauds.

Promissory Estoppel

The doctrine of **promissory estoppel**, or **equitable estoppel**, is another equitable exception to the strict application of the Statute of Frauds. The version of promissory estoppel in the *Restatement (Second) of Contracts* provides that if parties enter into an oral contract that should be in writing under the Statute of Frauds, the oral promise is enforceable against the promisor if three conditions are met: (1) The promise induces action or forbearance of action by another, (2) the reliance on the oral promise was foreseeable, and (3) injustice can be avoided only by enforcing the oral promise.[8] Where this doctrine applies, the promisor is *estopped* ("prevented") from raising the Statute of Frauds as a defense to the enforcement of the oral contract.

promissory estoppel (equitable estoppel)

An equitable doctrine that prevents the withdrawal of a promise by a promisor if it will adversely affect a promisee who has adjusted his or her position in justifiable reliance on the promise. An equitable doctrine that permits enforcement of oral contracts that should have been in writing. It is applied to avoid injustice.

PARALEGAL PERSPECTIVE

Kim A. Spitzmiller is a graduate of Caldwell College and has been a paralegal for over 25 years in the field of intellectual property. In 1997, she formed her own consulting firm in Bridgewater, New Jersey, specializing in trademark. She supports a multitude of clients in the pharmaceutical, medical device, chemical, personal care, and food industries.

Working in the field of trademark law requires a number of skills and points of reference. Oftentimes conflicts arise between parties that are seeking to register similar trademarks. One type of resolution to this type of conflict is having the parties enter into a contract called a Consent or Co-Existence Agreement.

Preparing or reviewing this type of contract involves understanding and evaluating not only the written words but those terms that are unwritten or implied. It is important to interpret what obligations are being conveyed within the contract and how that may affect and/or restrict future marketing of products covered under the trademarks of both parties. Although it is difficult to predict the future, I work closely with the client's marketing department to ensure that I have a clear understanding of the possibilities of product and industry expansion, as well as a feel for the competition in the marketplace.

Another type of contract frequently used involves licensing. Although the same attention to the stated versus unstated terms is important, it is also imperative to ensure that the licensor exercises quality control over a licensee's goods and services. If this is not done, in some countries, the trademark may become vulnerable to attack by the licensee or a third party. In addition, the drafting of terms covering length of time, royalties, exclusivity and proper trademark usage are specific clauses that I get involved with drafting.

ETHICS SPOTLIGHT

PROMISSORY ESTOPPEL

The grape growers case in the Ethics Spotlight on page 155 was used to illustrate raising a Statute of Frauds argument. As the discussion that follows show, issues in that same case also illustrate the doctrine of Promissory Estoppel.

Bronco Wine Company (Bronco) crushed grapes and sold them for use in bulk wines. It purchased the grapes it needed from various grape growers. Bronco entered into an oral

---

[8]*Restatement (Second) of Contracts*, Section 139.

contract with Allied Grape Growers (Allied), a cooperative corporation of many grape growers, to purchase 850 tons of Carnelian grapes from Allied for delivery the next year.

The following year's grape crop was very large, and there was a glut of foreign wines on the market. Thus, the price of grapes and wines decreased substantially. Bronco accepted and paid for one shipment of Carnelian grapes from Allied but refused to accept the rest. By the time Bronco rejected the highly perishable grapes, it was too late for Allied to resell the grapes to another buyer.

Allied sued Bronco to recover damages for breach of contract. Bronco defended, arguing that the Statute of Frauds applied to the Bronco–Allied contract and because the contract was oral Bronco did not have to perform the contract. Allied argued that the equity doctrine of promissory estoppel applied and excused the writing requirement in this case. The trial court held that the parties' oral contract did not violate the Statute of Frauds because Allied detrimentally relied on Bronco's promise to purchase the grapes. The jury awarded $3.4 million to Allied. Bronco appealed.

The court of appeal applied the doctrine of promissory estoppel and prohibited Bronco from raising the Statute of Frauds against enforcement of its oral promise to buy the grapes from Allied. The court stated, "In California, the doctrine of estoppel is proven where one party suffers an unconscionable injury if the Statute of Frauds is asserted to prevent enforcement of oral contracts. There is substantial evidence that Allied's loss was unconscionable given these facts. The Statute of Frauds should not be used in this instance to defeat the oral agreement reached by the parties in this case." The court of appeal affirmed the trial court's judgment, awarding $3.4 million of damages to Allied. *Allied Grape Growers v. Bronco Wine Co.,* 249 Cal. Rptr. 872 (Ct. App. 1988).

Law & Ethics Questions

1. Was a contract entered into in this case?
2. **Ethics** Was it ethical for Bronco to assert the Statute of Frauds to save it from performing the oral contract it had agreed to?
3. What does the equity doctrine of promissory estoppel provide?

Web Exercises

1. **Web** Visit the website of the Court of Appeal of California, Fifth Appellate District, at www.courtinfo.ca.us/courts/courtsofappeal.
2. **Web** Use www.google.com and find an article or case that describes a recent application of the doctrine of promissory estoppel.

■ FORMALITY OF THE WRITING

Some written commercial contracts are long, detailed documents that have been negotiated by the parties and drafted and reviewed by their lawyers. Others are preprinted forms with blanks that can be filled in to fit the facts of a particular situation.

A written contract does not, however, have to be either drafted by a lawyer or formally typed to be legally binding. Generally, the law only requires a writing containing the essential terms of the parties' agreement.

Example: Any writing—including letters, telegrams, invoices, sales receipts, checks, and handwritten agreements written on scraps of paper—can be an enforceable contract under this rule.

Required Signature

The Statute of Frauds and the UCC require a written contract, whatever its form, to be signed *by the party against whom enforcement is sought.* The signature of the person who is enforcing the contract is not necessary. Thus, a written contract may be enforceable against one party but not the other party.

Generally, the signature may appear anywhere on the writing. In addition, it does not have to be a person's full legal name.

Example: The person's last name, first name, nickname, initials, seal, stamp, engraving, or other symbol or mark (e.g., an X) that indicates the person's intent can be binding. The signature may be affixed by an authorized agent.

Integration of Several Writings

Both the common law of contracts and the UCC permit **integration of several writings** to form a single written contract. That is, the entire writing does not have to appear in one document to be an enforceable contract.

Integration may be by an *express reference* in one document that refers to and incorporates another document within it. This procedure is called **incorporation by reference**. Thus, what may often look like a simple one-page contract may actually be hundreds of pages in length.

Example: Credit cards, documents to open bank accounts, contracts with colleges and universities, and other contracts often incorporate by express reference such documents as the master agreement between the issuer and cardholders, subsequent amendments to the agreement, and such.

integration of several writings
Where several different writings or documents are considered to form one enforceable contract.

incorporation by reference
When integration is made by express reference in one document that refers to and incorporates another document within it.

CONTEMPORARY Issue

WHAT CONSTITUTES A SIGNATURE?

In the past, courts have accepted nicknames, first names, initials, symbols, and X's as proper signatures of a promisor. But what happens if the promisor does not actually sign the document? Can it be enforced? One court said yes. Consider the following facts.

MRLS Construction Corporation (MRLS), which was the construction manager on a building project, hired a subcontractor, Sime Construction Company (Sime), to work on the project. When Parma Tile, Mosaic & Marble Company, Inc. (Parma), refused to deliver tile to Sime unless MRLS guaranteed payment, MRLS sent the following fax to Parma: "MRLS would guarantee payment for goods delivered to the Nehemiah project in the event Sime Construction does not pay within terms."

The name MRLS was printed across the top of the unsigned fax. Parma delivered the tile to Sime and, when Sime failed to pay, billed MRLS in reliance on the purported guarantee. MRLS refused to pay. MRLS argued that there was no enforceable contract because the fax was not signed. Parma sued MRLS.

The court rejected this argument and held that the fax constituted an enforceable guarantee because the printed name MRLS appeared across the top of the fax. The court found that this satisfied the signature requirement of the Statute of Frauds. The court stated, "The Statute of Frauds was not meant to be utilized to evade an obligation intentionally incurred. MRLS should not be permitted to evade its obligation because of the current and extensive use of electronic transmissions in modern business transactions." *Parma Tile, Mosaic & Marble Company, Inc. v. Estate of Short,* New York Law Journal, December 10, 1992.

PARALEGAL PERSPECTIVE

Stephanie Runion is an honors graduate from Patricia Stevens College in St. Louis, Missouri. She works as the senior paralegal for the law office of Nathan S. Cohen, a family and domestic law firm in St. Louis.

I am a paralegal for an attorney who practices in general areas of law but focuses on family and domestic law. I assist the attorney in every aspect of the case from start to finish. I work with the attorney to create a wide range of documents and ensure that all documents are compliant with the local rules of court.

Contracts affect my work on a daily basis. I am responsible for drafting marital separation agreements, family court judgments, contracts for employment of the attorney in personal injury and workers' compensation cases, settlement agreements, and much more.

The attorney and our clients rely on my ability to pay close attention to detail when creating these various types of contracts to ensure that the ultimate goal of the parties is not misstated, the document complies with the rules of court, and the document contains no errors.

Without my overall experience and knowledge with regard to contracts and my willingness to continue to learn, my supervising attorney would have a much harder job. These skills have made me a valuable asset to the firm.

Several documents may be integrated to form a single written contract if they are somehow physically attached to each other to indicate a party's intent to show integration.

Example: Attaching several documents together with a staple, paper clip, or some other means may indicate integration. Placing several documents in the same container (e.g., an envelope) may also indicate integration. Such an action is called *implied integration.*

Interpreting Contract Words and Terms

When contracts are at issue in a lawsuit, courts are often called on to interpret the meaning of certain contract words or terms. The parties to a contract may define the words and terms used in their contract. Many written contracts contain a detailed definition section—usually called a **glossary**—that defines many of the words and terms used in the contract.

If the parties have not defined the words and terms of a contract, the courts apply the following **standards of interpretation:**

- *Ordinary* words are given their usual meaning according to the dictionary.
- *Technical words* are given their technical meaning, unless a different meaning is clearly intended.
- *Specific terms* are presumed to qualify *general terms.* For example, if a provision in a contract refers to the subject matter as "corn," but a later provision refers to the subject matter as "feed corn" for cattle, this specific term qualifies the general term.
- If both parties are members of the same trade or profession, words are given their meaning as used in the trade (i.e., *usage of trade*). If the parties do not want trade usage to apply, the contract must indicate that.
- Where a preprinted form contract is used, *typed words* in a contract prevail over *preprinted words. Handwritten words* prevail over both preprinted and typed words.
- If there is an ambiguity in a contract, the ambiguity will be resolved against the party who drafted the contract.

glossary
A detailed definition section in a written contract.

standards of interpretation
If the parties have not defined the words and terms of a contract, the courts apply those words and terms in the manner they normally are defined.

CAREER FRONT

Construction Law Paralegal Job Description

A construction law paralegal works with contracts in the following ways:

- Meet with client and obtain information about project history and current status.
- Review and obtain relevant documents located at city building department, including city meeting minutes, building applications, inspection reports, permits, and drawings.
- Obtain, organize, review, and summarize bid and contract documents and any amendments thereto.
- Obtain, organize, review, and summarize all subcontractor and vendor agreements and any amendments thereto.
- Obtain, review, and summarize all insurance policies and/or bonds issued for the project.
- Obtain, review, organize, and summarize project logs, daily reports, change orders, pay applications and certified payroll records.
- Obtain, review, and summarize documentation evidencing financial transactions between all entities involved in the project.
- Obtain and review relevant union contracts to ensure compliance with prevailing wage provisions.
- Prepare financial analysis and project summary.
- Interview construction manager.
- Interview representatives of subcontractors and vendors.
- Coordinate site visit/inspection; photograph site as necessary.
- Negotiate settlements with subcontractors and vendors.
- Work with experts to review and analyze project plans and specifications.
- Identify liens filed by contractor and/or subcontractors through review of county records.
- Draft mechanic's lien and obtain all documents supporting lien; coordinate filing of lien and distribution of notice of filing lien with appropriate entities/individuals.
- Obtain information about mechanic's lien(s) from county records. Obtain all necessary documents and information from lien holder to verify amount and validity of lien. Negotiate settlement of lien(s). Coordinate payment of lien(s) with client. Draft releases, including release of claims and release/satisfaction of mechanic's lien.

Source: Excerpted by permission from the National Association of Legal Assistants (www.nala.org) and the National Federation of Paralegal Associations, Inc. (www.paralegals.org).

Merger, or Integration, Clause

The parties to a written contract may include a clause stipulating that the contract is a complete integration and the exclusive expression of their agreement and that parol evidence may not be introduced to explain, alter, contradict, or add to the terms of the contract. This type of clause, called a **merger**, or **integration, clause**, expressly reiterates the parol evidence rule.

merger
Occurs when one corporation is absorbed into another corporation and ceases to exist.

■ PAROL EVIDENCE RULE

By the time a contract is reduced to writing, the parties usually have engaged in prior or contemporaneous discussions and negotiations or exchanged prior

parol evidence
Any oral or written words outside the four corners of the written contract.

parol evidence rule
A rule that says if a written contract is a complete and final statement of the parties' agreement, any prior or contemporaneous oral or written statements that alter, contradict, or are in addition to the terms of the written contract are inadmissible in court regarding a dispute over the contract. There are several exceptions to this rule.

complete integration
Where the written contract is a complete and final statement of the parties' agreement.

writings. Any oral or written words outside the *four corners* of the written contract are called **parol evidence**. *Parol* means "word."

The **parol evidence rule** was originally developed by courts as part of the common law of contracts. The UCC has adopted the parol evidence rule as part of the law of sales contracts.[9] The parol evidence rule states that if a written contract is a complete and final statement of the parties' agreement (i.e., a **complete integration**), any prior or contemporaneous oral or written statements that alter, contradict, or are in addition to the terms of the written contract are inadmissible in any court proceeding concerning the contract.[10] In other words, a completely integrated contract is viewed as the best evidence of the terms of the parties' agreement.

Exceptions to the Parol Evidence Rule

There are several major exceptions to the general rule excluding parol evidence. Parol evidence may be admitted in court if it:

- Shows that a contract is void or voidable (e.g., evidence that the contract was induced by fraud, misrepresentation, duress, undue influence, or mistake).
- Explains ambiguous language.
- Concerns *a prior course of dealing or course of performance* between the parties or a *usage of trade*.[11]

INTERNATIONAL LAW

Signatures in Foreign Countries

Americans, Europeans, and many others in the world use their personal hand-applied signatures on legal documents. In Japan, China, and other countries of Asia, however, individuals often do not use their hand-applied signatures to sign legal documents. Instead, they follow the age-old tradition of using a stamp as their signature. The stamp is a character or set of characters carved onto the end of a cylinder-shaped piece held in a person's hand. The owner places this end in ink and then applies this end to the document to be signed, leaving an imprint that serves as the owner's signature. In Japan this cylinder is called a *hanko*; in China it is called a *chop*. *Hankos* and *chops* are registered with the government. They can be made of ivory, jade, agate, gold, animal's horn, wood, or even plastic.

In societies that use personal signatures, if a signature is suspected of being forged, the victim can hire handwriting experts and use modern technology to prove it is not his or her signature. In Japan, China, and other countries where *hankos* and *chops* are used, it is much more difficult to prove forgery because anyone in possession of another's *hanko* or *chop* can apply it. Some people predict the demise of the *hanko* and *chop* because of the possible problem of fraud and the increased use of hand-applied signatures by younger persons in countries used to using the *hanko* and *chop*. Others predict the rich tradition of using a *hanko* or *chop* will continue.

[9]UCC Section 2-202.
[10]*Restatement (Second) of Contracts*, Section 213.
[11]UCC Sections 1-205, 2-202, and 2-208.

- *Fills in the gaps* in a contract (e.g., if a price term or time of performance term is omitted from a written contract, the court can hear parol evidence to imply the reasonable price or time of performance under the contract).
- Corrects an obvious clerical or typographical error. The court can *reform* the contract to reflect the correction.

INTERNET EXERCISES AND CASE QUESTIONS

Working the Web Internet Exercises

1. Earlier in this chapter, you were instructed to review *Stattuck v. Klotzbach*, a case that is part of contemporary contract law relating to e-mails and the Statute of Frauds. Other contemporary case law indicates that a buyer's e-mail of a firm offer on a seller's house can be sufficient for Statute of Frauds purposes. For a contemporary case where the court found no "meeting of the minds" occurred as to the terms of the sale of the house where "essential terms" were not included in the e-mail, find and review the case *Rosenfeld v. Zerneck*, 776 N.Y.S.2d 458 (App. Div. 2004).
2. For an overview of the developing law of e-commerce and digital signatures, see "Are Online Business Transactions Executed by Electronic Signatures Legally Binding?" at www.law.duke.edu/journals/dltr/ARTICLES/2001dltr0005.html
3. Although common law contract principles have general application, many contracts are regulated on an industrywide basis, by state statutes. See www.law.cornell.edu/topics/topic2.html#particular for examples.
4. For an overview of defenses to contract claims, see www.west.net/~smith/contracts.htm.

CHAPTER 6 SUMMARY

STATUTE OF FRAUDS, p. 154

Writing Requirement

Statute of Frauds. This state statute requires that the following contracts be in writing:

1. **Contracts involving the transfer of interests in real property.** This includes contracts for the sale of land, buildings and items attached to land, mortgages, leases for a term of more than one year, and express easements.
   a. *Part performance exception.* To avoid injustice, this exception permits the specific enforcement of oral contracts for the sale of land when they have been partially performed.
2. **Contracts that cannot be performed within one year of their formation.**
3. **Collateral contracts.** These contracts occur where one person promises to answer for the debts or duties of another person. Also called *guaranty contracts.*
   a. *Main purpose exception.* This exception permits enforcement of oral collateral promises if the main or leading purpose of the collateral promise is to benefit the guarantor.
4. **Promises made in consideration of marriage, such as prenuptial agreements.**
5. **Agents' contracts to sell real property.**
6. **Contracts for the sale of goods costing $500 or more.** [UCC §201]

Promissory Estoppel

Promissory estoppel is an equitable doctrine that prevents the application of the Statute of Frauds. It permits the enforcement of oral contracts that should otherwise be in writing under the Statute of Frauds to prevent injustice or unjust enrichment.

FORMALITY OF THE WRITING, p. 162

Sufficiency of the Writing

1. *Formality of the writing.* A written contract does not have to be formal or drafted by a lawyer to be enforceable. Informal contracts, such as handwritten notes, letters, and invoices, are enforceable contracts.
2. *Required signature.* The party against whom enforcement of the contract is sought must have signed the contract. The signature may be the person's full legal name, last name, first name, nickname, initials, or other symbol or mark.
3. *Integration of several writings.* Several writings may be integrated to form a contract. Integration may be by:
   a. *Express reference.* In this case, one document expressly incorporates another document.
   b. *Implied reference.* In this case, documents are physically attached by staple or by paper clip or are placed in the same envelope.

PAROL EVIDENCE RULE, p. 165

The Parol Evidence Rule

1. *Parol evidence.* Parol evidence consists of any oral or written words that are outside the four corners of a written contract.
2. *Parol evidence rule.* This rule provides that if a written contract is a complete integration, any prior or contemporaneous oral or written statements are inadmissible as evidence to alter or contradict the terms of the written contract.
3. *Exceptions to the parol evidence rule.* Parol evidence may be admitted in court to:
   a. Prove mistake, fraud, misrepresentation, undue influence, or duress.
   b. Explain ambiguous language.
   c. Explain a prior course of dealing or course of performance between the parties or a usage of trade.
   d. Fill in the gaps in a contract.
   e. Correct obvious clerical or typographical errors.

Interpretation of Contracts

The courts have developed the following rules for interpreting contracts:

1. *Ordinary words* are given their usual dictionary meaning.
2. *Technical words* are given their technical meaning, unless a different meaning is clearly intended.
3. *Specific terms* are presumed to qualify *general terms*.
4. *Typed words* prevail over *preprinted words; handwritten words* prevail over both preprinted and typed words.
5. Ambiguities in a contract are resolved against the party who drafted the contract.
6. Unless otherwise agreed, words are given their usual meaning in the trade if both parties are members of the same trade.

TERMS AND CONCEPTS

Complete integration   166
Deed of trust   155
Easement   155
Equal dignity rule   160
Glossary   164
Guarantor   158
Guaranty contract   158
Incorporation by reference   163
Integration of several writings   163
Lease   155
Life estate   155
"Main purpose" (leading object) exception   158
Merger   165
Modification   159
Mortgage   155
One-year rule   158
Original (primary) contract   158
Parol evidence   166
Parol evidence rule   166
Part performance   156
Prenuptial agreement   160
Promissory estoppel (equitable estoppel)   161
Promissory note   173
Real property   154
Section 201 of the Uniform Commercial Code (UCC)   159
Standards of interpretation   164
Statute of Frauds   154
UCC Statute of Frauds   159

CASE SCENARIO REVISITED

Now that you understand more about the Statute of Frauds and the doctrine of promissory estoppel, consider the case scenario from the beginning of the chapter. Do you think the Statute of Frauds will prevent Bell Enterprises from enforcing Gary Mc-Graw's oral promise to buy the silver? Does the doctrine of promissory estoppel prevent the application of the Statute of Frauds in this case? See *Atlantic Wholesale Co. v. Solondz*, 320 S.E.2d 720 (S.C. Ct. App. 1984) to help you with your answer.

CRITICAL LEGAL THINKING CASES

Critical Legal Thinking Case 6.1 *Statute of Frauds* Fritz Hoffman and Fritz Frey contracted the Sun Valley Company (Company) about purchasing a 1.64-acre piece of property known as the "Ruud Mountain Property," located in Sun Valley, Idaho, from the Company. Mr. Conger, a representative of the Company, was authorized to sell the property, subject to the approval of the executive committee of the Company. Conger reached an agreement on the telephone with Hoffman and Frey whereby they would purchase the property for $90,000, payable at 30 percent down, with the balance to be payable quarterly at an annual interest rate of 9.25 percent. The next day, Hoffman sent Conger a letter confirming the conversation.

The executive committee of the Company approved the sale. Sun Valley Realty prepared the deed of trust, note, seller's closing statement, and other loan documents. However, before the documents were executed by either side, Sun Valley Company sold all its assets, including the Ruud Mountain property, to another purchaser. When the new owner refused to sell the Ruud Mountain lot to Hoffman and Frey, they brought this action for specific performance of the oral contract. Who wins? *Hoffman v. Sun Valley Co.*, 628 P.2d 218 (Idaho 1981).

Critical Legal Thinking Case 6.2 *Real Property* Robert Briggs and his wife purchased a home located at 167 Lower Orchard Drive, Levittown, Pennsylvania. They made a down payment and borrowed the balance on a 30-year mortgage. Six years later, when the Briggs were behind on their mortgage payments, they entered into an oral contract to sell the house to Winfield and Emma Sackett if the Sacketts would pay the three months' arrearages on the loan and agree to make the future payments on the mortgage. Mrs. Briggs and Mrs. Sackett were sisters. The Sacketts paid the arrearages, moved into the house, and continued to live there. Fifteen years later, Robert Briggs filed an action to void the oral contract as in violation of the Statute of Frauds and evict the Sacketts from the house. Who wins? *Briggs v. Sackett*, 418 A.2d 586 (Pa. Super. Ct. 1980).

Critical Legal Thinking Case 6.3 *One-Year Contract* Robert S. Ohanian was vice president of sales for the West Region of Avis Rent a Car System, Inc. (Avis). Officers of Avis testified that Ohanian's performance in the West Region was excellent, and, in a depressed economic period, Ohanian's West Region stood out as the one region that was growing and profitable. In the fall of 1980, when Avis's Northeast Region was doing badly, the president of Avis asked Ohanian to take over that region. Ohanian was reluctant to do so because he and his family liked living in San Francisco, and he had developed a good team in the West Region, was secure in his position, and feared the politics of the Northeast Region. Ohanian agreed to the transfer only after the general manager of Avis orally told him "unless you screw up badly, there is no way you are going to get fired—you will never get hurt here in this company." Ohanian did a commendable job in the Northeast Region. Approximately one year later, at the age of 47, Ohanian was fired without cause by Avis. Ohanian sued Avis for breach of the oral lifetime contract. Avis asserted the Statute of Frauds against this claim. Who wins? *Ohanian v. Avis Rent a Car Sys., Inc.*, 779 F.2d 101 (2d Cir. 1985).

Critical Legal Thinking Case 6.4 *Guaranty Contract* David Brown met with Stan Steele, a loan officer with the Bank of Idaho (now First Interstate Bank) to discuss borrowing money from the bank to start a new business. After learning that he did not qualify for the loan on the basis of his own financial strength, Brown told Steele that his former employers, James and Donna West of California, might be willing to guarantee the payment of the loan. Steele talked to Mr. West, who orally stated on the telephone that he would personally guarantee the loan to Brown. Based on this guaranty, the bank loaned Brown the money. The bank sent a written guaranty to Mr. and Mrs. West for their signatures, but it was never returned to the bank. When Brown defaulted on the loan, the bank filed suit against the Wests to recover on their guaranty contract. Are the Wests liable? *First Interstate Bank of Idaho, N.A. v. West*, 693 P.2d 1053 (Idaho 1984).

Critical Legal Thinking Case 6.5 *Guaranty Contract* Six persons, including Benjamin Rosenbloom and Alfred Feiler, were members of the board of directors of the Togs Corporation. A bank agreed to loan the corporation $250,000 if the members of the board would personally guarantee the payment of the loan. Feiler objected to signing the guaranty to the bank because of other pending personal financial negotiations that the contingent liability of the guaranty might adversely affect. Feiler agreed with Rosenbloom and the other board members that if they were held personally liable on the guaranty, he would pay his one-sixth share of that amount to them directly. Rosenbloom and the other members of the board signed the personal guaranty with the bank, and the bank made the loan to the corporation. When the corporation defaulted on the loan, the five guarantors had to pay the loan amount to the bank. When they attempted to collect a one-sixth share from Feiler, he refused to pay, alleging that his oral promise had to be in writing under the Statute of Frauds. Does Feiler have to pay the one-sixth share to the other board members? *Feiler v. Rosenbloom*, 416 A.2d 1345 (Md. Ct. Spec. App. 1980).

Critical Legal Thinking Case 6.6 *Agent's Contract* Paul L. McGirr operated an Enco service station in Los Angeles that sold approximately 25,000 to 35,000 gallons of gasoline a month. McGirr telephoned Gulf Oil Corporation (Gulf) regarding an advertisement for dealers. McGirr met with Theodore Marks, an area representative of Gulf, to discuss the possibility of McGirr's operating a Gulf service station. McGirr asked Marks if Gulf had any good, high-producing units available. Marks replied that he had a station at the corner of Figueroa and Avenue 26 that sold about 200,000 gallons of gasoline a month. Marks told McGirr that this station would not be available for about 90 days because Gulf had to terminate the arrangement with the current operator of the station. Marks told McGirr that he could have the Figueroa station only if he also took a "dog" station on Garvey Avenue. McGirr agreed to take this station only if he also was assured he would get the Figueroa station. Marks assured him he would. When McGirr asked Marks for this assurance in writing, Marks stated that he did not have to put it in writing because he was the "kingpin in his territory." So they shook hands on the deal.

McGirr terminated his arrangement with Enco and moved to the Garvey Avenue station. He signed a written lease for the Garvey station, which was signed by Max Reed, Gulf's regional sales manager. Under the Statute of Frauds, the lease for a service station must be in writing. Nothing in writing was ever signed by the parties regarding the Figueroa station. A few months later, Marks was transferred to a different territory, and Gulf refused to lease the Figueroa station to McGirr. McGirr sued Marks and Gulf for breach of an oral contract. Is Marks or Gulf liable? *McGirr v. Gulf Oil Corp.*, 115 Cal. Rptr. 902 (Ct. App. 1974).

Critical Legal Thinking Case 6.7 *Sufficiency of a Writing* Irving Levin and Harold Lipton owned the San Diego Clippers Basketball Club, a professional basketball franchise. Levin and Lipton met with Philip Knight to discuss the sale of the Clippers to Knight. After the meeting, they all initialed a three-page handwritten memorandum that Levin had drafted during the meeting. The memorandum outlined the major terms of their discussion, including subject matter, price, and the parties to the agreement. Levin and Lipton forwarded to Knight a letter and proposed sale agreement. Two days later, Knight informed Levin that he had decided not to purchase the Clippers. Levin and Lipton sued Knight for breach of contract. Knight argued in defense that the handwritten memorandum was not enforceable because it did not satisfy the Statute of Frauds. Is he correct? *Levin v. Knight,* 865 F.2d 1271 (9th Cir. 1989).

ETHICS CASES

Ethics Case 6.1 American Broadcasting Company Merchandising, Inc., a subsidiary of American Broadcasting Company, Inc. (collectively, ABC), entered into a written contract with model Cheryl Tiegs whereby ABC would pay Tiegs $400,000 per year for the right to be the exclusive agent to license the merchandising of goods under her name. When ABC was unsuccessful in attracting licensing arrangements for Tiegs, a representative of ABC contacted Paul Sklar who had previous experience in marketing apparel and licensing labels. Sklar enlisted the help of Mark Blye, and together they introduced ABC and Tiegs to Sears, Roebuck and Company (Sears). This introduction led to an agreement among Sears, ABC, and Tiegs whereby Sears marketed a line of "Cheryl Tiegs" female apparel through Sears department stores and catalog sales. Blye and Sklar sued ABC for a finder's fee for introducing ABC to Sears. Because there was no express written or oral contract among ABC and Blye and Sklar, they alleged there was an implied-in-fact contract between the parties. Section 5-701 (a)(10) of the New York Statute of Frauds requires a finder's fee contract of the type in this case to be in writing. Who wins? Did ABC act ethically in this case? *Blye v. American Broad. Co. Merch., Inc.,* 476 N.Y.S.2d 874 (App. Div. 1984).

Ethics Case 6.2 Adolfo Mozzetti, who owned a construction company, orally promised his son, Remo, that if Remo would manage the family business for their mutual benefit and would take care of him for the rest of his life, he would leave the family home to Remo. Section 2714 of the Delaware Code requires contracts for the transfer of land to be in writing. Section 2715 of the Delaware Code requires testamentary transfers of real property to be in writing. Remo performed as requested—he managed the family business and took care of his father until the father died. When the father died, his will devised the family home to his daughter, Lucia M. Shepard. Remo brought an action to enforce his father's oral promise that the home belonged to him. The daughter argued that the will should be upheld. Who wins? Did the daughter act ethically in trying to defeat the father's promise to leave the property to the son? Did the son act ethically in trying to defeat his father's will? *Shepard v. Mozzetti,* 545 A.2d 621 (Del. 1988).

BRIEFING THE CASE WRITING ASSIGNMENT

Read Case A.6 in the Case Appendix (*Hampton v. Federal Express Corporation*). This case is excerpted from the court of appeals opinion. Review and brief the case. After briefing the case, you should be able to answer the following questions:

1. Why was the plaintiff suing the defendant? What amount of damages was the plaintiff suing for?
2. What did the written contract stipulate regarding the recovery of damages? Explain.
3. Was the written contract enforced by the court in this case?

PRACTICE TIP

You now know how to put together a simple contract and a letter contract. There are sometimes contracts that begin and end without the formality contained in either of those contracts. For instance, an agreement called a **promissory note** is an unconditional written promise by one party to pay money to another party. (Promissory notes are governed by UCC 3-104[e].) Here's an example of a promissory note form. You should also be aware that many legal documents may also require the signature and seal of a notary public.

promissory note
A two-party negotiable instrument that is an unconditional written promise by one party to pay money to another party.

Dated: _____

FOR VALUE RECEIVED, the undersigned, _____, promises to pay the order of _____ the sum of $_____ on _____, 20___, together with interest thereon at the rate of _____% *per annum* from the date hereof.

_____

STATE OF _____, _____ COUNTY, ss:

The foregoing instrument was acknowledged before me this _____ day of _____, 20___.

_____
Notary Public
State of _____

(Place Seal Here)

Commission expires _____

PARALEGAL PORTFOLIO EXERCISE

Being able to draft a simple promissory note for your attorney's review will be especially important when you are employed as a paralegal. Remember the facts in Chapter 4 regarding Kelly's purchase of a diamond ring from Sarah? Assume that Sarah agrees to give Kelly one year to pay the purchase price and, because Kelly is a friend, will only charge her 2% interest for that year. With this information in mind, and using the form in the Practice Tip, draft a promissory note for this transaction.

An honest man's word is as good as his bond.
—*Don Quixote*

Third-Party Rights and Discharge | CHAPTER 7

CASE SCENARIO

The law firm where you work as a paralegal is representing Maco, Inc. (Maco), a roofing contractor. In January 2006, Maco hired Brian Barrows as a salesperson. Barrows was assigned a geographic territory and was responsible for securing contracts for Maco within his territory. The employment contract provided that Barrows was to receive a 26 percent commission on the net profits from roofing contracts he obtained. The contract contained the following provision: "To qualify for payment of the commission, the salesperson must sell and supervise the job; the job must be completed and paid for; and the salesperson must have been in the continuous employment of Maco, Inc., during the aforementioned period." In July 2007, Barrows obtained a $129,603 contract with the Board of Education of Cook County for Maco to make repairs to the roof of the Hoover School in Evanston, Illinois. During the course of the work, Barrows visited the site more than 60 times. In January 2008, before the work was completed, Maco fired Barrows. Later, Maco refused to pay Barrows the commission when the project was completed and paid for. Barrows sued Maco to recover the commission.

■ CHAPTER INTRODUCTION

The parties to a contract are said to be in **privity of contract.** Contracting parties have a legal obligation to perform the duties specified in their contract. A party's duty of performance may be discharged by agreement of the parties, excuse of performance, or operation of law. If one party fails to perform as promised, the other party may enforce the contract and sue for breach.

privity of contract
The state of two specified parties being in a contract.

CHAPTER OBJECTIVES

After studying this chapter, you should be able to:

1. Describe assignment of contracts and what contract rights are assignable.

2. Define *intended beneficiary* and describe this person's rights under a contract.

3. Define *covenant*.

4. Distinguish among conditions precedent, conditions subsequent, and concurrent conditions.

5. Explain when the performance of a contract is excused because of objective impossibility or commercial impracticability.

PARALEGAL PERSPECTIVE

Della Wallace is a graduate of the Raritan Valley Community College's Paralegal Studies Program in New Jersey. She works as an environmental litigation paralegal for the law firm of DiFrancesco, Bateman, Coley, Yospin, Kunzman, Davis & Lehrer in Warren, New Jersey.

As an environmental litigation paralegal, I am responsible for locating any and all documents that will help substantiate the client's position. The use of contracts in the legal venue is essential to determine the course of action that best suits the client's defense strategy process. Many of our clients seek legal advice due to one or more forms of nondisclosure, misrepresentation, or fraud. The use of contracts in environmental matters provides evidence of fact.

A standard in the environmental litigation practice is the investigation of the indemnification clause. Document searches are used in conjunction with making the determination on how to assert responsibility for the cost of the remediation. The indemnification clause will identify the extent of liability for the parties of interest.

Once the preliminary investigations are performed, it is imperative to seek historical information such as names and addresses of previous owners or tenants of the contaminated property, the types of businesses that operated on the site and the dates of operation, current status information regarding the former owner or tenant, and whether the property is listed on the superfund site.

The optimal solution for a contaminated site would be the sale of the property to an entity that specializes in the remediation process. Brownfield's Land and Revitalization program is known for cleaning up and reinvesting in the properties.

With two exceptions, third parties do not acquire any rights under other people's contracts. The exceptions are (1) *assignees* to whom rights are subsequently transferred and (2) *intended third-party beneficiaries* to whom the contracting parties intended to give rights under the contract at the time of contracting.

This chapter discusses the rights of third parties under a contract, conditions to performance, and ways of discharging the duty of performance.

■ ASSIGNMENT OF RIGHTS

assignment of rights
The transfer by the parties of their contractual rights.

In many cases, the parties to a contract can transfer their rights under the contract to other parties. The transfer of contractual rights is called an **assignment of rights** or just an **assignment.**

Form of Assignment

assignor
The party who transfers the rights. The transferor in an assignment situation. The obligee who transfers the right.

assignee
The party to whom the right has been transferred. The transferee in an assignment situation. The party to whom rights have been transferred.

subsequent assignee (subassignee)
When an assignee transfers the rights under the contract to yet another person.

A party who owes a duty of performance is called the *obligor*. A party who is owed a right under a contract is called the *obligee*. An obligee who transfers the right to receive performance is called an **assignor.** The party to whom the right has been transferred is called the **assignee.** The assignee can assign the right to yet another person (called a **subsequent assignee,** or **subassignee**). Exhibit 7.1 illustrates these relationships.

Generally, no formalities are required for a valid assignment of rights. Although the assignor often uses the word *assign*, other words or terms, such as *sell, transfer, convey,* and *give*, are sufficient to indicate an intent to transfer a contract right.

Example: Suppose a retail clothing store purchases $5,000 worth of goods on credit from a manufacturer. Payment is due in 120 days. Assume the manufacturer needs cash before the 120-day period expires, so the manufacturer (assignor) sells

Exhibit 7.1 Assignment of a Right

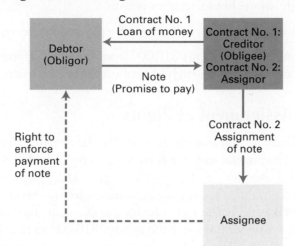

its right to collect the money to another party (assignee) for $4,000. If the retail store is given proper notice of the assignment, it must pay $5,000 to the assignee.

Rights That Can and Cannot Be Assigned

In the United States, public policy favors a free flow of commerce. Hence, most contract rights are assignable, including sales contracts and contracts for the payment of money.

The following types of contracts present special problems for assignments:

1. **Personal service contracts.** Contracts for the provision of personal services are generally not assignable.[1] For example, if an artist contracts to paint someone's portrait, the artist cannot send a different artist to do the painting without the prior approval of the person to be painted. The parties may agree that a personal service contract may be assigned. For example, many professional athletes' contracts contain a clause permitting assignability of the contract.

2. **Assignment of future rights.** Usually, a person cannot assign a currently nonexistent right that he or she expects to have in the future. For example, suppose a multimillion-dollar heiress signs a will, leaving all her property to her grandson. The grandson cannot assign his expected right to receive his inheritance.

3. ***Contracts where assignment would materially alter the risk.*** A contract cannot be assigned if the assignment would materially alter the risk or duties of the obligor. For example, suppose Laura Peters, who has a safe driving record, purchases automobile insurance from an insurance company. Her rights to be insured cannot be assigned to another driver because the assignment would materially alter the risk and duties of the insurance company.

4. ***Assignment of legal action.*** Legal actions involving personal rights cannot be assigned. For example, suppose Donald Matthews is severely injured by Alice Hollyfield in an automobile accident caused by her negligence.

personal service contracts
Contracts for providing personal services such as for an artist painting someone's portrait.

assignment of future rights
A currently nonexistent right that a party expects to have sometime in the future.

---

[1]*Restatement (Second) of Contracts*, Sections 311 and 318.

Matthews can sue Hollyfield to recover damages for his injuries. He cannot assign his right to sue her to another person.

A legal right that arises out of a breach of contract may be assigned.

Example: Suppose Andrea borrows $10,000 from the bank. If she defaults on the loan, the bank may assign the legal rights to collect the money to a collection agency.

Effect of an Assignment of Rights

Where there has been a valid assignment of rights, the assignee "stands in the shoes of the assignor." That is, the assignor is entitled to performance from the obligor. The unconditional assignment of a contract right extinguishes all the assignor's rights, including the right to sue the obligor directly for nonperformance.[2]

An assignee takes no better rights under the contract than the assignor had. For example, if the assignor has a right to receive $10,000 from a debtor, the right to receive this $10,000 is all that the assignor can assign to the assignee. An obligor can assert any defense he or she had against the assignor or the assignee. For example, an obligor can raise the defenses of fraud, duress, undue influence, minority, insanity, illegality of the contract, mutual mistake, or payment by worthless check of the assignor against enforcement of the contract by the assignee. The obligor can also raise any personal defenses (e.g., participation in the assignor's fraudulent scheme) he or she may have directly against the assignee.

In Case 7.1, the court held that an assignment was illegal.

CASE 7.1   ASSIGNING LEASES

Accrued Fin. Serv., Inc. v. Prime Retail, Inc., 298 F.3d 291 (4th Cir. 2002).

Facts

Accrued Financial Services, Incorporated (AFS), is a corporation engaged in the business of conducting lease audits on behalf of tenants in commercial buildings and factory outlet malls. AFS is paid a percentage—usually 40 to 50 percent—of the discrepancy overcharges that it discovers and collects as a result of its audits. The tenant signs a letter of agreement with AFS and assigns all legal causes of action it may have against the landlord to AFS. The assignment grants AFS the authority to file lawsuits in its name against landlords at its discretion. After AFS conducted an audit of Prime Retail, Incorporated (a landlord), on behalf of tenants who had signed assignment agreements, AFS brought a lawsuit against Prime Retail, asserting various claims of overcharges. The U.S. District Court dismissed the case, finding that the assignment of the tenants' claims to AFS violated public policy and were therefore illegal. AFS appealed.

Issue

Does the assignment by a tenant of its legal claims against a landlord violate public policy and is it therefore illegal?

---

[2]*Restatement (Second) of Contracts,* Section 317.

Language of the Court

These relationships between AFS and the tenants were essentially lawsuit-mining arrangements under which AFS "mined for" and prosecuted lawsuits with no regard for the informed wishes of the real parties in interest. AFS thus became a promoter of litigation principally for the sake of the fees that it would earn for itself and not for the benefit that it might produce for the tenant, the real party in interest. Under these arrangements, even though the tenant might conclude, after reviewing the facts uncovered, that a lawsuit would imprudently damage the landlord–tenant relationship—or that pursuing aggressive allegations would do more harm than good—the tenant lost the right to control its destiny. Because we see these broad assignments as nothing more than arrangements through which to intermeddle and stir up litigation for the purpose of making a profit, we conclude that they violate Maryland's strong public policy against stirring up litigation and are therefore void and unenforceable in Maryland.

Decision

The U.S. Court of Appeals held that the tenants' assignment of their legal causes of action against Prime Retail to AFS violated public policy and was therefore illegal and void. The Court of Appeals affirmed the decision of the district court.

Law & Ethics Questions

1. Why did the court of appeals find the tenants' assignments of their legal causes of action against Prime Retail to AFS illegal? How can these assignments be distinguished from typical contingency fee arrangements that plaintiffs' lawyers often have with clients?

2. **Ethics** Did AFS act ethically in this case?

3. What would be the consequences if a party's legal cause of action could be assigned to another party to pursue? Explain.

Notice of Assignment

When an assignor makes an assignment of a right under a contract, the assignee is under a duty to notify the obligor that (1) the assignment has been made and (2) performance must be rendered to the assignee. If the assignee fails to notify the obligor of the assignment, the obligor may continue to render performance to the assignor, who no longer has a right to it. The assignee cannot sue the obligor to recover payment because the obligor has performed according to the original contract. The assignee's only course of action is to sue the assignor for damages.

The result changes if the obligor is notified of the assignment but continues to render performance to the assignor. In such situations, the assignee can sue the obligor and recover payment. The obligor will then have to pay twice: once wrongfully to the assignor and then rightfully to the assignee. The obligor's only recourse is to sue the assignor for damages.

Anti-Assignment and Approval Clauses

Some contracts contain **anti-assignment clauses** that prohibit the assignment of rights under the contracts. Such clauses may be used if the obligor does not want

anti-assignment clause
A clause that prohibits the assignment of rights under the contract.

CAREER FRONT

Job Description: Personal Injury/Medical Malpractice/Product Liability Paralegal

A personal injury paralegal can be involved with contracts in the following ways:

- Draft client agreement for attorney review and client signature.
- Maintain file including documents involving contact with insurance carrier(s), client, health care provider(s), employer(s), and state/local agencies.
- Obtain, review, organize, and analyze medical records. If appropriate, compile medical notebook for each individual involved in action.
- Conduct computerized medical, scientific, and technical literature research. Analyze materials and prepare synopsis.
- Obtain and compile records relating to product history and information about similar products, including research and development, manufacture, patent/copyright filings, instructions for use, distribution, sales, and advertising documents.
- Attend site, product, accident, or vehicle inspection.
- As necessary and appropriate, interview doctors, nurses, and hospital personnel involved in patient care.
- Obtain, review, and organize damage information; calculate damages (medical expenses, lost wages, household expenses, insurance agreements, consortium claims, property damages); prepare, maintain, and update damage summaries.
- Prepare settlement proposals and agreements, including assembling information on the history of plaintiff and the nature and effect of injuries and damages.
- Develop information and acquire records for wrongful death (i.e., supporting evidence regarding sibling and/or child/parent economic claims).
- Obtain factual information about products, companies, and individuals from various resources, including government agencies.
- As necessary and appropriate, arrange medical examinations for client or opposing parties.
- Communicate with experts and provide copies of all relevant documentation regarding accident, product information, and/or medical care, including all summaries of same.
- Answer client questions; keep client updated on progress of case.
- Liaison with insurance adjusters; provide necessary information/documentation to adjusters.
- Interview experts and develop questions to ask experts. (Many times government experts will not volunteer information but will answer direct questions posed to them, so the paralegal needs to know what questions to ask.)
- Write demand letters.
- Prepare settlement statements and agreements.

Source: Excerpted by permission from the National Association of Legal Assistants (www.nala.org) and the National Federation of Paralegal Associations, Inc. (www.paralegals.org).

approval clause
A clause that permits the assignment of the contract only upon receipt of an obligor's approval.

to deal with or render performance to an unknown third party. Some contracts contain an **approval clause** that requires the obligor to approve any assignment. Many states prohibit the obligor from unreasonably withholding approval.

SUCCESSIVE ASSIGNMENTS OF THE SAME RIGHT

An obligee (the party who is owed a performance, money, a right, or another thing of value) has the right to assign a contract right or benefit to another party. If the obligee fraudulently or mistakenly makes successive assignments of the same right to a number of assignees, which assignee has the legal right to the assigned right? To answer this question, the following rules are applied:

- **The American rule** (or **New York rule**) provides that the first assignment *in time* prevails, regardless of notice. Most states follow this rule.
- **The English rule** provides that the first assignee to *give notice* to the obligor (the person who owes the performance, money, duty, or other thing of value) prevails.
- **The possession of tangible token rule** provides that under either the American or English rule, if the assignor makes successive assignments of a contract right that is represented by a tangible token, such as a stock certificate or a savings account passbook, the first assignee who receives delivery of the tangible token prevails over subsequent assignees. However, if the first assignee leaves the tangible token with the assignor, the subsequent assignee prevails. This is because the first assignee could have prevented the problem by having demanded delivery of the tangible token. In other words, physical possession of the tangible token is the pivotal issue.

■ DELEGATION OF DUTIES

Unless otherwise agreed, the parties to a contract can generally transfer the performance of their duties under the contract to other parties. This transfer is called the **delegation of duties,** or just **delegation.**

An obligor who transfers his or her duty is called a **delegator.** The party to whom the duty is transferred is the **delegatee.** The party to whom the duty is owed is the *obligee*. Generally, no special words or formalities are required to create a delegation of duties. Exhibit 7.2 illustrates the parties to a delegation of a duty.

delegation of duties
A transfer of contractual duties by the obligor to another party for performance.

delegator
The obligor who transferred his or her duty.

delegatee
The party to whom the duty has been transferred.

PARALEGAL PERSPECTIVE

Heather Fauber is a graduate of Saint Mary-of-the-Woods College's Paralegal Studies Program. She works as a paralegal in the Legal Department of Caterpillar Inc.

I am a paralegal in the commercial section of the legal department of Caterpillar Inc. My job entails preparing contracts for specific business units within the corporation and working with the mergers and acquisitions team. The contracts I work with vary from general confidentiality agreements to highly negotiated purchase agreements.

Under the supervision of an attorney, I work with our internal business unit contacts through contract negotiation, drafting, and execution. As drafts go back and forth between the parties to an agreement, I do preliminary reviews of the documents, noting errors and potential risks. My reviews save time for the attorney working on the matter.

As a member of the mergers and acquisitions team, when assigned to a deal, I take on a leadership role in coordinating the due diligence process for the team. I also assist with preparation, review, and execution of the necessary merger/acquisition documents. When necessary, I also perform administrative duties, such as formation and registration of subsidiary corporations and LLCs.

Paralegals are an invaluable part of corporate legal departments. I am able to act as a liaison between the business units and the attorneys, increasing productivity a great deal.

Exhibit 7.2 Delegation of a Duty

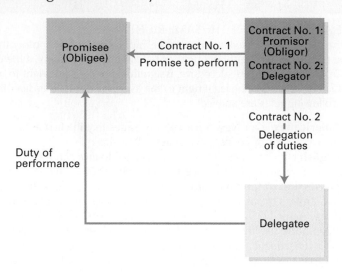

Duties That Can and Cannot Be Delegated

Often, contracts are entered into with companies or firms rather than with individuals. In such cases, a firm may designate any of its qualified employees to perform the contract. For example, if a client retains a firm of lawyers to represent her, the firm can *delegate* the duties under the contract to any qualified member of the firm. If the obligee has a substantial interest in having the obligor perform the acts required by the contract, however, duties may not be transferred.[3] This restriction includes obligations under the following types of contracts:

1. **Personal service contracts calling for the exercise of personal skills, discretion, or expertise.** For example, if Dr. Dre is hired to give a concert on a college campus, the Dixie Chicks cannot appear in his place.
2. **Contracts whose performance would materially vary if the obligor's duties were delegated.** For example, if a person hires an experienced surgeon to perform a complex surgery, a recent medical school graduate cannot be substituted in the operating room.

Effect of Delegation of Duties

If a delegation is valid, the delegator remains legally liable for the performance of the contract. If the delegatee does not perform properly, the obligee can sue the obligor-delegator for any resulting damages.

The question of the delegatee's liability to the obligee depends on whether there has been an *assumption of duties* or a *declaration of duties*. Where a delegation of duties contains the term *assumption* or other similar language, there is an **assumption of duties** by the delegatee. The delegatee is liable to the obligee for nonperformance. The obligee can sue either the delegator or the delegatee.

If the delegatee has not assumed the duties under a contract, the delegation of duties is called a **declaration of duties.** Here, the delegatee is not legally liable to the obligee for nonperformance. The obligee's only recourse is to sue the delegator. A delegatee who fails to perform his or her duties is liable to the delegator for damages arising from this failure to perform.

assumption of duties
When a delegation of duties contains the term assumption, I assume the duties, or other similar language; the delegatee is legally liable to the obligee for nonperformance.

declaration of duties
If the delegatee has not assumed the duties under a contract, the delegatee is not legally liable to the obligee for nonperformance.

---

[3]*Restatement (Second) of Contracts*, Section 318(2).

THE ETHICAL PARALEGAL

Unauthorized Practice of Law

The practice of law is limited to attorneys who are licensed and admitted to the bar. It is just that simple. No matter how skilled a paralegal is or how many years of experience he or she has, a paralegal *cannot* do any of the things generally understood to be "the practice of law." ABA Model Rule 5.5 deals with the unauthorized practice of law, or "UPL."[4]

The ethical paralegal knows there are four things the paralegal cannot do because they are UPL. In other words, these four things are considered "the practice of law":

1. Accept a case (i.e., tell the client the firm or lawyer will take their case);
2. Set a fee (i.e., evaluate the case and tell the client how much the fee will be for representation);
3. Give legal advice (this does not preclude the paralegal from giving *factual information*); and
4. Represent a client in court—except for some administrative agencies (however, of course the paralegal can still *assist* the attorney in court).[5]

Anti-Delegation Clause

The parties to a contract can include an **anti-delegation clause** indicating that the duties cannot be delegated. Anti-delegation clauses are usually enforced. Some courts, however, have held that duties that are totally impersonal—such as the payment of money—can be delegated despite such clauses.

anti-delegation clause
A clause that prohibits the delegation of duties under the contract.

Assignment and Delegation

An **assignment and delegation** occurs when there is a transfer of both rights and duties under a contract. If the transfer of a contract to a third party contains only language of assignment, the modern view holds that there is corresponding delegation of the duties of the contract.[6]

assignment and delegation
Transfer of both rights and duties under the contract.

■ THIRD-PARTY BENEFICIARIES

Third parties sometimes claim rights under others' contracts. Such third parties are either *intended* or *incidental beneficiaries*. Each of these designations is discussed here.

Intended Beneficiaries

When parties enter into a contract, they can agree that the performance of one of the parties should be rendered to or directly benefit a third party. Under such circumstances, the third party is called an **intended third-party beneficiary.** An

---

[4]Copies of the ABA Model Rules of Professional Conduct are available from Service Center, American Bar Association, 321 North Clark Street, Chicago, IL 60610, 1-800-285-2221. The Model Rules can also be viewed online at http://www.abanet.org/cpr/mrpc/mrpc_toc.html.

[5]For more on a paralegal representing a client before an administrative agency, see *Cleveland Bar Ass'n v. CompManagement, Inc.*, 818 N.E.2d 1181 (Ohio 2004) and *Cleveland Bar Ass'n v. CompManagement, Inc.*, 857 N.E.2d 95 (Ohio 2006).

[6]*Restatement (Second) of Contracts*, Section 328.

intended third-party beneficiary can enforce the contract against the party who promised to render performance.[7]

The beneficiary may be expressly named in the contract from which he or she is to benefit or may be identified by another means. For example, there is sufficient identification if a testator of a will leaves his estate to "all my children, equally."

Intended third-party beneficiaries may be classified as either *donee* or *creditor* beneficiaries. These terms are defined in the following sections. The *Restatement (Second) of Contracts* and many state statutes have dropped this distinction, however, and now refer to both collectively as *intended beneficiaries*.[8]

Donee Beneficiaries

donee beneficiary contract

A contract entered into with the intent to confer a benefit or gift on an intended third party.

promisee

One to whom promise has been made.

promisor

One who makes a promise.

donee beneficiary

The third party on whom the benefit is to be conferred.

When a person enters into a contract with the intent to confer a benefit or gift on an intended third party, the contract is called a **donee beneficiary contract.** A life insurance policy with a named beneficiary is an example of such a contract. These three persons are involved in such a contract:

1. The **promisee** (the contracting party who directs that the benefit be conferred on another)
2. The **promisor** (the contracting party who agrees to confer performance for the benefit of the third person)
3. The **donee beneficiary** (the third person on whom the benefit is to be conferred)

If the promisor fails to perform the contract, the donee beneficiary can sue the promisor directly.

Example: Brian Peterson hires a lawyer to draft his will. He directs the lawyer to leave all of his property to his best friend, Jeffrey Silverman. Assume that (1) Peterson dies and (2) the lawyer's negligence in drafting the will causes it to be invalid. Consequently, Peterson's distant relatives receive the property under the state's inheritance statute. Silverman can sue the lawyer for damages because he was the intended donee beneficiary of the will.

Example: A mother, the insured, buys a life insurance policy from a life insurance company and names her daughter as the beneficiary to be paid the life insurance proceeds if the mother dies. The daughter is the intended beneficiary of the contract between her mother and the life insurance company. Assume that the mother dies. If the life insurance company refuses to pay the life insurance proceeds to the daughter, the daughter can sue the life insurance company and recover the insurance proceeds. (see Exhibit 7.3).

Creditor Beneficiaries

creditor beneficiary contract

A contract that arises in the following situation: (1) a debtor borrows money, (2) the debtor signs an agreement to pay back the money plus interest, (3) the debtor sells the item to a third party before the loan is paid off, and (4) the third party promises the debtor that he or she will pay the remainder of the loan to the creditor.

The second type of intended beneficiary is the creditor beneficiary. A **creditor beneficiary contract** usually arises in the following situation:

1. A debtor borrows money from a creditor to purchase some item.
2. The debtor signs an agreement to pay the creditor the amount of the loan plus interest.
3. The debtor sells the item to another party before the loan is paid.
4. The new buyer promises the debtor that he or she will pay the remainder of the loan amount to the creditor.

---

[7]*Restatement (Second) of Contracts*, Section 302.
[8]*Restatement (Second) of Contracts*, Section 302(1)(b).

Exhibit 7.3 Donee Beneficiary Contract

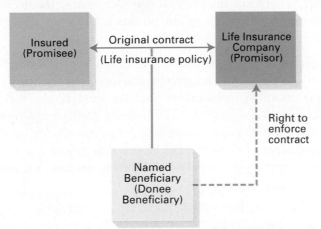

The creditor is the new intended creditor beneficiary to this second creditor.[9] The parties to the second contract are the original debtor (the promisee), the new party (the promisor), and the original creditor (the **creditor beneficiary**) (see Exhibit 7.4).

creditor beneficiary
Original creditor who becomes a beneficiary under the debtor's new contract with another party.

Exhibit 7.4 Creditor Beneficiary Contract

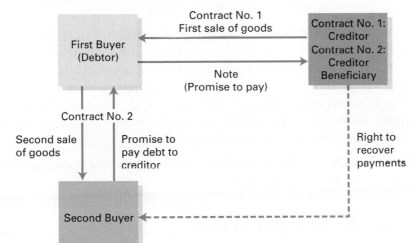

MARKETPLACE

Job Announcement: Medical Malpractice Paralegal

Plaintiff's medical malpractice firm seeks a paralegal with 5 years experience. The duties of this challenging position would include but are not limited to medical record organization, reviewing patient agreements, abstracting depositions/ summarizing medical records, deposition scheduling, initiating and responding to discovery requests, day-to-day file management, and trial preparation.

Medical/Nursing background a plus but not necessary. Must be proficient with litigation support and case management software. Excellent benefits package.

Send resume to:

---

[9]*Restatement (Second) of Contracts*, Section 302(1)(a).

If the promisor fails to perform according to the contract, the creditor beneficiary may either (1) enforce the original contract against the debtor-promisee or (2) enforce the new contract against the promisor. However, the creditor can collect only once.

Example: Suppose Big Hotels obtains a loan from City Bank to refurbish a hotel in Atlanta, Georgia. The parties sign a promissory note requiring the loan to be paid off in equal monthly installments over the next 10 years. Before the loan is paid, Big Hotels sells the hotel to ABC Hotels, another chain of hotels. ABC Hotels agrees with Big Hotels to complete the payments due on the City Bank loan. The bank has two options if ABC Hotels fails to pay: It can sue Big Hotels on the promissory note to recover the unpaid loan amount or it can use its status as a creditor beneficiary to sue ABC Hotels.

Incidental Beneficiaries

incidental beneficiary
A party who is unintentionally benefited by other people's contracts.

In many instances, the parties to a contract unintentionally benefit a third party when the contract is performed. In such situations, the third party is referred to as an **incidental beneficiary.** An incidental beneficiary has no rights to enforce or sue under other people's contracts. Generally, the public and taxpayers are only incidental beneficiaries to contracts entered into by the government on their behalf. As such, they acquire no right to enforce government contracts or to sue parties who breach these contracts.

Example: Suppose Heather owns a house on Residential Street. Her neighbor John owns the house next door. Heather contracts with a painting contractor to paint her house. The painting contractor breaches the contract and does not paint Heather's house. Although John may have benefited if Heather's house was painted, he is merely an incidental beneficiary and has no cause of action to sue the painting contractor for not painting Heather's house. Heather, of course, can sue the painting contractor for breach of contract.

Often the courts are asked to decide whether a third party is an intended or an incidental beneficiary, as in Case 7.2.

third-party beneficiary
A third person that the contracting parties intended should receive a benefit from the contract.

CASE 7.2 THIRD-PARTY BENEFICIARY

Bain v. Gillispie, 357 N.W.2d 47 (Iowa Ct. App. 1984).

Facts

James C. Bain, a college basketball referee, had a contract with the Big 10 Basketball Conference (Big 10) to referee various basketball games. During a game that took place on March 6, 1982, Bain called a foul on a University of Iowa player that permitted free throws by a Purdue University player. That player scored the point that gave Purdue a last-minute victory and eliminated Iowa from the Big 10 championship. Some Iowa fans, including John and Karen Gillispie, asserted that the foul call was clearly in error. The Gillispies operated a novelty store in Iowa City that sold University of Iowa sports memorabilia. They filed a complaint against Bain, alleging that his negligent refereeing constituted a breach of his contract with the Big 10 and destroyed a potential market for their products. The Gillispies sought $175,000 in compensatory damages plus exemplary damages. The trial court granted Bain's motion for summary judgment. The Gillispies appealed.

Issue

Were the Gillispies intended beneficiaries of the contract between Bain and the Big 10 Basketball Conference?

Language of the Court

The trial court found that there was no issue of material fact on the Gillispies' claim that they were beneficiaries under Bain's contract with the Big 10. Because the Gillispies would not be privy to the contract, they must be direct beneficiaries to maintain a cause of action, and not merely incidental beneficiaries.

A direct beneficiary is either a donee beneficiary or a creditor beneficiary. Gillispies make no claim that they are creditor beneficiaries of Bain, the Big 10 Athletic Conference, or the University of Iowa. The real test is said to be whether the contracting parties intended that a third person should receive a benefit that might be enforced in the courts. It is clear that the purpose of any promise that Bain might have made was not to confer a gift on the Gillispies. Likewise, the Big 10 did not owe any duty to the Gillispies such that they would have been donee beneficiaries. If a contract did exist between Bain and the Big 10, Gillispies can be considered nothing more than incidental beneficiaries and as such are unable to maintain a cause of action. Consequently, there is no genuine issue for trial that could result in Gillispies obtaining a judgment under a contract theory of recovery.

Decision

The appellate court held that the Gillispies were merely incidental beneficiaries of the contract between Bain and the Big 10 Basketball Conference. Therefore, they could not maintain their lawsuit for an alleged breach of that contract. The court of appeals affirmed the judgment of the trial court.

Law & Ethics Questions

1. Should the law allow incidental beneficiaries to recover damages for the breach of other people's contracts? Why or why not?
2. **Ethics** Did the Gillispies have a legitimate lawsuit in this case?
3. Do third parties have rights under many business contracts? Give some examples.

■ COVENANTS AND CONDITIONS

In contracts, parties make certain promises to each other. These promises may be classified as *covenants* or *conditions*. The difference between the two is discussed in the following paragraphs.

Covenants

A **covenant** is an unconditional promise to perform. Nonperformance of a covenant is a breach of contract that gives the other party the right to sue. For example, if Medcliff Corporation borrows $100,000 from a bank and signs a promissory note to repay this amount plus 10 percent interest in one year, this promise is a covenant. That is, it is an unconditional promise to perform.

covenant
An unconditional promise to perform.

condition

A qualification of a promise that becomes a covenant if it is met. There are three types of conditions: conditions precedent, conditions subsequent, and concurrent conditions.

condition precedent

A condition that must happen or be performed before some right dependent thereon accrues or some act dependent thereon is performed.

Conditions of Performance

A conditional promise (or qualified promise) is not as definite as a covenant. The promisor's duty to perform (or not perform) arises only if the **condition** does (or does not) occur.[10] It becomes a covenant if the condition is met, however.

Generally, contractual language such as *if*, *on condition that*, *provided that*, *when*, *after*, and *as soon as* indicates a condition. A single contract may contain numerous conditions that trigger or excuse performance. There are three types of conditions: *conditions precedent*, *conditions subsequent*, and *concurrent conditions*.

Condition Precedent

If a contract requires the occurrence (or nonoccurrence) of an event *before* a party is obligated to perform a contractual duty, there is a **condition precedent.** The happening (or nonhappening) of the event triggers the contract or duty of performance. If the event does not occur, no duty to perform arises because there is a failure of condition.

Example: Suppose Company B offers Joan Andrews a job as an industrial engineer upon her graduation from college. If Andrews graduates, the condition has been met. If the employer refuses to hire Andrews at that time, she can sue the employer for breach of contract. If Andrews does not graduate, however, Company B is not obligated to hire her because there has been a failure of condition.

CASE 7.3   CONDITION PRECEDENT

Architectural Systems, Inc. v. Gilbane Building Co., 760 F. Supp. 79 (D. Md. 1991).

Facts

Carley Capital Group (Carley) was the owner of a project in the city of Baltimore known as "Henderson's Wharf." The project was designed to convert warehouses into residential condominiums. On September 4, 1987, Carley hired Gilbane Building Company (Gilbane) to be the general contractor and construction manager for the project. Gilbane hired Architectural Systems, Inc. (ASI) as the subcontractor to perform drywall and acoustical tile work on the project. The subcontract included the following clause: "It is specifically understood and agreed that the payment to the trade contractor is dependent, as a condition precedent, upon the construction manager receiving contract payments from the owner."

Gilbane received periodic payments from Carley and paid ASI as work progressed. By late 1988, ASI had satisfactorily performed all of its obligations under the subcontract and submitted a final bill of $348,155 to Gilbane. Gilbane did not pay this bill because it had not received payment from Carley. On March 10, 1989, Carley filed for bankruptcy. ASI sued Gilbane seeking payment.

Issue

Must Gilbane pay ASI?

---

[10]*The Restatement (Second) of Contracts*, Section 224, defines a *condition* as "an event, not certain to occur, which must occur, unless its nonperformance is excused, before performance under a contract is due."

Language of the Court

ASI argues that it did not assume the credit risk simply by the inclusion of the statement "as a condition precedent" in the subcontract. It may not be sound business practice to accept such a business proposal but that is what occurred. The provision unambiguously declares that Gilbane is not obligated to pay ASI until it first received payment by the owner. The cause for the owner's nonpayment is not specifically addressed and could be due to a number of causes, including insolvency.

A provision that makes receipt of payment by the general contractor a condition precedent to its obligation to pay the subcontractor transfers from the general contractor to the subcontractor the credit risk of non-payment by the owner for any reason (at least for any reason other than the general owner's own fault), including insolvency of the owner.

Decision

The district court held that Gilbane was not obligated to pay ASI because the condition precedent to this payment—receipt of payment from Carley—had not occurred. The court granted summary judgment to Gilbane.

Law & Ethics Questions

1. What is the difference between a covenant and a condition precedent? Explain.

2. **Ethics** Did Gilbane act unethically in not paying ASI? Did ASI act unethically in suing Gilbane?

3. If the condition precedent had not been expressly provided in the subcontract, who would have borne the risk of Carley's default?

Condition Precedent Based on Satisfaction

Some contracts reserve the right to a party to pay for services provided by the other only if the services meet the first party's "satisfaction." The courts have developed two tests—the *personal satisfaction test* and the *reasonable person test*—to examine whether this special form of condition precedent has been met:

1. The **personal satisfaction test** is a *subjective* test that applies if the performance involves personal taste and comfort (e.g., contracts for decorating, tailoring, etc.). The only requirement is that the person given the right to reject the contract acts in good faith.

   Example: Suppose Gretchen employs an artist to paint her daughter's portrait. Assume the contract provides that the client does not have to pay for the portrait unless she is satisfied with it. Accordingly, Gretchen may reject the painting if she personally dislikes it, even though a reasonable person would be satisfied with it.

2. The **reasonable person test** is an *objective* test used to judge contracts involving mechanical fitness and most commercial contracts. Most contracts that require the work to meet a third person's satisfaction (e.g., engineer, architect) are judged by this standard.

Example: Suppose a large mail-order catalog business hires someone to install a state-of-the-art computer system that will handle its order entry and record-keeping functions. The system is installed and operates to industry standards. According to

condition precedent based on satisfaction
Clause in a contract that reserves the right to a party to pay for the items or services contracted for only if they meet his or her satisfaction.

personal satisfaction test
Subjective test that applies to contracts involving personal taste and comfort.

reasonable person test
Objective test that applies to commercial contracts and contracts involving mechanical fitness.

the reasonable person test, the company cannot reject the contract as not meeting its satisfaction.

Time of Performance as a Condition Precedent

Generally, there is a breach of contract if the contract is not performed when due. Nevertheless, if the other party is not jeopardized by the delay, most courts treat the delay as a minor breach and give the nonperforming party additional time to perform. Conversely, if the contract expressly provides that *"time is of the essence"* or similar language, performance by the stated time is an express condition. There is a breach of contract if the contracting party does not perform by the stated date.

Condition Subsequent

condition subsequent
A condition, if it occurs or doesn't occur, that automatically excuses the performance of an existing contractual duty to perform.

A **condition subsequent** exists when a contract provides that the occurrence or nonoccurrence of a specific event automatically excuses the performance of an existing duty to perform. For example, many employment contracts include a clause that permits the employer to terminate the contract if the employee fails a drug test.

Note that the *Restatement (Second) of Contracts* eliminates the distinction between conditions precedent and conditions subsequent. Both are referred to as "conditions."[11]

Concurrent Condition

concurrent condition
A condition that exists when the parties to a contract must render performance simultaneously; each party's absolute duty to perform is conditioned on the other party's absolute duty to perform.

Concurrent conditions arise when the parties to a contract must render performance simultaneously—that is, when each party's absolute duty to perform is conditioned on the other party's absolute duty to perform.

For example, suppose a contract to purchase goods provides that payment is due upon delivery. In other words, the buyer's duty to pay is conditioned on the seller's duty to deliver the goods, and vice versa. Recovery is available if one party fails to respond to the other party's performance.

Implied Condition

implied-in-fact condition
A condition that can be implied from the circumstances surrounding a contract and the parties' conduct.

Any of the previous types of conditions may be further classified as either express or implied conditions. An *express condition* exists if the parties expressly agree on it. An **implied-in-fact condition** is one that can be implied from the circumstances surrounding a contract and the parties' conduct. For example, a contract in which a buyer agrees to purchase grain from a farmer implies proper street access to the delivery site, proper unloading facilities, and the like.

■ DISCHARGE OF PERFORMANCE

A party's duty to perform under a contract may be discharged by *mutual agreement* of the parties, by *impossibility of performance*, or by *operation of law*. These methods of discharge are discussed next.

Discharge by Agreement

In many situations, the parties to a contract mutually decide to discharge their contractual duties. The different types of mutual agreement are discussed in the following paragraphs.

- *Mutual rescission*—If a contract is wholly or partially executory on both sides, the parties can agree to rescind (i.e., cancel) the contract.

---

[11]*Restatement (Second) of Contracts*, Section 224.

Concept Summary

Types of Conditions

Type of Condition	Description
Condition precedent	A specified event must occur or not occur before a party is obligated to perform contractual duties.
Condition subsequent	The occurrence or nonoccurrence of a specified event excuses the performance of an existing contractual duty to perform.
Concurrent condition	The parties to a contract are obligated to render performance simultaneously. Each party's duty to perform is conditioned on the other party's duty to perform.
Implied condition	An implied-in-fact condition is implied from the circumstances surrounding a contract and the parties' conduct.

ETHICS SPOTLIGHT

SATISFACTION CLAUSE: "I DON'T LIKE IT"

Commercial contracts often include "satisfaction clauses" that are designed to ensure that an appropriate quality of performance is received before the promisee is obligated to pay. But how satisfied must the contracting party be before there is an obligation to pay? Consider the following case.

General Motors Corporation hired Baystone Construction, Inc. (Baystone) to build an addition to a Chevrolet plant in Muncie, Indiana. Baystone, in turn, hired Morin Building Products Company (Morin) to supply and erect the aluminum walls for the addition. The contract required that the exterior siding of the walls be of "aluminum with a mill finish and stucco embossed surface texture to match finish and texture of existing metal siding." The contract also included a satisfaction clause. Morin put up the walls. The exterior siding did not give the impression of having a uniform finish when viewed in bright sunlight from an acute angle and General Motors' representative rejected it. Baystone removed Morin's siding and hired another subcontractor to replace it. General Motors approved the replacement siding. When Baystone refused to pay Morin the $23,000 balance owing on the contract, Morin brought suit against Baystone to recover this amount.

The trial court held in favor of Morin and permitted it to recover the balance from Baystone. The court of appeals affirmed. The court held that the objective reasonable person standard governed the satisfaction clauses in this commercial dispute.

The reasonable person standard applies to most contracts involving commercial quality, operative fitness, or mechanical utility that other knowledgeable persons can judge. The court of appeals held that Baystone was not justified in rejecting Morin's work under the reasonable person standard. The court stated, "The building for which the aluminum siding was intended was a factory. Aesthetic considerations were decidedly secondary to considerations of function and cost. The parties probably did not intend to subject Morin's rights to aesthetic whims." *Morin Building Products Co., Inc. v. Baystone Construction, Inc.*, 717 F. 2d 413 (7th Cir. 1983)

1. Do you think General Motors was justified in rejecting Morin's work in this case?
2. Should the law adopt the personal satisfaction test to judge compliance with satisfaction clauses in all instances? Why or why not?

Mutual rescission requires the parties to enter into a second agreement that expressly terminates the first one. Unilateral rescission of the contract by one of the parties without the other party's consent is not effective. Unilateral rescission of a contract constitutes a breach of that contract.

- *Substituted contract*—The parties to a contract may enter into a new contract that revokes and discharges a prior contract. The new contract is called a **substituted contract**. If one of the parties fails to perform his or her

mutual rescission
Where the parties enter into a second agreement that expressly terminates the first one.

substituted contract
A new contract that revokes and discharges a prior contract.

novation
An agreement that substitutes a new party for one of the original contracting parties and relieves the exiting party of liability on the contract.

accord and satisfaction
The settlement of a contract dispute.

accord
An agreement whereby the parties agree to accept something different in satisfaction of the original contract.

satisfaction
The performance of an accord.

impossibility of performance (objective impossibility)
Nonperformance that is excused if the contract becomes impossible to perform; must be objective impossibility, not subjective.

duties under a substituted contract, the nonbreaching party can sue to enforce its terms against the breaching party. The prior contract cannot be enforced against the breaching party because it has been discharged.

■ *Novation*—A novation agreement (commonly called **novation**) substitutes a third party for one of the original contracting parties. The new substituted party is obligated to perform the contract. All three parties must agree to the substitution. In a novation, the existing party is relieved of liability on the contract.

■ *Accord and satisfaction*—The parties to a contract may agree to settle a contract dispute by an **accord and satisfaction.** The agreement whereby the parties agree to accept something different in satisfaction of the original contract is called an **accord.**[12] The performance of an accord is called a **satisfaction.**

An accord does not discharge the original contract. It only suspends it until the accord is performed. Satisfaction of the accord discharges both the original contract and the accord. If an accord is not satisfied when it is due, the aggrieved party may enforce either the accord or the original contract.

Discharge by Impossibility

Under certain circumstances, the nonperformance of contractual duties is excused—that is, discharged—because of *impossibility of performance*.

Impossibility of performance (or **objective impossibility**) occurs if a contract becomes impossible to perform.[13] The impossibility must be objective impossibility ("it cannot be done") rather than subjective impossibility ("I cannot do it"). The following types of objective impossibility excuse nonperformance:

1. The death or incapacity of the promisor prior to the performance of a personal service contract.[14] For example, if a professional athlete dies prior to or during a contract period, his or her contract with the team is discharged.
2. The destruction of the subject matter of a contract prior to performance.[15] For example, if a building is destroyed by fire, the lessees are discharged from further performance unless otherwise provided in the lease.
3. A supervening illegality, which makes performance of the contract illegal.[16] For example, suppose an art dealer contracts to purchase native art found in a foreign country. The contract is discharged if the foreign country enacts a law forbidding native art from being exported from the country before the contract is performed.

CASE 7.4 PERSONAL SERVICE CONTRACTS

Parker v. Arthur Murray, Inc., 295 N.E.2d 487 (Ill. App. Ct. 1973).

Facts

In November 1959, Ryland S. Parker, a 37-year-old college-educated bachelor, went to the Arthur Murray Studios (Arthur Murray) in Oak Park, Illinois, to redeem a certificate entitling him to three free dancing lessons. At that time he

[12]*Restatement (Second) of Contracts*, Section 281.
[13]*Restatement (Second) of Contracts*, Section 261.
[14]*Restatement (Second) of Contracts*, Section 262.
[15]*Restatement (Second) of Contracts*, Section 263.
[16]*Restatement (Second) of Contracts*, Section 264.

lived alone in a one-room attic apartment. During the free lessons the instructor told Parker that he had "exceptional potential to be a fine and accomplished dancer." Parker thereupon signed a contract for more lessons. Parker attended lessons regularly and was praised and encouraged by his instructors despite his lack of progress. Contract extensions and new contracts for additional instructional hours were executed, which Parker prepaid. Each written contract contained the bold-type words, "NONCANCELLABLE CONTRACT." On September 24, 1961, Parker was severely injured in an automobile accident, rendering him incapable of continuing his dancing lessons. At that time he had contracted for a total of 2,734 hours of dance lessons, for which he had prepaid $24,812. When Arthur Murray refused to refund any of the money, Parker sued to rescind the outstanding contracts. The trial courts held in favor of Parker and ordered Arthur Murray to return the prepaid contract payments. Arthur Murray appealed.

Issue

Does the doctrine of impossibility excuse Parker's performance of the personal service contracts?

Language of the Court

Plaintiff was granted rescission on the ground of impossibility of performance. Defendants do not deny that the doctrine of impossibility of performance is generally applicable to the case at bar. Rather they assert that certain contract provisions bring the case within the Restatement's limitation that the doctrine is inapplicable if "the contract indicates a contrary intention." It is contended that such bold-type phrases as "NON-CANCELLABLE CONTRACT," "NON-CANCELLABLE NEGOTIABLE CONTRACT," and "I UNDERSTAND THAT NO REFUNDS WILL BE MADE UNDER THE TERMS OF THIS CONTRACT" manifested the parties' mutual intent to waive their respective rights to invoke the doctrine of impossibility.

This is a construction that we find unacceptable. Courts engage in the construction and interpretation of contracts with the sole aim of determining the intention of the parties. We need rely on no construction aids to conclude that plaintiff never contemplated that by signing a contract with such terms as "NON-CANCELLABLE" and "NO REFUNDS," he was waiving a remedy expressly recognized by Illinois courts. Although neither party to a contract should be relieved from performance on the ground that good business judgment was lacking, a court will not place upon language a ridiculous construction. We conclude that plaintiff did not waive his right to assert the doctrine of impossibility.

Suffice it to say that overwhelming evidence supported plaintiff's contention that he was incapable of continuing his lessons.

Decision

The appellate court held that the doctrine of impossibility of performance excused Parker's performance of the personal service contracts. Affirmed.

Law & Ethics Questions

1. Should the doctrine of impossibility excuse parties from performance of their contracts? Why or why not?

2. **Ethics** Did Arthur Murray act ethically in not returning Parker's money?

3. Why do you think Arthur Murray fought this case?

Force Majeure Clauses

force majeure clauses
Certain events, such as floods, earthquakes, or tornadoes, that will excuse nonperformance of a contract.

The parties may agree in a contract that certain events will excuse nonperformance of the contract. These clauses are called **force majeure clauses.**

Usually, force majeure clauses excuse nonperformance caused by natural disasters such as floods, tornadoes, earthquakes, and such. Modern clauses often excuse performance due to labor strikes, shortages of raw materials, and the like.

Commercial Impracticability

commercial impracticability
Nonperformance that is excused if an extreme or unexpected development or expense makes it impractical for the promisor to perform.

Many states recognize the doctrine of **commercial impracticability** as an excuse for nonperformance of contracts. Commercial impracticability excuses performance if an unforeseeable event makes it impractical for the promisor to perform. This doctrine has not yet been fully developed by the courts. It is examined on a case-by-case basis.

Example: A utility company enters into a contract to purchase uranium for its nuclear-powered generator from a uranium supplier at a fixed price of $1 million per year for five years. Suppose a new uranium cartel is formed worldwide, and the supplier must pay $3 million for uranium to supply the utility with each year's supply. In this case, the court would likely allow the supplier to rescind its contract with the utility, based on commercial impracticability. Note that it is not impossible for the supplier to supply the uranium.

Discharge by Operation of Law

statute of limitations
Statute that establishes the time period during which a lawsuit must be brought; if the lawsuit is not brought within this period, the injured party loses the right to sue.

discharge
Actions or events that relieve certain parties from liability on negotiable instruments. There are three methods of discharge: (1) payment of the instrument; (2) cancellation; and (3) impairment of the right of recourse. The termination of the legal duty of a debtor to pay debts that remain unpaid upon the completion of a bankruptcy proceeding. Creditors' claims that are not included in a Chapter 11 reorganization are discharged. A discharge is granted to a debtor in a Chapter 13 consumer debt adjustment bankruptcy only after all the payments under the plan are completed by the debtor.

Certain legal rules discharge parties from performing contractual duties. These rules are discussed in the following paragraphs.

- *Statutes of limitations*—Every state has a **statute of limitations** that applies to contract actions. Although the time periods vary from state to state, the usual period for bringing a lawsuit based on breach of contract is one to five years. The UCC provides that a cause of action based on a breach of sales or lease contract must be brought within four years after the cause of action accrues (UCC §2-725, UCC §2A-506).
- *Bankruptcy*—Bankruptcy, governed by federal law, is a means of allocating the debtor's nonexempt property to satisfy his or her debts. Debtors may also reorganize in bankruptcy. In most cases, the debtor's assets are insufficient to pay all the creditors' claims. In this case, the debtor receives a **discharge** of the unpaid debts. The debtor is then relieved of legal liability to pay the discharged debts.
- *Alteration of the contract*—If a party to a contract intentionally alters the contract materially, the innocent party may opt either to discharge the contract or to enforce it. The contract may be enforced either on its original terms or on the altered terms. A material alteration is a change in price, quantity, or some other important term.

CONTEMPORARY Issue

COMMERCIAL IMPRACTICABILITY

"[T]he focus of impracticability analysis is upon the nature of the agreement and the expectations of the parties."

Judge Nesbitt, *U.S. Court of Appeals for the Eleventh Circuit*

Sometimes, unforeseen circumstances make the performance of a contract highly impracticable or very expensive. Modern contract law, including the Uniform Commercial Code (UCC), recognizes the doctrine of commercial impracticability as excusing nonperformance in certain situations. Consider the following case.

Alimenta (U.S.A.), Inc. (Alimenta) entered into a contract with Cargill, Inc. (Cargill), under which Alimenta would purchase shelled edible peanuts from Cargill. The peanut crop had been planted in the fields at the time the contract was entered into. Cargill, which had contracts to purchase peanuts from peanut farmers, expected to make $3 million in profit from peanut sales.

Unfortunately, there was a severe drought that year, and the crop yield was substantially reduced. Thus, Cargill could deliver to Alimenta only about 65 percent of the promised peanuts. Cargill delivered the same percentage to all of its customers. Alimenta filed suit against Cargill for breach of contract. Cargill asserted that further performance under the contract was excused by the doctrine of commercial impracticability. At trial the jury rendered a verdict for Cargill. Alimenta appealed.

The trial court held that the drought in this case was unforeseen. The evidence showed that the shortage of peanuts was unprecedented. In fact, there had been a surplus of domestic peanuts for the preceding 20 years. The trial court found that it was not impossible for Cargill to fully perform the contract. Cargill could have gone into the market and purchased the peanuts, which were selling at a much higher price than contracted for, and delivered the peanuts to Alimenta. Cargill, however, had already suffered a $47-million loss on its peanut contract even without taking this step.

The court of appeals affirmed the trial court's ruling in favor of Cargill. The court held that Cargill was excused from further performance by the doctrine of commercial impracticability. The court stated that "the focus of impracticability analysis is upon the nature of the agreement and the expectations of the parties" and not on whether it is physically possible for the defendant to perform the contract. *Alimenta (U.S.A.), Inc. v. Cargill, Inc.,* 861 F.2d 650 (11th Cir. 1988).

Law & Ethics Questions

1. What does the doctrine of commercial impraticability provide? Explain.
2. How does the doctrine of commercial impracticability differ from impossibility of performance?
3. **Ethics** Did Cargill act ethically in this case? Why or why not?

Web Exercises

1. **Web** Visit the website for the U.S Court of Appeals for the Eleventh Circuit at www.ca11.uscourts.gov.
2. **Web** Visit the website of Cargill Corporation at www.cargill.com.
3. **Web** Use www.google.com and find the current price of peanuts on a commodities exchange.

INTERNET EXERCISES AND CASE QUESTIONS

Working the Web Internet Exercises

1. Which provision of the UCC permits assignment and delegation? An extensive overview of contract law can be found at the Contracts home page (Craig Smith, Santa Barbara College of Law) at www.west.net/~smith/contracts .htm. Review the "Third Party Rights" section.
2. Why does bankruptcy have the effect of discharging contractual obligations? See www.nolo.com and search for *bankruptcy*.
3. A good case can be lost because of a statute of limitations. These statutes vary by state and by type of claim. See www.nolo.com/encyclopedia/articles/cm/ timely.html for a summary of the statues and find your state law.

CHAPTER 7 SUMMARY

ASSIGNMENT OF RIGHTS, p. 176

Form of Assignment

1. *Assignment.* Assignment is transfer of contractual rights by a party to a contract to a third person.
2. *Assignor.* An assignor is a contract party who assigns the contractual rights.
3. *Assignee.* An assignee is a third person to whom contract rights are assigned.

Effect of Assignment

The assignee "stands in the shoes of the assignor" and is entitled to performance of the contract by the obligor.

Notice of Assignment

1. *Duty to notify.* The assignee must notify the obligor that (1) the assignment has been made and (2) performance must be rendered to the assignee.
2. *Failure to give notice.* If the assignee fails to give proper notice to the obligor and the obligor renders performance to the assignor, the assignee's only course of action to recover is from the assignor.

Anti-Assignment and Approval Clauses

1. *Anti-assignment clause.* This clause prohibits the assignment of rights under a contract.
2. *Approval clause.* This clause permits assignment of the contract only upon receipt of the obligor's approval.

Successive Assignments

If the obligee makes successive assignments of the same right, one of the following rules (depending on state law) applies:

1. *American rule.* Under this rule, the first assignment in time prevails, regardless of notice. Also called the *New York rule.*
2. *English rule.* Under this rule, the first assignee to give notice to the obligor prevails.

DELEGATION OF DUTIES, p. 181

Delegation of Duties

1. *Delegation.* Delegation is transfer of contractual duties by a party to a contract to a third person.
2. *Delegator.* The delegator is the party who transfers his or her contractual duties.
3. *Delegatee.* The delegatee is the third person to whom contractual duties are delegated.

Effect of Delegation

The effect of delegation depends on whether there has been:

1. *Assumption of duties.* The delegatee is liable to the obligee for nonperformance. The obligee may sue either the delegatee or the delegator.
2. *Declaration of duties.* The delegatee is not liable to the obligee for nonperformance. The obligee can sue only the delegator. The delegatee is liable to the delegator for any damages suffered by the delegator because of the delegatee's nonperformance.

Anti-Delegation Clause

This clause prohibits the delegation of duties under a contract.

THIRD-PARTY BENEFICIARIES, p. 183

Intended Beneficiaries

An intended beneficiary is a third person who is owed performance under other parties' contract. There are two types:

1. *Donee beneficiary.* This person is to be rendered performance gratuitously under a contract (for example, a beneficiary of a life insurance policy). A donee beneficiary may sue the promisor for nonperformance.
2. *Creditor beneficiary.* A creditor becomes a beneficiary to a contract between the debtor and a third party who agrees to perform the debtor's obligation. If the debt is not paid, the creditor may sue either (1) the debtor under the original contract or (2) the third party as a creditor beneficiary.

Incidental Beneficiaries

An incidental beneficiary is a third person who incidentally receives some benefit under other parties' contract but who has no rights to enforce it or to sue for its nonperformance.

COVENANTS AND CONDITIONS, p. 187

Covenants

Covenants are unconditional promises to perform. Nonperformance of a covenant is a breach of contract that gives the other party the right to sue.

Conditions of Performance

Condition. A promisor's duty to perform or not perform arises only if the *condition* does or does not occur. Also called a *qualified promise.* There are several types:

1. **Condition precedent.** This requires the occurrence or nonoccurrence of an event before a party is obligated to perform. Conditions precedent based on "satisfaction" are measured by one or two standards:
   a. *Personal satisfaction test.* The subjective intent of the decision maker applies if the performance involves personal taste or comfort.
   b. *Reasonable person test.* The objective intent of a reasonable person in the circumstances applies to contracts involving mechanical fitness or commercial contracts.
2. **Condition subsequent.** This provides that the occurrence or nonoccurrence of a specific event automatically excuses performance under a contract.
3. **Concurrent condition.** This arises when the parties to a contract must render performance simultaneously.
4. **Implied-in-fact condition.** This condition is implied from the circumstances surrounding a contract and the parties' conduct.

DISCHARGE OF PERFORMANCE, p. 190

Discharge by Agreement

1. **Mutual rescission.** The parties mutually agree to rescind an executory contract.
2. **Substituted contract.** The parties enter into a new contract that revokes a prior contract.
3. **Novation.** The parties agree to the substitution of a third party for one of the original parties. The exiting party is relieved of liability, and the entering party is obligated to perform the contract.
4. **Accord and satisfaction.** The parties agree to settle a contract dispute. The *satisfaction* of the *accord* discharges the original contract.

Discharge by Impossibility

1. **Impossibility of performance.** The contract is objectively impossible to perform because of an event.
2. **Commercial impracticability.** The contract is impractical for the promisor to perform because of an event.
3. **Force majeure clause.** The parties stipulate in the contract what events will excuse performance.

Discharge by Operation of Law

1. **Statute of limitations.** A contract that is not brought within the stipulated limitations period discharges contractual duties.
2. **Bankruptcy.** Discharge in bankruptcy relieves the debtor of legal liability to pay the discharged debts.
3. **Alteration of a contract.** If a party to a contract intentionally alters it materially, the innocent party may opt either to discharge the contract or enforce it on its original or altered terms.

TERMS AND CONCEPTS

Accord   192

Accord and satisfaction   192

Anti-assignment clause   179

Anti-delegation clause   183

Approval clause   180
Assignment and delegation   183
Assignment of future rights   177
Assignment of rights   176
Assignee   176
Assignor   176
Assumption of duties   182
Commercial impracticability   194
Concurrent condition   190
Condition   188
Condition precedent   188
Condition precedent based on satisfaction   189
Condition subsequent   190
Covenant   187
Creditor beneficiary   185
Creditor beneficiary contract   184
Declaration of duties   182
Delegatee   181
Delegator   181
Delegation of duties   181
Discharge   194
Donee beneficiary   184
Donee beneficiary contract   184
Force majeure clause   194
Implied-in-fact condition   190
Impossibility of performance (objective impossibility)   192
Incidental beneficiary   186
Mutual rescission   191
Novation   192
Personal satisfaction test   189
Personal service contract   177
Privity of contract   175
Promisee   184
Promisor   184
Reasonable person test   189
Satisfaction   192
Statutes of limitation   194
Subsequent assignee (subassignee)   176
Substituted contract   191
Third-party beneficiary   186

CASE SCENARIO REVISITED

Remember the case scenario at the beginning of the chapter involving the employment contract between Maco, Inc., and Brian Barrows? How are employment contracts different from other contracts? Is there anything in this contract that would bring about the excuse of a condition? Who do you think would win in this dispute? For more information on this situation, see the case the case *Barrows v. Maco, Inc.*, 419 N.E.2d 634 (Ill. App. Ct. 1981).

CRITICAL LEGAL THINKING CASES

Critical Legal Thinking Case 7.1 *Third Party* Eugene H. Emmick hired L. S. Hamm, an attorney, to draft his will. The will named Robert Lucas and others (Lucas) as beneficiaries. When Emmick died, it was discovered that the will was improperly drafted, violated state law, and was therefore ineffective. Emmick's estate was transferred pursuant to the state's intestate laws. Lucas did not receive the $75,000 he would have otherwise received had the will been valid. Lucas sued Hamm for breach of the Emmick–Hamm contract to recover what he would have received under the will. Who wins? *Lucas v. Hamm*, 364 P.2d 685 (Cal. 1961).

Critical Legal Thinking Case 7.2 *Third-Party Beneficiary* Angelo Boussiacos hired Demetrios Sofias, a general contractor, to build a restaurant for him. Boussiacos entered into a loan agreement with Bank of America (B of A) whereby B of A would provide the construction financing to build the restaurant. As is normal with most construction loans, the loan agreement provided that loan funds would be periodically disbursed by B of A to Boussiacos at different stages of construction, as requested by Boussiacos. Problems arose in the progress of the construction. When Boussiacos did not pay Sofias for certain work that had been done, Sofias sued B of A for breach of contract to collect payment directly from B of A. Can Sofias maintain the lawsuit against B of A? *Sofias v. Bank of America*, 218 Cal. Rptr. 388 (Ct. App. 1985).

Critical Legal Thinking Case 7.3 *Assignment* William John Cunningham, a professional basketball player, entered into a contract with Southern Sports Corporation, which owned the Carolina Cougars, a professional basketball team. The contract provided that Cunningham was to play basketball for the Cougars for a three-year period, commencing on October 2, 1971. The contract contained a provision that it could not be assigned to any other professional basketball franchise without Cunningham's approval. Subsequently, Southern Sports Corporation sold its assets, including its franchise and Cunningham's contract, to the Munchak Corporation (Munchak). There was no change in the location of the Cougars after the purchase. When Cunningham refused to play for the new owners, Munchak sued to enforce Cunningham's contract. Was Cunningham's contract assignable to the new owner? *Munchak Corp. v. Cunningham*, 457 F.2d 721 (4th Cir. 1972).

Critical Legal Thinking Case 7.4 *Assignment* In 1974, Berliner Foods Corporation (Berliner), pursuant to an oral contract, became a distributor for Häagen-Dazs ice cream. Over the next decade, both parties flourished as the marketing of high-quality, high-priced ice cream took hold. Berliner successfully promoted the sale of Häagen-Dazs to supermarket chains and other retailers in the Baltimore–Washington, DC, area. In 1983, the Pillsbury Company acquired Häagen-Dazs. Pillsbury adhered to the oral distribution agreement and retained Berliner as a distributor for Häagen-Dazs ice cream. In December 1985, Berliner entered into a contract and sold its assets to Dreyers, a manufacturer of premium ice cream that competed with Häagen-Dazs. Dreyers ice cream had previously been sold primarily in the western part of the United States. Dreyers attempted to expand its market to the east by choosing to purchase Berliner as a means to obtain distribution in the mid-Atlantic region. When Pillsbury learned of the sale, it advised Berliner that its distributorship for Häagen-Dazs was terminated. Berliner, which wanted to remain a distributor for Häagen-Dazs, sued Pillsbury for breach of contract, alleging that the oral distribution agreement with Häagen-Dazs and Pillsbury was properly assigned to Dreyers. Who wins? *Berliner Foods Corp. v. Pillsbury Co.*, 633 F. Supp. 557 (D. Md. 1986).

Critical Legal Thinking Case 7.5 *Anti-Assignment Clause* In 1976, the city of Vancouver, Washington, contracted with B & B Contracting Corporation (B & B) to construct a well pump at a city-owned water station. The contract contained the following anti-assignment clause: "The contractor shall not assign this contract or any part thereof, or any moneys due or to become due thereunder." The work was not completed on time, and the city withheld $6,510 as liquidated damages from the contract price. B & B assigned the claim to this money to Portland Electric and Plumbing Company (PEPCo). PEPCo, as the assignee, filed suit against the City of Vancouver, alleging that the city had breached its contract with B & B by wrongfully refusing to pay $6,510 to B & B. Can PEPCo maintain the lawsuit against the City of Vancouver? *Portland Elec. and Plumbing Co. v. City of Vancouver*, 627 P.2d 1350 (Wash. Ct. App. 1981).

Critical Legal Thinking Case 7.6 *Delegation of Duties* C. W. Milford owned a registered Quarterhorse named Hired Chico. In March 1969, Milford sold the horse to Norman Stewart. Recognizing that Hired Chico was a good stud, Milford included the following provision in the written contract that was signed by both parties: "I, C. W. Milford, reserve 2 breedings each year on Hired Chico registration #403692 for the life of this stud horse regardless of whom the horse may be sold to." The agreement was filed with the county court clerk of Shelby County, Texas. Stewart later sold Hired Chico to Sam McKinnie. Prior to purchasing the horse, McKinnie read the Milford–Stewart contract and testified that he understood the terms of the contract. When McKinnie refused to grant Milford the stud services of Hired Chico, Milford sued McKinnie for breach of contract. Who wins? *McKinnie v. Milford*, 597 S.W.2d 953 (Tex. App. 1980).

Critical Legal Thinking Case 7.7 *Condition* Shumann Investments, Inc. (Shumann), hired Pace Construction Corporation (Pace), a general contractor, to build "Outlet World of Pasco County." In turn, Pace hired OBS Company, Inc. (OBS), a subcontractor, to perform the framing, drywall, insulation, and stucco work on the project. The contract between Pace and OBS stipulated: "Final payment shall not become due unless and until the following conditions precedent to final payment have been satisfied... (c) receipt of final payment for subcontractor's work by contractor from owner." When Shumann refused to pay Pace, Pace refused to pay OBS. OBS sued Pace to recover payment. Who wins? *Pace Constr. Corp. v. OBS Co.*, 531 So. 2d 737 (Fla. Dist. Ct. App. 1988).

ETHICS CASES

Ethics Case 7.1 Pabagold, Inc. (Pabagold), a manufacturer and distributor of suntan lotions, hired Mediasmith, an advertising agency, to develop an advertising campaign for Pabagold's Hawaiian Gold Pabatan suntan lotion. In the contract, Pabagold authorized Mediasmith to enter into agreements with third parties to place Pabagold advertisements for the campaign and to make payments to these third parties for the Pabagold account. Pabagold agreed to pay Mediasmith for its services and to reimburse it for expenses incurred on behalf of Pabagold. The Pabagold–Mediasmith contract provided for arbitration of any dispute arising under the contract.

In April 1981, Mediasmith entered into a contract with Outdoor Services, Inc. (Outdoor Services), an outdoor advertising company, to place Pabagold ads on billboards owned by Outdoor Services. Outdoor Services provided the agreed-upon work and billed Mediasmith $8,545 for its services. Mediasmith requested payment of this amount from Pabagold so it could pay Outdoor Services. When Pabagold refused to pay, Outdoor Services filed a demand for arbitration as provided in the Pabagold–Mediasmith contract. Pabagold defended, asserting that Outdoor Services could not try to recover the money because it was not in privity of contract with Pabagold.

Did Pabagold act ethically in refusing to pay Outdoor Services? From a moral perspective, does it matter that Outdoor Services and Pabagold were not in privity of contract? Who wins? *Outdoor Serv., Inc. v. Pabagold, Inc.*, 230 Cal. Rptr. 73 (Ct. App. 1986).

Ethics Case 7.2   Indiana Tri-City Plaza Bowl (Tri-City) leased a building from Charles H. Glueck for use as a bowling alley. The lease provided that Glueck was to provide adequate paved parking for the building. The lease gave Tri-City the right to approve the plans for the construction and paving of the parking lot. When Glueck submitted paving plans to Tri-City, it rejected the plans and withheld its approval. Tri-City argued that the plans were required to meet its personal satisfaction before it had to approve them. Evidence showed that the plans were commercially reasonable in the circumstances. A lawsuit was filed between Tri-City and Glueck. Who wins? Was it ethical for Tri-City to reject the plans? *Indiana Tri-City Plaza Bowl v. Estate of Glueck*, 422 N.E.2d 670 (Ind. Ct. App. 1981).

BRIEFING THE CASE WRITING ASSIGNMENT

Read Case A.7 in Appendix A (*Chase Precast Corporation v. John J. Paonessa Company, Inc.*). This case is excerpted from the appellate court opinion. Review and brief the case. After briefing the case, you should be able to answer the following questions:

1. Who were the contracting parties and what did their contract provide?
2. Why did the defendant not complete the contract?
3. What does the doctrine of frustration of purpose provide?
4. Did the doctrine of frustration of purpose excuse the defendant's nonperformance?

PRACTICE TIP

The number of days in the contract is very often an important term—for repayment, delivery of goods, and the like. The number of days set out in the contract could refer to the days *before* something is to be done or *after* something is to be done. Depending on the contract, the provision regarding the date could read as set out in one of the following two examples:

_____ will pay half of the total amount due within the thirty days *prior to* the delivery of the goods.

_____ will pay the remaining half of the total amount due within the thirty days *following* the delivery of the goods.

Contracts must not be sports of an idle hour,
mere matters of pleasantry and badinage, never
intended by the parties to have any serious
effect whatsoever.

—*Lord Stowell*

Dalrymple v. Dalrymple,
2 Hag. Con. 54, at 105 (1811).

Remedies for Breach of Traditional and E–Contracts

CHAPTER **8**

CASE SCENARIO

The law firm where you work as a paralegal is representing L.C., Inc., a large maker of sportswear in the United States. L.C. is a well-known name in fashion, with sales of over $1 billion per year. The company distributes its products through 9,000 retail outlets in the United States. Another company, Fragrance, Inc., is a major producer of fragrances, toiletries, and cosmetics, with annual sales of more than $3 billion a year. L.C., wanted to promote its well-known name on perfumes and cosmetics, so it entered into a joint venture with Fragrance, Inc. Under the contract, L.C. would make available its names, trademarks, and marketing experience, and Fragrance would engage in the procurement and manufacture of the fragrances, toiletries, and cosmetics. The parties agreed to equally share the financial requirements of the joint venture. During its first year of operation, the joint venture had sales of more than $16 million. In the second year, sales increased to $26 million, making it one of the fastest growing fragrance and cosmetic lines in the country. It is now one year later and Fragrance has refused to continue procuring and manufacturing the line of fragrances and cosmetics for the joint venture. The Christmas season is fast approaching, and L.C. has been unable to obtain the necessary fragrances and cosmetics from any other source.

CHAPTER OBJECTIVES

After studying this chapter, you should be able to:

1. Explain how *complete performance* discharges contractual duties.

2. Identify *inferior performance* and the *material breach* of a contract.

3. Describe *compensatory, consequential,* and *nominal damages*.

4. Define the *equitable remedies* of specific performance, reformation, and injunction.

5. Describe *torts* associated with contracts.

■ CHAPTER INTRODUCTION

The three levels of performance of a contract are *complete*, *substantial*, and *inferior*. Complete (or strict) performance by a party discharges that party's duties under the contract. Substantial performance constitutes a minor breach of the contract. Inferior performance constitutes a material breach that impairs or destroys the essence of the contract. Various remedies may be obtained by a nonbreaching party if a **breach of contract** occurs—that is, if a contracting party fails to perform an absolute duty owed under a contract.[1]

The most common remedy for a breach of contract is an award of **monetary damages**, often called the "law remedy." If a monetary award does not provide adequate relief, however, the court may order any one of several **equitable remedies**, including specific performance, reformation, and injunction. Equitable remedies are based on the concept of fairness.

This chapter discusses breach of contract and the remedies available to the nonbreaching party.

breach of contract
If a contracting party fails to perform an absolute duty owed under a contract.

monetary damages
An award of money.

equitable remedies
Remedies based on the concept of fairness, such as specific performance, reformation, and injunction.

PARALEGAL PERSPECTIVE

Karen Billieu is a graduate of the Paralegal Studies Program at the University of Cincinnati. She has been a paralegal for seven years. She currently works in the areas of probate and estate planning for the law firm of Katz, Greenberger & Norton LLP in Cincinnati, Ohio.

In the area of estate planning, I am responsible for drafting wills, powers of attorney, and advance directives for the attorney's review. Many of our clients wish to create revocable or irrevocable trust agreements or family limited liability companies for asset protection and probate avoidance. Because these are contracts, I am required to ensure that each document meets the statutory requirements for all contracts and adequately accomplishes the client's testamentary wishes.

In the area of probate, I am responsible for assisting the attorney in ensuring the decedent's wishes are carried out or, in the case of intestacy, that the estate is distributed according to statute. This may involve the sale of real estate, automobiles, and other personal property; however, occasionally, the sale, distribution, or liquidation of a business interest is required. I review all real estate listing contracts and purchase contracts and prepare fiduciary deeds for the attorney's review. Where a business interest is involved, I initially review all partnership or incorporation documents and report any requirements for sale or transfer of interest to the attorney and then draft or review the contracts or other documents required to affect the sale or transfer, for the attorney's approval.

The attorney relies on me to identify areas of concern or unusual requirements, to research all statutory requirements, to be the main contact for clients, and to maintain the timely progression of the probate of a decedent's estate or the completion of a client's estate plan. In this way, we are able to provide a more efficient and cost-effective service to our clients.

■ PERFORMANCE AND BREACH

If a contractual duty has not been discharged (i.e., terminated) or excused (i.e., relieved of legal liability), the contracting party owes an absolute duty (i.e., covenant) to perform the duty. As mentioned in the chapter introduction, the three types of performance of a contract are *complete performance*, *substantial performance* (or minor breach), and *inferior performance* (or material breach). These concepts are discussed in the following paragraphs.

---

[1]*Restatement (Second) of Contracts*, Section 235(2).

Complete Performance

Most contracts are discharged by the **complete**, or **strict, performance** of the contracting parties. Complete performance occurs when a party to a contract renders performance exactly as required by the contract. A fully performed contract is called an **executed contract**.

Note that **tender of performance** also discharges a party's contractual obligations. *Tender* is an unconditional and absolute offer by a contracting party to perform his or her obligations under the contract.

Example: Suppose Ashley's Dress Shops, Inc. contracts to purchase dresses from a manufacturer for $25,000. Ashley's has performed its obligation under the contract once it tenders the $25,000 to the manufacturer. If the manufacturer fails to deliver the dresses, Ashley's can sue it for breach of contract.

Substantial Performance: Minor Breach

Substantial performance occurs when there has been a **minor breach** of contract. In other words, it occurs when a party to a contract renders performance that deviates slightly from complete performance. The nonbreaching party may try to convince the breaching party to elevate his or her performance to complete performance. If the breaching party does not correct the breach, the nonbreaching party can sue to recover *damages* by (1) deducting the cost to repair the defect from the contract price and remitting the balance to the breaching party or (2) suing the breaching party to recover the cost to repair the defect if the breaching party has already been paid (see Exhibit 8.1).

Example: Suppose Donald Trump contracts with Big Apple Construction Co. to have Big Apple construct an office building for $50 million. The architectural plans call for installation of three-ply windows in the building. Big Apple constructs the building exactly to plan except that it installs two-ply windows. There has been substantial performance. It would cost $300,000 to install the correct windows. If Big Apple agrees to replace the windows, its performance is elevated to complete performance, and Trump must remit the entire contract price. However, if Trump has to hire someone else to replace the windows, he may deduct this cost of repair from the contract price and remit the difference to Big Apple.

Inferior Performance: Material Breach

A **material breach** of a contract occurs when a party renders **inferior performance** of his or her contractual obligations that impairs or destroys the essence of the contract. There is no clear line between a minor breach and a material breach. A determination is made on a case-by-case basis.

Exhibit 8.1 Remedy Where There Has Been Substantial Performance (Minor Breach)

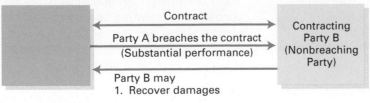

---

complete performance
Occurs when a party to a contract renders performance exactly as required by the contract; discharges that party's obligations under the contract.

executed contract
A contract that has been fully performed on both sides; a completed contract.

tender of performance
Tender is an unconditional and absolute offer by a contracting party to perform his or her obligations under the contract. Occurs when a party who has the ability and willingness to perform offers to complete the performance of his or her duties under the contract.

substantial performance
Performance by a contracting party that deviates only slightly from complete performance.

minor breach
A breach that occurs when a party renders substantial performance of his or her contractual duties.

material breach
A breach that occurs when a party renders inferior performance of his or her contractual duties.

inferior performance
Occurs when a party fails to perform express or implied contractual obligations that impair or destroy the essence of the contract.

Exhibit 8.2 Remedies Where There Has Been Inferior Performance (Material Breach)

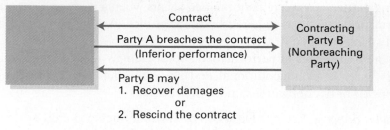

Where there has been a material breach of contract, the nonbreaching party may *rescind* the contract and seek restitution of any compensation paid under the contract to the breaching party. The nonbreaching party is discharged from any further performance under the contract.[2] Alternatively, the nonbreaching party may treat the contract as being in effect and sue the breaching party to recover *damages* (see Exhibit 8.2).

Example: Suppose a university contracts with a general contractor to build a new three-story building with classroom space for 1,000 students. However, the completed building can support the weight of only 500 students because the contractor used inferior materials. The defect cannot be repaired without rebuilding the entire structure. Because this is a material breach, the university may rescind the contract and require the removal of the building. The university is discharged of any obligations under the contract and free to employ another contractor to rebuild the building. Alternatively, the university could accept the building and deduct from the contract price damages caused by the defect.

Anticipatory Breach

anticipatory breach
A breach that occurs when one contracting party informs the other that he or she will not perform his or her contractual duties when due.

Anticipatory breach (or **anticipatory repudiation**) of contract occurs when the contracting party informs the other party in advance that he or she will not perform his or her contractual duties when due. This type of material breach can be expressly stated or implied from the conduct of the repudiator. Where there is an anticipatory repudiation, the nonbreaching party's obligations under the contract

---

Concept Summary

Types of Performance

Type of Performance	Legal Consequence
Complete performance	The contract is discharged.
Substantial performance (minor breach)	The nonbreaching party may recover damages caused by the breach.
Inferior performance (material breach)	The nonbreaching party may either (1) rescind the contract and recover restitution or (2) affirm the contract and recover damages.

---

[2]*Restatement (Second) of Contracts*, Section 241.

are discharged immediately. The nonbreaching party also has the right to sue the repudiating party when the anticipatory breach occurs; there is no need to wait until performance is due.[3]

In Case 8.1, the court found a breach of contract.

CASE 8.1 BREACH OF CONTRACT

Chodos v. West Publ'g Co., 292 F.3d 992 (9th Cir. 2002).

"Because West concedes that the manuscript was of high quality and that it declined to publish it solely for commercial reasons rather than because of any defect in its form and content, we hold as a matter of law that West breached its agreement with Chodos."

Judge Stephen Reinhardt, *U.S. Court of Appeals for the Ninth Circuit*

Facts

Rafael Chodos is a California attorney who specializes in the law of fiduciary duty, which includes a party's obligation to act honestly and with loyalty when performing his or her legal duties to another. Chodos sent a detailed proposal and table of contents to Bancroft-Whitney, the leading publisher of legal texts, to write a treatise on fiduciary duties. The editors at Bancroft-Whitney were enthusiastic about the proposal and sent Chodos a standard-form "author agreement" that set forth the terms of the publishing contract. Chodos was to be paid 15 percent of the gross revenues from the sales of the treatise. Chodos and Bancroft-Whitney signed the agreement.

For three years Chodos wrote the manuscript. He significantly limited the time spent on his law practice and spent over 3,600 hours writing the manuscript. During this time, Chodos worked with editors of Bancroft-Whitney in developing and editing the manuscript. Midway through this period, West Publishing Group purchased Bancroft-Whitney, and the two companies merged. The Bancroft-Whitney editors, now employed by West, continued to work with Chodos on editing and developing the manuscript. Three years after beginning, Chodos submitted the final manuscript to West. West editors suggested changes to the manuscript, which Chodos completed. West sent Chodos a letter, apologizing for delays in publication and assuring him publication would take place within three months.

However, one month after the promised publication date, Chodos received a letter from West's marketing department, stating that West had decided not to publish Chodos's manuscript because it did not "fit with [West's] current product mix" and because of concerns about its "market potential." West admitted, however, that the manuscript was of "high quality" and that its decision was not due to any literary shortcomings of Chodos's work. Chodos filed a lawsuit against West, alleging breach of contract. The U.S. District Court granted summary judgment in favor of West. Chodos appealed.

Issue

Did West Publishing breach the author agreement it had with Chodos?

---

[3]*Restatement (Second) of Contracts*, Section 253; UCC Section 2-610.

Language of the Court

The uncontroverted evidence in this case is that Chodos worked diligently in cooperation with West—indeed with West's encouragement—to produce a work that met the highest professional standard, and that he was successful in that venture. His performance was induced by an agreement that permitted rejection of the completed manuscript only for deficiencies in "form and content." Chodos thus labored to complete a work of high quality with the expectation that, if he did so, it would be published. He devoted thousands of hours of labor to the venture, and passed up substantial professional opportunities, only for West to decide that due to the vagaries of its internal reorganizations and changes in its business strategies or in the national economy or the market for legal treaties, his work, albeit admittedly of high quality, was for naught. It would be inequitable, if not unconscionable, for an author to be forced to bear this considerable burden solely because of his publisher's change of management, its poor planning, or its inadequate financial analyses at the time it entered into the contract, or even because of an unexpected change in the marketplace. Moreover, to allow a publisher to escape its contractual obligations for these reasons would be directly contrary to both the language and the spirit of the standard Author Agreement.

In sum, we reject the district court's determination that West acted within its discretion afforded it by the Author Agreement when it decided not to publish Chodos's manuscript. Because West concedes that the manuscript was of high quality and that it declined to publish it solely for commercial reasons rather than because of any defect in its form and content, we hold as a matter of law that West breached its agreement with Chodos.

Decision

The U.S. Court of Appeals held as a matter of law that West Publishing had breached its contract with Chodos. The court of appeals reversed the district court's summary judgment in favor of West, remanded the case to the U.S. District Court to enter summary judgment as to liability in Chodos's favor, and ordered further proceedings consistent with the opinion of the court of appeals.

Law & Ethics Questions

1. Should a court enforce the terms of a contract literally? Or should the court give contracts a broad interpretation, as requested by West Publishing?

2. **Ethics** Did West Publishing act ethically in this case? Should it have read Chodos's treatise on fiduciary duty before terminating its contract with Chodos?

3. If West Publishing wanted to reserve the right to terminate its contract with Chodos based on changes in its own marketing strategy, company reorganization, or changes in the marketplace, how should West have done so? What amount of money should West have paid Chodos?

Web Exercises

1. **Web** Visit the website of the Supreme Court of New York, Appellate Division, First Department, at www.courts.state.ny.us/courts/ad1.

2. **Web** Visit the website of West Group at www.westgroup.com.

3. **Web** Use www.google.com and find an article or case about a breach of a contract.

CAREER FRONT

Job Description: Business Formation Paralegal

A business formation paralegal can be involved with contracts relating to the formation of corporate entities in the following ways:

- Check name availability and reserve or register corporate name.
- Draft and file articles or certificate of incorporation.
- Draft bylaws.
- Draft notices of organizational meetings and resolutions to be adopted.
- Draft minutes of organizational meeting of incorporator(s), stockholders or board of directors, or written consents in lieu of meeting.
- Assemble and maintain corporate minute book.
- Order corporate seal.
- Draft documents necessary to issue stock certificates including subscription agreements, receipts, stock certificates, restrictive legends, investment letters, stock and stockholder registers, and trust agreements.
- Assist with the establishment of a bank account.
- Prepare and file application for federal employer identification number.
- Prepare and file appropriate state tax registrations, including workers' compensation and unemployment insurance.
- Prepare and file election by a small business corporation and draft stock-holder consents to such election.
- Prepare and file documents and forms necessary to secure appropriate local business licenses.
- Prepare and file assumed name certificates.
- Prepare and file appropriate applications for professional or special purpose corporations.
- Prepare and file appropriate Internal Revenue Service forms concerning the formation of nonprofit corporations.
- Draft employment agreements and confidentiality agreements for corporate officers and key employees.
- Draft stockholders agreement.
- Draft lease agreement.
- Draft buy-sell agreement.

Source: Excerpted by permission from the National Association of Legal Assistants (www.nala.org) and the National Federation of Paralegal Associations, Inc. (www.paralegals.org).

E-Commerce & Information Technology

Breach of an Internet Contract

A contract is a contract is a contract, even if it is over the Internet. Consider the following case. The Hotmail Corporation (Hotmail) is a Silicon Valley company that provides free e-mail on the Internet. Hotmail's online services allow its millions of registered subscribers to exchange e-mail messages on the Internet. The company registered the name "Hotmail" as a federal trademark and obtained the Internet domain name "hotmail.com." Every e-mail sent by a Hotmail subscriber automatically displays Hotmail's domain name and mark. To become a Hotmail subscriber, one must agree to abide by a Service Agreement by clicking an "accept" prompt on

(continued)

the computer screen. This click-wrap contract expressly prohibits subscribers from using Hotmail's services to send unsolicited commercial bulk e-mail, or "spam," or to send obscene or pornographic messages. The transmission of spam is a practice widely condemned by the Internet community.

In the fall of 1997, Hotmail discovered that defendants Van$ Money Pie Inc., ALS Enterprises, Inc., LCGM, Inc., and the Genesis Network, Inc., created Hotmail accounts that were facilitating their sending spam e-mail to Hotmail subscribers. The spam messages advertised pornography and "get-rich-quick" schemes, among other things. Hotmail was inundated with complaints from its subscribers who had received the spam, and faced the loss of customers as well as an overloading of its services from the spam e-mail.

Hotmail sued the defendants in district court for breach of contract and sought a preliminary injunction to enjoin the defendants from sending spam e-mail using Hotmail accounts, domain name, and mark. This district court agreed with Hotmail on its breach of contract claim, stating

> The evidence supports a finding that plaintiff Hotmail will likely prevail on its breach of contract claim and that there are at least serious questions going to the merits of this claim in that plaintiff has presented evidence of the following: that defendants obtained a number of Hotmail mail-boxes and access to Hotmail's services; that in so doing defendants agreed to abide by Hotmail's Terms of Service which prohibit using a Hotmail account for purposes of sending spam and/or pornography; that defendants breached their contract with Hotmail by using Hotmail's services to facilitate sending spam and/or pornogaphy; that Hotmail complied with the conditions of the contract except those from which its performance was excused; and that if defendants are not enjoined they will continue to create such accounts in violation of the Terms of Service.

The district court enforced the click-wrap contract and held the defendants in breach of Hotmail's Internet contract. The court issued a preliminary injunction prohibiting the defendants from using Hotmail accounts or Hotmail's domain name or mark to send spam. *Hotmail Corporation v. Van$ Money Pie, Inc.,* 47 U.S.P.Q. 1020 (N.D.Cal. 1998).

■ MONETARY DAMAGES

A nonbreaching party may recover **monetary damages** from a breaching party. Monetary damages are available whether the breach was minor or material. Several types of monetary damages may be awarded. These include *compensatory, consequential, liquidated,* and *nominal damages.*

Compensatory Damages

compensatory damages
An award of money intended to compensate a nonbreaching party for the loss of the bargain; they place the nonbreaching party in the same position as if the contract had been fully performed by restoring the "benefit of the bargain." Damages that are generally equal to the difference between the value of the goods as warranted and the actual value of the goods accepted at the time and place of acceptance.

Compensatory damages are intended to compensate a nonbreaching party for the loss of the bargain. In other words, they place the nonbreaching party in the same position as if the contract had been fully performed by restoring the "benefit of the bargain."

Example: Suppose Lederle Laboratories enters into a written contract to employ a manager for three years at a salary of $6,000 per month. Before work starts, the manager is informed that he or she will not be needed. This is a material breach of contract. Assume the manager finds another job, but it pays only $5,000 a month. The manager may recover $1,000 per month for 36 months (a total of $36,000) from Lederle Laboratories as compensatory damages. These damages place the manager in the same situation as if the contract with Lederle had been performed.

The amount of compensatory damages that will be awarded for breach of contract depends on the type of contract involved and which party breached the contract. The award of compensatory damages in some special types of contracts is discussed in the following paragraphs.

Sale of Goods

Compensatory damages for a breach of a sales contract involving goods are governed by the Uniform Commercial Code (UCC). The usual measure of damages for a breach of a sales contract is the difference between the contract price and the market price of the goods at the time and place the goods were to be delivered.[4]

Example: Suppose Revlon, Inc., contracted to buy a piece of equipment from Greenway Supply Co. for $20,000 and the equipment is not delivered. Revlon then purchases the equipment from another vendor but has to pay $25,000 because the current market price for the equipment has risen. Revlon can recover $5,000—the difference between the market price paid ($25,000) and the contract price ($20,000)—in compensatory damages.

Construction Contracts

A construction contract arises when the owner of real property contracts to have a contractor build a structure or do other construction work. The compensatory damages recoverable for a breach of a construction contract vary with the stage of completion the project is in when the breach occurs.

The contractor may recover the profits he or she would have made on the contract if the owner breaches the construction contract before construction begins.

Example: Suppose RXZ Corporation contracts to have the Ace Construction Co. build a factory for $1.2 million. It will cost Ace $800,000 in materials and labor to build the factory for RXZ. If RXZ Corporation breaches the contract before construction begins, Ace can recover $400,000 in "lost profit."

Example: Assume in the prior example that Ace Construction Co. had spent $300,000 on materials and labor before RXZ breached the contract. Here, Ace can recover $700,000—$400,000 lost profit plus $300,000 expended on materials and labor.

If the builder breaches a construction contract, either before or during construction, the owner can recover the increased cost above the contract price that he or she has to pay to have the work completed by another contractor.

Example: Suppose that in the previous instance Ace Construction Co., which had contracted to build the factory for RXZ for $1.2 million, breached the contract by refusing to build the factory. Assume that RXZ Corporation has to pay $1.5 million to have the same factory built by another contractor. RXZ can recover the increased cost of construction ($300,000) from Ace as compensatory damages.

Employment Contracts

An employee whose employer breaches an employment contract can recover lost wages or salary as compensatory damages. If the employee breaches the contract,

---

[4]UCC Sections 2-708 and 2-713.

THE ETHICAL PARALEGAL

Conflict of Interest

A conflict of interest exists whenever the attorney or any person represented by the attorney (i.e., a client) has interests adverse in any way to another client. Several ABA Model Rules—Rule 1.7 through Rule 1.13—address this essential element of loyalty in the attorney's relationship with the client. Paralegals can be of important assistance to the attorney and the law firm in making sure that conflict of interest checks are done.

However, a conflict of interest can be created in ways other than just the representation of two clients whose interests are adverse to each other. The acceptance of a gift can also be considered a conflict of interest in the attorney's dual role of *adviser* to a client and a *recipient* of a gift from a client.

Although the potential for conflict of interest is less when a client gives a paralegal a gift, the ethical paralegal knows to be cautious in these situations. A cautionary tale for this situation is set out in the case of *In Re Estate of Divine*, 635 N.E.2d 581 (Ill. App. Ct. 2004).

the employer can recover the costs to hire a new employee plus any increase in salary paid to the replacement.

Mitigation of Damages

mitigation of damages
When a contract has been breached, the law places a duty on the innocent non-breaching party to avoid and reduce the resulting damages.

If a contract has been breached, the law places a duty on the innocent nonbreaching party to take reasonable efforts to **mitigate** (i.e., avoid and reduce) the resulting damages. The extent of mitigation required depends on the type of contract involved.

If an employer breaches an employment contract, the employee owes a duty to mitigate damages by trying to find substitute employment. The employee is only required to accept *comparable employment*. The courts consider such factors as compensation, rank, status, job description, and geographic location in determining the comparability of jobs.

In Case 8.2, the court had to decide whether jobs were comparable.

CASE 8.2 MITIGATION OF DAMAGES

Parker v. Twentieth Century-Fox Film Corp., 474 P.2d 689 (Cal. 1970).

"The female lead as a dramatic actress in a Western-style motion picture can by no stretch of imagination be considered the equivalent of or substantially similar to the lead in a song-and-dance production."

Judge Burke, *Supreme Court of California*

Facts

Twentieth Century Fox Film Corporation (Fox), a major film production studio, entered into an employment contract with Shirley MacLaine Parker (Parker), an actress. Under the contract, Parker was to play the leading female role in a musical production called *Bloomer Girl*, to be filmed in Los Angeles. In the movie, Parker would be able to use her talents as a dancer and as an actress. The contract provided that Parker was to be paid guaranteed compensation of $53,571.42 per week for 14 weeks, for a total of $750,000. One month before filming was to start, Fox sent Parker a letter, notifying her it was not going to film *Bloomer Girl*. However, the letter offered Parker the leading female role in a film tentatively titled *Big Country*, which was a dramatic western to be filmed in Australia. The compensation Fox offered Parker was identical to that offered for *Bloomer Girl*. Fox gave Parker one week to accept. She did not, and the offer expired. Parker sued Fox to recover the guaranteed compensation provided in the *Bloomer Girl* contract. The trial court granted summary judgment to Parker. Fox appealed.

Issue

Was the job that Fox offered Parker in *Big Country* comparable employment that Parker was obligated to accept to mitigate damages?

Language of the Court

The general rule is that the measure of recovery by a wrongfully discharged employee is the amount of salary agreed upon for the period of service, less the amount that the employer affirmatively proves the employee has earned or with reasonable effort might have earned from other employment. However, before projected earnings from other employment opportunities not sought or accepted by the discharged employee can be applied, in mitigation, the employer must show that the other employment was comparable, or substantially similar, to that of which the employee has been deprived, the employee's rejection of or failure to seek other available employment of a different or inferior kind may not be resorted to in order to mitigate damages.

Applying the foregoing rules to the record in the present case, with all intendments in favor of the party opposing the summary judgment motion—here, defendant Fox—it is clear that the trial court correctly ruled that plaintiff's failure to accept defendant's tendered substitute employment could not be applied in mitigation of damages because the offer of the Big Country lead was of employment both different and inferior, and that no factual dispute was presented on that issue. The mere circumstances that Bloomer Girl was to be a musical review, calling upon plaintiff's talents as a dancer as well as an actress, and was to be produced in the City of Los Angeles, whereas Big Country was a straight dramatic role in a Western-type story taking place in an opal mine in Australia, demonstrates the difference in kind between the two employments. The female lead as a dramatic actress in a Western-style motion picture can by no stretch of imagination be considered the equivalent of or substantially similar to the lead in a song-and-dance production.

Decision

The supreme court held that the job that Fox offered to Parker in *Big Country* was not comparable employment to the role Fox had contracted Parker to play in *Bloomer Girl*. Therefore, Parker did not fail to mitigate damages by refusing to accept such employment. The supreme court affirmed the trial court's summary judgment in favor of Parker.

Law & Ethics Questions

1. Should nonbreaching parties be under a duty to mitigate damages caused by the breaching party? Why or why not?

2. **Ethics** Did Fox act ethically in this case? Did Parker?

3. Who is most likely to be able to mitigate damages when there is a breach of an employment contract: (1) the president of a large corporation, (2) a middle manager, or (3) a bank teller?

Web Exercises

1. **Web** Visit the Supreme Court of California at www.courtsinfo.ca.gov/courts/supreme.

2. **Web** Visit the website of Twentieth Century-Fox Film Corporation at www.foxmovies.com

3. **Web** Use www.google.com and find an article that discusses the doctrine of mitigation of damages.

Consequential Damages

consequential (special) damages
Foreseeable damages that arise from circumstances outside the contract. To be liable for these damages, the breaching party must know or have reason to know that the breach will cause special damages to the other party.

In addition to compensatory damages, a nonbreaching party can sometimes recover **consequential**, or **special, damages** from the breaching party. Consequential damages are *foreseeable* damages that arise from circumstances outside a contract. To be liable for consequential damages, the breaching party must know or have reason to know that the breach will cause special damages to the other party.

Example: Suppose Soan-Allen Co., a wholesaler, enters into a contract to purchase 1,000 men's suits for $150 each from Fabric Manufacturing Co., a manufacturer. Prior to contracting, the wholesaler tells the manufacturer that the suits will be resold to retailers for $225. The manufacturer breaches the contract by failing to manufacture the suits. The wholesaler cannot get the suits manufactured by anyone else in time to meet his contracts. He or she can recover $75,000 of lost profits on the resale contracts (1,000 suits × $75 profit) as consequential damages from the manufacturer because the manufacturer knew of this special damage to Soan-Allen Co. if it breached the contract.

CASE 8.3   LIQUIDATED DAMAGES

Super Valu Stores, Inc. v. Peterson, 506 So. 2d 317 (Ala. 1987).

Facts

Super Valu Stores, Inc. (Super Valu), a wholesale operator of supermarkets, developed a new concept for a market called "County Market." The basic concept of the County Market was that it must be the lowest-priced store in the marketplace and operate on a high-volume, low-profit margin structure. In 1981, Super Valu purchased a parcel of property in Oxford, Alabama, for the development of a County Market.

It planned to lease the store to an independent retailer to operate. Thomas J. Peterson, who was an executive of Super Valu, applied for the operator's position at the proposed store. In January 1984, Peterson was approved as the retail operator of the proposed Oxford County Market. On February 24, 1984, Peterson retired from Super Valu so that he could operate the new store. When Super Valu failed to construct and lease the store to Peterson, he sued Super Valu for breach of contract. The trial court held in favor of Peterson and awarded him $5 million in lost profits that would have been derived by him from the store. Super Valu appealed.

Issue

Are lost profits from an unestablished business recoverable as consequential damages even though it can be argued that they are inherently too speculative and conjectural?

Language of the Court

We are of the opinion that the jury's award of damages to Peterson is completely consistent with the law of Alabama and with the evidence in this case. Current Alabama law, like the law of other states, authorizes recovery of anticipated profits of an unestablished business, if proved with reasonable certainty. This general rule is applied in most states and is referred to as the "rule of reasonable certainty." This Court's explicit rationale for applying the reasonable certainty rule was its recognition that to disallow damages for loss of reasonably certain future profits would encourage breach of contract with new business. The rule in Alabama is that jury verdicts awarding lost profits will be affirmed if the plaintiff provides a basis upon which the jury could, with reasonable certainty, calculate the amount of profits that were lost as a result of defendant's wrongful actions.

The fundamental basis for Peterson's evidence as to damages was Super Valu's own projections of profits, produced in its normal course of business long before this dispute arose. These projections were the product of an intense, exhaustive process involving many different Super Valu personnel. Super Valu's projections resulted from the application of a scientific methodology that for many years had accurately predicted the future performance of stores associated with Super Valu. These projections were also based upon the prior successful performances of the Super Valu business system, of which the Oxford County Market would have become a standardized part. The jury could have found that Super Valu and Peterson relied upon these profit projections in making their initial decision to go forward with the Oxford County Market store.

Decision

The state supreme court held that lost profits from an unestablished business can be recovered as consequential damages if they can be determined with reasonable certainty. The court held that such damages were determined with reasonable certainty in this case and affirmed the trial court's judgment.

Law & Ethics Questions

1. Are lost profits too speculative to be awarded in breach of contract actions?

2. **Ethics** Did Super Valu act ethically by denying liability in this case?

3. If unestablished businesses could not recover lost profits, would there be more or fewer breaches of contract with such businesses?

Under certain circumstances, the parties to a contract may agree in advance to the amount of damages payable upon a breach of contract. These damages are called **liquidated damages**. To be lawful, the actual damages must be difficult or

liquidated damages
Damages to which parties to a contract agree in advance if the contract is breached. Damages that are specified in the contract rather than determined by the court. Damages that will be paid upon a breach of contract and that are established in advance

penalty
Punishment imposed by law (the penalty of imprisonment).

impracticable to determine, and the liquidated amount must be reasonable in the circumstances.[5] An enforceable liquidated damages clause is an exclusive remedy, even if actual damages are later determined to be different.

A liquidated damages clause is considered a **penalty** if actual damages are clearly determinable in advance or if the liquidated damages are excessive or unconscionable. If a liquidated damages clause is found to be a penalty, it is unenforceable. The nonbreaching party may then recover actual damages.

In Cases 8.4 and 8.5, the court had to decide whether a liquidated damages clause was enforceable.

CASE 8.4 LIQUIDATED DAMAGES

Uzan v. 845 UN Ltd. P'ship, 778 N.Y.S.2d 171 (App. Div. 2004).

> *"In his affidavit Donald Trump stated that he sought 25% down payments from pre-construction purchasers at the Trump World Tower because of the substantial length of time between contract signing and closing, during which period 845 UN had to keep the units off the market, and because of the obvious associated risks."*

> Judge Mazzarelli, *Supreme Court of New York, Appellate Division*

Facts

The Trump World Tower was a luxury condominium building to be constructed at 845 United Nations Plaza in Manhattan, New York. It would be New York City's highest residential building. 845 UN Limited Partnership (845 UN) began selling condominiums at the building before the building was constructed. Donald Trump is the managing general partner of 845 UN. The condominium offering plan required a nonrefundable down payment of 25 percent of the purchase price. The purchase contract provided that if a purchaser defaulted and did not complete the purchase, 845 UN could keep the 25 percent down payment as liquidated damages.

Cem Uzan and Hakan Uzan, brothers and Turkish billionaires, each contracted to purchase two condominium units on the top floors of the building. Cem and Hakan were both represented by attorneys and took two months of negotiations and many draft purchase agreements in which they obtained special consessions from 845 UN regarding the purchase of their units for a total cost of $32 million. Over the course of two years, while the building was being constructed, the brothers paid the 25 percent nonrefundable down payment of $8 million.

On September 11, 2001, before the building was complete, terrorists attacked New York City by flying two planes into the World Trade Center, the city's two tallest buildings, murdering thousands of people. Thereafter, the Uzans' attorneys delivered a letter to 845 UN stating,

> We believe that our clients are entitled to rescind their Purchase Agreements in view of the terrorist attack which occurred on September 11 and has not abated. In particular, our clients are concerned that the top floors in a "trophy" building, described as the tallest residential building in the world, will be an attractive terrorist target. The situation is further aggravated by the fact that the building

---

[5]*Restatement (Second) of Contracts*, Section 356(1).

bears the name of Donald Trump, perhaps the most widely known symbol of American capitalism. Finally, the United Nations complex brings even more attention to this location.

That day 845 UN sent Cem and Hakan default letters notifying them that they had 30 days to cure their default. Upon the expiration of the cure period, 845 UN terminated the four purchase agreements and kept the 25 percent down payments on the four condominiums as liquidated damages. Cem and Hakan sued 845 UN, alleging that the 25 percent nonrefundable down payment was an unenforceable and unconscionable penalty that should be returned to them. 845 UN defended, arguing that the 25 percent nonrefundable down payment was an enforceable liquidated damage clause. The trial court granted 845 UN partial summary judgment finding that Cem and Hakan had to forfeit a 10 percent down payment. 845 UN appealed.

Issue

Is the 25 percent nonrefundable down payment enforceable liquidated damages, or is it an unconscionable and unenforceable penalty?

Language of the Court

In his affidavit Donald Trump stated that he sought 25% down payments from preconstruction purchasers at the Trump World Tower because of the substantial length of time between contract signing and closing, during which period 845 UN had to keep the units off the market, and because of the obvious associated risks. Trump also affirmed that down payments in the range of 20% to 25% are standard practice in the new construction luxury condominium submarket in New York City.

It is clear that plaintiffs are not entitled to a return of any portion of their down payment. Here the 25% down payment was a specifically negotiated element of the contracts. There is no question that this was an arm's length transaction. The parties were sophisticated businesspeople, represented by counsel, who spent two months at the bargaining table before executing the amended purchase agreements.

Further, the record evidences that it is customary in the preconstruction luxury condominium industry for parties to price the risk of default at 25% of the purchase price. The purchase agreements included a detailed nonrefundable down payment clause to which plaintiffs' counsel had negotiated a specific amendment. That amendment allowed for the payment of 25% of the purchase price in three installments: 10% at contract, an additional 7 1/2% 12 months later, and a final 7 1/2% 18 months later. Clearly, plaintiffs were fully aware of and accepted the requirement of a nonrefundable 25% down payment for these luxury preconstruction condominiums.

The detailed provision concerning the nonrefundable deposit was integral to the transaction. If plaintiffs were dissatisfied with the 25% nonrefundable down payment provision in the purchase agreements, the time to have voiced objection was at the bargaining table. Because they chose to accept it, they are committed to its terms. Thus, upon plaintiffs' default and failure to cure, defendant was entitled to retain the full 25% down payments.

Decision

The appellate court held that the 25 percent nonrefundable down payment was an enforceable liquidated damage clause and not an unconscionable penalty. The appellate court, as a matter of law, granted 845 UN's motion for summary judgment, allowing 845 UN to keep Cem and Hakan's down payments, and dismissed their complaint.

Law & Ethics Questions

1. What are liquidated damages? What purpose is served by liquidated damages? Explain.

2. What is an unconscionable penalty? What are the consequences of finding that a liquidated damage clause is a penalty?

3. **Ethics** Was it ethical for Cem and Hakan to try to back out of the purchase agreements and get their money back? Do you think they had a good reason to do so?

4. What happened to the prices of high-rise condominiums and apartments in New York City after the terrorist attack?

5. **Ethics** Was it unethical for Donald Trump and 845 UN not to let Cem and Hakan rescind their purchase agreements and receive back their down payments?

Web Exercises

1. **Web** Visit the Supreme Court of New York, Appellate Division, First Department, at www.nycourts.gov/courts/ad1.

2. **Web** To view a photograph of the Trump World Tower in New York City, go to www.trumpworldtower.com.

3. **Web** Use www.google.com and find a video of the terrorist attack on the World Trade Center in New York City on September 11, 2001.

CASE 8.5 LIQUIDATED DAMAGES

California & Hawaii Sugar Co. v. Sun Ship, Inc., 794 F.2d 1433 (9th Cir. 1986).

"Promising to pay damages of a fixed amount, the parties normally have a much better sense of what damages can occur. Courts must be reluctant to over-rule their judgment."

Judge Noonan, *United States Court of Appeals for the Ninth Circuit*

Facts

The California and Hawaiian Sugar Company (C&H), a California corporation, is an agricultural cooperative owned by 14 sugar plantations in Hawaii. It transports raw sugar to its refinery in Crockett, California. Sugar is a seasonal crop, with about 70 percent of the harvest occurring between April and October. C&H requires reliable seasonal shipping of the raw sugar from Hawaii to California. Sugar stored on the ground or left unharvested suffers a loss of sucrose and goes to waste.

After C&H was notified by its normal shipper that it would be withdrawing its services at a specified date in the future, C&H commissioned the design of a large hybrid vessel—a tug of a catamaran design consisting of a barge attached to the tug. After substantial negotiation, C&H contracted with Sun Ship, Inc. (Sun Ship), a Pennsylvania corporation, to build the vessel for $25,405,000. The contract gave Sun Ship one and three-quarter years to build and deliver the ship to C&H. The contract also contained a liquidated damages clause calling for a payment of $17,000 per day for each day that the vessel was not delivered to C&H after the agreed-upon delivery date. Sun Ship did not complete the vessel until eight and a half months after the agreed-upon delivery date. Upon delivery, the vessel was commissioned and christened the *Moku Pahu*.

During the season the boat had not been delivered, C&H was able to find other means of shipping the crop from Hawaii to its California refinery. Evidence established that actual damages suffered by C&H because of the nonavailability of the vessel from Sun Ship were $368,000. When Sun Ship refused to pay the liquidated damages, C&H filed suit to require payment of $4,413,000 in liquidated damages under the contract. The district court entered judgment in favor of C&H and awarded the corporation $4,413,000 plus interest. Sun Ship appealed.

Issue

Is the liquidated damages clause enforceable, or is it a penalty clause that is not enforceable?

Language of the Court

Contracts are contracts because they contain enforceable promises, and absent some overriding public policy, those promises are to be enforced. Where each of the parties is content to take the risk of its turning out in a particular way, why should one be released from the contract, if there were no misrepresentation or other want of fair dealing? Promising to pay damages of a fixed amount, the parties normally have a much better sense of what damages can occur. Courts must be reluctant to over-rule their judgment. Where damages are real but difficult to prove, injustice will be done the injured party if the court substitutes the requirements of judicial proof for the parties own informed agreement as to what is a reasonable measure of damages. The liquidated damage clause here functions in lieu of a court's determination of the consequential damages suffered by C&H.

Proof of this loss is difficult. Whatever the loss, the parties had promised each other that $17,000 per day was a reasonable measure. The court must decline to substitute the requirements of judicial proof for the parties' own conclusion. The court will uphold the parties' bargain.

Decision

The court of appeals held that the liquidated damages clause was not a penalty and was therefore enforceable. The court of appeals affirmed the judgment of the district court in favor of C&H.

Law & Ethics Questions

1. Should liquidated damages clauses be enforced, or should nonbreaching parties be allowed to recover only actual damages caused by the breaching party?

2. **Ethics** Did either party act unethically in this case?

3. Do you think many businesses use liquidated damages clauses? Can you give some examples?

Web Exercises

1. **Web** Visit the website of the U.S. Court of Appeals for the Ninth Circuit at www.ca9.uscourts.gov.

2. **Web** Visit the website of C&H Sugar Company at www.chsugar.com.

3. **Web** Use www.google.com and find information about sugar plantations in Hawaii.

Nominal Damages

nominal damages
Damages awarded when the nonbreaching party sues the breaching party even though no financial loss has resulted from the breach; usually consists of $1 or some other small amount.

A nonbreaching party can sue a breaching party to a contract for nominal damages even if no financial loss resulted from the breach. **Nominal damages** are usually awarded in a small amount, such as $1. Cases involving nominal damages are usually brought on principle.

Example: Suppose Mary enters into an employment contract with Microhard Corporation. It is a three-year contract, and Mary is to be paid $100,000 per year. After Mary works for one year, Microhard Corporation fires Mary. The next day, Mary finds a better position at Microsoft Corporation, in the same city, paying $125,000 per year on a two-year contract. Mary has suffered no monetary damages but could bring a civil lawsuit against Microhard Corporation because of its breach and recover nominal damages ($1). Most courts disfavor nominal damage lawsuits because they use valuable court time and resources.

Enforcement of Remedies

writ of attachment
A document that orders a sheriff or other government officer to seize the breaching party's property, and to sell the property at auction to satisfy a judgment.

If a nonbreaching party brings a successful lawsuit against a breaching party to a contract, the court will enter a *judgment* in his or her favor. This judgment must then be collected. If the breaching party refuses to pay the judgment, the court may do the following:

- *Issue a writ of attachment*—A **writ of attachment** orders the sheriff or other government officer to seize property in the possession of the breaching

PARALEGAL PERSPECTIVE

Amy Gabbard graduated from the University of Arkansas Fort Smith with an A.A.S. in paralegal/legal assistance. She is certified by the National Association of Legal Assistants. She is currently employed as a real estate paralegal for Wal-Mart Stores, Inc.

I work for a large corporation handling real estate transactions from the initial purchase/lease of land through construction and the grand opening of stores. In my position, I deal with contracts daily. These contracts vary from purchase/lease agreements, development agreements, documents regarding covenants, and restrictions to letter agreements and easements.

Because I have over a hundred projects open at any given time, I take on the role of assisting my attorney in reviewing contracts as opposed to the initial drafting of them. It is important that I am aware of the elements of a contract, what constitutes consideration, the difference between words such as "shall" and "may," and the danger of ambiguous words such as "prefer." Overlooking something during this process could either void a contract or cause liability for the company.

Coming into the role of a real estate paralegal, I was apprehensive because I had no experience with real estate work. I relied on my strong background in contract law to succeed. Whether working in a position focusing on contracts or one focusing on another area of law, I feel the knowledge of contracts will be beneficial and useful to me in whatever I do.

Concept Summary

Types of Monetary Damages

Type of Damage	Description
Compensatory	Compensates a nonbreaching party for the loss of a bargain. It places the nonbreaching party in the same position as if the contract had been fully performed.
Consequential	Compensates a nonbreaching party for foreseeable special damages. The breaching party must have known or should have known that these damages would result from the breach.
Liquidated	Agreement by the parties in advance that sets the amount of damages recoverable in case of breach. These damages are lawful if they do not cause a penalty.
Nominal	Damages awarded against the breaching party even though the nonbreaching party has suffered no actual damages because of the breach. A small amount (e.g., $1) is usually awarded.

CONTEMPORARY Issue

JURISDICTION IN CONTEMPORARY CONTRACT LAW CASES

As a litigation paralegal knows, for a court to have personal jurisdiction over a defendant who is a nonresident, the defendant must be subject to a "long-arm statute." The extent of state long-arm statutes varies considerably among the states. However, most states specifically indemnify those types of contacts with the forum state that must be present for a court to exercise specific personal jurisdiction. E-mail and cyberspace issues have added a new dimension in determining jurisdiction in contract law cases.

Some states have created a sliding scale to determine jurisdiction issues arising out of these new technology issues. At one end are "active" websites where business is being done over the site and people in the forum state are encouraged or even enticed to interact with the website. At the other end are the "inactive" or "passive" websites where information is posted on a website. In those cases, the site is accesible to forum jurisdiction users, but there is no effort to do business nor do much more than make information available. The difficult cases are those in the middle, where there is some interaction or the possibility of interaction. Those cases require the courts to examine the level of interactivity and the commercialism of the website.

In one case, *CompuServe Inc. v. Patterson*,[6] the 6th Circuit required more than a passive website to establish minimum contacts for purposes of jurisdiction. In that case, the court found that Patterson had purposely availed himself of the laws of Ohio through his online activities. He entered into a contract with the plaintiff (the computer network service) in Ohio, used the plaintiff's Ohio-based service to market and sell his software, and maintained contacts with Ohio by sending messages by e-mail to the plaintiff in Ohio.

Although issues relating to long-arm jurisdiction issues created by e-mail and cyberspace may not yet be totally settled, the perceived outcome of the CompuServe case is that an individual who uses a computer network service to market a product should expect that disputes can be brought in the service's home state.

---

[6]*CompuServe, Inc. v. Patterson*, 89 F.3d 1257 (6th Cir. 1996), *rehearing en banc denied*, No. 95-3452, 1996 U.S. App. LEXIS 24796, at *1 (6th Cir. Sept. 19, 1996).

writ of garnishment
A document that orders the breaching party's wages, bank accounts, or other property held by a third party be paid over to the nonbreaching party to satisfy a judgment.

party that he or she owns and to sell the property at auction to satisfy the judgment.

■ *Issue a writ of garnishment*—A **writ of garnishment** orders that wages, bank accounts, or other property of the breaching party in the hands of third parties be paid over to the nonbreaching party to satisfy the judgment. Federal and state laws limit the amount of the breaching party's wages or salary that can be garnished.

■ RESCISSION AND RESTITUTION

rescission
An action to rescind (undo) the contract. Rescission is available if there has been a material breach of contract, fraud, duress, undue influence, or mistake.

restitution
Returning of goods or property received from the other party to rescind a contract; if the actual goods or property is not available, a cash equivalent must be made.

Rescission is an action to undo a contract. It is available where there has been a material breach of contract, fraud, duress, undue influence, or mistake. Generally, to rescind a contract, the parties must make **restitution** of the consideration they received under the contract.[7] Restitution consists of returning the goods, property, money, or other consideration received from the other party. If possible, the actual goods or property must be returned. If the goods or property have been consumed or are otherwise unavailable, restitution must be made by conveying a cash equivalent. The rescinding party must give adequate notice of the rescission to the breaching party. Rescission and restitution restore the parties to the positions they occupied prior to the contract.

Example: Suppose Filene's Department Store contracts to purchase $100,000 of goods from a sweater manufacturer. The store pays $10,000 as a down payment, and the first $20,000 of goods are delivered. The goods are materially defective, and the defect cannot be cured. This breach is a material breach. Filene's can rescind the contract. The store is entitled to receive its down payment back from the manufacturer, and the manufacturer is entitled to receive the goods back from the store. In Case 8.6, the court had to decide whether to order the rescission of a contract.

CASE 8.6   RESCISSION OF A CONTRACT

Hickman v. Bates, 889 So. 2d 1249 (La. App. 2004).

> *"The Court finds that Keith's failure to inform his young, limited, first cousin was intentional and was done to obtain an advantage over her. That is, of divesting her interest in 45 acres in Bienville Parish and 236 acres in Madison Parish for a pittance."*

> Judge Caraway, *Court of Appeal of Louisiana*

Facts

Patricia Dianne Hickman inherited half interests to two pieces of real property when her mother died. One of the properties, in Bienville Parish, Louisiana, contained 45 acres of woodland. The second property, in Madison Parish, Louisiana, contained approximately 236 acres of land and a house. Patricia was 20 years old and had a mental condition that required medication. Patricia, who lived separately from her parents, received a telephone call from her father, Joe Hickman, to come and visit him. Joe was ill with cancer and lived with his sister Christine Bates and her husband. They are parents of Keith Bates, Patricia's first cousin.

---

[7]*Restatement (Second) of Contracts*, Section 370.

The day after Patricia arrived, Joe informed Patricia that an important concern of his was for her to sell her interests in the two pieces of property to Keith Bates and his wife Sheila (the Bates). Joe expressed his doubts that Patricia would be able to maintain the properties and expressed his interest in keeping the property in the family. Patricia agreed to sell the properties to the Bates for $500. Patricia signed legal documents that had previously been drawn by an attorney prior to her arrival.

Subsequently, through a friend, Patricia sued the Bates to rescind the contracts selling her interest in the two pieces of property to them, alleging fraud. Expert testimony at trial valued the Madison Parish property at $259,000 and the Bienville Parish property at $20,700. The trial court found fraud and rescinded the contracts. The trial court did not, however, award Patricia attorneys fees. Both sides appealed.

Issue

Should the sales contracts be rescinded because of fraud and should Patricia be awarded attorneys fees?

Language of the Court

A contract is formed by the consent of the parties. However, consent may be vitiated by error, fraud, or duress. Fraud is a misrepresentation or a suppression of the truth made with the intention either to obtain an unjust advantage for one party or to cause a loss or inconvenience to the other. Fraud need only be proven by a preponderance of the evidence and may be established by circumstantial evidence.

In its very thorough and well-reasoned oral ruling, the trial court made the following findings of fact concerning its determination of fraud: "The court finds that Patricia's intellectual abilities are limited, both from her lack of education and from her mental condition that requires medicine. Considering her situation, her youth, she was then 20 years old, and her limited abilities, as well as her lack of prior knowledge of the purpose of the visit, and her father's illness, and the fact that she trusted her father and her cousin, the Court finds that Keith had a responsibility to make sure Patricia was informed fully about the transactions and make sure that she understood everything she was doing and the import of everything she was doing, including the fact that she would own nothing, and including the price considerations involved before she signed those documents. The Court finds that Keith's failure to inform his young, limited, first cousin was intentional and was done to obtain an advantage over her. That is, of divesting her interest in 45 acres in Bienville Parish and 236 acres in Madison Parish for a pittance."

We can discern no manifest error in these determinations. Accordingly, we find that the trial court committed no error in rescinding the sales on the ground of fraud. This portion of the judgment is affirmed. We reverse the trial court's ruling denying attorney fees and grant Patricia reasonable attorney fees through the time of this appeal in the amount of $12,000. Costs of this appeal are assessed to defendants-appellants.

Decision

The court of appeal affirmed the trial court's finding of fraud and its judgment rescinding the sales contracts by which Patricia sold her interests in the two properties to the Bates. The court of appeal reversed the trial court's denial of an award of attorney fees to Patricia and awarded $12,000 in attorney fees to Patricia.

Law & Ethics Questions

1. Describe the rescission of a contract.

2. Define fraud. Do you think fraud occurred in this case?

3. **Ethics** Did Patricia's father, Joe Hickman, and her first cousin, Keith Bates, act ethically in this case?

4. **Ethics** Did Patricia need the court's help in this case?

Web Exercises

1. **Web** Visit the website of the Court of Appeal of Louisiana, Second Circuit, at www.lacoa2.org.

2. **Web** Visit the websites of Bienville Parish, Louisiana, at www.lapage.com/parishes/bienv.htm, and Madison Parish, Louisiana, at www.lapage.com/parishes/madis.htm.

3. **Web** Use www.google.com and find a case where a contract was rescinded.

CONTEMPORARY Issue

MUST A WEDDING RING BE RETURNED IF THE ENGAGEMENT IS BROKEN OFF?

"[T]he inherent weaknesses in any fault-based system lead us to adopt a no-fault approach to resolution of engagement ring disputes."

Judge Newman

When a man and woman are in love, the man often asks the woman to marry him and presents her with an engagement ring. But engagements do not always lead to weddings and are sometimes broken off by one of the parties. Who gets the engagement ring? Does the woman get to keep the ring, or can the man recover it? Consider the following case.

Rodger Lindh (Rodger) proposed marriage to Janis Surman (Janis) and presented her with a diamond ring he purchased for $17,400. She accepted his proposal and ring. Discord developed in their relationship, however. Seven months after the engagement, Rodger called off the engagement. He asked Janis to return the engagement ring, but when she refused, Rodger sued her, seeking recovery of the ring. The Pennsylvania trial court and appellate court applied a no-fault rule and held that Janis must return the ring to Rodger. Janis appealed to the Pennsylvania Supreme Court.

The Pennsylvania Supreme Court noted that Janis favored the "fault" rule for deciding who gets the ring in a broken engagement case. Under this rule, if *she* breaks off the engagement, *he* gets the ring back; if *he* breaks off the engagement, *she* gets to keep the ring. Although noting that some states still follow this rule, the Pennsylvania Supreme Court stated that Pennsylvania would not follow the fault rule. The court noted that the process of determining who is "wrong" and who is "right" is difficult in modern relationships and that this would require parties to aim bitter and unpleasant accusations at each other.

Instead, the Pennsylvania Supreme Court decided to follow the modern, objective no-fault rule, which holds that an engagement ring must be returned to the donor, no matter who breaks off the engagement. The court stated,

(continued)

Courts that have applied no-fault principles to engagement ring cases have borrowed from the policies of their respective legislatures that have moved away from the notion of fault in their divorce statutes. We agree with those jurisdictions that have looked toward the development of no-fault divorce law for a principle to decide engagement ring cases, and the inherent weaknesses in any fault-based system lead us to adopt a no-fault approach to resolution of engagement ring disputes. We believe that the benefits from the certainty of our rule outweigh its negatives, and that a strict no-fault approach is less flawed than a fault-based theory.

The Pennsylvania Supreme Court affirmed the judgment of the lower courts, awarding the engagement ring to Rodger. *Lindh v. Surman*, 742 A.2d 643 (Pa. 1999).

Law & Ethics Questions

1. What does the fault rule regarding the return of engagement rings provide? Is there any difficulty in applying this rule? Explain.
2. What does the objective rule regarding the return of engagement rings provide?
3. **Ethics** Was it ethical for Roger to sue to get the engagement ring back when he broke off the engagement?
4. **Ethics** Was it ethical for Janis to keep the engagement ring after the engagement had been broken off?

Web Exercises

1. **Web** Visit the Supreme Court of Pennsylvania at www.courts.state.pa.us/ IndexSupreme.asp.
2. **Web** Use www.google.com and find what your state's law is regarding the return of an engagement ring if the engagement is broken off.

■ EQUITABLE REMEDIES

Equitable remedies are available if a breach of contract cannot be adequately compensated through a legal remedy. They are also available to prevent unjust enrichment. The most common equitable remedies are *specific performance, reformation,* and *injunction.*

Specific Performance

An award of **specific performance** orders the breaching party to perform the acts promised in a contract. The courts have the discretion to award this remedy if the subject matter of the contract is unique.[8]

Example: Specific performance is available to enforce land contracts because every piece of real property is considered unique. Works of art, antiques, and items of sentimental value, rare coins, stamps, heirlooms, and such also fit the requirement for uniqueness. Most other personal property does not.

Specific performance of personal service contracts is not granted because the courts would find it difficult or impracticable to supervise or monitor performance of such a contract.

Example: Brad contracts with Michael Angelo to paint a life-size portrait of Angie. Subsequently, Michael refuses to paint the painting. Brad cannot sue

specific performance
A remedy that orders the breaching party to perform the acts promised in the contract; usually awarded in cases where the subject matter is unique, such as in contracts involving land, heirlooms, and paintings. Judgment of the court ordering a licensor to specifically perform the license by making the contracted-for unique information available to the licensee. A decree of the court that orders a seller or lessor to perform his or her obligations under the contract; usually occurs when the goods in question are unique, such as art or antiques.

---

[8]*Restatement (Second) of Contracts*, Section 359.

Michael to paint the painting because specific performance would not be ordered. Brad could sue to recover any payments he has made to Michael.

Example: Brad contracts with Michael Angelo to paint a life-size portrait of Angie. Michael paints the painting, but, because he wants to keep his masterpiece, Michael refuses to deliver it to Brad. In this case, Brad can sue for specific performance and recover possession of the unique painting.

CONTEMPORARY Issue

HARD DEALING FOR THE HARD ROCK CAFE

In the 1970s, Peter Morton operated a popular restaurant and tourist attraction in England known as the "Hard Rock Cafe." At that time, Milton Okun of the United States inquired about investing in the business. Morton declined Okun's offer but indicated that if he contemplated expanding the business to the United States, he would contact Okun. In December 1981, Morton located a site suitable for a Hard Rock Cafe in Los Angeles, California. Morton contacted Okun and offered him stock in the general partnership. An agreement was executed on March 2, 1982, whereby Okun contributed $100,000 in exchange for a 20 percent interest in the general partnership. Paragraph 9 of the agreement gave Okun the option to participate in future Hard Rock Cafes with the same 20 percent interest.

After Morton raised funds from limited partners, the Hard Rock Cafe opened in the Beverly Center in Los Angeles and was a commercial success. As a result, Morton decided to exploit the San Francisco market. Per their agreement, Morton offered Okun a 20 percent interest, which Okun accepted.

In 1984, while Morton was finalizing plans for operating a Hard Rock Cafe in Chicago, Illinois, Morton and Okun had a disagreement. Morton advised Okun that he planned to exclude Okun from participating in the venture. Okun offered to participate on the terms of their 1982 agreement. Morton rejected that offer and proceeded with the development of restaurants in Houston, Honolulu, and Chicago without offering Okun a general partnership interest in these ventures. Okun sued Morton for breach of contract, seeking an order of specific performance of their 1982 agreement. The trial court held in favor of Okun and ordered specific performance of the contract. Morton appealed.

Can the 1982 agreement between Morton and Okun be specifically performed?

The court of appeals noted that as a whole, the terms of the agreement were sufficient to establish from the outset the ways in which future ventures were to be financed, owned, and operated by the parties. The fundamental structure of all such undertakings was to be based on the 20/80 ratio established for the creation of the L.A. Hard Rock Cafe. The court stated that although the agreement admittedly does not deal in specifics, neither law nor equity requires that every term and condition be set forth in the contract. In light of the fact that neither defendant nor plaintiff could predict with any degree of certainty the success of the Los Angeles operation, it is not surprising that Paragraph 9 was drafted broadly enough to accommodate changing circumstances and unforeseen developments.

Defendant asserts, however, that specific performance should not have been granted because enforcement of the contract will require continuous and protracted judicial supervision. The courts of this state have generally followed this "archaic" rule. This case merely involves the offering of an opportunity to

(continued)

participate in a business venture and the concomitant payment of capital and expenses for that participation.

The court stated, "We are not here concerned with the day-to-day management of any particular Hard Rock Cafe or related enterprises that would require the close and ongoing cooperation of the parties or the court." The defendant retains the discretion under the terms of the judgment to structure each venture as he pleases so long as he maintains the 20/80 ratio and does nothing to interfere with or burden plaintiff's right to participate in the deal. Under these circumstances, the court concluded that the decree of specific performance is not unduly burdensome nor requires inordinate supervision by the trial court.

The appellate court held that the subject matter of the agreement between Morton and Okun was unique and therefore that the agreement can be specifically enforced. *Okun v. Morton*, 203 Cal. App. 3d, 850 (1998).

In Case 8.7, the court had to decide whether to issue an order of specific performance.

CASE 8.7   SPECIFIC PERFORMANCE

Alba v. Kaufmann, 810 N.Y.S.2d 539 (App. Div. 2006).

"[T]he case law reveals that the equitable remedy of specific performance is routinely awarded in contract actions involving real property, on the premise that each parcel of real property is unique."

Judge Crew, *Supreme Court of New York, Appellate Division*

Facts

Jean-Claude Kaufmann owned approximately 37 acres of real property located in Rensselaer County, New York. The property is located in a wooded area and improved with a nineteenth-century farmhouse. Kaufmann and his spouse, Christine Cacace, reside in New York City and use the property as a weekend or vacation home. After Kaufmann and Cacace lost their jobs, their financial situation prompted Kaufmann to list the property for sale for $350,000.

Richard Alba and his spouse (Albas) were shown the property and offered the full asking price. The parties executed a contract for sale and the Albas paid a deposit, obtained a mortgage commitment, and procured a satisfactory house inspection and title insurance. A date for closing the transaction was set. Prior to closing, Cacace sent the Albas an e-mail indicating that she and Kaufmann had "a change of heart" and no longer wished to go forward with the sale. Albas sent a reply e-mail stating their intent to go forward with the scheduled closing. Cacace responded with another e-mail informing the Albas she had multiple sclerosis and alleging that the "remorse and dread" over the impending sale was making her ill. When Kaufmann refused to close, the Albas sued, seeking specific performance, and moved for summary judgment. The supreme court denied the motion. The Albas appealed.

Issue

Was an order of specific performance of the real estate contract warranted in this case?

Language of the Court

There must be a reversal. In order to establish their entitlement to summary judgment, the Albas were required to demonstrate that they substantially performed their contractual obligations and were ready, willing and able to fulfill their remaining obligations, that Kaufmann was able but unwilling to convey the property and that there is no adequate remedy at law. The Albas plainly discharged that burden here. After executing the underlying contract, the Albas paid a deposit, obtained a mortgage commitment, demonstrated that they had the financial wherewithal to purchase what was to be for them a vacation home, obtained a satisfactory home inspection and procured title insurance. In short, the record demonstrates that the Albas were ready, willing and able to close and, but for Kaufmann's admitted refusal to do so, would have consummated the transaction.

As to the remedy the Albas seek, the case law reveals that the equitable remedy of specific performance is routinely awarded in contract actions involving real property, on the premise that each parcel of real property is unique. Although certain defenses do exist including, insofar as is relevant here, unreasonable hardship, the court's discretion to grant or deny specific performance of a contract for the sale of realty is not unlimited; unless the court finds that granting a decree of specific performance would be a drastic or harsh remedy, or work injustice, the court must direct specific performance. Moreover, volitional unwillingness, as distinguished from good faith inability, to meet contractual obligations furnishes neither a ground for cancellation of the contract nor a defense against its specific performance.

Even accepting, for purposes of this discussion, that the alleged exacerbation of Cacace's symptoms is both genuine and causally related to the proposed sale of property, as she is not a party to the contract, her connection to the transaction is simply too attenuated for Kaufmann to claim undue hardship. In our view, permitting a third party who is not a signatory to a real estate contract, such as a spouse or, potentially, a child, sibling, or parent, to assert, via the titled owner, an undue hardship claim by voicing objection to or otherwise contending that the proposed sale is simply too much to bear would interject uncertainty and chaos into the otherwise orderly world of contract law. Simply put, permitting a defendant to raise an undue hardship defense under the circumstances present here would place a nearly impossible burden upon potential purchasers of real property namely, to ascertain whether any of the signatories' relatives had any potential objection to the sale in question.

Decision

The appellate court reversed the supreme court's denial of Albas' motion for summary judgment. The appellate court, as a matter of law, granted the Albas' motion for summary judgment and ordered Kaufmann to specifically perform the real estate contract.

Law & Ethics Questions

1. What does the doctrine of specific performance provide? Explain.

2. **Ethics** Was it ethical for the seller, Kaufman, to try to back out of the contract?

3. **Ethics** Should the Albas' knowledge of Cacace's health problems have led them not to sue for specific performance?

Web Exercises

1. **Web** Vist the website of the Supreme Court of New York, Appellate Division, Third Department, at www.courts.state.ny.us/ad3.

2. **Web** Use www.google.com and find an article or case where the doctrine of specific performance has been applied.

Reformation

Reformation is an equitable doctrine that permits the court to rewrite a contract to express the parties' true intentions.

Example: Suppose a clerical error is made during the typing of a contract, and both parties sign the contract without discovering the error. If a dispute later arises, the court can reform the contract to correct the clerical error to read as the parties originally intended.

reformation
An equitable doctrine that permits the court to rewrite a contract to express the parties' true intentions.

Quasi-Contract

A **quasi-contract** (also called *quantum meruit* or an *implied-in-law contract*) is an equitable doctrine that permits the recovery of compensation even though no enforceable contract exists between the parties because of lack of consideration, the Statute of Frauds has run out, or the like. Such contracts are imposed by law to prevent unjust enrichment. Under quasi-contract, a party can recover the reasonable value of the services or materials provided.

Example: Suppose a physician stops to render aid to an unconscious victim of an automobile accident. That physician could recover the reasonable value of his or her services from that person.

quasi-contract
An obligation created by the law to avoid unjust enrichment in the absence of an agreement between the parties.

Injunction

An **injunction** is a court order that prohibits a person from doing a certain act. To obtain an injunction, the requesting party must show that he or she will suffer irreparable injury if the injunction is not issued.

Example: Suppose a professional football team enters into a five-year employment contract with a "superstar" quarterback. During this five-year period, the quarterback

injunction
A court order that prohibits a person from doing a certain act.

Concept Summary

Types of Equitable Remedies

Type of Equitable Remedy	Description
Specific performance	Court orders the breaching party to perform the acts promised in the contract. The subject matter of the contract must be unique.
Reformation	A court rewrites a contract to express the parties' true intentions. It is usually used to correct clerical errors.
Injunction	A court prohibits a party from doing a certain act. Injunctions are available in contract actions only in limited circumstances.

MARKETPLACE

Job Announcement: Corporate Paralegal Hire

Corporate legal department of a NASDAQ-listed company is searching for an experienced paralegal with a general corporate, securities, intellectual property, and governance background. Qualified applicants will have a minimum of 7 years experience with progressive responsibility, and specific expertise, in:

- Preparing resolutions, minutes, by-laws, articles of incorporation, written consent agreements, and similar corporate governance documents for attorney review and execution;
- Identifying the requirements for, and preparing, all or certain substantive portions of all of the Company's public disclosure filings including Forms 3, 4, 8-K, 10-Q, 10-K, and Schedule 14(A);
- Contract administration;
- Supporting the Corporate Secretary by maintaining corporate records including minute books, stock and stock-based compensation records for company officers and directors, and administering the compensation payment program and the Company's related disclosure obligations;
- Managing bankruptcy claims on behalf of the Company with responsibility for the entire bankruptcy life-cycle, from filing a proof of claim to negotiating settlement agreements with the trustee; including preparing periodic reports on the status of claims for Company management;
- Managing the Company's intellectual property program and directing outside IP counsel as appropriate; and
- Document management

The successful candidate will also demonstrate:

- Strong listening and writing skills and an ability to see beyond a defined role and a strong understanding of how the paralegal position fits into the overall success of the Legal Department;
- A meticulous attention to detail;
- An ability to work in an environment that is unpredictable and with minimal supervision;
- A professional attitude and ability to function well as part of a small corporate legal team; and
- A sense of humor.

A degree from an accredited 4-year undergraduate institution and a paralegal certificate are required.

Please e-mail CV to:

---

breaches the contract and enters into a contract to play for a competing team. Here, the first team can seek an injunction to prevent the quarterback from playing for the other team.

■ TORTS ASSOCIATED WITH CONTRACTS

tort
A wrong. There are three categories: (1) intentional torts, (2) unintentional torts (negligence), and (3) strict liability.

The recovery for breach of contract is usually limited to contract damages. A party who can prove a contract-related **tort,** however, may also recover tort damages. Tort damages include compensation for personal injury, pain and suffering, emotional distress, and possibly punitive damages.

Generally, **punitive damages** are not recoverable for breach of contract. They are recoverable, however, for certain tortious conduct that may be associated with the nonperformance of a contract. These actions include fraud, intentional conduct, and other egregious conduct. Punitive damages are in addition to actual damages and may be kept by the plaintiff. Punitive damages are awarded to punish the defendant, to deter the defendant from similar conduct in the future, and to set an example for others.

The major torts associated with contracts are *intentional interference with contractual relations* and *breach of the implied covenant of good faith and fair dealing.*

punitive damages
Damages that are awarded to punish the defendant, to deter the defendant from similar conduct in the future, and to set an example for others.

Intentional Interference with Contractual Relations

A party to a contract may sue any third person who intentionally interferes with the contract and causes that party injury. The third party does not have to have acted with malice or bad faith. This tort, which is known as the tort of **intentional interference with contractual relations**, usually arises when a third party induces a contracting party to breach a contract with another party. The following elements must be shown:

1. A valid, enforceable contract between the contracting parties
2. Third-party knowledge of this contract
3. Third-party inducement to breach the contract

A third party can contract with the breaching party without becoming liable for this tort if a contracting party has already breached the contract because the third party cannot be held to have induced a preexisting breach.

intentional interference with contractual relations
A tort that arises when a third party induces a contracting party to breach the contract with another party.

CONTEMPORARY Issue

THE MEANING OF A HANDSHAKE

There is a substantial danger of being found liable for tortious conduct and being assessed punitive damages if one intentionally interferes with another's contract. Consider the celebrated case of *Texaco, Inc. v. Pennzoil Co.,* 729 S.W.2d 768 (Tex. App. 1987).

The saga began in 1983, when Pennzoil tried to buy up 20 percent of Getty Oil's (Getty) outstanding stock for $100 per share. At that time, about 40 percent of Getty's outstanding stock was owned by the Sarah C. Getty Trust (Trust), 11.8 percent was owned by the J. Paul Getty Museum in Los Angeles (Museum), and the rest was held by other investors.

On January 1, 1984, the head of the Trust met with representatives of Pennzoil. Pennzoil decided to make a play for total control of Getty by offering investors a buyout price of $110 per share. The Trust accepted a resolution approving Pennzoil's offer on January 3, 1984. Two days later, Getty, Pennzoil, the Trust, and the Museum issued a joint press release announcing that the parties had "agreed in principle" to a merger of Getty with Pennzoil. The parties shook hands and hoisted glasses of champagne to toast the deal. Nothing in writing had yet been signed by the parties, however.

Forty-eight hours later, the party was over. Texaco, Inc. (Texaco), had been tipped that Getty was for sale. Representatives of Texaco met secretly with some trustees of the Trust and officials from the Museum about how Texaco could structure a takeover of Getty. A written deal was reached whereby Texaco would purchase shares held by the Museum and the Trust for $125 per share

(continued)

and therby acquire more than 50 percent of Getty's outstanding shares in a $10-billion deal. Texaco completed its takeover of Getty.

Not surprisingly, Pennzoil was not pleased with Texaco's maneuver. On February 8, 1985, Pennzoil filed suit in Texas alleging that Texaco had tortiously interfered with its agreement with Getty. Pennzoil argued its handshake deal with Getty was a contract. It cited a Texas oil industry custom according to which handshakes were gentlemen's agreements that were to be honored. Texaco asserted that the argument wouldn't get Pennzoil to first base because the contract had to be formalized in writing to be enforceable.

Before the trial even began, Texaco accused Pennzoil's lawyer of impropriety for having given a $10,000 campaign contribution to the state court judge who was presiding in the case. Another Texas judge found no reason for the trial court judge to withdraw.

After a hard-fought trial, the jury held that the handshake between the Getty and Pennzoil people did count as a contract and that a definitive written agreement was unnecessary to seal the deal. After finding that such an agreement had indeed been reached, the jury moved on to the question of whether the tactics Texaco used to reach its takeover agreement were tortious. The jury found that Texaco had intentionally interfered with Pennzoil's agreement with Getty.

With the issue of liability resolved, the jury awarded a mind-boggling amount of money: $7.53 billion in actual damages. The jury heaped another $3 billion in punitive damages onto Pennzoil's award. This was the largest judgment in history. Texaco's appeals succeeded in getting the punitive damages reduced to $1 billion. Ultimately, to avoid the judgment, Texaco declared bankruptcy. Texaco emerged from bankruptcy one year later after the parties agreed to settle the entire matter for $3 billion. It is estimated that Pennzoil's lawyer, who had taken the case on contingency, earned a fee of approximately $600 million.

ETHICS SPOTLIGHT

INTERFERENCE WITH A CONTRACT

Ricardo E. Brown Jr., known as "Kurupt," was an unknown teenage rap singer who lived with his father. In 1989, Lamont Brumfield, a promoter of young rappers, "discovered" Kurupt. Lamont introduced his brother Kenneth Brumfield, who owned a music publishing business, to Kurupt. Beginning in 1990 Lamont produced demos for Kurupt, set up photo shoots, booked him to sing at many clubs, and paid for Kurupt's clothing and personal and living expenses. Kurupt lived with Lamont after Kurupt's father kicked him out of the house. In 1991, Lamont obtained recording work for Kurupt with the rap group SOS. In November 1991, Kurupt signed an exclusive recording agreement with Lamont's company, an exclusive publishing agreement with Kenneth's company, and a management agreement with Kenneth for an initial term of three years, with an additional option term. These contracts gave Kurupt 7 percent royalties on sales. The Brumfields spent at least $65,000 to support and promote Kurupt, often borrowing money from family and friends to do so.

Andre Young, known as Dr. Dre, invited Lamont, Kenneth, and Kurupt to a picnic, where he introduced them to Marion Knight, the owner of Death Row Records, Inc. The Brumfields and Kurupt made it clear to Dr. Dre and Knight that the Brumfields had exclusive contracts with Kurupt. After Kurupt performed at the picnic, Dr. Dre invited Kurupt to his house to record songs for Dr. Dre's album *Chronic*. In December 1992, *Chronic* was released by Death Row Records, Inc., and sold millions of copies. The Brumfields continued to promote Kurupt and to take care of his living expenses. When Dr. Dre invited Kurupt to go on tour to promote the *Chronic* album, Kurupt told the Brumfields he was going to visit family in Philadelphia but instead went on tour for four weeks. In 1993, Kurupt worked on another Death Row Records album. In May 1994, Kenneth exercised his option and renewed his management agreement with Kurupt.

Despite the multimillion-dollar profit of the *Chronic* album, the Brumfields were paid nothing by Death Row Records. At the end of 1994, Death Row moved Kurupt out of the condominium he shared with Lamont and into a house. While cleaning out the condominium, Lamont found papers showing that Death Row Records had paid Kurupt advances beginning in April 1993.

The evidence showed that Kurupt had breached the contracts he had with the Brumfields and had earned approximately $1.5 million in royalties from Death Row records for his work on the *Chronic* album and many other albums. The court held there was evidence that Death Row Records had caused Kurupt to breach these contracts and was therefore liable for the tort of intentional interference with a contract. The court held that defendant Death Row Records, Inc., had committed the tort of intentionally interfering with the contracts that the Brumfields had with rapper Kurupt. The court awarded $5,519,000 to the Brumfields, including $1.5 million in punitive damages to Lamont and $1 million in punitive damages to Kenneth. The judgment of the superior court was upheld by the Court of Appeals of California. *Brumfield v. Death Row Records, Inc.*, No. B149561, 2003 LEXIS 7843, at *1 (Cal. Ct. App. Unpub. Aug. 19, 2003).

Breach of the Implied Covenant of Good Faith and Fair Dealing

Several states have held that a **covenant of good faith and fair dealing** is implied in certain types of contracts. Under this covenant, the parties to a contract are not only held to the express terms of the contract but are also required to act in "good faith" and deal fairly in all respects in obtaining the objective of the contract. A breach of this implied covenant is a tort for which tort damages are recoverable. This tort, which is sometimes referred to as the **tort of bad faith**, is an evolving area of the law.

In Case 8.8, the court found a bad faith tort and awarded punitive damages.

convenant of good faith and fair dealing
Under this implied covenant, the parties to a contract not only are held to the express terms of the contract but are also required to act in "good faith" and deal fairly in all respects in obtaining the objective of the contact.

tort of bad faith
A breach of the requirement that the parties act and deal fairly in all respects in obtaining the objective of the contract.

CASE 8.8   BAD FAITH TORT

O'Neill v. Gallant Ins. Co., 769 N.E.2d 100 (Ill. App. Ct. 2002).

"Where an insurer is pursued for its refusal to settle a claim, "bad faith" lies in an insurer's failure to give at least equal consideration to the insured's interests when the insurer arrives at a decision on whether to settle the claim."

Judge Clyde L. Kuehn, *Appellate Court of Illinois*

Facts

On Halloween Day Christine Narvaez drove her automobile onto the parking lot of a busy supermarket. Narvaez had her two-year-old grandchild with her. The youngster was riding, unconstrained, in a booster seat. Narvaez saw a friend and decided to stop for a brief chat. She parked the car and exited the car, leaving the keys in the ignition and the motor running. The youngster crawled behind the wheel, slipped the car into gear, and set it in motion. The car struck Marguerite O'Neill, a woman in her eighties, pinned her between the Narvaez car and another car, and slowly crushed the woman's trapped body.

O'Neill was pried loose and airlifted to a hospital trauma center. O'Neill suffered a crushed hip, a broken arm, and four cracked ribs, and she lost more than 40 percent of her blood supply as a result of internal bleeding. She spent one month in the hospital intensive care unit and had to be placed in a nursing home and was deprived of the ability to live independently.

Narvaez carried the $20,000 minimum amount of liability insurance allowed by law. She was insured by Gallant Insurance Company. O'Neill's medical bills totaled $105,000. O'Neill sued Narvaez and her insurance company, Gallant. O'Neill's attorney demanded the policy limit of $20,000 from Gallant in settlement of O'Neill's claim and offered a complete release from liability for Narvaez. Three Gallant insurance adjusters, its claims manager, and the lawyer of the law firm representing Gallant for the case all stated to John Moss, Gallant's executive vice president, that Gallant should accept the settlement offer. Moss rejected their advice and refused to settle the case.

One year later, on the eve of trial, Moss offered to settle for the $20,000 policy limit, but O'Neill then refused. The case went to trial, and the jury returned a verdict against Narvaez of $731,063. Gallant paid $20,000 of this amount, closed its file, and left Narvaez liable for the $711,063 excess judgment. To settle her debt to O'Neill, Narvaez assigned her claims against Gallant to O'Neill. O'Neill then sued Gallant for a bad faith tort for breaching the covenant of good faith and fair dealing that Gallant owed to Narvaez to settle the case. The jury found Gallant liable for a bad faith tort and awarded O'Neill $710,063 ($1,000 short of the judgment in the first trial) in actual damages and $2.3 million in punitive damages. Gallant appealed.

Issue

Was Gallant liable for a bad faith tort?

Language of the Court

Where an insurer is pursued for its refusal to settle a claim, "bad faith" lies in an insurer's failure to give at least equal consideration to the insured's interests when the insurer arrives at a decision on whether to settle the claim. A significant part of the evidence presented against Gallant consisted of the pattern of conduct engaged in by Gallant over the five years leading up to this bad-faith action. O'Neill presented 44 known cases where Gallant's Illinois customers suffered excess judgments after Gallant passed up the opportunity to settle within the policy limits. Most of the excess judgments occurred on John Moss's watch. The dollar amount by which the excess judgments exceeded policy limits totaled $10,849,313.

The jury's finding of bad faith was not against the manifest weight of the evidence. We must side with O'Neill and against Gallant on the extent to which the evidence established the existence of reprehensible conduct on the part of Narvaez's insurance provider. If the term "reprehensible" means shameful, i.e., conduct deserving of severe reproach, Gallant's treatment of Narvaez and others who bought insurance from it, was truly reprehensible.

Decision

The appellate court held that Gallant was liable for a bad faith tort and upheld the trial court's judgment, awarding O'Neill $710,063 in actual damages and $2.3 million in punitive damages.

Law & Ethics Questions

1. Define the tort of breach of the implied covenant of good faith and fair dealing. Why is it called the "bad faith" tort?

2. **Ethics** Did Gallant act ethically in this case?

3. **Ethics** Will the implied covenant of good faith and fair dealing make insurance companies act more ethically toward their customers? Explain.

Web Exercises

1. **Web** Visit the website of the Appellate Court of Illinois at www.state.il.us/court/appellatecourt.

2. **Web** Use www.google.com and find an article or case that discusses a bad faith tort.

INTERNET EXERCISES AND CASE QUESTIONS

Working the Web Internet Exercises

1. Visit "LII: Law About ... Remedies" at www.law.cornell.edu/topics/remedies.html and "LII: Law About ... Commercial Law" at www.law.cornell.edu/topics/commercial.html, which includes information on consumer credit, damages, debtors and creditors, injunctions, and remedies.

2. Determine whether the following are provided in your state's UCC:
   - Good faith and reasonableness requirement
   - Right to stop goods in transit
   - Right to cover

CHAPTER 8 SUMMARY

PERFORMANCE AND BREACH, p. 206

Levels of Performance

1. *Complete performance.* A party in complete performance renders performance exactly as required by the contract. That party's contractual duties are discharged.

2. *Substantial performance.* A party in substantial performance renders performance that deviates only slightly from complete performance. There is a *minor breach*. The nonbreaching party may recover damages caused by the breach.

3. *Inferior performance.* A party in inferior performance fails to perform express or implied contractual duties that impair or destroy the essence of the contract. There is a *material breach*. The nonbreaching party may either (1) rescind the contract and recover restitution or (2) affirm the contract and recover damages.

Anticipatory Breach

In an anticipatory breach, one contracting party informs the other party—by express words or by conduct—that he or she will not perform his or her contractual duties when due. This gives an immediate cause of action to the nonbreaching party to sue for breach of contract. It is also called *anticipatory repudiation*.

MONETARY DAMAGES, p. 212

Monetary Damages

1. *Compensatory damages.* These damages compensate a nonbreaching party for the loss of a contract. They restore the "benefit of the bargain" to the nonbreaching party as if the contract had been fully performed.
2. *Consequential damages.* These are foreseeable damages that arise from circumstances outside the contract and of which the breaching party either knew or had reason to know. They are also called *special damages.*
3. *Nominal damages.* These are small damages awarded to a nonbreaching party who has suffered no financial loss because of the defendant's breach of contract. They are usually awarded on principle.
4. *Liquidated damages.* These are damages payable upon breach of contract that are agreed on in advance by the contracting parties. Liquidated damages substitute for actual damages. For a liquidated damage clause to be lawful, the following two conditions must be met:
   a. The actual damages must be extremely difficult or impracticable to determine.
   b. The liquidated amount must be a reasonable estimate of the harm that would result from the breach.

A liquidated damage clause is considered a *penalty* if actual damages are clearly determinable in advance or the liquidated damages are excessive or unconscionable. A penalty is unenforceable and the nonbreaching party may recover actual damages.

Mitigation of Damages

The law places a duty on a nonbreaching party to take reasonable efforts to avoid or reduce the resulting damages from a breach of contract. To mitigate a breach of an employment contract, the nonbreaching party must only accept "comparable" employment.

RESCISSION AND RESTITUTION, p. 224

Rescission and Restitution

Rescission is an action by a nonbreaching party to undo a contract. It is available upon the material breach of a contract. The parties must make restitution of the consideration they have received from the other party. Rescission and restitution restore the parties to the positions they occupied prior to the contract.

EQUITABLE REMEDIES, p. 227

Equitable Remedies

Equitable remedies are available if a nonbreaching party cannot be adequately compensated by a legal remedy or to prevent unjust enrichment.

1. *Specific performance.* This court order requires the breaching party to perform his or her contractual duties. It is available only if the subject matter of the contract is *unique.*
2. *Reformation.* Reformation permits the court to rewrite a contract to express the parties' true intention. It is available to correct clerical and mathematical errors.
3. *Injunction.* This court order prohibits a person from doing a certain act. The requesting party must show that he or she will suffer irreparable injury if the injunction is not granted.

TORTS ASSOCIATED WITH CONTRACTS, p. 232

Types of Torts Associated with Contracts

1. *Intentional interference with contractual relations.* When this tort is committed, a third party intentionally interferes with another party's contract and induces the other party to that contract to breach it, causing the nonbreaching party injury.
2. *Breach of the implied covenant of good faith and fair dealing.* When this tort is committed, a party to a contract does not act in good faith or fails to deal fairly in achieving the object of the contract. This duty is implied in only certain contracts (e.g., insurance contracts). It is also called the *tort of bad faith.*

Tort Damages

1. *Compensatory damages.* These include compensation for personal injury, pain and suffering, emotional distress, and other injuries caused by the defendant's tortious conduct.
2. *Punitive damages.* These are recoverable against a defendant for intentional or egregious conduct. They are awarded to punish the defendant, to deter the defendant from similar conduct in the future, and to set an example for others.

TERMS AND CONCEPTS

Anticipatory breach (anticipatory repudiation) 208

Breach of contract 206

Compensatory damages 212

Complete (strict) performance 207

Consequential (special) damages 216

Covenant of good faith and fair dealing 235

Equitable remedies 206

Executed contract 207

Inferior performance 207

Injunction 231

Intentional interference with contractual relations 233

Liquidated damages 217

Material breach 207

Minor breach 207

Mitigation of damages 214

Monetary damages 206

Nominal damages 222

Penalty 218

Punitive damages 233

Quasi-contract 231

Reformation 231

Rescission 224

Restitution 224

Specific performance 227

Substantial performance 207

Tender of performance 207

Tort 232

Tort of bad faith 235

Writ of attachment 222

Writ of garnishment 224

CASE SCENARIO REVISITED

Remember the case scenario at the beginning of the chapter involving L.C., Inc.? Now that you know more about the concept of specific performance, do you think it is an appropriate remedy in this situation? To help you with your answer, see the case *Liz Claiborne, Inc. v. Avon Prod., Inc.*, 530 N.Y.S.2d 425 (App. Div. 1988).

CRITICAL LEGAL THINKING CASES

Critical Legal Thinking Case 8.1 *Performance* Louis Haeuser, who owned several small warehouses, contracted with Wallace C. Drennen, Inc. (Drennen), to construct a road to the warehouses. The contract price was $42,324. After Drennen completed the work, some cracks appeared in the road, causing improper drainage. In addition, "birdbaths" that accumulated water appeared in the road. When Haeuser refused to pay, Drennen sued to recover the full contract price. Haeuser filed a cross complaint to recover the cost of repairing the road. Who wins? *Wallace C. Drennen, Inc. v. Haeuser*, 402 So. 2d 771 (La. App. 1981).

Critical Legal Thinking Case 8.2 *Anticipatory Repudiation* Muhammad Ali (Ali), a professional heavyweight boxer, successfully defended his heavyweight boxing championship of the world by defeating Ken Norton. Shortly after the fight, Ali held a press conference and, as he had done on several occasions before, announced his retirement from boxing. At that time Ali had beaten every challenger except Duane Bobick, whom he had not yet fought. Subsequently, Madison Square Garden Boxing, Inc. (MSGB), a fight promoter, offered Ali $2.5 million if he would fight Bobick. Ali agreed, stating, "We are back in business again." MSGB and Ali signed a fighters' agreement, and MSGB paid Ali a $125,000 advance payment. The fight was to take place in Madison Square Garden. Three months before the fight was to take place, Ali told MSGB that he was retiring from boxing and would not fight Bobick in February. Must MSGB wait until the date performance is due to sue Ali for breach of contract? *Madison Square Garden Boxing, Inc. v. Muhammad Ali*, 430 F. Supp. 679 (N.D. Ill. 1977).

Critical Legal Thinking Case 8.3 *Damages* Hawaiian Telephone Company entered into a contract with Microform Data Systems, Inc. (Microform), for Microform to provide a computerized assistance system that would handle 15,000 calls per hour with a one-second response time and with a "nonstop" feature to allow automatic recovery from any component failure. The contract called for installation of the host computer no later than mid-February of the next year. Microform was not able to meet the initial installation date, and at that time, it was determined that Microform was at least nine months away from providing a system that met contract specifications. Hawaiian Telephone canceled the contract and sued Microform for damages. Did Microform materially breach the contract to allow recovery of damages? *Hawaiian Tel. Co. v. Microform Data Sys. Inc.*, 829 F.2d 919 (9th Cir. 1987).

Critical Legal Thinking Case 8.4 *Damages* Raquel Welch was a movie actress who appeared in about 30 films over a 15-year period. She was considered a sex symbol, and her only serious dramatic role was as a roller derby queen in *Kansas City Bomber*. During that time period, Michael Phillips and David Ward developed a film package based on the John Steinbeck novella *Cannery Row*. Metro-Goldwyn-Mayer Film Company (MGM) accepted to produce the project and entered into a contract with Welch to play the leading female character, a prostitute named Suzy. At 40 years old, Welch relished the chance to direct her career toward more serious roles. Welch was to receive $250,000 from MGM, with payment divided into weekly increments during filming. Filming began, but three weeks later MGM fired Welch and replaced her with another actress, Debra Winger. Welch sued MGM to recover the balance of the $194,444 that remained unpaid under the contract. Who wins? *Welch v. Metro-Goldwyn-Mayer Film Co.*, 254 Cal. Rptr. 645 (Ct. App. 1988).

Critical Legal Thinking Case 8.5 *Damages* Ptarmigan Investment Company (Ptarmigan), a partnership, entered into a contract with Gundersons, Inc. (Gundersons), a South Dakota corporation in the business of golf course construction. The contract provided that Gundersons would construct a golf course for Ptarmigan for a contract price of $1,294,129. Gundersons immediately started work and completed about a third of the work by about three months later, when bad weather forced cessation of most work. Ptarmigan paid Gundersons for the work to that date. In the following spring, Ptarmigan ran out of funds and was unable to pay for the completion of the golf course. Gundersons sued Ptarmigan and its individual partners to recover the lost profits it would have made on the remaining two thirds of the contract. Can Gundersons recover these lost profits as damages? *Gundersons, Inc. v. Ptarmigan Inv. Co.*, 678 P.2d 1061 (Colo. Ct. App. 1983).

Critical Legal Thinking Case 8.6 *Liquidated Damages* H. S. Perlin Company, Inc. (Perlin), and Morse Signal Devices of San Diego (Morse) entered into a contract whereby Morse agreed to provide burglar and fire alarm service to Perlin's coin and stamp store. Perlin paid $50 per month for this service. The contract contained a liquidated damages clause limiting Morse's liability to $250 for any losses incurred by Perlin based on Morse's failure of service. Six years after the burglary system was installed, a burglary occurred at Perlin's store. Before entering the store, the burglars cut a telephone line that ran from the burglar system in Perlin's store to Morse's central location. When the line was cut, a signal indicated the interruption of service at Morse's central station. Inexplicably, Morse took no further steps to investigate the interruption of service at Perlin's store. The burglars stole stamps and coins with a wholesale value of $958,000, and Perlin did not have insurance against this loss. Perlin sued Morse to recover damages. Is the liquidated damages clause enforceable? *H.S. Perlin Co. v. Morse Signal Devices of San Diego*, 258 Cal. Rptr. 1 (Ct. App. 1989).

Critical Legal Thinking Case 8.7 *Liquidated Damages* United Mechanical Contractors, Inc. (UMC), an employer, agreed to provide a pension plan for its unionized workers. UMC was to make monthly payments into a pension fund administered by the Idaho Plumbers and Pipefitters Health and Welfare Fund (Fund). Payments were due by the 15th of each month. The contract between UMC and the Fund contained a liquidated damages clause that provided if payments due from UMC were received later than the 20th of the month, liquidated damages of 20 percent of the required contribution would be assessed against

UMC. In one month, the fund received UMC's payment on the 24th. The Fund sued UMC to recover $9,245.23 in liquidated damages. Is the liquidated damages clause enforceable? *Idaho Plumbers & Pipefitters Health & Welfare Fund v. United Mech. Contractors, Inc.*, 875 F.2d 212 (9th Cir. 1989).

Critical Legal Thinking Case 8.8 *Injunction* Anita Baker, a then-unknown singer, signed a multiyear recording contract with Beverly Glen Music, Inc. (Beverly Glen). Baker recorded for Beverly Glen a record album that was moderately successful. After having some difficulties with Beverly Glen, Baker was offered a considerably more lucrative contract by Warner Communications, Inc. (Warner). Baker accepted the Warner offer and informed Beverly Glen that she would not complete their contract because she had entered into an agreement with Warner. Beverly Glen sued Baker and Warner, and it sought an injunction to prevent Baker from performing as a singer for Warner. Is an injunction an appropriate remedy in this case? *Beverly Glen Music, Inc. v. Warner Commc'ns, Inc.*, 224 Cal. Rptr. 260 (Ct. App. 1986).

Critical Legal Thinking Case 8.9 *Intentional Interference with Contractual Relations* Pacific Gas and Electric Company (PG & E) entered into a contract with Placer County Water Agency (Agency) to purchase hydroelectric power generated by the Agency's Middle Fork American River Project. The contract was not terminable until 2013. As energy prices rose during the 1970s, the contract became extremely valuable to PG & E. The price PG & E paid for energy under the contract was much lower than the cost of energy from other sources. Ten years later, Bear Stearns & Company (Bear Stearns), an investment bank and securities underwriting firm, learned of the Agency's power contract with PG & E. Bear Stearns offered to assist the Agency in an effort to terminate the power contract with PG & E in exchange for a share of the Agency's subsequent profits and the right to underwrite any new securities issued by the Agency. Bear Stearns also agreed to pay the legal fees incurred by the Agency in litigation concerning the attempt to get out of the PG & E contract. Who wins and why? *Pacific Gas & Elec. Co. v. Bear Stearns & Co.*, 791 P.2d 587 (Cal. 1990).

ETHICS CASES

Ethics Case 8.1 Walgreen Company began operating a pharmacy in the Southgate Mall in Milwaukee when the mall opened. It had a lease for a 30-year term that contained an exclusivity clause in which the landlord, Sara Creek Property Company (Sara Creek), promised not to lease space in the mall to anyone else who wanted to operate a pharmacy or a store containing a pharmacy. With 11 years left on the Walgreen-Sara Creek lease, after its anchor tenant went broke, Sara Creek informed Walgreen that it intended to lease the anchor tenant space to Phar-Mor Corporation. Phar-Mor, a "deep discount" chain, would occupy 100,000 square feet, of which 12,000 square feet would be occupied by a pharmacy the same size as Walgreen's. The entrances to the two stores would be within a few hundred feet of each other. Walgreen sued Sara Creek for breach of contract and sought a permanent injunction against Sara Creek's leasing the anchor premises to Phar-Mor. Do the facts of this case justify the issuance of a permanent injunction? Did Sara Creek act ethically in not living up to the contract with Walgreen? *Walgreen Co. v. Sara Creek Prop. Co.*, 966 F.2d 273 (7th Cir. 1992).

Ethics Case 8.2 Rosina Crisci owned an apartment building in which Mrs. DiMare was a tenant. One day while DiMare was descending a wooden staircase on the outside of the apartment building, she fell through the staircase and was left hanging 15 feet above the ground until she was rescued. Crisci had a $10,000 liability insurance policy on the building from the Security Insurance Company (Security) of New Haven, Connecticut. DiMare sued Crisci and Security for $400,000 for physical injuries and psychosis suffered from the fall. Prior to trial, DiMare agreed to take $10,000 in settlement of the case. Security refused this settlement offer. DiMare reduced her settlement offer to $9,000, of which Crisci offered to pay $2,500. Security again refused to settle the case. The case proceeded to trial, and the jury awarded DiMare and her husband $110,000. Security paid $10,000, pursuant to the insurance contract, and Crisci had to pay the difference. Crisci, a widow of 70 years of age, had to sell her assets, became dependent on her relatives, declined in physical health, and suffered from hysteria and suicide attempts. Crisci sued Security for tort damages for breach of the implied covenant of good faith and fair dealing. Did Security act in bad faith? *Crisci v. Security Ins. Co. of New Haven, Conn.*, 426 P.2d 173 (Cal. 1967).

BRIEFING THE CASE WRITING ASSIGNMENT

Read Case A.8 in Appendix A (*E. B. Harvey & Company, Inc. v. Protective Systems, Inc.*). This case is excerpted from the appellate court opinion. After briefing the case, you should be able to answer the following questions:
1. What were Protective Systems' duties under the contract?
2. What amount of damages was Protective Systems liable for under the express terms of the contract?
3. Was Protective Systems negligent in this case?
4. What policy considerations did the court cite in upholding the liquidated damage clause?

PRACTICE TIP

A process sometimes known as "redlining" helps track changes made to drafts of a contract during the negotiation process. The paralegal must assist the attorney by making sure the other side does not make changes to the contract that go unnoticed. The redlining or "track changes" feature should be activated in the word processing software so changes are reviewed. Additionally, the paralegal should be certain that every new draft of the contract is dated. Redlining and dating are critical to ensure there is nothing in the contract that has not been thoroughly reviewed by the attorney.

Through the use of chat rooms, any person with a phone line can become a town crier with a voice that resonates farther than it could from any soapbox. Through the use of Web pages, mail exploders, and newsgroups, the same individual can become a pamphleteer.

–Justice Stevens

Reno v. American Civil Liberties Union,
521 U.S. 844 (1997).

E-Contracts and Internet Law | CHAPTER 9

CASE SCENARIO

The law firm where you work as a paralegal is representing James Holmes. James corresponded back and forth by e-mail with Gregory Lindblad regarding the purchase of a real estate parcel owned by James. In one of the last e-mails, James indicated that the price of $530,000 was final. Based on what he believed was an agreed-upon contract, James then applied for and received a mortgage loan for another parcel of real estate to which he planned to move.

■ CHAPTER INTRODUCTION

The use of the Internet and the World Wide Web, and the sale of goods and services through **e-commerce,** has exploded. Large and small businesses sell goods and services over the Internet through websites and registered **domain names.** Consumers and businesses can purchase almost any good or service they want over the Internet, using such sites as Amazon.com, eBay, and others. Businesses and individuals may register domain names to use on the Internet. Anyone who infringes on these rights may be stopped from doing so and is liable for damages.

In addition, software and information may be licensed either by physically purchasing the software or information and installing it on a computer or by merely downloading the software or information directly into the computer.

Many legal scholars and lawyers argued that traditional rules of contract law do not adequately meet the needs of Internet transactions and software and information licensing. These concerns led to an effort to create new contract law for electronic transactions. After much debate, the National Conference of Commissioners

e-commerce
The sale of goods and services by computer over the Internet.

domain name
A unique name that identifies an individual's or company's website .

CHAPTER OBJECTIVES

After studying this chapter, you should be able to:

1. Describe Internet domain names and how domain names are protected by the Anticybersquatting Consumer Protection Act.

2. Define an *e-contract* and a *software license.*

3. Describe the provisions of the Uniform Computer Information Transactions Act (UCITA).

4. Describe the provisions of the Federal Electronics Signatures Act and the Electronic Signature in Global and National Commerce Act.

5. Describe the federal laws that protect against cyber crimes.

Uniform Electronic Transactions Act (UETA)
A model act that—along with the UCITA—provides uniform and comprehensive rules for contracts involving computer information transactions and software and information licenses.

Uniform Computer Information Transactions Act (UCITA)
A model act that provides uniform and comprehensive rules for contracts involving computer information transactions and software and information licenses.

on Uniform State Laws developed the **Uniform Electronic Transactions Act (UETA)** and the **Uniform Computer Information Transactions Act (UCITA)**. These model acts provide uniform and comprehensive rules for contracts involving **computer information transactions** and software and information licenses.

The federal government has also enacted many federal statutes that regulate the Internet and e-commerce. Federal law has been passed that regulates the Internet and protects personal rights while using the Internet. In addition, many new federal criminal statutes were enacted to protect against cyber crimes.

This chapter covers Internet law, domain names, e-contracts, licensing of software, privacy laws, and criminal laws that regulate the Internet and online commerce. Most importantly, this chapter also covers the operation of Web businesses and explains how the UETA and UCITA and other laws regulate the creation, transfer, and enforcement of e-commerce and informational rights licensing contracts.

PARALEGAL PERSPECTIVE

Raeann Bromark is a graduate of Norwalk Community College's Paralegal Studies Program in Norwalk, CT. She works as a project paralegal for the law firm of Edward Angell Palmer & Dodge, L.L.P., in Stamford, CT.
I work in a law firm that represents clients in the areas of real estate, corporate, intellectual property, and litigation. My job involves working on any project that is needed throughout the office.

When I assist in the real estate area, I draft for attorney review all of the documents required to perform a closing. These documents include, but are not limited to, contracts needed, such as the purchase agreement, the deeds, and lease assignments.

When I am needed in the Corporate Department, I draft the paperwork to form new companies such as limited liability companies and corporations. I also draft the necessary documents needed for a merger and acquisition such as purchase agreements and lease assignments, both of which are contracts.

In intellectual property I do research needed to prepare trademarks and patents. Then I draft the trademark and patent paperwork for attorney review.

In addition to drafting contracts for attorney review, the attorneys I work with want me to review all contracts to ensure they are free from mistakes.

Based on my experience, regardless of the type of law paralegals work in, they will be dealing with some sort of contract.

computer information transactions
Under UCITA Section 102(a)(II), a computer information transaction "is an agreement to create, transfer, or license computer information or informational rights."

Internet
A collection of millions of computers that provide a network of electronic connections between computers.

■ THE INTERNET AND THE WORLD WIDE WEB

The **Internet**, or **Net**, is a collection of millions of computers that provide a network of electronic connections between the computers. Individuals and businesses use the Internet and the World Wide Web for communication of information and data, much of it related to commercial transactions and the resulting e-contracts.

The Internet

The Internet's evolution helped usher in the Information Age of today. The Internet began in 1969 when the U.S. Department of Defense created electronic communications for military and national defense purposes. Building on this start, in the 1980s the National Science Foundation, the federal government's main scientific and technical agency, established the Net to facilitate high-speed communications among research centers at academic and research institutions around the world.

Eventually, individuals and businesses began using the Internet for communication of information and data. In 1980, fewer than 250 computers were hooked to the Internet. Growth was rapid in the late 1990s and into the early 2000s, and today several hundred million computers are connected to the Internet.

The World Wide Web

The **World Wide Web** consists of millions of computers that support a standard set of rules for the exchange of information called hypertext transfer protocol (HTTP). Web-based documents are formatted using common coding languages. Businesses and individuals can hook up to the Web by registering with a service such as America Online (AOL).

Individuals and businesses can have their own websites. A website is composed of electronic documents known as Web pages. Websites and pages are stored on servers throughout the world, which are operated by **Internet service providers (ISPs).** They are viewed by using Web browsing software such as Microsoft Internet Explorer and Netscape Navigator. Each website has a unique online address.

The Web has made it extremely attractive to conduct commercial activities online. Companies such as Amazon.com and eBay are e-commerce powerhouses that sell all sorts of goods and services. Existing brick-and-mortar companies, such as Wal-Mart, Merrill Lynch, and Dell Computers, sell their goods and services online as well. E-commerce over the Web will continue to grow dramatically each year.

World Wide Web
An electronic connection of millions of computers that support a standard set of rules for the exchange of information.

Internet service providers (ISPs)
An operator maintaining a server upon which individuals and businesses can have their own websites.

INTERNET & TECHNOLOGY

Free Speech and the Internet

"Through the use of chat rooms, any person with a phone line can become a town crier with a voice that resonates farther than it could from any soapbox."

Justice Stevens

In 1997, the U.S. Supreme Court decided *Reno v. American Civil Liberties Union,* a major case involving free-speech rights over the Internet. In the case, the U.S. Supreme Court held that portions of a federal statute enacted by Congress, entitled the Communications Decency Act (CDA), that was designed to protect minors from "indecent transmissions" over the Internet, violated the free speech clause of the First Amendment to the U.S. Constitution.

In its decision, the Supreme Court recognized the importance and uniqueness of the Internet and issued an opinion guaranteeing the users of the Internet the highest constitutional free-speech protection. Excerpt of the language from the U.S. Supreme Court's opinion follows:

The Internet is an international network of interconnected computers. The Internet has experienced extraordinary growth. Individuals can obtain access to the Internet from many different sources, generally hosts themselves or entities with a host affiliation. Most colleges and universities provide access for their students and faculty; many corporations provide their employees with access through an office network. Several major national "online services" offer access to their own extensive proprietary networks as well as a link to the much larger resources of the Internet.

Anyone with access to the Internet may take advantage of a wide variety of communication and information retrieval methods. These methods are constantly evolving and difficult to categorize precisely. But, as presently constituted, those

(continued)

most relevant to this case are electronic mail ("e-mail"), automatic mailing list services ("mail exploders," sometimes referred to as "listservs"), "newsgroups," "chat rooms," and the "World Wide Web." All of these methods can be used to transmit text; most can transmit sound, pictures, and moving video images. Taken together, these tools constitute a unique medium—known to its users as "cyberspace"—located in no particular geographical location but available to anyone, anywhere in the world, with access to the Internet.

Each medium of expression may present its own problems. Thus, some of our cases have recognized special justifications for regulation of the broadcast media that are not applicable to other speakers. In these cases, the Court relied on the history of extensive government regulation of the broadcast medium, the scarcity of available frequencies at its inception, and its "invasive" nature. Those factors are not present in cyberspace. Neither before nor after the enactment of the CDA have the vast democratic fora of the Internet been subject to the type of government supervision and regulation that has attended the broadcast industry. Moreover, the Internet is not as "invasive" as radio or television. The District Court specifically found that "communications over the Internet do not invade an individual's home or appear on one's computer screen unbidden. Users seldom encounter content by accident." It also found that "almost all sexually explicit images are preceded by warnings as to the content," and cited testimony that "odds are slim that a user would come across a sexually explicit site by accident."

Unlike the conditions that prevailed when Congress first authorized regulation of the broadcast spectrum, the Internet can hardly be considered a "scarce" expressive commodity. It provides relatively unlimited, low-cost capacity for communication of all kinds. This dynamic, multifaceted category of communication includes not only traditional print and news services, but also audio, video, and still images, as well as interactive, real-time dialogue. Through the use of chat rooms, any person with a phone line can become a town crier with a voice that resonates farther than it could from any soapbox. Through the use of Web pages, mail exploders, and newsgroups, the same individual can become a pamphleteer. As the District Court found, "the content on the Internet is as diverse as human thought."

Systems have been developed to help parents control the material that may be available on a home computer with Internet access. A system may either limit a computer's access to an approved list of sources that have been identified as containing no adult material, it may block designated inappropriate sites, or it may attempt to block messages containing identifiable objectionable features. Although parental control software currently can screen for certain suggestive words or for known sexually explicit sites, it cannot now screen for sexually explicit images. Nevertheless, the evidence indicates that a reasonably effective method by which parents can prevent their children from accessing sexually explicit and other material which parents may believe is inappropriate for their children will soon be available.

The Government may not reduce the adult population to only what is fit for children. The CDA, casting a far darker shadow over free speech, threatens to torch a large segment of the Internet community. Notwithstanding the legitimacy and importance of the congressional goal of protecting children from harmful materials, we agree with the three-judge District Court that the statute abridges "the freedom of speech" protected by the First Amendment

Source: Reno v. American Civil Liberties Union, 521 U.S. 844 (1997).

Law & Ethics Questions

1. What did the federal Communications Decency Act (CDA) enacted by Congress try to do?
2. **Ethics** Should parents be responsible for their children's access to the Internet?
3. Do you agree with the following statement of the U.S. Supreme Court? "The Government may not reduce the adult population to only what is fit for children. The CDA . . . threatens to torch a large segment of the Internet community."

(continued)

E-Mail

Electronic mail, or **e-mail**, is one of the most widely used applications for communication over the Internet. Using e-mail, individuals around the world can instantaneously communicate in electronic writing with one another. Each person can have an e-mail address that identifies him or her by a unique address. E-mail will continue to grow in use in the future as it replaces some telephone and paper correspondence and increases new communication between persons.

In Case 9.1, the court addressed the liability of an ISP.

electronic mail (e-mail)
Electronic written communication between individuals using computers connected to the Internet.

CASE 9.1   INTERNET LAW

John Doe v. GTE Corp., 347 F.3d 655 (7th Cir. 2003).

"[A] web host cannot be classified as an aider and abettor of criminal activities conducted through access to the Internet."

Judge Easterbrook, *United States Court of Appeals for the Seventh Circuit*

Facts

Someone secretly took video cameras into the locker room and showers of the Illinois State football team. Videotapes showing these undressed players were displayed at the website univ.youngstuds.com operated by Franco Productions. The Internet name concealed the name of the person responsible. The GTE Corporation, an ISP, provided a high-speed connection and storage space on its server so the content of the website could be accessed. The nude images passed over GTE's network between Franco Productions and its customers. The football players sued Franco Productions and GTE for monetary damages. Franco Productions defaulted when it could not be located. Franco Productions was ordered to pay over $500 million in damages, though there is little hope of collection. The U.S. District Court dismissed the case against GTE. The football players appealed.

Issue

Is GTE Corporation, as the ISP, liable for damages to the plaintiff football players?

Language of the Court

The district court's order dismissing the complaint rests on 47 U.S.C. Section 230 (c)(1), a part of the federal Communications Decency Act of 1996. This subsection provides: *"No provider or user of an interactive computer service shall be treated as the publisher or speaker of any information provided by another information content provider." Just as the telephone company is not liable as an aider and abettor for tapes or narcotics sold by phone, and the Postal Service is not liable for tapes sold (and delivered) by mail, so a web host cannot be classified as an aider and abettor of criminal activities conducted through access to the Internet. GTE is not a "publisher or speaker" as Section 230(c)(1) uses those terms. Therefore, GTE cannot be liable under any state-law theory to the persons harmed by Franco's material.*

Decision

The court of appeals held that GTE Corporation, as an ISP, was not liable for the nude videos of the football players transmitted over its system by Franco Productions. The court of appeals affirmed the district court's order, dismissing the plaintiff football players' lawsuit against GTE.

Law & Ethics Questions

1. Why do you think Congress enacted Section 230(c)(1)? Explain.

2. **Ethics** Did the owner of Franco Productions act ethically in this case?

3. Will the taking and posting on the Internet of unconsented-to photographs of others escalate? Explain.

Web Exercises

1. **Web** Visit the U.S. Court of Appeals for the Seventh Circuit at www.ca7 .uscourts.gov.

2. **Web** Go to www.google.com and find an article that discusses free speech over the Internet.

■ DOMAIN NAMES

Most businesses conduct e-commerce by using websites that can be located on the Internet under domain names. Each website is identified by a unique Internet *domain name.*

Example: The domain name for the publisher of this book is www.prenhall.com.

Domain names can be registered. The first step in registering a domain name is to determine whether any other party already owns the name. For this purpose, InterNIC maintains a "Whois" database that contains the domain names that have been registered. The InterNIC website is located online at www.internic.net.

Domain names can also be registered at Network Solutions, Inc.'s, website, which is located at www.networksolutions.com, as well as at other sites. An applicant must complete a registration form, which can be done online. It costs less than $50 to register a domain name for one year, and the fee may be paid by credit card online.

Exhibit 9.1 lists the most commonly used top-level extensions for domain names.

Exhibit 9.1 Commonly Used Top-Level Extensions for Domain Names

- **.com.** This extension represents the word *commercial* and is the most widely used extension in the world. Most businesses prefer a .com domain name because it is a highly recognized business symbol.
- **.net.** This extension represents the word *network*, and it is most commonly used by ISPs, Web-hosting companies, and other businesses that are directly involved in the infrastructure of the Internet. Some businesses also choose domain names with a .net extension.
- **.org.** This extension represents the word *organization* and is primarily used by nonprofit groups and trade associations.
- **.info.** This extension signifies a resource website. It is an unrestricted global name that may be used by businesses, individuals, and organizations.
- **.biz.** This extension is used for small-business websites.
- **.us.** This extension is for U.S. websites. Many businesses choose this extension, which is relatively new.
- **.cc.** This extension was originally the country code for Coco Keeling Islands, but it is now unrestricted and may be registered by anyone from any country. It is often registered by businesses.
- **.bz.** This extension was originally the country code for Belize, but it is now unrestricted and may be registered by anyone from any country. It is commonly used by small businesses.
- **.name.** This new extension is for individuals, who can use it to register personalized domain names.
- **.museum.** This extension enables museums, museum associations, and museum professionals to register websites.
- **.coop.** This extension represents the word *cooperative* and may be used by cooperative associations around the world.
- **.aero.** This extension is exclusively reserved for the aviation community. It enables organizations and individuals in that community to reserve websites.
- **.pro.** This extension is available to professionals, such as doctors, lawyers, consultants, and other professionals.
- **.edu.** This extension is for educational institutions.

Web Exercises

1. Web go to www.networksolutions.com. See if your name is available in the .com and .name extensions.
2. Think up a name you would like to use for a business. Go to www.networksolutions.com and see if this business name is available in the .com extension.

INTERNET & TECHNOLOGY

Domain Name Anticybersquatting Act

In November 1999, the U.S. Congress enacted, and the president signed, the **Anticybersquatting Consumer Protection Act** [15 U.S.C. Section 1125(d)]. The act was specifically aimed at cybersquatters who register Internet domain names of famous companies and people and hold them hostage by demanding ransom payments from the famous company or person.

In the past, trademark law was of little help in this area, either because the famous person's name was not trademarked or because, even if the name was trademarked, trademark law required distribution of goods or services to find infringement, and most cybersquatters did not distribute goods or services but merely sat on the Internet domain name.

The 1999 act has two fundamental requirements: (1) The name must be famous and (2) the domain name must have been registered in bad faith. Thus, the law prohibits the act of cybersquatting itself if it is done in *bad faith.*

The first issue in applying the statute is whether the domain name is someone else's famous name. Trademarked names qualify; nontrademarked names—such as those of famous actors, actresses, singers, sports stars, politicians, and

(continued)

Anticybersquatting Consumer Protection Act
A law specifically aimed at "cybersquatters"—persons who register Internet domain names of famous companies and people and hold them hostage by demanding ransom payments from the famous companies or people.

such—are also protected. In determining bad faith, the law provides that courts may consider the extent to which the domain name resembles the holder's name or the famous person's name, whether goods or services are sold under the name, the holder's offer to sell or transfer the name, and whether the holder has acquired multiple Internet domain names of famous companies and persons.

The act provides for the issuance of cease-and-desist orders and injunctions by the court. In addition, the law adds monetary penalties: A plaintiff has the option of seeking statutory damages of between $1,000 and $300,000 in lieu of proving damages. The Anticybersquatting Consumer Protection Act gives owners of trademarks and persons with famous names a new weapon to attack the kidnapping of Internet domain names by cyberpirates.

Example: The Academy Award–winning actress Julia Roberts won back the domain name juliaroberts.com because it had been registered in bad faith by another party. The singer Sting was not so lucky because the word *sting* is generic, allowing someone else to register and keep the domain name sting.com.

In Case 9.2, the court applied the federal anticybersquatting act.

CASE 9.2   DOMAIN NAME

E. & J. Gallo Winery v. Spider Webs Ltd., 286 F.3d 270 (5th Cir. 2002).

"Spider Webs has no intellectual property rights or trademark in the name 'ernestandjuliogallo,' aside from its registered domain name."

Judge Jolly, *United States Court of Appeals for the Fifth Circuit*

Facts

Ernest & Julio Gallo Winery (Gallo) is a famous maker of wines located in California. The company registered the trademark "Ernest & Julio Gallo" in 1964 with the U.S. Patent and Trademark Office. The company has spent over $500 million promoting its brand name and has sold more than four billion bottles of wine. Its name has taken on a secondary meaning as a famous trademark name. In 1999, Steve, Pierce, and Fred Thumann created Spider Webs Ltd., a limited partnership, to register Internet domain names. Spider Webs registered more than 2,000 Internet domain names, including ernestandjuliogallo.com. Spider Webs is in the business of selling domain names. Gallo filed suit against Spider Webs Ltd. and the Thumanns, alleging violation of the federal Anticybersquatting Consumer Protection Act (ACPA). The U.S. District Court held in favor of Gallo and ordered Spider Webs to transfer the domain name ernestandjuliogallo.com to Gallo. Spider Webs Ltd. appealed.

Issue

Did Spider Webs Ltd. and the Thumanns act in bad faith in registering the Internet domain name ernestandjuliogallo.com?

Language of the Court

Spider Webs does not appeal the holdings that Gallo had a valid registration in its mark, that the mark is famous and distinctive, and that the domain name registered by Spider Webs is identical or confusingly similar to Gallo's mark. However, Spider Webs argues that they did not act with a "bad faith intent to profit," as required by the ACPA.

Spider Webs has no intellectual property rights or trademark in the name "ernestandjuliogallo," aside from its registered domain name. The domain name does not contain the name of Spider Webs or any of the other defendants. Spider Webs had no prior use or any current use of the domain name in connection with the bona fide offering of goods or services. Steve Thumann admitted that the domain name was valuable and that they hoped Gallo would contact them so that they could "assist" Gallo in some way. There is uncontradicted evidence that Spider Webs was engaged in commerce in the selling of domain names and that they hoped to sell this domain name some day.

There was evidence presented that Gallo's mark is distinctive and famous. Further, Gallo registered the mark, which is a family name, thirty-eight years ago, and other courts have found that "'Gallo' has clearly become associated with wine in the United States such that its evolution to 'secondary meaning' status may not be seriously questioned." The circumstances of this case all indicate that Spider Webs knew Gallo had a famous mark in which Gallo had built up goodwill, and that they hoped to profit from this by registering "ernestandjuliogallo.com" and waiting for Gallo to contact them so they could "assist" Gallo. In sum, the factors strongly support a finding of bad faith.

Decision

The U.S. Court of Appeals held that the name Ernest and Julio Gallo was a famous trademark name and that Spider Web Ltd. and the Thumanns acted in bad faith when they registered the Internet domain name ernestandjuliogallo .com. The U.S. Court of Appeals upheld the U.S. District Court's decision, ordering the defendants to transfer the domain name to plaintiff E. & J. Gallo Winery.

Law & Ethics Questions

1. What does the Anticybersquatting Consumer Protection Act (ACPA) provide? Explain.

2. **Ethics** Did the defendants act ethically in registering so many Internet domain names? What was the motive of the defendants?

3. How valuable is a company's trademark name? Does the ACPA protect that value? Explain.

Web Exercises

1. **Web** Visit the website of the U.S. Court of Appeals for the Fifth Circuit at www.ca5.uscourts.gov.

2. **Web** Visit the website of the E. & J. Gallo Winery at www.gallo.com.

INTERNET & TECHNOLOGY

World Intellectual Property Organization (WIPO)

An international arbitration and mediation center where domain owners can bring actions to recover a domain name.

Armani Outmaneuvered for Domain Name

G. A. Modefine S. A. is the owner of the famous "Armani" trademark, under which it produces and sells upscale and high-priced apparel. The Armani label is recognized worldwide. But Modefine was surprised when it tried to register for the domain name armani.com and found that it had already been taken. Modefine brought an arbitration action in the **World Intellectual Property Organization (WIPO)**, an international arbitration and mediation center, against the domain name owner to recover the armani.com domain name. To win, Modefine had to prove the domain name was identical or confusingly similar to its trademark, the owner who registered the name did not have a legitimate interest in the name, and the owner registered the name in bad faith.

The person who owned the domain name, Anand Ramnath Mani, appeared at the proceeding and defended his ownership rights. The arbitrator found that Modefine's trademark and Mr. Mani's domain name were identical but held that Mr. Mani had a legitimate claim to the domain name. The arbitrator wrote that it is "common practice for people to register domain names which are based upon initials and a name, acronyms or otherwise variants of their full names." The court rejected Modefine's claim that Mr. Mani's offer to sell the name for $1,935 constituted bad faith. The arbitrator ruled against Modefine and permitted Mr. Mani to own the domain name armani.com. *G. A. Modefine S.A. v. A. R. Mani*, No. D2001-0537 WIPO (2001).

Law & Ethics Questions

1. **Ethics** Did Mr. Anand Ramnath Mani have a legitimate reason for having registered the domain name www.armani.com?
2. **Ethics** Did G. A. Modefine S. A., the owner of the "Armani" trademark, have a legitimate claim to recover the domain name armani.com? Explain.

Web Exercise

1. **Web** Go to the website www.armani.com. Who owns this website today?

INTERNET & TECHNOLOGY

Domain Names Sold for Millions

What is a domain name worth? In some cases, plenty. Take the case of the domain name www.business.com. This name, which was originally registered as a domain name for less than $50, was sold to another purchaser for $150,000 in 1996. Many people at the time thought this was an outrageous sum to pay for a domain name—that is, until the second purchaser turned around and resold the name to ECompanies for $7,500,000.

Other domain names have been sold at high prices too.

Example: The domain name www.altavista.com was purchased by Compaq Computer for its Internet search engine. Other domain names sold for high prices include www.wine.com for $3 million, www.bingo.com for $1.1 million, www.wallstreet.com for $1 million, and www.drugs.com for $800,000.

(continued)

The highest price paid for a domain name was paid for the domain name www.sex.com. Gary Kremen had purchased the name in 1996 for next to nothing. In 2006, Kremen sold the name to Escom for the record price of $14 million.

As commerce over the Internet increases, unregistered memorable domain names become harder to find. The sale of the better domain names has increased, with multimillion-dollar price tags being paid for the most desirable names—which were originally registered for less than $100.

Web Exercise

1. **Web** Use www.google.com and find an article that discusses the sale of a domain name. What was the domain name, and what price was it sold for?

CAREER FRONT

Business Franchise Paralegal

A business franchise paralegal can be involved with contracts in the following ways:

- Draft franchise agreement and related agreements/contracts.
- Draft Federal Trade Commission (FTC) disclosure statements and franchise offering circulars.
- Compile information for inclusion in FTC disclosure statements and franchise offering circulars.
- File offering circulars, annual reports, and amendments in registration states.
- File notices of intent to sell franchises/business opportunities or exemption notices in registration states.
- Communicate with state regulators about registration/disclosure requirements.
- Review and file advertising/promotional materials with registration states.
- Administer disclosure process of prospective franchisees.
- Draft franchise documents for execution.
- Communicate with client or franchisee about execution of documents.
- Communicate with client or franchisee about compliance with franchise agreement.
- Draft default notices to franchisees.
- Monitor franchisee compliance with terms of franchise and other agreements.
- Write policies for disclosure and franchising processes.
- Monitor activities of franchise salespeople.
- Prepare earnings claims information to give to franchisees.
- Review requests for transfer of franchise and prepare documents for execution.
- Draft documents for repurchasing franchise business.
- Draft documents for terminating franchise agreement.
- Maintain repository and/or database of franchise activity.
- Review and draft documents for franchisee financing.

Source: Excerpted by permission from the National Association of Legal Assistants (www.nala.org) and the National Federation of Paralegal Associations, Inc. (www.paralegals.org).

■ E-CONTRACTS

E-mail and the Web have exploded as means of personal and business communication. In the business environment, e-mail and the Web are sometimes the methods used to negotiate and agree on contract terms and to send and agree to a final contract. Are e-mail and Web contracts enforceable? Assuming all the elements to establish a contract are present, an **e-mail** or **Web contract** is valid and enforceable. The main problem in a lawsuit seeking to enforce an e-mail or Web contract is evidence, but this problem, which exists in almost all lawsuits, can be overcome by printing out the e-mail or Web contract and its prior e-mail or Web negotiations, if necessary.

Electronic Signature in Global and National Commerce Act (SIGN Act)
A federal statute designed to recognize electronic contracts as meeting the writing requirement of the Statute of Frauds for most contracts.

INTERNET & TECHNOLOGY

E-Contracts Writing Requirement

In 2000, the federal government enacted the **Electronic Signature in Global and National Commerce Act (SIGN Act)**. This act is a federal statute enacted by Congress and therefore has national reach. The act is designed to place the world of electronic commerce on a par with the world of paper contracts in the United States.

One of the main features of the act is that it recognizes electronic contracts as meeting the writing requirement of the Statute of Frauds for most contracts. Statutes of Frauds are state laws that require certain types of contracts to be in writing. The 2000 federal act provides that electronically signed contracts cannot be denied effect because they are in electronic form or delivered electronically. The act also provides that record retention requirements are satisfied if the records are stored electronically.

The federal law was passed with several provisions to protect consumers. First, consumers must consent to receiving electronic records and contracts. Second, to receive electronic records, consumers must be able to demonstrate they have access to the electronic records. Third, businesses must tell consumers they have the right to receive hard-copy documents of their transaction.

Law & Ethics Questions

1. What do state Statutes of Frauds provide?
2. What does the federal SIGN Act provide regarding electronic contracts? Explain.
3. **Ethics** Does the rule of the federal act promote fraud? Why or why not?

INTERNET & TECHNOLOGY

E-Signatures

In the past, signatures have been hand-applied by the person signing the document. No more. In the electronic commerce world, it is now "What is your mother's maiden name?" "Slide your smart card in the sensor," or "Look into the iris scanner." But are electronic signatures sufficient to form an enforceable contract? In 2000, the federal government stepped into the breach and enacted the Electronic Signature in Global and National Commerce Act (SIGN Act).

(continued)

One of the main features of this federal law is that it recognizes an *electronic signature*, or *e-signature*. The act gives an e-signature the same force and effect as a pen-inscribed signature on paper. The act is technology neutral, however, in that the law does not define or decide which technologies should be used to create a legally binding signature in cyberspace. Loosely defined, a *digital signature* is some electronic method that identifies an individual. The challenge is to make sure that someone who uses a digital signature is the person he or she claims to be. The act provides that a digital signature can basically be verified in one of three ways:

1. By something the signatory knows, such as a secret password, pet's name, and so forth
2. By something a person has, such as a smart card, which looks like a credit card and stores personal information
3. By biometrics, which uses a device that digitally recognizes fingerprints or the retina or iris of the eye

The verification of electronic signatures is creating a need for the use of scanners and methods for verifying personal information.

Law & Ethics Questions

1. What is a digital signature?
2. Does the SIGN Act give legal effect to an e-signature?
3. **Ethics** Does the SIGN Act, by recognizing e-signatures, promote fraud? Why or why not?

PARALEGAL PERSPECTIVE

Cynthia A. Laquinta is a certified paralegal employed by the company Koppers, Inc., in Pittsburgh, Pennsylvania. She graduated from the Paralegal Institute at Duquesne in Pittsburgh.

While working as a litigation paralegal in a corporate law department, my knowledge of contract law is deepened with every claim and lawsuit. A contract is nothing more than an agreement to exchange valuable items between two or more parties; however, it is vital to conducting business. I depend on contracts when defending the corporation's position in claims and lawsuits.

When I review a claim for any potential liability on the part of our corporation, I am also reviewing the claim for a source of outside liability or indemnification by a third party. Applicable contracts with our vendors must be reviewed at the onset of a claim or litigation to determine if any indemnification is available from another party. Indemnification from a third party will eliminate or reduce the liability of our corporation, thus reducing our expenses and exposure.

For example, each of our insurance policies is a contract and requires a review and analysis for each claim; our contracts with our transportation and supply vendors often determine the extent of potential liability we may have in a particular claim.

When drafting contracts with our vendors, one of the cornerstones of the terms and conditions is to ensure our interests are protected and full indemnification is provided by our vendors and third parties. This requires the corporate law department to work closely with the corporation's manufacturing and logistics departments in drafting and negotiating contracts.

Our in-house and outside counsel depend on me to consider all sources of the corporation's extent of liability and potential methods of indemnification or remuneration; contracts are a major source during my search.

■ SOFTWARE AND E-LICENSING

Much of the new cyberspace economy is based on electronic contracts and the licensing of computer information. E-commerce created problems for forming contracts over the Internet, enforcing e-commerce contracts, and providing consumer protection. To address these problems, in 1999 the National Conference of Commissioners on Uniform State Laws (a group of lawyers, judges, and legal scholars) drafted the Uniform Computer Information Transactions Act (UCITA). This model act establishes a uniform and comprehensive set of rules that govern the creation, performance, and enforcement of computer information transactions. A computer information transaction is an agreement to create, transfer, or license computer information or information rights [UCITA § 102(a)(11)].

The UCITA does not become law until a state's legislature enacts it as a state statute. Most states have adopted e-commerce and licensing statutes similar to many of the provisions of the UCITA as their law for computer transactions and the licensing of software and informational rights. The UCITA will be used as the basis for discussing state laws that affect computer, software, and licensing contracts.

Unless displaced by the UCITA, state law and equity principles, including principal and agent law, fraud, duress, mistake, trade secret law, and other state laws, supplement the UCITA [UCITA § 114]. Any provisions of the UCITA preempted by federal law are unenforceable to the extent of the preemption [UCITA § 105(a)].

E-Commerce & Information Technology

The Uniform Electronic Transactions Act (UETA)

To avoid impeding the growth of electronic commerce, there is a substantial need for a uniform law that regulates certain aspects of contracting over the Internet. To this end, the National Conference of Commissioners on Uniform State Laws promulgated the **Uniform Electronic Transactions Act (UETA)**. This model act is designed to create uniform laws for electronic records and electronic signatures. The goal of the act is to place electronic records and signatures on the same level as paper contracts and written signatures. Thus, electronic contracts should be as enforceable, as well as avoidable, as paper contracts.

The UETA applies only to transactions between parties who have agreed to conduct their transactions by electronic means. Whether the parties agree to conduct a transaction by electronic means is determined from the context and surrounding circumstances, including the parties' conduct, customer initiation of Internet communications, and such [UETA § 5].

Once a transaction is determined to be covered by the UETA, the UETA recognizes two main concepts. First, the UETA states that an *electronic record* satisfies the requirement for a contract and also the requirement for writing where the contract is required to be in writing by the Statute of Frauds. Second, the UETA recognizes that an *electronic signature* is a signature that is enforceable equal to a written signature on a paper contract [UETA § 2]. In addition, the UETA specifies that as the law requires a record or signature to be notarized, acknowledged, or made under oath, the requirement is satisfied by an electronic signature of the authorized person, provided all information required in the notarization, acknowledgement, and so forth, is included [UETA § 11].

The UETA supports the increased use of electronic commerce by assuring that electronic records receive legal recognition on a par with paper contracts and that electronic signatures are treated equally to signatures written on paper. The UETA does not displace existing contract law concerning offer and acceptance, consideration, reliance, mistake, fraud, undue influence, duress, duties of care, and other contract requirements or defenses. The UETA does not become law until a state adopts the model act as its own statute. States are expected to adopt the UETA to provide uniformity of law for enforcing electronic records and signatures as contracts.

Licensing of Informational Rights

Intellectual property and information rights are extremely important assets of many individuals and companies. Patents, trademarks, copyrights, trade secrets, data, software programs, and such, constitute valuable intellectual property and information rights.

The owners of intellectual property and information rights often wish to transfer limited rights in the property or information to parties for specified purposes and limited duration. The agreement that is used to transfer such limited rights is called a **license**, defined as follows [UCITA § 102(a)(40)]:

> *License means a contract that authorizes access to, or use, distribution, performance, modification, or reproduction of, information or information rights, but expressly limits the access or uses authorized or expressly grants fewer than all rights in the information, whether or not the transferee has title to a licensed copy. The term includes an access contract, a lease of a computer program, and a consignment of a copy.*

The parties to a license are the licensor and the licensee. The **licensor** is the party who owns the intellectual property or information rights and obligates himself or herself to transfer rights in the property or information to the licensee. The **licensee** is the party who is granted limited rights in or access to the intellectual property of information rights [UCITA § 102(a)(41), (42)]. Exhibit 9.2 illustrates a licensing arrangement.

A license grants the contractual rights expressly described in the license and the right to use any information rights within the licensor's control that are necessary to exercise the expressly described rights [UCITA § 307(a)].

Exclusive License

A license can grant the licensee the exclusive rights to use the information. An **exclusive license** means that for the specified duration of the license, the licensor will not grant to any other person rights in the same information [UCITA § 307(f)(2)].

license
A contract that transfers limited rights in intellectual property and informational rights. Grants a person the right to enter upon another's property for a specified and usually short period of time.

licensor
The owner of intellectual property or informational rights who transfers rights in the property or information to the licensee.

licensee
The party who is granted limited rights in or access to intellectual property or informational rights owned by the licensor.

exclusive license
A license that grants the licensee exclusive rights to use informational rights for a specified duration.

Exhibit 9.2 Licensing Arrangement

Licensor

License
(transfer of rights in
intellectual property
or information)

Licensee

INTERNET & TECHNOLOGY

Click-Wrap Licenses

In the past, most business and consumer contracts consisted of written agreements signed by both parties. With the advent of the Internet, many online contracts no longer fit this traditional mode. Take click-wrap licenses, for example. A **click-wrap license** is a contract used by many software companies to sell their software over the Internet or in physical packages where the software is later installed on a computer.

The software company, called the licensor, typically displays a series of dialogue boxes on the computer screen that state the terms of the agreement before the software is downloaded or installed by the potential licensee. The terms of a software click-wrap license are typically not negotiable, and the licensee (the person who is granted the license) indicates his or her acceptance by clicking on a prompt button on the screen labeled "I accept" or "I agree." Click-wrap licenses contain terms of the agreement, disclaimers of warranties, guarantees for the protection of trademarks and trade secrets, and other provisions that would normally be contained in a paper license. Click-wrap agreements provide a fast, inexpensive, and convenient way for licensors to mass-market their software to users without requiring paper contracts or physical signatures.

A question recently presented to the courts is whether click-wrap licenses are enforceable. The courts have held that a party is considered to have manifested her consent to enter into a contract by her physical action of using a mouse to click the "I Agree" prompt button for the click-wrap license.

The new Uniform Computer Information Transactions Act (UCITA) specifically provides that a licensee who has the opportunity to review the terms of the license is bound by those terms if the licensee "manifests assent" before or during the party's initial use of or access to the licensor's software [UCITA § 210(a)]. Thus, under the modern e-commerce interpretation of the law of contracts, popular click-wrap licenses are enforceable contracts between software licensors and user licensees.

Law & Ethics Questions

1. What is a click-wrap license? Explain.
2. Have you ever licensed software over the Internet? If so, did you read the click-wrap license before ordering the software?
3. **Ethics** Should a click-wrap license be enforced against the licensee? Wy or why not?

MARKETPLACE

Job Announcement: Corporate Securities Paralegal

A national corporation for food and beverages has an immediate opening for an experienced Corporate and Securities Paralegal in its corporate office.

Primary responsibilities include the following: filings and assistance with drafting & filing of Section 16 other SEC forms, conducting due diligence for and drafting proxy materials, Annual Meeting preparation, drafting board/stockholder consent agreements and minutes and other director and officer related materials, compliance with NYSE listing standards, planning for and preparation of materials for the board and board committees, maintaining subsidiaries in compliance

(continued)

with corporate governance rules. Must have knowledge of Corporate and Securities laws, contract law, and remain current on proposed/enacted legislation affecting public company practices. More than three years experience as a securities paralegal with a law firm or corporate legal department is preferred, but all strong candidates will be considered. Four-year college degree strongly preferred.

The corporation is an equal opportunity employer and will only contact the most qualified candidates.

Please e-mail resume to:

Licensing Agreement

A licensor and a licensee usually enter into a written **licensing agreement** that expressly states the terms of their agreement. Licensing agreements tend to be very detailed and comprehensive contracts. This is primarily because of the nature of the subject matter and the limited uses granted in the intellectual property or informational rights.

licensing agreement
Detailed and comprehensive written agreement between the licensor and licensee that sets forth the express terms of their agreement.

E-Commerce & Information Technology

Software and Information Access Contracts

Sometimes instead of transferring a copy of information to a licensee, a software license grants the licensee the right to access information in the possession of the licensor. This type of license is called an **access contract**. Access contracts provide for access by the licensee to the information for an agreed-upon time or number of uses. The licensee's access to the information must be available at times and in a manner that complies with the express terms of the license. If such terms are not stated in the agreement, access by the licensee shall be at times and in a manner that is reasonable for the particular type of contract in light of ordinary standards of the business, trade, or industry.

The licensee's right of access is to information as periodically modified and updated by the licensor. A change in the content of the information is not a breach of contract unless the change conflicts with express terms in the license. An occasional failure to have access available is not a breach of contact if it is either (1) normal in the business, trade, or industry or (2) is caused by scheduling downtime; reasonable periods of failure of equipment, communications, or computer programs; or reasonable needs for maintenance [UCITA § 611].

access contract
Where a software licensor grants the licensee the right to access information in the possession of the licensor for an agreed-upon time or for a number of uses.

INTERNET & TECHNOLOGY

Counteroffers Ineffectual Against Electronic Agents

In today's e-commerce, many sellers use electronic agents to sell goods and services. An *electronic agent* is any telephonic or computer system established by a seller to accept orders. Voice mail and web page order systems are examples of electronic agents.

In the past, when humans dealt with each other face to face, by telephone, or in writing, their negotiations might have consisted of an exchange of several offers and counteroffers until agreed-upon terms were reached and a contract was

(continued)

formed. Each new counteroffer extinguished the previous offer and became a new viable offer. Most electronic agents do not have the ability to evaluate and accept counteroffers or to make counteroffers. The UCITA recognizes this limitation and provides that a contract is formed if an individual takes action that causes the electronic agent to cause performance or promise benefits to the individual. Thus, counteroffers are not effective against electronic agents [UCITA § 206(a)].

Example: "Birdie" is an electronic ordering system for placing orders for electronic information sold by the Green Company, a producer of computer software and electronic information. Freddie Calloway dials the Green Company's toll-free telephone number and orders new software for $1,000, using the Birdie voice mail electronic ordering system. Freddie enters the product code and description, his mailing address and credit card information, and other data needed to complete the transaction, but at the end of the order states, "I will accept this software if, after two weeks of use, I am satisfied with the software." Because Freddie has placed the order with an electronic agent, Freddie has ordered the software, and his counteroffer is ineffectual.

Licensing Information Technology Rights

The Uniform Computer Information Transactions Act (UCITA) creates contract law for the licensing of information technology rights. The UCITA will be used for discussing the licensing of information rights in the following paragraphs.

Formation of a Contract

A contract may be formed in any manner that shows agreement, including an offer and acceptance, conduct of both parties, or operation of electronic agents [UCITA § 202(a)]. An offer to make a contract invites acceptance in any manner and by any medium reasonable under circumstances. If an offer is received, the offer may be accepted by either promptly promising to ship a copy or shipping a copy of it. If an offer in an electronic message evokes an electronic message accepting the offer, a contract is formed when an electronic acceptance is received [UCITA § 203].

A transaction covered by the UCITA is not subject to the Statute of Frauds, which requires contracts to be in writing, or by other state laws [UCITA § 201(f)].

Acceptance with Varying Terms   A party can expressly make an offer conditional on agreement by the other party to all the terms of the offer. Acceptance by the other party of all the terms creates a contract, but varying the terms in the purported acceptance does not create a contract [UCITA § 205].

If an offer has not been made conditional on acceptance of all the terms, and the party purporting to accept has varied the terms of the offer in his or her acceptance, the following rules apply: If the transaction is between merchants, the purposed additional nonmaterial terms offered by the offeree become part of the contract unless the original offeror gives notice of objections to these terms within a reasonable time after receiving them. If one of the parties is not a merchant, varying the terms of an offer by the offeree is a rejection of the offer and constitutes a counteroffer. Any material alteration of the terms of the offer by the offeree, even between merchants, rejects the offer and no contract is formed [UCITA § 204].

Title to Copy   Title to a copy of the software or electronic information is determined by the license. In many licenses, the licensor reserves title to a copy; in other licenses, title to the copy transfers to the licensee. A licensee's right under the license to possess, control, and use a copy is governed by the license [UCITA § 502(a)].

THE ETHICAL PARALEGAL

Reporting Misconduct

ABA Rule 8.3 deals with reporting professional misconduct.[1] This rule descended from another ABA ethics rule referred to as "The Fink Rule." The idea is that an attorney has the duty to expose corrupt or dishonest conduct in order to maintain the integrity of the legal profession.

Don't forget that the ABA Model Rules themselves do not carry the weight of law. What is important—at least in regard to what is enforceable by law—are the ethics rules the paralegal's state has adopted on reporting misconduct. Therefore, ethical paralegals should know what their particular state law says about reporting misconduct to the appropriate authority.

Authenticating the Record

If a contract requires payment of a contract fee of $5,000 or more, the contract is enforceable against a party only if that party authenticated the record [UCITA § 201(a)]. **Authenticate** means either signing the contract or executing an electronic symbol, sound, or message attached to, included in, or linked with the record [UCITA § 102(a)(6)].

An electronic authentication is attributed to a person if it was the act of that person or his or her electronic agent [UCITA § 213]. Authentication may be proven in any manner, including a showing that a party made use of information or access that could have been available only if he or she engaged in operations that authenticated the record [UCITA § 108]. Authentication may be shown by using an **attribution procedure** to verify the electronic authentication and to detect errors or changes in electronic authentication. This procedure requires the use of codes, algorithms, identifying words or numbers, encryption, callback, or other acknowledgment [UCITA § 102(a)(5)].

Example: Yuan uses the Internet and places an order to license software for her computer from License.com, Inc., through its electronic website ordering system. The web page order form asks Yuan to type her name, address, telephone number, credit card information, computer information, and a personal identification number. The electronic agent requests that Yuan verify this information a second time before accepting the order, which Yuan does. Only after doing so does License.com, Inc.'s, electronic agent place the order and send an electronic copy of the software to Yuan's computer, where she installs the new software program. There has been authentication of Yuan's signature and a proper attribution procedure to verify the authentication.

Confirmation Letter   If the parties to a contract are merchants and the contract fee is $5,000 or more, the contract may be enforced even without authentication if one party to the contract sends a record confirming the contract and the other party does not reject the confirmation within 10 days after receiving it [UCITA § 201(d)].

authenticate
Signing the contract or executing an electronic symbol, sound, or message attached to, included in, or linked with the record.

attribution procedure
A procedure using codes, algorithms, identifying words or numbers, encryption, callback, or other acknowledgment to verify an authentication of a record.

---

[1]Copies of the ABA Model Rules of Professional Conduct are available from Service Center, American Bar Association, 321 North Clark Street, Chicago, IL 60610, 1-800-285-2221. The Model Rules can also be viewed online at http://www.abanet.org/cpr/mrpc/mrpc_toc.html.

Performance

A party to a licensing agreement owes a duty to perform in a manner that conforms to the contract. Each party owes a duty to tender performance when performance is due. **Tender of performance** occurs when a party who has the ability and willingness to perform offers to complete the performance of his or her duties under the contract [UCITA § 601].

A software license requires the delivery of software, information, or data from the licensor to the licensee. The parties may designate in their contract the place for the electronic or physical delivery of a copy of the information. If no place is stated in the contract, the place of delivery is the licensor's place of business [UCITA § 606].

Example: Maria enters into a licensing agreement to license electronic information from DataBase, Inc. DataBase, Inc., notifies Maria that a copy of the electronic information she has licensed is available for her to download from its website; DataBase, Inc., has tendered performance. Maria offers to pay DataBase, Inc., the licensing fee by credit card; Maria has tendered performance.

Risk of Loss of the Copy   When the copy is delivered electronically or is not delivered by a carrier, the risk of loss of the copy passes to the licensee upon its receipt of the copy.

If a copy is delivered from the licensor to the licensee by a carrier, one of two rules applies: (1) If the agreement requires the licensor to deliver the copy to a particular destination, the risk of loss remains with the licensor until the copy is tendered at the designated destination, or (2) if the agreement does not require the licensor to deliver the copy to a particular destination, the risk of loss transfers to the licensee when the licensor delivers the copy to the carrier [UCITA § 614].

Acceptance of a Copy   A licensee who has been tendered a copy by the licensor is deemed to have accepted the copy if the licensee (1) signifies that the tender was conforming, (2) acts with respect to the copy in a manner that signifies the tender was conforming, (3) retains a copy despite its nonconformity, (4) commingles the copy or information with other copies or information, (5) obtains a substantial benefit for the copy that cannot be returned, or (6) acts in a manner inconsistent with the licensor's ownership of the copy [UCITA § 610].

Excuse of Performance   The UCITA provides that a party's delay in performance or nonperformance under a license agreement is excused if the performance has been made impracticable. The UCITA stipulates that delay or nonperformance is made *impracticable* by (1) the occurrence of a contingency whose nonoccurrence was a basic assumption on which the contract was made or (2) compliance with any domestic or foreign statute or governmental rule. Where there is a delay or nonperformance excused by impracticability, there is no breach of contract.

A party claiming the excuse of impracticability must reasonably notify the other party that there has been a delay in performance. If an excuse affects only part of the party's capacity to perform, the party claiming the excuse shall allocate performance among its customers in any manner that is fair and reasonable and notify the other party of the quota it is to receive. Whenever a party is notified there is a delay or nonperformance caused by impracticability, that party may terminate the contract and thereby be discharged from the unperformed portion of the contract [UCITA § 615].

Example: Zeke, a foreign national and businessperson, enters into a licensing agreement to license certain informational rights from Zendex Corporation, a corporation located in the United States. Zeke is to take possession of the information

tender of performance
Tender is an unconditional and absolute offer by a contracting party to perform his or her obligations under the contract. Occurs when a party who has the ability and willingness to perform offers to complete the performance of his or her duties under the contract.

when it is made available to him on Zendex's website, and he will be able to download it to his computer. Prior to the delivery of the informational rights, however, the U.S. Congress enacts a statute restricting the exporting of the type of information that Zeke has contracted to receive. In this instance Zendex's performance is excused because its performance of the contract has been made illegal by government statute.

Warranties

Certain warranties may attach to a license of informational rights because either the licensor has made express warranties or the law has imposed one or more implied warranties. The law, however, permits some of these warranties to be disclaimed if certain requirements are met.

Warranties of Noninterference and Noninfringement

A licensor of information warrants that no third person holds any claim or interest in the information or claim of infringement or misappropriation that would interfere with the license's use or enjoyment of the information [UCITA § 401].

Example: Antoine licenses a certain database from Data.com, Inc., for three years to use in his business. After using the database for a short time, Antoine receives notice from a court to desist from using the database because the data infringes a copyright held by Information.com, Inc. Here, there has been a breach of the warranty of noninfringement by Data.com, Inc.; Antoine can recover damages from Data.com, Inc., for the breach of this warranty.

Express Warranty

Licensors are not required to do so, but they often make express warranties concerning the quality of their software or information. An **express warranty** is any affirmation of fact or promise by the licensor about the quality of its software or information. An express warranty can result from a description of the information, advertising, samples or models, demonstrations of the final product, and such. An express warranty is not created by the licensor's statements of opinion [UCITA § 402].

Example: Info, Inc., has developed software for predicting the price of securities sold on NASDAQ and warrants that its software is free from defects. Info, Inc. will pay $10,000 liquidated damages and replace the software free of charge if it does not perform correctly within the first year of use. Here, Info, Inc., has made an express warranty about the quality of its information. Financial Times, Inc., a financial services company, licenses the software from Info, Inc., but after three months of use the software fails. Info, Inc., owes Financial Times, Inc., $10,000 and a free replacement copy of the software [UCITA § 406(a)].

express warranty
Any affirmation of fact or promise by the licensor about the quality of its software or information. A warranty that is created when a seller or lessor makes an affirmation that the goods he or she is selling or leasing meet certain standards of quality, description, performance, or condition.

Implied Warranty of Merchantability of the Computer Program

The law implies that a merchant licensor warrants the computer program is fit for the ordinary purposes for which the computer program is used. This warranty is called the **implied warranty of merchantability of the computer program**. This implied warranty includes a warranty that the copies of the computer program have been adequately packaged and labeled, and that the program conforms to any promises or affirmations of fact made on the container or label [UCITA § 403].

Example: Juan licenses a software program from Medi, Inc., to sort data and information from his extensive databases and to run with other software and database programs used in his medical supplies business. The licensing agreement and label on the Medi software program state that the copy of the license program has been

implied warranty of merchantability of the computer program
An implied warranty that the copies of the computer program are within the parameters permitted by the licensing agreement, that the computer program has been adequately packaged and labeled, and that the program conforms to any promises or affirmations of fact on the container or label.

tested and will run without error. Juan installs the software, but every third or fourth time he runs it, it fails to operate properly and shuts down his computer and other programs. There has been a breach of the implied warranty of the merchantability of the computer program because the Medi software does not fall within the parameters of the licensing agreement or affirmation of fact on the label. Juan can recover remedies from Medi, Inc.

Implied Warranty of Informational Content   A merchant who collects, compiles, processes, provides, or transmits informational content warrants to the licensee that there is no inaccuracy in the informational content caused by the merchant's failure to perform with reasonable care. This warranty is called the **implied warranty of informational content** [UCITA § 404].

implied warranty of informational content
An implied warranty that there is no inaccuracy in the informational content caused by the merchant-licensor's failure to perform with reasonable care.

Example: Christine licenses a database of historical and current interest-rate information from DataMarket, Inc.; the information is updated daily by DataMarket. Christine uses the information to make extensive bond investments for her clients. She uses the information one day to make certain investments. It turns out, however, that DataMarket, Inc., made several accidental errors in inputting the interest-rate data, thus causing an error in Christine's calculations and decisions. Here there has been a breach of implied warranty of informational content because the licensor, DataMarket, Inc., failed to perform with reasonable care. Christine can seek remedies against DataMarket, Inc.

Implied Warranty of Fitness for a Particular Purpose   A licensor that has a reason to know of any particular purpose for which the computer information is required and knows that the licensee is relying on the licensor's skill or judgment to select or furnish suitable information warrants that the information is fit for the licensee's purpose. This warranty is called the **implied warranty of fitness for a particular purpose** [UCITA § 405].

implied warranty of fitness for a particular purpose
An implied warranty that information is fit for the licensee's purpose that applies if the licensor (1) knows of any particular purpose for which the computer information is required and (2) knows that the licensee is relying on the licensor's skill or judgment to select or furnish suitable information.

Example: Ahmad, who operates a large Internet order-taking and delivery business, contacts IMB, Inc., a large software developer, about licensing software to operate his business. Ahmad tells the IMB representative about the volume of his business and his business needs and informs the IMB representative that he is relying on her to select the software for Ahmad, which she installs. The software, however, is inadequate to handle Ahmad's business needs. Here there has been a breach of implied warranty of fitness for a particular purpose. Ahmad may pursue remedies against IMB, Inc.

General Disclaimer of Warranties   The UCITA permits a licensor to disclaim all implied warranties by expressions like "as is" or "with all faults" or other language that in common understanding calls the licensee's attention to the disclaimer and makes plain there are no implied warranties [UCITA § 406(c)]. All of the implied warranties are also disclaimed by stating, "Except for express warranties stated in this contract, if any, this 'information' [or 'computer program'] is provided with all faults, and the entire risk as to satisfactory quality, performance, accuracy, and effort is with the user," or by using words of similar import [UCITA § 406 (b)(3)]. General disclaimers must be conspicuous.

■ BREACH OF LICENSE AGREEMENTS

The parties to a contract for the licensing of information owe a duty to perform the obligations stated in the contract. If a party fails to perform as required, there is a breach of the contract. Breach of contract by one party to a licensing agreement gives the nonbreaching party certain rights, including the right to recover damages or other remedies [UCITA § 701].

Adequate Assurance of Performance

Each party to a license agreement expects to receive due performance from the other party. If any reasonable grounds arise prior to the performance date that make one party think the other party might not deliver performance when due, the aggrieved party may demand adequate assurance of due performance from the other party. Until such assurance is received, the aggrieved party may, if commercially reasonable, suspend performance until assurance is received. Failure to provide assurance within 30 days permits the aggrieved party to repudiate the contract [UCITA § 708].

Licensee's Refusal of Defective Tender

If the licensor tenders a copy that is a material breach of the contract, the nonbreaching party to whom tender is made may either (1) refuse the tender, (2) accept the tender, or (3) accept any commercially reasonable units and refuse the rest [UCITA § 704].

Licensee's Revocation of Acceptance

If a licensee has accepted tender of a copy where the nonconformity is a material breach, the licensee may later revoke his or her acceptance if (1) acceptance was made because discovery was difficult at the time of tender but was then later discovered or (2) the nonconformity was discovered at the time of tender but the licensor agreed to cure the defect, and the defect has not been reasonably cured [UCITA § 707].

INTERNET & TECHNOLOGY

Consumers Saved from Electronic Errors

The UCITA provides that consumers are not bound by their unilateral electronic errors if the consumer:

1. Promptly upon learning of the error notifies the licensor of the error.
2. Does not use or receive any benefit from the information, or make the information or benefit available to a third party.
3. Delivers all copies of the information to the licensor or destroys all copies of the information, pursuant to reasonable instructions from the licensor.
4. Pays all shipping, reshipping, and processing costs of the licensor. [UCITA § 217]

The UCITA does not relieve a consumer of his or her electronic error if the other party provides a reasonable method to detect and correct or avoid the error. Thus, many sellers establish methods whereby the buyer must verify the information and purchase order a second time before an electronic order is processed. This procedure strips the consumer of the defense of UCITA Section 217. Section 217 of the UCITA applies only to consumers who make electronic errors in contracting. Electronic errors by nonconsumers are handled under the common law of contracts or the Uniform Commercial Code (UCC), whichever applies.

Example: Kai, a consumer, intends to order 10 copies of a video game over the Internet from Cybertendo, a video game producer. In fact, Kai makes an error

(continued)

and orders 110 games. The electronic agent maintaining Cybertendo's website's ordering process electronically disburses 110 games. The next morning Kai discovers his mistake and immediately e-mails Cybertendo, describing the mistake and offering to return or destroy the copies at his expense. When Kai receives the games, he returns the 110 copies unused. Under the UCITA, Kai has no contract obligation for 110 copies but bears the cost of returning them to Cybertendo or destroying them if Cybertendo instructs him to do so. However, if Cybertendo's website's electronic ordering system had asked Kai to confirm his order of 110 copies of the purchase order, and Kai had confirmed the original order of 110 copies, Kai would have had to pay for the 110 copies, even if his confirmation had been in error.

■ REMEDIES FOR BREACH

The UCITA provides certain *remedies* to an aggrieved party upon the breach of a licensing agreement. A party may not recover more than once for the same loss, and his or her remedy (other than liquidated damages) may not exceed the loss caused by the breach [UCITA § 801]. The UCITA provides that a cause of action must be commenced within one year after the breach was or should have been discovered, but not more than five years after the breach actually occurred [UCITA § 805]. Remedies are discussed in the following paragraphs.

Cancellation

cancellation
The termination of a contract by a contracting party upon the material breach of the contract by the other party. A buyer or lessee may cancel a sales or lease contract if the seller or lessor fails to deliver conforming goods or repudiates the contract or if the buyer or lessee rightfully rejects the goods or justifiably revokes acceptance of the goods.

If there has been a material breach of a contract that has not been cured or waived, the aggrieved party may cancel the contract. **Cancellation** is effective when the canceling party notifies the breaching party of the cancellation. Upon cancellation, the breaching party in possession or control of copies, information, documentation, or other materials that are the property of the other party must use commercially reasonable efforts to return them or hold them for disposal on instructions from the other party. All obligations that are executory on both sides at the time of cancellation are discharged [UCITA § 802(a) and (b)].

Upon cancellation of a license, the licensor has the right to have all copies of the licensed information returned by the licensee and to prevent the licensee from continuing to use the licensed information.

Licensor's Damages

licensor's damages
If a licensee breaches a contract, the licensor may sue and recover monetary damages from the licensee caused by the breach.

If a licensee breaches a contract, the licensor may recover **licensor's damages**. The licensor may sue and recover from the licensee monetary damages caused by the breach, plus any consequential and incidental damages [UCITA § 808]. A licensor can recover *lost profits* caused by the licensee's failure to accept or complete performance of the contract. Lost profits is a proper measure of damages in this case because the licensor has effectively unlimited capability to make access available to others so there will be no license to substitute to reduce damages owed by the breaching licensee.

Example: iSuperSoftware.com licenses a master disk of its software program to Distributors, Inc., to make and distribute 10,000 copies of the software. This is a nonexclusive license, and the license fee is $1 million. It costs iSuperSoftware.com $15 to produce the disk. If Distributors, Inc., refuses the disk and breaches the contract, iSuperSoftware.com can recover $1 million less $15 as damages for the profits lost on the transaction.

Licensor's Right to Cure

Unlike the common law of contracts, the UCITA provides that a licensor has the **right to cure** a breach of a license in certain circumstances. A breach of contract may be cured if (1) the time of performance of the contract has not expired and the licensor makes conforming performance within the time of performance; (2) the time of performance has expired but the licensor had reasonable grounds to believe the performance would be acceptable, in which case the licensor has a reasonable time to make conforming performance; or (3) the licensor makes conforming performance before the licensee cancels the contract. In all three situations, the licensor must reasonably notify the licensee of the intent to cure [UCITA § 703(a)].

right to cure
A licensor has the right to cure a contract under certain conditions.

INTERNET & TECHNOLOGY

Electronic Self-Help

Just like normal contracts, electronic licenses can be breached by licensees. If such a breach occurs, the licensor can resort to remedies provided in the UCITA. Sections 815 and 816 of the UCITA provide that a licensor can resort to electronic self-help if a breach occurs—for example, if the licensee fails to pay the license fee. Such electronic self-help can consist of activating disabling bugs and time bombs that have been embedded in the software or information that will prevent the licensee from further using the software or information.

Section 816 provides that a licensor is entitled to use electronic self-help only if the following requirements are met:

1. The licensee must specifically agree to the inclusion in the license of self-help as a remedy. There must be a specific self-help option to which the licensee assents.
2. The licensor must give the licensee at least 15 days' notice prior to the disabling action. The notice period allows the licensee to make lawful adjustments to minimize the effects of the licensor's self-help or to seek a judicial remedy to combat the use of the self-help.
3. The licensor may not use self-help if it would cause a breach of the peace, risk personal injury, cause significant damage or injury to information other than the licensee's information, result in injury to the public health or safety, or cause grave harm to national security.

A licensor who violates these provisions and uses self-help improperly is liable for damages. This liability cannot be disclaimed.

Licensee's Damages

When a licensor breaches a contract, the licensee may sue and recover monetary damages from the licensor. The amount of the damages depends on the facts of the situation. This is called the **licensee's damages**. Upon the licensor's breach, the licensee may either (1) cover by purchasing other electronic information from another source and recover the difference between the value of the promised

licensee's damages
The amount of monetary compensation the licensee can recover when the licensor breaches a contract.

cover
Right of a buyer or lessee to purchase or lease substitute goods if a seller or lessor fails to make delivery of the goods or repudiates the contract or if the buyer or lessee rightfully rejects the goods or justifiably revokes their acceptance. The licensee's right to engage in a commercially reasonable substitute transaction after the licensor has breached the contract.

performance from the licensor and the cost of cover or (2) not cover and recover the value of the performance from the licensor. **Cover** means engaging in a commercially reasonable substitute transaction. The licensee may obtain an award of consequential and incidental damages in either case. A licensee cannot obtain excessive or double recovery [UCITA § 809].

Example: Auction.com is an Internet company that operates an online auction service. Auction.com enters into a contract with MicroHard, Inc., a software producer, for a site license to use MicroHard, Inc.'s software. Auction.com agrees to pay $500,000 as an initial license fee and $10,000 per month for the license duration of three years. Before Auction.com pays any money under the license, MicroHard, Inc., breaches the contract and does not deliver the software. Auction.com covers by licensing commercially similar software from another software company for the payment of a $600,000 initial licensing fee and $11,000 per month for the license duration of three years. Under the facts of this case, Auction.com can recover from MicroHard, Inc., $100,000 for the increased initial fee and $36,000 for the increased monthly costs for breach of contract.

Licensee Can Obtain Specific Performance

specific performance
A remedy that orders the breaching party to perform the acts promised in the contract; usually awarded in cases where the subject matter is unique, such as in contracts involving land, heirlooms, and paintings. Judgment of the court ordering a licensor to specifically perform the license by making the contracted-for unique information available to the licensee. A decree of the court that orders a seller or lessor to perform his or her obligations under the contract.

The UCITA provides the remedy of **specific performance** if the parties have agreed to this remedy in their contract or if the agreed-upon performance is unique. The test of uniqueness requires the court to examine the total situation that characterizes the contract [UCITA § 811].

Example: Nedra enters into a licensing agreement to obtain access to certain informational rights from Info, Inc., for a specified monthly license fee. The data are proprietary to Info, Inc., and are not available from any other vendor. If Info, Inc., breaches the license and refuses to give Nedra access to the information, Nedra can sue and obtain an order of specific performance whereby the court orders Info, Inc., to make the contracted-for information available to Nedra for duration of the license.

Liquidation of Damages

liquidated damages
Damages to which parties to a contract agree in advance if the contract is breached. Damages that are specified in the contract rather than determined by the court. Damages that will be paid upon a breach of contract and that are established in advance

The parties to a license may provide that damages for breach of contract may be liquidated. **Liquidated damages** are damages specified in the contract rather than determined by the court. The amount of liquidated damages must be reasonable in light of the loss anticipated at the time of contracting or the anticipated difficulties of proving loss in the event of breach. The fixing of unreasonably large liquidated damages is void [UCITA § 804].

■ LIMITATION OF REMEDIES

The UCITA provides that the parties to an agreement may limit the remedies available for breach of the contract. This is done by including provisions in the contract. Remedies may be restricted to the return of copies and repayment of the licensing fee or limited to the repair or replacement of the nonconforming copies. Limitations of remedies in licenses subject to the UCITA are enforceable unless they are unconscionable [UCITA § 803].

In Case 9.3, the court upheld a limitation-of-remedies clause in a software license.

CASE 9.3   REMEDIES

M.A. Mortenson Co. v. Timberline Software Corp., 970 P.2d 803 (Wash. Ct. App. 1999).

> "We find that Mortenson's installation and use of the software
> manifested its assent to the terms of the license."
>
> Judge Webster, *Court of Appeals of Washington*

Facts

The Timberline Software Corporation (Timberline) produces software programs that are used by contractors to prepare bids to do work on construction projects. The M.A. Mortenson Company (Mortenson), a contractor, had been using Timberline software for some time without any problem. Timberline introduced an advanced version of its bidding software program called *Precision*. Mortenson, as the licensee, entered into a license agreement with Timberline, the licensor, to license the use of the Precision software. Timberline delivered the software to Mortenson, and a Timberline representative installed the software on Mortenson's computer. The software license agreement contained the following terms, which were printed on the outside of the envelope in which the software disks were packaged and on the inside cover of the user's manual, and they also appear on the introductory computer screen each time the software program is executed:

> *Carefully read the following terms and conditions before using the programs. Use of the programs indicates your acknowledgement that you have read this license, understand it, and agree to be bound by its terms and conditions. If you do not agree to these terms and conditions, promptly return the programs and user manuals to the place of purchase and your purchase price will be refunded. You agree that your use of the program acknowledges that you have read this license, understand it, and agree to be bound by its terms and conditions.*
>
> *Limitation of remedies and liability: neither Timberline nor anyone else who has been involved in the creation, production, or delivery of the programs or user manuals shall be liable to you for any damages of any type, including but not limited to any lost profits, lost savings, loss of anticipated benefits, or other incidental or consequential damages arising out of the use or inability to use such programs, whether arising out of contract, negligence, strict tort, or under any warranty, or otherwise, even if Timberline has been advised of the possibility of such damages or for any other claim by any other party. Timberline's liability for damages in no event shall exceed the license fee paid for the right to use the programs.*

Mortenson used the Precision software and prepared a bid to do contracting work for the Harborview Hospital project. While preparing the bid, the program aborted at least five times before Mortenson's employees finished the bid. Subsequently, Mortenson claimed that its bid was $2 million under what it should have been had the Precision software program worked correctly. Mortenson sued Timberline to recover consequential damages, arguing that the Precision software calculated an inaccurate bid. Timberline defended, alleging that the limitation-of-remedies clause in the software license prevented Mortenson's lawsuit. Mortenson countered that the limitation-of-remedies clause was unconscionable and therefore unenforceable. The trial court granted summary judgment to Timberline and dismissed the lawsuit. Mortenson appealed.

Issue

Was the limitation-of-remedies clause in the Timberline software license unconscionable?

Language of the Court

We hold that the terms of the present license agreement are part of the contract as formed between the parties. We find that Mortenson's installation and use of the software manifested its assent to the terms of the license and that it is bound by all terms of that license that are not found to be illegal or unconscionable.

Considering all the circumstances surrounding the transaction in the case, the limitations clause is not unconscionable. The introductory screen warned that use of the program was subject to a license. This warning placed Mortenson on notice that use of the software was governed by a license. Mortenson had reasonable opportunity to learn and understand the terms of the agreement. The limitations provision was not hidden in a maze of fine print but appeared in all capital letters. Finally such limitations provisions are widely used in the computer software industry.

Decision

The court of appeals held that the limitation-of-remedies clause in the software license was conspicuous and not unconscionable, and it therefore prohibited Mortenson's lawsuit to recover consequential damages from Timberline. The court of appeals affirmed the trial court's grant of summary judgments to Timberline that dismissed the case.

Law & Ethics Questions

1. What does the doctrine of unconscionability provide? Does the doctrine serve any useful purpose?

2. **Ethics** Did Timberline act ethically when it included a limitation-of-remedies clause in its software license?

3. What would be the business consequences if limitation-of-remedies clauses in software licenses were all held to be per se illegal?

Web Exercises

1. **Web** Visit the Court of Appeals of Washington, Division One, at www. courts.wa.gov.

2. **Web** Use www.google.com. Find a software license and determine if it has a limitation-of-remedies clause in it.

Electronic Communications Privacy Act (ECPA)
A federal law that, with some exceptions, makes it a crime to intercept an electronic communication.

■ ONLINE PRIVACY

E-mail, computer data, and other electronic communications are sent daily by millions of people using computers and the Internet. Recognizing how the use of computer and electronic communications raise special issues of privacy, the federal government enacted the **Electronic Communications Privacy Act (ECPA)**.

The ECPA makes it a crime to intercept an electronic communication at the point of transmission, while in transit, when stored by a router or server, or after receipt by the intended recipient. An electronic communication includes any transfer of signals, writings, images, sounds, data, or intelligence of any nature. The ECPA makes it illegal to access stored e-mail as well as e-mail in transmission.

The ECPA provides that stored electronic communications may be accessed without violating the law by the following:

1. The party or entity providing the electronic communication service. The primary example would be an employer who can access stored e-mail communications of employees using the employer's service.
2. Government and law enforcement entities that are investigating suspected illegal activity. Disclosure would be required only pursuant to a validly issued warrant.

The ECPA provides for criminal penalties. In addition, the ECPA provides that an injured party may sue for civil damages for violations of the ECPA.

Law & Ethics Questions

1. What does the Electronic Communications Privacy Act (ECPA) prohibit? Explain.

2. Does the use of electronic communications make it easier to violate privacy rights?

3. **Ethics** Should one expect to have lessened privacy rights for electronic communications?

■ CYBER CRIMES

The advent of the computer and the Internet created an ability of persons to engage in a new form of crimes called cyber crimes. This new technology allowed criminals to commit existing crimes using a new medium.

Fraud can now be perpetrated over the Internet. In addition, the Internet has allowed criminals to engage in new crimes as well. The police, law enforcement agencies, Congress, and the courts have had to address these new cyber crimes. In response, Congress has enacted several new federal statutes that define criminal behavior using computers and the Internet. The courts have had to interpret and apply these new statutes, as well as applying existing criminal statutes to this new medium of crime.

⌨ INTERNET & TECHNOLOGY

Counterfeit Access Device and Computer Fraud and Abuse Act

The **Counterfeit Access Device and Computer Fraud and Abuse Act of 1984**, as amended, makes it a federal crime to access a computer knowingly to obtain (1) restricted federal government information, (2) financial records of financial institutions, and (3) consumer reports of consumer reporting agencies. The act also makes it a crime to use counterfeit or unauthorized access devices, such as cards or code numbers, to obtain things of value or transfer funds or to traffic in such devices [Public Law 98–473, Title II].

Counterfeit Access Device and Computer Fraud and Abuse Act of 1984
A federal law that makes it a crime to access restricted government and other information by computer for unauthorized purposes.

Electronic Funds Transfer Act

A law regulating the payment and deposit of funds by electronic transfer.

INTERNET & TECHNOLOGY

Electronic Funds Transfer Act

The **Electronic Funds Transfer Act** regulates the payment and deposit of funds using electronic funds transfers, such as direct deposit of payroll and Social Security checks in financial institutions, transactions using automated teller machines (ATMs), and such. The act makes it a federal crime to use, furnish, sell, or transport a counterfeit, stolen, lost, or fraudulently obtained ATM card, code number, or other device used to conduct electronic funds transfers. The act imposes criminal penalties of imprisonment and the assessment of criminal fines [15 U.S.C. § 1693].

INTERNET & TECHNOLOGY

Cyber Identity Fraud

For centuries, some people—for various purposes, mostly financial—have attempted to take the identities of other persons. Today, taking on the identity of another can be extremely lucrative, earning the spoils of another's credit cards, bank accounts, Social Security benefits, and such. The use of new technology—computers and the Internet—has made such identity fraud even easier. But a victim of such fraud is left with funds stolen, a dismantled credit history, and thousands of dollars in costs trying to straighten out the mess. Identity fraud is the fastest-growing financial fraud in America.

Identity Theft and Assumption Deterrence Act of 1998

A federal law making it a federal felony to commit identity fraud or theft.

To combat such fraud, Congress passed the **Identity Theft and Assumption Deterrence Act of 1998**. This act criminalizes identity fraud, making it a federal felony punishable with prison sentences ranging from 3 to 25 years. The act also appoints a federal administrative agency, the Federal Trade Commission (FTC), to help victims restore their credit and erase the impact of the imposter. Law enforcement officials suggest the following steps to protect against identity fraud: Never put your Social Security number on any document unless it is legally required, obtain and review copies of your credit report at least twice each year, and use safe passwords (e.g., other than family names and birthdays) on bank accounts and other accounts that require personal identification numbers (PINs).

Law & Ethics Questions

1. What is identity fraud? Explain.
2. How does the Internet make it easier for criminals to commit identity theft?

Web Exercises

1. **Web** Visit the website of the Federal Trade Commission (FTC) at www.ftc.gov. Find information about protecting yourself from identity theft.
2. **Web** Use www.google.com and find an article about a recent identity theft case.

INTERNET & TECHNOLOGY

Information Infrastructure Protection Act (IIP Act)

The Internet and Information Age ushered in a whole new world for education, business, and consumer transactions. But what followed was a rash of cyber crimes. Prosecutors and courts wrestled over how to apply existing laws written in a nondigital age to new Internet-related abuses.

In 1996, Congress responded by enacting the **Information Infrastructure Protection Act (IIP Act)**. In this federal law, Congress addressed computer-related crimes as distinct offenses. The IIP Act provides protection for any computer attached to the Internet.

The IIP Act makes it a federal crime for anyone intentionally to access and acquire information from a protected computer without authorization. The IIP Act does not require that the defendant accessed a protected computer for commercial benefit. Thus, persons who transmit a computer virus over the Internet or hackers who trespass into Internet-connected computers may be criminally prosecuted under the IIP Act. Even merely observing data on a protected computer without authorization is sufficient to meet the requirement that the defendant has accessed a protected computer. Criminal penalties for violating the IIP Act include imprisonment and fines.

The IIP Act gives the federal government a much-needed weapon for directly prosecuting cyber crooks, hackers, and others who enter, steal, destroy, or look at others' computer data without authorization.

Law & Ethics Questions

1. What does the Information Infrastructure Protection Act (IIP Act) provide? Explain.
2. **Ethics** Is it hard to get caught violating the IIP Act?

Information Infrastructure Protection Act (IIP Act)
A federal law making it a federal crime to access and acquire information from a protected computer without authorization.

State Criminal Laws

Often, larceny statutes cover only the theft of tangible property. Because computer software, programs, and data are intangible property, they are not covered by some existing state criminal statutes. To compensate for this, many states have either modernized existing laws to include computer crime or amended existing penal codes to make certain abuses of computers a criminal offense. Computer trespass, the unauthorized use of computers, tampering with computers, and the unauthorized duplication of computer-related materials are usually forbidden by these acts (See New York Session Laws, 1986, Chapter 514).

Our growing reliance on computers has made us more aware of the risks associated with losing the data stored on them. As a result, it is likely that the safety of the nation's ever-expanding computer networks will be legislated even more in the future.

INTERNET & TECHNOLOGY

Computer Hacker Found Guilty of Cyber Crime

In "techie" circles, Kevin D. Mitnick became the underground icon of computer hackers. During a decade's reign, Mitnick terrorized the federal government, universities, and such high-tech companies as Sun Microsystems, Novell Corporation, MCI Communications, Digital Equipment Corporation, and others by breaking

(continued)

into their computer systems. Mitnick used his computer skills to penetrate his victim's computer systems to steal secret information and wreak havoc with their software and data.

Mitnick, a self-taught computer user, has a history of computer-related crime. As a 17-year-old, he was placed on probation for stealing computer manuals from a Pacific Bell Telephone switching center in Los Angeles. Mitnick was next accused of breaking into federal government and military computers. He has also been accused of breaking into the nation's telephone and cellular telephone networks, stealing thousands of data files and trade secrets from corporate targets, obtaining at least 20,000 credit card numbers of some of the country's richest persons, and sabotaging government, university, and private computer systems around the nation. Mitnick was arrested and convicted of computer crimes and served time in prison.

Upon release from prison, he was put on probation and placed in a medical program to treat his compulsive addiction to computers, which included a court order not to touch a computer or modem. Mitnick dropped out of sight and evaded federal law enforcement officials for several years as he continued a life of computer crime.

Mitnick's next undoing came when he broke into the computer of Tsutomu Shimomura, a researcher at the San Diego Supercomputer Center. Shimomura, a cybersleuth who advises the FBI and major companies on computer and Internet security, made it his crusade to catch the hacker who broke into his computer. Shimomura watched electronically as Mitnick invaded other computers across the country, but he could not physically locate Mitnick because he disguised his whereabouts by breaking into telephone company computers and rerouting all his computer calls. Eventually, Shimomura's patient watching paid off as he traced the electronic burglar to Raleigh, North Carolina. Shimomura flew to Raleigh, where he used a cellular-frequency-direction-finding antenna to locate Mitnick's apartment. The FBI was notified and an arrest warrant was obtained from a judge at his home. The FBI arrested Mitnick at his apartment. Mitnick was placed in jail without bail pending the investigation of his case.

Mitnick's computer crimes spree has been estimated to have cost his victims several hundreds of millions of dollars in losses. Mitnick has not been accused of benefiting financially from his deeds. Subsequently, Mitnick entered into a plea agreement with federal prosecutors. The U.S. District Court judge sentenced Kevin Mitnick to 46 months in prison, including time served, and ordered him to pay $4,125 in restitution to the companies he victimized. The judge called this a token amount but did not order a larger restitution because she believed Mitnick would not be able to pay more. After seving his time in jail, Mitnick was released from prison. As part of the sentencing, Mitnick cannot use electronic devices, from PCs to cellular telephones, during an additional probationary period following his release from prison. Mitnick is now acting as a consultant to businesses advising them how to protect themselves from computer hackers. See *United States v. Mitnick*, No. 97-50365, 1998 U.S. App. LEXIS 10836, at *1 (9th Cir. May 20, 1998).

Law & Ethics

1. What is a computer hacker?
2. Is it a crime to hack into other person's or entity's computers and either steal important and confidential information or just cause damages to the computer system and its contents?
3. **Ethics** Why do many computer hackers do what they do?
4. Should Mitnick have been given a greater sentence in this case? Why or why not?

INTERNET EXERCISES AND CASE QUESTIONS

Working the Web Internet Exercises

1. For a discussion of the Federal Dilution Act, featuring Barbie, Elvis, and Coca-Cola, see cyber.law.harvard.edu/property/respect/antibarbie.html.
2. For an overview of the Federal Electronic Signatures Act, explore the law review article "Are Online Business Transactions Executed by Electronic Signatures Legally Binding?" at www.law.duke.edu/journals/dltr/Articles/2001dltr0005.html.
3. Domain name dispute resolution procedures are presented in great detail at www.icann.org/dndr/udrp/policy.htm. Check this site for everything from an overview to sample pleading forms.

CHAPTER 9 SUMMARY

INTERNET, p. 246

The Internet and World Wide Web

1. *Internet.* The Internet is a collection of millions of computers that provide a network of electronic connections between computers.
2. *World Wide Web.* The Web is an electronic collection of computers that support a standard set of rules for the exchange of information called hypertext transfer protocol (HTTP).
3. *Electronic mail (e-mail).* E-mail is electronic written communication between individuals using computers connected to the Internet.

DOMAIN NAMES, p. 250

Domain Name

1. *Domain name.* A domain name is a unique name that identifies an individual's or a company's website.
2. *Domain name registration.* Domain names are registered by filing the appropriate form with a domain name registration service and paying the appropriate fee.

Anticybersquatting Act

1. *Anticybersquatting Consumer Protection Act.* This federal statute permits a court to issue cease-and-desist orders and injunctions and to award monetary damages against anyone who has registered a domain name (1) of a famous name or (2) in bad faith.

E-CONTRACTS, p. 256

E-Mail and Web Contracts

Contracts may be formed electronically over the Internet using e-mail and the World Wide Web.

Electronic Signatures

The Electronic Signature in Global and National Commerce Act (E-Sign Act). This federal statute (1) recognizes electronic contracts as meeting the writing requirement of the Statute of Frauds and (2) recognizes and gives electronic signatures—e-signatures—the same force and effect as pen-inscribed signatures on paper.

SOFTWARE AND E-LICENSING, p. 257

License

1. *License.* A license is a contract that transfers limited rights in intellectual property and informational rights.
2. *Licensor.* The owner of intellectual property or informational rights who transfers rights in the property or information to the licensee is called a licensor.
3. *Licensee.* The party who is granted limited rights or access to intellectual property or informational rights owned by the licensor is called a licensee.
4. *Licensing agreement.* A licensing agreement is a detailed and comprehensive written agreement between the licensor and the licensee that sets forth the express terms of their agreement.
5. *Access contract.* An access contract is a type of license that grants the licensee access to the licensed information for an agreed-upon time or number of uses.

ONLINE PRIVACY, p. 272

Electronic Privacy

Electronic Communications Privacy Act. This federal statute makes it a crime to intercept an "electronic communication" at the point of transmission, while in transit, when stored by a router or server, or after receipt by the intended recipient.

CYBER CRIMES, p. 273

Cyber crimes are those crimes committed by using computer technology and the Internet. These crimes could be crimes that already exist and new cyber crimes enacted into law.

1. *Counterfeit Access Device and Computer Fraud and Abuse Act.* This federal statute makes it a crime to knowingly access a computer to obtain specified information.
2. *Electronic Funds Transfer Act.* This federal statute makes it a crime to use, furnish, sell, or transport a counterfeit, stolen, lost, or fraudulently obtained ATM card, code number, or device used to conduct electronic funds transfers.
3. *Identity Theft and Assumption Deterrence Act.* This federal statute makes it a crime to engage in identity theft.
4. *Information Infrastructure Protection Act (IIP Act).* This federal statute makes it a crime to intentionally access and obtain information from a protected computer without authorization.

TERMS AND CONCEPTS

Access contract   261
Anticybersquatting Consumer Protection Act   251
Attribution procedure   263
Authenticate   263
Cancellation   268
Computer information transactions   246
Counterfeit Access Device and Computer Fraud and Abuse Act   273
Cover   270
Domain name   245
E-commerce   245

Electronic Communications Privacy Act (ECPA)   272
Electronic Funds Transfer Act   274
Electronic mail (e-mail)   249
Electronic Signature in Global and National Commerce Act (SIGN Act)   256
Exclusive license   259
Express warranty   265
Identity Theft and Assumption Deterrence Act of 1988   274
Implied warranty of fitness for a particular purpose   266
Implied warranty of informational content   266
Implied warranty of merchantability of the computer program   265
Information Infrastructure Protection Act (IIP Act)   275
Internet (Net)   246
Internet service provider (ISP)   247
License   259
Licensee   259
Licensee's damages   269
Licensing agreement   261
Licensor   259
Licensor's damages   268
Liquidated damages   270
Right to cure   269
Specific performance   270
Tender of performance   264
Uniform Computer Information Transactions Act (UCITA)   246
Uniform Electronic Transactions Act (UETA)   246
World Intellectual Property Organization (WIPO)   254
World Wide Web   247

CASE SCENARIO REVISITED

Remember the case of James and Gregory at the beginning of the chapter? Now that you understand more about the relevance of e-mails to the law of contracts, as well as the issues of a "writing" and specific performance, who do you think would prevail if Gregory refused to complete the contract for the sale of James's real estate? The case of *Lindblad v. Holmes*, No. BACV2004-00469, 2004 Mass. LEXIS 631, at*1 (Super. Ct. Nov. 24, 2004) may help you with your analysis.

CRITICAL LEGAL THINKING CASES

Critical Legal Thinking Case 9.1 *Domain Name*   Francis Net, a freshman in college and a computer expert, browses websites for hours each day. One day, she thinks to herself, "I can make money registering domain names and selling them for a fortune." She has recently seen an advertisement for Classic Coke, a cola drink produced and marketed by Coca-Cola Company. Coca-Cola Company has a famous trademark on the term *Classic Coke* and has spent millions of dollars advertising this brand and making the term famous throughout the United States and the world. Francis goes to the website www.networksolutions.com, an Internet domain name registration service, to see if the Internet domain name classiccoke.com has been taken. She discovers that it is available, so she immediately registers the Internet domain name classiccoke.com for herself and pays the $70 registration fee with her credit card. Coca-Cola Company decides to register the Internet domain name classiccoke.com, but when it checks at the Network Solutions website, it discovers that Francis Net has already registered the Internet domain name. Coca-Cola Company contacts Francis, who demands $500,000 for the name. Coca-Cola Company sues Francis to prevent Francis from using the Internet domain name classiccoke.com and to recover it from her under the federal ACPA. Who wins?

This critical thinking case is a hypothetical. However, a somewhat similar issue regarding website names was dealt with in the case *Coca-Cola Co. v. Purdy*, No. 02-1782 ADM/JGL, 2005 U.S. Dist. LEXIS 1226, at *1 (D.Minn. Jan. 28, 2005). In the *Purdy* case, the Coca-Cola-like website in question was actually an anti-abortion site. The court ordered a permanent injunction against the usage of this website name. As a critical thinking exercise, find and read the *Purdy* case. Distinguish the facts, the laws applied, and the outcomes of these two cases.

Critical Legal Thinking Case 9.2 *E-Mail Contract* The Little Steel Company is a small steel fabricator that makes steel parts for various metal machine shop clients. When Little Steel Company receives an order from a client, it must locate and purchase 10 tons of a certain grade of steel to complete the order. The Little Steel Company sends an e-mail message to West Coast Steel Company, a large steel company, inquiring about the availability of 10 tons of the described grade of steel. The West Coast Steel Company replies by e-mail that it has available the required 10 tons of steel and quotes $450 per ton. The Little Steel Company's purchasing agent replies by e-mail that the Litle Steel Company will purchase the 10 tons of described steel at the quoted price of $450 per ton. The e-mails are signed electronically by the Little Steel Company's purchasing agent and the selling agent of the West Coast Steel Company. When the steel arrives at the Little Steel Company's plant, the Little Steel Company rejects the shipment, claiming the defense of the Statute of Frauds. The West Coast Steel Company sues the Little Steel Company for damages. Who wins?

Critical Legal Thinking Case 9.3 *Contract* Einstein Financial Analysts, Inc. (EFA), has developed an electronic database that has recorded the number of plastic pails manufactured and sold in the United States since plastic was first invented. Using this data and a complicated patented software mathematical formula developed by EFA, a user can predict with 100 percent accuracy (historically) how the stock of each of the companies of the Dow Jones industrial average will perform on any given day of the year. William Buffet, an astute billionaire investor, wants to increase his wealth, so he enters into an agreement with EFA whereby he is granted the sole right to use the EFA data (updated daily) and its financial model for the next five years. Buffet pays EFA $100 million for the right to the data and mathematical formula. After using the data and software formula for one week, Buffet discovers that EFA has also transferred the right to use the EFA plastic pail database and software formula to his competitor. Buffet sues EFA. What type of arrangement have EFA and Buffet entered into? Who wins?

Critical Legal Thinking Case 9.4 *License* An Internet firm called Info.com, Inc., licenses computer software and electronic information over the Internet. Info.com has a website, info.com, where users can license Info.com software and electronic information. The website is operated by an electronic agent; a potential user enters Info.com's website and looks at software and electronic information that is available from Info.com. Mildred Hayward pulls up the Info.com. website on her computer and decides to order a certain type of Info.com software. Hayward enters the appropriate product code and description; her name, mailing address, and credit card information; and other data needed to complete the order for a three-year license at $300 per month; the electronic agent has Hayward verify all the information a second time. When Hayward has completed verifying the information, she types at the end of her order, "I accept this electronic software only if after I have used it for two months I still personally like it." Info.com's electronic agent delivers a copy of the software to Hayward, who downloads the copy of the software onto her computer. Two weeks later, Hayward sends the copy of the software back to Info.com, stating, "Read our contract: I personally don't like this software; cancel my license." Info.com sues Hayward to recover the license payments for three years. Who wins?

This critical thinking case is a hypothetical. However, a somewhat similar issue was dealt with in the case *ProCD, Inc. v. Zeidenberg*, 86 F.3d 1447 (7th Cir. 1996). In the *ProCD* case, the defendant chose to ignore the licensing agreement restricting its use to noncommercial purposes. The court found that the original licensing agreement was binding. As a critical thinking exercise, find and read the *ProCD* case. Distinguish the facts, the laws applied, and the outcomes of these two cases.

Critical Legal Thinking Case 9.5 *Electronic Signature* David Abacus uses the Internet to order license software for his computer from Inet.License, Inc. (Inet), through Inet's electronic website ordering system. Inet's web page order form asks David to type in his name, mailing address, telephone number, e-mail address, credit card information, computer location information, and personal identification number. Inet's electronic agent requests that David verify the information a second time before it accepts the order, which David does. The license duration is two years, at a license fee of $300 per month. Only after receiving the verification of information does Inet's electronic agent place the order and send an electronic copy of the software program to David's computer, where he installs the new software program. David later refuses to pay the license fee due Inet because he claims his electronic signature and information were not authentic. Inet sues David to recover the license fee. Is David's electronic signature enforceable against him?

Critical Legal Thinking Case 9.6 *License* Tiffany Pan, a consumer, intends to order three copies of a financial software program from iSoftware, Inc. Tiffany, using her computer, enters iSoftware's website isoftware.com and places an order with the electronic agent taking orders for the website. The license provides for a duration of three years at $300 per month for each copy of the software program. Tiffany enters the necessary product code and description; her name, mailing address, and credit card information; and other data necessary to place the order. When the electronic order form prompts Tiffany to enter the number of copies of the software program she is ordering, Tiffany mistakenly types in "30." Isoftware's electronic agent places the order and ships 30 copies of the software program to Tiffany. When Tiffany receives the 30 copies of the software program, she ships them back to iSoftware with a note stating, "Sorry, there has been a mistake. I only meant to order 3 copies of the software, not 30." When iSoftware bills Tiffany for the license fees for the 30 copies, Tiffany refuses to pay. iSoftware sues Tiffany to recover the license fees for 30 copies. Who wins?

This critical thinking case is a hypothetical. A similar, but still different, software licensing issue was dealt with in the case *1-A Equip. Co. v. Icode, Inc.*, 2003 Mass. App. Div. 30 (Dist. Ct. 2003). In the *1-A* case, the court found that a forum selection clause (i.e., where a lawsuit had to be filed) located in the license agreement was binding. As a critical thinking exercise, find and read the *1-A* case. Distinguish the facts, the laws applied, and the outcomes of these two cases.

Critical Legal Thinking Case 9.7 *License*   Silvia Miofsky licenses a software program from Accura.com, Inc., to sort information from a database to be used in Silvia's financial planning business. The license is for three years, and the license fee is $500 per month. The new software program from Accura.com will be run in conjunction with other software programs and databases used by Silvia in her business. The licensing agreement between Accura.com and Silvia and the label on the software package state that the copy of the licensed software program has been tested by Accura.com and will run without error. Silvia installs the copy of Accura.com's software, but every fifth or sixth time the program is run, it fails to operate properly and shuts down Silvia's computer and other programs. Silvia sends the software, marked *defective*, back to Accura.com. When Accura.com bills Silvia for the unpaid license fees for the three years of the license, Silvia refuses to pay. Accura.com sues Silvia to recover the license fees under the three-year license. Who wins?

This critical thinking case is a hypothetical. However, a similar issue was dealt with in the case *Performance Chevrolet, Inc. v. Market Scan Info. Sys., Inc.*, No. CV-04-244-S-BLW, 2007 U.S. Dist. LEXIS 23257, at *1 (D. Idaho Mar. 29, 2007). In the *Performance Chevrolet* case, the purchased software did not provide daily updates as promised. As a result, the court found that the software provider had breached the contract. As a critical thinking exercise, find and read the *Performance Chevrolet* case. Distinguish the facts, the laws applied, and the outcomes of these two cases.

Critical Legal Thinking Case 9.8 *License*   Metatag, Inc., is a developer and distributor of software and electronic information rights over the Internet. Metatag produces a software program called Virtual 4-D Links; a user of the program merely types in the name of a city and address anywhere in the world, and the computer transports the user there and creates a four-dimensional space and a sixth sense unknown to the world before. The software license is nonexclusive, and Metatag licenses its Virtual 4-D Link to millions of users worldwide. Nolan Bates, who has lived alone with his mother too long, licenses the Virtual 4-D Link program for five years for a license fee of $350 per month. Bates uses the program for two months before his mother discovers why he has had a smile on his face lately. Bates, upon his mother's urging, returns the Virtual 4-D Link software program to Metatag, stating he is canceling the license. Metatag sues Bates to recover the unpaid license fees. Who wins?

ETHICS CASES

Ethics Case 9.1   BluePeace.org is a new environmental group that has decided that expounding its environmental causes over the Internet is the best and most efficient way to spend its time and money to advance its environmental causes. To draw attention to its websites, BluePeace.org comes up with catchy Internet domain names. One is macyswearus.org, another is exxonvaldezesseals.org, and another is generalmotorscrashesdummies.org. The macyswearus.org website first shows beautiful women dressed in mink fur coats sold by Macy's Department Stores and then goes into graphic photos of minks being slaughtered and skinned and made into the coats. The exxonvaldezesseals.org website first shows a beautiful, pristine bay in Alaska, with the *Exxon Valdez* oil tanker quietly sailing through the waters, and then it shows photos of the ship breaking open and spewing forth oil and then seals who are gooey with oil, suffocating and dying on the shoreline. The website generalmotorscrashesdummies.org shows a General Motors automobile involved in normal crash tests with dummies followed by photographs of automobile accident scenes where adults and children lie bleeding and dying after an accident involving General Motors automobiles. Macy's Department Stores, the Exxon Oil Company, and the General Motors Corporation sue BluePeace.org for violating the federal ACPA. Who wins? Has BluePeace.org acted unethically in this case?

This critical thinking case is a hypothetical case dealing with a "bait and switch" issue in a website name. A different sort of website name issue—regarding *cybersquatting*—was dealt with in the case *Porsche Cars N. Am., Inc. v. Spencer*, No. CIV. S-00-471 GEN PAN, 2000 U.S. Dist. LEXIS 7060, at *1 (E.D. Cal. May 18, 2000). In that case, the defendant had rushed to reserve numerous domain names. The court in the *Porsche* case granted a preliminary injunction against the defendant's use of the website name at issue. As a critical thinking exercise, find and read the *Porsche* case. Distinguish the facts, the laws applied, and the outcomes of these two cases.

Ethics Case 9.2   Apricot.com is a major software developer that licenses software to be used over the Internet. One of its programs, called Match, is a search engine that searches personal ads on the Internet and provides a match for users for potential dates and possible marriage partners. Nolan Bates subscribes to the Match software program from Apricot.com. The license duration is five years, with a license fee of $200 per month. For each subscriber, Apricot.com produces a separate web page that shows photos of the subscriber and personal data. Bates places a photo of himself with his mother, with the caption, "Male, 30 years old, lives with mother, likes quiet nights at home." Bates licenses the Apricot.com Match software and uses it 12 hours each day, searching for his Internet match. Bates does not pay Apricot.com the required monthly licensing fee for any of the three months he uses the software. After using the Match software but refusing to pay Apricot.com its licensing fee, Apricot.com activates the disabling bug in the software and disables the Match software on Bates's computer. Apricot.com does this with no warning to Bates. It then sends a letter to Bates stating, "Loser, the license is canceled!" Bates sues Apricot.com for disabling the Match software program. Who wins? Did Bates act ethically? Did Apricot.com act ethically?

BRIEFING THE CASE WRITING ASSIGNMENT

Read Case A.9 in Appendix A (*Toys "R" Us, Inc. v. Abir*). This case is excerpted from the federal district court opinion. Review and brief the case. After briefing the case, you should be able to answer the following questions:

1. Who was the plaintiff? Who was the defendant?
2. How did the Internet domain names of both parties influence the court's decision?

PRACTICE TIP

Many bar associations and legal experts recommend using 'Plain English' language in the contract. The theory is that by using 'Plain English' fewer disputes will ensue over the terms of the contract. In other words, the language won't be ambiguous, but, rather, the contract's meaning will be totally clear to all of the parties involved.

The 'Plain English' theory is discussed in more detail on several websites. A couple of those websites are:

http://www.michbar.org/generalinfo/plainenglish/columns/147.html
http://www.languageandlaw.org/PLAINENGLISH.HTM

Domestic and International Sales and Lease Contracts

PART TWO

Chapter 10   Formation of Sales and Lease Contracts

Chapter 11   Performance of Sales and Lease Contracts

Chapter 12   Remedies for Breach of Sales and Lease Contracts

Chapter 13   Sales and Lease Warranties

Commercial law lies within a narrow compass, and is far purer and freer from defects than any other part of the system.

—*Henry Peter Brougham*

House of Commons, February 7, 1828

Formation of Sales and Lease Contracts

CASE SCENARIO

The law firm where you work as a paralegal is representing Jane Wilson who leased a pickup truck from World Leasing, Inc. Jane had experience in business and had signed contracts before. In the past, Wilson had read the contracts before signing them. When signing the contract for the lease of the truck, however, Jane did not take the opportunity to read the lease. She signed a statement declaring she had read and understood the lease. The lease contained a provision that made Jane responsible for payments on the truck even if the truck was destroyed. Several months after leasing the truck, Jane was involved in a two-vehicle collision. The pickup truck was destroyed. World Leasing, Inc., has demanded to be paid for the balance of the lease.

■ CHAPTER INTRODUCTION

Most tangible items—such as books, clothing, and tools—are considered *goods*. In medieval times, merchants gathered at fairs in Europe to exchange such goods. Over time, certain customs and rules evolved for enforcing contracts and resolving disputes. These customs and rules, which were referred to as the "Law Merchant," were enforced by "fair courts" established by the merchants. Eventually, the customs and rules of the Law Merchant were absorbed into the common law.

Toward the end of the 1800s, England enacted a statute (the Sales of Goods Act) that codified the common law rules of commercial transactions. In the United States, laws governing the sale of goods also developed. In 1906, the **Uniform Sales Act** was promulgated in the United States. This act was enacted in many states.

Uniform Sales Act
A law governing sales of goods that was adopted by most states. It was later subsumed within Article 2 of the Uniform Commercial Code.

CHAPTER OBJECTIVES

After studying this chapter, you should be able to:

1. Define sales contracts governed by Article 2 of the UCC.

2. Define lease contracts governed by Article 2A of the UCC.

3. Apply the basic UCC principles of good faith and reasonableness.

4. Describe the formation of sales and lease contracts.

5. Define the UCC's firm offer rule, additional terms rule, and written confirmation rule.

Uniform Commercial Code
Comprehensive statutory scheme that includes laws that cover aspects of commercial transactions.

Article 2 (Sales)
A section of the Uniform Commercial Code that deals with the sale of goods.

intangible property
Rights that cannot be reduced to physical form such as stock certificates, certificates of deposit, bonds and copyrights.

Article 2A (Leases)
Article of the UCC that governs lease of goods.

It was quickly outdated, however, as mass production and distribution of goods developed in the twentieth century.

In 1949, the National Conference of Commissioners on Uniform State Laws promulgated a comprehensive statutory scheme called the **Uniform Commercial Code (UCC)**. The UCC covers most aspects of commercial transactions. The most important section of the UCC—as it relates to contract law—is Article 2.

Note that **Article 2 (Sales)** of the UCC deals with the sale of *goods*, not real property (real estate), services, or **intangible property**. **Article 2A (Leases)** of the UCC governs personal property leases. These articles are intended to provide clear, easy-to-apply rules that place the risk of loss of the goods on the party most able to either bear the risk or insure against it. The rules of the UCC may vary depending on whether the buyer or the seller is a merchant.

The UCC does not *replace* the common law of contracts. The common law of contracts continues to govern if the UCC is silent on an issue.

This chapter discusses sales and lease contracts. Other articles of the UCC are discussed in subsequent chapters.

PARALEGAL PERSPECTIVE

Cathy D. Canny is a senior litigation paralegal at Dann Pecar Newman & Kleiman, P.C., in Indianapolis, Indiana. She is a graduate of Saint Mary-of-the-Woods College in Saint Mary-of-the-Woods, Indiana. She holds a bachelor of arts degree in paralegal studies, and she also obtained a minor in business administration.

Many of our cases involve contract disputes. From the initial client conference, to drafting or responding to complaints, through the discovery stage, and preparing for and assisting at trial, my knowledge of contract law is extremely important. My work often involves some sort of contract. Types of contracts that I may see in cases include employment agreements, severance and release agreements, noncompete contracts, shareholder agreements, contracts between customer and vendor, and purchase contracts, to name just a few.

From simple contracts to those that are complex, my attorneys depend on me to have substantive knowledge. I am able to review the contracts to identify the parts that are relevant and those that are in contention. Then, I look at the applicable law and fact gather for preparation of the case. This enables my attorneys to have more reliance on me, which frees up their time for other tasks they must accomplish.

Knowledge of contract law has given me invaluable expertise to better assist my attorneys in our litigation cases. There are so many areas of litigation, and it is imperative that I, as a paralegal, have practice knowledge of substantive areas of law. It also enables me to assist attorneys in other practice areas, such as bankruptcy, real estate, and corporate law. This makes me a very well-rounded paralegal and an asset to my law firm.

Paralegals are an integral part of the legal services team. With effective utilization by attorneys at my firm, our clients benefit and the law firm improves its profitability.

■ UNIFORM COMMERCIAL CODE (UCC)

One of the major frustrations of business persons conducting interstate business is that they are subject to the laws of each state in which they operate. To address this problem, the National Conference of Commissioners on Uniform State Laws in 1949 promulgated the Uniform Commercial Code (UCC).

LANDMARK LAW

THE UNIFORM COMMERCIAL CODE (UCC)

The UCC is a **model act** drafted by the American Law Institute and the National Conference of Commissioners on Uniform State Law. This model act contains uniform rules that govern commercial transactions. For the UCC, or any part of the UCC, to become law in a state, that state needs to enact the UCC as its commercial law statute. Every state (except Louisiana, which has adopted only parts of the UCC) has enacted the UCC or the majority of the UCC as a commercial statute.

The UCC is divided into articles, with each article establishing uniform rules for a particular facet of U.S. commerce. The articles of the UCC are listed below and are discussed in the chapters in Part II of this book.

The UCC is continually being revised to reflect changes in modern commercial practices and technology. Article 2, which establishes rules that govern the sale of goods, was recently amended. Article 2A was added to govern leases of

personal property, and Article 4A was added to regulate the use of wire transfers in the banking system. Articles 3 and 4, which cover the creation and transfer of negotiable instruments and the clearing of checks through the banking system, were substantially amended in 1990. Article 9, which covers secured transactions in personal property, has also been revised.

Web Exercises

1. **Web** To view the list of articles to the UCC, go to www.law.cornell.edu/ucc/index/htm.
2. **Web** Visit the website of the National Conference of Commissioners on Uniform State Laws at www.nccusl.org.
3. **Web** Visit the website of the American Law Institute at www.ali.org.

Article 1	General Provisions
Article 2	Sales
Article 2A	Leases
Article 3	Negotiable Instruments
Article 4	Bank Deposits and Collections
Article 4A	Funds Transfers
Article 5	Letters of Credit
Article 6	Bulk Transfers
Article 7	Documents of Title
Article 8	Investment Securities
Article 9	Secured Transactions
Revised Article 9	Secured Transactions

■ ARTICLE 2 (SALES)

All states except Louisiana have adopted some version of Article 2 (Sales) of the UCC. Article 2 is also applied by federal courts to sales contracts governed by federal law. Article 2 has recently been revised. This article, referred to as **Revised Article 2**, has been adopted by some states.

What Is a Sale?

Article 2 of the UCC applies to transactions in goods [UCC 2-102]. All states have held that Article 2 applies to the sale of goods. A **sale** consists of the passing of title from a seller to a buyer for a price [UCC 2-106(1)].

model act
A statute proposed to legislatures for adoption (e.g., the Model Probate Code proposed by the National Conference of Commissioners of Uniform Laws).

Revised Article 2
A recent revision of Article 2 to the Uniform Commercial Code that deals with the sale of goods.

sale
The passing of title from a seller to a buyer for a price. Also called a conveyance.

Exhibit 10.1 Sales Transaction

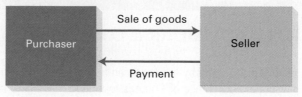

Example: The purchase of a computer is a sale subject to Article 2, whether the computer was paid for by cash, credit card, or other form of consideration (see Exhibit 10.1)

What Are Goods?

goods
Tangible things that are movable at the time of their identification to the contract.

Goods are defined as tangible things that are movable at the time of their identification to a contract [UCC 2-105(1)]. Specially manufactured goods and the unborn young of animals are examples of goods. Certain items are not considered goods and not subject to Article 2:

1. Money and intangible items, such as stocks, bonds, and patents, are not tangible goods.
2. Real estate is not a tangible good because it is not movable [UCC 2-105(1)]. Minerals, structures, growing crops, and other things that are severable from real estate may be classified as goods subject to Article 2, however.

Example: The sale and removal of a chandelier in a house is a sale of goods subject to Article 2 because its removal would not materially harm the realty. The sale and removal of the furnace, however, would be a sale of real property because its removal would cause material harm [UCC 2-107(2)].

Goods Versus Services

mixed sale
A sale that involves the provision of a service and a good in the same transaction.

Contracts for the provision of services—including legal services, medical services, and dental services—are not covered by Article 2. Sometimes, however, a sale involves both the provision of a service and a good in the same transaction. This sale is referred to as a **mixed sale**. Article 2 applies to mixed sales only if the goods are the predominant part of the transaction. The UCC provides no guidance for deciding cases based on mixed sales; therefore, the courts decide these issues on a case-by-case basis, using the common law of contracts.

In Case 10.1, the court had to decide whether a sale was of a good or a service.

CASE 10.1 GOOD OR SERVICE

Hector v. Cedars-Sinai Med. Ctr., 225 Cal. Rptr. 595 (Ct. App. 1986).

"The essence of the relationship between a hospital and its patients does not relate essentially to any product or piece of equipment it uses but to the professional services it provides."

Judge Spencer, *Court of Appeal of California*

Facts

Frances Hector entered Cedars-Sinai Medical Center (Cedars-Sinai), Los Angeles, California, for surgery on her heart. During the operation, a pacemaker was installed. The pacemaker, manufactured by American Technology, Inc., was installed at Cedars-Sinai by Hector's physician, Dr. Eugene Kompaniez. The pacemaker was defective, causing injury to Hector. Hector sued Cedars-Sinai under Article 2 of the UCC for breach of warranty. The trial court held that the sale was primarily a sale of a service and not of goods; therefore, the UCC did not apply. The trial court granted Cedars-Sinai motion for summary judgment and dismissed Hector's lawsuit. Hector appealed.

Issue

Is the installation of a pacemaker by a hospital a sale of a good subject to Article 2 of the UCC?

Language of the Court

The physician's services depend upon his skill and judgment derived from his specialized training, knowledge, experience, and skill. A doctor diagnosing and treating a patient normally is not selling either a product or insurance. A hospital is not ordinarily engaged in the business of selling any of the products or equipment it uses in providing such services. The essence of the relationship between a hospital and its patients does not relate essentially to any product or piece of equipment it uses but to the professional services it provides.

Testimony indicates that Cedars-Sinai does not routinely stock pacemakers, nor is it in the business of selling, distributing, or testing pacemakers. The treatment provided by Cedars-Sinai in relation to implantation of pacemakers includes pre- and post-operative care, nursing care, a surgical operating room, and technicians. As a provider of services rather than a seller of a product, the hospital is not subject to liability for a defective product provided to the patient during the course of his or her treatment.

Decision

The court of appeal held that Cedars-Sinai was a provider of medical services and not a seller of goods. Therefore, Cedars-Sinai was not liable for breach of warranty under the UCC because the UCC did not apply. The court of appeal affirmed the decision of the trial court.

Law & Ethics Questions

1. Should the UCC be extended to service providers?
2. **Ethics** Was it ethical for the hospital to deny liability in this case?
3. Could American Technology, Inc., be held liable to the plaintiff in this case? Why do you think the plaintiff sued Cedars-Sinai in this case?

Web Exercises

1. **Web** Visit the website of the Courts of Appeal of California to find the Second Appellate District, at www.courtinfo.ca.gov/courts.

2. **Web** Visit the website of Cedars-Sinai Medical Center at www.csmc.edu.

3. **Web** Use www.google.com and find an article that discusses the use of Article 2 (Sales) in your state.

Who Is a Merchant?

merchant
A person who (1) deals in the goods of the kind involved in the transaction or (2) by his or her occupation holds himself or herself out as having knowledge or skill peculiar to the goods involved in the transaction.

Generally, Article 2 of the UCC applies to all sales contracts, whether they involve merchants or not. However, Article 2 contains several provisions that either apply only to merchants or impose a greater duty on merchants. UCC 2-104(1) defines a **merchant** as (1) a person who deals in the goods of the kind involved in the transaction or (2) a person who by his or her occupation holds himself or herself out as having knowledge or skill peculiar to the goods involved in the transaction. For example, a sporting goods dealer is a merchant with respect to sporting goods but is not if he sells his lawn mower to a neighbor. The courts disagree as to whether farmers are merchants within this definition.

PARALEGAL PERSPECTIVE

Fern Burnett currently works as a paralegal at the corporate offices of Valley Yellow Pages in Fresno, California. Among the degrees she has earned is an A.S. degree in paralegalism from Fresno City College in Fresno, California, where she now teaches legal research and writing. She currently works as corporate paralegal for the Valley Yellow Pages in Fresno.

As the company's corporate paralegal, I work daily with the general counsel and other corporate officers and managers to review, draft, revise, or advise on contracts.

Housing our employees in sales offices throughout the state involves securing leases and insurance policies, and reviewing subordination, nondisturbance, and attornment agreements. My work also involves analyzing contracts with independent contractors and utility corporations.

Because the company sells advertisement, customer contracts are fundamental to any lawsuit or dispute that may arise. Essential to the functioning of the corporation are agreements for payment, contracts for services with companies for graphics, publishing, distribution, and website creation and management.

The corporation must also enter into contracts with companies for employee services (i.e., medical insurance, retirement accounts, and disability benefits).

Under the supervision of the general counsel, I handle contracts and agreements in a very practical way to help word agreements without using archaic legalese, and I help to ensure that the best interests of the corporation and its employees are met.

◼ ARTICLE 2A (LEASES)

Personal property leases are a billion-dollar industry. Consumer leases of automobiles or equipment and commercial leases of such items as aircraft and industrial machinery fall into this category. In the past, these transactions were governed by a combination of common law principles, real estate law, and reference to Article 2. Some of these legal rules and concepts do not quite fit a lease transaction.

Uniform Commercial Code—Leases
Article 2A of the UCC directly addresses personal property leases including the formation, performance, and default of leases in goods.

Article 2A of the UCC was promulgated in 1987. This article, which is cited as the **Uniform Commercial Code—Leases**, directly addresses personal property leases [UCC 2A-101]. It establishes a comprehensive, uniform law covering the formation, performance, and default of leases in goods [UCC 2A-102, 2A-103(h)].

Article 2A is similar to Article 2. In fact, many Article 2 provisions were changed to reflect leasing terminology and practices that carried over to Article 2A.

Definition of a Lease

A **lease** is a transfer of the right to the possession and use of the named goods for a set term in return for certain consideration [UCC 2A-103(1)(i)(x)]. The leased goods can be anything from a hand tool leased to an individual for a few hours to a complex line of industrial equipment leased to a multinational corporation for a number of years.

In an ordinary lease, the **lessor** is the person who transfers the right of possession and use of goods under the lease [UCC 2A-103(1)(p)]. The **lessee** is the person who acquires the right to possession and use of goods under a lease [UCC 2A-103(1)(n)].

Example: Dow Chemical Company decides to lease robotic equipment to manufacture most of its products. Ingersoll-Rand Corporation, which manufactures robotic equipment, enters into a lease contract to lease robotic equipment to Dow Chemical. Ingersoll-Rand is the lessor, and Dow Chemical is the lessee (see Exhibit 10.2).

Finance Lease

A **finance lease** is a three-party transaction consisting of a lessor, a lessee, and a **supplier** (or vendor). The lessor does not select, manufacture, or supply the goods. Instead, the lessor acquires title to the goods or the right to their possession and use in connection with the terms of the lease [UCC 2A-103(1) (g)].

Example: JetBlue Airways, a commercial air carrier, decides to acquire a new airplane. Boeing Company manufactures the airplane JetBlue wants to acquire. To finance the airplane acquisition, JetBlue goes to City Bank, which purchases the airplane from Boeing, and City Bank then leases the airplane to JetBlue. City Bank is the lessor, JetBlue is the lessee, and Boeing is the supplier. City Bank does not take physical delivery of the airplane; the airplane is delivered by Boeing directly to JetBlue (see Exhibit 10.3).

lease
A contract for the exclusive possession of lands or tenements for a determinate period; a contract by which the lessor grants the lessee the exclusive right to possess and use personal property of the lessor for a specified period.

lessor
The person who transfers the right of possession and use of goods under the lease.

lessee
The person who acquires the right to possession and use of goods under a lease.

finance lease
A three-party transaction consisting of the lessor, the lessee, and the supplier.

supplier
One engaged in the business of making products available to consumers; all persons in the chain of production and distribution of a consumer product.

Exhibit 10.2 Lease

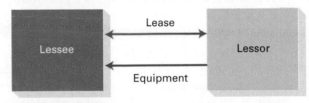

Exhibit 10.3 Finance Lease

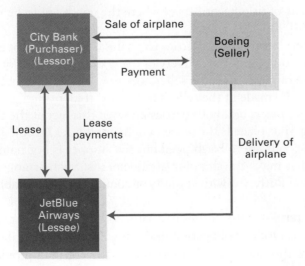

■ FORMATION OF SALES AND LEASE CONTRACTS: OFFER

As with general contracts, the formation of sales and lease contracts requires an offer and an acceptance. The UCC-established rules for each of these elements often differ considerably from common law.

A contract for the sale or lease of goods may be made in any manner sufficient to show agreement, including conduct by both parties that recognizes the existence of a contract [UCC 2-204, (1), 2A-204(1)]. Under the UCC, an agreement sufficient to constitute a contract for the sale or lease of goods may be found even though the moment of its making is undetermined [UCC 2-204 (2), 2A-204 (2)].

Open Terms

Sometimes the parties to a sale or lease contract leave open a major term in the contract. The UCC is tolerant of open terms. According to UCC 2-204(3) and 2A-204(3), the contract does not fail because of indefiniteness if (1) the parties intended to make a contract and (2) there is a reasonably certain basis for giving an appropriate remedy. In effect, certain **open terms** are permitted to be "read into" a sale or lease contract. This rule is commonly referred to as the **gap-filling rule**.

Some examples of terms that are commonly left open are the following:

open term
A section of a sales or lease contract on which the parties are allowed to "read into" the meaning of that section.

gap-filling rule
A rule that says an open term can be "read into" a contract.

open price term
Where a sales contract does not contain a specific price; a "reasonable price" is implied at the time of delivery.

- *Open price term*—If a sales contract does not contain a specific price (**open price term**), a "reasonable price" is implied at the time of delivery. The contract may provide that a price is to be fixed by a market rate (e.g., commodities market), as set or recorded by a third person or agency (e.g., a government agency), or by another standard, either upon delivery or on a set date. If the agreed-upon standard is unavailable when the price is to be set, a reasonable price is implied at the time of delivery of the goods [UCC 2-305(1)].

  A seller or buyer who reserves the right to fix a price must do so in good faith [UCC 2-305(2)]. When one of the parties fails to fix an open price term, the other party may opt either (1) to treat the contract as canceled or (2) to fix a reasonable price for the goods [UCC 2-305(3)].

- *Open payment term*—If the parties to a sales contract do not agree on payment terms, payment is due at the time and place at which the buyer is to receive the goods. If delivery is authorized and made by way of document of title, payment is due at the time and place at which the buyer is to receive the document of title, regardless of where the goods are to be received [UCC 2-310].

- *Open delivery term*—If the parties to a sales contract do not agree to the time, place, and manner of delivery of the goods, the place for delivery is the seller's place of business. If the seller does not have a place of business, delivery is to be made at the seller's residence. If identified goods are located at some other place, and both parties know of this fact at the time of contracting, that place is the place of delivery [UCC 2-308].

  Where goods are to be shipped but the shipper is not named, the seller is obligated to make the shipping arrangements. Such arrangements must be made in good faith and within limits of commercial reasonableness [UCC 2-311(2)].

- *Open time term*—If the parties to a sales contract do not set a specific time of performance for any obligation under the contract, the contract must be performed within a reasonable time. If the sales contract provides for successive performance over an unspecified period of time, the contract is valid for a reasonable time [UCC 2-309].

- *Open assortment term*—If the assortment of goods to a sales contract is left open, the buyer is given the option of choosing those goods.

Example: Suppose Macy's contracts to purchase 1,000 dresses from Liz Claiborne, Inc. The contract is silent as to the assortment of colors of the dresses. The buyer may pick the assortment of colors for the dresses from the seller's stock. The buyer must make the selection in good faith and within limits set by commercial reasonableness [UCC 2-311(2)].

MARKETPLACE

Job Announcement: Labor Litigation Paralegal

A national drugstore chain is seeking a paralegal to assist attorneys primarily with respect to labor, employment, and wage and hour litigation matters. The paralegal will assist attorneys with discovery assignments, case management, and employment contract review.

Qualified candidate must have a paralegal certificate with a college degree preferred. At least 3 years of labor and employment law paralegal experience with a law firm or corporate law department is required. General office experience and PC proficiency (Microsoft Office, Access a plus) are essential. Experience as a paralegal and database experience are a plus.

Come work with an industry leader! We offer a competitive salary and excellent benefits package including medical, dental, profit sharing 401(k), stock purchase plan, and store discounts.

For immediate consideration, apply online at:

CONTEMPORARY Issue

UCC "FIRM OFFER" RULE

Recall that the common law of contracts allows the offeror to revoke an offer any time prior to its acceptance. The only exception allowed by the common law is an *option contract* (i.e., where the offeree pays the offeror consideration to keep the offer open).

The UCC recognizes another exception, which is called the **firm offer rule**. This rule states that a *merchant* who (1) offers to buy, sell, or lease goods and (2) gives a written and signed assurance on a separate form that the offer will be held open cannot revoke the offer for the time stated or, if no time is stated, for a reasonable time. The maximum amount of time permitted under this rule is three months [UCC 2-205, 2A-205].

Example: On June 1, a merchant-seller offers to sell a Mercedes-Benz to a buyer for $50,000. The merchant-seller signs a written assurance to keep that offer open until August 30. On July 1, the merchant-seller sells the car to another buyer. On August 21, the original offeree tenders $50,000 for the car. The merchant-seller is liable to the original offeree for breach of contract.

firm offer rule
Under the UCC, a merchant who offers to buy, sell, or lease goods and who gives a written and signed assurance that the offer will be held open cannot revoke the offer for the time stated or a reasonable time.

Consideration

The formation of sales and lease contracts requires consideration. However, the UCC changes the common law rule that requires the modification of a contract to be supported by new consideration. An agreement modifying a sales or lease contract needs no consideration to be binding [UCC 2-209(1), 2A-208(1)].

Modification of a sales or lease contract must be made in good faith [UCC 1-203]. As in the common law of contracts, modifications are not binding if they are obtained through fraud, duress, extortion, and such.

■ FORMATION OF SALES AND LEASE CONTRACTS: ACCEPTANCE

Both common law and the UCC provide that a contract is created when the offeree (i.e., the buyer or lessee) sends an acceptance to the offeror, not when the offeror receives the acceptance. For example, a contract is made when the acceptance letter is delivered to the post office. The contract remains valid even if the post office loses the letter.

Unless otherwise unambiguously indicated by language or circumstance, an offer to make a sales or lease contract may be accepted in any manner and by any reasonable medium of acceptance [UCC 2-206(1)(a), 2A-206(1)]. Applications of this rule are discussed in the following paragraphs.

Methods of Acceptance

The UCC permits acceptance by any reasonable manner or method of communication.

Example: A seller sends a telegram to a proposed buyer, offering to sell the buyer certain goods. The buyer responds by mailing a letter of acceptance to the seller. In most circumstances, mailing the letter of acceptance would be considered reasonable. If the goods were extremely perishable or if the market for the goods were very volatile, however, a faster means of acceptance (such as a telegram) might be warranted.

If an order or other offer to buy goods requires prompt or current shipment, the offer is accepted if the seller (1) promptly promises to ship the goods or (2) promptly ships either conforming or nonconforming goods [UCC 2-206(1)(b)]. The shipment of conforming goods signals acceptance of the buyer's offer.

Acceptance of goods occurs after the buyer or lessee has a reasonable opportunity to inspect them and signifies that (1) the goods are conforming, (2) he or she will take or retain the goods in spite of their nonconformity, or (3) he or she fails to reject the goods within a reasonable time after tender or delivery [UCC 2-513(1), 2A-515(1)].

Accommodation Shipment

accommodation
A shipment that is offered to the buyer as a replacement for the original shipment when the original shipment cannot be filled.

A shipment of nonconforming goods does not constitute an acceptance if the seller reasonably notifies the buyer that the shipment is offered only as an **accommodation** to the buyer [UCC 2-206(1)(b)]. For example, suppose a buyer offers to purchase 500 red candles from a seller. The seller's red candles are temporarily

CONTEMPORARY Issue

UCC PERMITS ADDITIONAL TERMS

Under common law's **mirror image rule**, an offeree's acceptance must be on the same terms as the offer. The inclusion of additional terms in the acceptance is considered a counteroffer rather than an acceptance. Thus, the offeror's original offer is extinguished.

UCC 2-207(1) is more liberal than the mirror image rule. It permits definite and timely expression of acceptance or written confirmation to operate as an acceptance even though they contain terms that are additional to or different from the offered terms, unless the acceptance is expressly conditional on assent to such terms. This rule differs for merchants and nonmerchants.

If one or both parties to a sales contract are nonmerchants, any additional terms are considered **proposed additions** to the contract. The proposed additions do not constitute a counteroffer or extinguish the original offer. If the offeree's proposed additions are accepted by the original offeror, they become part of the contract. If they are not accepted, the sales contract is formed on the basis of the terms of the original offer [UCC 2-207(2)].

Example: A salesperson at a Lexus dealership offers to sell a top-of-the-line coupe to a buyer for $64,000. The buyer replies, "I accept your offer, but I would like to have a satellite radio in the car." The satellite radio is a proposed addition to the contract. If the salesperson agrees, the contract between the parties consists of the terms of the original offer plus the additional term regarding the satellite radio. If the salesperson rejects the proposed addition, the sales contract consists of the terms of the original offer because the buyer made a definite expression of acceptance.

mirror image rule
States that for an acceptance to exist, the offeree must accept the terms as stated in the offer.

proposed additions
If one or both parties to the contract are nonmerchants, any additional terms do not constitute a counteroffer or extinguish the original offer. If the offeree's proposed conditions are accepted by the original offeror, they become part of the contract. If they are not accepted, the sales contract is formed on the basis of the original offer.

THE ETHICAL PARALEGAL

Avoid the Appearance of Impropriety

The ethical paralegal knows to avoid unethical and improper acts. However, the ethical rules require legal professionals to do more. Legal professionals must avoid even the *appearance* of having done something unethical and improper. This is called the avoidance of the *appearance of impropriety*.

The appearance of impropriety is often raised in situations where attorneys move between law firms (ABA Model Rule 1.10) and where there are issues of improper influence on a tribunal (ABA Model Rule 3.5).[1] Because even an innocent act can take on the appearance of impropriety, ethical paralegals should always be aware of how their actions—even if innocent—might be interpreted by an observer.

out of stock. The seller sends the buyer 500 green candles and notifies the buyer that these candles are being sent as an accommodation. The seller has not accepted (or breached) the contract. The accommodation is a counteroffer from the seller to the buyer. The buyer is free either to accept or to reject the counteroffer.

---

[1]Copies of the ABA Model Rules of Professional Conduct are available from Service Center, American Bar Association, 321 North Clark Street, Chicago, IL 60610, 1-800-285-2221. The Model Rules can also be viewed online at http://www.abanet.org/cpr/mrpc/mrpc_toc.html.

CONTEMPORARY Issue

"BATTLE OF THE FORMS"

When merchants negotiate sales contracts, they often exchange preprinted forms. These boilerplate forms usually contain terms that favor the drafter. Thus, an offeror who sends a standard form contract as an offer to the offeree may receive an acceptance drafted on the offeree's own form contract. This scenario—commonly called the **battle of the forms**—raises important questions: Is there a contract? If so, what are its terms? The UCC provides guidance in answering these questions.

Under UCC 2-207(2), If both parties are merchants, any additional terms contained in an acceptance become part of the sales contract unless (1) the offer expressly limits acceptance to the terms of the offer, (2) the additional terms materially alter the terms of the original contract, or (3) the offeror notifies the offeree that he or she objects to the additional terms within a reasonable time after receiving the offeree's modified acceptance.

The most important point in the battle of the forms is that there is no contract if the additional terms so materially alter the terms of the original offer that the parties cannot agree on the contract. This fact-specific determination is made by the courts on a case-by-case basis.

battle of the forms
Where the parties to a contract go back and forth with each other trying to get the other to agree to their standard contract form.

■ UCC STATUTE OF FRAUDS

The UCC includes Statute of Frauds provisions that apply to all sales and lease contracts. All contracts for the sale of goods costing $500 or more and lease contracts involving payments of $1,000 or more must be in writing [UCC 2-201(1), 2A-201(1)]. The writing must be sufficient to indicate that a contract has been made between the parties. Except as discussed in the paragraphs that follow, the writing must be signed by the party against whom enforcement is sought or by his or her authorized agent or broker. If a contract falling within these parameters is not written, it is unenforceable.

Example: A seller orally agrees to sell her computer to a buyer for $550. When the buyer tenders the purchase price, the seller asserts the Statute of Frauds and refuses to sell the computer to him. The seller is correct. The contract must be in writing to be enforceable because the contract price for the computer exceeds $499.99.

Exceptions to the Statute of Frauds

In three situations, a sales or lease contract that would otherwise be required to be in writing is enforceable even if it is not in writing [UCC 2-201(3), UCC 2A-201(4)]:

specially manufactured goods
Goods manufactured specifically for the buyer.

1. **Specially manufactured goods**—Buyers and lessees often order specially manufactured goods. If a contract to purchase or lease such goods is oral, the buyer or lessee may not assert the Statute of Frauds against the enforcement of the contract if (1) the goods are not suitable for sale or lease to others in the ordinary course of the seller's or the lessor's business and (2) the seller or lessor has made either a substantial beginning of the manufacture of the goods or commitments for their procurement.

2. **Admissions in pleadings or court**—If the party against whom enforcement of an oral sales or lease contract is sought admits in pleadings, testimony, or otherwise in court that a contract for the sale or lease of goods was made, the oral contract is enforceable against that party. However, the contract is only enforceable as to the quantity of goods admitted.

3. **Part acceptance**—An oral sales or lease contract that should otherwise be in writing is enforceable to the extent to which the goods have been received and accepted by the buyer or lessee.

Example: A lessor orally contracts to lease 100 personal computers to a lessee. The lessee accepts the first 20 computers tendered by the lessor. This action is part acceptance. The lessee refuses to take delivery of the remaining 80 computers. Here, the lessee must pay for the 20 computers she originally received and accepted. The lessee does not have to accept or pay for the remaining 80 computers.

admissions in pleadings or court
When a party admits in pleadings, testimony, or otherwise in court that a contract for the sale or lease of goods was made, the oral contract is enforceable against that party.

part acceptance
When a sales or lease contract is oral but should have been in writing, the contract is enforceable only to the extent to which the goods have been received and accepted by the buyer or lessee.

CONTEMPORARY Issue

UCC WRITTEN CONFIRMATION RULE

If both parties to an oral sales or lease contract are merchants, the Statute of Frauds requirement can be satisfied if (1) one of the parties to an oral agreement sends a written confirmation of the sale or lease within a reasonable time after contracting and (2) the other merchant does not give written notice of an objection to the contract within 10 days after receiving the confirmation. This situation is true even though the party receiving the written confirmation has not signed it. The only stipulations are that the confirmation be sufficient and that the party to whom it was sent has reason to know its contents [UCC 2-201(2)].

Example: A merchant-seller in Chicago orally contracts by telephone to sell goods to a merchant-buyer in Phoenix for $25,000. Within a reasonable time after contracting, the merchant-seller sends a sufficient written confirmation to the buyer. The buyer, who has reason to know the contents of the confirmation, fails to object to the contents of the confirmation in writing within 10 days after receiving it. The Statute of Frauds has been met, and the buyer cannot thereafter raise it against enforcement of the contract.

When Written Modification Is Required

Oral modification of a contract is not enforceable if the parties agree that any modification of the sales or lease contract must be signed in writing [UCC 2-209(2), 2A-208(2)]. In the absence of such an agreement, oral modifications to sales and lease contracts are binding if they do not violate the Statute of Frauds.

If the oral modification brings the contract within the Statute of Frauds, it must be in writing to be enforceable.

Example: A lessor and lessee enter into an oral lease contract for the lease of goods at a rent of $450. Subsequently, the contract is modified by raising the rent to $550. Because the modified contract rent is more than $499.99, the contract comes under the UCC Statute of Frauds, and the modification must be in writing to be enforceable.

CAREER FRONT

Criminal Law Paralegal

A criminal law paralegal can be involved with contracts in the following ways:

- Prepare client agreement for attorney to undertake representation of client's case.
- Prepare and file motion for bond reduction.
- Arrange for bail.
- Gather information for plea bargain agreement and prepare changes or plea for arraignment.
- Obtain discovery (police reports, search warrant, and affidavits) and interview witnesses.
- Examine physical evidence and tangible objects.
- Examine and photograph scene of alleged crime.
- Analyze case based on documents and information obtained.
- Prepare for preliminary hearing or grand jury presentation.
- Draft demurrer.
- As necessary and appropriate, draft motions to change venue, set aside indictment, to suppress, for acquittal, for civil compromise, for diversion, in limine, for return of property, to postpone trial, to disqualify judge, and to withdraw as attorney of record.
- Arrange civil compromise.
- Prepare documents concerning work release.
- Draft trial memorandum.
- Attend conference with prosecutor.
- Draft motions in arrest of judgment, for new trial, for release pending new trial, for appeal.
- Prepare sentencing information and work with probation officers.
- Draft petition for leniency for probation.
- Research law about appealable issues.
- Draft assignments of error and arguments.

Source: Excerpted by permission from the National Association of Legal Assistants (www.nala.org) and the National Federation of Paralegal Associations, Inc. (www.paralegals.org).

Parol Evidence

parol evidence rule
A rule that says if a written contract is a complete and final statement of the parties' agreement, any prior or contemporaneous oral or written statements that alter, contradict, or are in addition to the terms of the written contract are inadmissible in court regarding a dispute over the contract. There are several exceptions to this rule.

course of performance
The history of previous conduct of the parties regarding the contract in question.

The **parol evidence rule** states that when a sales or lease contract is evidenced by a writing that is intended to be a final expression of the parties' agreement or a confirmatory memorandum, the terms of the writing may not be contradicted by evidence of (1) a prior oral or written agreement or (2) a contemporaneous oral agreement (i.e., parol evidence) [UCC 2-202, 2A-202]. This rule is intended to ensure certainty in written sales and lease contracts.

Occasionally, the express terms of a written contract are not clear on their face and must be interpreted. In such cases, reference may be made to certain sources outside the contract. These sources are construed together when they are consistent with each other. If that is unreasonable, they are considered in descending order of priority [UCC 2-208(2), 2A-207(2)]:

1. **Course of performance**—The previous conduct of the parties regarding the contract in question.

ETHICS SPOTLIGHT

A CHICKEN FARMER GETS PLUCKED

Sometimes the Statute of Frauds, which was designed to prevent fraud, is used by a party to try to back out of an oral sales contract. Consider the following case.

Perdue Farms, Inc. sells dressed poultry under the brand name "Perdue Roasters." Motts, Inc. of Mississippi entered into an oral contract with Perdue to purchase 1,500 boxes of roasters from Perdue at a stated price. Motts was to pick up the roasters at Perdue's Maryland plant. Motts entered into a contract to resell the roasters to Dairyland, Inc. Motts sent a letter to Perdue confirming the oral agreement. Perdue received the confirmation and did not object to it. When Motts's truck arrived at Perdue's Maryland plant to pick up the roasters, Perdue informed Motts's drivers that the roasters would not be loaded unless complete payment was made before delivery. Under previous contracts between the parties, payment was due seven days after delivery. Perdue informed Motts that the roasters would not be sold to Motts on credit. Perdue then sold the roasters directly to Dairyland.

Motts sued Perdue to recover damages for breach of the sales contract. Perdue denied liability, arguing the contract had to be in writing under the UCC Statute of Frauds because it was over $500. Motts argued that the situation fell under the written confirmation rule exception to the UCC Statute of Frauds.

The district court agreed with Motts. UCC-2-201(2) binds merchants to oral sales contracts if one sends the other a confirmation letter that is not objected to within 10 days after its receipt. Both parties in this case were merchants, and Perdue did not object to Motts's confirmation letter within the 10-day period. The court denied Perdue the Statute of Frauds defense and made Motts's confirmation letter enforceable against Perdue. See *Perdue Farms, Inc. v. Motts, Inc. of Miss.,* 459 F. Supp. 7 (N.D. Miss. 1978).

Law & Ethics Questions

1. What does the UCC Statute of Frauds provide?
2. What does the UCC written confirmation rule provide? Explain.
3. **Ethics** Did Perdue act ethically in this case? Why do you think Perdue did not want to meet its agreement with Motts?

Web Exercises

1. **Web** Visit the website of Perdue Farms, Inc. at www.perdue.com.
2. **Web** Use www.google.com and find an article that discusses the UCC Statute of Frauds.

---

2. **Course of dealing**—The conduct of the parties in prior transactions and contracts.
3. **Usage of trade**—Any practice or method of dealing that is regularly observed or adhered to in a place, a vocation, a trade, or an industry.

Example: A cattle rancher contracts to purchase corn from a farmer. The farmer delivers feed corn to the rancher. The rancher rejects this corn and demands delivery of corn that is fit for human consumption. Ordinarily, usage of trade would be the first source of interpretation of the word *corn*. If the parties had prior dealings, though, the use of the term in their prior dealings would become the primary source of interpretation.

course of dealing
A sequence of previous acts and conduct between the parties to a particular transaction, which fairly establishes a common basis of understanding for interpreting their communications and other conduct.

usage of trade
A regularly observed or adhered to practice or method of dealing in a particular trade or industry.

Concept Summary

Comparison of Contract Law and the Law of Sales

Topic	Common Law of Contracts	UCC Law of Sales
Definiteness	Contract must contain all the material terms of the parties' agreement.	The UCC gap-filling rule permits terms to be implied if the parties intended to make a contract [UCC 2-204].
Irrevocable offers	Option contracts.	Option contracts. Firm offers by merchants to keep an offer open are binding up to three months without any consideration [UCC 2-205].
Counteroffers	Acceptance must be a mirror image of the offer. A counteroffer rejects and terminates the offer.	Additional terms of an acceptance become part of the contract if (1) they do not materially alter the terms of the offer and (2) the offeror does not object within a reasonable time after reviewing the acceptance [UCC 2-207].
Statute of Frauds	Writing must be signed by the party against whom enforcement is sought.	Writing may be enforced against a party who has not signed it if (1) both parties are merchants, (2) one party sends a written confirmation of oral agreement within a reasonable time after contracting, and (3) the other party does not give written notice of objection within 10 days after receiving the confirmation [UCC 2-201].
Modification	Consideration is required.	Consideration is not required [UCC 2-209].

E-Commerce & Information Technology

Unfair and Deceptive Acts over the Internet

Federal Trade Commission (FTC)
Federal government agency empowered to enforce federal franchising rules. Federal administrative agency empowered to enforce the Federal Trade Commission Act and other federal consumer protection statutes.

Section 5
Prohibits unfair and deceptive practices.

Little did Congress know over 80 years ago when it passed the **Federal Trade Commission Act** that Section 5 of the act would be used to prosecute fraud over the Internet. **Section 5** prohibits "unfair and deceptive" acts affecting commerce. The FTC has demonstrated recently that old laws can learn new tricks. Consider the following case.

Powerful search engines have been developed to allow surfers to browse the Internet and connect to websites in which they are interested. Certain scammers came up with a scheme where they would entice unwitting surfers to connect to their porn sites and not be able to get out. The scheme worked as follows. The

(continued)

scammers made fake copies of over 25 million popular websites such as the *Harvard Business Review, Japanese Friendship Gardens*, and others. Search engines trolling the Web for new pages found these websites and added them to their listings. The scammers added to the faked web pages an extra bit of coding so that as soon as surfers found the bogus web page, it rerouted—"page-jacked"—them to the scammer's porn website. Once there, the user was "mouse-trapped" at the porn site and efforts to escape led only to new porn pages. The porn site operators made money by selling advertisements, and ad prices were often based on the number of hits on the site.

The Federal Trade Commission (FTC), a federal government agency, investigated and sued porn site operators in federal court for violating Section 5 of the FTC Act. The court found that the porn site operators had engaged in unfair and deceptive practices in violation of Section 5, issued an injunction to shut down the porn sites, and ordered the operators not to engage in such conduct in the future.

INTERNATIONAL LAW

Letters of Credit in International Trade

The major risks in any business transaction involving the sale of goods are that (1) the seller will not be paid after delivering the goods and (2) the buyer will not receive the goods after paying for them. These risks are even more acute in international transactions, where the buyer and seller may not know each other, the parties are dealing at long distance, and the judicial systems of the parties' countries may not have jurisdiction to decide a dispute if one should arise. The irrevocable **letter of credit** has been developed to manage these risks in international sales. The function of a letter of credit is to substitute the credit of a recognized international bank for that of the buyer.

An irrevocable letter of credit works this way. Suppose a buyer in one country and a seller in another country enter into a contract for the sale of goods. The buyer goes to his or her bank and pays the bank a fee to issue a letter of credit in which the bank agrees to pay the amount of the letter (which is the amount of the purchase price of the goods) to the seller's bank if certain conditions are met. These conditions are usually the delivery of documents indicating that the seller has placed the goods in the hands of a shipper. The buyer is called the **account party**, the bank that issues the letter of credit is called the **issuing bank**, and the seller is called the **beneficiary** of the letter of credit.

The issuing bank then forwards the letter of credit to a bank that the seller has designated in his or her country. This bank, which is called the **correspondent** or **confirming bank**, relays the letter of credit to the seller. Now that the seller sees that he or she is guaranteed payment, he or she makes arrangements to ship the goods and receives a **bill of lading** from the carrier proving so. The seller then delivers these documents to the confirming bank. The confirming bank examines the documents and, if it finds them in order, pays the seller and forwards the documents to the issuing bank. By this time, the buyer has usually paid the amount of the purchase price to the issuing bank (unless an extension of credit has been arranged), and the issuing bank then charges the buyer's account. The issuing bank forwards the bill of lading and other necessary documents to the buyer, who then picks up the goods from the shipper when they arrive.

If the documents (e.g., bill of lading, proof of insurance) conform to the conditions specified in the letter of credit, the issuing bank must pay the letter of credit. If the account party does not pay the issuing bank, the issuing bank's only recourse is to sue the account party to recover damages.

(continued)

letter of credit
A written instrument addressed by one person to another requesting the latter to give credit to the person in whose favor it is drawn.

account party
The buyer in regard to a letter of credit.

issuing bank
The institution that issues the letter of credit.

beneficiary
A person or organization designated in the will that receives all or a portion of the testator's property at the time of the testator's death. The person who is to receive the life insurance proceeds when the insured dies. Person for whose benefit a trust is created.

correspondent
A securities firm, bank, or other financial organization that regularly performs services for another in a place or market to which the other does not have direct access (a correspondent on an exchange; correspondent bank).

bill of lading
A document of title that is issued by a carrier when goods are received for transportation.

Article 5 (Letters of Credit)
A section of the UCC that governs letters of credit unless otherwise agreed to by the parties.

Uniform Customs and Practices for Documentary Credits (UCP)
Rules created by the International Chamber of Commerce which govern the formation and performance of letters of credit.

Article 5 (Letters of Credit) of the UCC governs letters of credit unless otherwise agreed by the parties. The International Chamber of Commerce has promulgated the **Uniform Customs and Practices for Documentary Credits (UCP)**, which contains rules governing the formation and performance of letters of credit. Although the UCP is neither a treaty nor a legislative enactment, most banks incorporate the terms of the UCP in letters of credit they issue.

INTERNET EXERCISES AND CASE QUESTIONS

Working the Web Internet Exercises

1. Find the major differences in the rules of contract formation under the common law and UCC Article 2. Visit "Legal Information Institute (LII) Sales Law Overview" at www.law.cornell.edu/topics/sales.html.
2. Do the rules change when the parties are both merchants?
3. Although a contract can be created under UCC Article 2 even when several terms are omitted, generally one term must be included for a contract to be deemed valid by a court. Which term is it?

CHAPTER 10 SUMMARY

UNIFORM COMMERCIAL CODE, p. 288

The Uniform Commercial Code (UCC)

The Uniform Commercial Code (UCC) is a *model act* that contains uniform rules that govern commercial transactions.

State Adoption of the UCC

Most states have enacted all or part of the UCC as their commercial law statute.

ARTICLE 2 (SALES), p. 289

Article 2 (Sales)

Article 2 of the UCC applies to transactions in goods [UCC 2-102].

1. *Goods.* Goods are tangible things that are movable at the time of their identification in a sales contract [UCC 2-105(1)].
2. *Scope of Article 2.* Article 2 applies to all sales contracts, whether they involve merchants or not.

ARTICLE 2A (LEASES), p. 292

Article 2A (Leases)

Article 2A of the UCC applies to personal property leases of goods [UCC 2A-101].

1. *Lease.* A lease is a transfer of the right to the possession and use of the named goods for a set term in return for certain consideration.
2. *Parties to a lease:*
   a. *Lessor.* A person who transfers the right of possession and use of goods is a lessor [UCC 2A-103(1)(p)].
   b. *Lessee.* A person who acquires the right to possession and use of goods is a lessee [UCC 2A-103(1)(n)].

3. *Finance lease.* A finance lease is a three-party transaction of the lessor, the lessee, and the supplier of the leased goods. The parties to a finance lease are:
   a. *Lessor.* The lessor acquires title to the goods from the supplier and leases the goods to the lessee. The lessor is often a bank or another creditor.
   b. *Lessee.* The lessee is the person who acquires the right to possession and use of the goods.
   c. *Supplier.* The supplier is the third party who supplies the goods. The supplier usually sells the goods to the lessor.

FORMATION OF SALES AND LEASE CONTRACTS: OFFER, p. 294

Open terms. If the parties leave open a major term in a sales or lease contract, the UCC permits the following terms to be read into the contract:

1. Price term
2. Payment term
3. Delivery term
4. Time term
5. Assortment term

This is commonly called the *gap-filling rule* [UCC 2-204(3), 2A-204(3)].

Firm Offer Rule

The firm offer rule is a UCC rule that says a merchant who (1) makes an offer to buy, sell, or lease goods and (2) assures the other party in a separate writing that the offer will be held open cannot revoke the offer for the time stated, or if no time is stated, for a reasonable time [UCC 2-205, 2A-205].

FORMATION OF SALES AND LEASE CONTRACTS: ACCEPTANCE, p. 296

Accommodation shipment. This is a shipment offered to the buyer by the seller as a replacement for the original shipment when the original shipment cannot be filled. The buyer may either accept or reject this shipment [UCC 2-206(1)(b)].

Additional Terms Permitted

The UCC permits an acceptance of a sales contract to contain additional terms and still to act as an acceptance rather than a counteroffer in certain circumstances. The following UCC rules apply [UCC 2-207(2)]:

1. *One or both parties are nonmerchants.* The additional terms are considered proposed additions to the contract. If the offeree's proposed terms are accepted by the offeror, they become part of the contract. If they are not accepted, the sales contract is formed on the basis of the terms of the original offer.
2. *Both parties are merchant.* The additional terms contained in the acceptance become part of the sales contract *unless* (1) the offer expressly limits the acceptance to the terms of the offer, (2) the additional terms materially alter the original contract, or (3) the offerer notifies the offeree that he or she objects to the additional terms within a reasonable time after receiving the offeree's modified acceptance. There is no contract if the additional terms so materially alter the terms of the original offer that the parties cannot agree on the contract.

UCC STATUTE OF FRAUDS, p. 298

The UCC Statute of Frauds requires contracts for the sale of goods costing $500 or more and lease contracts involving payments of $1,000 or more to be in writing [UCC 2-201(1), 2A-201(1)].

Exceptions to the Statute of Frauds. The UCC recognizes the following exceptions to the Statute of Frauds where a sales or lease contract that is required to be in writing is enforceable even though it is not in writing:

1. *Specially manufactured goods.* In these contracts, the goods are not suitable for sale or lease to others in the ordinary course of business and the seller or lessor has made either a substantial beginning of manufacture of the goods or commitments for their procurement.
2. *Admissions in pleadings or court.* A party admits in pleadings, testimony, or otherwise in court that he or she has entered into a contract.
3. *Part acceptance.* An oral sales or lease contract is enforceable to the extent to which the goods have been received and accepted by the buyer or lessee.

Written Confirmation Rule

If both parties to an oral sales or lease contract are merchants, the Statute of Frauds requirements are satisfied if (1) one of the parties sends a *written confirmation* of the sale to the other within a reasonable time after contracting and (2) the other merchant does not give written notice of an objection to the contract within 10 days after receiving the confirmation [UCC 2-201(2)].

TERMS AND CONCEPTS

Accommodation shipment 296
Account party 303
Admissions in pleadings or court 299
Article 2 (Sales) 288
Article 2A (Leases) 288
Article 5 (Letters of Credit) 304
Battle of the forms 298
Beneficiary 303
Bill of lading 303
Correspondent (confirming bank) 303
Course of dealing 301
Course of performance 300
Federal Trade Commission Act 302
Finance lease 293
Firm offer rule 295
Gap-filling rule 294
Goods 290
Intangible property 288
Issuing bank 303
Lease 293
Lessee 293
Lessor 293

Letter of credit 303

Merchant 292

Mirror image rule 297

Mixed sale 290

Model act 289

Open price term 294

Open term 294

Parol evidence rule 300

Part acceptance 299

Proposed additions 297

Revised Article 2 289

Sale 289

Section 5 302

Specially manufactured goods 298

Supplier 293

Uniform Commercial Code (UCC) 288

Uniform Commercial Code—Leases 292

Uniform Customs and Practices for Documentary Credits (UCP) 304

Uniform Sales Act 287

Usage of trade 301

CASE SCENARIO REVISITED

Recall the case scenario at the beginning of the chapter involving Jane Wilson and her lease of a pickup truck from World Leasing, Inc. Do you think this lease was unconscionable? Does the fact that Jane did not read the contract affect the outcome of this case? To help you with your decision, read the case *Wilson v. World Omni Leasing, Inc.*, 540 So. 2d 713 (Ala. 1989).

CRITICAL LEGAL THINKING CASES

Critical Legal Thinking Case 10.1 *Merchant*   Mark Hemphill was a football player at Southern Illinois State University. As a member of the team, Hemphill was furnished with a uniform and helmet. He was injured while playing football for the school. Hemphill claimed that his helmet was defective and contributed to his injuries. Hemphill's attorneys suggested that he sue the university's athletic director, Sayers, and the head football coach, Shultz. The attorneys told Hemphill that he might be able to recover for his injuries based on several provisions of the Uniform Commercial Code. The attorneys specifically suggested that he use the UCC provisions that impose certain obligations on merchants. Hemphill brought suit against Sayers and Shultz. Does Article 2 apply to this case? *Hemphill v. Sayers*, 552 F. Supp. 685 (S.D. Ill. 1982).

Critical Legal Thinking Case 10.2 *Good or Service*   Mr. Gulash lived in Shelton, Connecticut. He wanted an above-ground swimming pool installed in his backyard. Gulash contacted Stylarama, Inc. (Stylarama), a company specializing in the sale and construction of pools. The two parties entered into a contract that called for Stylarama to "furnish all labor and materials to construct a Wavecrest brand pool, and furnish and install a pool with vinyl liners." The total cost for materials and labor was $3,690. There was no breakdown in the contract of costs between labor and materials. After the pool was installed, its sides began bowing out, the 2 by 4-inch wooden supports for the pool rotted and misaligned, and the entire pool became tilted. Gulash brought suit, alleging that Stylarama had violated several provisions of Article 2 of the UCC. Is this transaction one involving goods, making it subject to Article 2? *Gulash v. Stylarama*, 364 A.2d 1221 (Conn. Super. Ct. 1975).

Critical Legal Thinking Case 10.3 *Statute of Frauds* St. Charles Cable TV (St. Charles) was building a new cable television system in Louisiana. It contacted Eagle Comtronics, Inc. (Eagle), by phone and began negotiating to buy descrambler units for its cable system. These units would allow St. Charles's customers to receive the programs they had paid for. Although no written contract was ever signed, St. Charles ordered several thousand descramblers. The descramblers were shipped to St. Charles, along with a sales acknowledgment form. St. Charles made partial payment for the descramblers before discovering that some of the units were defective. Eagle accepted a return of the defective scramblers. St. Charles then attempted to return all the descramblers, asking that they be replaced by a newer model. When Eagle refused to replace all the old descramblers, St. Charles stopped paying Eagle. Eagle sued St. Charles, claiming that no valid contract existed between the parties. Is there a valid sales contract? *St. Charles Cable TV v. Eagle Comtronics, Inc.*, 687 F. Supp. 820 (S.D.N.Y. 1988).

Critical Legal Thinking Case 10.4 *Firm Offer* Gordon Construction Company (Gordon) was a general contractor in the New York City area. Gordon planned on bidding for the job of constructing two buildings for the Port Authority of New York. In anticipation of its own bid, Gordon sought bids from subcontractors. E. A. Coronis Associates (Coronis), a fabricator of structured steel, sent a signed letter to Gordon. The letter quoted a price for work on the Port Authority project and stated that the price could change, based on the amount of steel used. The letter contained no information other than the price Coronis would charge for the job. One month later, Gordon was awarded the Port Authority project. Four days later, Coronis sent Gordon a telegram, withdrawing its offer. Gordon replied that it expected Coronis to honor the price it had previously quoted to Gordon. When Coronis refused, Gordon sued. Gordon claimed that Coronis was attempting to withdraw a firm offer. Who wins? *E.A. Coronis Assoc. v. Gordon Constr. Co.*, 216 A.2d 246 (N.J. Super. Ct. App. Div. 1966).

Critical Legal Thinking Case 10.5 *Battle of the Forms* Dan Miller was a commercial photographer who had taken a series of photographs that had appeared in the *New York Times*. *Newsweek* magazine wanted to use the photographs. When a *Newsweek* employee named Dwyer phoned Miller, he was told that 72 images were available. Dwyer said he wanted to inspect the photographs and offered a certain sum of money for each photo *Newsweek* used. The photos were to remain Miller's property. Miller and Dwyer agreed to the price and the date for delivery. *Newsweek* sent a courier to pick up the photographs. Along with the photos, Miller gave the courier a delivery memo that set out various conditions for the use of the photographs. The memo included a clause that required *Newsweek* to pay $1,500 each if any of the photos were lost or destroyed. After *Newsweek* received the package, it decided it no longer needed Miller's work. When Miller called to have the photos returned, he was told they had all been lost. Miller demanded that *Newsweek* pay him $1,500 for each of the 72 lost photos. Assuming the court finds Miller and *Newsweek* to be merchants, are the clauses in the delivery memo part of the sales contract? *Miller v. Newsweek, Inc.*, 660 F. Supp. 852 (D. Del. 1987).

Critical Legal Thinking Case 10.6 *Open Terms* Alvin Cagle was a potato farmer in Alabama who had had several business dealings with the H. C. Schmieding Produce Co. (Schmieding). Several months before harvest, Cagle entered into an oral sales contract with Schmieding. The contract called for Schmieding to pay the market price at harvest time for all the red potatoes that Cagle grew on his 30-acre farm. Schmieding asked that the potatoes be delivered during the normal harvest months. As Cagle began harvesting his red potatoes, he contacted Schmieding to arrange delivery. Schmieding told the farmer that no contract had been formed because the terms of the agreement were too indefinite. Cagle demanded that Schmieding buy his crop. When Schmieding refused, Cagle sued to have the contract enforced. Has a valid sales contract been formed? *H.C. Schmieding Produce Co. v. Cagle*, 529 So. 2d 243 (Ala.1988).

Critical Legal Thinking Case 10.7 *Statute of Frauds* Collins was a sales representative of Donzi Marine Corp. (Donzi), a builder of light speedboats. Collins met Wallach, the owner of a retail boat outlet, at a marine trade show. Collins offered him a Donzi dealership, which would include the right to purchase and then market Donzi speedboats. Wallach tendered a check for $50,000 to Collins. Collins accepted the check, but neither party ever signed a written contract. Wallach ordered several boats. Donzi terminated the dealership because it had found another boat dealer willing to pay more for the franchise. Wallach sued Donzi for breach of contract. Is the contract enforceable under the UCC? *Wallach Marine Corp. v. Donzi Marine Corp.*, 675 F. Supp. 838 (S.D.N.Y. 1987).

ETHICS CASES

Ethics Case 10.1 Kurt Perschke was a grain dealer in Indiana. Perschke phoned Ken Sebasty, the owner of a large wheat farm, and offered to buy 14,000 bushels of wheat for $1.95 a bushel. Sebasty accepted the offer. Perschke said that he could send a truck for the wheat on a date stated six months later. On the day of the phone call, Perschke's office manager sent a memorandum to Sebasty, stating the price and quantity of wheat that had been contracted for. One month before the scheduled delivery, Perschke called Sebasty to arrange for the loading of the wheat. Sebasty stated that no contract had been made. When Perschke brought suit, Sebasty claimed the contract was unenforceable because of the Statute of Frauds. Was it ethical for Sebasty to raise the Statute of Frauds as a defense? Assuming both parties are merchants, who wins the suit? *Sebasty v. Perschke*, 404 N.E.2d 1200 (Ind. Ct. App. 1980).

Ethics Case 10.2 Alex Abatti was the sole owner of A&M Produce Company (A&M), a small farming company located in California's Imperial Valley. Although Abatti had never grown tomatoes, he decided to do so. He sought the advice of FMC Corporation (FMC), a large diversified manufacturer of farming and other equipment, as to what kind of equipment he would need to process the tomatoes. An FMC representative recommended a certain type of machine, which A&M purchased from FMC pursuant to a form sales contract provided by FMC. Within the fine print, the contract contained one clause that disclaimed any warranty liability by FMC and a second clause that stated FMC would not be liable for consequential damages if the machine malfunctioned.

A&M paid $10,680 down toward the $32,041 purchase price, and FMC delivered and installed the machine. A&M immediately began experiencing problems with the machine. It did not process the tomatoes quickly enough. Tomatoes began piling up in front of the belt that separated the tomatoes for weight sizing. Overflow tomatoes had to be sent through the machine at least twice, causing damage to them. Fungus spread through the damaged crop. Because of these problems, the machine had to be continually started and stopped, which significantly reduced processing speed.

A&M tried on several occasions to get additional equipment from FMC, but on each occasion its request was rejected. Because of the problems with the machine, A&M closed its tomato operation. A&M finally stated, "Let's call the whole thing off" and offered to return the machine if FMC would refund A&M's down payment. When FMC rejected this offer and demanded full payment of the balance due, A&M sued to recover its down payment and damages. It alleged breach of warranty caused by defect in the machine. In defense, FMC pointed to the fine print of the sales contract, stating that the buyer waived any rights to sue it for breach of warranty or to recover consequential damages from it.

Was it ethical for FMC to include waiver of liability and waiver of consequential damage clauses in its form contract? Did A&M act morally in signing the contract and then trying to get out from under its provisions? Legally, are the waiver clauses so unconscionable as to not be enforced? *A&M Produce Co. v. FMC Corp.*, 186 Cal. Rptr. 114 (Ct. App. 1982).

BRIEFING THE CASE WRITING ASSIGNMENT

Read Case A.10 in Appendix A (*Cafazzo v. Cent. Med. Health Serv., Inc.*). This case is excerpted from the Supreme Court of Pennsylvania's opinion. Review and brief the case. After briefing the case, you should be able to answer the following questions:
1. What was the plaintiff suing for? Explain.
2. What issue was presented to the court? Why was this issue important? Explain.
3. How did the court decide this case?

PRACTICE TIP

Sometimes, rather than reciting and reciting again contract provisions, specific provisions that are consistent from one agreement to another can be incorporated by using a "shortcut." Here is an example:

As used in this Agreement, the terms _____ and _____ as defined in the Purchase Agreement will have the same meanings as in this Agreement.

Note: Whenever using such a shortcut, the paralegal must carefully check the second document to make sure all of the terms from the first document are a proper fit. If not, then the best solution may be to eliminate the shortcut and draft the entire provision to suit the second document.

A lawyer without history or literature is a mechanic, a mere working mason: if he possesses some knowledge of these, he may venture to call himself an architect.

—**Sir Walter Scott**

Guy Mannering, Chapter 37 (1815)

Performance of Sales and Lease Contracts | CHAPTER 11

CASE SCENARIO

The law firm where you work as a paralegal is representing Cherry Creek Dodge, Inc. (Cherry Creek). Cherry Creek sold a 1985 Dodge Ramcharger to Executive Leasing of Colorado (Executive Leasing). Executive Leasing, which was in the business of buying and selling cars, paid for the Dodge with a draft. Cherry Creek maintained a security interest in the car until the draft cleared. The same day that Executive Leasing bought the Dodge, it sold the car to Bruce and Peggy Carter. The Carters paid in full for the Dodge with a cashier's check, and the vehicle was delivered to them. The Carters had no of knowledge the financial arrangement between Executive Leasing and Cherry Creek. The draft that Executive Leasing gave Cherry Creek was worthless.

■ CHAPTER INTRODUCTION

Under common law, the rights and obligations of the buyer, the seller, and third parties were determined based on who held technical title to the goods. Article 2 of the Uniform Commercial Code (UCC) establishes precise rules for determining the *passage of title* in sales contracts. Other provisions of Article 2 apply, irrespective of title, except as otherwise provided [UCC 2-401].

Common law placed the *risk of loss* to goods on the party who held title to the goods. Article 2 of the UCC rejects this notion and adopts concise rules for risk of loss that are not tied to title. It also gives the parties to the sales contract the right to *insure* the goods against loss if they have an "insurable interest" in the goods. Title, risk of loss, and insurable interest are discussed in this chapter.

CHAPTER OBJECTIVES

After studying this chapter, you should be able to:

1. Identify when title to goods passes in shipment and destination contracts.

2. Define shipment and delivery terms.

3. Describe who bears the risk of loss when goods are lost or damaged in shipment.

4. Identify who bears the risk of loss when goods are stolen and resold.

5. Define *good faith purchaser for value* and *buyer in the ordinary course of business*.

■ IDENTIFICATION AND PASSAGE OF TITLE

The identification of goods is rather simple. It means distinguishing the goods named in a contract from the seller's or lessor's other goods. The seller or lessor retains the risk of loss of the goods until he or she identifies them to a sales or lease contract. Further, UCC 2-401(1) and 2-501 prevent title to goods from passing from the seller to the buyer unless the goods are identified to the sales contract. In a lease transaction, title to the leased goods remains with the lessor or a third party. It does not pass to the lessee.

The identification of goods and the passage of title are discussed in the following paragraphs.

Identification of Goods

identification of goods
Distinguishing the goods named in the contract from the seller's or lessor's other goods.

Identification of goods can be made at any time and in any manner explicitly agreed to by the parties to a contract. In the absence of such an agreement, the UCC mandates when identification occurs [UCC 2-501(1), 2A-217].

Already existing goods are identified when the contract is made and names the specific goods sold or leased.

Example: A piece of farm machinery, a car, or a boat is identified when its serial number is listed on the sales or lease contract.

Goods that are part of a larger mass of goods are identified when the specific merchandise is designated.

Example: If a food processor contracts to purchase 150 cases of oranges from a farmer who has 1,000 cases of oranges, the buyer's goods are identified when the seller explicitly separates or tags the 150 cases.

future goods
Goods not yet in existence (ungrown crops, unborn stock animals).

Future goods are goods not yet in existence. For example, unborn young animals (such as unborn cattle) are identified when the young are conceived. Crops to be harvested are identified when the crops are planted or otherwise become growing crops. Future goods other than crops and unborn young are identified when the goods are shipped, marked, or otherwise designated by the seller or lessor as the goods to which the contract refers.

Passage of Title

Once the goods that are the subject of a contract exist and have been identified, title to the goods may be transferred from the seller to the buyer. Article 2 of the UCC establishes precise rules for determining the passage of title in sales contracts. (As mentioned earlier, lessees do not acquire title to the goods they lease.)

Under UCC 2-401(1), **title** to goods passes from the seller to the buyer in any manner and on any conditions explicitly agreed upon by the parties. If the parties do not agree to a specific time, title passes to the buyer when and where the seller's performance with reference to the physical delivery is completed. This point in time is determined by applying the rules discussed in the following paragraphs [UCC 2-401(2)].

title
Legal, tangible evidence of ownership of goods.

Shipment and Destination Contracts

A **shipment contract** requires the seller to ship the goods to the buyer via a common carrier. The seller is required to (1) make proper shipping arrangements and (2) deliver the goods into the carrier's hands. Title passes to the buyer at the time and place of shipment [UCC 2-401(2)(a)].

A **destination contract** requires the seller to deliver the goods either to the buyer's place of business or to another destination specified in the sales contract. Title passes to the buyer when the seller tenders delivery of the goods at the specified destination [UCC 2-401(2)(b)].

shipment contract
A contract that requires the seller to ship the goods to the buyer via a common carrier. The buyer bears the risk of loss during transportation. A sales contract that requires the seller to send the goods to the buyer, but not a specifically named destination.

destination contract
A sales contract that requires the seller to deliver conforming goods to a specific destination. The seller bears the risk of loss during transportation. A contract that requires the seller to deliver the goods either to the buyer's place of business or to another destination specified in the sales contract.

Delivery of Goods Without Moving Them

Sometimes a sales contract authorizes goods to be delivered without requiring the seller to move them. In other words, the buyer might be required to pick up goods from the seller. In such situations, the time and place of the passage of title depends on whether the seller is to deliver a **document of title** (i.e., a warehouse receipt or bill of lading) to the buyer. If a document of title is required, title passes when and where the seller delivers the document to the buyer [UCC 2-401(3) (a)].

Example: If the goods named in the sales contract are located at a warehouse, title passes when the seller delivers to the buyer a warehouse receipt representing the goods.

If (1) no document of title is needed and (2) the goods are identified at the time of contracting, title passes at the time and place of contracting [UCC 2-401(3) (b)]. For example, if the buyer signs a sales contract to purchase bricks from the seller, and the contract stipulates that the buyer will pick up the bricks at the seller's place of business, title passes when the contract is signed by both parties. This situation is true even if the bricks are not picked up until a later date.

document of title
An actual piece of paper, such as warehouse receipt or bill of lading, that is required in some transactions of pick up and delivery. A negotiable instrument developed to represent the interests of the different parties in a transaction that uses storage or transportation between the parties.

■ RISK OF LOSS: NO BREACH OF SALES CONTRACT

In the case of sales contracts, common law placed the risk of loss of goods on the party who had title to the goods. Article 2 of the UCC rejects this notion and allows the parties to a sales contract to agree among them who will bear the risk of loss if the goods subject to the contract are lost or destroyed. If the parties do not have a specific agreement concerning the assessment of the risk of loss, the UCC mandates who will bear the risk.

Carrier Cases: Movement of Goods

Unless otherwise agreed, goods that are shipped via carrier (e.g., railroad, ship, truck) are considered to be sent pursuant to a *shipment contract* or a *destination contract*. Absent any indication to the contrary, sales contracts are presumed to be shipment contracts rather than destination contracts.

Shipment Contracts

A shipment contract requires the seller to ship goods conforming to the contract to a buyer via a carrier. The risk of loss passes to the buyer when the seller delivers the conforming goods to the carrier. The buyer bears the risk of loss of the goods during transportation [UCC 2-509(1) (a)].

Shipment contracts are created in two ways. The first requires the use of the term *shipment contract*. The second requires the use of one of the following delivery terms: FOB, FAS, CIF, or C & F.

Destination Contracts

A sales contract that requires the seller to deliver conforming goods to a specific destination is a destination contract. Such a contract requires the seller to bear the risk of loss of the goods during their transportation. Thus, with the exception of a no-arrival, no-sale contract, the seller is required to replace any goods lost in transit. The buyer does not have to pay for destroyed goods. The risk of loss does not pass until the goods are tendered to the buyer at the specified destination [UCC 2-509(1)(b)].

Unless otherwise agreed, destination contracts are created in two ways. The first method requires the use of the term *destination contract*. The alternative method requires the use of the following delivery terms: FOB *place of destination*, ex-ship, or no-arrival, no-sale contract.

CONTEMPORARY Issue

FOB
Free on board. The seller must bear the expense and risk of loss until the goods are put in the carrier's possession.

FAS
Free alongside. The seller bears the expense and risk of loss until the goods are alongside a named vessel or the dock designated.

CIF
Cost, insurance, and freight. Pricing terms indicating the cost for which the seller is responsible.

C & F
Cost and freight. Pricing terms indicating the cost for which the seller is responsible.

FOB place of destination
The seller bears the expense and risk of loss until the goods are tendered to the buyer.

ex-ship (from the carrying vessel)
The seller bears the expense and risk of loss until the goods are unloaded.

no-arrival, no-sale contract
The seller bears the expense and risk of loss during transportation only.

SHIPPING TERMS

The following are commonly used shipping terms:

- **FOB (free on board) point of shipment** (e.g., FOB Anchorage, Alaska) requires the seller to arrange to ship goods and put the goods in the carrier's possession. The seller bears the expense and risk of loss until this is done [UCC 2-319(1)(a)].
- **FAS (free alongside)** or **FAS (vessel) port of shipment** (e.g., *The Gargoyle*, New Orleans) requires the seller to deliver and tender the goods alongside the named vessel or on the dock designated and provided by the buyer. The seller bears the expense and risk of loss until this is done [UCC 2-319(2)(a)].
- **CIF (cost, insurance, and freight)** and **C & F (cost and freight)** are pricing terms that indicate the cost for which the seller is responsible. These terms require the seller to bear the expense and the risk of loss of loading the goods on the carrier [UCC 2-320(1)(3)].
- **FOB place of destination** (e.g., FOB Miami, Florida) requires the seller to bear the expense and risk of loss until the goods are tendered to the buyer at the place of destination [UCC 2-319(1) (b)].
- **Ex-ship (from the carrying vessel)** requires the seller to bear the expense and risk of loss until the goods are unloaded from the ship at its port of destination [UCC 2-322(1) (b)].
- **No-arrival, no-sale contract** requires the seller to bear the expense and risk of loss of the goods during transportation. However, the seller is under no duty to deliver replacement goods to the buyer because there is no contractual stipulation that the goods will arrive at the appointed destination [UCC 2-324(a) (b)].

THE ETHICAL PARALEGAL

Working to Improve the Legal System

The "Public Serve" ethics rules (ABA Model Rule 6.1, 6.2, 6.3, and 6.4) deal with the responsibility of legal professionals to improve the legal system.[1] For attorneys, fulfilling this responsibility can take place by providing pro bono service, accepting court appointments, becoming a member of a legal services organization, and/or engaging in law reform activities.

Paralegals can also help improve the legal system for the public—and improve the paralegal profession in the process. Ethical paralegals engage in pro bono work, participate in continuing legal education, seek involvement in professional paralegal organizations, conduct themselves ethically, and act with integrity.

Noncarrier Cases: No Movement of Goods

Sometimes a sales contract stipulates that the buyer is to pick up the goods, at either the seller's place of business or another specified location. This type of arrangement raises a question: Who bears the risk of loss if the goods are destroyed or stolen after the contract date and before the buyer picks up the goods from the seller? The UCC provides two different rules for this situation. One applies to *merchant-sellers* and the other to *nonmerchant-sellers* [UCC 2-509(3)].

Merchant-Seller

If the seller is a merchant, the risk of loss does not pass to the buyer until the goods are received. In other words, a merchant-seller bears the risk of loss between the time of contracting and the time the buyer picks up the goods.

Example: On June 1, Tyus Motors, a merchant, contracts to sell a new automobile to a consumer. Tyus Motors keeps the car for a few days after contracting to prep it. During this period, the car is destroyed by fire. Under the UCC, Tyus Motors bears the risk of loss because of its merchant status.

Nonmerchant-Seller

Nonmerchant-sellers pass the risk of loss to the buyer upon "tender of delivery" of the goods. Tender of delivery occurs when the seller (1) places or holds the goods available for the buyer to take delivery and (2) notifies the buyer of this fact.

Example: On June 1, a nonmerchants contracts to sell his automobile to his next-door neighbor. Delivery of the car is tendered on June 3, and the buyer is notified of this. The buyer tells the seller he will pick up the car "in a few days." The car is destroyed by fire before the buyer picks it up. In this situation, the buyer bears the risk of loss because (1) the seller is a nonmerchant and (2) delivery was tendered on June 3. If the car were destroyed on June 2—that is, before delivery was tendered—the seller would bear the risk of loss.

Goods in the Possession of a Bailee

Goods sold by a seller to a buyer are sometimes in the possession of a **bailee** (e.g., a warehouse). If such goods are to be delivered to the buyer without the seller

bailee
A holder of goods who is not a seller or a buyer (e.g., a warehouse or common carrier).

---

[1]Copies of the ABA Model Rules of Professional Conduct are available from Service Center, American Bar Association, 321 North Clark Street, Chicago, IL 60610, 1-800-285-2221. The Model Rules can also be viewed online at http://www.abanet.org/cpr/mrpc/mrpc_toc.html.

moving them, the risk of loss passes to the buyer when (1) the buyer receives a negotiable document of title (such as a warehouse receipt or bill of lading) covering the goods, (2) the bailee acknowledges the buyer's right to possession of the goods, or (3) the buyer receives a nonnegotiable document of title or other written direction to deliver *and* has a reasonable time to present the document or direction to the bailee and demand the goods. If the bailee refuses to honor the document or direction, the risk of loss remains on the seller [UCC 2-509(2)].

MARKETPLACE

Job Announcement: Commercial Litigation Paralegal

Satellite office of a large national law firm seeks an experienced commercial litigation paralegal to manage commercial based cases. Will handle complex litigation from discovery though trial, including managing electronic discovery, document management, and drafting settlement agreements.

Pay to $95K. Not heavy OT. Must have at least 5 years of experience as a commercial litigation paralegal with a large law firm. Must have experience using litigation technology. Experience at trial strongly preferred.

Please e-mail your resume to:

CONTEMPORARY Issue

EFFECT OF BANKRUPTCY ON EXECUTORY CONTRACTS AND UNEXPIRED LEASES

executory contract
A contract that has not yet been fully performed. With Court approval, executory contracts may be rejected by a debtor in bankruptcy.

In a Chapter 11 bankruptcy the debtor is given the opportunity to accept or reject certain executory contracts and unexpired leases. An **executory contract**, or **unexpired lease**, is a contract or lease that has not been fully performed. For example, a contract to purchase or supply goods at a later date is an executory contract; a 20-year office lease that has 8 years left until it is completed is an unexpired lease. Other executory contracts and unexpired leases may include consulting contracts, contracts to purchase or provide services, equipment leases, warehouse leases, and such.

Under the Bankruptcy Code, the debtor-in-possession (or trustee) in a Chapter 11 proceeding is given authority to assume or reject executory contracts. In general, the debtor rejects unfavorable executory contracts and assumes favorable executory contracts. Court approval is necessary to reject an executory contract. The debtor is not liable for damages caused by the rejection of executory contracts and unexpired leases in bankruptcy. Note that executory contracts and unexpired leases may also be rejected in Bankruptcy Chapter 7, Chapter 12, and Chapter 13 proceedings.

Example: Suppose Import Corporation files for Chapter 11 reorganization bankruptcy. After a review of its executory contracts and unexpired leases, the corporation identifies the following unfavorable executory contracts and unexpired leases: a contract to purchase goods from a supplier that has 2 years left, a contract to deliver services to a customer that has 1 year left, a lease for office space that has 10 years left, and an equipment lease for trucks that has 3 years left. Import Corporation can reject all these contracts and leases, with the court's approval. Import Corporation is not liable for any damages caused by its rejection of these executory contracts and unexpired leases.

RISK OF LOSS: CONDITIONAL SALES

Sellers of ten entrust possession of goods to buyers on a trial basis. These transactions are classified as *sales on approval*, *sales or returns*, and *consignment* transactions [UCC 2-326].

Sale on Approval

In a **sale on approval**, there is no sale unless and until the buyer accepts the goods. A sale on approval occurs when a merchant (e.g., a computer store) allows a customer to take the goods (e.g., an Apple computer) home for a specified period of time (e.g., three days) to see if they fit the customer's needs. The prospective buyer may use the goods to try them out during this time.

Acceptance of the goods occurs if the buyer (1) expressly indicates acceptance, (2) fails to notify the seller of rejection of the goods within the agreed-upon trial period (or, if no time is agreed upon, a reasonable time), or (3) uses the goods inconsistently with the purpose of the trial (e.g., the customer resells the computer to another person).

The goods are not subject to the claims of the buyer's creditors until the buyer accepts them. In a sale on approval, the risk of loss and title to the goods remain with the seller. They do not pass to the buyer until acceptance [UCC 2-327(1)].

sale on approval
A type of sale in which there is no actual sale unless and until the buyer accepts the goods.

Sale or Return

In a **sale or return contract**, the seller delivers goods to a buyer with the understanding that the buyer may return them if they are not used or resold within a stated period of time (or within a reasonable time, if no specific time is stated). The sale is considered final if the buyer fails to return the goods within the specified time or reasonable time if no time is specified. The buyer has the option of returning all the goods or any commercial unit of the goods.

Example: Suppose a fashion designer delivers 10 dresses to a fashion boutique on a sale or return basis. The boutique pays $10,000 ($1,000 per dress). If the boutique does not resell the dresses within three months, it may return the unsold garments to the designer. At the end of three months, the boutique has sold 4 of the dresses. The remaining 6 dresses may be returned to the designer. The boutique can recover the compensation paid for the returned dresses.

In a sale or return contract, the risk of loss and title to the goods pass to the buyer when the buyer takes possession of the goods. In the previous example, if the dresses were destroyed while they were at the boutique, the boutique owner would be responsible for paying the designer for them [UCC 2-327(2)]. Goods sold pursuant to a sale or return contract are subject to the claims of the buyer's creditors while the goods are in the buyer's possession.

sale or return contract
A contract that says that the seller delivers goods to a buyer with the understanding that the buyer may return them if they are not used or resold within a stated or reasonable period of time.

Consignment

In a **consignment**, a seller (the **consignor**) delivers goods to a buyer (the **consignee**) to sell. The consignee is paid a fee if he or she sells the goods on behalf of the consignor. A consignment is treated as a sale or return under the UCC. Whether the goods are subject to the claims of the buyer's creditors usually depends on whether the seller files a financing statement as required by Article 9 of the UCC. If the seller filed a financing statement, the goods are subject to the claims of the seller's creditors. If the seller failed to file

consignment
An arrangement where a seller (the consignor) delivers goods to a buyer (the consignee) for sale.

consignor
The person shipping the goods. The bailor.

consignee
The person to whom the bailed goods are to be delivered.

such statement, the goods are subject to the claims of the buyer's creditors [UCC 2-326(3)].

In Case 11.1 the court had to assess risk of loss in a conditioned sale situation.

CASE 11.1 CONDITIONAL SALE

Prewitt v. Numismatic Funding Corp., 745 F.2d 1175 (8th Cir. 1984).

"Under the provisions of the UCC relating to risk of loss, as adopted in Missouri, the risk of loss remains with the seller."

Judge Bright, *United States Court of Appeals for the Eighth Circuit*

Facts

Numismatic Funding Corporation (Numismatic), with its principal place of business in New York, sells rare and collector coins by mail throughout the United States. Frederick R. Prewitt, a resident of St. Louis, Missouri, responded to Numismatic's advertisement in the *Wall Street Journal*. Prewitt received several shipments of coins from Numismatic via the mails. These shipments were "on approval" for 14 days. Numismatic gave no instructions as to the method for returning unwanted coins. Prewitt kept and paid for several coins and returned the others to Numismatic, fully insured, via FedEx. Numismatic mailed Prewitt 28 gold and silver coins worth over $60,000 on a 14-day approval. Thirteen days later, Prewitt returned all the coins via certified mail and insured them for the maximum allowed, $400. Numismatic never received the coins. Prewitt brought this action seeking a declaratory judgment as to his nonliability. Numismatic filed a counterclaim. The district court awarded Prewitt a declaratory judgment of nonliability. Numismatic appealed.

Issue

Who bears the risk of loss, Prewitt or Numismatic?

Language of the Court

The trial court determined, and the parties do not dispute, that the delivery of coins between seller Numismatic and buyer Prewitt constituted a sale "on approval." Under the provisions of the UCC relating to risk of loss, as adopted in Missouri, the risk of loss remains with the seller.

Appellant Numismatic contends that the parties impliedly agreed to shift the risk of loss to Prewitt. It argues that an agreement by Prewitt to assume the risk of loss arose by implication from the prior course of dealing between the parties in which Prewitt had returned coins fully insured via Federal Express. The trial court found that Numismatic shipped the coins to Prewitt through the U.S. Postal Service and that no instructions on the method of return were ever given by Numismatic. In light of this finding, and the absence of any specific evidence in the record indicating that the parties had agreed upon a method of return, we reject Numismatic's contention that there was an understanding between the parties that Prewitt would return the coins fully insured via Federal Express.

Decision

The court of appeals held that the transaction in question was a sale on approval and that under UCC 2-327(1), Numismatic, the owner of the coins, bore the risk of their loss during the return shipment from Prewitt. The court of appeals affirmed the decision of the district court.

Law & Ethics Questions

1. Do you agree with how the UCC assesses risk of loss in sale on approval transactions?

2. **Ethics** Should Prewitt have fully insured the coins before sending them back to Numismatic?

3. How could Numismatic have protected its interests in this case?

Web Exercises

1. **Web** Visit the U.S. Court of Appeals for the Eighth Circuit at www.ca8 .uscourts.gov.

2. **Web** Use www.google.com and find an article that discusses conditional sales.

PARALEGAL PERSPECTIVE

Andrea Powell is the risk manager for Merillat Industries, LLC, in Adrian, Michigan. She received an associate's degree in legal assisting technology from the University of Toledo, Ohio, and a bachelor's degree in business administration from Lourdes College in Sylvania, Ohio.

As risk manager, I lead the review and negotiation of contract provisions of supplier, sales, and business contracts to ensure adherence with prudent risk management practices.

I establish standard contract requirements for dealers, vendors, subcontractors, and suppliers. I review business contract agreements to ensure appropriate risk transfer, insurance, and indemnification provisions.

I'm also responsible for all contract management including reviewing, analysis, drafting, and negotiating changes. In this role, I work with all departments throughout the organization including sales, marketing, finance, and field operations. I am often called on to communicate with senior management regarding terms and obligations that will impact the organization.

▧ RISK OF LOSS: BREACH OF SALES CONTRACT

The risk of loss rules just discussed applies where there is no breach of contract. Separate risk of loss rules apply to situations involving breach of a sales contract [UCC 2-510].

Seller in Breach

A seller breaches a sales contract if he or she tenders or delivers nonconforming goods to the buyer. If the goods are so nonconforming that the buyer has the right to reject them, the risk of loss remains on the seller until (1) the defect or nonconformity is cured or (2) the buyer accepts the nonconforming goods.

Example: A buyer orders 1,000 talking dolls from a seller. The contract is a shipment contract, which normally places the risk of loss during transportation on the buyer. The seller ships nonconforming dolls that cannot talk. The goods are destroyed in transit. The seller bears the risk of loss because he breached the contract by shipping nonconforming goods.

Buyer in Breach

A buyer breaches a sales contract if he or she (1) refuses to take delivery of conforming goods, (2) repudiates the contract, or (3) otherwise breaches the contract. A buyer who breaches a sales contract before the risk of loss would normally pass to him or her bears the risk of loss of any goods identified to the contract. The risk of loss rests on the buyer for only a commercially reasonable time. The buyer is only liable for any loss in excess of insurance recovered by the seller.

■ RISK OF LOSS: LEASE CONTRACTS

The parties to a lease contract may agree as to who will bear the risk of loss of the goods if they are lost or destroyed. If the parties do not so agree, the UCC supplies the following risk of loss rules:

1. In the case of an ordinary lease, the risk of loss is retained by the lessor. If the lease is a finance lease, the risk of loss passes to the lessee [UCC 2A-219].
2. If a tender of delivery of goods fails to conform to the lease contract, the risk of loss remains with the lessor or supplier until cure or acceptance [UCC 2A-220(1)(a)].

CONTEMPORARY Issue

INSURING AGAINST LOSS OF GOODS

To protect against financial loss that would occur if goods were damaged, destroyed, lost, or stolen, the parties to sales and lease contracts should purchase insurance against such loss. If the goods are then lost or damaged, the insured party receives reimbursement from the insurance company for the loss.

To purchase insurance, a party must have an *insurable interest* in the goods. A seller has an insurable interest in goods as long as he or she retains title or has a security interest in the goods. A lessor retains an insurable interest in the goods during the term of the lease. A buyer or lessee obtains an insurable interest in the goods when they are identified in the sales or lease contract. Both the buyer and seller, or the lessee and lessor, can have an insurable interest in the goods at the same time [UCC 2-501 and 2A-218].

To obtain and maintain proper insurance coverage on goods, a contacting party should:

- Determine the value of goods subject to the sales or lease contract.
- Purchase insurance from a reputable insurance company to cover the goods subject to the contract.
- Maintain the insurance by paying the premiums when they are due.
- Immediately file the proper claim and supporting documentation with an insurance company if the goods are damaged, destroyed, lost, or stolen.

CAREER FRONT

Job Description: Labor/Employment

A labor/employment paralegal can be involved with contracts in the following ways:

- Draft position papers to Equal Employment Opportunity Commission (EEOC). Obtain and assemble documents and labor contracts pursuant to EEOC's request for information.
- Conduct factual investigation; that is, obtain documents from various sources within the company; obtain files from government agencies; trace witnesses; pursue relevant facts.
- Prepare case outlines.
- Handle Freedom of Information Act requests and other requests for employee information.
- Analyze information and assist in preparing affirmative action plans.
- Draft performance evaluation forms for the client.
- Conduct research and develop materials for employee policy manual.
- Monitor state and federal regulations, such as OSHA and Americans with Disabilities Act, to ensure compliance by client.
- Assist with factual and legal research concerning status of employees and applicable payroll exemptions.
- Maintain repository of applicable union contracts for client and assist with activities ensuring compliance with contract provisions.
- Pursuant to local authority, gather factual information and attend unemployment compensation hearings.

Source: Excerpted by permission from the National Association of Legal Assistants (www.nala.org) and the National Federation of Paralegal Associations, Inc. (www.paralegals.org).

■ SALES BY NONOWNERS

Sometimes people sell goods even though they do not hold valid title to them. The UCC anticipated many of the problems this situation could cause and established rules concerning the title, if any, that could be transferred to the purchasers.

Void Title and Lease: Stolen Goods

In a case where a buyer purchases goods or a lessee leases goods from a thief who has stolen them, the purchaser does not acquire title to the goods and the lessee does not acquire any leasehold interest in the goods. The real owner can reclaim the goods from the purchaser or lessee [UCC 2-403(1)]. This is called **void title**.

Example: Suppose someone steals a truckload of Sony television sets that are owned by Sears. The thief resells the televisions to City-Mart, which does not know the goods were stolen. If Sears finds out where the televisions are, it can reclaim them. Because the thief had no title in the goods, title was not transferred to City-Mart. City-Mart's only recourse is against the thief, if he or she can be found.

void title
A thief acquires no title to the goods he or she steals.

Voidable Title: Sales or Lease of Goods to Good Faith Purchasers for Value

voidable title
Title that a purchase has if the goods were obtained by (1) fraud, (2) a check that is later dishonored, or (3) impersonating another person.

good faith purchaser for value
A person to whom good title can be transferred from a person with voidable title. The real owner cannot reclaim goods from a good faith purchaser for value.

good faith subsequent lessee
A person to whom a lease interest can be transferred from a person with voidable title. The real owner cannot reclaim the goods from the subsequent lessee until the lease expires.

entrustment rule
A UCC section allowing certain merchants to transfer all rights in goods, including title.

buyer in the ordinary course of business
A person who in good faith and without knowledge of another's ownership or security interest in goods buys the goods in the ordinary course of business from a person in the business of selling goods of that kind [UCC 1-201(9)].

A seller or lessor has **voidable title** to goods if the goods were obtained by fraud, if a check is later dishonored, or if he or she impersonates another person. A person with voidable title to goods can transfer good title to a **good faith purchaser for value** or a **good faith subsequent lessee**. A good faith purchaser or lessee for value is someone who pays sufficient consideration or rent for the goods to the person he or she honestly believes has good title to those goods [UCC 2-201(1), 1-201(44)(d)]. The real owner cannot reclaim goods from such a purchaser [UCC 2-403(1)].

Example: Suppose a person buys a Rolex watch from his neighbor for nearly fair market value. It is later discovered that the seller obtained the watch from a jewelry store with a "bounced check." The jewelry store cannot reclaim the watch because the second purchaser purchased the watch in good faith and for value.

Assume instead that the purchaser bought the watch from a stranger for far less than fair market value. It is later discovered the seller obtained the watch from a jewelry store by fraud. The jewelry store can reclaim the watch because the second purchaser was not a good faith purchaser for value.

Entrustment Rule

The **entrustment rule** found in UCC 2-403(2) holds that if an owner *entrusts* the possession of his or her goods to a merchant who deals in goods of that kind, the merchant has the power to transfer all rights (including title) in the goods to a **buyer in the ordinary course of business**. The real owner cannot reclaim the goods from this buyer.

Example: Kim Jones brings her computer into the Computer Store to be repaired. The Computer Store both sells and services computers. Jones leaves (entrusts) her computer at the store until it is repaired. The Computer Store sells her computer to Harold Green. Green, a buyer in the ordinary course of business, acquires title to the computer. Jones cannot reclaim the computer from Green. Her only recourse is against the Computer Store.

The entrustment rule also applies to leases. If a lessor entrusts the possession of his or her goods to a lessee who is a merchant who deals in goods of that kind, the merchant-lessee has the power to transfer all the lessor's and lessee's rights in the goods to a buyer or sublessee in the ordinary course of business [UCC 2A-305(2)].

In Case 11.2 the court had to decide whether a purchaser was a buyer in the ordinary course of business.

CASE 11.2 BUYER IN THE ORDINARY COURSE OF BUSINESS

Lindholm v. Brant, No. X05CV020189393, 2005 Conn. LEXIS 2366, at *1 (Super. Ct. Aug. 29, 2005), aff'd, 925 A.2d 1048 (Conn. 2007).

"Any entrusting of possession of goods to a merchant who deals in goods of that kind gives him power to transfer all rights of the entruster to a buyer in ordinary course of business."

Judge Rogers, *United States Court of Appeals for the Eighth Circuit*

Facts

In 1962, Andy Warhol, a famous artist, created a silkscreen on canvas entitled *Red Elvis*. *Red Elvis* consisted of 36 identical faces of Elvis Presley with a red background and is approximately 5.75 feet in height and 4.35 feet in width. Kerstin Lindholm was an art collector who, for 30 years, had been represented by Anders Malmberg, an art dealer. In 1987, with the assistance and advice of Malmberg, Lindholm purchased Red Elvis for $300,000.

In 1996, the Guggenheim Museum in New York City decided to sponsor an Andy Warhol exhibition. The staff of the Guggenheim contacted Malmberg to see if Lindholm was willing to lend *Red Elvis* to the exhibition. Lindholm agreed and *Red Elvis* was placed in the Gugenheim exhibition. Once the Guggenheim exhibition was completed in 2000, Malmberg told Lindholm he could place *Red Elvis* on loan to the Louisana Museum in Denmark if Lindholm agreed. By letter dated March 20, 2000, Lindholm agreed and gave permission to Malmberg to obtain possession of *Red Elvis* from the Guggenheim Museum and place it on loan to the Louisana Museum. Instead of placing *Red Elvis* on loan to the Louisana Museum, Malmberg, claiming ownership to *Red Elvis*, immediately contracted to sell *Red Elvis* to Peter M. Brant, an art collector, for $2.9 million. Brant had his lawyer do a UCC lien search and search of the Art Loss Registry related to *Red Elvis*. These searches revealed no claims or liens against *Red Elvis*.

Brant paid $2.9 million to Malmberg and received an invoice of sale and possession of *Red Elvis*. Subsequently, Lindholm discovered the fraud. Lindholm brought a civil lawsuit in the state of Connecticut against Brant to recover *Red Elvis*. Brant argued that he was a buyer in the ordinary course of business because he purchased *Red Elvis* from an art dealer to whom Lindholm had entrusted *Red Elvis*, and there he had a claim that was superior to Lindholm's claim of ownership.

Issue

Was Brant a buyer in the ordinary course of business who had a claim of ownership to *Red Elvis* that was superior to that of the owner Lindholm?

Language of the Court

The Brant defendants have pleaded a special defense to all counts that Brant is a buyer in the ordinary course pursuant to Conn. Gen. Stat. Sections 42a-2-403(2) and (3). A person with voidable title has power to transfer a good title to a good faith purchase for value. Any entrusting of possession of goods to a merchant who deals in goods of that kind gives him power to transfer all rights of the entruster to a buyer in ordinary course of business. "Entrusting" includes any delivery and any acquiescence in retention of possession regardless of any condition expressed between the parties to the delivery or acquiescence and regardless of whether the procurement of the entrusting or the possessor's disposition of the goods have been such as to be larcenous under the criminal law.

That statutory provision sets forth the circumstances in which an innocent, good faith purchaser of goods who acquires them from a dealer in goods of that kind has a right to the goods superior to the rights of the owner/entrustor of the goods. This special defense requires the Brant defendants to show that Brant was a buyer in the ordinary course.

K. Lindholm's March 20, 2000 letter constituted an entrustment of Red Elvis to a merchant, Malmberg. Once K. Lindholm entrusted Red Elvis to Malmberg she gave him the power to transfer all of her rights as the entruster to a buyer in the ordinary course.

Plaintiff's expert, Hoffeld, admitted that the Art Loss Registry is the best recognized mechanism for determining whether a piece of art is stolen. Accordingly, it was reasonable in investigating title for Brant to search the Art Loss Registry and the UCC liens to determine if there were any claims on Red Elvis.

Neither Brant nor his attorneys were focused on the possibility that Malmberg was simply stealing the painting from K. Lindholm. Based on Brant's lawyer's failure to identify to Brant that this might be an outright theft by Malmberg and based on Malmberg's excellent reputation in the art world as well as the fact that the Guggenheim released the painting to Malmberg, it was reasonable for Brant to believe that Malmberg had title to the painting when Malmberg physically delivered the painting to the agreed-upon bonded warehouse.

After considering all of the evidence, the court finds that pursuant to Conn. Gen. Stat. Section 42a-2-403 Brant took good title to Red Elvis. *Specifically, Brant purchased* Red Elvis *from Malmberg in good faith and in the ordinary course of business. Brant honestly believed Malmberg owned* Red Elvis *when he purchased the painting from him. Brant also observed reasonable commercial standards of fair dealing in the art industry when he purchased* Red Elvis *from Malmberg. Accordingly, because Brant has proven his special defense of being a buyer in the ordinary course, judgment will enter in favor of the defendants on all counts.*

Decision

The court held that Brant was a buyer in the ordinary course of business who obtained ownership to *Red Elvis* when he purchased the stolen *Red Elvis* from Malmberg. The court held that Brant's claim of ownership as a buyer in the ordinary course of business was superior to Lindholm's claim of ownership because Lindholm had entrusted *Red Elvis* to an art dealer who sold the stolen *Red Elvis* to Brant.

Law & Ethics Questions

1. What does the rule of buyer in the ordinary course of business provide regarding the purchase of stolen property? Explain.
2. Did Lindholm entrust *Red Elvis* to Malmberg, an art dealer? What could be the consequence of entrusting property to a merchant who sells the type of property that is entrusted to him?
3. **Ethics** Did Malmberg act ethically in this case? Did he act criminally?
4. **Ethics** Did Linholm have a good case to try to recover *Red Elvis* from Brant?

Web Exercises

1. **Web** Visit the website of the Superior Court of Connecticut at www.jud .state.ct.us.
2. **Web** Use www.google.com and find a short biography of Andy Warhol.
3. **Web** Visit the website of the Guggenheim Museum in New York City at www.guggenheim.org.
4. **Web** Use www.google.com and find a picture of *Red Elvis*.

CORN FARMERS GET SHUCKED

The entrustment rule is raised in the following case. Robert, David, and Hazel Schluter (Schluters) are grain farmers in Starbuck, Minnesota. They often hired a specific trucker to haul their grain to the public grain elevator, United Farmers Elevator, to whom they would sell their grain. On some occasions, the Schluters would sell their grain to the trucker, who would then resell the grain to the elevator or others. In the case at hand, the Schluters hired the trucker to haul their corn to the elevator. When the trucker got to the elevator, he represented that he owned the corn and sold it to the elevator for $288,000. The trucker absconded with the money.

The Schluters sued the elevator to recover payment for their corn. Who owns the corn, the Schluters or the elevator? The trail court applied the entrustment rule and held that the elevator had title to the corn as a buyer in the ordinary course of business. The appellate court stated.

> It is undisputed the trucker bad for several years bought and sold grain in the farmers' area, and the elevator had done business with the trucker not only as a hauler of grain belonging to others but also as a seller of grain belonging to himself. Thus, he was known in the area as a buyer and seller. This combination of the trucker's own conduct over time and his reputation in the area are sufficient to qualify him as a merchant of grain under the UCC, since he dealt in goods of the kind or otherwise held himself out as having knowledge or skill as a grain buyer and seller.

Under these facts, the trucker was a "merchant" and the farmers entrusted their grain to him. The undisputed facts show the farmers entrusted their grain to an independent trucker who was also a merchant, thereby empowering him to transfer ownership to the elevator as a buyer in the ordinary course of business. Under the UCC entrustment rule the elevator owned the corn. [*Schluter v. United Farmers Elevator*, 479 N.W.2d 82 (Minn.App.1992)].

1. Did the trucker act ethically in this case?
2. Do you think the UCC entrustment rule places loss on the right party? Explain.

Concept Summary

Passage of Title by Nonowner Third Parties

Type of Transaction	Title Possessed by Seller	Innocent Purchaser	Purchaser Acquires Title to Goods
Goods acquired by theft are resold.	Void title	Good faith purchaser for value	No. Original owner may reclaim the goods.
Goods acquired by fraud or dishonored check are resold.	Voidable title	Good faith purchaser for value	Yes. Purchaser takes free of claim of original owner.
Goods entrusted by owner to merchant who deals in that type of good are resold.	No title	Buyer in the ordinary course of business	Yes. Purchaser takes free of claim of original owner.
Creditor possesses security interest in goods that are sold.	Good title	Buyer in the ordinary course of business	Yes. Purchaser takes free of creditor's security interest.

INTERNATIONAL LAW

International Trade Terms

Trade abbreviations such as FOB and CIF are widely used in international contracts. The most widely used trade terms are those published by the International Chamber of Commerce. Called *Incoterms*, they are well known throughout the world. Their use in international sales is encouraged by trade councils, courts, and international lawyers. The UN Convention on Contracts for the International Sale of Goods (CISG) allows parties to incorporate trade terms of their choosing.

Parties who adopt the *Incoterms* or any other trade terms in their international contracts should make sure they express their desire clearly. For example, a contract might refer to FOB *(Incoterms 1990)* or CIF *(U.S. UCC)*.

CONTEMPORARY Issue

Article 6 (Bulk Sales)
The section of the UCC that governs when an owner transfers a major part of a business's material, merchandise, inventory, or equipment not in the ordinary course of business.

bulk transfer
When an owner transfers a major part of a business's material, merchandise, inventory, or equipment not in the ordinary course of business.

BULK SALES LAW DUMPED

Article 6 (Bulk Sales) of the UCC establishes rules that were designed to prevent fraud when there is a bulk transfer of goods. A **bulk transfer** occurs when an owner transfers a major part of a business's material, merchandise, inventory, or equipment not in the ordinary course of business. This usually occurs upon the sale of the assets of a business.

If there ia a bulk transfer of assets, Article 6 requires that (1) the seller furnish the buyer with a list of all of the creditors of the business, and (2) the buyer notify all of the listed creditors at least 10 days before taking possession of or paying for the goods, whichever occurs first. The buyer is not responsible for or liable to unlisted creditors [UCC 6-105].

If all of the requirements of Article 6 are met, the buyer receives title to the goods free of all claims of the seller's creditors. If the requirements of Article 6 are not met, the goods in the buyer's possession are subject to the claims of the seller's creditors for six months after the date of the possession [UCC 6-111].

In 1988, after much review, the National Conference of Commissioners on Uniform State Laws (NCCUSL) and the American Law Institute (ALI) reported that the regulation of bulk sales was no longer necessary. Consequently, they withdrew their support for Article 6 and encouraged states that had enacted the Article to repeal it.

The report criticized the bulk transfer law for adding costs—without corresponding benefits—to business transactions. The report claimed that it was unfair to impose liability on an innocent buyer because a dishonest seller failed to pay its creditors. The committee then stated that changing laws and economics, as well as improved communications, made it more difficult for merchants to sell their merchandise and abscond with the proceeds. Further, the report noted that modern jurisdiction laws make it easier to obtain and enforce judgments against debtors who have left the state.

Recognizing that some state legislatures may wish to continue to regulate bulk transfers, the committee also promulgated a revised version of Article 6.

INTERNET EXERCISES AND CASE QUESTIONS

Working the Web Internet Exercises

1. Find UCC Article 2 as adopted in your jurisdiction. Review the seller's remedies under UCC 2-703. See www.law.cornell.edu/uniform/ucc.html#a2.
2. When may the buyer revoke acceptance? See UCC 2-608(1).
3. Review UCC 2-712. What is the connection between *cover* and *mitigation of damages?*

CHAPTER 11 SUMMARY

IDENTIFICATION AND PASSAGE OF TITLE, p. 314

Identification

Identification distinguishes the goods named in the contract from the seller's or lessor's other goods [UCC 2-501(1)].

Passage of Title

1. *Passage of title by agreement.* Title to goods of a sales contract passes from the seller to the buyer in any manner and on any conditions explicitly agreed upon by the parties.
2. *Passage of title where there is no agreement.* If the parties have no agreement as to the passage of title, title passes according to the following UCC rules [UCC 2-401(2)]:
   a. *Shipment contract.* Requires the seller to ship the goods to the buyer via a common carrier. Title passes to the buyer at the time and place of shipment.
   b. *Destination contract.* Requires the seller to deliver the goods to the buyer's place of business or other designated destination. Title passes to the buyer when the seller tenders delivery of the goods at the specified destination.
   c. *Goods that do not move.* If a sales contract authorizes the goods to be delivered without requiring the seller to move them, title passes at the time and place of contracting, unless a document of title is required, in which case title passes when the seller delivers the document of title to the buyer.
3. *Passage of title in lease contracts.* Title to the leased goods remains with the lessor or a third party. Title does not pass to the lessee.

RISK OF LOSS: NO BREACH OF SALES CONTRACT, p. 315

1. *Agreement.* The parties to a sales contract may agree among themselves as to who will bear the risk of loss of goods if they are lost or destroyed.
2. *No agreement.* If the parties to a sales contract do not have a specific agreement concerning the assessment of risk of loss, the UCC mandates who will bear the risk [UCC 2-509].

Carrier Cases: Movement of Goods

1. *Shipment contract.* With a shipment contract, the risk of loss passes to the buyer when the seller delivers conforming goods to a carrier. The buyer bears the risk of loss during transportation.
2. *Destination contract.* With a destination contract, the risk of loss does not pass to the buyer until the goods are tendered to the buyer at the designated destination. The seller bears the risk of loss during transportation.

Shipping Terms

Sales contracts often contain the following shipping terms:

1. FOB (free on board) point of shipment
2. FAS (free alongside) or FAS (vessel) port of shipment
3. CIF (cost, insurance, and freight) and C & F (cost and freight)
4. FOB place of destination
5. Ex-ship (from the carrying vessel)
6. No-arrival, no-sale contract

Noncarrier Cases: No Movement of Goods

If the buyer is to pick up the goods from the seller's place of business or other specified location, the following UCC rules apply:

1. **Merchant-seller.** If the seller is a merchant, the risk of loss does not pass to the buyer until the goods are received by the buyer. The merchant-seller bears the risk of loss between the time of contracting and the time the buyer picks up the goods.
2. **Nonmerchant-seller.** If the seller is a nonmerchant, risk of loss passes to the buyer upon tender of delivery of the goods by the seller (i.e., the seller holds the goods available for the buyer to take delivery).

RISK OF LOSS: CONDITIONAL SALES, p. 319

Conditional Sales

Sellers often entrust goods to a buyer on a trial basis. The following UCC rules for risk of loss apply [UCC 2-327]:

1. **Sale on approval.** Occurs when a merchant allows a customer to take the goods for a specified period of time to try the goods. There is no sale unless and until the buyer accepts the goods. The risk of loss remains with the seller and does not transfer to the buyer until acceptance.
2. **Sale or return.** Occurs when a seller delivers goods to a buyer with the understanding that the buyer may return them if they are not used or resold during a stated period of time. The risk of loss passes to the buyer when the buyer takes possession of the goods.
3. **Consignment.** Occurs when a seller (*consignor*) delivers goods to a buyer (*consignee*) to sell. The risk of loss passes to the consignee when the consignee takes possession of the goods.

RISK OF LOSS: BREACH OF SALES CONTRACT, p. 321

Risk of Loss: Breach of Sales Contract

If there has been a *breach of a sales contract*, the UCC rules concerning risk of loss apply [UCC 2-510].

Seller in Breach

If a seller breaches a sales contract by tendering or delivering nonconforming goods, the risk of loss to the goods remains with the seller until (1) the defect or nonconformity is cured or (2) the buyer accepts the nonconforming goods.

Buyer in Breach

If a buyer breaches a sales contract by refusing to take delivery of conforming goods or repudiating the contract before the risk of loss would normally transfer to him or her, the buyer bears the risk of loss of any goods identified in the contract for a reasonable commercial time.

RISK OF LOSS: LEASE CONTRACTS, p. 322

1. *Agreement.* The parties to a lease contract may agree as to who will bear the risk of loss of the goods if they are lost or destroyed.
2. *No agreement.* If the parties do not have an agreement concerning the assessment of risk of loss, the following UCC rules for risk of loss apply [UCC 2A-219, 2A-220]:
    a. *Ordinary lease.* The risk of loss is retained by the lessor.
    b. *Finance lease.* The risk of loss passes to the lessee.
    c. *Breach of contract.* If a tender of delivery of goods fails to conform to the lease contract, the risk of loss remains with the lessor or supplier until acceptance or cure.

SALES BY NONOWNERS, p. 323

Sales by Nonowners

If a person sells goods that he or she does not hold valid title to, the buyer acquires rights in the goods under the UCC [UCC 2-403].

Void Title and Lease: Stolen Goods

A thief acquires no title to goods he or she steals. A person who purchases stolen goods does not acquire title to the goods. Any such title is call *void title*. The real owner can reclaim the goods from the purchaser. The purchaser's recourse is to recover from the thief.

Voidable Title: Sale or Lease of Goods to Good Faith Purchasers for Value

If goods are obtained by fraud, with a check that is later dishonored, or through impersonation of another person, the perpetrator acquires *voidable title* to the goods. If the perpetrator sells or leases the goods to a *good faith purchaser or lessee for value*—a person who pays sufficient consideration or rent for the goods and honestly believes the seller or lessor has good title to the goods—the buyer or lessee acquires good title to the goods. The real owner's recourse is against the perpetrator who acquired the goods from him or her.

Entrustment Rule

If an owner entrusts possession of his or her goods to a merchant who deals in goods of that kind (e.g., for repair) and the merchant sells those goods to a *buyer in the ordinary course of business* (e.g., a customer of the merchant), the buyer acquires title to the goods. The real owner's recourse is against the merchant who sold his or her goods. This rule is called the *entrustment rule.*

TERMS AND CONCEPTS

Article 6 (Bulk Sales)   328
Bailee   317
Bulk transfer   328
Buyer in the ordinary course of business   324
C & F (cost and freight)   316
CIF (cost, insurance, and freight)   316

Consignee 319

Consignor 319

Consignment 319

Destination contract 315

Document of title 315

Entrustment rule 324

Executory contract (unexpired lease) 318

Ex-ship (from the carrying vessel) 316

FAS (free alongside) or FAS (vessel) port of shipment 316

FOB place of destination 316

FOB (free on board) point of shipment 316

Future goods 314

Good faith purchaser for value 324

Good faith subsequent lessee 324

Identification of goods 314

No-arrival, no-sale contract 316

Sale on approval 319

Sale or return contract 319

Shipment contract 315

Title 315

Void title 323

Voidable title 324

CASE SCENARIO REVISITED

Remember the case scenario at the beginning of the chapter involving Cherry Creek Dodge, Inc. and Executive Leasing of Colorado? Is there any way this dispute might have been prevented? What will happen if Cherry Creek attempts to recover the vehicle from the Carters? Who wins? To help you with your answer, see *Cherry Creek Dodge, Inc. v. Carter*, 733 P.2d 1024 (Wyo. 1987).

CRITICAL LEGAL THINKING CASES

Critical Legal Thinking Case 11.1 *Identification of Goods* The Big Knob Volunteer Fire Company (Fire Co.) agreed to purchase a fire truck from Hamerly Custom Productions (Hamerly), which was in the business of assembling various component parts into fire trucks. Fire Co. paid Hamerly $10,000 toward the price two days after signing the contract. Two weeks later, it gave Hamerly $38,000 more toward the total purchase price of $53,000. Hamerly bought an engine chassis for the new fire truck on credit from Lowe and Meyer Garage (Lowe and Meyer). After installing the chassis, Hamerly painted the Big Knob Fire Department's name on the side of the cab. Hamerly never paid for the engine chassis, and the truck was repossessed by Lowe and Meyer. The Fire Co. sought to recover the fire truck from Lowe and Meyer. Although the Fire Co. was the buyer of a fire truck, Lowe and Meyer questioned whether any goods had ever been identified in the contract. Were they? *Big Knob Volunteer Fire Co. v. Lowe & Meyer Garage*, 487 A.2d 953 (Pa. Super. Ct. 1985).

Critical Legal Thinking Case 11.2 *Passage of Title*   New England Yacht Sales (Yacht Sales) sold a yacht to Robert Pease. Pease paid for the yacht in full, and Yacht Sales delivered to him a marine bill of sale. The marine bill of sale stated that Yacht Sales was transferring "all of its right, title, and interest" in the yacht to Pease. The yacht never left the Connecticut shipyard that Yacht Sales rented. During the winter, Yacht Sales did repair work on the yacht. In the spring, Yacht Sales delivered the yacht to Pease in Rhode Island. At issue in this case was when the sales tax was due to the state of Connecticut—October 18, 1980, or May 8, 1981. When did the title actually pass? *New England Yacht Sales v. Commissioner of Revenue Serv.*, 504 A.2d 506 (Conn. 1986).

Critical Legal Thinking Case 11.3 *Stolen Goods*   John Torniero was employed by Michaels Jewelers, Inc. (Michaels). During the course of his employment, Torniero stole pieces of jewelry, including several diamond rings, a sapphire ring, a gold pendant, and several loose diamonds. Over a period of several months, Torniero sold individual pieces of the stolen jewelry to G&W Watch and Jewelry Corporation (G&W). G&W had no knowledge of how Torniero obtained the jewels. Torniero was arrested when Michaels discovered the thefts. After Torniero admitted that he had sold the stolen jewelry to G&W, Michaels attempted to recover it from G&W. G&W claimed title to the jewelry as a good faith purchaser for value. Michaels challenged G&W's claim to title in court. Who wins? *United States v. Michaels Jewelers, Inc.*, No. N 85-242 (JAC), 1985 U.S. Dist. LEXIS 15142, at *1 (D. Conn. Oct. 8, 1985).

Critical Legal Thinking Case 11.4 *Passage of Title*   J. A. Coghill owned a Rolls-Royce Corniche automobile, which he sold to a man claiming to be Daniel Bellman. Bellman gave Coghill a cashier's check for $94,500. When Coghill tried to cash the check, his bank informed him that the check had been forged. Coghill reported the vehicle as stolen. Subsequently, Barry Hyken responded to a newspaper ad listing a Rolls-Royce Corniche for sale. Hyken went to meet the seller of the car, the man who claimed to be Bellman, in a parking lot. When Hyken asked why the car was advertised as a 1980 model when it was in fact a 1979, Bellman replied that it was a newspaper mistake. Hyken agreed to pay $62,000 for the car. When Hyken asked to see Bellman's identification, Bellman provided documents with two different addresses. Bellman explained that he was in the process of moving. Although there seemed to be some irregularities in the title documents to the car, Hyken took possession anyway. Three weeks later, the Rolls-Royce Corniche was seized by the police. Hyken sued to get it back. Who wins? *Landshire Food Serv., Inc. v. Coghill*, 709 S.W.2d 509 (Mo. Ct. App. 1986).

Critical Legal Thinking Case 11.5 *Entrustment Rule*   Fuqua Homes, Inc. (Fuqua) is a manufacturer of prefabricated houses. MMM was a partnership created by two men named Kirk and Underhill. MMM operated as a dealer of prefabricated homes. On seven occasions before the disputed transactions occurred, MMM had ordered homes from Fuqua. MMM was contacted by Kenneth Ryan, who wanted to purchase a 55-foot modular home. MMM called Fuqua and ordered a prefabricated home that met Ryan's specifications. Fuqua delivered the home to MMM and retained a security interest in it until MMM paid the purchase price. MMM installed the house on Ryan's property and collected full payment from Ryan. Kirk and Underhill then disappeared, taking Ryan's money with them. Fuqua was never paid for the prefabricated home it had manufactured. Ryan had no knowledge of the dealings between MMM and Fuqua. Fuqua claimed title to the house based on its security interest. Who has title to the home? *Fuqua Homes, Inc. v. Evanston Bldg. & Loan Co.*, 370 N.E.2d 780 (Ohio Ct. App. 1977).

Critical Legal Thinking Case 11.6 *Risk of Loss*   All America Export-Import Corp. (All America) placed an order for several thousand pounds of yarn with A.M. Knitwear (Knitwear). On June 4, All America sent Knitwear a purchase order. The purchase order stated the terms of the sale, including language that stated the price was FOB the seller's plant. A truck hired by All America arrived at Knitwear's plant. Knitwear turned the yarn over to the carrier and notified All America that the goods were now on the truck. The truck left Knitwear's plant and proceeded to a local warehouse. Sometime during the night, the truck was hijacked and all the yarn was stolen. All America had paid for the yarn by check but stopped payment on it when it learned the goods had been stolen. Knitwear sued All America, claiming it must pay for the stolen goods because it bore the risk of loss. Who wins? *A.M. Knitwear v. All Am., Etc.*, 359 N.E.2d (N.Y. 1976).

Critical Legal Thinking Case 11.7 *Risk of Loss*   Mitsubishi International Corporation (Mitsubishi) entered into a contract with Crown Door Company (Crown) that called for Mitsubishi to sell 12 boxcar loads of plywood to Crown. According to the terms of the contract, Mitsubishi would import the wood from Taiwan and deliver it to Crown's plant in Atlanta. Mitsubishi had the wood shipped from Taiwan to Savannah, Georgia. At Savannah, the plywood was loaded onto trains and hauled to Atlanta. When the plywood arrived in Atlanta, it was discovered that the railroad had been negligent in loading the train. The negligent loading had caused the cargo to shift during the trip, and the shifting had caused extensive damage to the wood. Who bore the risk of loss? *Georgia Port Auth. v. Mitsubishi Int'l Corp.*, 274 S.E.2d 699 (Ga. Ct. App. 1980).

Critical Legal Thinking Case 11.8 *Risk of Loss*   Martin Silver ordered two rooms of furniture from Wycombe, Meyer & Co., Inc. (Wycombe), a manufacturer and seller of custom-made furniture. On February 23, 1982, Wycombe sent invoices to Silver, advising him the furniture was ready for shipment. Silver tendered payment in full for the goods and asked that one room of furniture be shipped immediately and the other be held for shipment on a later date. Before any instructions were received as to the second room of furniture, it was destroyed in a fire. Silver and his insurance company attempted to recover the money he had paid for the destroyed furniture. Wycombe refused to return the payment, claiming the risk of loss was on Silver. Who wins? *Silver v. Wycombe, Meyer & Co.*, 477 N.Y.S.2d 288 (N.Y. Civ. Ct. 1984).

Critical Legal Thinking Case 11.7 *Insurable Interest*   Donald Hayward signed a sales contract with Dry Land Marina, Inc. (Dry Land). The contract was for the purchase of a 30-foot Revel Craft Playmate Yacht for $10,000. The contract called for Dry Land to install a number of options on Hayward's yacht and then deliver it to him. Before taking delivery of the yacht, Hayward signed a security agreement in favor of Dry Land and a promissory note. Several weeks later, a fire swept through Dry Land's showroom. Hayward's yacht was among the goods destroyed in the fire. Who had an insurable interest in the yacht? *Hayward v. Potsma*, 188 N.W.2d 31 (Mich. Ct. App. 1971).

ETHICS CASES

Ethics Case 11.1   Raceway Auto Auction (Raceway), New York, sold an Oldsmobile automobile to Triangle Auto Sales (Triangle). Triangle paid for the car with a check. Raceway delivered possession of the car to Triangle. Thereafter, Triangle's check bounced because of insufficient funds. In the meantime, Triangle sold the car to Campus Auto Sales (Campus), Rhode Island, which sold it to Charles Motor Co., Inc. (Charles), Rhode Island, which sold it to Lee Oldsmobile-Cadillac, Inc. (Lee Oldsmobile), Maine, which sold it to Stephanie K. LeBlanc of Augusta, Maine. When Triangle's check bounced, Raceway reported the car as stolen. Four months after she purchased the car, Stephanie was stopped by the Maine police, who seized the car. To maintain good relations with its customer, Lee Oldsmobile paid Raceway to obtain the certificate of title to the automobile and then sued Charles to recover. Did Triangle Auto Sales act ethically in this case? Did Charles Motor Co. obtain valid title to the automobile? *Lee Oldsmobile-Cadillac, Inc. v. Labonte*, D.C.A. No. 77-260, C.A. No. 76-2663, 1980 R.I. LEXIS 190, at *1 (Super. Ct. Oct. 15, 1980).

Ethics Case 11.2 Executive Financial Services, Inc. (EFS), purchased three tractors from Tri-County Farm Company (Tri-County), a John Deere dealership owned by Gene Mohr and James Loyd. The tractors cost $48,000, $19,000, and $38,000. EFS did not take possession of the tractors but instead left the tractors on Tri-County's lot. EFS leased the tractors to Mohr-Loyd Leasing (Mohr-Loyd), a partnership between Mohr and Loyd, with the understanding and representation by Mohr-Loyd that the tractors would be leased out to farmers. Instead of leasing the tractors, Tri-County sold them to three different farmers. EFS sued and obtained judgment against Tri-County, Mohr-Loyd, and Mohr and Loyd personally for breach of contract. Because that judgment remained unsatisfied, EFS sued the three farmers who bought the tractors to recover the tractors from them. Did Mohr and Loyd act ethically in this case? Who owns the tractors, EFS or the farmers? *Executive Fin. Serv., Inc. v. Pagel*, 715 P.2d 381 (Kan. 1986).

BRIEFING THE CASE WRITING ASSIGNMENT

Read Case A.11 in Appendix A (*Burnett v. Purtell*). This case is excerpted from the court of appeals opinion. Review and brief the case. In your brief, be sure to answer the following questions.

1. Who were the plaintiff and defendant? Were they merchants?
2. Describe the sales transaction.
3. Was there tender of delivery of the goods? Why is this issue important to the outcome of the case?
4. Who bore the risk of loss when the goods were destroyed?

PRACTICE TIP

As you have already learned, sometimes contracts don't go smoothly. Sometimes there is a breach of the contract, which may lead to litigation. The Federal Rules of Civil Procedure and almost all state rules have been revised to include rules on E-Discovery in litigation matters.

Review the case *PSEG Power N.Y., Inc. v. Alberici Constructors, Inc.*, No. 1:05-CV-657 (DNH/RFT), 2007 U.S. Dist. LEXIS 66767 (N.D.N.Y. Sept. 7, 2007). In this breach of contract case, the defendant sought production of all electronically stored e-mails relating to the contract along with their corresponding attachments. The court relied on Fed.R.Civ.P. 34(b) in its discussion of this E-Discovery issue.

Trade and commerce, if they were not made of india-rubber, would never manage to bounce over obstacles which legislators are continually putting in their way.

—*Henry D. Thoreau*
Resistance to Civil Government (1849)

Remedies for Breach of Sales and Lease Contracts

CASE SCENARIO

The law firm where you work as a paralegal is representing Dr. and Mrs. Sedmak (Sedmaks). The Sedmaks are collectors of Chevrolet Corvettes. The couple saw an article in *Vette Vues* magazine concerning a new limited-edition Corvette. The limited edition was designed to commemorate the selection of the Corvette as the official pace car of the Indianapolis 500. Chevrolet was manufacturing only 6,000 of these pace cars. The Sedmaks visited Charlie's Chevrolet, Inc. (Charlie's), a local Chevrolet dealer. Charlie's was to receive only one limited-edition car, which the sales manager agreed to sell to the Sedmaks for the sticker price of $35,000. When the Sedmaks went to pick up and pay for the car, they were told that because of the great demand for the limited edition, it was going to be auctioned to the highest bidder.

■ CHAPTER INTRODUCTION

Usually, the parties to a sales or lease contract owe a duty to perform the **obligations** specified in their agreement [UCC 2-301, 2A-301]. The seller's or lessor's general obligation is to transfer and deliver the goods to the buyer or lessee. The buyer's or lessee's general obligation is to accept and pay for the goods.

    When one party *breaches* a sales or lease contract, the UCC provides the injured party with a variety of prelitigation and litigation remedies. These remedies

obligation
An action a party to a sales or lease contract is required by law to carry out.

CHAPTER OBJECTIVES

After studying this chapter, you should be able to:

1. Describe the performance of sales and lease contracts.

2. List and describe the seller's remedies for the buyer's breach of a sales contract.

3. List and describe the buyer's remedies for the seller's breach of a sales contract.

4. List and describe the lessor's remedies for the lessee's breach of a lease contract.

5. List and describe the lessee's remedies for the lessor's breach of a lease contract.

are designed to place the injured party in as good a position as if the breaching party's contractual obligations were fully performed [UCC 1-106(1), 2A-401(1)]. The best remedy depends on the circumstances of the particular case.

The performance of obligations and remedies available for breach of sales and lease contracts are discussed in this chapter.

PARALEGAL PERSPECTIVE

Cathy Lynn Davis is a certified paralegal with a specialty in civil litigation. She currently works for Wilkerson & Bryan, P.C., in Montgomery, Alabama, where she handles a variety of matters, including both telecommunications and administrative law and civil litigation matters. Cathy holds an associate's degree in legal studies, a bachelor's degree in management of human resources, and a master's degree in criminal justice, all from Faulkner University in Montgomery, Alabama.

Throughout my career, I have worked for a plaintiff's firm, an insurance defense firm, and am currently working in a firm that specializes in, among other things, utility law.

Presently, I perform a variety of tasks for our clients, including contract review. In that regard, I interact with clients to ensure that all parties are kept apprised of the status of the negotiations, research various provisions, and track multiple drafts and revisions of complex agreements exchanged by the parties. Upon occasion, I assist our attorneys in arbitration of disputes related to these matters.

Although my legal background is primarily in litigation, I have found contract work to be just as challenging, particularly when assisting in the drafting process to avoid future litigation or other disputes. It is my greatest challenge to obtain complete disclosures from our clients and assist in creating a contract that reduces the risk of a dispute for the agreement's duration.

■ SELLER'S AND LESSOR'S PERFORMANCE

tender of delivery
The obligation of the seller to transfer and deliver goods to the buyer in accordance with the sales contract.

Tender of delivery, or the transfer and delivery of goods to the buyer or lessee in accordance with a sales or lease contract, is the seller's or lessor's basic obligation [UCC 2-301]. Tender of delivery requires the seller or lessor to (1) put and hold conforming goods at the buyer's or lessee's disposition and (2) give the buyer or lessee any notification reasonably necessary to enable delivery of goods. The parties may agree as to the time, place, and manner of delivery. If there is no special agreement, tender must be made at a reasonable hour, and the goods must be kept available for a reasonable period of time.

Example: The seller cannot telephone the buyer at 12:01 A.M. and say the buyer has 15 minutes to accept delivery [UCC 2-503(1), 2A-508(1)].

Unless otherwise agreed or unless the circumstances permit either party to request delivery in lots, the goods named in the contract must be tendered in a single delivery. Payment of a sales contract is due upon tender of delivery unless an extension of credit between the parties has been arranged. If the goods are rightfully delivered in lots, the payment is apportioned for each lot [UCC 2-307]. Lease payments are due in accordance with the terms of the lease contract.

Place of Delivery

Many sales and lease contracts state where the goods are to be delivered. Often, the contract will say that the buyer or lessee must pick up the goods from the seller or lessor. If the contract does not expressly state where the delivery will take place, the UCC stipulates place of delivery on the basis of whether a carrier is involved.

Noncarrier Cases

Unless otherwise agreed, the place of delivery is the seller's or lessor's place of business. If the seller or lessor has no place of business, the place of delivery is the seller's or lessor's residence. If the parties have knowledge at the time of contracting that identified goods are located in some other place, that place is the place of delivery.

Example: If the parties contract regarding the sale of wheat that is located in a silo, the silo is the place of delivery [UCC 2-308].

Sometimes the goods are in the possession of a bailee (e.g., a warehouse) and are to be delivered without being moved. In such cases, tender of delivery occurs when the seller either (1) tenders to the buyer a negotiable document of title covering the goods, (2) produces acknowledgment from the bailee of the buyer's right to possession of the goods, or (3) tenders a nonnegotiable document of title or a written direction to the bailee to deliver the goods to a buyer. The seller must deliver all such documents in correct form [UCC 2-503(4) and (5)].

Carrier Cases

Unless the parties have agreed otherwise, if delivery of goods to a buyer is to be made by carrier, the UCC establishes different rules for *shipment contracts* and *destination contracts*. These rules are described in the paragraphs that follow.

Shipment Contracts

Sales contracts that require the seller to send the goods to the buyer, but not to a specifically named destination, are called **shipment contracts**. Under such contracts, the seller must do all the following [UCC 2-504]:

1. Put the goods in the carrier's possession and contract for the proper and safe transportation of the goods.
2. Obtain and promptly deliver or tender in correct form any documents (a) necessary to enable the buyer to obtain possession of the goods, (b) required by the sales contract, or (c) required by usage of trade.
3. Promptly notify the buyer of the shipment.

The buyer may reject the goods if a material delay or loss is caused by the seller's failure to make a proper contract for the shipment of goods or properly notify the buyer of the shipment.

Example: If a shipment contract involves perishable goods and the seller fails to ship the goods via a refrigerated carrier, the buyer may rightfully reject the goods if they spoil during transit.

shipment contract
A contract that requires the seller to ship the goods to the buyer via a common carrier. The buyer bears the risk of loss during transportation. A sales contract that requires the seller to send the goods to the buyer, but not a specifically named destination.

Destination Contracts

A sales contract that requires the seller to deliver goods to the buyer's place of business or another specified destination is a **destination contract**. Unless otherwise agreed, destination contracts require delivery to be tendered at the buyer's place of business or other location specified in the sales contract. Delivery must be at a reasonable time and in a reasonable manner and with proper notice to the buyer. Appropriate documents of title must be provided by the seller to enable the buyer to obtain the goods from the carrier [UCC 2-503].

destination contract
A sales contract that requires the seller to deliver conforming goods to a specific destination. The seller bears the risk of loss during transportation. A contract that requires the seller to deliver the goods either to the buyer's place of business or to another destination specified in the sales contract.

Perfect Tender Rule

A seller or lessor is under a duty to deliver conforming goods. If the goods or tender of delivery fails in any respect to conform to the contract, the buyer or lessee

perfect tender rule
A rule that says if the goods or tender of a delivery fail in any respect to conform to the contract, the buyer may opt either (1) to reject the whole shipment, (2) to accept the whole shipment, or (3) to reject part and accept part of the shipment.

may opt either (1) to reject the whole shipment, (2) to accept the whole shipment, or (3) to reject part and accept part of the shipment. This option is referred to as the **perfect tender rule** [UCC 2-601, 2A-509].

Example: A sales contract requires the seller to deliver 100 shirts to a buyer. When the buyer inspects the delivered goods, it is discovered that 99 shirts conform to the contract and 1 shirt does not conform. Pursuant to the perfect tender rule, the buyer may reject the entire shipment. If a buyer accepts nonconforming goods, the buyer may seek remedies against the seller.

Exceptions to the Perfect Tender Rule

The UCC alters the perfect tender rule in the following situations:

1. *Agreement of the parties*—The parties to the sales or lease contract may agree to limit the effect of the perfect tender rule. For example, they may decide that (1) only the defective or nonconforming goods may be rejected, (2) the seller or lessor may replace nonconforming goods or repair defects, or (3) the buyer or lessee will accept nonconforming goods with appropriate compensation from the seller or lessor.
2. *Substitution of carriers*—The UCC requires the seller to use a commercially reasonable substitute if (1) the agreed-upon manner of delivery fails or (2) the agreed-upon type of carrier becomes unavailable [UCC 2-614(1)].

Example: A sales contract specifies delivery of goods by Mac Trucks, Inc., a common carrier, but a labor strike prevents delivery by this carrier. The seller must use any commercially reasonable substitute (such as another truck line or the rails). The buyer cannot reject the delivery because there is a substitute carrier. Unless otherwise agreed, the seller bears any increased cost of the substitute performance.

Cure

cure
An opportunity to repair or replace defective or nonconforming goods.

The UCC gives a seller or lessor who delivers nonconforming goods an opportunity to **cure** the nonconformity. Although the term *cure* is not defined by the UCC, it generally means an opportunity to repair or replace defective or nonconforming goods [UCC 2-508, 2A-513].

A cure may be attempted if the time for performance has not expired and the seller or lessor notifies the buyer or lessee of his or her intention to make a conforming delivery within the contract time.

Example: A lessee contracts to lease a BMW 850i automobile from a lessor for delivery July 1. On June 15, the lessor delivers a BMW 740i to the lessee, and the lessee rejects it as nonconforming. The lessor has until July 1 to cure the nonconformity by delivering the BMW 850i specified in the contract.

A cure may also be attempted if the seller or lessor had reasonable grounds to believe the delivery would be accepted. The seller or lessor may have a further reasonable time to substitute a conforming tender.

Example: A buyer contracts to purchase 100 red dresses from a seller for delivery July 1. On July 1, the seller delivers 100 blue dresses to the buyer. In the past, the buyer has accepted different-colored dresses than those ordered. This time, though, the buyer rejects the blue dresses as nonconforming. The seller has a reasonable time after July 1 to deliver conforming red dresses to the buyer.

In Case 12.1, a seller attempted to cure a defective delivery.

CASE 12.1 CURE

Joc Oil USA, Inc. v. Consolidated Edison Co. of N.Y., 443 N.E.2d 932 (N.Y. 1982).

> *"Therefore, prior to delivery and at the time Joc Oil made its offer to cure by tendering a new conforming shipment, it had cause to believe that the original shipment would have been accepted by the buyer 'with or without money allowance.'"*
>
> Judge Fuchsberg, *Court of Appeals of New York*

Facts

Joc Oil USA, Inc. (Joc Oil) contracted to purchase low-sulfur fuel oil from an Italian oil refinery. The Italian refinery issued a certificate to Joc Oil, indicating that the sulfur content of the oil was 0.50 percent. Joc Oil entered into a sales contract to sell the oil to Consolidated Edison Company of New York, Inc. (Con Ed). Con Ed agreed to pay an agreed-upon price per barrel for oil not to exceed 0.50 percent sulfur. When the ship delivering the oil arrived, it discharged the oil into three Con Ed storage tanks. A report issued by Con Ed stated that the sulfur content of the oil was 0.92 percent. Joc Oil then made an offer to cure the defect by substituting a conforming shipment of oil already on a ship that was to arrive within two weeks. Con Ed rejected Joc Oil's offer to cure. Joc Oil sued Con Ed for breach of contract. The trial court held that under the circumstances of this case, Joc Oil had the right to cure the defect in delivery and that Con Ed breached the contract by refusing to permit this cure. The court entered judgment against Con Ed and awarded Joc Oil $1,385,512 in damages plus interest and the costs of this action. The appellate division court affirmed the judgment. Con Ed appealed.

Issue

Did Joc Oil have a right to cure the defect in the delivery?

Language of the Court

Joc Oil had "reasonable grounds to believe" that the original shipment would be "acceptable" to Con Ed. Moreover, although Joc Oil had no predelivery knowledge of the 0.92% sulfur content disclosed after delivery, it would still have believed that such a shipment would have been acceptable to Con Ed based upon its prior knowledge of Con Ed purchase and use practices during this period of oil scarcity and volatile pricing. Prior to delivery and at the time Joc Oil made its offer to cure by tendering a new conforming shipment, it had cause to believe that the original shipment would have been accepted by the buyer "with or without money allowance" [UCC 2-508(2)].

Decision

The court of appeals held that Joc Oil had made a reasonable and timely offer to cure that was improperly rejected by Con Ed. The court of appeals affirmed the prior court's judgment, awarding Joc Oil $1,385,512 in damages plus interest and costs.

Law & Ethics Questions

1. Should the law recognize the right to cure a defective tender of goods? Why or why not?

2. **Ethics** Did Con Ed act ethically in this case? Did Joc Oil?

3. Why do you think Con Ed rejected Joc Oil's offer to cure the defect in delivery? Explain.

Web Exercises

1. **Web** Visit the website of the Court of Appeals of New York at www .nycourts.gov.

2. **Web** Visit the website of Consolidated Edison Company of New York at www.coned.com.

3. **Web** Use www.google.com and find an article that discusses the UCC's rule concerning curing a defective delivery of a good.

Installment Contracts

installment contract
A contract that requires or authorizes the goods to be delivered and accepted in separate lots.

An **installment contract** requires or authorizes goods to be delivered and accepted in separate lots. Such a contract must contain a clause that states "each delivery in a separate lot" or equivalent language.

Example: A contract in which the buyer orders 100 shirts, to be delivered in four equal installments of 25 items, is an installment contract.

The UCC alters the perfect tender rule with regard to installment contracts. The buyer or lessee may reject the entire contract only if the nonconformity or default with respect to any installment or installments substantially impairs the value of the entire contract. The buyer or lessee may reject any nonconforming installment if the value of the installment is impaired and the defect cannot be cured. Thus, in each case, the court must determine whether the nonconforming installment impairs the value of the entire contract or only that installment [UCC 2-612, 2A-510].

Destruction of Goods

The UCC provides that if goods identified in a sales or lease contract are totally destroyed without the fault of either party before the risk of loss passes to the buyer or the lessee, the contract is void. Both parties are then excused from performing the contract.

If the goods are only partially destroyed, the buyer or lessee may inspect the goods and then choose either to treat the contract as void or to accept the goods. If the buyer or lessee opts to accept the goods, the purchase price or rent will be reduced to compensate for damages [UCC 2-613, 2A-221].

Example: A buyer contracts to purchase a sofa from a seller. The seller agrees to deliver the sofa to the buyer's home. The truck delivering the sofa is hit by an automobile, and the sofa is totally destroyed. Because the risk of loss has not passed to the buyer, the contract is voided, and the buyer does not have to pay for the sofa.

GOOD FAITH AND REASONABLENESS

Generally, the common law of contracts only obligates the parties to perform according to the express terms of their contract. There is no breach of contract unless the parties fail to meet these terms.

Recognizing certain situations may develop that are not expressly provided for in a contract or that strict adherence to the terms of a contract without doing more may not be sufficient to accomplish the contract's objective, the Uniform Commercial Code (UCC) adopts two broad principles that govern the performance of sales and lease contracts: *good faith* and *reasonableness*.

UCC 1-203 states, "Every contract or duty within this Act imposes an obligation of good faith in its performance or enforcement." Although both parties owe a duty of good faith in the performance of a sales or lease contract, merchants are held to a higher standard of good faith than nonmerchants. Nonmerchants are held to the subjective standard of honesty in fact, whereas merchants are held to the objective standard of fair dealing in the trade [UCC 2-103(1)(b)].

The words *reasonable* and *reasonably* are used throughout the UCC to establish the duties of performance by the parties to sales and lease contracts. For example, unless otherwise specified, the parties must act within a "reasonable" time [UCC 1-204(1)(2)]. As another example, if the seller does not deliver the goods as contracted, the buyer may make "reasonable" purchases to cover (i.e., obtain substitute performance) [UCC 2-712(1)]. The term *commercial reasonableness* is used to establish certain duties of merchants under the UCC. Articles 2 and 2A of the UCC do not specifically define the terms *reasonable* and *commercial reasonableness*. Instead, these terms are defined by reference to the course of performance or the course of dealing between the parties, usage of trade, and such.

Note that the concepts of good faith and reasonableness extend to the "spirit" of the contract as well as the contract terms. The underlying theory is that the parties are more apt to perform properly if their conduct is to be judged against these principles. This is a major advance in the law of contracts.

Law & Ethics Questions

1. **Ethics** Do the UCC concepts of *good faith* and *reasonableness* enhance ethical conduct?
2. Should the concept of *good faith* be implied in every contract? Why or why not?

■ BUYER'S AND LESSEE'S PERFORMANCE

Once the seller or lessor has properly tendered delivery, the buyer or lessee is obligated to accept and pay for the goods in accordance with the sales or lease contract. If there is no agreement, the provisions of the UCC control.

Right of Inspection

Unless otherwise agreed, the buyer or lessee has the right to inspect goods that are tendered, delivered, or identified in the sales contract prior to accepting or paying for them. If the goods are shipped, the inspection may take place after their arrival. If the inspected goods do not conform to the contract, the buyer or lessee may reject them without paying for them [UCC 2-513(1), 2A-515(1)].

The parties may agree as to the time, place, and manner of inspection. If there is no such agreement, the inspection must occur at a reasonable time and place and in a reasonable manner. Reasonableness depends on the circumstances of the case, common usage of trade, prior course of dealing between the parties, and such. If the goods conform to the contract, the buyer pays for the inspection. If the goods

COD (cash on delivery)
Buyers must pay for the goods upon delivery without the right to inspect them first.

are rejected for nonconformance, the cost of inspection can be recovered from the seller [UCC 2-513(2)].

Buyers who agree to **COD (cash on delivery)** deliveries are not entitled to inspect the goods before paying for them. In certain sales contracts (e.g., cost, insurance, and freight [CIF] contracts), payment is due from the buyer upon receipt of documents of title, even if the goods have not yet been received. In such a case, the buyer is not entitled to inspect the goods before paying for them [UCC 2-513(3)].

THE ETHICAL PARALEGAL

Candor and Honesty

The ethical paralegal knows that complete honesty is required in every aspect of his or her professional career. Of particular note to the paralegal is the honesty and candor required before a tribunal (i.e., the court) as set out in ABA Model Rule 3.3.[1]

At first blush, it might not seem that this rule is so important to the paralegal because it is almost always the attorney who is appearing before the court. However, there are several circumstances where the paralegal is responsible for work that ultimately is presented to the court.

Many paralegals have the responsibility of legal research and writing. The ethical paralegal knows that all of the law must be presented to the court. In other words, if the paralegal finds a case in his or her legal research that conflicts with a client's position, that case must still be disclosed to the court. Working with the attorney, the paralegal should be able to find a way to distinguish that case in a way that might still favor the client.

Payment

Goods that are accepted must be paid for [UCC 2-607(1)]. Unless the parties to a contract agree otherwise, payment is due from a buyer when and where the goods are delivered, even if the place of delivery is the same as the place of shipment. Buyers often purchase goods on credit extended by the seller. Unless the parties agree to other terms, the credit period begins to run from the time the goods are shipped [UCC 2-310]. A lessee must pay lease payments in accordance with the lease contract [UCC 2A-516(1)].

The goods can be paid for in any manner currently acceptable in the ordinary course of business (check, credit card, or the like) unless the seller demands payment in cash or unless the contract names a specific form of payment. If the seller requires cash payment, the buyer must be given an extension of time necessary to procure the cash. If the buyer pays by check, payment is conditional on the check being honored (paid) when it is presented to the bank for payment [UCC 2-511].

Acceptance

acceptance
Acquiescence (acceptance of guilt).

Acceptance occurs when the buyer or lessee takes any of the following actions after a reasonable opportunity to inspect the goods: (1) signifies to the seller or lessor in words or by conduct that the goods are conforming or that the buyer or lessee

---

[1]Copies of the ABA Model Rules of Professional Conduct are available from Service Center, American Bar Association, 321 North Clark Street, Chicago, IL 60610, 1-800-285-2221. The Model Rules can also be viewed online at http://www.abanet.org/cpr/mrpc/mrpc_toc.html.

will take or retain the goods despite their nonconformity or (2) fails effectively to reject the goods within a reasonable time after their delivery or tender by the seller or lessor. Acceptance also occurs if a buyer acts inconsistently with the seller's ownership rights in the goods.

Example: Acceptance occurs if the buyer resells the goods delivered by the seller [UCC 2-606(1), 2A-515(1)].

Buyers and lessees may only accept delivery of a "commercial unit," a unit of goods that commercial usage deems is a single whole for purpose of sale. Thus, it may be a single article (such as a machine), a set of articles (such as a suite of furniture or an assortment of sizes), a quantity (such as a bale, a gross, or a carload), or any other unit treated in use or in the relevant market as a single whole. Acceptance of a part of any commercial unit is acceptance of the entire unit [UCC 2-606(2), 2A-515(2)].

Revocation of Acceptance

A buyer or lessee who has accepted goods may subsequently *revoke* his or her acceptance if (1) the goods are nonconforming, (2) the nonconformity substantially impairs the value of the goods to the buyer or lessee, and (3) one of the following factors is shown: (a) the seller's or lessor's promise to a timely cure of the nonconformity is not met, (b) the goods were accepted before the nonconformity was discovered and the nonconformity was difficult to discover, or (c) the goods were accepted before the nonconformity was discovered and the seller or lessor assured the buyer or lessee that the goods were conforming.

Revocation of acceptance is not effective until the seller or lessor is so notified. In addition, the revocation must occur within a reasonable time after the buyer or lessee discovers or should have discovered the grounds for the revocation. The revocation, which must be of a lot or commercial unit, must occur before there is any substantial change in the condition of the goods (e.g., before perishable goods spoil) [UCC 2-608(1), 2A-517(1)].

revocation of acceptance
Where the buyer or lessee who has accepted goods subsequently withdraws that acceptance.

■ SELLER'S AND LESSOR'S REMEDIES

Various remedies are available to sellers and lessors if a buyer or lessee breaches a contract. These remedies are discussed in the paragraphs that follow.

Right to Withhold Delivery

Delivery of goods may be *withheld* if the seller or lessor is in possession of them when the buyer or lessee breaches the contract. This remedy is available if the buyer or lessee wrongfully rejects or revokes acceptance of the goods, fails to make a payment when due, or repudiates the contract. If part of the goods under the contract have been delivered when the buyer or lessee materially breaches the contract, the seller or lessor may withhold delivery of the remainder of the affected goods [UCC 2-703(a), 2A-523(1)(c)].

A seller or lessor who discovers the buyer or lessee is insolvent before the goods are delivered may refuse to deliver as promised unless the buyer or lessee pays cash for the goods [UCC 2-702(1), 2A-525(1)]. Under the UCC, a person is insolvent when he or she (1) ceases to pay his or her debts in the ordinary course of business, (2) cannot pay his or her debts as they become due, or (3) is insolvent within the meaning of the federal bankruptcy law [UCC 1-201(23)].

Right to Stop Delivery of Goods in Transit

stop delivery of the goods

When a seller or lessor, upon learning of a buyer's or lessee's insolvency, stops goods from being delivered while they are in transit.

Often, sellers and lessors employ common carriers and other bailees (e.g., warehouses) to hold and deliver goods to buyers and lessees. The goods are considered to be *in transit* while they are in possession of these carriers or bailees. A seller or lessor that learns of the buyer's or lessee's insolvency while the goods are in transit may **stop delivery of the goods**, irrespective of the size of the shipment.

Essentially, the same remedy is available if the buyer or lessee repudiates the contract, fails to make payment when due, or otherwise gives the seller or lessor some other right to withhold or reclaim the goods. In these circumstances, however, the delivery can be stopped only if it constitutes a carload, a truckload, a planeload, or a larger express or freight shipment [UCC 2-705(1), 2A-526(1)].

The seller or lessor must give sufficient notice to allow the bailee, by reasonable diligence, to prevent delivery of the goods. After receipt of notice, the bailee must hold and deliver the goods according to the directions of the seller or lessor. The seller is responsible for all expenses borne by the bailee in stopping the goods [UCC 2-705(3), 2A-526(3)].

Goods may be stopped in transit until the buyer or lessee obtains possession of the goods or the carrier or other bailee acknowledges that it is holding the goods for the buyer or lessee [UCC 2-705(2), 2A-526(2)].

Right to Reclaim Goods

reclamation

The right of a seller or lessor to demand the return of goods from the buyer or lessee under specified situations.

In certain situations, a seller or lessor may demand the return of the goods it sold or leased that are already in the possession of the buyer or lessee. In a sale transaction, **reclamation** is permitted in two situations. If the goods are delivered in a credit sale and the seller then discovers the buyer was insolvent, the seller has 10 days within which to demand that the goods be returned [UCC 2-507(2)]. If the buyer misrepresented his or her solvency in writing within three months before delivery [UCC 2-702(2)] or paid for goods in a cash sale with a check that bounces [UCC 2-507(2)], the seller may reclaim the goods at any time.

A lessor may reclaim goods in the possession of the lessee if the lessee is in default of the contract [UCC 2A-525(2)].

To exercise a right of reclamation, the seller or lessor must send the buyer or lessee a written notice demanding return of the goods. The seller or lessor may not use self-help to reclaim the goods if the buyer or lessee refuses to honor his or her demand. Instead, appropriate legal proceedings must be instituted.

Right to Dispose of Goods

disposition of goods

A seller or lessor who is in possession of goods at the time the buyer or lessee breaches or repudiates the contract may in good faith resell, release, or otherwise dispose of the goods in a commercially reasonable manner and recover damages, including incidental damages, from the buyer or lessee.

If a buyer or lessee breaches or repudiates a sales or lease contract before the seller or lessor has delivered the goods, the seller or lessor may resell or re-lease the goods and recover damages from the buyer or lessee [UCC 2-703(d), 2-706(1), 2A-523(1)(e), 2A-527(1)]. This right also arises if the seller or lessor has reacquired the goods after stopping them in transit.

The **disposition of the goods** by the seller or lessor must be made in good faith and in a commercially reasonable manner. The goods may be disposed of as a unit or in parcels in a public or private transaction. The seller or lessor must give the buyer or lessee reasonable notification of his or her intention to dispose of goods unless the goods threaten to quickly decline in value or are perishable. The party who buys or leases the goods in good faith for value takes the goods free of any rights of the original buyer or lessee [UCC 2-706(5), 2A-527(4)].

The seller or lessor may recover any damages incurred on the disposition of the goods. In the case of a sales contract, damages are defined as the difference between the disposition price and the original contract price. In the case of a lease contract, damages are the difference between the disposition price and the rent the original lessee would have paid.

The profit does not revert to the original buyer or lessee if the seller or lessor disposes of the goods at a higher price than the buyer or lessee contracted to pay. The seller or lessor may also recover any **incidental damages** (reasonable expenses incurred in stopping delivery, transportation charges, storage charges, sales commission, and the like [UCC 2-710, 2A-530]) incurred on the disposition of the goods [UCC 2-706(1), 2A-527(2)].

Example: A buyer contracts to purchase a racehorse for $20,000. When the seller tenders delivery, the buyer refuses to accept the horse or pay for it. The seller, in good faith, and in a commercially reasonable manner, resells the horse to a third party for $17,000. Incidental expenses of $500 are incurred on the resale. The seller can recover $3,500 from the original buyer: the $3,000 difference between the resale price and the contract price and $500 for the incidental expenses.

incidental damages
When goods are resold or released, incidental damages are reasonable expenses incurred in stopping delivery, transportation charges, storage charges, sales commissions, and so on.

Unfinished Goods

Sometimes a sales or lease contract is breached or repudiated before the goods are finished. In such a case, the seller or lessor may choose either (1) to cease manufacturing the goods and resell them for scrap or salvage value or (2) to complete the manufacture of the goods and resell, re-lease, or otherwise dispose of them to another party [UCC 2-704(2), 2A-524(2)]. The seller or lessor may recover damages from the breaching buyer or lessee.

Right to Recover the Purchase Price or Rent

In certain circumstances, the UCC provides that a seller or lessor may sue the buyer or lessee to **recover the purchase price or rent** stipulated in the sales or lease contract. This remedy is available in the following situations:

1. The buyer or lessee accepts the goods but fails to pay for them when the price or rent is due.
2. The buyer or lessee breaches the contract after the goods have been identified in the contract and the seller or lessor cannot resell or dispose of them.
3. The goods are damaged or lost after the risk of loss passes to the buyer or lessee [UCC 2-709(1), 2A-529(1)].

recovery of the purchase price or rent
A seller or lessor may recover the contracted-for purchase price or rent from the buyer or lessee if the buyer or lessee (1) fails to pay for accepted goods, (2) breaches the contract and the seller or lessor cannot dispose of the goods, or if (3) the goods are damaged or lost after the risk of loss passes to the buyer or lessee.

To recover the purchase price or rent, the seller or lessor must hold the goods for the buyer or lessee. If resale or other disposition of the goods becomes possible prior to the collection of the judgment, however, the seller or lessor may resell or dispose of them. In such situations, the net proceeds of any disposition must be credited against the judgment [UCC 2-709(2), 2A-529(2) and (3)]. The seller or lessor may also recover incidental damages from the buyer or lessee.

Right to Recover Damages for Breach of Contract

If a buyer or lessee repudiates a sales or lease contract or wrongfully rejects tendered goods, the seller or lessor may sue to **recover the damages** caused by the buyer's or lessee's breach. Generally, the amount of damages is calculated as the difference between the contract price (or rent) and the market price (or rent) of the goods at the time and place the goods were to be delivered to the buyer or lessee plus incidental damages [UCC 2-708(1), 2A-528(1)].

If the preceding measure of damage will not put the seller or lessor in as good a position as performance of the contract would have, the seller or lessor can seek

recovery of damages
A seller or lessor may recover damages measured as the difference between the contract price (or rent) and the market price (or rent) at the time and place the goods were to be delivered, plus incidental damages, from a buyer or lessee who repudiates the contract or wrongfully rejects tendered goods.

348 CHAPTER 12

recovery of lost profits
When the buyer breaches performance of the contract and the seller seeks damages for profits they would have received from the full performance of the contract.

cancellation
The termination of a contract by a contracting party upon the material breach of the contract by the other party. A buyer or lessee may cancel a sales or lease contract if the seller or lessor fails to deliver conforming goods or repudiates the contract or if the buyer or lessee rightfully rejects the goods or justifiably revokes acceptance of the goods.

to **recover any lost profits** that would have resulted from the full performance of the contract plus an allowance for reasonable overhead and incidental damages [UCC 2-708(2), 2A-528(2)].

Right to Cancel a Contract

A seller or lessor may cancel a sales or lease contract if the buyer or lessee breaches that contract by rejecting or revoking acceptance of the goods, failing to pay for the goods, or repudiating all or any part of the contract. The **cancellation** may refer only to the affected goods or to the entire contract if the breach is material [UCC 2-703(f), 2A-523(1)(a)].

A seller or lessor who rightfully cancels a sales or lease contract by notifying the buyer or lessee is discharged of any further obligations under that contract. The buyer's or lessee's duties are not discharged, however. The seller or lessor retains the right to seek damages for the breach [UCC 2-106(4), 2A-523(3)].

CONTEMPORARY Issue

LOST VOLUME SELLER

Should a seller be permitted to recover the profits it lost on a sale to a defaulting buyer if the seller sold the goods to another buyer? It depends. If the seller had only one item or a limited number of items and could produce no more, the seller cannot recover lost profits from the defaulting buyer. This is because the seller made those profits on the sale of the item to the new buyer. If, however, the seller could have produced more of the item, the seller is a "lost volume seller." In this situation, the seller can make the profit from the sale of the item to the new buyer and sue the defaulting buyer to recover the profit it would have made from this sale. This is because the seller would have realized profits from two sales—the sale to the first buyer who defaulted and the second sale to the new buyer.

Concept Summary
Seller's and Lessor's Remedies

Location of Possession of Goods	Seller's or Lessor's Remedies at Time of Buyer's Breach
Goods in the possession of the seller	1. Withhold delivery of the goods [UCC 2-703(a), 2A-523(1)(c)]. 2. Demand payment in cash if the buyer is insolvent [UCC 2-702(1), 2A-525(1)]. 3. Resell or re-lease the goods and recover the difference between the contract or lease price and the resale or re-lease price [UCC 2-706, 2A-527]. 4. Sue for breach of contract and recover as damages either: a. The difference between the market price and the contract price [UCC 2-708(1), 2A-528(1)] or b. Lost profits [UCC 2-708(2), 2A-528(2)]. 5. Cancel the contract [UCC 2-703(f), 2A-523(1)(a)].

(continued)

| Goods in the possession of a carrier or bailee | 1. Stop goods in transit [UCC 2-705(1), 2A-526(1)].
  a. Carload, truckload, planeload, or larger shipment if the buyer is solvent.
  b. Any size shipment if the buyer is insolvent. |
| Goods in the possession of the buyer | 1. Sue to recover the purchase price or rent [UCC 2-709(1), 2A-525(1)].

2. Reclaim the goods [UCC 2-507(2), 2A-525(2)].
  a. The seller delivers goods in cash sale, and the buyer's check is dishonored.
  b. The seller delivers goods in a credit sale, and the goods are received by an insolvent buyer. |

MARKETPLACE

Business Law Paralegal: Job Announcement

Local corporation seeking to hire a business law paralegal. The ideal candidate understands and is educated in general business law concepts with exposure to entity formation, operating agreements, general contracts for products and services, periodic preparation of litigation briefs as well as various administrative office tasks such as Web research and data collection/entry.

Required is a minimum of an associate's degree in paralegal studies from an American Bar Association approved program, or a bachelor's degree coupled with a certificate in paralegal studies. Preferred is at least three years prior experience as a paralegal in a law firm, corporate legal department, or government agency. Strong writing, communication, and documentation skills are needed. International business, contracts, and commodity or financial trading experience is also a plus.

Interested candidates should submit a resume to:

■ BUYER'S AND LESSEE'S REMEDIES

The UCC provides a variety of remedies to a buyer or lessee upon the seller's or lessor's breach of a sales or lease contract. These remedies are discussed in the following paragraphs.

Right to Reject Nonconforming Goods or Improperly Tendered Goods

If the goods or the seller's or lessor's tender of delivery fails to conform to a sales or lease contract in any way, the buyer or lessee may (1) reject the whole, (2) accept the whole, or (3) accept any commercial unit and reject the rest. If the buyer or lessee chooses to reject the goods, he or she must identify defects that are ascertainable by reasonable inspection. Failure to do so prevents the buyer or lessee from relying on those defects to justify the rejection if the defect could have been cured by a seller or lessor who was notified in a timely manner [UCC 2-601, 2A-509]. Nonconforming or improperly tendered goods must be rejected within a reasonable time after their delivery or tender. The seller or lessor must be notified of the rejection. The buyer or lessee must hold any rightfully rejected goods with reasonable care for a reasonable time [UCC 2-602(2), 2A-512(1)].

If the buyer or lessee is a merchant and the seller or lessor has no agent or place of business at the market where the goods are rejected, the merchant-buyer or merchant-lessee must follow any reasonable instructions received from the seller or lessor with respect to the rejected goods [UCC 2-603, 2A-511]. If the seller or lessor gives no instructions and the rejected goods are perishable or will quickly decline in value, the buyer or lessee may make reasonable efforts to sell them on the seller's or lessor's behalf [UCC 2-604, 2A-512].

Any buyer or lessee who rightfully rejects goods is entitled to reimbursement from the seller or lessor for reasonable expenses incurred in holding, storing, reselling, shipping, and otherwise caring for the rejected goods.

Right to Recover Goods from an Insolvent Seller or Lessor

If a buyer or lessee makes partial or full payment for goods before they are received and the seller or lessor becomes insolvent within 10 days after receiving the first payment, the buyer or lessee may *recover the goods* from the seller or lessor. To do so, the buyer or lessee must tender the unpaid portion of the purchase price or rent due under the sales or lease contract. Only conforming goods that are identified in the contract may be recovered [UCC 2-502, 2A-522]. This remedy is often referred to as **capture**.

capture
The process by which a buyer or lessee can recover goods when seller or lessor becomes insolvent within 10 days of receiving the buyer's or lessee's first payment.

Right to Obtain Specific Performance

If goods are unique or the remedy at law is inadequate, a buyer or lessee may obtain **specific performance** of a sales or lease contract. A decree of specific performance orders the seller or lessor to perform the contract. Specific performance is usually used to obtain possession of works of art, antiques, rare coins, and other unique items [UCC 2-716(1), 2A-521(1)].

Example: A buyer enters into a sales contract to purchase a specific Rembrandt painting from a seller for $10 million. When the buyer tenders payment, the seller refuses to sell the painting to the buyer. The buyer may bring an equity action to obtain a decree of specific performance from the court, ordering the seller to sell the painting to the buyer.

specific performance
A remedy that orders the breaching party to perform the acts promised in the contract; usually awarded in cases where the subject matter is unique, such as in contracts involving land, heirlooms, and paintings. Judgment of the court ordering a licensor to specifically perform the license by making the contracted-for unique information available to the licensee.

Right to Cover

A buyer or lessee may exercise the **right to cover** by purchasing or renting substitute goods if the seller or lessor fails to make delivery of the goods or repudiates the contract or if the buyer or lessee rightfully rejects the goods or justifiably revokes their acceptance. The buyer's or lessee's cover must be made in good faith and without unreasonable delay. If the exact commodity is not available, the buyer or lessee may purchase or lease any commercially reasonable substitute.

A buyer or lessee who rightfully covers may sue the seller or lessor to recover as damages the difference between the cost of cover and the contract price or rent. The buyer or lessee may also recover incidental and consequential damages, less expenses saved (such as delivery costs) [UCC 2-712, 2A-518]. The UCC does not require a buyer or lessee to cover when a seller or lessor breaches a sales or lease contract. Failure of the buyer or lessee to cover does not bar the buyer from other remedies against the seller.

right to cover
When a buyer or lessee purchases or rents substitute goods.

PARALEGAL PERSPECTIVE

Karen Wasil is the chief compliance officer for NorthPointe Capital, LLC, in Troy, Michigan. She received her paralegal degree from the University of Toledo in Toledo, Ohio.

I am the chief compliance officer for NorthPointe Capital, LLC, a registered investment adviser. Contracts are an integral part of our company. We must have an investment contract and guidelines describing our agreement with the client to establish an account and invest the client's money.

Contracts are the backbone of every aspect of our business, including electronic trading, custody of the money, e-mail retention, auditors, disaster recovery, software, and employee benefit agreements. If you are drafting a contract for a client, remember that the clients should review the contract to be sure they are capable of complying with the representations and not agreeing to something they think is "boilerplate." You should be aware there are regulatory restrictions on some contracts (i.e., investment advisory) that will not allow the assignment of a contract or may require shareholder approval before an assignment can be completed. In addition, contracts are part of the mandatory books and records that the regulators want to see when they conduct an examination of a company.

I agree with the saying "If it is not in writing then it is not part of the contract." So many times salespeople sell the product, but when it comes to the contract they are unable to put the representations into the contract.

Do not be afraid to ask for changes to the contract even if someone tells you, "This is our standard agreement." You may be surprised at what you are able to negotiate.

Right to Replevy Goods

A buyer or lessee may replevy (recover) goods from a seller or lessor who is wrongfully withholding them. The buyer or lessee must show that he or she was unable to cover or that attempts at cover will be unavailing. Thus, the goods must be scarce, but not unique. **Replevin** actions are available only as to goods identified in a sales or lease contract [UCC 2-716(3), 2A-521(3)].

replevin
An action by a buyer or lessor to recover scarce goods wrongfully withheld by a seller or lessor.

Example: On January 1, IBM contracts to purchase monitors for computers from a seller for delivery on June 1. IBM intends to attach the monitors to a new computer that will be introduced on June 30. On June 1, the seller refuses to sell the monitors to IBM because it can get a higher price from another buyer. IBM tries to cover but cannot. IBM may successfully replevy the monitors from the seller.

Right to Cancel a Contract

If a seller or lessor fails to deliver conforming goods, repudiates the contract, or if the buyer or lessee rightfully rejects the goods or justifiably revokes acceptance of the goods, the buyer or lessee may *cancel* the sales or lease contract. The contract may be canceled with respect to the affected goods or, if there is a material breach, the whole contract may be canceled. A buyer or lessee who rightfully cancels a contract is discharged from any further obligations on the contract and retains his or her rights to other remedies against the seller or lessor [UCC 2-711(1), 2A-508(1)(a)].

Right to Recover Damages for Nondelivery or Repudiation

If a seller or lessor fails to deliver the goods or repudiates the sales or lease contract, the buyer or lessee may recover *damages*. The measure of damages is the difference between the contract price (or original rent) and the market price (or rent) at the time the buyer or lessee learned of the breach. Incidental and consequential damages, less expenses saved, can also be recovered [UCC 2-713, 2A-519].

Example: Fresh Foods Company contracts to purchase 10,000 bushels of soybeans from Sunshine Farms for $5 per bushel. Delivery is to occur on August 1. On August 1 the market price of soybeans is $7 per bushel. Sunshine Farms does not deliver the soybeans. Fresh Foods decides not to cover and to do without the soybeans. Fresh Foods sues Sunshine for market value minus the contract price damages. It can recover $20,000 ($7 market price minus $5 contract price multiplied by 10,000 bushels) plus incidental damages less expenses saved because of Sunshine's breach. Fresh Foods cannot recover consequential damages because it did not attempt to cover.

Right to Recover Damages for Accepted Nonconforming Goods

damages for accepted nonconforming goods
A buyer or lessee may accept nonconforming goods and recover the damages caused by the breach from the seller or lessor or deduct the damages from any part of the purchase price or rent still due under the contract.

A buyer or lessee may accept nonconforming goods from a seller or lessor. The acceptance does not prevent the buyer or lessee from suing the seller or lessor to recover the **damages for accepted nonconforming goods** and any loss resulting from the seller's or lessor's breach. Incidental and consequential damages may also be recovered. The buyer or lessee must notify the seller or lessor of the nonconformity within a reasonable time after the breach was or should have been discovered. Failure to do so bars the buyer or lessee from any recovery. If the buyer or lessee accepts nonconforming goods, he or she may deduct all or any part of damages resulting from the breach from any part of the purchase price or rent still due under the contract [UCC 2-714(1), 2A-516(1)].

Example: A retail clothing store contracts to purchase 100 designer dresses for $100 per dress from a seller. The buyer pays for the dresses prior to delivery. After the dresses are delivered, the buyer discovers that 10 of the dresses have flaws in them. The buyer may accept these nonconforming dresses and sue the seller for reasonable damages resulting from the nonconformity.

Concept Summary

Buyer's and Lessee's Remedies

Situation	Buyer's or Lessee's Remedy
Seller or lessor refuses to deliver the goods or delivers nonconforming goods that the buyer or lessee does not want.	1. Reject nonconforming goods [UCC 2-601, 2A-509]. 2. Revoke acceptance of nonconforming goods [UCC 2-608, 2A 517(1)]. 3. Cover [UCC 2-712, 2A-518]. 4. Sue for breach of contract and recover damages [UCC 2-713, 2A-519]. 5. Cancel the contract [UCC 2-711(1), 2A-508(1)(a)].
Seller or lessor tenders nonconforming goods and the buyer or lessee accepts them.	1. Sue for ordinary damages [UCC 2-714(1), 2A-516(1)]. 2. Deduct damages from the unpaid purchase or rent price [UCC 2-714(1), 2A-516(1)].
Seller or lessor refuses to deliver the goods and the buyer or lessee wants them.	1. Sue for specific performance [UCC 2-716(1), 2A-521(1)]. 2. Replevy the goods [UCC 2-716(3), 2A-521(3)]. 3. Recover the goods from an insolvent seller or lessor [UCC 2-502, 2A-522].

CAREER FRONT

Job Description: Trust Paralegal

A trust paralegal can be involved with contracts in the following ways:

- Draft inter vivos trust agreements for attorney review.
- Review wills for creation and direction of testamentary trusts; review court orders for creation and direction of statutory trusts.
- Maintain financial records of trusts.
- Obtain tax identification number for trust.
- Coordinate periodic income and principal distributions from trusts.
- Correspond and communicate with trusts' grantors and beneficiaries.
- Coordinate the transfer of assets into trusts, including bank accounts, stock transfers, and real estate deeds.
- Make income payments to trust beneficiaries.
- Draft fiduciary tax returns.
- Perform an investment analysis; with the trustee's approval, employ advisers or assistants as required.
- Draft agreements for the employment of advisers or assistants.
- Perform routine trust accounting.
- As appropriate, prepare disclaimers in the beneficiary's interests.
- Advise the trustee of trust responsibilities.
- Distribute trust assets at termination of the trust.
- Draft petitions and proposed orders as necessary.
- Draft inventories, accounts, and petitions for those trusts requiring adjudication.
- Draft trust distribution settlement agreements.
- Draft fiduciary income tax returns for trusts; inform trusts' beneficiaries of the tax liability of their distributions via IRS Schedules K-1.
- Draft intangible property tax returns for trusts and estates.
- Draft pleadings registering or terminating trusts and appointing or substituting trustees.
- Prepare schedule of allocations to trusts under will.
- Analyze and make investment recommendations to attorney for estate planning.

Source: Excerpted by permission from the National Association of Legal Assistants (www.nala.org) and the National Federation of Paralegal Associations, Inc. (www.paralegals.org).

ADDITIONAL PERFORMANCE ISSUES

UCC Articles 2 (Sales) and 2A (Leases) contain several other provisions that affect the parties' performance of a sales or lease contract. These provisions are discussed in the following paragraphs.

Assurance of Performance

Each party to a sales or lease contract expects that the other party will perform his or her contractual obligations. If one party to a contract has reasonable grounds to believe the other party either will not or cannot perform his or her contractual obligations, an **adequate assurance** of due performance may be demanded in writing. If it is commercially reasonable, the party making the demand may suspend his or her performance until adequate assurance of due performance is received from the other party [UCC 2-609, 2A-401].

assurance of performance
Where each party expects that the other party will perform his or her contractual obligations.

adequate assurance
When a party has reasonable grounds to believe the other party will not perform his or her contractual obligations, they may demand a writing assuring them that performance will occur.

Example: A buyer contracts to purchase 1,000 bushels of wheat from a farmer. The contract requires delivery on September 1. In July, the buyer learns that floods have caused substantial crop loss in the area of the seller's farm. The farmer receives the buyer's written demand for adequate assurance on July 15. The farmer fails to give adequate assurance of performance. The buyer may suspend performance and treat the sales contract as having been repudiated.

Anticipatory Repudiation

anticipatory repudiation
The repudiation of a sales or lease contract by one of the parties prior to the date set for performance.

Occasionally, a party to a sales or lease contract repudiates the contract before his or her performance is due under the contract. If the repudiation impairs the value of the contract to the aggrieved party, it is called **anticipatory repudiation**. Mere wavering on performance does not meet the test for anticipatory repudiation.

If an anticipatory repudiation occurs, the aggrieved party can (1) await performance by the repudiating party for a commercially reasonable time (e.g., until the delivery date or shortly thereafter) or (2) treat the contract as having been breached at the time of the anticipatory repudiation, which gives the aggrieved party an immediate cause of action. In either case, the aggrieved party may suspend performance of his or her obligations under the contract [UCC 2-610, 2A-402].

An anticipatory repudiation may be retracted before the repudiating party's next performance is due if the aggrieved party has not (1) canceled the contract, (2) materially changed his or her position (e.g., purchased goods from another party), or (3) otherwise indicated the repudiation is considered final. The retraction may be made by any method that clearly indicates the repudiating party's intent to perform the contract [UCC 2-611, 2A-403].

Statute of Limitations

statute of limitations
Statute that establishes the time period during which a lawsuit must be brought; if the lawsuit is not brought within this period, the injured party loses the right to sue.

The UCC **statute of limitations** provides that an action for breach of any written or oral sales or lease contract must commence within four years after the cause of the action accrues. The parties may agree to reduce the limitations period to one year, but they cannot extend it beyond four years.

Agreements Affecting Remedies

The parties to a sales or lease contract may agree on remedies in addition to or in substitution for the remedies provided by the UCC.

Example: The parties may limit the buyer's or lessee's remedies to repair and replacement of defective goods or parts or to the return of the goods and repayment (refund) of the purchase price or rent. The remedies agreed on by the parties are in addition to the remedies provided by the UCC unless the parties expressly provide that they are exclusive. If an exclusive remedy fails of its essential purpose (e.g., there is an exclusive remedy of repair but there are no repair parts available), any remedy may be had, as provided in the UCC.

liquidated damages
Damages to which parties to a contract agree in advance if the contract is breached. Damages that are specified in the contract rather than determined by the court.

The UCC permits parties to a sales or lease contract to establish in advance the damages that will be paid upon a breach of the contract. Such preestablished damages, called **liquidated damages**, substitute for actual damages. In a sales or lease contract, liquidated damages are valid if they are reasonable in light of the anticipated or actual harm caused by the breach, the difficulties of proof of loss, and the inconvenience or nonfeasibility of otherwise obtaining an adequate remedy [UCC 2-718(1), 2A-504].

ETHICS SPOTLIGHT

UNCONSCIONABLE CONTRACT

UCC Article 2 (Sales) and Article 2A (Leases) have adopted the equity doctrine of **unconscionability**. Under this doctrine, a court may determine as a matter of law that a contract is unconscionable. To prove unconscionability, there must be proof that the parties had substantial unequal bargaining power, that the dominant party misused its power in contracting, and that it would be manifestly unfair or oppressive to enforce the contract. This sometimes happens where a dominant party uses a preprinted form contract and the terms of the contract are unfair or oppressive.

If a court finds a contract or any clause in a contract is unconscionable, the court may refuse to enforce the contract, or it may enforce the remainder of the contract without the unconscionable clause, or it may so limit the application of any unconscionable clause as to avoid any unconscionable result [UCC 2-302, 2A-108]. Unconscionability is sometimes found in a consumer lease if the consumer has been induced by unconscionable conduct to enter into the lease. The doctrine of unconscionability also applies to Web contracts.

unconscionability
Where there is unequal bargaining power between the parties such that it would be manifestly unfair to enforce the contract.

Law & Ethics Questions

1. **Ethics** Does the doctrine of unconscionability encourage ethical behavior? Explain.
2. Is the doctrine of unconscionability necessary? Explain.

INTERNET EXERCISES AND CASE QUESTIONS

Working the Web Internet Exercises

1. Visit "LII: Law About . . . Remedies" at www.law.cornell.edu/topics/remedies .html and "LII: Law About . . . Commercial Law" at www.law.cornell.edu/ topics/commercial.html, which includes information on consumer credit, damages, debtors and creditors, injunctions, and remedies.
2. Determine whether the following are provided in your state's UCC:
   - Good faith and reasonableness requirement
   - Right to stop goods in transit
   - Right to cover

CHAPTER 12 SUMMARY

SELLER'S AND LESSOR'S PERFORMANCE, p. 338

Tender of Delivery

Tender of delivery requires the seller or lessor to (1) put and hold *conforming goods* at the buyer's or lessee's disposition and (2) give the buyer or lessee any notification reasonably necessary to enable the buyer or lessee to take delivery of the goods [UCC 2-503(1), 2A-508(1)].

Place of Delivery

1. *Agreement.* The parties may agree in the sales or lease contract as to the place of delivery.
2. *No agreement.* If there is no agreement in the contract as to place of delivery, the following UCC rules apply:
   a. *Noncarrier cases.* The place of delivery is the seller's or lessor's place of business, unless the seller or lessor has no place of business, in which case the place of delivery is the seller's or lessor's residence.

    b. *Carrier cases:*
       i. *Shipment contracts.* The sales contract requires the seller to send goods to the buyer by carrier. Delivery occurs when the seller puts the goods in the carrier's possession [UCC 2-504].
      ii. *Destination contracts.* The sales contract requires the seller to deliver the goods to the buyer's place of business or other destination. Delivery occurs when the goods reach this destination [UCC 2-503].

Perfect Tender Rule

The seller or lessor is under a duty to deliver *conforming goods* to the buyer or lessee. If the goods or tender of delivery fail in any respect to conform to the contract, the buyer or lessee may opt to (1) reject the whole shipment, (2) accept the whole shipment, or (3) reject part and accept part of the shipment [UCC 2-601, 2A-509]. *Exceptions to the perfect tender rule:*

1. *Agreement of the parties.* The parties may agree to limit the effect of the perfect tender rule.
2. *Substitution of carriers.* A seller must use a commercially reasonable substitute if the agreed upon manner of delivery fails or the agreed upon type of carrier becomes unavailable [UCC 2-614(1)].
3. *Cure.* A seller or lessor who delivers nonconforming goods has the opportunity to *cure* the nonconformity by repairing or replacing defective or nonconforming goods if the time for performance has not expired and the seller or lessor notifies the buyer or lessee of his or her intention to make a conforming delivery within the contract time [UCC 2-508, 2A-513].
4. *Installment contracts.* The buyer or lessee may reject any nonconforming installment if the value of the installment is impaired and the defect cannot be cured. The buyer or lessee may reject the entire contract upon the tender of a nonconforming installment only if the nonconformity substantially impairs the value of the entire contract [UCC 2-612, 2A-510].
5. *Destruction of goods.* If goods identified in the contract are totally destroyed without fault of either party before the risk of loss passes to the buyer or lessee, the seller or lessor is excused from performance [UCC 2-613].

General Obligations

The UCC has adopted the following broad principles that govern the performance of sales and lease contracts:

1. *Good faith.* Parties to a sales or lease contract must perform their contract obligations in *good faith* [UCC 1-203].
2. *Reasonableness.* Many UCC provisions require parties to take *reasonable* steps or to act *reasonably* in performing contract obligations.
3. *Commercial reasonableness.* Some provisions of the UCC require merchants to use *commercial reasonableness* in the performance of their contract obligations.

BUYER'S AND LESSEE'S OBLIGATIONS AND PERFORMANCE, p. 343

Right of Inspection

Unless otherwise agreed, the buyer or lessee has the right to inspect goods that are tendered, delivered, or identified in the sales or lease contract prior to accepting or paying for them [UCC 2-513(1), 2A-515(1)].

Payment

Duty to pay. Goods accepted by the buyer or lessee must be paid for in accordance with the terms of the sales or lease contract. Unless otherwise agreed, payment or rent is due when and where the goods are delivered [UCC 2-310, 2A-516(1)].

Acceptance

Acceptance occurs when the buyer or lessee takes one of the following actions [UCC 2-606, 2A-515]:

1. Signifies in words or by conduct that the goods are conforming or that the goods will be taken or retained despite their nonconformity.
2. Fails to reject the goods within a reasonable time after their delivery by the seller or lessor.
3. Acts inconsistently with the seller's ownership rights in the goods.

Buyers and lessees may only accept delivery of a *commercial unit.*

SELLER'S AND LESSOR'S REMEDIES, p. 345

Right to Withhold Delivery

Delivery of goods may be withheld if the seller or lessor discovers the buyer or lessee is insolvent before the goods are delivered [UCC 2-703(a), 2A-523(1)(c)].

Demand payment in cash. If the seller or lessor discovers the buyer or lessee is insolvent, he or she may refuse to deliver the goods unless payment is rendered in cash [UCC 2-702(1), 2A-525(1)].

Right to Stop Delivery of Goods in Transit

If the goods are in transit or in the bailee's possession, the seller or lessor may stop delivery (1) of a carload, a truckload, or a planeload of goods if the buyer or lessee repudiates the contract, fails to make a payment when due, or otherwise breaches the contract or (2) of any size shipment if the buyer or lessee becomes insolvent [UCC 2-705(1), 2A-526(1)].

Right to Reclaim Goods

A seller or lessor may reclaim goods in the possession of the buyer or lessee if:

1. The goods are delivered in a credit sale and the seller then discovers that the buyer was insolvent [UCC 2-000].
2. The buyer misrepresented his or her solvency in writing within three months before delivery or paid for goods in a cash sale with a check that bounces [UCC 2-702(2) and 507(2)].

Right to Dispose of Goods

If a buyer or lessee breaches or repudiates the sales or lease contract before the seller or lessor has delivered the goods, the seller or lessor may resell or release the goods and recover damages from the buyer or lessee. Damages are calculated as the difference between the disposition price or rent and the original contract price or rent [UCC 2-706(1), 2A-527(1)].

Right to Recover the Purchase Price or Rent

If the buyer or lessee accepts the goods but fails to pay for them when the contract price or rent is due, the seller or lessor may sue to recover the contracted-for purchase price or rent from the buyer or lessee [UCC 2-709(1), 2A-529(1)].

Right to Recover Damages for Breach of Contract

If a buyer or lessee repudiates a sales or lease contract, the seller or lessor may sue to recover the damages caused by the breach. Damages are calculated as the difference between the original contract price (or rent) and the market price (or rent) of the goods at the time and place the goods were to be delivered, or lost profits [UCC 2-708(1), 2-708(2), 2A-528(1), 2A-528(2)].

Right to Cancel the Contract

The seller or lessor may cancel the sales or lease contract if the buyer or lessee breaches the contract. The seller or lessor is discharged of any further obligations under the canceled contract [UCC 2-106(4), 2A-523(3)].

BUYER'S AND LESSEE'S REMEDIES, p. 349

Seller or Lessor Refuses to Deliver the Goods or Delivers Nonconforming Goods Lessee Does Not Want

1. *Reject nonconforming goods.* If the goods or the seller's or lessor's tender of delivery fails to conform to a sales or lease contract in any way, the buyer or lessee may (1) reject the whole, (2) accept the whole, or (3) accept any commercial unit and reject the rest [UCC 2-601, 2A-509].
2. *Revoke acceptance of nonconforming goods.* A buyer or lessee who has accepted goods may subsequently revoke his or her acceptance if (1) the goods are nonconforming, (2) the nonconformity substantially impairs the value of the goods to the buyer or lessee, and (3) one of the following factors is shown:
   a. The seller's or lessor's promise to reasonably cure the nonconformity is not met,
   b. The goods were accepted before the nonconformity was discovered and the nonconformity was difficult to discover, or
   c. The goods were accepted before the nonconformity was discovered and the seller or lessor assured the buyer or lessee that the goods were conforming [UCC 2-608(1), 2A-517(1)].
3. *Cover.* If the seller or lessor fails to make delivery of goods or repudiates a sales or lease contract or if the buyer or lessee rightfully rejects the goods or justifiably revokes their acceptance, the buyer or lessee may cover by purchasing or renting substitute goods from another party. The buyer or lessee may recover from the seller or lessor damages calculated as the difference between the cost of cover and the original contract price or rent [UCC 2-712, 2A-518].
4. *Sue for breach of contact and recover damages.* If a seller or lessor fails to deliver the goods or repudiates a sales or lease contract, the buyer or lessee may recover damages from the seller or lessor. Damages are calculated as the difference between the contract price (or original rent) and the market price (or rent) at the time the buyer or lessee learned of the breach [UCC 2-713, 2A-519].
5. *Cancel the contract.* A buyer or lessee may cancel a sales or lease contract if the seller or lessor fails to deliver conforming goods or repudiates the contract or if the buyer or lessee rightfully rejects the goods or justifiably revokes acceptance of the goods. The buyer or lessee is discharged from any further obligations under the canceled contract [UCC 2-711(1), 2A-508(1)(a)].

Seller or Lessor Tenders Nonconforming Goods and Buyer or Lessee Accepts Them

1. *Sue for damages.* If a buyer or lessee accepts nonconforming goods from a seller or lessor, the buyer or lessee may recover as damages any loss resulting from the seller's or lessor's breach [UCC 2-714(1), 2A-516(1)].

2. ***Deduct damages from unpaid purchase price or rent.*** If a seller or lessor breaches the sales or lease contract and the buyer or lessee accepts nonconforming goods, the buyer or lessee may deduct all or any part of the damages resulting from the breach from any part of the price or rent still due under the sales or lease contract [UCC 2-714(1), 2A-516(1)].

Seller or Lessor Refuses to Deliver the Goods and Buyer or Lessee Wants Them

1. ***Specific performance.*** If the goods are unique or the remedy at law in inadequate, a buyer or lessee may obtain a decree of specific performance that orders the seller or lessor to perform the sales or lease contract [UCC 2-716(1), 2A-521(1)].
2. ***Replevy the goods.*** A buyer or lessee may replevy (recover) scarce goods from a seller or lessor who is wrongfully withholding them [UCC 2-716(3), 2A-521(3)].
3. ***Recover the goods from an insolvent seller or lessor.*** If the buyer or lessee makes partial or full payment for the goods before they are received and the seller or lessor becomes insolvent within 10 days after receiving the first payment, the buyer or lessee may recover the goods from the seller or lessor [UCC 2-502, 2A522].

Unconscionable Sales and Lease Contracts

If a sales or lease contract or any clause in it is *unconscionable*, the court may either refuse to enforce the contract or limit the application of the unconscionable clause [UCC 2-302, 2A-108].

ADDITIONAL PERFORMANCE ISSUES, p. 353

Assurance of Performance

If one party to a sales or lease contract has reasonable grounds to believe the other party either will not or cannot perform his or her contractual obligations, he or she may demand in writing an adequate assurance of performance from the other party. The party making the demand may suspend his or her performance until adequate assurance of performance is received [UCC 2-609, 2A-401].

Anticipatory Repudiation

Anticipatory repudiation occurs when a party to a sales or lease contract repudiates the contract before his or her performance is due. The aggrieved party can (1) await performance when due or (2) treat the contract as having been breached at the time of the anticipatory repudiation [UCC 2-610, 2A-402].

Statute of Limitations

The UCC provides that an action for breach of any written or oral sales or lease contract must commence within four years after the cause of action accrues. The parties may agree to reduce the limitations period to one year, but they cannot extend it beyond four years [UCC 2-725, 2A-506].

Agreements Affecting Remedies

1. ***Limitations on remedies.*** The parties to a sales or lease contract may agree on remedies in addition to or in substitution for the remedies provided by Article 2 or 2A of the UCC [UCC 2-719(1), 2A-503(1)].
2. ***Unconscionable limitations.*** Any agreement concerning the limitation or exclusion of damages that is found to be unconscionable is unenforceable. With respect to consumer goods, a limitation of consequential damages

for personal injuries is prima facie unconscionable [UCC 2-719(3), 2A-503(3)].

3. *Liquidated damages.* The parties to a sales or lease contract may establish in advance the damages that will be paid upon a breach of the contract [UCC 2-718(1), 2A-504].

TERMS AND CONCEPTS

Acceptance   344

Adequate assurance   353

Anticipatory repudiation   354

Assurance of performance   353

Cancellation   348

Capture   350

COD (cash on delivery)   344

Cure   340

Damages for accepted nonconforming goods   352

Destination contract   339

Disposition of goods   346

Incidental damages   347

Installment contract   342

Liquidated damages   354

Obligations   337

Perfect tender rule   340

Reclamation   346

Recovery of damages   347

Recovery of lost profits   348

Recovery of purchase price or rent   347

Replevin   351

Revocation of acceptance   345

Right to cover   350

Shipment contract   339

Specific performance   350

Statute of limitations   354

Stop delivery of the goods   346

Tender of delivery   338

Unconscionability   355

CASE SCENARIO REVISITED

Remember the case at the beginning of the chapter where Dr. and Mrs. Sedmak had agreed to purchase a limited edition Corvette from a dealership but the dealership decided to auction off the car instead? Knowing what you now know about specific performance, do you think this would be a good case under that theory? If so, who would win? To help you with your answer, see the case of *Sedmak v. Charlie's Chevrolet, Inc.*, 622 S.W.2d 694 (Mo. Ct. App. 1981).

CRITICAL LEGAL THINKING CASES

Critical Legal Thinking Case 12.1 *Nonconforming Goods* The Jacob Hartz Seed Company, Inc. (Hartz), bought soybeans for use as seed from E. R. Coleman. Coleman certified that the seed had an 80 percent germination rate. Hartz paid for the beans and picked them up from a warehouse in Card, Arkansas. After the seed was transported to Georgia, a sample was submitted for testing to the Georgia Department of Agriculture. When the department reported a germination level of only 67 percent, Coleman requested that the seed be retested. The second set of tests reported a germination rate of 65 percent. Hartz canceled the contract after the second test, and Coleman reclaimed the seed. Hartz sought a refund of the money it had paid for the seed, claiming the soybeans were nonconforming goods. Who wins? *Jacob Hartz Seed Co. v. Coleman*, 612 S.W.2d 91 (Ark. 1981).

Critical Legal Thinking Case 12.2 *Right to Cure* Connie R. Grady purchased a new Chevrolet Chevette from Al Thompson Chevrolet (Thompson). Grady gave Thompson a down payment on the car and financed the remainder of the purchase price through General Motors Acceptance Corporation (GMAC). Grady picked up the Chevette. The next day, the car broke down and had to be towed back to Thompson. Grady picked up the repaired car one day later. The car's performance was still unsatisfactory in that the engine was hard to start, the transmission slipped, and the brakes had to be pushed to the floor to function. Two weeks later, Grady again returned the Chevette for servicing. When she picked up the car that evening, the engine started, but the engine and brake warning lights came on. This pattern of malfunction and repair continued for another two months. Grady wrote a letter to Thompson, revoking the sale. Thompson repossessed the Chevette. GMAC sued Grady to recover its money. Grady sued Thompson to recover her down payment. Thompson claimed that Grady's suit was barred because the company was not given adequate opportunity to cure. Who wins? *General Motors Acceptance Corp. v. Grady*, 501 N.E.2d 68 (Ohio Ct. App. 1985).

Critical Legal Thinking Case 12.3 *Revocation of Acceptance* Roy E. Farrar Produce Company (Farrar) was a packer and shipper of tomatoes in Rio Arriba County, New Mexico. Farrar contacted Wilson, an agent and salesman for International Paper Company (International), and ordered 21,500 tomato boxes for $.64 per box. The boxes were to each hold between 20 and 30 pounds of tomatoes for shipping. When the boxes arrived at Farrar's plant, 3,624 of them were immediately used to pack tomatoes. When the boxes were stacked, they began to collapse and crush the tomatoes contained within them. The produce company was forced to repackage the tomatoes and store the unused tomato boxes. Farrar contacted International and informed it that it no longer wanted the boxes because they could not perform as promised. International claimed that Farrar had accepted the packages and must pay for them. Who wins? *International Paper Co. v. Farrar*, 700 P.2d 642 (N.M. 1985).

Critical Legal Thinking Case 12.4 *Commercial Impracticality* Charles C. Campbell was a farmer who farmed some 600 acres in the vicinity of Hanover, Pennsylvania. In the spring, Campbell entered into a contract with Hostetter Farms, Inc. (Hostetter), a grain dealer with facilities in Hanover. The sales agreement called for Campbell to sell Hostetter 20,000 bushels of No. 2 yellow corn at

$1.70 per bushel. Delivery was made five months later in the fall. Unfortunately, the summer was an unusually rainy one, and Campbell could not plant part of his crop because of the wet ground. After the corn was planted, part of the crop failed due to the excessive rain. As a result, Campbell delivered only 10,417 bushels. Hostetter sued Campbell for breach of contract. Campbell asserted the defense of commercial impracticability. Who wins? *Campbell v. Hostetter Farms, Inc.*, 380 A.2d 463 (Pa. Super. Ct. 1977).

Critical Legal Thinking Case 12.5 *Right to Reclaim Goods* Archer Daniels Midland Company (Archer) sold ethanol for use in gasoline. Archer sold 80,000 gallons of ethanol on credit to Charter International Oil Company (Charter). The ethanol was shipped to Charter's facility in Houston. Charter became insolvent sometime during that period. Archer sent a written notice to Charter, demanding the return of the ethanol. At the time Charter received the reclamation demand, it had only 12,000 gallons of ethanol remaining at its Houston facility. When Charter refused to return the unused ethanol, Archer sued to recover the ethanol. Who wins? *Archer Daniels Midland v. Charter Int'l Oil Co.*, 60 B.R. 854 (M.D. Fla. 1986).

Critical Legal Thinking Case 12.6 *Right to Resell Goods* Meuser Material & Equipment Company (Meuser) was a dealer in construction equipment. Meuser entered into an agreement with Joe McMillan for the sale of a bulldozer to McMillan. The agreement called for Meuser to deliver the bulldozer to McMillan's residence in Greeley, Colorado. McMillan paid Meuser with a check. Before taking delivery, McMillan stopped payment on the check. Meuser entered into negotiations with McMillan in an attempt to get McMillan to abide by the sales agreement. During this period, Meuser paid for the upkeep of the bulldozer. When it became apparent that further negotiations would be fruitless, Meuser began looking for a new buyer. Fourteen months after the original sale was supposed to have taken place, the bulldozer was resold for less than the original contract price. Meuser sued McMillan to recover the difference between the contract price and the resale price as well as for the cost of upkeep on the bulldozer for 14 months. Who wins? *McMillan v. Meuser Material & Equip. Co.*, 541 S.W.2d 911 (Ark. 1976).

Critical Legal Thinking Case 12.7 *Right to Recover Purchase Price* C. R. Daniels, Inc. (Daniels), entered into a contract for the design and sale of grass catcher bags for lawn mowers to Yazoo Manufacturing Company, Inc. (Yazoo). Daniels contracted to design grass catcher bags that would fit the "S" series mower made by Yazoo. Yazoo provided Daniels with a lawn mower to design the bag. After Yazoo approved the design of the bags, it issued a purchase order for 20,000 bags. Daniels began to ship the bags. After accepting 8,000 bags, Yazoo requested that the shipments stop. Officials of Yazoo told Daniels it would resume accepting shipments in a few months. Despite several attempts, Daniels could not get Yazoo to accept delivery of the remaining 12,000 bags. Daniels sued Yazoo to recover the purchase price of the grass bags still in its inventory. Who wins? *C.R. Daniels, Inc. v. Yazoo Mfg. Co.*, 641 F. Supp. 205 (S.D. Miss. 1986).

Critical Legal Thinking Case 12.8 *Right to Recover Lost Profits* Saber Energy, Inc. (Saber), entered into a sales contract with Tri-State Petroleum Corporation (Tri-State). The contract called for Saber to sell Tri-State 110,000 barrels of gasoline per month for six months. Saber was to deliver the gasoline through the Colonial pipeline in Pasadena, Texas. The first 110,000 barrels were delivered on time. On August 1, Saber was informed that Tri-State was canceling the contract.

Saber sued Tri-State for breach of contract and sought to recover its lost profits as damages. Tri-State admitted its breach but claimed that lost profits is an inappropriate measure of damages. Who wins? *Tri-State Petroleum Corp. v. Saber Energy, Inc.*, 845 F.2d 575 (5th Cir. 1988).

Critical Legal Thinking Case 12.9 *Right to Cover* Kent Nowlin Construction, Inc. (Nowlin) was awarded a contract by the state of New Mexico to pave a number of roads. After Nowlin was awarded the contract, it entered into an agreement with Concrete Sales & Equipment Rental Company, Inc. (C & E). C&E was to supply 20,000 tons of paving material to Nowlin. Nowlin began paving the roads, anticipating C&E's delivery of materials. On the delivery date, however, C&E shipped only 2,099 tons of paving materials. Because Nowlin had a deadline to meet, the company contracted with Gallup Sand and Gravel Company (Gallup) for substitute material. Nowlin sued C&E to recover the difference between the higher price it had to pay Gallup for materials and the contract price C&E had agreed to. C&E claims it is not responsible for Nowlin's increased costs. Who wins? *Concrete Sales & Equip. Rental Co. v. Kent Nowlin Constr., Inc.*, 746 P.2d 645 (N.M. 1987).

ETHICS CASES

Ethics Case 12.1 Ruby and Carmen Ybarra purchased a new double-wide mobile home from Modern Trailer Sales, Inc. (Modern). Modern delivered the mobile home to the Ybarras. A few days after delivery, portions of the floor began to rise and bubble, creating an unsightly and troublesome situation for the Ybarras. The Ybarras complained to Modern about the floor as soon as they discovered the defects. Modern sent repairmen to cure the defective floor on at least three occasions, but each time they were unsuccessful. The Ybarras continued to complain about the defects. The Ybarras continued to rely on Modern's assurances it was able and willing to repair the floor. After four years of complaints, the Ybarras sued to revoke their acceptance of the sales contract. Did the Ybarras properly revoke their acceptance of the sales contract? Did Modern act ethically in this case? Did the Ybarras? *Ybarras v. Modern Trailer Sales, Inc.*, 609 P.2d 331 (N.M. 1980).

Ethics Case 12.2 Allsopp Sand and Gravel (Allsopp) and Lincoln Sand and Gravel (Lincoln) were both in the business of supplying sand to construction companies. In March 1986, Lincoln's sand dredge became inoperable. To continue in business, Lincoln negotiated a contract with Allsopp to purchase sand over the course of a year. The contract called for the sand to be loaded on Lincoln's trucks during Allsopp's regular operating season (March through November). Loading at other times was to be done by "special arrangement." By November 1986, Lincoln had taken delivery of a quarter of the sand it had contracted for. At that point, Lincoln requested that several trucks of sand be loaded in December. Allsopp informed Lincoln it would have to pay extra for this special arrangement. Lincoln refused to pay extra, pointing out the sand was already stockpiled at Allsopp's facilities. Allsopp also offered to supply an employee to supervise the loading. Negotiations between the parties broke down, and Lincoln informed Allsopp it did not intend to honor the remainder of the contract. Allsopp sued Lincoln. Was it commercially reasonable for Lincoln to demand delivery of sand during December? Did Lincoln act ethically in this case? *Allsopp Sand & Gravel v. Lincoln Sand & Gravel*, 525 N.E.2d 1185 (Ill. App. Ct. 1988).

BRIEFING THE CASE WRITING ASSIGNMENT

Read Case A.12 in Appendix A (*LNS Investment Co., Inc. v. Phillips 66 Co.*). This case is excerpted from the district court opinion. Review and brief the case. After briefing the case, you should be able to answer the following questions:
1. What did the sales contract provide?
2. Was the contract performed?
3. What is the issue in this case?
In whose favor did the court rule?

PRACTICE TIP

Labor union agreements, franchise agreements, leases, and other commercial contracts often contain *arbitration clauses* that require disputes arising out of the contract be submitted to arbitration. In arbitration, the parties choose an impartial third party to hear and decide the dispute. This neutral party is called the *arbitrator*. Arbitrators are usually members of the American Arbitration Association (AAA) or another arbitration association. You can learn more about the AAA by going to its website at www.adr.org.

Some details should be clarified before drafting an arbitration clause:

- Will this be *binding* arbitration? Or do the parties retain the right to challenge the result in court?
- How is the arbitrator to be chosen?
- How is the arbitrator paid?
- What is the timeline for arbitration?
- Should the amount of an award for damages be specified in the contract?
- Will damages be limited to foreseeable damages? Or will indirect damages be agreed to as well?

A sample arbitration agreement might be as simple as the following:

"The parties agree to submit any disputes arising from this agreement to final and binding arbitration under the Rules of the American Arbitration Association."

PARALEGAL PORTFOLIO EXERCISE

Using the information about arbitration from the Practice Tip, the American Arbitration Association's website, and other information on *arbitration clauses* you find on the Internet, draft the following:
1. A basic arbitration clause
2. A binding arbitration clause
3. A more complicated arbitration clause that includes references to:
   a. How the arbitrator is chosen and paid.
   b. The timeline for the arbitration.
   c. How damages are to be calculated.

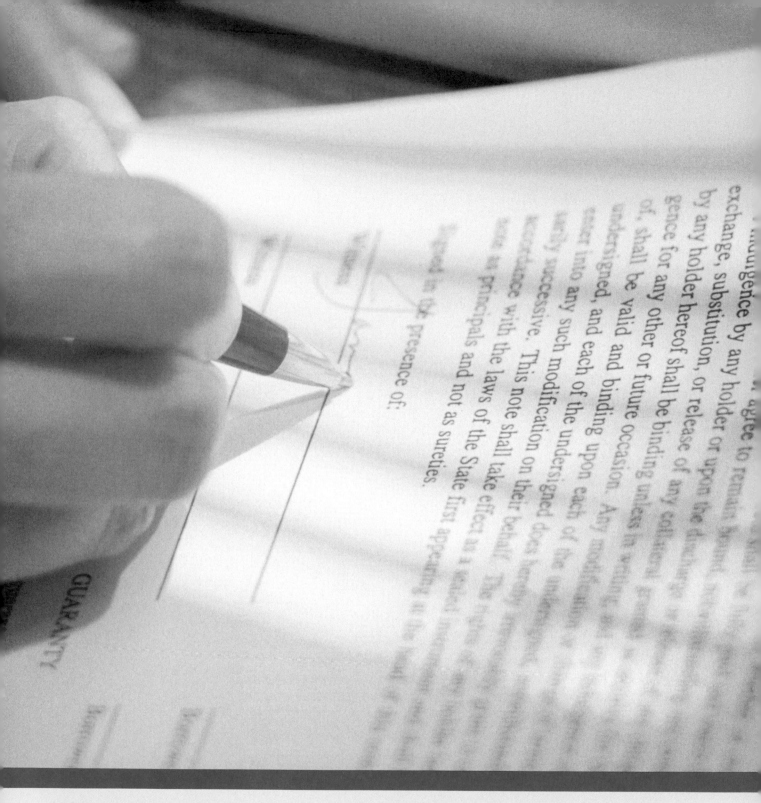

When a manufacturer engages in advertising in order to bring his goods and their quality to the attention of the public and thus to create consumer demand, the representations made constitute an express warranty running directly to a buyer who purchases in reliance thereon. The fact that the sale is consummated with an independent dealer does not obviate the warranty.

—Justice Francis

Henningsen v. Bloomfield Motors, Inc., 161 A.2d 69 (N.J. 1960).

Sales and Lease Warranties | CHAPTER 13

CASE SCENARIO

The law firm where you work as a paralegal is representing Jack Crothers. Jack went to Norm's Auto Sales (Norm's) to buy a used car. Maurice Boyd, a salesman at Norm's, showed Jack a Dodge automobile. While running the car's engine, Boyd told Jack that the Dodge "had a rebuilt carburetor" and "runs good." After listening to the sales pitch, Jack bought the car. As Jack was driving the Dodge the next day, the car suddenly went out of control and crashed into a tree. Jack was seriously injured. The cause of the crash was an obvious defect in the Dodge's accelerator linkage.

■ CHAPTER INTRODUCTION

The doctrine of *caveat emptor*—let the buyer beware—governed the law of sales and leases for centuries. Finally, the law recognized that consumers and other purchasers and lessees of goods needed greater protection. Article 2 of the Uniform Commercial Code (UCC), which has been adopted in whole or in part by 50 states, establish certain **warranties** that apply to the sale of goods. Article 2A of the UCC, which has been adopted in many states, establish warranties that apply to lease transactions.

Warranties are the buyer's or lessee's assurance that the goods meet certain standards. Warranties, which are based on contract law, may be either *expressly* stated or *implied* by law. If the seller or lessor fails to meet a warranty, the buyer or lessee can sue for breach of warranty. Sales and lease warranties are discussed in this chapter.

warranty
A buyer's or lessee's assurance that the goods meet certain standards. A representation of the insured that is expressly incorporated in the insurance contract.

CHAPTER OBJECTIVES

After studying this chapter, you should be able to:

1. Identify and describe express warranties.
2. Describe the implied warranty of merchantability.
3. Describe the implied warranty of fitness for a particular purpose.
4. Identify warranty disclaimers and determine when they are unlawful.
5. Describe the warranties of good title and no infringements.

367

PARALEGAL PERSPECTIVE

Stephannie Keefe Gambill is a graduate of Saint Mary-of-the Woods College and has a bachelor of arts degree in paralegal studies. She is the paralegal for the City of Terre Haute Legal Department in Terre Haute, Indiana.

My supervisor is the mayor-appointed city attorney. The Legal Department is responsible for representing all of the municipal departments, which include transit and sewage treatment utilities, human resources, information technology, engineering, finance, police, fire, street, and park departments. This office also represents the mayor and the city council. Statutory law governs almost all functions of municipal government. Therefore, I must be aware of the constantly changing statutory requirements to ensure that the City remains compliant.

The City purchases land or easements for the construction of sanitary lift stations, sewer laterals, or public walking trails. I am responsible for working with appraisers, contacting property owners, drafting notification letters, purchase agreements, and deeds, and completing the transfers.

The City maintains collective bargaining agreements with six unions that are renegotiated and amended annually. In addition, the individual departments consistently purchase new equipment or contract for specialized services. Those contracts are all reviewed by the Legal Department. I work closely with the attorney and the individual departments to ensure that the contracts are prepared accurately to reflect the specific needs of the department.

Providing legal services for such a diversity of organizations, needs, and interests, I get to see it all!

■ EXPRESS WARRANTY

express warranty
Any affirmation of fact or promise by the licensor about the quality of its software or information. A warranty that is created when a seller or lessor makes an affirmation that the goods he or she is selling or leasing meet certain standards of quality, description, performance, or condition.

Express warranties, which are the oldest form of warranty, are created when a seller or lessor affirms that the goods he or she is selling or leasing meet certain standards of quality, description, performance, or condition.[1] Express warranties can be either written, oral, or inferred from the seller's conduct.

It is not necessary to use formal words such as *warrant* or *guarantee* to create an express warranty. Express warranties can be made by mistake because the seller or lessor does not have to intend specifically to make the warranty.[2]

Sellers and lessors are not required to make such warranties. Generally, express warranties are made to entice consumers and others to buy or lease their products. That is why these warranties are often in the form of advertisements, brochures, catalogs, pictures, illustrations, diagrams, blueprints, and so on.

An express warranty is created when the seller or lessor indicates the goods will conform to:

1. All *affirmations of fact or promise* made about them.

   Example: Statements such as "This car will go 100 miles per hour" or "This house paint will last at least five years."

2. Any *description* of them.

   Example: Terms such as *Idaho potatoes* and *Michigan cherries.*

3. Any *model* or *sample* of them.

   Example: A model oil drilling rig or a sample of wheat taken from a silo.

---

[1]UCC 2-313(1), 2A-210(1).
[2]UCC 2-313(2), 2A-210(2).

Basis of the Bargain

Buyers and lessees can recover for breach of an express warranty if the warranty was a contributing factor—not necessarily the sole factor—that induced the buyer to purchase the product or the lessee to lease the product. This is known as the **basis of the bargain.**[3] The UCC does not define the term *basis of the bargain*, so this test is broadly applied by the courts. Generally, all statements by the seller or lessor prior to or at the time of contracting are presumed to be part of the basis of the bargain unless good reason is shown to the contrary. Postsale statements that modify the contract are part of the basis of the bargain.

Generally, a retailer is liable for the express warranties made by manufacturers of goods it sells. Manufacturers are not liable for express warranties made by wholesalers and retailers unless the manufacturer authorizes or ratifies the warranty.

basis of the bargain
All statements by the seller or lessor prior to or at the time of contracting.

Statements of Opinion

Many express warranties arise during the course of negotiations between a buyer and a seller (or lessor and lessee). The seller's or lessor's **statements of opinion** (i.e., **puffing**) or commendation of the goods do not create an express warranty.[4] It is often difficult to determine whether the seller's statement is an affirmation of fact (which creates an express warranty) or a statement of opinion (which does not create a warranty). An affirmation of the *value* of goods does not create an express warranty.[5]

puffing
A seller's opinion on the quality of goods; usually overpraise, exaggeration, or hype.

Example: A used car salesperson's statement that "This is the best used car available in town" does not create an express warranty because it is an opinion and mere puffing. However, a statement such as "This car has been driven only 20,000 miles" is an express warranty because it is a statement of fact. Statements such as "This painting is worth a fortune" or "Others would gladly pay $20,000 for this car" do not create an express warranty because these are a statement of value and not a statement of fact.

In Case 13.1, the court had to decide whether an express warranty had been created.

CASE 13.1   EXPRESS WARRANTY

Daughtrey v. Ashe, 413 S.E.2d 336 (Va. 1992).

"The trial judge found that the diamonds were of a grade substantially less than v.v.s."

Judge Whiting, *Supreme Court of Virginia*

Facts

W. Hayes Daughtrey consulted Sidney Ashe, a jeweler, about the purchase of a diamond bracelet as a Christmas present for his wife. Ashe showed Daughtrey a diamond bracelet that he had for sale for $15,000. When Daughtrey decided to purchase the bracelet, Ashe completed and signed an appraisal form that stated that the diamonds were "H color and v.v.s. quality." (V.v.s. is one of the highest ratings in a quality classification employed by jewelers.) After Daughtrey paid for the bracelet, Ashe put the bracelet and the appraisal form in a box. Daughtrey gave the bracelet to his wife as a

---

[3]UCC 2-313(1), 2A-210(1).
[4]UCC 2-313(2).
[5]UCC 2-313(2).

Christmas present. One year later, when another jeweler looked at the bracelet, Daughtrey discovered that the diamonds were of substantially lower grade than v.v.s. Daughtrey filed a specific performance suit against Ashe to compel him to replace the bracelet with one mounted with v.v.s. diamonds or pay appropriate damages. The trial court denied relief for breach of warranty. Daughtrey appealed.

Issue

Was an express warranty made by Ashe regarding the quality of the diamonds in the bracelet?

Language of the Court

We consider whether Ashe's statement of the grade of the diamonds was an express warranty. The Court contends that Ashe's statement of the grade of the diamonds is a mere opinion and, thus, cannot qualify as an express warranty.

It is not necessary to the creation of an express warranty that the seller use formal words such as "warrant" or "guarantee" or that he have a specific intention to make a warranty. Here, Ashe did more than give a mere opinion of the value of the goods; he specifically described them as diamonds of "H color and v.v.s. quality." Ashe did not qualify his statement as a mere opinion. And, if one who has superior knowledge makes a statement about the goods sold and does not qualify the statement as his opinion, the statement will be treated as a statement of fact. The trial judge found that the diamonds were of a grade substantially less than v.v.s.

Given these considerations, we conclude that Ashe's description of the goods was more than his opinion; rather, he intended it to be a statement of a fact. Therefore, the court erred in holding that the description was not an express warranty.

Decision

The appellate court held that an express warranty had been created. The trial court's decision was reversed, and the case was remanded for a determination of appropriate damages to be awarded to Daughtrey.

Law & Ethics Questions

1. What is the remedy when an express warranty has been breached? Is the remedy sufficient?

2. **Ethics** Did Ashe act ethically in denying that his statement created an express warranty?

3. Do businesses have to make express warranties? Why do businesses make warranties about the quality of their products?

Web Exercises

1. **Web** Visit the website of De Beers International at www.debeers.com. Find the rating system for the quality of diamonds.

2. **Web** Visit the website of the Supreme Court of Virginia at www.courts.state .va.us.

3. **Web** Use www.google.com and find an article about the De Beers monopoly and the mining of diamonds.

CAREER FRONT

Job Description: Employee Benefits Paralegal

An employee benefits paralegal works with contracts in numerous ways, such as the following:

- Draft and design qualified plan documents and trust agreements, including amendments and restatements, to comply with law and regulations or client requests.
- Develop and review summary plan descriptions.
- Draft deferred compensation plans, including nonqualified executive compensation and stock option plans.
- Draft welfare benefit plans, including cafeteria plans, medical reimbursement plans, dependent care assistance plans, and health-care plans.
- Draft affiliate adoption statement.
- Draft administrative documents and agreements, including notification of participation, election to participate, beneficiary designation, qualified joint and survivor annuity and qualified preretirement survivor annuity waivers and application for benefits, and election to contribute.
- Draft summary annual report.
- Draft benefit and/or compensation statement.
- Draft loan request forms, including loan agreements and consents, if appropriate, and purpose of loan verification for participant loans.
- Draft board of directors resolutions for plan adoption, adoption of amendments, contribution amounts, and other actions required to be taken by the board.
- Draft and file application for IRS determination letter.
- Assist client in preparing and filing annual report (5500 series and related schedules).
- Monitor progress of new plans and amendments to verify required actions occur on schedule.
- Review and interpret regulations issued by government agencies to determine their application and relevance to client plans.
- Assist in preparing and coordinate general notice mailings to clients about potential impact of new legal developments upon plans.
- Research interpretive questions on prohibited transactions for qualified and nonqualified plans.
- Calculate employer contributions and forfeitures and allocate to participant accounts.
- Determine earnings adjustments and allocate to participant accounts.
- Calculate participants' years of service for eligibility and vesting.
- Calculate benefit for terminated participants.

Source: Excerpted by permission from the National Association of Legal Assistants (www.nala.org) and the National Federation of Paralegal Associations, Inc. (www.paralegals.org).

Damages Recoverable for Breach of Warranty

Where there has been a breach of warranty, the buyer or lessee may sue the seller or lessor to recover **compensatory damages**. The amount of recoverable compensatory damages is generally equal to the difference between (1) the value of the goods as warranted and (2) the actual value of the goods accepted at the time and

compensatory damages
An award of money intended to compensate a nonbreaching party for the loss of the bargain; they place the nonbreaching party in the same position as if the contract had been fully performed by restoring the "benefit of the bargain." Damages that are generally equal to the difference between the value of the goods as warranted and the actual value of the goods accepted at the time and place of acceptance.

place of acceptance.[6] A purchaser or lessee can recover for personal injuries that are caused by a breach of warranty.

Example: Suppose a used car salesperson warrants that a used car has been driven only 20,000 miles. If true, that would make the car worth $10,000. The salesperson gives the buyer a "good deal" and sells the car for $8,000. Unfortunately, the car was worth only $4,000 because it was actually driven 100,000 miles. The buyer discovers the breach of warranty and sues the salesperson for damages. The buyer can recover $6,000 ($10,000 warranted value minus $4,000 actual value). The contract price ($8,000) is irrelevant to this computation.

Example: Suppose Frances Gordon purchases new tires for her car, and the manufacturer expressly warrants the tires against blowout for 50,000 miles. Suppose one of the tires blows out after being used only 20,000 miles, causing severe injury to Gordon. She can recover personal injury damages from the manufacturer because of the breach of warranty.

■ IMPLIED WARRANTY

In addition to express warranties made by a manufacturer or seller, the law sometimes implies warranties to the sale or lease of goods. Implied warranties are not expressly stated in the sales or lease contract but instead are implied by law. The most common forms of implied warranties are the *implied warranty of merchantability*, the *implied warranty of fitness for human consumption*, and the *implied warranty of fitness for a particular purpose*. Each one of these warranties are covered in the following discussion.

Implied Warranty of Merchantability

If the seller or lessor of a good is a merchant with respect to goods of that kind, the sales contract contains an **implied warranty of merchantability** unless it is properly disclaimed.[7] This requires the following standards to be met:

- ■ *The goods must be fit for the ordinary purposes for which they are used.*

  Example: A chair must be able to safely perform the function of a chair. If a normal-size person sits in a chair that has not been tampered with, and the chair collapses, there has been a breach of the implied warranty of merchantability. If, however, the same person is injured because he or she uses the chair as a ladder and it tips over, there is no breach of implied warranty because serving as a ladder is not the ordinary purpose of a chair.

- ■ *The goods must be adequately contained, packaged, and labeled.*

  Example: The implied warranty of merchantability applies to the milk bottle as well as to the milk inside the bottle.

- ■ *The goods must be of an even kind, quality, and quantity within each unit*—All the goods in a carton, package, or box must be consistent.

- ■ *The goods must conform to any promise or affirmation of fact made on the container or label*—The goods must be capable of being used safely in accordance with the instructions on the package or label.

implied warranty of merchantability
Unless properly disclosed, a warranty that is implied that sold or leased goods are fit for the ordinary purpose for which they are sold or leased, and other assurances.

---

[6]UCC 2-714(2), 2A-508(4).
[7]UCC 2-314(1), 2A-212(1).

- *The quality of the goods must pass without objection in the trade*—Other users of the goods should not object to their quality.
- *Fungible goods must meet a fair average or middle range of quality*—To be classified as a certain grade, grain or ore must meet the average range of quality of that grade.

fungible
Goods consisting of identical and interchangeable particles or components.

Note that the implied warranty of merchantability does not apply to sales or leases by nonmerchants or casual sales.

Example: The implied warranty of merchantability applies to the sale of a lawn mower sold by a merchant who is in the business of selling lawn mowers. It does not apply when one neighbor sells a lawn mower to another neighbor.

Case 13.2 raised the issue of implied warranty of merchantability.

CASE 13.2 IMPLIED WARRANTY OF MERCHANTABILITY

Denny v. Ford Motor Co., 662 N.E.2d (N.Y. 1995).

> *"The law implies a warranty by a manufacturer that places its product on the market that the product is reasonably fit for the ordinary purpose for which it was intended."*
>
> Judge Titone, *Court of Appeals of New York*

Facts

Nancy Denny purchased a Bronco II, a small utility vehicle manufactured by Ford Motor Company. Denny testified that she purchased the Bronco II for use on paved city and suburban streets, not for off-road use. On June 9, 1986, when Denny was driving the vehicle on a paved road, she slammed on the brakes in an effort to avoid a deer that had walked directly into her motor vehicle's path. The Bronco II rolled over, and Denny was severely injured. Denny sued Ford Motor Company to recover damages for breach of the implied warranty of merchantability.

Denny alleged that the Bronco II presented a significantly higher risk of occurrence of rollover accidents than did ordinary passenger vehicles. Denny introduced evidence at trial that showed that the Bronco II had a low stability index because of its high center of gravity, narrow tracks, and shorter wheel base, as well as the design of its suspension system. Ford countered that the Bronco II was intended as an off-road vehicle and not designed to be used as a conventional passenger automobile on paved streets. The trial court found Ford liable and awarded Denny $1.2 million in damages. Ford appealed.

Issue

Did Ford Motor Company breach the implied warranty of merchantability?

Language of the Court

Plaintiff introduced a Ford marketing manual that predicted many buyers would be attracted to the Bronco II because utility vehicles were suitable to "contemporary lifestyles" and were "considered fashionable" in some suburban areas. According to this manual, the sales presentation of the Bronco II should take into account the vehicle's "suitability for commuting and for suburban and city driving." Additionally, the vehicle's ability to switch between two-wheel and four-wheel drive would "be particularly appealing to women who may be concerned about driving in snow and ice with their children." Plaintiff testified that the perceived safety benefits of its four-wheel drive capacity was what attracted her to the Bronco II. She was not at all interested in its off-road use.

The law implies a warranty by a manufacturer that places its product on the market that the product is reasonably fit for the ordinary purpose for which it was intended. If it is, in fact, defective and not reasonably fit to be used for its intended purpose, the warranty is breached. Plaintiff's proof focused on the sale of the Bronco II for suburban driving and everyday road travel. Plaintiff also adduced proof that the Bronco II's design characteristics made it unusually susceptible to rollover accidents when used on paved roads. All of this evidence was useful in showing that routine highway and street driving was the "ordinary purpose" for which the Bronco II was sold and that it was not "fit"—or safe—for that purpose. Thus, under the evidence in this case, a rational fact finder could have concluded that the vehicle was not safe for the "ordinary purpose" of daily driving for which it was marketed and sold.

Decision

The court of appeals held that Ford had breached the implied warranty of merchantability and upheld the jury award for the plaintiff.

Law & Ethics Questions

1. What is an implied warranty of merchantability? Explain.

2. What is the public policy underlying an implied warranty?

3. **Ethics** Did Ford act ethically in defending that the Bronco II was sold only as an off-road vehicle? Was this argument persuasive?

4. What are the business implications of this decision? Do you think that utility vehicles such as the Bronco II have a higher rollover danger than normal passenger automobiles?

Web Exercises

1. **Web** Visit the website of Ford Motor Company at www.ford.com. Does Ford still make a Bronco class of vehicle?

2. **Web** Visit the website of the Court of Appeals of New York, at www.courts .state.ny.us.

3. **Web** Use www.google.com and find an article about the rollover problem of Ford Bronco vehicles.

Implied Warranty of Fitness for Human Consumption

implied warranty of fitness for human consumption
A warranty that applies to food or drink consumed on or off the premises of restaurants, grocery stores, fast-food outlets, and vending machines.

The common law implied a special warranty—the **implied warranty of fitness for human consumption**—to food products. The UCC incorporates this warranty, which applies to food and drink consumed on or off the premises, within the implied warranty of merchantability. Restaurants, grocery stores, fast-food outlets, and vending-machine operators are all subject to this warranty. States use one of the following two tests in determining whether there has been a breach of the implied warranty of fitness for human consumption:

- *Foreign substance test*—Under the **foreign substance test,** a food product is unmerchantable if a foreign object in that product causes injury to a person.

    Example: The warranty would be breached if an injury was caused by a nail in a cherry pie. If the same injury was caused by a cherry pit in the pie, the pie would not be unmerchantable.

- *Consumer expectation test*—The majority of states have adopted the modern **consumer expectation test** to determine the merchantability of food products.

    Example: Under this implied warranty, if a person is injured by a chicken bone while eating fried chicken, the injury is not actionable.

    Example: The implied warranty would be breached if a person was injured by a chicken bone while eating a chicken salad sandwich. This is because a consumer would expect that the food preparer would have removed all bones from the chicken.

foreign substance test
A test to determine merchantability based on foreign objects that are found in food.

consumer expectation test
A test to determine merchantability based on what the average consumer would expect to find in food products.

Implied Warranty of Fitness for a Particular Purpose

The UCC contains an implied **warranty of fitness for a particular purpose**. This implied warranty is breached if the goods do not meet the buyer's or lessee's expressed needs. The warranty applies to both merchant and nonmerchant sellers and lessors.

The warranty of fitness for a particular purpose is implied at the time of contracting if:

1. The seller or lessor has reason to know the particular purpose for which the buyer is purchasing the goods or the lessee is leasing the goods.
2. The seller or lessor makes a statement that the goods will serve this purpose.
3. The buyer or lessee relies on the seller's or lessor's skill and judgment and purchases or leases the goods.[8]

Example: Susan Logan wants to buy lumber to build a house, so she goes to Winter's lumberyard. Logan describes to Winter the house she intends to build. She also tells Winter that she is relying on him to select the right lumber. Winter selects the lumber, and Logan buys it and builds the house. Unfortunately, the house collapses because the lumber was not strong enough to support it. Logan can sue Winter for breach of the implied warranty of fitness for a particular purpose.

Case 13.3 raises the issue of implied warranty of fitness for a particular purpose.

implied warranty of fitness for a particular purpose
An implied warranty that information is fit for the licensee's purpose that applies if the licensor (1) knows of any particular purpose for which the computer information is required and (2) knows that the licensee is relying on the licensor's skill or judgment to select or furnish suitable information.

CASE 13.3   IMPLIED WARRANTY OF FITNESS FOR
A PARTICULAR PURPOSE

Mack Massey Motors, Inc. v. Garnica, 814 S.W.2d 167 (Tex. Ct. App. 1991).

"*A claim of warranty of fitness requires that goods serve their particular purpose.*"

Judge Fuller, *Court of Appeals of Texas*

Facts

Felicitas Garnica sought to purchase a vehicle capable of towing a 23-foot Airstream trailer she had on order. She went to Mack Massey Motors, Inc. (Massey

[8]UCC 2-315, 2A-213.

Motors), to inquire about purchasing a Jeep Cherokee that was manufactured by Jeep Eagle. After Garnica explained her requirements to the sales manager, he called the Airstream dealer concerning the specifications of the trailer Garnica was purchasing. The sales manager advised Garnica that the Jeep Cherokee could do the job of pulling the trailer. After purchasing the vehicle, Garnica claimed it did not have sufficient power to pull the trailer. She brought the Jeep Cherokee back to Massey Motors several times for repairs for a slipping transmission. Eventually, she was told to go to another dealer. The drive shaft on the Jeep Cherokee twisted apart at 7,229 miles. Garnica sued Massey Motors and Jeep Eagle for damages, alleging breach of the implied warranty of fitness for a particular purpose. The jury returned a verdict in favor of Garnica. Massey Motors and Jeep Eagle appealed.

Issue

Did the defendants make and breach an implied warranty of fitness for a particular purpose?

Language of the Court

In the instant case, the service provided by Massey Motors' sales staff included undertaking the responsibility of checking with the Airstream dealer and thereafter representing that the Jeep Cherokee, with an automatic transmission, was suitable for pulling the Airstream. Massey Motors' sales manager testified he knew the intended purpose for Mrs. Garnica's use of the proposed vehicle and that he undertook to investigate the specifications of the Airstream. After having undertaken the inquiry, he recommended the Jeep Cherokee as being suitable for the purposes Mrs. Garnica was seeking—that of towing the Airstream trailer she had on order.

A claim of warranty of fitness requires that goods serve their particular purpose. The evidence supported the jury determination that the Jeep Cherokee simply was exceeding its towing capacity and that Massey Motors had misrepresented the fact that this was the proper vehicle suitable for towing the Airstream trailer. In light of Massey Motors' superior knowledge and expertise concerning Mrs. Garnica's inquiry and reliance, the evidence was sufficient to support the jury's finding.

Decision

The appellate court held that Massey Motors had made and breached an implied warranty of fitness for a particular purpose but Jeep Eagle had not.

Law & Ethics Questions

1. Should the law recognize the implied warranty of fitness for a particular purpose? Or should buyers be held to know their own requirements?

2. **Ethics** Did Massey Motors act unethically in this case?

3. Do you think damages should have been awarded in this case?

Web Exercises

1. **Web** Visit the website of Chrysler LLC at www.chryslerllc.com. Does the company still sell Jeep vehicles?

2. **Web** Visit the website of Airstream, Inc. at www.airstream.com. Look for an Airstream that is 23 feet long, the size of the Airstream in this case.

3. **Web** Visit the website of the Court of Appeals of Texas, Eighth Circuit, at www.8thcoa.courts.state.tx.us.

4. **Web** Use www.google.com and find an article that discusses the safety of Jeep vehicles.

Concept Summary

Express and Implied Warranties of Quality

Type of Warranty	How Created	Description
Express warranty	Made by the seller or lessor.	Affirms that the goods meet certain standards of quality, description, performance, or condition [UCC 2-313(1), 2A-210(1)].
Implied warranty of merchantability	Implied by law if the seller or lessor is a merchant.	Implies that the goods: 1. Are fit for the ordinary purposes for which they are used. 2. Are adequately contained, packaged, and labeled. 3. Are of an even kind, quality, and quantity within each unit. 4. Conform to any promise or affirmation of fact made on the container or label. 5. Pass without objection in the trade. 6. Meet a fair, average, or middle range of quality for fungible goods [UCC 2-314(1), 2A-212(1)].
Implied warranty of fitness for a particular purpose	Implied by law.	Implies that the goods are fit for the purpose for which the buyer or lessee acquires the goods if: 1. The seller or lessor has reason to know the particular purpose for which the goods will be used. 2. The seller or lessor makes a statement that the goods will serve that purpose, and 3. The buyer or lessee relies on the statement and buys or leases the goods [UCC 2-315, UCC 2A-213].

PARALEGAL PERSPECTIVE

Andrea A. Zwegat is a senior paralegal specializing in intellectual property at the Lubrizol Corporation in Wickliffe, Ohio. She manages the worldwide trademark portfolio for Lubrizol and its subsidiaries. She has a bachelor of arts degree from Hiram College and a Certificate in Legal Studies from Ursuline College. She has also published articles in the Ohio State Bar Association's Bar Bulletin, National Paralegal Reporter, *and Cleveland Association of Paralegals'* NewsCAPsule.

I work for a large international chemical corporation. I handle various types of agreements concerning intellectual property. To resolve trademark disputes, I assist in the preparation of trademark settlement and coexistence agreements. These agreements are important to keep the integrity of our trademarks and eliminate confusion in the marketplace.

Trademark rights are also granted in trademark licenses, distributorship, and sales representation agreements. I assist with the process to ensure trademark exhibits for these types of agreements are accurate and properly marked with the ™ or ®. I also assist in due diligence for merger and acquisitions, verifying the trademark information is accurate prior to the deal closing.

Previously I drafted confidentiality agreements ensuring Lubrizol's trade secrets were protected. This involved getting an information sheet from the business groups, analyzing the type of information to be protected, understanding the direction of the flow of confidential information, and determining the proper agreement template to use.

I make a significant contribution by gathering necessary information, making sure trademark information is accurate, saving time for the attorneys, and providing timely and cost-effective services to the corporation.

■ WARRANTY DISCLAIMER

warranty disclaimer
Statements that negate express and implied warranties.

Warranties can be *disclaimed* or limited. If an *express warranty* is made, it can be limited only if the **warranty disclaimer** and the warranty can be reasonably construed with each other.

All implied warranties of quality may be disclaimed by expressions such as *as is*, *with all faults*, or other language that makes it clear to the buyer there are no implied warranties. This type of disclaimer is often included in sales contracts for used products. If the preceding language is not used, disclaimers of the *implied warranty of merchantability* must specifically mention the term *merchantability*. These disclaimers may be oral or written.

The *implied warranty of fitness for a particular purpose* may be disclaimed in general language, without specific use of the term *fitness*.

Example: Language such as "There are no warranties that extend beyond the description on the fact hereof" is sufficient to disclaim the fitness warranty. The disclaimer must be in writing.

MARKETPLACE

Job Announcement: Litigation Paralegal

National law firm seeks a litigation paralegal with 4+ years of experience.

Responsibilities include initial client interviews, preparing client retainer contracts, case investigation, preparation of factual summaries/analysis for use by attorneys, abstracting medical records and depositions, trial preparation, and maintenance and organization of case files. Heavy client contact, excellent communication skills a must. Ideal candidate must be highly organized, detail oriented, able to work independently, and computer literate with Microsoft Office products. Paralegal certificate required. We offer a competitive salary & excellent benefits! ONLY qualified applicants, please.

Send resume w/salary requirements to:

Conspicuous Display of Disclaimer

Written disclaimers must be conspicuously displayed to be valid. The courts construe **conspicuous** as noticeable to a reasonable person.[9]

Example: A heading printed in capital letters or typeface that is larger or in a different style than the rest of the body of a sales or lease contract is considered conspicuous. Different-color type is also considered conspicuous.

conspicuous
A requirement that warranty disclaimers be noticeable to the average person.

INTERNET & TECHNOLOGY

Warranty Disclaimers in Software Licenses

Most software companies license their software to users. A software license is a complex contract that contains the terms of the license. Most software licenses contain a warranty disclaimer and limitation on liability clauses that limit the licensor's liability if the software malfunctions. Disclaimer of warranty and limitation on liability clauses that are included in a typical software license appear below.

> #### SOFTWARE.COM, INC. LIMITATION AND WAIVERS OF WARRANTIES, REMEDIES, AND CONSEQUENTIAL DAMAGES
>
> **Limited Warranty.** Software.com, Inc. warrants that (a) the software will perform substantially in accordance with the accompanying written materials for a period of 90 days from the date of receipt, and (b) any hardware accompanying the software will be free from defects in materials and workmanship under normal use and service for a period of one year from the date of the receipt. Any implied warranties on the software and hardware are limited to 90 days and one (1) year, respectively. Some states do not allow limitations on duration of an implied warranty, so the above limitation may not apply to you.
>
> **Customer Remedies.** Software.com, Inc.'s entire liability and your exclusive remedy shall be, at Software.com, Inc.'s option, either (a) return of the price paid or (b) repair or replacement of the software or hardware that does not meet Software.com, Inc.'s Limited Warranty and that is returned to Software.com, Inc. with a copy of your receipt. This Limited Warranty is void if failure of the software or hardware has resulted from accident, abuse, or misapplication. Any replacement software will be warranted for the remainder of the original warranty or 30 days, whichever is longer. These remedies are not available outside the United States of America.
>
> **No Other Warranties.** Software.com, Inc. disclaims all other warranties, either express or implied, including but not limited to implied warranties of merchantability and fitness for a particular purpose, with respect to the software, the accompanying written materials, and any accompanying hardware. This Limited Warranty gives you specific legal rights. You may have others, which vary from state to state.

(continued)

---

[9]UCC 2-316, 2A-214.

> **NO LIABILITY FOR CONSEQUENTIAL DAMAGES.** In no event shall Software.com, Inc. or its suppliers be liable for any damages whatsoever (including, without limitation, damages for loss of business profits, business interruption, loss of business information, or other pecuniary loss) arising out of the use of or inability to use this Software.com, Inc. product, even if Software.com, Inc. has been advised of the possibility of such damages. Because some states do not allow the exclusion or limitation of liability for consequential or incidental damages, the above limitation may not apply to you.

LANDMARK LAW

MAGNUSON-MOSS WARRANTY ACT PROTECTS CONSUMERS

In 1975, Congress enacted the **Magnuson-Moss Warranty Act**, which covers written warranties relating to *consumer* products.[10] This federal act is administered by the Federal Trade Commission (FTC). Commercial and industrial transactions are not governed by the act.

The act does not require a seller or lessor to make express written warranties. However, persons who do make such warranties are subject to the provisions of the act. If the warrantor chooses to make an express warranty, the Magnuson-Moss Warranty Act requires that the warranty be labeled as either "full" or "limited."

To qualify as a **full warranty**, the warrantor must guarantee free repair or replacement of the defective product. The warrantor must indicate whether there is a time limit on the full warranty (e.g., "full 36-month warranty"). In a **limited warranty**, the warrantor limits the scope of a full warranty in some way (e.g., a return of the purchase price or replacement or such). The fact that the warranty is full or limited must be conspicuously displayed. The disclosures must be in "understandable language."

A consumer may bring a civil action against a defendant for violating the provisions of the act. A successful plaintiff can recover damages, attorneys' fees, and other costs incurred in bringing the action. The act authorizes warrantors to establish an informal dispute resolution procedure. The procedure must be conspicuously described in the written warranty. Aggrieved consumers must assert their claims through this procedure before they can take legal action.

The act does not create any implied warranties. It does, however, modify the state law of implied warranties in one crucial respect: Sellers or lessors who make express written warranties relating to consumer products are forbidden from disclaiming or modifying the implied warranties of merchantability and fitness for a particular purpose. A seller or lessor may set a time limit on implied warranties, but this time limit must correspond to the duration of any express warranty.

Law & Ethics Questions

1. What is the underlying purpose of the Magnuson-Moss Warranty Act? Explain.
2. **Ethics** Do you think that the Magnuson-Moss Warranty Act will cause sellers of products to consumers to act more ethically? Why or why not?

Web Exercises

1. **Web** Use www.google.com and find an article that discusses the protections to consumers afforded by the Magnuson-Moss Warranty Act.

Magnuson-Moss Warranty Act
A United States federal law (15 U.S.C. § 2301 *et seq.*). Enacted in 1975, it is the federal statute that governs warranties on consumer products.

limited warranty
A product guarantee that is limited or restricted in some way.

■ SPECIAL WARRANTIES OF TITLE AND POSSESSION

The UCC imposes special warranties on sellers and lessors of goods.

These include a *warranty of good title*, a *warranty of no security interests*, a *warranty of no infringements*, and a *warranty of no interference*. These warranties are discussed in the following paragraphs.

---

[10]15 U.S.C Sections 2301-2312.

Warranty of Good Title

Unless properly disclaimed, sellers of goods warrant they have valid title to the goods they are selling and the transfer of title is rightful [UCC 2-312(1)(a)]. This is called the **warranty of good title**. Persons who transfer goods without proper title breach this warranty.

Example: Ingersoll-Rand owns a heavy-duty crane. A thief steals the crane and sells it to Turner Corp. Turner does not know the crane is stolen. If Ingersoll-Rand discovers Turner has the equipment, it can reclaim it. Turner, in turn, can recover against the thief for breach of the warranty of title. This is because the thief impliedly warranted that he or she had good title to the equipment and the transfer of title to Turner was rightful.

Warranty of No Security Interests

Under the UCC, sellers of goods automatically warrant that the goods they sell are delivered free from any third-party security interests, liens, or encumbrances that are unknown to the buyer [UCC 2-312(1)(b)]. This is called the **warranty of no security interests.**

Example: Albert Connors purchases a refrigerator on credit from Trader Horn's, an appliance store. The store takes back a security interest in the refrigerator. Before completely paying off the refrigerator, Connors sells it to a friend for cash. The friend has no knowledge of the store's security interest. After Connors misses several payments, the appliance store repossesses the refrigerator. Connors's friend may recover against him based on his breach of warranty of no security interests in the goods [UCC 2-312(1)(b)].

The warranties of good title and no security interests may be excluded or modified by specific language [UCC 2-312(2)]. For example, specific language such as "seller hereby transfers only those rights, title, and interest as he or she has in the goods" is sufficient to disclaim these warranties. General language such as "as is" or "with all faults" is not specific enough to be a disclaimer to the warranties of good title and no security interests. The special nature of certain sales (e.g., sheriffs' sales) tells the buyer that the seller is not giving title warranties with the sale of the goods.

Warranty of No Infringements

Unless otherwise agreed, a seller or lessor who is a merchant regularly dealing in goods of the kind sold or leased automatically warrants that the goods are delivered free of any third-party patent, trademark, or copyright claim [UCC 2-312(3), 2A-211(2)]. This is called the **warranty against infringement.**

Example: Adams & Co., a manufacturer of machines that make shoes, sells a machine to Smith & Franklin, a shoe manufacturer. Subsequently, Alice Jones claims she has a patent on the machine. Jones proves her patent claim in court. Jones notifies Smith & Franklin that the machine can no longer be used without permission (and, perhaps, the payment of a fee). Smith & Franklin may rescind the contract with Adams & Co. based on the breach of the no infringement warranty.

Warranty of No Interference

When goods are leased, the lessor warrants that no person holds a claim or an interest in the goods that arose from an act or omission of the lessor that will interfere with

warranty of good title
Sellers warrant that they have valid title to the goods they are selling and that the transfer of title is rightful.

warranty of no security interests
Sellers of goods warrant that the goods they sell are delivered free from any third-party security interests, liens, or encumbrances that are unknown to the buyer.

warranty of no infringement
An implied promise that there are no interferences or interventions that will affect the contract.

warranty against infringements
A seller or lessor who is a merchant who regularly deals in goods of the kind sold or leased automatically warrants that the goods are delivered free of any third-party patent, trademark, or copyright claim.

warranty of no interference
An implied promise that there are no conflicts that will encroach upon a contract.

the lessee's enjoyment of his or her leasehold interest [UCC 2A-211(1)]. This is referred to as the **warranty of no interference,** or the **warranty of quiet possession.**

Example: Suppose Occidental Petroleum leases a piece of heavy equipment from Aztec Drilling Co. Aztec later gives a security interest in the equipment to City Bank as collateral for a loan. If Aztec defaults on the loan and City Bank repossesses the equipment, Occidental can recover damages from Aztec for breach of the warranty of no interference.

THE ETHICAL PARALEGAL

Advertising and Solicitation

An attorney being allowed to advertise his or her legal services to the public is a relatively recent event. Before the case of *Bates v. Arizona*, attorneys could not advertise on television or on billboards.[11] Although there are still cases dealing with misleading or otherwise unethical advertising, for the most part, advertising is now fully permitted by attorneys.

However, *solicitation* by attorneys is another matter. Where advertising is directed to the public at large, solicitation is directed to a specific invidual by letter, telephone, or in person. ABA Rule 7.3 prohibits attorneys and their employees from soliciting clients in most circumstances.[12] The ethical paralegal should read the case of *Idaho State Bar v. Jenkins*, 816 P.2d 335 (1991) to understand more fully the intricacies of the prohibition against solicitation.

INTERNET EXERCISES AND CASE QUESTIONS

Working the Web Internet Exercises

1. Review an example of Colorado's UCC provisions at www.law.cornell.edu/uniform/ucc.html and study the warranty provisions and how they work.
2. UCC Article 2 provides for disclaimers of warranties. Find the provisions of the Magnuson-Moss Warranty Act and review the various disclaimers. Do you think disclaimers are a good idea? See "LII Law About . . . Sales Law" at www.law.cornell.edu/topics.html for a summary of the warranties under UCC Article 2.

CHAPTER 13 SUMMARY

EXPRESS WARRANTY, p. 368

Express Warranty

An express warranty is an affirmation by a seller or lessor that the goods he or she is selling or leasing meet certain standards of quality, description, performance, or condition.

---

[11]433 U.S. 350 (1977).

[12]Copies of the ABA Model Rules of Professional Conduct are available from Service Center, American Bar Association, 321 North Clark Street, Chicago, IL 60610, 1-800-285-2221. The Model Rules can also be viewed online at http://www.abanet.org/cpr/mrpc/mrpc_toc.html.

IMPLIED WARRANTY, p. 372

Implied Warranty of Merchantability

Implied warranty of merchantability is implied by law in sales and lease transactions. It requires that the goods:

1. Be fit for the ordinary purposes for which they are used.
2. Be adequately contained, packaged, and labeled.
3. Be of an even kind, quality, and quantity within each unit.
4. Conform to any promise or affirmation of fact made on the container or label.
5. Pass without objection in the trade.
6. Meet a fair or middle range of quality if the goods are fungible.

Implied Warranty of Fitness for Human Consumption

Implied warranty of fitness for human consumption is a warranty implied by law that food products are fit for human consumption. States apply one of the two following tests:

1. *Foreign substance test.* A food is unmerchantable if a foreign object in the food caused the plaintiff's injury.
2. *Consumer expectation test.* A food is unmerchantable if an object in the food that a consumer would not expect to be there caused the plaintiff's injury. The UCC incorporates this warranty within the implied warranty of merchantability.

Implied Warranty of Fitness for a Particular Purpose

Implied warranty of fitness for a particular purpose is a warranty by a seller or lessor that the goods will meet the buyer's or lessee's expressed needs.

WARRANTY DISCLAIMER, p. 378

1. **Express warranties.** Express warranties can be limited if the warranty and disclaimer can be reasonably construed with each other.
2. **Implied warranties:**
   a. *Disclaimer.* An implied warranty can be disclaimed by expressions like *as is, with all faults,* or such language. If such language is not used, implied warranties are disclaimed as follows:
      i. *Implied warranty of merchantability.* This is an oral or written disclaimer that mentions the word *merchantability.*
      ii. *Implied warranty of fitness for a particular purpose.* This is a written disclaimer of general language.
3. **Conspicuousness.** Written disclaimers must be conspicuously displayed to be enforceable.

MAGNUSON-MOSS WARRANTY ACT, p. 380

This act is a federal statute that covers written warranties that apply to *consumer* products.

1. **Full and limited warranties.** If a good costs more than $10 and the warrantor makes an express warranty, the warranty must be labeled *full* or *limited.*
   a. *Full warranty.* A full warranty guarantees free repair or replacement of a defective product. A time limit may be placed on the warranty.
   b. *Limited warranty.* A limited warranty limits the scope of a full warranty in some way (e.g., return of the purchase price).

2. *Limitation on disclaiming implied warranties.* If a seller or lessor makes an express warranty, he or she cannot disclaim or modify the implied warranties of merchantability and fitness for a particular purpose. A time limit may be placed on implied warranties but must correspond to the duration of the express warranty.

SPECIAL WARRANTIES OF TITLE AND POSSESSION, p. 380

1. *Warranty of Good Title* A warranty in which the seller warrants that he or she has valid title to the goods being sold and the transfer of title is rightful.
2. *Warranty of No Security Interests* A warranty in which sellers of goods warrant that the goods they sell are delivered free from any third-party security interests, liens, or encumbrances unknown to the buyer.
3. *Warranty of No Infringements* An automatic warranty of a seller or lessor who is a merchant who regularly deals in goods of the kind sold or leased warrants that the goods are delivered free of any third-party patent, trademark, or copyright claim.
4. *Warranty of No Interference* A warranty in which the lessor warrants that no person holds a claim or interest in the goods that arose from an act or omission of the lessor that will interfere with the lessee's enjoyment of his or her leasehold interest.

TERMS AND CONCEPTS

Basis of the bargain   369
Compensatory damages   371
Conspicuous   379
Consumer expectation test   375
Express warranty   368
Foreign substance test   375
Fungible   373
Implied warranty of fitness for human consumption   374
Implied warranty of fitness for a particular purpose   375
Implied warranty of merchantability   372
Limited warranty   380
Magnuson-Moss Warranty Act   380
Statements of opinion (puffing)   369
Warranty   367
Warranty against infringement   381
Warranty disclaimer   378
Warranty of good title   381
Warranty of no security interests   381
Warranty of no infringements (warranty of quiet possession)   381
Warranty of no interference   382

CASE SCENARIO REVISITED

Remember the situation at the beginning of the chapter regarding Jack Crothers and his purchase of a Dodge from Norm's Auto Sales? Now that you understand more about sales and lease warranties, who do you think would win if a lawsuit was brought? For help with your answer, see *Crothers v. Norm's Auto Sales*, 384 N.W.2d 562 (Minn. Ct. App. 1986).

CRITICAL LEGAL THINKING CASES

Critical Legal Thinking Case 13.1 *Warranty of Title* When James Redmond wanted to purchase an automobile, he spoke to a salesman at Bill Branch Chevrolet, Inc. (Bill Branch). The salesman offered to sell Redmond a blue Chevrolet Caprice for $6,200. The car was to be delivered to Redmond's residence. Redmond gave the salesman $1,000 cash and received a receipt in return. The next day, the salesman delivered the car to Redmond, and Redmond paid the remaining amount due. The salesman gave Redmond a printed sales contract that reflected the payments made, with no balance due. One month later, Redmond called Bill Branch and asked for the title papers to the car. Redmond was told the car had been reported stolen prior to the sale and he could not receive title until he contacted Bill Branch's insurance company. Redmond sued Bill Branch Chevrolet, Inc. Is Bill Branch liable? *Bill Branch Chevrolet v. Redmond*, 378 So. 2d 319 (Fla. Dist. Ct. App. 1980).

Critical Legal Thinking Case 13.2 *Express Warranty* Gloria Crandell purchased a used Coronado clothes dryer from Larkin and Jones Appliance Company (Larkin and Jones). The dryer, displayed on the sales floor, had a tag affixed to it that described the machine as a "quality reconditioned unit" that was "tag tested" and "guaranteed." In addition to these written statements, a salesman assured Crandell that the dryer carried a 90-day guarantee for "workmanship, parts, and labor." Crandell bought the dryer because of the guarantee and the low price. Two weeks after the machine was delivered, Crandell asked her son to put a blanket in the dryer to dry. Twenty minutes later, she noticed smoke pouring into her bedroom. By the time Crandell reached the laundry room, the machine was engulfed in flames. A defect in the clothes dryer had caused the fire. Crandell sued Larkin and Jones for breach of an express warranty. Is there an express warranty? *Crandell v. Larkin & Jones Appliance Co.*, 334 N.W.2d 31 (S.D. 1983).

Critical Legal Thinking Case 13.3 *Implied Warranty of Merchantability* Geraldine Maybank took a trip to New York City to visit her son and her two-year-old grandson. She borrowed her daughter's camera for the trip. Two days before leaving for New York, Maybank purchased a package of G. T. E. Sylvania Blue Dot flash cubes at a Kmart store, owned by the S. S. Kresge Company. On the carton of the package were words to the effect that each bulb was safety coated. Upon arriving in New York, Maybank decided to take a picture of her grandson. She opened the carton of flash cubes and put one on the camera. When Maybank pushed down the lever to take a picture, the flash cube exploded. The explosion knocked her glasses off and caused cuts to her left eye. Maybank was hospitalized for eight days. Maybank sued S. S. Kresge Company. Who wins? *Maybank v. S.S. Kresge Co.*, 266 S.E.2d 409 (N.C. Ct. App. 1980).

Critical Legal Thinking Case 13.4 *Implied Warranty of Fitness for Human Consumption* Tina Keperwes went to a Publix Supermarket (Publix) in Florida and bought a can of Doxsee brand clam chowder. Keperwes opened the can of soup and prepared it at home. While eating the chowder, she bit down on a clam shell and injured one of her molars. Keperwes filed suit against Publix and Doxsee for breach of an implied warranty. In the lawsuit, Keperwes alleged that the clam chowder "was not fit for use as food, but was defective, unwholesome, and unfit for human consumption" and "was in such condition as to be dangerous to life and health." At the trial, Doxsee's general manager testified as to the state-of-the-art methods Doxsee uses in preparing its chowder. Are Publix and Doxsee liable for the injury to Keperwes's tooth? *Keperwes v. Publix Supermarkets, Inc.*, 534 So. 2d 872 (Fla. Dist. Ct. App. 1988).

Critical Legal Thinking Case 13.5 *Disclaimer of Warranty*   Automatic Sprinkler Corporation of America (Automatic Sprinkler) wished to purchase a dry chemical fire protection system from Ansul Company (Ansul). An Ansul representative gave Automatic Sprinkler a proposal on the company's behalf. The proposal was a document five pages long. Each page included printed information describing the fire extinguisher system. Only the fifth and last page had printing on the back. The information on the back of page 5 contained a limited five-year warranty that covered only the replacement of defective parts. The limited warranty concluded with this statement: "This warranty is in lieu of all other warranties express or implied." Automatic Sprinkler purchased the system and installed it in a client's building. Several years later, a fire broke out in the building, and the Ansul fire extinguisher system failed to discharge. Automatic Sprinkler sued Ansul for a breach of an implied warranty of merchantability. Ansul claimed that all warranties except the limited five-year warranty were disclaimed. Is Ansul's disclaimer enforceable? *Insurance Co. of N. Am. v. Automatic Sprinkler*, 423 N.E.2d 151 (Ohio 1981).

Critical Legal Thinking Case 13.6 *Disclaimer of Warranty*   Cole Energy Development Company (Cole Energy) wanted to lease a gas compressor for use in its business of pumping and selling natural gas and began negotiating with the Ingersoll-Rand Company (Ingersoll-Rand). On December 5, 1983, the two parties entered into a lease agreement for a KOA gas compressor. The lease agreement contained a section labeled "WARRANTIES." Part of the section read:

There are no implied warranties of merchantability or fitness for a particular purpose contained herein.

The gas compressor that was installed failed to function properly. As a result, Cole Energy lost business. Cole Energy sued Ingersoll-Rand for the breach of an implied warranty of merchantability. Is Ingersoll-Rand liable? *Cole Energy Dev. Co. v. Ingersoll-Rand Co.*, 678 F. Supp. 208 (C.D. Ill. 1988).

ETHICS CASES

Ethics Case 13.1   Brian Keith, an actor, attended a boat show in Long Beach, California. At the boat show, Keith obtained sales literature on a sailboat called the "Island Trader 41" from a sales representative of James Buchanan, a seller of sailboats. One sales brochure described the vessel as "a picture of sure-footed seaworthiness." Another brochure called the sailboat "a carefully well-equipped and very seaworthy live-aboard vessel." One month later, Keith purchased an Island Trader 41 sailboat from Buchanan for a total purchase price of $75,610. After delivery of the sailboat, a dispute arose in regard to the seaworthiness of the vessel. Keith sued Buchanan for breach of warranty. Buchanan defended, arguing that no warranty had been made. Is it ethical for Buchanan to try to avoid being held accountable for statements of quality about the product that were made in the sales brochures given Keith? Should sales puffing be considered to create an express warranty? Why or why not? Who wins this case? *Keith v. Buchanan*, 220 Cal. Rptr. 392 (Ct. App. 1985).

Ethics Case 13.2   Peter Troy, president and owner of Troy's Custom Smoking Co., Inc. (Troy's), contacted Peter Bader, president of Swan Island Sheet Metal Works, Inc. (Swan Island), and asked Bader if Swan Island could manufacture two stainless-steel gas-burner crab cookers for Troy's. Troy explained to Bader the planned use of the cooker and some of the special needs a crab cooker must satisfy. That is, the crab is cooked by dropping it into boiling water, allowing the water to recover to a rolling boil, and boiling the crab for 10 minutes. If the recovery time exceeds 10 minutes, or if the cooker cannot sustain a rolling boil, the crab is immersed too long in hot water and the finished product is unpalatable. Troy and Bader were equally unknowledgeable about gas-burner cookers, but Bader assured Troy that he would hire an expert to assist in manufacturing a crab cooker to meet Troy's needs.

Bader sent Troy a brochure illustrating the type of burner the expert had selected to meet Troy's needs. Troy ordered the cooker, which was delivered to Troy's Beaverton, Oregon, store. Within a week or two after delivery, Troy complained to Swan Island concerning the cooker's performance. The cooker cooked too slowly, and the pilot light and burner were difficult to light and keep lit. Swan Island attempted but could not correct the defects. For four months, Troy's cooked crab in the Swan Island cooker. Because of the poor performance of the cooker, Troy's ruined a substantial amount of crab and had to obtain cooked crab from another outlet to serve its customers. Troy's notified Swan Island to pick up the crab cooker. Swan Island sued Troy's to recover the purchase price of the cooker. Troy's filed a counterclaim against Swan Island to rescind the contract and recover damages. Did Swan Island breach an implied warranty of fitness for a particular purpose? Did Swan Island act ethically in denying liability in this case? *Swan Island Sheet Metal Works, Inc. v. Troy's Custom Smoking Co.*, 619 P.2d 1326 (Or. Ct. App. 1980).

BRIEFING THE CASE WRITING ASSIGNMENT

Read Case A.13 in Appendix A (*Cate v. Dover Corporation*). This case is excerpted from a court of appeals opinion. Review and brief the case. After briefing the case, you should be able to answer the following questions:

1. What did the warranty section of the contract provide?
2. What type of warranty was involved in this case?
3. What is the issue in the case?
4. In whose favor did the court rule?

PRACTICE TIP

It is especially important for a paralegal to have a general understanding of the warranty provisions of the UCC when working with a contract subject to the UCC. It is not sufficient to simply omit any unwanted warranties from the written contract. The UCC provides for implied warranties, so simply not mentioning warranties does not eliminate them. The code is specific in its requirements for disclaiming warranties. So the paralegal must be aware that there are times that a warranty disclaimer is a necessary part of the contract.

Contract Relationships and Special Forms

PART THREE

Chapter 14   Relationship of Tort Law to Contract Law

Chapter 15   Special Forms of Contracts

A manufacturer is strictly liable in tort when an article he places on the market, knowing that it is to be used without inspection for defects, proves to have a defect that causes injury to a human being.

—*Justice Traynor*

Greenman v. Yuba Power Product, Inc., 377 P.2d 897 (Cal. 1963).

Relationship of Tort Law to Contract Law

CHAPTER 14

CASE SCENARIO

The law firm where you work as a paralegal is representing Virginia Burke. Burke purchased a bottle of "Le Domaine" champagne manufactured by Almaden Vineyards, Inc. At home, she removed the wine seal from the top of the bottle but did not remove the plastic cork. She set the bottle on the counter, intending to serve it in a few minutes. Shortly thereafter, the plastic cork spontaneously ejected from the bottle, ricocheted off the wall, and struck Burke in the left lens of her eyeglasses, shattering the lens and driving pieces of glass into her eye. The champagne bottle did not contain any warning of this danger. Evidence showed that Almaden had previously been notified of the spontaneous ejection of the cork from its champagne bottles.

◼ CHAPTER INTRODUCTION

If a product defect causes injury to purchasers, lessees, users, or bystanders, the injured party may recover damages under certain contract law theories. The injured party may also be able to recover for his or her injuries under certain tort law doctrines. These tort doctrines include negligence, misrepresentation, and the modern theory of strict liability.

The liability of manufacturers, sellers, lessors, and others for injuries caused by defective products is commonly referred to as **products liability**. The various tort principles that permit injured parties to a contract to recover damages caused by defective products are discussed in this chapter.

products liability
The liability of manufacturers, sellers, and others for the injuries caused by defective products.

CHAPTER OBJECTIVES

After studying this chapter, you should be able to:

1. Understand the relationship of tort law to contract law.

2. Define the doctrine of *strict liability*.

3. Identify and describe defects in manufacture and design.

4. Identify and describe defects of failure to warn and failure to provide adequate packaging.

5. Describe the damages recoverable in a product liability lawsuit.

PARALEGAL PERSPECTIVE

Jennifer Wallace is a certified paralegal and a certified Florida legal assistant. She earned an AS degree in legal studies from Hillsborough Community College and is pursuing her BS degree in legal studies from Florida Gulf Coast University. She works at the law firm of Rory B. Weiner, P.A., in Brandon, Florida, in the areas of commercial litigation, wills and trusts, small business law, and real estate.

Here's a reality check: Without written contracts, most paralegals wouldn't have a job. Think about it—contracts are everywhere: real estate, insurance, settlements, business, and don't forget the retainer agreement!

Paralegals are invaluable when assisting in the writing and reviewing of contracts. They offer a second set of "ears" or "eyes" in listening and interpreting what clients want in their contracts and how they want it expressed.

Paralegals should understand their state's legal requirements and any statutory requirements. Only attorneys may interpret the law, but paralegals should understand these basic requirements and make sure to spot them when reviewing the contract.

Some contracts contain the necessary elements to be enforceable and others are poorly written and vulnerable to attack. Paralegals must educate themselves about the elements of a clear and enforceable contract and use that knowledge as a resource in assisting the attorney. In this case, knowledge *is* power.

■ PRODUCT LIABILITY

The law provides that persons injured by products, and heirs of persons killed by products, may bring tort actions to recover for damages. The plaintiff may rely on several traditional tort theories, including negligence and material misrepresentation of the defendant. In addition, in certain circumstances a plaintiff can assert the relatively modern tort doctrine of strict liability. If a violation of strict liability has been found, the plaintiff may recover compensatory damages but also may be able to recover punitive damages if the defendant's conduct has been reckless or intentional.

■ NEGLIGENCE AND FAULT

Depending on the circumstances of the case, persons who are injured by defective products may be able to recover damages under the tort theories of *negligence* and *misrepresentation*. Both theories require the defendant to be *at fault* for causing the plaintiff's injuries. These theories are discussed in the paragraphs that follow.

Negligence

negligence
A tort related to defective products where the defendant has breached a duty of due care and caused harm to the plaintiff. Failure of a corporate director or officer to exercise the duty of care while conducting the corporation's business.

A person injured by a defective product may bring an action for **negligence** against the negligent party. To be successful, the plaintiff must prove that the defendant breached a duty of due care to the plaintiff and thereby caused the plaintiff's injuries. Failure to exercise due care includes failing to assemble the product carefully, negligent product design, negligent inspection or testing of the product, negligent packaging, failure to warn of the dangerous propensities of the product, and such. Note that in a negligence lawsuit, only a party who was actually negligent is liable to the plaintiff.

The plaintiff and the defendant do not have to be in privity of contract.[1] For example, in the landmark case *MacPherson v. Buick Motor Co.*,[2] the court held that an injured consumer could recover damages from the manufacturer of a product even though the consumer was not in a contract with the manufacturer from which he had purchased the product. The plaintiff generally bears the difficult burden of proving that the defendant was negligent.

Example: Assume the purchaser of a motorcycle is injured in an accident. The accident occurred because a screw was missing from the motorcycle. How does the buyer prove who was negligent? Was it the manufacturer, which left the screw out during the assembly of the motorcycle? Was it the retailer, who negligently failed to discover the missing screw while preparing the motorcycle for sale? Was it the mechanic, who failed to replace the screw after repairing the motorcycle? Negligence remains a viable, yet difficult, theory on which to base a product liability action.

In Case 14.1, the court held a defendant manufacturer liable for negligence in a product liability lawsuit.

CASE 14.1   FAILURE TO WARN

Benedi v. McNeil-P.P.C., Inc., 66 F.3d 1378 (4th Cir. 1995).

Facts

Antonio Benedi consumed three to four glasses of wine a night during the week and sometimes more on the weekend. On February 5, 1993, Benedi began taking Extra-Strength Tylenol in normal doses for flu-like aches. On February 10, 1993, Benedi was admitted to the hospital in a coma and near death due to liver and kidney failure. On the night of February 12, 1993, Benedi underwent an emergency liver transplant. Because of the transplant, Benedi would have to undergo kidney dialysis in the future. Blood tests performed shortly after Benedi's admission to the hospital revealed that he suffered from acetaminophen (Tylenol) toxicity, which is caused by the combination of Tylenol and too much alcohol. The bottle from which Benedi took the Tylenol did not contain a warning of the dangers of the combination of Tylenol and excessive alcohol consumption. Benedi sued McNeil-P.P.C., Incorporated (McNeil), the manufacturer of Tylenol, for negligent failure to warn. The jury found McNeil negligent and awarded Benedi $7,850,000 in compensatory damages. McNeil appealed.

Issue

Is McNeil liable for negligent failure to warn?

Language of the Court

At trial, Benedi called two liver disease specialists who both testified that a warning of the possible danger to heavy drinkers from combining alcohol and acetaminophen should have

[1] *Restatement (Second) of Torts*, Section 395.
[2] *MacPherson v. Buick Motor Co.*, 111 N.E. 1050 (N.Y. 1916).

been placed on the Tylenol label since the mid-1980s. These experts described exactly how the alcohol-acetaminophen mixture can become a toxin in the liver. They cited numerous treatises and articles published in medical journals prior to 1993 that described the increased risk of liver injury when acetaminophen is combined with alcohol. One of plaintiff's experts referred to sixty reports that McNeil had received by the end of 1992 documenting cases of liver injury associated with combining therapeutic doses of Tylenol with alcohol. Because Benedi's experts presented sufficient evidence on the issue of causation, the district judge properly submitted that issue to the jury. It was the jury's role to assess the weight and credibility of the evidence, and the jury found that Benedi proved causation. We find that ample evidence existed from which a reasonable jury could find for Benedi.

Decision

The Court of Appeals affirmed the jury's verdict awarding plaintiff Benedi $7,850,000 against McNeil for negligent failure to warn.

> **Note:** In the summer of 1993 (after Benedi's injury), McNeil included a warning on Tylenol that persons who regularly consume three or more alcoholic drinks a day should consult a physician before using Tylenol.

Law & Ethics Questions

1. What elements are necessary to prove negligence? Do you think McNeil was negligent in this case? Do you think jurors are sophisticated enough to evaluate and judge scientific evidence?

2. **Ethics** Did McNeil act ethically in failing to put a warning on Tylenol? Do you think a warning was warranted?

3. What will be the implication of this case to manufacturers of pain-killing drugs? Will consumers be better off because of this decision? Explain.

Misrepresentation

intentional misrepresentation
Intentionally defrauding another person out of money, property, or something else of value. When a seller or lessor fraudulently misrepresents the quality of a product and a buyer is injured thereby. Occurs when one person consciously decides to induce another person to rely and act on a misrepresentation. Also called fraud. Occurs when an agent makes an untrue statement that he or she knows is not true.

misrepresentation
An assertion that is made that is not in accord with the facts.

doctrine of strict liability in tort
A tort doctrine that makes manufacturers, distributors, wholesalers, retailers, and others in the chain of distribution of a defective product liable for the damages caused by the defect irrespective of fault.

A buyer or lessee who is injured because a seller or lessor fraudulently misrepresented the quality of a product can sue the seller for the tort of **intentional misrepresentation,** or **fraud.** Recovery is limited to persons who were injured because they relied on the **misrepresentation**.

Intentional misrepresentation occurs when a seller or lessor either (1) affirmatively misrepresents the quality of a product or (2) conceals a defect in it. Because most reputable manufacturers, sellers, and lessors do not intentionally misrepresent the quality of their products, fraud is not often used as the basis for product liability actions.

■ STRICT LIABILITY

In the landmark case ***Greenman v. Yuba Power Products, Inc.,***[3] the California Supreme Court adopted the **doctrine of strict liability in tort** as a basis for prod-

---

[3] *Greenman v. Yuba Power Prod., Inc.,* 377 P.2d 897 (Cal. 1963).

uct liability actions. Most states have now adopted this doctrine as a basis for product liability actions. The doctrine of strict liability removes many of the difficulties for the plaintiff associated with other theories of product liability. This section examines the scope of the strict liability doctrine.

Liability Without Fault

Unlike negligence, strict liability does not require the injured person to prove that the defendant breached a duty of care. **Strict liability** is **liability without fault**. A seller can be found strictly liable even though he or she has exercised all possible care in the preparation and sale of his or her product.

strict liability
Liability without fault.

The doctrine of strict liability applies to sellers and lessors of products who are engaged in the business of selling and leasing products. Casual sales and transactions by nonmerchants are not covered. Thus a person who sells a defective product to a neighbor in a casual sale is not strictly liable if the product causes injury.

Strict liability applies only to products, not services. In hybrid transactions involving both services and products, the dominant element of the transaction dictates whether strict liability applies.

Example: In a medical operation that requires a blood transfusion, the operation would be the dominant element, and strict liability would not apply. Strict liability may not be disclaimed.

All in the Chain of Distribution Are Liable

All parties in the **chain of distribution** of a defective product are *strictly liable* for the injuries caused by that product. Thus all manufacturers, distributors, wholesalers, retailers, lessors, and subcomponent manufacturers may be sued under the doctrine of strict liability in tort. This view is based on public policy. Lawmakers presume that sellers and lessors will insure against the risk of a strict liability lawsuit and spread the cost to their consumers by raising the price of products.

chain of distribution
All manufacturers, distributors, wholesalers, retailers, lessors, and subcomponent manufacturers involved in a transaction.

Example: Suppose a subcomponent manufacturer produces a defective tire and sells it to a truck manufacturer. The truck manufacturer places the defective tire on one of its new-model trucks. The truck is distributed by a distributor to a retail dealer. Ultimately, the retail dealer sells the truck to a buyer. The defective tire causes an accident in which the buyer is injured. All the parties in the tire's chain of distribution can be sued by the injured party; in this case, the liable parties are the subcomponent manufacturer, the truck manufacturer, the distributor, and the retailer.

A defendant who has not been negligent but who is made to pay a strict liability judgment can bring a separate action against the negligent party in the chain of distribution to recover its losses. In the preceding example, for instance, the retailer could sue the manufacturer to recover the strict liability judgment assessed against it.

Exhibit 14.1 compares the doctrines of negligence and strict liability.

Parties Who Can Recover for Strict Liability

Because strict liability is a tort doctrine, privity of contract between the plaintiff and the defendant is not required. In other words, the doctrine applies even

Exhibit 14.1 Negligence and Strict Liability Compared

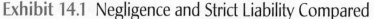

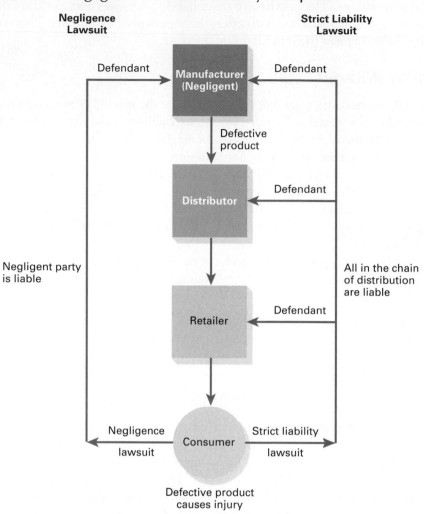

CONTEMPORARY Issue

RESTATEMENT OF TORTS DEFINITION OF STRICT LIABILITY

RESTATEMENT (SECOND) OF TORTS

The most widely recognized articulation of the doctrine of strict liability in tort is found in Section 402A of the *Restatement (Second) of Torts*, which provides:

1. *One who sells any product in a defective condition unreasonably dangerous to the user or consumer or to his property is subject to liability for physical harm thereby caused to the ultimate user or consumer, or to his property, if*
   a. *the seller is engaged in the business of selling such a product, and*
   b. *it is expected to and does reach the user or consumer without substantial change in the condition in which it is sold.*
2. *The rule stated in Subsection (1) applies although*
   a. *the seller has exercised all possible care in the preparation and sale of his product, and*
   b. *the user or consumer has not bought the product from or entered into any contractual relation with the seller.*

(continued)

RESTATEMENT (THIRD) OF TORTS

In 1997, the American Law Institute (ALI) adopted the *Restatement (Third) of Torts: Product Liability*. This new *Restatement* includes the following definition of defect:

> A product is defective when, at the time of sale or distribution, it contains manufacturing defect, is defective in design, or is defective because of inadequate instructions or warnings.
>
> A product:
>
> a. contains a manufacturing defect when the product departs from its intended design even though all possible care was exercised in the preparation and marketing of the product;
> b. is defective in design when the foreseeable risks of harm posed by the product could have been reduced or avoided by the adoption of a reasonable alternative design by the seller or other distributor, or a predecessor in the commercial chain of distribution, and the omission of the alternative design renders the product not reasonably safe;
> c. is defective because of inadequate instructions or warnings when the foreseeable risks of harm posed by the product could have been reduced or avoided by the provision of reasonable instructions or warnings by the seller or other distributor, or a predecessor in the commercial chain of distribution, and the omission of the instructions or warnings renders the product not reasonably safe.

if the injured party had no contractual relations with the defendant. Under strict liability, sellers and lessors are liable to the ultimate user or consumer. Users include the purchaser or lessee, family members, guests, employees, customers, and persons who passively enjoy the benefits of the product (e.g., passengers in automobiles).

Most jurisdictions have judicially or statutorily extended the protection of strict liability to bystanders. The courts have stated that bystanders should be entitled to even greater protection than a consumer or user. This is because consumers and users have the opportunity to inspect for defects and to limit their purchases to articles manufactured by reputable manufacturers and sold by reputable retailers, whereas bystanders do not have the same opportunity.

Damages Recoverable for Strict Liability

The damages recoverable in a strict liability action vary by jurisdiction. Damages for personal injuries are recoverable in all jurisdictions that have adopted the doctrine of strict liability, although some jurisdictions limit the dollar amount of the award. Property damage is recoverable in most jurisdictions, but economic loss (e.g., lost income) is recoverable in only a few jurisdictions. **Punitive damages,** monetary damages awarded to punish the defendant, are generally allowed if the plaintiff can prove the defendant either intentionally injured him or her or acted with reckless disregard for his or her safety.

punitive damages
Damages that are awarded to punish the defendant, to deter the defendant from similar conduct in the future, and to set an example for others.

PARALEGAL PERSPECTIVE

Ron J. Taylor works as a corporate paralegal in the legal department for The Williams Companies, Inc. in Tulsa, Oklahoma. He is a graduate of the University of Tulsa's Paralegal Studies Program. Ron is also a member of both TALA and NALA.

I'm a member of the legal department of a large energy company that represents its own internal clients. Under the supervision of attorneys, I perform tasks for many clients involving multiple areas of law (i.e., litigation, acquisition and divestitures, employment, corporate, finance and treasury, regulatory, and research on records information management).

At the onset of any matter, regardless of the area of law, I'm responsible for matter setup. Matter setup includes planning a budget, drafting a case assessment, engaging outside counsel, and more. As the matter setup process progresses, I schedule client interviews and meetings to discuss the details of the case and collect client documents. At this point in our process, I likely will have most of the required information to draft or review many of the agreements that follow.

Some of the many agreements that I've drafted and reviewed for supervising attorneys are engagement letters, purchase and sale agreements, destruction notices, letters of conveyances, lease agreements, assessment agreements, EEOC notices, HSR filings, due diligence loan agreements, FERC filings, and others.

Supervising attorneys appreciate my talents and expect the very best of my expertise on every project. Because nearly every document that I draft is an agreement of some sort, the supervising attorney expects me to identify, correct, or suggest any changes for clarity that I come across in an agreement. I have a lot of pride in being a noteworthy member of the legal department where goals and processes are set to streamline costs.

■ DEFECTIVE PRODUCT

product defects
In a strict liability lawsuit, the injured party must show that the product that caused the injury was defective.

To recover for strict liability, the injured party must first show that the product that caused the injury was somehow *defective*. (Remember that the injured party does not have to prove who caused the product to become defective.) Plaintiffs can allege multiple **product defects** in one lawsuit. A product can be found to be defective in many ways. The most common types of defects are *defects in manufacture*, *design*, and *packaging*, and *failure to warn*. These defects are discussed in the following paragraphs.

Defect in Manufacture

defect in manufacture
A defect that occurs when the manufacturer fails to (1) properly assemble a product, (2) properly test a product, or (3) adequately check the quality of the product.

A **defect in manufacture** occurs when the manufacturer fails to (1) properly assemble a product, (2) properly test a product, or (3) adequately check the quality of a product.

Example: American Ladder Company designs, manufactures, and sells ladders. American Ladder Company manufactures a ladder, but a worker at the company fails to put one of the screws in the ladder that would support one of the steps of the ladder. The ladder is sold to Weingard Distributor, a wholesaler, which sells it to Reynolds Hardware Store, which sells the ladder to Heather, a consumer. When Heather is on the ladder, painting her house, the step of the ladder breaks because of the missing screw, and Heather falls and is injured. The missing screw is an example of a defect in manufacture. Under the doctrine of strict liability, American Ladder Company, Weingard Distributor, and Reynolds Hardware Store are liable to Heather.

The Case 14.2 is a classic example involving a defect in manufacture.

CASE 14.2   DEFECT IN MANUFACTURE

Shoshone Coca-Cola Bottling Co. v. Dolinski, 420 P.2d 855 (Nev. 1966).

"In the case at hand, Shoshone contends that insufficient proof was offered to establish that the mouse was in the bottle of 'Squirt' when it left Shoshone's possession."

Judge Thompson, *Supreme Court of Nevada*

Facts

Leo Dolinski purchased a bottle of Squirt, a soft drink, from a vending machine at a Sea and Ski plant, his place of employment. Dolinski opened the bottle and consumed part of its contents. He immediately became ill. Upon examination, it was found that the bottle contained the decomposed body of a mouse, mouse hair, and mouse feces. Dolinski visited a doctor and was given medicine to counteract nausea. Dolinski suffered physical and mental distress from consuming the decomposed mouse and thereafter possessed an aversion to soft drinks. The Shoshone Coca-Cola Bottling Company (Shoshone) had manufactured and distributed the Squirt bottle. Dolinski sued Shoshone, basing his lawsuit on the doctrine of strict liability. The state of Nevada had not previously recognized the doctrine of strict liability. However, the trial court adopted the doctrine of strict liability, and the jury returned a verdict in favor of the plaintiff. Shoshone appealed.

Issue

Should the state of Nevada judicially adopt the doctrine of strict liability? If so, was there a defect in the manufacture of the Squirt bottle that caused the plaintiff's injuries?

Language of the Court

In our view, public policy demands that one who places upon the market a bottled beverage in a condition dangerous for use must be held strictly liable to the ultimate user for injuries resulting from such use, although the seller has exercised all reasonable care.

Our acceptance of strict tort liability against the manufacturer and distributor of a bottled beverage does not mean that the plaintiff is relieved of the burden of proving a case. He must still establish that his injury was caused by a defect in the product and that such defect existed when the product left the hands of the defendant.

In the case at hand, Shoshone contends that insufficient proof was offered to establish that the mouse was in the bottle of "Squirt" when it left Shoshone's possession. The plaintiff offered the expert testimony of a toxicologist who examined the bottle and contents on the day the plaintiff drank from it. It was his opinion that the mouse "had been dead for a long time" and that the dark stains (mouse feces) that he found on the bottom of the bottle must have been there before the liquid was added. The jury apparently preferred the latter evidence that traced cause to the defendant.

Decision

The Supreme Court of Nevada adopted the doctrine of strict liability and held that the evidence supported the trial court's finding of a defect in manufacture. The supreme court affirmed the trial court's decision in favor of plaintiff Dolinski.

Law & Ethics Questions

1. Should the courts adopt the theory of strict liability? Why or why not?

2. **Ethics** Was it ethical for Shoshone to argue it was not liable to Dolinski?

3. **Ethics** Should all parties in the chain of distribution of a defective product—even parties that are not responsible for the defect—be held liable under the doctrine of strict liability? Or should liability be based only on fault?

Web Exercises

1. **Web** Visit the website of PepsiCo at www.pepsico.com. Can you find any information on the manufacture of Squirt soda?

2. **Web** Visit the website of the Supreme Court of Nevada at www.nvsupremecourt.us.

3. **Web** Use www.google.com and find an article about strict liability as it applies to product defects.

CAREER FRONT

Job Description: Corporate Contracts Paralegal

A corporate contracts paralegal can be involved with contracts in the following ways:

- Responsible for the day-to-day processing of builder contracts and other contractual agreements
- Build and maintain relationships with internal and external customers
- Manage lease process
- Facilitate communications between builders, company, and parent company
- Manage/Facilitate daily contract process
  a. Review and modify contract
  b. Record to contract log
  c. Track metric on contracts
  d. Scan contract for electronic filing
  e. Send contract to the customer
  f. Follow up on executed copies of contract
- Assist in contract negotiation, writing contract addendums and protecting the company's legal rights under contract
- Manage/Facilitate daily lease process
- Assist in monitoring and managing general liability claims and legal matters
- Assist in monitoring construction defect and other litigation
- Communicate effectively with parent company
- Understand customers' requirements, resolve issues, and build good relationships internally and externally
- Be an active part of the team working to reduce/limit risk exposure
- Participate in continuous improvement activities

Source: Excerpted by permission from the National Association of Legal Assistants (www.nala.org) and the National Federation of Paralegal Associations, Inc. (www.paralegals.org).

Defect in Design

A **defect in design** can support a strict liability action.

Example: Design defects include toys that are designed with removable parts that could be swallowed by children, machines and appliances designed without proper safeguards, and trucks and other vehicles designed without warning devices to let people know the vehicle is backing up.

In evaluating the adequacy of a product's design, the courts apply a risk-utility analysis and consider the gravity of the danger posed by the design, the likelihood that injury will occur, the availability and cost of producing a safer alternative design, the social utility of the product, and other factors.

In Cases 14.3 and 14.4, the courts had to decide whether there was a design defect.

defect in design
A defect that occurs when a product is improperly designed.

CASE 14.3   DEFECT IN DESIGN

Lakin v. Senco Prod., Inc., 925 P.2d 107 (Or. Ct. App. 1996).

"Thus, it was foreseeable—indeed, highly likely given the SN325's recoil and 'bump fire' potential—that serious injury could occur to someone when the nail gun double fired."

Judge Haselton, *Court of Appeals of Oregon*

Facts

Senco Products, Inc. (Senco), manufactures and markets a variety of pneumatic nail guns, including the SN325 nail gun, which discharges 3.25-inch nails. The SN325 uses special nails designed and sold by Senco. The SN325 discharges a nail only if two trigger mechanisms are activated; that is, the user must both squeeze the nail gun's finger trigger and press the nail gun's muzzle against a surface, activating the bottom trigger, or safety. The SN325 can fire up to nine nails per second if the trigger is continuously depressed and the gun is bounced along the work surface, constantly reactivating the muzzle safety/trigger.

John Lakin was using a Senco SN325 nail gun to help build a new home. When attempting to nail two-by-fours under the eaves of the garage, Lakin stood on tiptoe and raised a two-by-four over his head. As he held the board in position with his left hand and the nail gun in his right hand, he pressed the nose of the SN325 up against the board, depressed the safety, and pulled the finger trigger to fire the nail into the board. The gun fired the first nail and then, in a phenomenon known as "double firing," immediately discharged an unintended second nail that struck the first nail. The gun recoiled violently backward toward Lakin and, with Lakin's finger still on the trigger, came into contact with his cheek. That contact activated the safety/trigger, causing the nail gun to fire a third nail. This third nail went through Lakin's cheekbone and into his brain.

The nail penetrated the frontal lobe of the right hemisphere of Lakin's brain, blocked a major artery, and caused extensive tissue damage. Lakin was unconscious for several days and ultimately underwent multiple surgeries. He suffers permanent brain damage and is unable to perceive information from the left hemisphere of the brain. He also suffers partial paralysis of the left side of his body. Lakin has undergone a radical personality change and is prone to violent outbursts. He is unable to obtain employment. Lakin's previously warm and loving relationship with his wife and four children has been permanently altered. He can no longer live with his family and instead resides in a supervised group home for brain-injured persons. Lakin and his wife sued Senco for strict liability based on design defect. The trial court found Senco liable and awarded $5,323,413 to Lakin, $876,000 to his wife, and $4 million in punitive damages against Senco. Senco appealed.

Issue

Is Senco liable to Lakin for strict liability based on a design defect in the SN325 that allowed it to double-fire?

Language of the Court

The evidence disclosed that the SN325 double-fired once in every 15 firings. Defendant rushed the SN325's production in order to maintain its position in the market, modifying an existing nail gun model so that it could shoot longer nails, without engaging in additional testing to determine whether the use of longer nails in that model would increase the prevalence of double fire. A reasonable juror could plausibly infer that conscious profit/market share motives underlay the failure to engage in adequate product research, development, and testing.

After reviewing the entire record, we conclude that the amount of damages awarded was within the range that a rational juror would be entitled to award. Before John Lakin's injury, defendant knew from numerous complaints that it was highly probable that the SN325 would "double fire." Thus, it was foreseeable—indeed, highly likely given the SN325's recoil and "bump fire" potential—that serious injury could occur to someone when the nail gun double fired.

Decision

The court of appeals applied a risk-utility analysis and held that the SN325 was defectively designed. The court affirmed the award of damages to Lakin and his wife.

Legal & Ethics Questions

1. Do you think the utility served by the nine-nail-per-second SN325 outweighed its risk of personal injury?
2. **Ethics** Did Senco act in conscious disregard of safety factors when it designed, manufactured, and sold the SN325 nail gun?
3. **Ethics** Do you think the award of punitive damages was warranted in this case?

Web Exercises

1. **Web** Visit the website of Senco Products, Inc. at www.senco.com. Can you find descriptions of the nail guns it now sells?
2. **Web** Visit the website of the Court of Appeals of Oregon at www.ojd.state.or.us/courts.
3. **Web** Use www.google.com and find an article about the dangers of using nail guns.

CASE 14.4   DESIGN DEFECT

Higgins v. Intex Recreation Corp., 99 P.3d 421 (Wash. Ct. App. 2004).

> "Now, the ride down a snow-covered hill backward at 30 miles per hour may be a thrill. But it has very little social value when compared to the risk of severe injury."
>
> Judge Sweeney, *Court of Appeals of Washington*

Facts

The Intex Recreation Corporation designed and sold the Extreme Sno-Tube II. This snow tube is ridden by a user down snow-covered hills and can reach a speed of 30 miles per hour. The snow tube has no steering device, and therefore a rider may end up spinning and going down a hill backward.

Dan Falkner bought an Extreme Sno-Tube II and used it sledding the same day. During Falkner's second run, the tube rotated him backward about a quarter to a third of the way down the hill. A group of parents, including Tom Higgins, stood near the bottom of the hill. Higgins saw seven-year old Kyle Potter walking in the path of Falkner's speeding Sno-Tube. Higgins ran and grabbed Potter to save him from harm, but while doing so the Sno-Tube hit Higgins and threw him into the air. Higgins landed on his forehead, which snapped his head back. The impact severed Higgins's spinal cord and left him quadriplegic.

Higgins sued Intex for damages based on strict liability. Evidence was introduced at trial that showed the Sno-Tube could rotate while going down hill and it had no guiding mechanism and no steering device. Evidence also showed that Intex made a Sno-Boggan that went just as fast but did not rotate because of ridges on the bottom of the device. The jury found a design defect in the Sno-Tube and held Intex liable for 35 percent of Higgins's damages.

Issue

Was the Extreme Sno-Tube II defectively designed, thus supporting the judgment against Intex?

Language of the Court

There are two tests for determining whether a product is defective. The risk-utility test requires a showing that the likelihood and seriousness of harm outweigh the burden on the manufacturer to design a product that would have prevented that harm and would not have impaired the product's usefulness. The consumer-expectation test requires a showing that the product is more dangerous than the ordinary consumer would expect. This test focuses on the reasonable expectation of the consumer.

A plaintiff can satisfy its burden of proving an alternative design by showing that another product more safely serves the same function as the challenged product. There is evidence in this record from which a jury could conclude that the placement of ribs or ridges on the bottom of the Sno-Tube, like those used on Intex's Sno-Boggan, would keep the rider from facing downhill. The rider could then see obstacles and direct the tube. All this could be done without sacrificing speed. This is enough to prove an alternative safer design. Now, the ride down a snow-covered hill backward at 30 miles per hour may be a thrill. But it has very little social value when compared to the risk of severe injury. We do not think the Sno-Tube is a product that is necessary regardless of the risks involved to the user. We find ample evidence to support this verdict, applying the risk-utility test.

We next take up Intex's assertion that the tube was not unsafe to an extent beyond that which would be contemplated by the ordinary consumer. Again, we find ample evidence in this record to support the Higgins's assertion to the contrary. And a reasonable jury could easily infer that the average consumer may expect the Sno-Tube to rotate. But he or she might not expect that it would continue in a backward position. Here, the Sno-Tube is inexpensive. But so is Intex's Sno-Boggan. And the Sno-Boggan provides a fast ride but not a blind high-speed ride. A jury could then find that a reasonable consumer would expect that a snow sliding product would not put him or her in a backward, high-speed slide. We find ample evidence in favor of the plaintiffs applying the consumer-expectation test.

Decision

The court of appeals held that the Sno-Tube was defectively designed and affirmed the judgment in favor of Higgins against Intex.

Law & Ethics Questions

1. What is a design defect? Explain.

2. What does the risk-utility test require? What does the consumer-expectation test require?

3. **Ethics** Should Intex have placed a ridge on the bottom of the Sno-Tube or equipped it with a steering device to make it safer?

4. Would you have found for or against Intex in this case? Explain.

Web Exercises

1. **Web** Visit the website of Intex Recreation Corporation at www.intexcorp .com. Does the company still sell any type of snow-tube devices?

2. **Web** Visit the website of the Court of Appeals of Washington at www .courts.wa.gov.

3. **Web** Use www.google.com and find an article about the dangers of snow tubing.

Crashworthiness Doctrine

crashworthiness doctrine
A doctrine that says automobile manufacturers are under a duty to design automobiles so they take into account the possibility of harm from a person's body striking something inside the automobile in the case of a car accident.

When an automobile is involved in an accident, the driver or passengers often are not injured by the blow itself. Instead, they are injured when their bodies strike something inside their own automobile (e.g., the dashboard or the steering wheel). This is commonly referred to as the "second collision." The courts have held that automobile manufacturers are under a duty to design automobiles to take into account the possibility of this second collision. This is called the **crashworthiness doctrine**. Failure to design an automobile to protect occupants from foreseeable dangers caused by a second collision subjects the manufacturer and dealer to strict liability.

ETHICS SPOTLIGHT

DESIGN DEFECT IN POOL EQUIPMENT

Lorenzo Peterson was swimming in a swimming pool with a friend at an apartment complex. Lorenzo watched as his friend swam to the bottom of the pool, slid an unattached drain cover away, and then slid it back. Lorenzo thought his friend had hidden something inside the drain, so he swam to the bottom of the pool. Lorenzo slid the drain cover aside and stuck his arm inside the drain. The 300 to 400 pounds of pull of the drain pump held Lorenzo trapped underwater. At least seven people tried to free Lorenzo to no avail. When the police arrived, they broke down the door to the pool equipment room and turned off the drain pump.

Lorenzo was trapped underwater for 12 minutes, which left him irreversibly brain damaged. Lorenzo, through his relatives, sued Sta-Rite Industries, Inc., the manufacturer of the drain, under the doctrine of strict liability to recover damages for Lorenzo's injuries. The plaintiff alleged that the underwater pool drain was defectively designed because it did not contain a shutoff mechanism. Evidence at trial showed that Sta-Rite's drain covers are designed to screw down, but often a drain cover becomes loose. Further evidence showed there had been more than 20 prior suction-entrapment accidents involving Sta-Rite's drain covers and pumps.

Previously, experts had designed a pool drain pump with a mechanism that would automatically shut off a pool drain pump when it detected it was pulling more than it should. Sta-Rite did not install such safety features on its drain pumps, however. After hearing the evidence, including seeing a video of a typical day in the life of Lorenzo after the accident, the jury took less than two hours to return a verdict against Sta-Rite. The jury found that a design defect existed in Sta-Rite's pool drain equipment and awarded Lorenzo $32 million for past and future medical expenses and $72 million for pain and suffering. *Sta-Rite Indus., Inc. v. Peterson*, 837 So. 2d 988 (Fla. Dist. Ct. App. 2003).

Law & Ethics Questions

1. **Ethics** Do you think Sta-Rite acted unethically in its conduct? Why or why not?
2. **Ethics** Was the award of $104 million warranted? Explain

Web Exercises

1. **Web** Visit the website of the Court of Appeals of Florida at www.flcourts.org.
2. **Web** Use www.google.com and find an article about someone being injured in a pool accident.

Failure to Warn

Certain products are inherently dangerous and cannot be made any safer and still accomplish the task for which they are designed. For example, certain useful drugs cause side effects, allergies, and other injuries to some users. Many machines and appliances include dangerous moving parts that, if removed, would defeat the purpose of the machine or appliance. Manufacturers and sellers of such products are under a *duty to warn* users about such a product's dangerous propensities. A proper and conspicuous warning placed on the product insulates the manufacturer and others in the chain of distribution from strict liability. **Failure to warn** of these dangerous propensities is a defect that will support a strict liability action.

failure to warn
A defect that occurs when a manufacturer does not place a warning on the packaging of products that could cause injury if the danger is unknown.

Example: The Universal Drug Corporation develops a new drug that has tremendous success in preventing and treating a certain type of cancer. The drug, however, has a 3 percent probability of causing an increased risk of heart disease in patients who take the drug. The drug cannot be made any safer and still have its cancer treatment effects. The Universal Drug Corporation owes a duty to warn potential users of its drug of these heart-related risks. If it fails to do so and a user suffers a heart attack because of use of the drug, the Universal Drug Corporation would be held strictly liable for failure to warn.

In Cases 14.4, 14.5, and 14.6, the court had to decide whether there was a failure to warn.

CASE 14.5   DESIGN DEFECT

Karlsson v. Ford Motor Co., 45 Cal. Rptr. 3d 265 (Ct. App. 2006).

"This is a chance for you to say, 'Hey Ford, if you know about a problem that is taking place, than do something about it.'"

Plaintiff's Lawyer, *Court of Appeals of California*

Facts

Five-year-old Johan Karlsson was riding in a Ford Windstar minivan with his mother, uncle, and four siblings. The Windstar minivan was designed and manufactured by Ford Motor Company. The Windstar had three rows of seating and provided combination lap belt and shoulder harnesses for all of the seats but one, the center seat of the rear third row bench, where Johan was seated. Instead of the so-called three-point harness worn by the others, Johan was provided only a lap belt.

The Karlssons were driving on Interstate 5 when the driver of the tractor-trailer in front of them dozed off and rear-ended a truck in front of him. A 15-ton steel coil fell off the tractor-trailer and struck the Karlssons' minivan. The six Karlssons who were wearing the shoulder harnesses were injured but made full recoveries. Johan suffered severe spinal injuries and was left a paraplegic.

The tractor-trailer was owned by TransContinental Transport (TCT). Johan sued TCT and Ford Motor Company. Johan settled with TCT for $10 million. Johan sued Ford to recover damages for strict liability, alleging design defect and failure to warn. The jury awarded Johan over $30 million in economic damages, pain and suffering, and punitive damages. Ford appealed.

Issue

Was there a design defect in the Windstar minivan and did Ford fail to warn of the defect?

Language of the Court

Johan's injuries were consistent with something physicians call seat belt syndrome, when a passenger restrained by only a lap belt jackknives over at the waist due to the force of the collision. Had Johan been wearing a three-point restraint, his injuries would have been no more severe than the other occupants of the Windstar. Johan's mother testified that she adjusted Johan's lap belt for him before starting the trip, making sure it fit snugly and rested on his hips.

The jury in this case was instructed on the theories of: (1) design defect under the risk-benefit approach; and (2) failure to warn. Under the design defect theory, Johan argued to the jury that Ford could have and should have installed a seat belt in the rear bench center seat that included some type of shoulder harness. Under the failure to warn theory, Johan argued to the jury that Ford did not adequately warn of the need to wear the lap belt properly, or of the magnitude of the harm that might follow as a result. Ford's primary defense was that the collision was a severe one and that Johan's seat belt was not properly adjusted.

The one comment to which Ford raised an objection came at the very end of Johan's rebuttal argument. After Johan's lawyer said, "This is your chance that maybe companies won't try to destroy...," Ford counsel cut him off with an objection. That objection was overruled, and Johan's lawyer then said, "This is a chance for you to say, 'Hey Ford, if you know about a problem that is taking place, than do something about it." Johan's lawyer concluded his argument soon after.

Decision

The court of appeals affirmed the trial court's judgment in favor of plaintiff Johan Karlsson against Ford Motor Company

Law & Ethics Questions

1. What is a design defect? Explain.

2. What constitutes failure to warn? Explain.

3. **Ethics** Did Ford Motor Company act ethically in this lawsuit?

Web Exercises

1. **Web** Visit the website of Ford Motor Company at www.ford.com. To learn about Ford vehicles, including minivans, go to www.fordvehicles.com

2. **Web** Visit the California Court of Appeal at www.courtinfo.ca.gov/courts/courtsofappeal. Click on "2nd District."

3. **Web** Use www.google.com and find an article that discusses strict liability.

CASE 14.6 FAILURE TO WARN

Crosswhite v. Jumpking, Inc., 411 F. Supp. 2d 1228 (D. Or. 2006).

> *"Plaintiff must present evidence that the trampoline was defectively designed. The burden of proof that the product was defective at the time it left the hands of the particular seller is upon the inured plaintiff."*

> Judge Aiken, *United States District Court for the District of Oregon*

Facts

One day, Gary Crosswhite was jumping on a trampoline with another boy. The trampoline was owned by Jack and Misty Urbach. The 14-foot round-shaped "backyard" trampoline was manufactured by Jumpking, Inc. While on the trampoline, Crosswhite attempted a back flip and accidentally landed on his head and neck. The force of the fall caused a fracture in Crosswhite's spine resulting in paraplegia. Crosswhite was 16 years old at the time of the injury.

Crosswhite filed a lawsuit in U.S. District Court against Jumpking to recover damages for strict liability based on design defect and failure to warn of the danger of using the trampoline. Defendant Jumpking filed a motion for summary judgment.

Issue

Is defendant Jumpking liable for strict liability to Crosswhite based on either defect in design or failure to warn?

Language of the Court

Plaintiff must present evidence that the trampoline was defectively designed. The burden of proof that the product was defective at the time it left the hands of the particular seller is upon the injured plaintiff; and unless evidence can be produced which will support the conclusion that it was then defective the burden will not be sustained. Plaintiff has not submitted any evidence to meet this burden. There can be no dispute that an ordinary consumer buys and uses a trampoline to jump on it, and a design that allows for such activity is exactly that which is contemplated by an ordinary consumer or user of a trampoline. Plaintiff's complaint against the defendant seems to be that all trampolines are defectively designed and should be banned from the marketplace. Given Oregon's objective standard and the facts that plaintiff was a 16-year-old, with a 3.6 grade point average in high school, with over six years experience with trampolines, I find that plaintiff was capable of appreciating the risks associated with jumping and performing flips on a trampoline.

Defendant's trampoline is manufactured with nine warning labels that are affixed to various trampoline components. In addition to these nine warning labels, defendant also provides a large laminated warning placard that is designed to be attached by the consumer to the metal frame near the ladder upon which jumpers mount the trampoline. Defendant further provides consumers with a detailed User Manual and a videotape that instructs both users and supervisors about safe and responsible trampoline use. However, defendant did affix those warnings to the trampoline as well as on a large warning placard attached to the trampoline at the point of entry or mounting. Specifically, warnings attached to the trampoline frame leg stated:

!WARNING

DO NOT LAND ON HEAD OR NECK. PARALYSIS OR DEATH CAN RESULT, EVEN IF YOU LAND IN THE MIDDLE OF THE TRAMPOLINE MAT (BED). TO REDUCE THE CHANCE OF LANDING ON YOUR HEAD OR NECK, DO NOT DO FLIPS.

!WARNING

ONLY ONE PERSON AT A TIME ON THE TRAMPOLINE. MULTIPLE JUMPERS INCREASE THE CHANCES OF LOSS OF CONTROL, COLLISION, AND FALLING OFF. THIS CAN RESULT IN BROKEN HEAD, NECK, BACK OR LEG.

I find that defendant's warnings were adequate as a matter of law.

Decision

The U.S. District Court held there was no design defect or failure to warn by defendant Jumpking. The district court granted summary judgment to Jumpking and dismissed the plaintiff's lawsuit.

Law & Ethics Questions

1. Do you think there was a design defect in the design of the trampoline? Why or why not?

2. Do you think there was a failure to warn about the dangers of using the trampoline? Why or why not?

3. **Ethics** With the inherent dangers of using a trampoline, should all trampolines be barred from the marketplace? Why or why not?

Web Exercises

1. **Web** Go to the website of Jumpking, Inc. at www.jumpking.com to view what a trampoline looks like.

2. **Web** Visit the website of the U.S. District Court for Oregon at www.ord .uscourts.gov.

3. **Web** Use www.google.com and find an article about someone else being injured using a trampoline.

CASE 14.7 FAILURE TO WARN

Glenn v. Overhead Door Corp., 935 So. 2d 1074 (Miss. Ct. App. 2006).

> *"Jolie could have easily avoided exposing Brittany to dangerous levels of carbon monoxide by not leaving her in a car unattended for an extended period of time with the engine running and the garage door down."*

> Judge Chandler, *Court of Appeals of Mississippi*

Facts

Jolie Glenn placed her three-year old daughter, Brittany, in a car with the engine running while it was parked in her garage with the garage door closed. Glenn went back into the house, sat down, and fell asleep. When she awoke, she realized Brittany was not with her. Jolie went into the garage and saw that the garage door was closed. Brittany was in the car and had died as a result of carbon monoxide poisoning. Overhead Door Corporation had manufactured the garage door and the garage door opener used by Jolie to open and close the garage door.

Malcolm Glenn, Jolie's ex-husband and Brittany's father, sued Overhead Door for strict liability, alleging design defect and failure to warn. Glenn argued that Overhead Door should have designed its garage door opener with a sensor that would determine when carbon monoxide had gotten too high in a garage and then alert the car owner. Glenn also alleged that Overhead Door had failed to warn a user of its overhead garage door opener that if the car was left running and the garage door was closed, carbon monoxide could build up to dangerous levels in the garage. The trial court granted summary judgment to Overhead Door.

Issue

Was Overhead Door liable for strict liability for either design defect or failure to warn?

Language of the Court

Jolie could have easily avoided exposing Brittany to dangerous levels of carbon monoxide by not leaving her in a car unattended for an extended period of time with the engine running and the garage door down. Proving that a manufacturer did not warn of some potential danger does not, by itself, create an issue of fact. In order to create a triable issue regarding failure to warn, the plaintiff must show that the user was ignorant of the danger warned against. Manufacturers and distributors have no duty to warn of dangers that are open and obvious or if the hazard associated with the product is common knowledge to the ordinary observer or consumer.

Malcolm argues that there is a genuine issue as to whether Overhead Door should have warned of the dangers of carbon monoxide poisoning because Jolie Glenn testified that it never crossed her mind that her daughter could die from carbon monoxide poisoning. However, she did testify that she knew a person should never leave a child unattended in a car with the engine running. She also testified that she knew and appreciated the danger of [**11] carbon monoxide poisoning and that she knew the garage door would not open automatically. She needed no other warning.

Decision

The court of appeals held that Overhead Door was not strictly liable for design defect or failure to warn. The court of appeals affirmed the trial court's grant of summary judgment in favor of Overhead Door.

Law & Ethics Questions

1. Do you think there was a design defect in this case? Explain.

2. Do you think there was a failure to warn in this case? Explain.

3. **Ethics** Was it ethical for the plaintiff in this case to sue Overhead Door based on the facts of this case?

4. **Ethics** Did Overhead Door owe a duty to design its garage door opener with a sensor to alert of high levels of carbon monoxide? Why or why not?

5. **Ethics** Did Overhead Door owe a duty to warn the owners of its garage doors and garage door openers of the danger of carbon monoxide poisoning? Why or why not?

Web Exercises

1. **Web** Visit the website of the Court of Appeals of Mississippi at www.mssc.state.ms.us.

2. **Web** Visit the website of Overhead Door Corporation at www.overheaddoor.com. Does the company sell any garage door openers with sensors on them to detect levels of carbon monoxide poisoning?

3. **Web** Use www.google.com and find an article about the safety of garage doors and garage door openers.

Defect in Packaging

Manufacturers owe a duty to design and provide safe packages for their products. This duty requires manufacturers to provide packages and containers that are tamperproof or clearly indicate if they have been tampered with. Certain manufacturers, such as drug manufacturers, owe a duty to place their products in containers that cannot be opened by children. A manufacturer's failure to meet this duty—a **defect in packaging**—subjects the manufacturer and others in the chain of distribution of the product to strict liability.

In Case 14.8, the court had to decide whether there was defective packaging.

defect in packaging
A defect that occurs when a product has been placed in packaging that is insufficiently tamperproof.

CASE 14.8 DEFECT IN PACKAGING

Elsroth v. Johnson & Johnson, 700 F. Supp. 151 (S.D.N.Y. 1998).

> *"We return, however, to the fundamental premise: no packaging can boast of being tamperproof."*

Judge Goettel, *United States District Court for the Southern District of New York*

Facts

Harriet Notarnicola purchased a box of Extra-Strength Tylenol capsules from a Bronxville, New York, grocery store owned by The Great Atlantic & Pacific Tea Co. (A&P). The Tylenol was manufactured by McNeil Consumer Products Co., a division of McNeilab, Inc. (McNeil), under the name Johnson & Johnson. Diane Elsroth was visiting her boyfriend, Michael Notarnicola, for a week at the home of Michael's parents. Late one night, Diane complained of a headache. Michael went to the kitchen, opened the box and plastic container of Extra-Strength Tylenol purchased by his mother at the A&P store, and returned with two capsules and a glass of water for Diane. A short time after ingesting the capsules, Diane retired. Her dead body was found the next day. The medical examiner concluded that the Tylenol capsules ingested by Diane had been contaminated by a lethal dose of potassium cyanide. The murder remains unsolved, but evidence shows that the Tylenol bottle had been tampered with after the product left the manufacturer's control. An unknown third party purchased the Tylenol, breached the packaging, substituted cyanide for some of the medicine contained in several of the gelatin capsules, somehow resealed the container and box in such a way that the tampering was not readily detectable, and placed the contaminated box on the shelf of the A&P store. John Elsroth, administrator of Diane's estate, brought this strict liability action against McNeil and A&P, seeking $1 million in compensatory damages and $92 million in punitive damages.

Issue

Was there a defect in packaging that would support an action for strict liability?

Language of the Court

Following issuance of the rule, the makers of Tylenol have marketed the product in tamper-resistant packaging with the following features: (1) a foil seal glued to the mouth of the container or bottle, (2) a "shrink seal" around the neck and cap of the container, and (3) a sealed box (the end flaps of which are glued shut) in which the product and container are placed. As one McNeil official put it, tampering by "the Rembrandt kind of criminals" could not be prevented by this type of packaging. McNeil was also operating under the constraint, as recognized by the Food and Drug Administration (FDA), that no packaging could prevent this kind of "exotic" tampering—tamperproof packaging is not possible.

The packaging alternative designed by McNeil employed not one, not two, but three of the tamper-resistant features. When all of these factors are thrown into the mix, we find, as a matter of law, that under a utility/risk analysis this packaging was in a condition reasonably contemplated by the ultimate consumer and was not unreasonably dangerous for its intended use. If there are better tamper-resistant features available that would be feasible for use here, plaintiff has not described them. We return, however, to the fundamental premise: no packaging can boast of being tamperproof.

Decision

The court held there was not a defect in packaging. The defendants are not therefore strictly liable for Elsroth's death.

Law & Ethics Questions

1. Should manufacturers be forced to make tamperproof packaging for their products? Is this possible? What would be the expense?

2. **Ethics** Did any of the parties in the case act unethically? Explain.

3. **Ethics** Do you think the plaintiff's seeking $92 million in punitive damages was warranted?

Web Exercises

1. **Web** Visit the website of Johnson & Johnson at www.jnj.com.

2. **Web** Visit the website of the U.S. District Court for the Southern District of New York at www.nysd.uscourts.gov.

3. **Web** Use www.google.com and find an article about the liability of manufacturers for failing to provide safe packaging.

MARKETPLACE

Job Announcement: Construction Litigation Paralegal

Large law firm seeks an experienced litigation paralegal to work on large construction-based cases. The paralegal will handle construction litigation from discovery through trial/mediation/arbitration. Pay to $85K + OT.

The successful candidate must have at least 4 years of experience as a litigation paralegal with a large law firm. Experience at trial, arbitration, and/or mediation required. Construction litigation experience strongly preferred, but not required. Strong writing skills and ability to review construction contracts, draft legal documents, and draft settlement agreements required. Must have experience using Casemap and/or Concordance.

Please e-mail your resume to:

Failure to Provide Adequate Instructions

Sellers are responsible to provide adequate instructions for the safe assembly and use of the products they sell.

Failure to provide adequate instructions for the safe assembly and use of a product is a defect that subjects the manufacturer and others in the chain of distribution to strict liability.

Other defects include inadequate testing of products, inadequate selection of component parts or materials, and improper certification of the safety of a product. The concept of "defect" is an expanding area of the law.

failure to provide adequate instructions
A defect that occurs when a manufacturer does not provide detailed directions for safe assembly and use of a product.

Punitive Damages

In product liability cases, a court can award *punitive damages* if it finds the defendant's conduct was committed with intent or reckless disregard for human life. Punitive damages are meant to punish the defendants and to send a message to the defendant (and other companies) that such behavior will not be tolerated. However, with large punitive damage awards making the headlines, companies began asking themselves when are punitive damages too much. The U.S. Supreme Court has addressed this issue.

In Case 14.9, the Supreme Court was asked to overturn a large award of punitive damages.

CASE 14.9   PUNITIVE DAMAGES

Philip Morris USA v. Williams, 549 U.S. 346 (2007).

> "In our view, the Constitution's Due Process Clause forbids a State to use
> a punitive damages award to punish a defendant for injury that it inflicts
> upon nonparties or those whom they directly represent, i.e., injury that it
> inflicts upon those who are, essentially, strangers to the litigation."
>
> Justice Breyer, *Supreme Court of the United States*

Facts

Jesse Williams was a heavy cigarette smoker. He favored Marlboro-brand cigarettes, which are produced by Philip Morris USA. Williams died because of his cigarette smoking. William's personal representative sued Philip Morris, alleging the company had engaged in deceit and had knowingly led Williams to believe cigarette smoking was safe.

At trial, the jury held that Philip Morris had engaged in deceit. The jury awarded $821,000 in compensatory damages and $79.5 million in punitive damages. In reaching its decision on punitive damages, the jury was permitted to consider harm caused to others who were not parties to the lawsuit. The trial court judge held that the $79.5 million in punitive damages was excessive and reduced it to $32 million. Both sides appealed.

The Oregon Court of Appeals rejected Philip Morris's arguments and restored the $79.5 million jury award. The Oregon Supreme Court denied review. The case was appealed to the U.S. Supreme Court.

Issue

Did the Oregon court unconstitutionally punish the defendant Philip Morris USA by allowing the jury to consider harm to nonparty victims when awarding punitive damages to the plaintiff?

Language of the U.S. Supreme Court

In our view, the Constitution's Due Process Clause forbids a State to use a punitive damages award to punish a defendant for injury that it inflicts upon nonparties or those whom they directly represent, i.e., injury that it inflicts upon those who are, essentially, strangers to the litigation. For one thing, the Due Process Clause prohibits a State from punishing an individual without first providing that individual with an opportunity to present every available defense. A defendant threatened with punishment for injuring a nonparty victim has no opportunity to defend against the charge, by showing, for example in a case such as this, that the other victim was not entitled to damages because he or she knew that smoking was dangerous or did not rely upon the defendant's statements to the contrary.

To permit punishment for injuring a nonparty victim would add a near standardless dimension to the punitive damages equation. How many such victims are there? How seriously were they injured? Under what circumstances did injury occur? The trial will not likely answer such questions as to nonparty victims. The jury will be left to speculate. And the fundamental due process concerns to which our punitive damages cases refer—risks of arbitrariness, uncertainty and lack of notice—will be magnified. We can find no authority supporting the use of punitive damages awards for the purpose of punishing a defendant for harming others.

Respondent argues that she is free to show harm to other victims because it is relevant to a different part of the punitive damages constitutional equation, namely, reprehensibility. That is to say, harm to others shows more reprehensible conduct. Philip Morris, in turn, does not deny that a plaintiff may show harm to others in order to demonstrate reprehensibility. Nor do we. Evidence of actual harm to nonparties can help to show that the conduct that harmed the plaintiff also posed a substantial risk of harm to the general public, and so was particularly reprehensible. A jury may not go further than this and use a punitive damages verdict to punish a defendant directly on account of harms it is alleged to have visited on nonparties.

Decision

The U.S. Supreme Court held that the Oregon court had applied the wrong standard in permitting the jury to award $79.5 million of punitive damages against Philip Morris. The Supreme Court remanded the case so the Oregon court could apply the correct standard stated by the U.S. Supreme Court in determining an award of punitive damages against Philip Morris.

Law & Ethics Questions

1. What does the constitutional doctrine of due process provide? Explain.

2. **Ethics** Does Philip Morris act ethically in selling cigarettes that knowingly cause cancer and other diseases and early death to many smokers?

3. **Ethics** What are the purposes of allowing the award of punitive damages? Do you think punitive damages have a deterrent effect?

4. **Ethics** In your opinion, do you think the award of $79.5 million of punitive damages was warranted in this case? How much, if any, would you have awarded?

5. **Social responsibility** Does Philip Morris USA act socially responsibly enough by trying to dissuade people from smoking? Should it have this burden at all? Explain.

Web Exercises

1. **Web** Visit the website of Philip Morris USA at www.philipmorrisusa.com. Does the company still sell the Marlboro brand of cigarette?

2. **Web** Visit the website of the U.S. Supreme Court at www.supremecourtus .gov. Can you find any documents related to this case?

3. **Web** Use www.google.com and find an article that discusses the dangers of smoking.

4. **Web** Use www.google.com and find an advertisement for the Marlboro-brand cigarette.

■ DEFENSES TO PRODUCT LIABILITY

Defendants in strict liability or negligence actions may raise several defenses to the imposition of liability. These defenses are discussed in the paragraphs that follow.

Generally Known Dangers

Certain products are inherently dangerous and known to the general population to be so. Sellers are not strictly liable for failing to warn of **generally known dangers**.

Example: It is a known fact that guns shoot bullets. Manufacturers of guns do not have to place a warning on the barrel of a gun warning of this generally known danger.

> **generally known dangers**
> A defense that acknowledges that certain products are inherently dangerous and are known to the general population to be so.

Government Contractor Defense

Many defense and other contractors manufacture products (e.g., rockets, airplanes, and such) to government specification. Most jurisdictions recognize a **government contractor defense** to product liability actions. To establish this defense, a government contractor must prove that (1) the precise specifications for the product were provided by the government, (2) the product conformed to those specifications, and (3) the contractor warned the government of any known defects or dangers of the product.

> **government contractor defense**
> A defense that says a contractor who was provided specifications by the government is not liable for any defect in the product that occurs as a result of those specifications.

Example: Assume an airplane manufacturer becomes a government contractor when it is hired to manufacture a fighter airplane to specifications provided by the U.S. Air Force. If the airplane proves defective because of its design, crashes, and causes injury, the manufacturer can escape liability by asserting the government contractor defense if the manufacturer either did not know of the defect or knew of the defect and warned the government of the defect.

Assumption of the Risk

Theoretically, the traditional doctrine of **assumption of the risk** is a defense to a product liability action. For this defense to apply, the defendant must prove that (1) the plaintiff knew and appreciated the risk and (2) the plaintiff voluntarily assumed the risk. In practice, the defense assumption of the risk is narrowly applied by the courts.

> **assumption of the risk**
> A defense a defendant can use against a plaintiff who knowingly and voluntarily enters into or participates in a risky activity that results in injury. A defense in which the defendant must prove that (1) the plaintiff knew and appreciated the risk and (2) the plaintiff voluntarily assumed the risk

Billing Practices

In many law firms, the paralegals working there have what are called "billable hours." In other words, the time the paralegal spends on a client's case is billable to that client. Unfortunately, because of the pressure on them to meet billable hour requirements, there have been a number of cases involving overbilling and billing abuse practices by paralegals.[4]

Excessive legal fees and billing abuses contribute to the low esteem in which the legal profession is sometimes held. However, the ethical paralegal knows that dishonest billing practices are not only unethical but also illegal. The ethical paralegal should never engage in this sort of practice and should not continue to work for a law firm that engages in such conduct.

Misuse of the Product

misuse
A defense that relieves a seller of product liability if the user abnormally misused the product. Products must be designed to protect against foreseeable misuse.

abnormal misuse
Considerably irregular or an atypical level of usage.

Sometimes users are injured when they misuse a product. If a user brings a product liability action, the defendant-seller may be able to assert **misuse of the product** as a defense. Whether the defense is effective depends on whether the misuse was foreseeable. The seller is relieved of product liability if the plaintiff has **abnormally misused** the product—that is, if there has been an *unforeseeable misuse* of the product. However, the seller is liable if there has been a *foreseeable misuse* of the product. This reasoning is intended to provide an incentive for manufacturers to design and manufacture safer products.

Correction of a Product Defect

A manufacturer that produces a defective product and later discovers said defect must 1) notify purchasers and users of the defect and (2) correct the defect. Most manufacturers faced with this situation recall the defective product and either repair the defect or replace the product.

The seller must make reasonable efforts to notify purchasers and users of the defect and the procedure to correct it. Reasonable efforts normally consist of sending letters to known purchasers and users and placing notices in newspapers and magazines of general circulation. If a user ignores the notice and fails to have the defect corrected, the seller may raise this as a defense against further liability with respect to the defect. Many courts have held that reasonable notice is effective even against users who did not see the notice.

Supervening Event

supervening event
An alteration or modification of a product by a party in the chain of distribution that absolves all prior sellers from strict liability.

For a seller to be held strictly liable, the product it sells must reach the consumer or user "without substantial change" in its condition. Under the doctrine of **supervening**, or **intervening, event,** the original seller is not liable if the product is materially altered or modified after it leaves the seller's possession and the alteration or modification causes an injury. A supervening event absolves all prior sellers in the chain of distribution from strict liability.

---

[4]*Brown v. Hammond*, 810 F. Supp. 644 (E.D. Pa. 1993).

Example: A manufacturer produces a safe piece of equipment. It sells the equipment to a distributor, which removes a safety guard from the equipment. The distributor sells it to a retailer, who sells it to a buyer. The buyer is injured because of the removal of the safety guard. The manufacturer can raise the defense of supervening event against the imposition of liability. However, the distributor and retailer are strictly liable for the buyer's injuries.

ETHICS SPOTLIGHT

GENERAL MOTORS LIABLE FOR DESIGN DEFECT

On Christmas Eve, Patricia Anderson was driving her Chevrolet Malibu automobile, manufactured by the General Motors Corporation (GM), home from church. Her four young children, ages one through nine, and a neighbor, were also in the car. The Chevy Malibu was stopped at a stoplight at 89th Place and Figueroa Street in Los Angeles when a drunken driver plowed his car into the back of the Malibu at 50 to 70 mph. The Malibu burst into flames as its gas tank ruptured and ignited. Although no one died in the crash, the occupants of the Malibu were severely burned. Many required substantial and multiple skin grafts.

The two injured women and four injured children sued GM for product liability. They alleged that the fuel tank of the Chevy Malibu was defectively designed and placed too close to the rear bumper. GM countered that the tragic accident was the fault of the drunken driver who struck the Malibu. The accident victims produced evidence that showed GM knew the car's fuel tank design was unsafe but had not changed the design because of cost. The Chevy Malibu was one of GM's A-Class cars, which also included the Pontiac Grand Am, the Oldsmobile Cutlass, and the Chevrolet Monte Carlo, all of which had similar fuel tank designs. The plaintiffs produced GM memos that said it would cost GM $8.59 per vehicle to produce and install a safer fuel tank design but it would cost the company only an estimated $2.40 per car not to fix the cars and pay damages to injured victims.

After a 10-week trial, the jurors returned a verdict of $107 million in compensatory damages to the plaintiffs for injuries, disfigurement, and pain and suffering caused to them by the accident. The jury then tacked on $4.9 billion as punitive damages to punish GM. This was the largest amount ever awarded in a personal injury lawsuit. After the trial, one juror stated, "We're just like numbers. Statistics. That's something that is wrong."

GM asked the trial judge to throw out the trial. GM claimed the jury was prejudiced by repetitive personal attacks on GM as a "soulless company" and its lawyers as "hired guns" who consumed "cappuccinos and designer muffins." GM did not convince the judge that such animosity influenced the jury.

In its post-trial motions, GM argued that the award of damages, specifically the $4.9 billion in punitive damages, was the result of bias and prejudice of the jury and asked the trial court judge to reduce the award of damages. The trial court judge let the compensatory damage award stand but reduced the award of punitive damages to $1 billion.

Law & Ethics Questions

1. **Ethics** Did GM's "cost–benefit" memos have much bearing on the outcome of the lawsuit? Explain.
2. **Ethics** Do you think GM deserved to be punished with punitive damages? Was the amount of punitive damages awarded appropriate? Explain.

Critical Thinking Exercise

A similar case involving GM was *Self v. General Motors Corp.*, 116 Cal. Rptr. 575 (Ct. App. 1974). The circumstances in the *Self* case are very similar to the case just discussed. In the *Self* case, a Chevrolet station wagon was involved in a traffic accident and the gas tank exploded. The injured parties sued GM on the basis of strict liability of poor design. However, the case was muddied by the character and preaccident behavior of the plaintiffs. There is also an interesting discussion of strict liability. In the *Self* case there was no mention of punitive damages.

As an exercise in critical thinking, find and read the *Self* case. Then distinguish the facts, the laws applied, and the outcomes of these two cases.

Web Exercises

1. **Web** Visit the website of General Motors Corporation at www.gm.com.
2. **Web** Use www.google.com and find an article discussing a case of strict liability where punitive damages were awarded.

Statute of Limitations and Statute of Repose

statute of limitations
Statute that establishes the time period during which a lawsuit must be brought; if the lawsuit is not brought within this period, the injured party loses the right to sue.

Most states have **statutes of limitations** that require an injured person to bring an action within a certain number of years from the time that he or she was injured by a defective product. This limitation period varies from state to state. Failure to bring an action within the appropriate time relieves the defendant of liability.

In most jurisdictions, the statute of limitations does not begin to run until the plaintiff suffers an injury. This subjects sellers and lessors to exposure for an unspecified period of time because a defective product may not cause an injury for years, or even decades, after it was sold.

statute of repose
A statute that limits the seller's liability to a certain number of years from the date when the product was first sold.

Some states have enacted **statutes of repose**. Statues of repose limit the seller's liability to a certain number of years from the date when the product was first sold. The period of repose varies from state to state.

Concept Summary

Statute of Limitation and Statute of Repose

Statute	Begins to Run
Statute of limitations	When the plaintiff suffers injury
Statute of repose	When the product is first sold

Contributory Negligence and Comparative Fault

contributory negligence
An unreasonable act or omission by the part victim (plaintiff) which, along with the defendant's negligence, is the proximate cause of the injury.

Sometimes a person who is injured by a defective product is negligent and contributes to his or her own injuries. The defense of **contributory negligence** bars an injured plaintiff from recovering from the defendant in a negligence action. However, this doctrine generally does not bar recovery in strict liability actions.

comparative fault
The measurement of damages by percentage. The victim's damages are reduced proportionate to the amount of negligence attributable to the victim.

Many states have held that the doctrine of **comparative fault** applies to strict liability actions. Under this doctrine, a plaintiff who is contributory negligent for his or her injuries is responsible for a *proportional share* of the damages. In other words, the damages are apportioned between the plaintiff and the defendant.

Example: Suppose an automobile manufacturer produces a car with a hidden defect and a consumer purchases the car from an automobile dealer. Assume the consumer is injured in an automobile accident in which the defect is found to be 75 percent responsible for the accident and the consumer's own reckless driving is found to be 25 percent responsible. The plaintiff suffers $1 million worth of injuries. Under the doctrine of *contributory negligence*, the plaintiff would recover nothing from the defendants. Under the doctrine of *comparative negligence*, the plaintiff would recover $750,000 from the defendants.

Concept Summary
Contributory Negligence and Comparative Fault

Doctrine	Description
Contributory negligence	A person partially responsible for causing his or her own injuries may not recover anything from the manufacturer or seller of a defective product that caused the remainder of the person's injuries.
Comparative fault	A person partially responsible for causing his or her own injuries is responsible for a proportional share of the damages. The manufacturer or seller of the defective product is responsible for the remainder of the plaintiff's damages.

INTERNET EXERCISES AND CASE QUESTIONS

Working the Web Internet Exercises

1. Find statistics on the most frequent type of product liability cases filed in your jurisdiction. Start with the consumer product safety data at www.cpsc.gov/library/data.html.
2. What is the statute of limitations on product liability in your jurisdiction for strict liability? See the *Restatement of Torts* Section 402A, at www.law.cornell.edu/topics/products_liability.html, which contains an overview of product liability law, with links to key primary and secondary sources.
3. Does your state have a statute of repose for product liability cases?

CHAPTER 14 SUMMARY

PRODUCT LIABILITY, p. 392

Misrepresentation

A seller or lessor fraudulently misrepresents the quality of a product, and the plaintiff relies on the misrepresentation and is injured thereby.

Negligence

A seller or lessor breaches his or her duty of due care by producing a defective product that causes injury to the plaintiff. Privity of contract between the seller or lessor and the plaintiff is not required.

STRICT LIABILITY, p. 394

Strict Liability in Tort

A manufacturer or seller who sells a defective product is liable to the ultimate user who is injured thereby. All in the chain of distribution are liable, irrespective of fault; sometimes called *vertical liability*.

DEFECTIVE PRODUCT, p. 398

The Concept of Defect

1. Defect in manufacture
2. Defect in design
3. Failure to warn
4. Defect in packaging
5. Failure to provide adequate instructions for assembly of a product
6. Other defects

DEFENSES TO PRODUCT LIABILITY, p. 415

Defenses to Product Liability

A manufacturer or seller is not liable for damages caused by a product it manufactures or sells if one of the following defenses applies:

1. *Supervening event.* The product was materially altered or modified after it left the seller's possession and the alteration or modification caused an injury. Also called *intervening event.*
2. *Generally known dangers.* A seller is not liable for failing to warn about inherent dangers in products that are known to the general population.
3. *Government contractor defense.* A manufacturer produces a product to government specifications and warns the government of any known defects in the specific design.
4. *Correction of a defect.* A manufacturer or seller who learns about a defect in a product it has sold notifies purchasers and users of the defect and corrects the defect.
5. *Assumption of the risk.* The plaintiff knew and appreciated the risk and voluntarily assumed the risk.
6. *Misuse of the product:*
   a. *Abnormal misuse.* The seller is not liable for injuries caused by the abnormal misuse of the product by the plaintiff. Also called *unforeseeable misuse.*
   b. *Foreseeable misuse.* The seller is liable for injuries caused by the foreseeable misuse of a product. The manufacturer must design products to be safe for foreseeable misuses.

Statutes of Limitations and Repose

1. *Statute of limitations.* An injured person must bring a product liability lawsuit within a specified period of time after being injured by a defective product.
2. *Statute of repose.* A person must bring a product liability lawsuit within a specified period of time after a defective product was first purchased or leased.

Contributory and Comparative Negligence

1. *Contributory negligence.* A person who is partially responsible for causing his or her own injuries may not recover anything from the manufacturer or seller of a defective product that caused the remainder of the person's injuries.
2. *Comparative negligence.* A person who is partially responsible for causing his or her own injuries is responsible for a proportional share of the damages. The manufacturer or seller of the defective product is responsible for the remainder of the plaintiff's damages. Also called *comparative fault.*

TERMS AND CONCEPTS

Abnormal misuse (unforeseeable misuse) 416
Assumption of the risk 415
Chain of distribution 395
Comparative fault 418
Contributory negligence 418
Crashworthiness doctrine 404
Defect in design 401
Defect in manufacture 398
Defect in packaging 411
Doctrine of strict liability in tort 394
Failure to provide adequate instructions 413
Failure to warn 405
Generally known dangers 415
Government contractor defense 415
Intentional misrepresentation (fraud) 394
Misrepresentation 394
Misuse 416
Negligence 392
Product defects 398
Products liability 391
Punitive damages 397
Statute of limitations 418
Statute of repose 418
Strict liability 395
Supervening event 416

CASE SCENARIO REVISITED

Remember the case at the beginning of the chapter in which Virginia Burke was injured by the champagne bottle cork? Now that you know more about the relationship of strict liability to contract law, if Burke sued Almaden to recover damages for strict liability is Almaden liable? To help you with your answer, see the case *Burke v. Almaden Vineyards, Inc.*, 150 Cal. Rptr. 419 (Ct. App. 1978).

CRITICAL LEGAL THINKING CASES

Critical Legal Thinking Case 14.1 *Strict Liability* Jeppesen and Company produces charts that graphically display approach procedures for airplanes landing at airports. These charts are drafted from tabular data supplied by the Federal Aviation Administration (FAA), an agency of the U.S. government. By law, Jeppesen cannot construct charts that include information different from that supplied by the FAA. One day, the pilot of an airplane owned by World Airways was on descent to land at the Cold Bay, Alaska, airport. The pilot was using an instrument approach procedure chart published by Jeppesen. The airplane crashed into a mountain near Cold Bay, killing all six crew members and destroying the aircraft. Evidence showed that the FAA data did not include the mountain. The heirs of the deceased crew members and World Airways brought a strict liability action against Jeppesen. Does the doctrine of strict liability apply to this case? Is Jeppesen liable? *Brocklesby v. Jeppesen & Co.*, 767 F.2d 1288 (9th Cir. 1985).

Critical Legal Thinking Case 14.2 *Failure to Warn* The Emerson Electric Co. manufactures and sells a product called the Weed Eater XR-90. The Weed Eater is a multipurpose weed-trimming and brush-cutting device. It consists of a handheld gasoline-powered engine connected to a long drive shaft, at the end of which can be attached various tools for cutting weeds and brush. One such attachment is a 10-inch circular saw blade capable of cutting through growth up to 2 inches in diameter. When this saw blade is attached to the Weed Eater, approximately 270 degrees of blade edge are exposed when in use. The owner's manual contained the following warning: "Keep children away. All people and pets should be kept at a safe distance from the work area, at least 30 feet, especially when using the blade." Donald Pearce, a 13-year-old boy, was helping his uncle clear an overgrown yard. The uncle was operating a Weed Eater XR-90 with the circular saw blade attachment. When Pearce stooped to pick up something off the ground about 6 to 10 feet behind and slightly to the left of where his uncle was operating the Weed Eater, the saw blade on the Weed Eater struck something near the ground. The Weed Eater kicked back to the left and cut off Pearce's right arm to the elbow. Pearce, through his mother, Charlotte Karns, sued Emerson to recover damages under strict liability. Is Emerson liable? *Karns v. Emerson Elec. Co.*, 817 F.2d 1452 (10th Cir. 1987).

Critical Legal Thinking Case 14.3 *Crashworthiness Doctrine* One night Verne Prior, while driving on U.S. 101 under the influence of alcohol and drugs at a speed of 65 to 85 mph, crashed his automobile into the left rear of a Chevrolet station wagon stopped on the shoulder of the freeway because of a flat tire. Christine Smith was sitting in the passenger seat of the parked car when the accident occurred. In the crash, the Chevrolet station wagon was knocked into a gully, where its fuel tank ruptured. The vehicle caught fire, and Smith suffered severe burn injuries. The Chevrolet station wagon was manufactured by General Motors Corporation. Evidence showed that the fuel tank was located in a vulnerable position in the back of the station wagon, outside the crossbars of the frame. Evidence further showed that if the fuel tank had been located underneath the body of the station wagon, between the crossbars of the frame, it would have been well protected in the collision. Smith sued General Motors for strict liability. Was the Chevrolet station wagon a defective product? *Smith v. General Motors Corp.*, 116 Cal. Rptr. 575 (Ct. App. 1974).

Critical Legal Thinking Case 14.4 *Misuse* The Wilcox-Crittendon Company manufactured harnesses, saddles, bridles, leads, and other items commonly used for horses, cattle, and other ranch and farm animals. One such item was a stallion or cattle tie, a 5-inch-long iron hook with a 1-inch ring at one end. The tongue on the ring opened outward to allow the hook to be attached to a rope or another object. In 1964, a purchasing agent for United Airlines, who was familiar with this type of hook because of earlier experiences on a farm, purchased one of them from Keystone Brothers, a harness and saddlery wares outlet located in San Francisco, California. Four years later, on March 28, 1968, Edward Dosier, an employee of United Airlines, was working to install a new grinding machine at a United Airlines maintenance plant. As part of the installation process, Dosier attached the hook to a 1,700-pound counterweight and raised the counterweight into the air. While the counterweight was suspended in the air, Dosier reached under the counterweight to retrieve a missing bolt. The hook broke, and the counterweight fell and crushed Dosier's arm. Dosier sued Wilcox-Crittendon for strict liability. Who wins? *Dosier v. Wilcox-Crittendon Co.*, 119 Cal. Rptr. 135 (Ct. App. 1975).

ETHICS CASES

Ethics Case 14.1   Celestino Luque lived with his cousins Harry and Laura Dunn in Millbrae, California. The Dunns purchased a rotary lawn mower from Rhoads Hardware. The lawn mower was manufactured by Air Capital Manufacturing Company and distributed by Garehime Corporation. Neighbors asked Luque to mow their lawn. While Luque was cutting the lawn, he noticed a small carton in the path of the lawn mower. Luque left the lawn mower in a stationary position with its motor running and walked around the side of the lawn mower to remove the carton. As he did so, he slipped on the wet grass and fell backward. Luque's left hand entered the unguarded hole of the lawn mower and was caught in its revolving blade, which turns at 175 miles per hour and 100 revolutions per second. Luque's hand was severely mangled and lacerated. The word *Caution* was printed above the unguarded hole on the lawn mower. Luque sued Rhoads Hardware, Air Capital, and Garehime Corporation for strict liability. The defendants argued that strict liability does not apply to *patent* (obvious) defects. Was it ethical for the defendants to argue they were not liable for patent defects? Would patent defects ever be corrected if the defendants' contention was accepted by the court? Who wins? *Luque v. McLean*, 501 P.2d 1163 (Cal. 1972).

BRIEFING THE CASE WRITING ASSIGNMENT

Read Case A.14 in Appendix A (*Horn v. General Motors Corporation*). This case is excerpted from a court of appeals opinion. Review and brief the case. After briefing the case, you should be able to answer the following questions:
1. What were the plaintiff's contentions upon appeal?
2. What theory of tort law was applied in this case?
3. What was the decision of the court?
4. Were damages awarded to the plaintiff?

PRACTICE TIP

Nearly all American jurisdictions have passed *lemon laws*. (Only Alabama, Arkansas, Idaho, South Carolina, and South Dakota do not have statutory lemon laws.) These are laws that provide protection in new car disputes in which the automobile was flawed from the beginning. The lemon laws recognize the "disparity of bargaining power" in the parties in vehicle purchase. The lemon laws are generally in addition to common law contract rights and UCC remedies.[5] The acts also supplement the Magnuson-Moss Warranty Act of 1975, federal legislation that protects consumers.

Remember: A "lemon" problem is severe, substantial, and resistant to repair. The lemon laws are not to remedy wear and tear or minor flaws. Paralegals should locate the lemon law statute in their jurisdiction. Remember that proving the case calls for substantial record collection and documentation. The following are the elements of most lemon law statutes:

1. A warranty breach exists.

2. The breach is substantial and material.

3. Repair efforts were permitted a particular number of times.

4. The automobile has been out of service more than a particular number of days or months.

5. The manufacturer or dealer has been put on notice.

6. Attempts have been made to arbitrate.

PARALEGAL PORTFOLIO EXERCISE

Locate the so-called lemon law for your state (or if in a state without a lemon law, locate the law in another state). In a memo titled "Lemon Law," describe (1) legislative intent of the law, (2) what constitutes a "significant defect" under the law, and (3) the time frame for corrective action.

---

[5]For example, UCC section 2-601 in which a buyer may refuse to accept, or section 2-608 in which a buyer may revoke acceptance.

The great object of the law is to encourage commerce.

—*Judge Chambre*

Beale v. Thompson, 12 U.S. 70 (1814).

Special Forms of Contracts | CHAPTER 15

CASE SCENARIO

The law firm where you work as a paralegal is representing Leroy Behlman. Leroy and 18 other football fans from Connecticut and New York decided to attend Super Bowl XII in New Orleans. They entered into contracts with Octagon Travel Center, Inc. (Octagon), a tour operator, and paid $399 each for transportation, lodging, and a ticket to Super Bowl XII. They purchased the tour package through Universal Travel Agency, Inc. (Universal), a travel agency that acts as a broker for a number of airline companies and tour operators. The individual contracts, however, were between the football fans and Octagon. When they arrived in New Orleans, no tickets to Super Bowl XII were forthcoming.

■ CHAPTER INTRODUCTION

There are special forms of contracts of which the paralegal should be aware. An in-depth discussion of these special forms of contracts—such as negotiable instruments, agency contracts, and labor contracts—is outside the scope of this textbook. However, because it is important that you have a general understanding of these contracts, an overview of these special forms of contracts is contained in this chapter.

■ NEGOTIABLE INSTRUMENTS

One special form of contract is a **negotiable instrument** (sometimes called **commercial paper**). This type of contract is important for conducting business and

negotiable instrument
Commercial paper that must meet these requirements: (1) be in writing, (2) be signed by the maker or drawer, (3) be an unconditional promise or order to pay, (4) state a fixed amount of money, (5) not require any undertaking in addition to the payment of money, (6) be payable on demand or at a definite time, and (7) be payable to order or to bearer. A special form of contract that satisfies the requirement established by Article 3 of the UCC. Also called commercial paper.

CHAPTER OBJECTIVES

After studying this chapter, you should be able to:

1. Distinguish between negotiable and nonnegotiable instruments.

2. Describe an agency contract and the liability it creates on a third party.

3. Understand the term *collective bargaining agreement*.

4. Identify the effect of bankruptcy on labor contracts.

personal affairs. In fact, in the United States, modern commerce could not continue without them. Examples of negotiable instruments include checks (such as the one that may have been used to pay for this book) and promissory notes (such as the one executed by a borrower of money to pay for tuition). An overview of the functions and types of negotiable instruments is covered in the following discussion.

Functions of Negotiable Instruments

To qualify as a negotiable instrument, a document must meet certain requirements established by Article 3 of the Uniform Commercial Code (UCC). If these requirements are met, a transferee who qualifies as a *holder in due course* (HDC) takes the instrument free of many defenses that can be asserted against the original payee. In addition, the document is considered an ordinary contract that is subject to contract law.

The concept of *negotiation* is important to the law of negotiable instruments. The primary benefit of a negotiable instrument is that it can be used as a substitute for money. As such, it must be freely transferable to subsequent parties. Technically, a negotiable instrument is negotiated when it is originally issued. The term *negotiation*, however, is usually used to describe the transfer of negotiable instruments to subsequent transferees.

Types of Negotiable Instruments

Revised Article 3 recognizes four kinds of instruments: drafts, checks, promissory notes, and certificates of deposit. Each of these is discussed in the following paragraphs.

Drafts

draft
A three-party instrument that is an unconditional written order by one party that orders the second party to pay money to a third party.

A **draft**, which is a three-party instrument, is an unconditional written order by one party (the **drawer**) that orders a second party (the **drawee**) to pay money to a third party (the **payee**) [UCC 3-104(e)]. The drawee must be obligated to pay the drawer money before the drawer can order the drawee to pay this money to a third party (the payee).

drawer of a draft
The party who writes the order for a draft.

For the drawee to be liable on a draft, the drawee must accept the drawer's written order to pay it. Acceptance is usually shown by the written word *accepted* on the face of the draft, along with the drawee's signature and the date. The drawee is called the **acceptor** of the draft because his or her obligation changes from that of having to pay the drawer to that of having to pay the payee. After the drawee accepts the draft, it is returned to the drawer or the payee. The drawer or the payee, in turn, can freely transfer it as a negotiable instrument to another party.

drawee of a draft
The party who must pay the money stated in the draft. Also called the acceptor of a draft.

acceptor
Someone who becomes liable on a draft by their acceptance of it.

Example: Mary Owens owes Hector Martinez $1,000. Martinez writes out a draft that orders Owens to pay this $1,000 to Cindy Choy. Owens agrees to this change of obligation and accepts the draft. Martinez is the drawer, Owens is the drawee, and Choy is the payee.

time draft
A draft payable at a designated future date.

A draft can be either a time draft or a sight draft. A **time draft** is payable at a designated future date. For example, language such as "pay on January 1, 2008" or "pay 120 days after date" creates a time draft (see Exhibit 15.1). A **sight draft** is payable on sight. A sight draft is also called a **demand draft**. For example, language such as "on demand pay" or "at sight pay" creates a sight draft. A draft can be both a time and a sight draft. Such a draft would provide that it is payable at a stated

sight draft
A draft payable on sight. Also called a demand draft.

demand draft
An order to pay a certain sum of money that expressly states it is payable on demand, on presentation, or on sight.

Exhibit 15.1 Time Draft

Payee

Sun Valley, Idaho   1414

One hundred and twenty (120) days after date *January 3,* 20 *08*

PAY TO THE
ORDER OF   *Kneadery Restaurant, Inc.* $ *10,000.00*

Ten Thousand and no/100   Dollars
VALUE RECEIVED AND CHARGE THE SAME TO ACCOUNT OF

Hank's Bank
100 Elkhorn Road
Sun Valley, Idaho 83353

MEMO

⑈:000000000⑈: 0000000000⑈ 1414

Michael Martin
Michael Martin

Drawee   Drawer

time after sight. For example, this type of draft is created by language such as "payable 90 days after sight."

Checks

A **check** is a distinct form of draft. It is unique in that it is drawn on a financial institution (the drawee) and is payable on demand [UCC 3-104(f)]. In other words, a check is an order to pay (see Exhibit 15.2). Most businesses and many individuals have checking accounts at financial institutions.

Like other drafts, a check is a three-party instrument. A customer who has a checking account and writes (draws) a check is the **drawer**. The financial institution on which the check is written is the **drawee**. And the party to whom the check is written is the **payee**.

check
An order by the drawer to the drawee bank to pay a specified sum of money from the drawer's checking account to the named payee (or holder). A distinct form of draft drawn on a financial institution and payable on demand.

drawer of a check
The checking account holder and writer of the check.

drawee of a check
The bank where the drawer has his or her account.

Exhibit 15.2 Check

Payee

Florence Cheeseman   16-4/1220   **1483**
123 Main Street
Westminster, NV 76543   *January 3,* 20 *07*

PAY TO THE
ORDER OF   *Gregory Cheeseman* $ *100.00*

One hundred and no/100   DOLLARS

SECURITY PACIFIC NATIONAL BANK
Wilshire-Highland Office
4929 Wilshire Blvd., Los Angeles, CA 90010

MEMO *college textbooks*   *Florence Cheeseman*

⑈:000000000⑈: 0000000000⑈ 1483   1483

Drawee   Drawer

Exhibit 15.3 Promissory Note

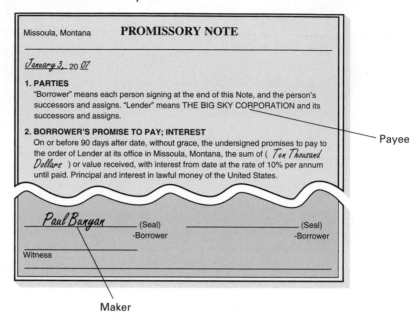

promissory note
A two-party negotiable instrument that is an unconditional written promise by one party to pay money to another party.

maker of a note
The party who makes the promise to pay (borrower).

time note
A note payable at a specific time.

demand note
A note payable on demand.

installment note
An agreement to pay a portion of a debt at successive periods until paid in full.

collateral
Security against repayment of the note that lenders sometimes require; can be a car, a house, or other property. The property that is subject to the security interest.

mortgage note
A promise to pay that secures the debt obligation.

collateral note
A note secured by personal property.

certificate of deposit (CD)
A two-party negotiable instrument that is a special form of note created when a depositor deposits money at a financial institution in exchange for the institution's promise to pay back the amount of the deposit plus an agreed-upon rate of interest upon the expiration of a set time period agreed upon by the parties.

Promissory Notes

A **promissory note** (or **note**) is an unconditional written promise by one party to pay money to another party [UCC 3-104(e)]. It is a two-party instrument (see Exhibit 15.3), not an order to pay. Promissory notes usually arise when one party borrows money from another. The note is evidence of (1) the extension of credit and (2) the borrower's promise to repay the debt.

A party who makes a promise to pay is the **maker of a note** (i.e., the borrower). The party to whom the promise to pay is made is the **payee** (i.e., the lender). A promissory note is a negotiable instrument that the payee can freely transfer to other parties.

The parties are free to design the terms of a note to fit their needs. For example, notes can be payable at a specific time (**time notes**) or on demand (**demand notes**). Notes can be made payable to a named payee or to "bearer." They can be payable in a single payment or in installments. The latter are called **installment notes**. Most notes require the borrower to pay interest on the principal.

Lenders sometimes require the maker of a note to post security for the repayment of the note. This security, which is called **collateral**, may be in the form of automobiles, houses, securities, or other property. If the maker fails to repay the note when it is due, the lender can foreclose and take the collateral as payment for the note. Notes are often named after the security that underlies the note. For example, notes secured by real estate are called **mortgage notes**, and notes secured by personal property are called **collateral notes**.

Certificates of Deposit

A **certificate of deposit (CD)** is a special form of note created when a depositor deposits money at a financial institution in exchange for the institution's promise to pay back the amount of deposit plus an agreed on rate of interest upon the expiration of a set time period agreed on by the parties [UCC 3-104(j)].

Exhibit 15.4 Certificate of Deposit

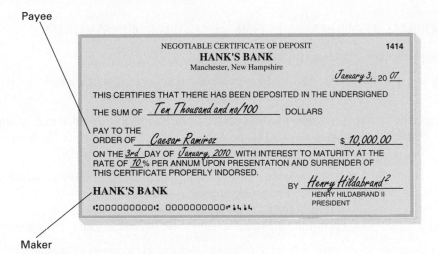

Payee

Maker

The financial institution is the borrower (the **maker**), and the depositor is the lender (the **payee**). A CD is a two-party instrument (see Exhibit 15.4). Note that a CD is a promise to pay, not an order to pay.

Unlike a regular passbook savings account, a CD is a negotiable instrument. CDs under $100,000 are commonly referred to as **small CDs**. CDs of $100,000 or more are usually called **jumbo CDs**.

small CD
A certificate of deposit under $100,000.

jumbo CD
A certificate of deposit in a very large denomination, usually at a minimum of $100,000. Also called negotiable certificates of deposit, these large investments are usually considered low-risk, stable investments for large investors.

Concept Summary

Types of Orders to Pay

Order to Pay	Parties	Description
1. Draft	Drawer	Person who issues a draft.
	Drawee	Person who owes money to a drawer; person who is ordered to pay a draft and accepts the draft.
	Payee	Person to whom a draft is made payable.
2. Check	Drawer	Owner of a checking account at a financial institution; person who issues a check.
	Drawee	Financial institution where drawer's checking account is located; party who is ordered to pay a check.
	Payee	Person to whom a check is made payable.
3. Promissory note	Maker	Party who issues a promissory note; this is usually the borrower.
	Payee	Party to whom a promissory note is made payable; this is usually the lender.
4. Certificate of deposit (CD)	Maker	Financial institution that issues a CD.
	Payee	Party to whom a CD is made payable; this is usually the depositor.

CONTEMPORARY Issue

FORMAL REQUIREMENTS FOR A NEGOTIABLE INSTRUMENT

Requirement	Description
Writing	Writing must be permanent and portable. Oral or implied instruments are nonnegotiable [UCC 3-104(d)].
Signed by maker or drawer	Signature must appear on the face of the instrument. It may be any mark intended by the signer to be his or her signature. Signature may be by an authorized representative [UCC 3-104(a)].
Unconditional promise or order to pay	Instrument must be an unconditional promise or order to pay [UCC 3-104(a)]. Permissible notations listed in UCC 3-106(a) do not affect the instrument's negotiability. If payment is conditional on the performance of another agreement, the instrument is nonnegotiable.
Fixed amount of money	Fixed amount: The amount required to discharge an instrument must be on the face of the instrument [UCC 3-104(a)]. Amount may include payment of interest and costs of collection. Revised Article 3 provides that variable interest rate notes are negotiable instruments.
	In money: Amount must be payable in U.S. or foreign country's currency. If payment is to be made in goods, services, or nonmonetary items, the instrument is nonnegotiable [UCC 3-104(a)].
Cannot require any undertaking in addition to the payment of money	A promise or an order to pay cannot state any other undertaking to do an act in addition to the payment of money [UCC 3-104(a)(3)]. A promise or an order may include authorization or power to protect collateral, dispose of collateral, waive any law intended to protect the obligee, and the like.
Payable on demand or at a definite time	Payable on demand: Payable at sight, upon presentation, or when no time for payment is stated [UCC 3-108(a)].
	Payable at a definite time: Payable at a definite date or before a stated date, a fixed period after a stated date, or at a fixed period after sight [UCC 3-108(b) and (c)]. An instrument payable only upon the occurrence of an uncertain act or event is nonnegotiable

THE ETHICAL PARALEGAL

Disruptive Courtroom Tactics

ABA Model Rule 3.5 deals with impartiality and decorum in the courtroom.[1] Although because of their role in representing the client in court, it is normally an attorney who might be involved with disruptive courtroom tactics or dirty tricks, paralegals must be aware of what constitutes courtroom decorum.

Paralegals working in civil litigation and criminal law frequently attend court proceedings with their attorneys. Because the paralegal has such a level of

(continued)

---

[1]Copies of the ABA Model Rules of Professional Conduct are available from Service Center, American Bar Association, 321 North Clark Street, Chicago, IL 60610, 1-800-285-2221. The Model Rules can also be viewed online at http://www.abanet.org/cpr/mrpc/mrpc_toc.html.

involvement and interest in the case, it is sometimes difficult to listen to the other side or hear a witness state something the paralegal knows not to be true. However, the ethical paralegals know they must not react to these untrue statements by rolling their eyes or making faces. Although the court might first warn the paralegal that his or her conduct was offensive, the judge could immediately charge the paralegal with contempt if he or she so chooses. Depending on the severity of the paralegal's behavior, such a contempt charge could result in a fine or even a jail term.

INTERNATIONAL LAW

Negotiable Instruments Payable in Foreign Currency

The UCC expressly provides that an instrument may state it is payable in foreign money [UCC 3-107]. For example, an instrument "payable in 10,000 yen in Japanese currency" is a negotiable instrument governed by Article 3 of the UCC.

Unless the instrument states otherwise, an instrument payable in foreign currency can be satisfied by the equivalent in U.S. dollars, as determined on the due date. The conversion rate is the current bank-offered spot rate at the place of payment on the due date. The instrument can expressly provide that it is payable only in the stated foreign currency. In that case, the instrument cannot be paid in U.S. dollars.

PARALEGAL PERSPECTIVE

Tracey A. Williams graduated from Roane State Community College with an associate of applied science degree in paralegal studies and received her bachelor's degree in organizational management from Tusculum College. She is a paralegal and trustee assistant with the law firm of Mostoller, Stulberg & Whitfield in Oak Ridge, Tennessee. She was certified as a bankruptcy assistant in 2004 by the Association of Bankruptcy Judicial Assistants (ABJA).

During my seven years as a paralegal, I have worked in different areas of law and all of them have dealt with contracts. In my current position as a trustee assistant, I oversee the administration of bankruptcy estates in which my attorney is appointed trustee. This involves reviewing the case for potential assets and liquidating them for a monetary distribution to creditors.

Through the process of finding assets I must review different types of contracts. On a daily basis I review security agreements, deeds of trust, promissory notes, land contracts, UCCs, and MDAs to determine the validity of the document. I must be able to locate defects and inconsistencies in the documents.

In liquidating assets I draft, for approval by my attorney, different types of contracts, such as promissory notes and deeds of trust. I also review listing agreements with real estate agents, contracts for sale on real estate, and settlement agreements with creditors. I need to understand warranty deeds, quit claim deeds, divorce documents, wills, and trust agreements in an effort to determine the type and validity of the transfer.

By knowing and understanding different types of contracts, I am able to save my attorney time and make a successful and meaningful contribution to my attorney and firm.

MARKETPLACE

■ AGENCY CONTRACTS

If businesspeople had to conduct all their business personally, the scope of their activities would be severely curtailed. Partnerships would not be able to operate, corporations could not act through managers and employees, and sole proprietorships would not be able to hire employees. The use of agents (or agency), which allows one person to act on behalf of another, solves this problem.

The many examples of agency relationships include a salesperson who sells goods for a store, an executive who works for a corporation, a partner who acts on behalf of a partnership, an attorney who is hired to represent a client, a real estate broker who is employed to sell a house, and so on. Agency is governed by a large body of common law known as **agency law**. The ability of the agent to contract for the principal is discussed in this section.

Agency Formation

Agency relationships are formed by the mutual consent of a principal and an agent. A party who employs another person to act on his or her behalf is called a **principal**. A party who agrees to act on behalf of another is called an **agent**. The principal–agent relationship is commonly referred to as an **agency**. This relationship is depicted in Exhibit 15.5.

Persons Who Can Initiate an Agency Relationship

Any person who has the capacity to contract can appoint an agent to act on his or her behalf. Generally, persons who lack **contractual capacity**, such as insane

agency law
The large body of common law that governs agency; a mixture of contract law and tort law.

principal
A person who authorizes an agent to sign a negotiable instrument on his or her behalf. The party who employs another person to act on his or her behalf.

agent
A person who has been authorized to sign a negotiable instrument on behalf of another person. The party who agrees to act on behalf of another.

agency
The principal-agent relationship: the fiduciary relationship "which results from the manifestation of consent by one person to another that the other shall act in his behalf and subject to his control, and consent by the other so to act."

contractual capacity
The legal qualification or competency to understand the nature and effects of one's acts so as to enter into a contract.

Exhibit 15.5 Principal–Agent Relationship

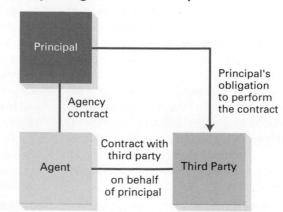

persons and minors, cannot appoint agents. However, the court can appoint a legal guardian or another representative to handle the affairs of insane persons, minors, and others who lack capacity to contract. With court approval, these representatives can enter into enforceable contracts on behalf of the persons they represent.

An agency can be created only to accomplish a lawful purpose. Agency contracts created for illegal purposes or against public policy are void and unenforceable. For example, a principal cannot hire an agent to kill another person. Some agency relationships are prohibited by law. For example, unlicensed agents cannot be hired to perform the duties of certain licensed professionals (e.g., doctors, lawyers).

Principal–Agent Relationship

A **principal–agent relationship** is formed when an employer hires an employee and gives that employee authority to act and enter into contracts on his or her behalf. The extent of this authority is governed by any express agreement between the parties and implied from the circumstances of the agency. For example, the president of a corporation usually has the authority to enter into major contracts on the corporation's behalf, and a supervisor on the corporation's assembly line may have the authority only to purchase the supplies necessary to keep the line running.

principal–agent relationship
An employer hires an employee and gives that employee authority to act and enter into contracts on his or her behalf.

Employer–Employee Relationship

An **employer–employee relationship** exists when an employer hires an employee to perform some form of physical service. For example, a welder on General Motors Corporation's assembly line is employed in an employer–employee relationship because he performs a physical task.

An employee is not an agent unless he or she is specifically empowered to enter into contracts on the principal employer's behalf. Employees may only enter into contracts that are within the scope of their employment. The welder in the previous example is not an agent because he cannot enter into contracts on behalf of General Motors Corporation. If the company empowered him to enter into contracts, he would become an agent.

employer–employee relationship
A relationship that results when an employer hires an employee to perform some form of physical service.

Contract Liability to Third Parties

A principal who authorizes an agent to enter into a contract with a third party is liable on the contract. Thus the third party can enforce the contract against the principal and recover damages from the principal if the principal fails to perform it.

Concept Summary

Kinds of Agency Relationships

Type of Relationship	Description
Principal–agent	The agent has authority to act on behalf of the principal as authorized by the principal and implied from the agency. An employee is often the agent of his employer.
Employer–employee	The employer has the right to control the physical conduct of the employee.

The agent can also be held liable on the contract in certain circumstances. Imposition of such liability depends on whether the agency is classified as (1) *fully disclosed*, (2) *partially disclosed*, or (3) *undisclosed*.

Fully Disclosed Agency

fully disclosed agency
Where the fact that the agent is acting on behalf of an agency is fully revealed and free from secrecy.

A **fully disclosed agency** results if a third party entering into a contract knows (1) that the agent is acting as an agent for a principal and (2) the actual identity of the principal. The third party has the requisite knowledge if the principal's identity is disclosed to the third party by either the agent or some other source.

In a fully disclosed agency, the contract is between the principal and the third party. Thus the principal, who is called a *fully disclosed principal*, is liable on the contract. The agent, however, is not liable on the contract because the third party relied on the principal's credit and reputation when the contract was made. An agent is liable on the contract if he or she guarantees that the principal will perform the contract.

The agent's signature on a contract entered into on the principal's behalf is important. It can establish the agent's status and, therefore, his or her liability. For instance, in a fully disclosed agency, the agent's signature must clearly indicate that he or she is acting as an agent for a specifically identified principal. Examples of proper signatures include "Allison Adams, agent for Peter Perceival," "Peter Perceival, by Allison Adams, agent," and "Peter Perceival, by Allison Adams."

Example: Poran Kawamara decides to sell her house and hires Mark Robbins, a real estate broker, to list and sell the house for a price of $1 million. They agree that Mark will disclose the existence of the agency and the identity of the principal to interested third parties. This is a fully disclosed agency. Mark shows the house to Heather, a prospective buyer, and discloses to Heather that he is acting as an agent for Poran. Heather makes an offer for the house at the $1 million asking price. Mark signs the contract with Heather on behalf of Poran by signing "Mark Robbins, agent for Poran Kawamara." Poran is liable on the contract with Heather, but Mark is not liable on the contract with Heather.

Partially Disclosed Agency

partially disclosed agency
Where the agency is partially disclosed, both the Agent and the Principal are bound.

A **partially disclosed agency** occurs if the agent discloses his or her agency status but does not reveal the principal's identity and the third party does not know the principal's identity from another source. The nondisclosure may be because (1) the principal instructs the agent not to disclose his or her identity to the third party or (2) the agent forgets to tell the third party the principal's identity. In this kind of agency, the principal is called a *partially disclosed principal*.

In a partially disclosed agency, both the principal and the agent are liable on third-party contracts. This is because the third party must rely on the agent's reputation, integrity, and credit because the principal is unidentified. If the agent is made to pay the contract, the agent can sue the principal for indemnification. The third party and the agent can agree to relieve the agent's liability. A partially disclosed agency can be created either expressly or by mistake.

Example: Assume a principal employs an agent to purchase a business on its behalf. The principal and agent expressly agree the agent will disclose the existence of the agency to third parties but will not disclose the identity of the principal. The agent finds a business for sale, and he discloses to the seller that he is acting as an agent but does not disclose the identity of the principal. The seller agrees to sell the business, and the agent signs "Allison Adams, agent." Here, there is a partially disclosed agency. The principal is liable on the contract with the third-party seller; the agent is also liable on the contract with the third-party seller.

If instead a principal and an agent agree the agent will represent the principal to purchase a business and that the agent will disclose the existence of the agency and the identity of the principal to third parties, this is a fully disclosed agency. Suppose the agent finds a suitable business for the principal and contracts to purchase the business on behalf of the principal, but the agent mistakenly signs the contract with the third party "Allison Adams, agent." This is a partially disclosed agency. The principal is liable on the contract with the third party, and the agent is also liable.

Undisclosed Agency

An **undisclosed agency** occurs when the third party is unaware of either the existence of an agency or the principal's identity. The principal is called an *undisclosed principal*. Undisclosed agencies are lawful. They are often used when the principal feels the terms of the contract would be changed if his or her identity were known. For example, a wealthy person may use an undisclosed agency to purchase property if he thinks the seller would raise the price of the property if his identity was revealed.

In an undisclosed agency, both the principal and the agent are liable on the contract with the third party. This is because the agent, by not divulging that he or she is acting as an agent, becomes a principal to the contract. The third party relies on the reputation and credit of the agent in entering into the contract. If the principal fails to perform the contract, the third party can recover against the principal of the agent. If the agent is made to pay the contract, he or she can recover indemnification from the principal. An undisclosed agency can be created either expressly or by mistake.

Example: Assume the Walt Disney Company wants to open a new theme park in Chicago but needs to first acquire land for the park. Disney employs an agent to work on its behalf to acquire the needed property, with an express agreement that the agent will not disclose the existence of the agency to a third-party seller. If a seller agrees to sell the needed land and the agent signs her name "Allison Adams," without disclosing the existence of the agency, it is an undisclosed agency. Disney is liable on the contract with the third-party seller, and so is the agent.

Suppose instead that Disney hires an agent to purchase land on its behalf and they agree the agent will represent Disney in a fully disclosed agency—that is, the agent is to disclose the existence of the agency and the identity of the principal to the third-party seller. If the agent locates a third-party seller who is willing to enter into a contract to sell the land but the agent mistakenly signs the contract "Allison Adams," without disclosing the agency to the third party, it is an undisclosed agency. Disney is liable on the contract with the third-party seller, and the agent is also liable.

Agent Exceeding the Scope of Authority

An agent who enters into a contract on behalf of another party impliedly warrants that he or she has the authority to do so. This is called the agent's **implied warranty of authority**. If the agent exceeds the scope of his or her authority, the principal is not liable on the contract unless the principal *ratifies* it. The agent, however, is liable to the third party for breaching the implied warranty of authority. To recover, the third party must show (1) reliance on the agent's representation and (2) ignorance of the agent's lack of status.

Example: Suppose Sam, Sara, Satchel, Samantha, and Simone form a rock band called SSSS. SSSS is just a voluntary association without any legal status. Sam

undisclosed agency
Where the agency is undisclosed, both the Agent and the Principal are bound.

implied warranty of authority
An agent who enters into a contract on behalf of another party impliedly warrants that he or she has the authority to do so.

enters into a contract with Rocky's Musical Instruments to purchase instruments and equipment for the band on credit and signs the contract, "Sam, for SSSS." When SSSS fails to pay the debt, Rocky's can sue Sam and recover. Sam must pay the debt because he breached his implied warranty of authority when he acted as an agent for a *nonexistent principal*; that is, the purported principal was not a legal entity on which liability could be imposed.

Concept Summary
Contract Liability of Principals and Agents to Third Parties

Type of Agency	Principal Liable	Agent Liable
Fully disclosed	Yes	No, unless the agent (1) acts as a principal or (2) guarantees the performance of the contract
Partially disclosed	Yes	Yes, unless the third party relieves the agent's liability
Undisclosed	Yes	Yes
Nonexistent	No, unless the principal ratifies the contract	Yes, the agent is liable for breaching the implied warranty of authority

Agent's Misrepresentation

intencional misrepresentation
Intentionally defrauding another person out of money, property, or something else of value. When a seller or lessor fraudulently misrepresents the quality of a product and a buyer is injured thereby. Occurs when one person consciously decides to induce another person to rely and act on a misrepresentation. Also called fraud. Occurs when an agent makes an untrue statement that he or she knows is not true.

Intentional misrepresentations are also known as **fraud** or **deceit**. They occur when an agent makes statements that he or she knows are not true. An *innocent misrepresentation* occurs when an agent negligently makes a misrepresentation to a third party.

A principal is liable for the intentional and innocent misrepresentations made by an agent acting within the scope of employment. The third party can either (1) rescind the contract with the principal and recover any consideration paid or (2) affirm the contract and recover damages.

Example: Assume that (1) a car salesperson is employed to sell the principal's car and (2) the principal tells the agent the car was repaired after it was involved in a major accident. If the agent intentionally tells the buyer the car was never involved in an accident, the agent has made an intentional misrepresentation. Both the principal and the agent are liable for this misrepresentation.

Agent Distinguished from an Independent Contractor

independent contractor
A person who contracts with another to do something for him who is not controlled by the other nor subject to the other's right to control with respect to his physical conduct in the performance of the undertaking. [Restatement (Second) of Agency].

Principals often employ outsiders—that is, persons and businesses who are not employees—to perform certain tasks on their behalf. These persons and businesses are called **independent contractors**. For example, lawyers, doctors, dentists, consultants, stockbrokers, architects, certified public accountants, real estate brokers, and plumbers are examples of people who commonly act as independent contractors. The party that employs an independent contractor is called a *principal*.

Example: Jin is a lawyer who has her own law firm and specializes in real estate law. Raymond, a real estate developer, hires Jin to represent him in the purchase of land. Raymond is the principal, and Jin is the independent contractor.

Liability for an Independent Contractor's Contracts

A principal can authorize an independent contractor to enter into contracts. Principals are bound by the authorized contracts of their independent contractors. For example, suppose a client hires a lawyer as an independent contractor to represent her in a civil lawsuit against a defendant to recover monetary damages. If the client authorizes the lawyer to settle a case within a certain dollar amount and the lawyer does so, the settlement agreement is binding.

If an independent contractor enters into a contract with a third party on behalf of the principal without express or implied authority from the principal to do so, the principal is not liable on the contract.

PARALEGAL PERSPECTIVE

Kristen A. Leeb is employed as a corporate paralegal for Hand Held Products, Inc., in Skaneateles Falls, New York. She received her paralegal education in the Certified Legal Assistant Program at Syracuse University in Syracuse, New York.

A contract is an agreement between competent parties, based on the genuine consent of the parties, supported by consideration made for a lawful objective in a form required by law, if any. When I learned these elements of a contract, I didn't realize that contracts would be prevalent in so many areas of law.

I find the contract aspect of the paralegal role to be most interesting and challenging. My first paralegal position involved complex contract litigation; thus my interest was enhanced and my skills perfected in this area. Today I report directly to the general counsel of a worldwide corporation. This corporate paralegal position requires knowledge and skills in contract drafting and review in the following areas: corporate work, subsidiary matters, mergers and acquisitions, litigation, sale of products and services, environmental, intellectual property, real property, research, and operational policies and procedures.

 ## CAREER FRONT

Job Description: Municipal Paralegal

A municipal paralegal can be involved with contracts in the following ways:

- Track cases;
- Record keeping and logging case information;
- Respond to inquiries and complaints;
- Ensure deadlines are met;
- Prepare correspondence and subpoenas;
- Perform pretrial preparation;
- Research the law on various municipal issues for municipal attorney's review;
- Prepare for trial and municipal attorney's argument of cases before courts or quasi-judicial bodies;
- Assist municipal attorney with appearances in courts to argue motions, writs, and other proceedings;
- Gather evidence;
- Conduct general research into legal matters;
- Draft briefs, motions, legal opinions, affidavits, memoranda, city contracts, and other legal papers for municipal attorney's review;
- Assist with witness preparation;
- Review city contracts for compliance with statute and policy.

Source: Excerpted by permission from the National Association of Legal Assistants (www.nala.org) and the National Federation of Paralegal Associations, Inc. (www.paralegals.org).

Agency Termination

An agency contract is similar to other contracts in that it can be terminated either by an act of the parties or by operation of law. These different methods of termination are discussed next. Note that once an agency relationship is terminated, the agent can no longer represent the principal or bind the principal to contracts.

Termination of an Agency Contract by Acts of the Parties

The parties to an agency contract can terminate the agency contract by agreement or by their actions. These are the four methods of termination of an agency contract by acts of the parties:

1. *Mutual Agreement*—As with any contract, the parties to an agency contract can mutually agree to terminate their agreement. By doing so, the parties relieve each other of any further rights, duties, obligations, or powers provided for in the agency contract. Either party can propose the termination of an agency contract.
2. *Lapse of Time*—Agency contracts are often written for a specific period of time. The agency terminates when the specified time period elapses. Suppose, for example, that the principal and agent enter into an agency contract "beginning January 1, 2008, and ending December 31, 2010." The agency automatically terminates on December 31, 2010. If the agency contract does not set forth a specific termination date, the agency terminates after a reasonable time has elapsed. The courts often look to the custom of an industry in determining the reasonable time for the termination of the agency.
3. *Purpose Achieved*—A principal can employ an agent for the time it takes to accomplish a certain task, purpose, or result. Such agencies automatically terminate when they are completed. For example, suppose a principal employs a licensed real estate broker to sell his house. The agency terminates when the house is sold and the principal pays the broker the agreed-upon compensation.
4. *Occurrence of a Specified Event*—An agency contract can specify that the agency exists until a specified event occurs. The agency terminates when the specified event happens. For example, if a principal employs an agent to take care of her dog until she returns from a trip, the agency terminates when the principal returns from the trip.

Termination of an Agency Contract by Operation of Law

Agency contracts can be terminated by operation of law as well as by agreement of the parties. The six methods of terminating an agency relationship by operation of law are as follows:

1. *Death*—The death of either the principal or the agent terminates an agency relationship. This rule is based on the old legal principle that because a dead person cannot act, no one can act for him or her. Note that the agency terminates even if one party is unaware of the other party's death. An agent's actions that take place after the principal's death do not bind the principal's estate.
2. *Insanity*—The insanity of either the principal or the agent generally terminates an agency relationship. A few states have modified this rule to provide that a contract entered into by an agent on behalf of an insane principal is enforceable if (a) the insane person has not been adjudged

insane, (b) the third party does not have knowledge of the principal's insanity at the time of contracting, and (c) the enforcement of the contract will prevent injustice.

3. **Bankruptcy**—An agency relationship is terminated if the principal is declared bankrupt. Bankruptcy requires the filing of a petition for bankruptcy under federal bankruptcy law.[2] With a few exceptions, neither the appointment of a state court receiver nor the principal's financial difficulties or insolvency terminates the agency relationship. The agent's bankruptcy usually does not terminate an agency unless the agent's credit standing is important to the agency relationship.

4. **Impossibility**—An agency relationship terminates if a situation arises that makes its fulfillment impossible. The following circumstances can lead to termination on this ground:

   a. *The loss or destruction of the subject matter of the agency.* For example, assume a principal employs an agent to sell his horse, but the horse dies before it is sold. The agency relationship terminates at the moment the horse dies.

   b. *The loss of a required qualification.* For example, suppose a principal employs a licensed real estate agent to sell her house, and the real estate agent's license is revoked. The agency terminates at the moment the license is revoked.

   c. *A change in the law.* For example, suppose a principal employs an agent to trap alligators. If a law is passed that makes trapping alligators illegal, the agency contract terminates when the law becomes effective.

5. **Changed Circumstances**—An agency terminates when there is an unusual change in circumstances that would lead the agent to believe the principal's original instructions should no longer be valid. For example, a principal employs a licensed real estate agent to sell a farm for $100,000. The agent thereafter learns that oil has been discovered on the property and makes it worth $1 million. The agency terminates because of this change in circumstances.

6. **War**—The outbreak of war between the principal's country and the agent's country terminates an agency relationship between the parties. Such an occurrence usually makes the performance of the agency contract impossible.

■ LABOR CONTRACTS

Before the Industrial Revolution, the doctrine of laissez-faire governed the employment relationship in this country. Generally, this meant that employment was subject to the common law of contracts and agency law. In most instances, employees and employers had somewhat equal bargaining power.

This changed dramatically when the country became industrialized in the late 1800s. For one thing, large corporate employers had much more bargaining power than their employees. For another, the issues of child labor, unsafe working conditions, long hours, and low pay caused concern. Both federal and state legislation sought to protect workers' rights, and labor unions were made lawful. Today, labor law is a mixture of contract law, agency law, and government regulation.

This section discusses labor law and collective bargaining agreements as they relate to contract law.

---

[2]See the discussion on bankruptcy later in this chapter.

Labor Law

In the 1880s, few laws protected workers against employment abuses. The workers reacted by organizing unions in an attempt to gain bargaining strength. Unlike unions in many European countries, unions in the United States did not form their own political party. By the early 1900s, employers used violent tactics against workers who were trying to organize into unions. The courts generally sided with employers in such disputes.

The **American Federation of Labor (AFL)** was formed in 1886, under the leadership of Samuel Gompers. Only skilled craft workers such as silversmiths and artisans were allowed to belong. In 1935, John L. Lewis formed the **Congress of Industrial Organizations (CIO)**. The CIO permitted semiskilled and unskilled workers to become members. In 1955, the AFL and CIO combined to form the **AFL-CIO**. Individual unions (such as the United Auto Workers and United Steel Workers) may choose to belong to the AFL-CIO, but not all unions opt to join.

Today, approximately 15 percent of private-sector wage and salary workers belong to labor unions. Many government employees also belong to unions.

American Federation of Labor (AFL)
One of the first federations of labor unions in the United States.

Congress of Industrial Organizations (CIO)
A federation of unions that organized workers in industrial unions in the United States and Canada from 1935 to 1955. The CIO was more aggressive and militant than the American Federation of Labor (AFL). The CIO merged with the AFL in 1955.

AFL-CIO
The 1955 combination of the AFL and the CIO.

LANDMARK LAW

FEDERAL LABOR UNION STATUTES

In the early 1900s, members of the labor movement lobbied Congress to pass laws to protect their rights to organize and bargain with management. During the Great Depression of the 1930s, several statutes were enacted to give workers certain rights and protections. Other statutes have been added since then. These are the major federal statutes in this area:

- *Norris–LaGuardia Act.* Enacted in 1932, this act stipulates that it is legal for employees to organize.[3]
- *National Labor Relations Act (NLRA).* This act, also known as the Wagner Act, was enacted in 1935.[4] The NLRA establishes the right of employees to form, join, and assist labor organizations; to bargain collectively with employers; and to engage in concerted activity to promote these rights.
- *Labor–Management Relations Act.* In 1947, Congress enacted the Labor–Management Relations Act (the Taft-Hartley Act).[5] This act (1) expands the activities that labor unions can engage in, (2) gives employers the right to engage in free-speech efforts against unions prior to a union election, and (3) gives the president of

the United States the right to seek an injunction (for up to 80 days) against a strike that would create a national emergency.
- *Labor–Management Reporting and Disclosure Act.* Congress enacted the Labor-Management Reporting and Disclosure Act of 1959 (the Landrum-Griffin Act).[6] This act regulates internal union affairs and establishes the rights of union members.
- *Railway Labor Act.* The Railway Labor Act of 1926, as amended in 1934, covers employees of railroad and airline carriers.[7]

NATIONAL LABOR RELATIONS BOARD (NLRB)

The National Labor Relations Act created the **National Labor Relations Board (NLRB)**. The NLRB is an administrative body comprised of five members appointed by the president and approved by the Senate. The NLRB oversees union elections, prevents employers and unions from engaging in illegal and unfair labor practices, and enforces and interprets certain federal labor laws. The decisions of the NLRB are enforceable in court.

National Labor Relations Board (NLRB)
A federal administrative agency that oversees union elections, prevents employers and unions from engaging in illegal and unfair labor practices, and enforces and interprets certain federal labor laws.

[3] 29 U.S.C. §§ 101–110, and 113–115.
[4] 29 U.S.C. §§ 151–169.
[5] 29 U.S.C. §§ 141 *et seq.*
[6] 29 U.S.C. §§ 401 *et seq.*
[7] 45 U.S.C. §§ 151–162, and 181–188.

In Case 15.1, the U.S. Supreme Court addressed the issue of whether an employer had to allow nonemployee union organizers on its property.

CASE 15.1 ORGANIZING A UNION

Lechmere, Inc. v. NLRB, 499 U.S. 918 (1991).

Facts

Lechmere, Inc. (Lechmere), owned and operated a retail store in the Lechmere Shopping Plaza in Newington, Connecticut. Thirteen smaller stores were located between Lechmere's store and the parking lot, which was owned by Lechmere. In June 1987, the United Food and Commercial Workers Union, AFL-CIO (Union), attempted to organize Lechmere's 200 employees, none of whom belonged to a union. After a full-page advertisement in a local newspaper drew little response, nonemployee union organizers entered Lechmere's parking lot and began placing handbills on windshields of cars parked in the employee section of the parking lot. Lechmere's manager informed the organizers that Lechmere prohibited solicitation or handbill distribution of any kind on the property and asked them to leave. They did so, and Lechmere personnel removed the handbills. Union organizers renewed their handbill effort in the parking lot on several subsequent occasions, but each time, they were asked to leave, and the handbills were removed. Union filed a grievance with the NLRB. The NLRB ruled in favor of Union and ordered Lechmere to allow handbill distribution in the parking lot. The court of appeals affirmed. Lechmere appealed to the U.S. Supreme Court.

Issue

May a store owner prohibit nonemployee union organizers from distributing leaflets in a shopping mall parking lot owned by the store?

Court's Reasoning

The U.S. Supreme Court cited the general rule that an employer cannot be compelled to allow distribution of union literature by nonemployee union organizers on its property. The Supreme Court noted, however, that an exception applies if the employees would otherwise live and work beyond the reach of reasonable union efforts to communicate with them. The Court held that this exception did not apply in this case. The Court cited the fact that the employees lived in a metropolitan area and that the union could advertise in the media and could stand on the public area adjoining Lechmere's parking lot to inform the employees of the union's organizational effort. The Supreme Court concluded, "Access to employees, not success in winning them over, is the critical issue."

Decision

The U.S. Supreme Court held that under the facts of this case, Lechmere could prohibit nonemployee union organizers from distributing leaflets to employees in the store's parking lot. The Supreme Court reversed the decision of the court of appeals.

Law & Ethics Questions

1. Should property rights take precedence over a union's right to organize employees?

2. **Ethics** Is it ethical for an employer to deny union organizers access to company property to conduct their organization efforts? Is it ethical for union organizers to demand this as a right?

3. What implications does this case have for business? Is this a pro- or antibusiness decision?

Collective Bargaining

Once a union has been elected, the employer and the union discuss the terms of employment of union members and try to negotiate a labor contract that embodies these terms. The act of negotiating this labor contract is called **collective bargaining**. The resulting labor contract is called a **collective bargaining agreement**. The employer and the union must negotiate with each other in good faith. Among other things, this prohibits making take-it-or-leave-it proposals.

The subjects of collective bargaining are classified as follows:

- *Compulsory subjects*—Wages, hours, and other terms and conditions of employment are compulsory subjects of collective bargaining. Fringe benefits, health benefits, retirement plans, work assignments, safety rules, and the like, are included in this category.
- *Illegal subjects*—Subjects such as closed shops and discrimination are illegal subjects and may not be negotiated.
- *Permissive subjects*—Subjects that are not compulsory or illegal are permissive subjects of collective bargaining. These include such issues as the size and composition of the supervisory force, location of plants, corporate reorganizations, and the like. These subjects may be bargained for if the company and union agree to do so.

Effect of Bankruptcy on Labor Contracts

Similar to the earlier discussion regarding the effect of a bankruptcy on agency contracts, **labor contracts** can be profoundly affected by bankruptcy law. For instance, even after the company and the union have bargained in good faith to establish a labor contract, a company filing for Chapter 11 bankruptcy can petition the bankruptcy court to reject and/or modify that collective bargaining agreement. The effect of a bankruptcy on the labor contract is discussed in this section.

Debtors, normally companies, filing for Chapter 11 reorganization sometimes have collective bargaining agreements with labor unions that require the payment of agreed-upon wages and other benefits to union member-employees for some agreed-upon period in the future. Debtors also often have contracts to pay union and nonunion retired employees and their dependents medical, surgical, hospitalization, dental, and death benefits (retiree benefits). What happens to those labor contracts when a company files bankruptcy is an important issue in the paralegal's study of contract law.

Debtors using bankruptcy reorganization as a tool to avoid collective bargaining agreements was a serious issue when the U.S. Supreme Court held, in *NLRB v. Bildisco & Bildisco*, that collective bargaining agreements are "executory contracts" and thus subject to rejection. After that Supreme Court decision, Congress amended the

collective bargaining
The act of negotiating contract terms between an employer and the members of a union.

collective bargaining agreement
The resulting contract from a collective bargaining procedure.

labor contract
Also called a collective bargaining agreement that applies to the employees a union represents. The collective bargaining agreement defines the terms and conditions of employment for represented employees.

Bankruptcy Code to prevent debtors from *misusing* Chapter 11 to reject collective bargaining agreements.[8] Although this is a very complicated issue, you should remember that if certain circumstances are met—including that the debtor's financial situation under the Chapter 11 is clearly benefited by rejecting the collective bargaining agreement—the labor contract *can* be modifed or even rejected *NLRB v. Bildisco & Bildisco*, 465 U.S. 513 (1984).

Another important point to remember is that the burden of proof in these collective bargaining matters is on the bankruptcy trustee. Until the collective bargaining agreement is ruled on by the court, it remains in force. An important case on collective bargaining agreements and bankruptcy is *In Re Unimet Corp.*, 842 F.2d 879 (6th Cir. 1988), cert. denied, 488 U.S. 828 (1989).

CONTEMPORARY Issue

CHAPTER 11 DEBTOR CAN REJECT COLLECTIVE BARGAINING AGREEMENT

If the Chapter 11 debtor wishes to reject the collective bargaining agreement, the Bankruptcy Code requires the following multistep process:

1. The debtor makes a proposal to the union or representative that sets forth its proposed modifications.
2. The debtor meets with the union or representative to discuss the proposal and confers in good faith in an attempt to reach a mutually satisfactory modification.
3. The union or representative refuses to accept the proposal without good cause.

If these steps have been taken, the court holds a hearing. The court may order the rejection of the collective bargaining agreement or modification of retiree benefits if it finds that the "balance of equities" favors rejection or modification of the labor contract and that rejection or modification is necessary to the reorganization of the company in the bankruptcy.

INTERNET EXERCISES AND CASE QUESTIONS

Working the Web Internet Exercises

1. Does your state have special laws covering digital signatures? See the law review article "Couriers Without Luggage: Negotiable Instruments and Digital Signature," by Jane Kaufman Winn, at www.law.sc.edu/sclr/vo149-4-winn.pdf.
2. Visit Nolo Press at www.nolo.com/category/ic_home.html to find general information regarding the classification of independent contractors versus employees.
3. One way to create an agency is to execute a power of attorney. See smallbiz.biz.findlaw.com/bookshelf/sblg/sblgchp13_f.html for information and www.njlaws.com/power_of_attorney.htm for a form.
4. For an overview of labor law, see "Labor and Employment Law," at jurist.law.pitt.edu/sg_lab.htm.
5. After September 11, a number of airlines—Delta, Northwest, and United—filed for bankruptcy protection. Under United's Chapter 11 reorganization plan, the airline was permitted to drop its four pension plans that covered

---

[8]The collective bargaining agreement section only applies in Chapter 11 cases under Section 1113 of the Bankruptcy Abuse Prevention and Consumer Protection Act of 2005.

120,000 current and retired United workers. As a result, employees lost thousands of dollars from their pensions each year. For more on United's bankruptcy, go to www.usatoday.com and search under "United Airlines."

CHAPTER 15 SUMMARY

NEGOTIABLE INSTRUMENTS, p. 427

Negotiable instrument. A special form of contract that satisfies the requirement established by Article 3 of the UCC. Also called *commercial paper.*

Instrument. Term that means *negotiable instrument.*

Article 3 of the UCC. A model code that establishes rules for the creation of, transfer of, enforcement of, and liability on negotiable instruments.

Draft. A three-party instrument that is an unconditional written order by one party that orders the second party to pay money to a third party.

Drawer of a draft. The party who writes an order for a draft.

Drawee of a draft. The party who must pay the money stated in a draft. Also called the *acceptor* of a draft.

payee of a draft
The party who receives the money from a draft.

Payee of a draft. The party who receives the money from a draft.

Check. A distinct form of draft drawn on a financial institution and payable on demand.

Drawer of a check. The checking account holder and writer of a check.

Drawee of a check. The financial institution where a drawer has his or her account.

payee of a check
The party to whom the check is written.

Payee of a check. The party to whom a check is written.

Promissory note. A two-party negotiable instrument that is an unconditional written promise by one party to pay money to another party.

Maker of a note. The party who makes a promise to pay (borrower).

payee of a note
The party to whom the promise to pay is made (lender).

Payee of a note. The party to whom a promise to pay is made (lender).

Collateral. Security against repayment of a note that lenders sometimes require; can be a car, a house, or other property.

Certificate of deposit (CD). A two-party negotiable instrument that is a special form of note created when a depositor deposits money at a financial institution in exchange for the institution's promise to pay back the amount of the deposit plus an agreed-upon rate of interest upon the expiration of a set time period agreed upon by the parties.

maker of a CD
The bank (borrower).

Maker of a CD. The financial institution that issues a CD (borrower).

payee of a CD
The depositor (lender).

Payee of a CD. The party to whom a CD is made payable; usually the depositor (lender).

Permanency requirement. A requirement of negotiable instruments that says they must be in a permanent state, such as written on ordinary paper.

Portability requirement. A requirement of negotiable instruments that says they must be able to be easily transported between areas.

signature requirement
A negotiable instrument must be signed by the drawer or maker. Any symbol executed or adopted by a party with a present intent to authenticate a writing qualifies as his or her signature.

Signature requirement. A requirement that states a negotiable instrument must be signed by the drawer or maker. Any symbol executed or adopted by a party with a present intent to authenticate a writing qualifies as his or her signature.

AGENCY CONTRACTS, p. 434

Agency law. The large body of common law that governs agency; a mixture of contract law and tort law.

Principal. A party who employs another person to act on his or her behalf.

Agent. A party who agrees to act on behalf of another.

Agency. The principal–agent relationship; the fiduciary relationship which results from the manifestation of consent by one person to another that the other shall act in his behalf and subject to his control, and consent by the other so to act.

Principal–agent relationship. A relationship formed when an employer hires an employee and gives that employee authority to act and enter into contracts on his or her behalf.

Employer–employee relationship. A relationship that results when an employer hires an employee to perform some form of physical service.

Independent contractor. A person or business that is not an employee but is employed by a principal to perform a certain task on his behalf.

Power of attorney. An express agency agreement that is often used to give an agent the power to sign legal documents on behalf of the principal.

LABOR CONTRACTS, p. 441

Federal Labor Statutes

Federal labor statutes include the following:

1. *Norris-LaGuardia Act.* This act made it legal for employees to organize.
2. *National Labor Relations Act.* This act established the right of employees to form, join, and assist labor unions. Also called the *Wagner Act* or *NLRA.*
3. *Labor-Management Relations Act.* This act expanded the activities labor unions could engage in, gave employers free speech rights to oppose unionization, and gave the president the right to seek injunctions against strikes that would create a national emergency. Also called the *Taft-Hurley Act.*
4. *Labor-Management Reporting and Disclosure Act.* Called labor's "bill of rights," this act gives union members the right to nominate candidates for union offices and vote in union elections. Also called the *Landrum-Griffin Act.*
5. *Railway Labor Act.* This act governs union rights of railroad and airline employees.

National Labor Relations Board (NLRB)

This federal administrative agency is empowered to administer federal labor law, oversee union elections, and decide labor disputes.

Organizing a Union

1. *Section 7 of the NLRA.* This section gives employees the right to join together and form a union.
2. *Appropriate bargaining union.* An appropriate bargaining union is a group of employees that a union is seeking to represent.

Collective Bargaining

Collective bargaining is a process whereby the union and employer negotiate the terms and conditions of employment for the covered employee union members.

1. *Collective bargaining agreement.* This is a contract resulting from collective bargaining.

Subjects of Collective Bargaining

1. *Compulsory subjects.* Compulsory subjects are wages, hours, and other terms and conditions of employment (e.g., vacations, medical benefits).

2. ***Illegal subjects.*** Illegal subjects are subjects that may not be negotiated (e.g., discrimination).
3. ***Permissive subjects.*** Permissive subjects are not compulsory or illegal (e.g., closing of plants).

TERMS AND CONCEPTS

Acceptor   428
AFL-CIO   442
Agency law   434
Agent   434
Agency   434
American Federation of Labor (AFL)   442
Certificate of deposit (CD)   430
Check   429
Collateral   430
Collateral note   430
Collective bargaining   444
Collective bargaining agreement   444
Congress of Industrial Organizations (CIO)   442
Contractual capacity   434
Demand draft   428
Demand note   430
Draft   428
Drawee of a draft   428
Drawee of a check   429
Drawer of a check   429
Drawer of a draft   428
Employer–employee relationship   435
Fully disclosed agency   436
Implied warranty of authority   437
Independent contractor   438
Installment note   430
Intentional misrepresentations (fraud or deceit) 438
Jumbo CD   431
Labor contract   444
Maker of a note   430
Maker of a CD   446
Mortgage note   430
National Labor Relations Board (NLRB)   442
Negotiable instrument (commercial paper)   427
Partially disclosed agency   436
Payee of a CD   446
Payee of a check   446
Payee of draft   446

Payee of a note   446

Principal   434

Principal–agent relationship   435

Promissory note (note)   430

Sight draft   428

Signature requirement   446

Small CD   431

Time draft   428

Time note   430

Undisclosed agency   437

CASE SCENARIO REVISITED

Remember the case scenario at the beginning of the chapter involving Leroy Behlman and the other football fans who contracted with Octagon Travel Center, Inc., for tickets to the Super Bowl? Now that you know more about agency law and the agent's ability to contract, do you believe Universal is liable? For assistance in answering this question, look at the case *Behlman v. Universal Travel Agency, Inc.*, 496 A.2d 962 (Conn. App. Ct. 1985).

CRITICAL LEGAL THINKING CASES

Critical Legal Thinking Case 15.1 *Negotiable Instrument: Note*   On August 17, 1979, Sandra McGuire and her husband entered into a contract to purchase the inventory, equipment, accounts receivable, and name of "Becca's Boutique" from Pascal and Rebecca Tursi. Becca's Boutique was a clothing store owned as a sole proprietorship by the Tursis. The McGuires agreed to purchase the store for $75,000, with a down payment of $10,000 and the balance to be paid by October 5, 1979. The promissory note signed by the McGuires read: "For value received, Thomas J. McGuire and Sandra A. McGuire, husband and wife, do promise to pay to the order of Pascal and Rebecca Tursi the sum of $65,000." Is the note an order to pay or a promise to pay? *P.P. Inc. v. McGuire*, 509 F. Supp. 1079 (D.N.J. 1981).

Critical Legal Thinking Case 15.2 *Creation of an Agency*   Renaldo, Inc., d.b.a. Baker Street, owns and operates a nightclub in Georgia. On the evening in question, plaintiff Ginn became "silly drunk" at the nightclub and was asked by several patrons and the manager to leave the premises. The police were called, and Ginn left the premises. When Ginn realized his jacket was still in the nightclub, he attempted to reenter the premises. He was met at the door by the manager, who refused him admittance. When Ginn persisted, an unidentified patron, without the approval of the manager, pushed Ginn, who lost his balance and fell backward. To break his fall, Ginn put his hand against the door jamb. The unidentified patron slammed the door on Ginn's hand and held it shut for several minutes. Ginn, who suffered severe injuries to his right hand, sued the nightclub for damages. Was the unidentified patron an agent of the nightclub? *Ginn v. Renaldo, Inc.*, 359 S.E.2d 390 (Ga. Ct. App. 1987).

Critical Legal Thinking Case 15.3 *Student Loan Agreements and Bankruptcy*   Woodcock graduated from law school and finished his MBA in

1983. His student loans came due nine months later. Because he was a part-time student until 1990, he requested that payment be deferred, which the lender incorrectly approved. He was not in a degree program, so payment should not have been deferred under the terms of the loan. Woodcock filed for bankruptcy in 1992, more than seven years after the loans first became due. So that debt would be discharged unless there was an "applicable suspension of the repayment period." Should Woodcock's student loan contract be discharged through filing for bankruptcy? *Woodcock v. Chemical Bank*, 144 F.3d 1340 (10th Cir. 1998).

ETHICS CASES

Ethics Case 15.1 Mullins Enterprises, Inc. (Mullins), was a business operating in the state of Kentucky. To raise capital, Mullins obtained loans from Corbin Deposit Bank & Trust Company (Corbin). Between 1971 and 1975, Corbin made eight loans to Mullins. Mullins executed a promissory note setting out the amount of the debt, the dates and times of installment payments, and the date of final payment and delivered it to the bank each time a loan was made. The notes were signed by an officer of Mullins. In 1980, a dispute arose between Mullins and Corbin as to the proper interpretation of the language contained in the notes. The bank contended that the notes were demand notes. Mullins claimed the notes were time instruments. Did Corbin or Mullins act unethically in this case? Or was this just a legal dispute? Who wins? *Corbin Deposit Bank & Trust Co. v. Mullins Enter., Inc.*, 641 S.W.2d 760 (Ky. Ct. App. 1982).

Ethics Case 15.2 Mike J. Rogers, owner of Arkansas Parts and Equipment Company (Arkansas Parts), invited Paul Mollenhour to be an officer of the business. Rogers wanted Mollenhour to join the business because his strong financial position would allow Rogers to secure operating financing more easily. With Mollenhour's assistance, Arkansas Parts secured financing in 1986. On February 19, 1986, Arkansas Parts executed a revolving credit note with State First National Bank of Texarkana (State First) in the amount of $150,000. The note was signed as follows:

/s/Mike Rogers

_____

Mike Rogers, Individually

/s/Dave Mollenhour, V. Pres.

_____

Dave Mollenhour, Individually

EQUIPMENT CO., INC.

_____

by: /s/Mike Rogers

_____

Mike Rogers, President

by: /s/Dave Mollenhour, V. Pres.

_____

Dave Mollenhour, Vice President and Secretary

The note stipulated that the parties were jointly and severally obligated to State First. After Arkansas Parts defaulted on the note, State First sued Arkansas Parts and Rogers and Mollenhour, individually. Mollenhour claimed he is not liable because his signature indicated his representative capacity. Who wins? Did Mollenhour act ethically in this case? *Mollenhour v. State First Nat'l Bank of Texarkana*, 769 S.W.2d 28 (Ark. Ct. App. 1989).

Ethics Case 15.3   The Hagues, husband and wife, owned a 160-acre tract they decided to sell. On March 19, 1976, they entered into a listing agreement with Harvey C. Hilgendorf, a licensed real estate broker, which gave Hilgendorf the exclusive right to sell the property for a period of 12 months. The Hagues agreed to pay Hilgendorf a commission of 6 percent of the accepted sale price if a bona fide buyer was found during the listing period.

By letter on August 13, 1976, the Hagues terminated the listing agreement with Hilgendorf. Hilgendorf did not acquiesce to the Hagues' termination, however. On September 30, 1976, Hilgendorf presented an offer to the Hagues from a buyer willing to purchase the property at the full listing price. The Hagues ignored the offer and sold the property to another buyer. Hilgendorf sued the Hagues for breach of the agency agreement. Did the Hagues act ethically in this case? Who wins the lawsuit? *Hilgendorf v. Hague*, 293 N.W.2d 272 (Iowa 1980).

BRIEFING THE CASE WRITING ASSIGNMENT

Read Case A.15 in the Case Appendix (*Simpson v. Norwesco, Inc.*, 583 F.2d 1007 (8th Cir. 1978). This case is excerpted from the court of appeals opinion. Review and brief the case. After briefing the case, you should be able to answer the following questions:

1. Who was the plaintiff? Who was the defendant?
2. What did the defendant do that caused the plaintiff to file this action?
3. What is an unfair labor practice?
4. Did the court find an unfair labor practice in this case?

PRACTICE TIP

As you saw in the section on labor law, the filing of a bankruptcy can have serious implications on a collective bargaining agreement. Although that is an important effect, you should be aware that a bankruptcy can lead to the automatic termination of other relationships and other contracts as well.

In October 2005, the Bankruptcy Abuse Prevention and Consumer Protection Act of 2005 (BAPCPA) took effect. This revision led to some of the most comprehensive changes to bankruptcy law in over 25 years. Because of the BAPCPA's effect on contracts, you should have some familiarity with this law, no matter the area of law in which you work.

First of all, remember that the discharge of a contract as a result of a bankruptcy happens not by anything the parties do but, rather, by operation of law. As you learned in previous chapters, contracts that have obligations due on both sides are "executory contracts." In bankruptcy Chapters 7, 11 and 13 cases,[9] BAPCPA sets out time limits for accepting or rejecting executory contracts. So, again, it is not the *filing* of the bankruptcy that terminates a contract, it is either the explicit rejection of the contract or the passage of a deadline that terminates the contract,

---

[9]A bankruptcy "Chapter 7" case is the most familiar form of bankruptcy. This is where the debtor's nonexempt property is sold for cash, the cash is distributed to the creditors, and any unpaid debts are discharged. In a "Chapter 11" bankruptcy case, there is a reorganization of the debtor's financial affairs under the supervision of the Bankruptcy Court. Most times, a Chapter 11 bankruptcy case is filed by a company or a corporation. The "Chapter 13" is a rehabilitation form of bankruptcy that permits the courts to supervise the debtor's plan for the payment of unpaid debts in installments.

if the debtor or the other party(s) *both* have some obligation remaining under the agreement.

For an example, think about a cell phone contract. If a debtor with a cell phone contract files a bankruptcy case (usually a Chapter 7 or a Chapter 13), the debtor either has to assume the cell phone contract explicitly (in other words, agree to continue to pay on the contract after the bankruptcy case is over) or the cell phone contract is rejected automatically at the conclusion of the bankruptcy case.

But if the bankruptcy court finds that the cell phone contract is *executory*, the contract remains in force. BAPCPA sets deadlines for assumption or rejection of executory contracts.

Some executory contracts can't be assumed where the services are "personal" to the debtor. For example, a recording contract for a major recording artist who filed bankruptcy could not be enforced, even though it was executory. The bankruptcy court could not force the singer to continue to perform under his or her contract with the recording studio.

LIST OF CASES REPORTED

1-A Equip. Co. v. Icode, Inc., 2003 Mass. App. Div. 30 (Dist. Ct. 2003). 281

A&M Produce Co. v. FMC Corp., 186 Cal. Rptr. 114 (Ct. App. 1982). 310

A.M. Knitwear v. All Am., Etc., 359 N.E.2d (N.Y. 1976). 334

Accrued Fin. Serv., Inc. v. Prime Retail, Inc., 298 F.3d 291 (4th Cir. 2002). 178

Alba v. Kaufmann, 810 N.Y.S.2d 539 (App. Div. 2006). 229

Alden v. Presley, 637 S.W.2d 862 (Tenn. 1982). 70

Alimenta (U.S.A.), Inc. v. Cargill, Inc., 861 F.2d 650 (11th Cir. 1988). 195

Allied Grape Growers v. Bronco Wine Co., 203 Cal. App. 3d 432 (1988). 155, 162

Allsopp Sand & Gravel v. Lincoln Sand & Gravel, 525 N.E.2d 1185 (Ill. App. Ct. 1988). 363

Alston v. Monk, 373 S.E.2d 463 (N.C. Ct. App. 1988). 123

Archer Daniels Midland v. Charter Int'l Oil Co., 60 B.R. 854 (M.D. Fla. 1986). 362

Architectural Systems, Inc. v. Gilbane Bldg. Co., 760 F. Supp. 79 (D.Md. 1991). 188

Aronowicz v. Nalley's, Inc., 106 Cal. Rptr. 424 (Ct. App. 1972). 87

Atlantic Wholesale Co. v. Solondz, 320 S.E.2d 720 (S.C. Ct. App. 1984). 169

Bain v. Gillispie, 357 N.W.2d 47 (Iowa Ct. App. 1984). 186

Barnes v. Treece, 549 P.2d 1152 (Wash. Ct. App. 1976). 144

Barrows v. Maco, Inc., 419 N.E.2d 634 (Ill. App. Ct. 1981). 200

Bates v. Arizona, 433 U.S. 350 (1977). 382

Beachcomber Coins, Inc. v. Boskett, 400 A.2d 78 (N.J. Sup. Ct. App. Div. 1979). 147

Beale v. Thompson, 12 U.S. 70 (1814). 426

Beavers v. Weatherly, 299 S.E.2d 730 (Ga. 1983). 122

Behlman v. Universal Travel Agency, Inc., 496 A.2d 962 (Conn. App. Ct. 1985). 449

Benedi v. McNeil-P.P.C., Inc., 66 F.3d 1378 (4th Cir. 1995). 393

Berliner Foods Corp. v. Pillsbury Co., 633 F. Supp. 557 (D. Md. 1986). 201

Beverly Glen Music, Inc. v. Warner Commc'ns, Inc., 224 Cal. Rptr. 260 (Ct. App. 1986). 242

Bickham v. Washington Bank & Trust Co., 515 So. 2d 457 (La. App. 1987). 30

Big Knob Volunteer Fire Co. v. Lowe & Meyer Garage, 487 A.2d 953 (Pa. Super. Ct. 1985). 332

Bill Branch Chevrolet v. Redmond, 378 So. 2d 319 (Fla. Dist. Ct. App. 1980). 385

Blye v. American Broad. Co. Merch., Inc., 476 N.Y.S.2d 874 (App. Div. 1984). 172

Bobby Floars Toyota, Inc. v. Smith, 269 S.E.2d 320 (N.C. Ct. App. 1980). 122

Briggs v. Sackett, 418 A.2d 586 (Pa. Super. Ct. 1980). 170

Brocklesby v. Jeppesen & Co., 767 F.2d 1288 (9th Cir. 1985). 422

Brown v. Hammond, 810 F. Supp. 644 (E.D. Pa. 1993). 416

Brumfield v. Death Row Records, Inc., No. B149561, 2003 Cal. LEXIS 7843, at *1 (Ct. App. Unpub. Aug. 19, 2003). 235

Burke v. Almaden Vineyards, Inc., 150 Cal. Rptr. 419 (Ct. App. 1978). 421

Burnett v. Purtell, No. 91-L-094, 1992 Ohio LEXIS 3467, at *1 (Ct. App. June 30, 1992). 478

Cafazzo v. Cent. Med. Health Serv., Inc., 668 A.2d 521 (Pa. 1995). 477

California & Haw. Sugar Co. v. Sun Ship, Inc., 794 F.2d 1433 (9th Cir. 1986). 220

Campbell v. Carr, 603 S.E.2d 625 (S.C. Ct. App. 2004). 101

Campbell v. Hostetter Farms, Inc., 380 A.2d 463 (Pa. Super. Ct. 1977). 362

Campbell v. McClure, 227 Cal. Rptr. 450 (Ct. App. 1986). 147

Carnival Leisure Indus., Ltd. v. Aubin, 938 F.2d 624 (5th Cir. 1991), *rev'd*, 53 F.3d 716 (5th Cir. 1995). 471

Cate v. Dover Corp., 776 S.W.2d 680 (Tex. App. 1989), *rev'd*, 790 S.W.2d 559 (Tex. 1990). 480

Cerdes v. Wright, 408 So. 2d 926 (La. App. 1981). 65

Chase Precast Corp. v. John J. Paonessa Co., 566 N.E.2d 603 (Mass. 1991). 474

Chenard v. Marcel Motors, 387 A.2d 596 (Me. 1978). 31

Cherry Creek Dodge, Inc. v. Carter, 733 P.2d 1024 (Wyo. 1987). 332

Chodos v. West Publ'g Co., 292 F.3d 992 (9th Cir. 2002). 209

City of Everett v. Mitchell, 631 P.2d 366 (Wash. 1981). 10

Cleveland Bar Ass'n v. CompManagement, Inc., 818 N.E.2d 1181 (Ohio 2004). 183

Cleveland Bar Ass'n v. CompManagement, Inc., 857 N.E.2d 95 (Ohio 2006). 183

Coca-Cola Co. v. Purdy, No. 02-1782 ADM/JGL, 2005 U.S. Dist. LEXIS 1226, at *1 (D. Minn. Jan. 28, 2005). 280

Cole Energy Dev. Co. v. Ingersoll-Rand Co., 678 F. Supp. 208 (C.D. Ill. 1988). 386

CompuServe, Inc. v. Patterson, 89 F.3d 1257 (6th Cir. 1996), *rehearing en banc denied*, No. 95-3452, 1996 U.S. App. LEXIS 24796, at *1 (6th Cir. Sept. 19, 1996). 223

Concrete Sales & Equip. Rental Co. v. Kent Nowlin Constr., Inc., 746 P.2d 645 (N.M. 1987). 363

Congregation Kadimah Toras-Moshe v. DeLeo, 540 N.E.2d 691 (Mass. 1989). 470

Continental Airlines, Inc. v. McDonnell Douglas Corp., 264 Cal. Rptr. 779 (Ct. App. 1989). 472

Cooper v. Smith, 800 N.E.2d 372 (Ohio Ct. App. 2003). 71

Corbin Deposit Bank & Trust Co. v. Mullins Enter., Inc., 641 S.W.2d 760 (Ky. Ct. App. 1982). 450

Crandell v. Larkin & Jones Appliance Co., 334 N.W.2d 31 (S.D. 1983). 385

C.R. Daniels, Inc. v. Yazoo Mfg. Co., 641 F. Supp. 205 (S.D. Miss. 1986). 362

Crisci v. Security Ins. Co. of New Haven, Conn., 426 P.2d 173 (Cal. 1967). 243

Crosswhite v. Jumpking, Inc., 411 F. Supp. 2d 1228 (D. Or. 2006). 407

Crothers v. Norm's Auto Sales, 384 N.W.2d 562 (Minn. Ct. App. 1986). 385

Dalrymple v. Dalrymple, 2 Hag. Con. 54, at 105 (1811). 204

Daughtrey v. Ashe, 413 S.E.2d 336 (Va. 1992). 369

Dees v. Saban Entm't, Inc., 131 F.3d 146 (9th Cir. 1997). 39

Dempsey v. Norwegian Cruise Line, 972 F.2d 998 (9th Cir. 1992). 87

Denny v. Ford Motor Co., 662 N.E.2d (N.Y. 1995). 373

Deupree v. Butner, 522 So. 2d 242 (Ala. 1988). 147

In re Estate of Divine, 635 N.E.2d 581 (Ill. App. Ct. 2004). 214

Dosier v. Wilcox-Crittendon Co., 119 Cal. Rptr. 135 (Ct. App. 1975). 423

Dovydenas v. The Bible Speaks, 869 F.2d 628 (1st Cir. 1989). 142

E.A. Coronis Assoc. v. Gordon Constr. Co., 216 A.2d 246 (N.J. Super. Ct. App. Div. 1966). 308

E. & J. Gallo Winery v. Spider Webs Ltd., 286 F.3d 270 (5th Cir. 2002). 252

E.B. Harvey & Co. v. Protective Sys., Inc., No. CA No. 840, 1989 Tenn. LEXIS 105, at *1 (Ct. App. Feb. 19, 1989). 475

Eckstein v. Eckstein, 379 A.2d 757 (Md. Ct. Spec. App. 1978). 148

Edmond's of Fresno v. MacDonald Group, Ltd., 217 Cal. Rptr. 375 (Ct. App. 1985). 64

Ellefson v. Megadeth, Inc., No. 04 Civ. 5395 (NRB), 2005 U.S. Dist. LEXIS 545, at *1 (S.D.N.Y. Jan. 12, 2005). 56

Elsroth v. Johnson & Johnson, 700 F. Supp. 151 (S.D.N.Y. 1998). 411

Executive Fin. Serv., Inc. v. Pagel, 715 P.2d 381 (Kan. 1986). 335

Feiler v. Rosenbloom, 416 A.2d 1345 (Md. Ct. Spec. App. 1980). 171

First Baptist Church of Moultrie v. Barber Contracting Co., 377 S.E.2d 717 (Ga. Ct. App. 1989). 149

First Interstate Bank of Idaho, N.A. v. West, 693 P.2d 1053 (Idaho 1984). 171

Flood v. Fiduciary & Guar. Life Ins. Co., 394 So. 2d 1311 (La. App. 1981). 107

Frasier v. Carter, 432 P.2d 32 (Idaho 1968). 86

Fuqua Homes, Inc. v. Evanston Bldg. & Loan Co., 370 N.E.2d 780 (Ohio Ct. App. 1977). 333

Galloway v. Galloway, 281 N.W.2d 804 (N.D. 1979). 122

G. A. Modefine S.A. v. A. R. Mani, No. D2001-0537 WIPO (2001). 254

Gann v. Morris, 596 P.2d 43 (Ariz. Ct. App. 1979). 123

Georgia Port Auth. v. Mitsubishi Int'l Corp., 274 S.E.2d 699 (Ga. Ct. App. 1980). 334

General Motors Acceptance Corp. v. Grady, 501 N.E.2d 68 (Ohio Ct. App. 1985). 361

Ginn v. Renaldo, Inc., 359 S.E.2d 390 (Ga. Ct. App. 1987). 449

Glende Motor Co. v. Superior Court, 205 Cal. Rptr. 682 (Ct. App. 1984). 64

Glenn v. Overhead Door Corp., 935 So. 2d 1074 (Miss. Ct. App. 2006). 409

Goodwest Rubber Corp. v. Munoz, 170 Cal. App. 3d 919 (1985). 88

Greenman v. Yuba Power Prod., Inc., 377 P.2d 897 (Cal. 1963). 390, 394

Gulash v. Stylarama, 364 A.2d 1221 (Conn. Super. Ct. 1975). 308

Gundersons, Inc. v. Ptarmigan Inv. Co., 678 P.2d 1061 (Colo. Ct. App. 1983). 241

Halbman v. Lemke, 298 N.W.2d 562 (Wis. 1980). 122

Hamer v. Sidwa, 27 N.E. 256 (N.Y. 1891). 68

Hampton v. Federal Express Corp., 917 F.2d 1119 (8th Cir. 1990). 473

Hawaiian Tel. Co. v. Microform Data Sys. Inc., 829 F.2d 919 (9th Cir. 1987). 241

Hayward v. Potsma, 188 N.W.2d 31 (Mich. Ct. App. 1971). 334

H.C. Schmieding Produce Co. v. Cagle, 529 So. 2d 243 (Ala.1988). 309

Hector v. Cedars-Sinai Med. Ctr., 225 Cal. Rptr. 595 (Ct. App. 1986). 290

Hemphill v. Sayers, 552 F. Supp. 685 (S.D. Ill. 1982). 307

Henningsen v. Bloomfield Motors, Inc., 161 A.2d 69 (N.J. 1960). 366

Hickman v. Bates, 889 So. 2d 1249 (La. App. 2004). 224

Higgins v. Intex Recreation Corp., 99 P.3d 421 (Wash. Ct. App. 2004). 403

Hilgendorf v. Hague, 293 N.W.2d 272 (Iowa 1980). 451

Hoffman v. Red Owl Stores, Inc., 26 Wis. 2d 683 (1965). 89

Hoffman v. Sun Valley Co., 628 P.2d 218 (Idaho 1981). 170

Horn v. Gen. Motors Corp., 551 P.2d 398 (Cal. 1976). 481

Hotmail Corp. v. Van$ Money Pie, Inc., 1998 U.S. Dist. LEXIS 10729, at *1 (N.D. Cal. Apr. 16, 1998). 212

H.S. Perlin Co. v. Morse Signal Devices of San Diego, 258 Cal. Rptr. 1 (Ct. App. 1989). 241

Hume v. United States, 132 U.S. 406 (1889). 90

Hunt v. McIlory Bank & Trust, 616 S.W.2d 759 (Ark. Ct. App. 1981). 63

Hydrotech Sys. Ltd. v. Oasis Waterpark, 803 P.2d 370 (Cal. 1991). 112

Idaho Plumbers & Pipefitters Health & Welfare Fund v. United Mech. Contractors, Inc., 875 F.2d 212 (9th Cir. 1989). 242

Idaho State Bar v. Jenkins, 816 P.2d 335 (1991). 382

Indiana Tri-City Plaza Bowl v. Estate of Glueck, 422 N.E.2d 670 (Ind. Ct. App. 1981). 202

Insurance Co. of N. Am. v. Automatic Sprinkler, 423 N.E.2d 151 (Ohio 1981). 386

International Paper Co. v. Farrar, 700 P.2d 642 (N.M. 1985). 361

Jacob Hartz Seed Co. v. Coleman, 612 S.W.2d 91 (Ark. 1981). 361

James v. Turilli, 473 S.W.2d 757 (Mo. Ct. App. 1971). 65

J.C. Durick Ins. v. Andrus, 424 A.2d 249 (Vt. 1980). 64

Jenkins v. Tuneup Masters, 235 Cal. Rptr. 214 (Ct. App. 1987). 64

Joc Oil USA, Inc. v. Consolidated Edison Co. of N.Y., 443 N.E.2d 932 (N.Y. 1982). 341

John Doe v. GTE Corp., 347 F.3d 655 (7th Cir. 2003). 249

Jones v. Flight Sport Aviation, Inc., 623 P.2d 370 (Colo. 1981). 96

Karlsson v. Ford Motor Co., 45 Cal. Rptr. 3d 265 (Ct. App. 2006). 406

Karns v. Emerson Elec. Co., 817 F.2d 1452 (10th Cir. 1987). 422

Kaszuba v. Zientara, 506 N.E.2d 1 (Ind. 1987). 124

Keith v. Buchanan, 220 Cal. Rptr. 392 (Ct. App. 1985). 387

Keperwes v. Publix Supermarkets, Inc., 534 So. 2d 872 (Fla. Dist. Ct. App. 1988). 386

Koch v. Spaulding, 529 N.E.2d 19 (Ill. App. Ct. 1988). 123

Krysa v. Payne, 176 S.W.3d 150 (Mo. Ct. App. 2005). 134

Lakin v. Senco Prod., Inc., 925 P.2d 107 (Or. Ct. App. 1996). 401

Landsberg v. Selchow & Richter Co., 802 F.2d 1193 (9th Cir. 1986). 22

Landshire Food Serv., Inc. v. Coghill, 709 S.W.2d 509 (Mo. Ct. App. 1986). 333

Lechmere, Inc. v. NLRB, 499 U.S. 918 (1991). 443

Lee Oldsmobile-Cadillac, Inc. v. Labonte, D.C.A. No. 77-260, C.A. No. 76-2663, 1980 R.I. LEXIS 190, at *1 (Super. Ct. Oct. 15, 1980). 335

Levin v. Knight, 865 F.2d 1271 (9th Cir. 1989). 172

Lim v. The.TV Corp. Int'l, 121 Cal. Rptr. 2d 323 (Ct. App. 2002). 44

Lindblad v. Holmes, No. BACV2004-00469, 2004 Mass. LEXIS 631, at*1 (Super. Ct. Nov. 24, 2004). 279

Lindh v. Surman, 742 A.2d 643 (Pa. 1999). 227

Lindholm v. Brant, No. X05CV020189393, 2005 Conn. LEXIS 2366, at *1 (Super Ct. Aug. 29, 2005), *aff'd*, 925 A.2d 1048 (Conn. 2007). 324

Liz Claiborne, Inc. v. Avon Prod., Inc., 530 N.Y.S.2d 425 (App. Div. 1988). 240

LNS Inv. Co. v. Phillips 66 Co., 731 F. Supp. 1484 (D. Kan. 1990). 479

Lucas v. Hamm, 364 P.2d 685 (Cal. 1961). 200

Lucy v. Zehmer, 84 S.E.2d 516 (Va. 1954). 63

Luque v. McLean, 501 P.2d 1163 (Cal. 1972). 423

Mack Massey Motors, Inc. v. Garnica, 814 S.W.2d 167 (Tex. Ct. App. 1991). 375

MacPherson v. Buick Motor Co., 111 N.E. 1050 (N.Y. 1916). 393

Madison Square Garden Boxing, Inc. v. Muhammad Ali, 430 F. Supp. 679 (N.D. Ill. 1977). 240

M.A. Mortenson Co. v. Timberline Software Corp., 970 P.2d 803 (Wash. Ct. App. 1999). 271

Marder v. Lopez, 450 F.3d 445 (9th Cir. 2006). 36

Mark Realty, Inc. v. Rogness, 418 So. 2d 373 (Fla. Dist. Ct. App. 1982). 467

Marvin v. Marvin, 557 P.2d 106 (Cal. 1976). 30

Maybank v. S.S. Kresge Co., 266 S.E.2d 409 (N.C. Ct. App. 1980). 385

McGirr v. Gulf Oil Corp., 115 Cal. Rptr. 902 (Ct. App. 1974). 171

McKinnie v. Milford, 597 S.W.2d 953 (Tex. App. 1980). 201

McLaughlin v. Heikkila, 697 N.W.2d 231 (Minn. Ct. App. 2005). 47

McMillan v. Meuser Material & Equip. Co., 541 S.W.2d 911 (Ark. 1976). 362

Mesaros v. United States, 845 F.2d 1576 (Fed. Cir. 1988). 41

Miller v. Newsweek, Inc., 660 F. Supp. 852 (D. Del. 1987). 309

Mollenhour v. State First Nat'l Bank of Texarkana, 769 S.W.2d 28 (Ark. Ct. App. 1989). 450

Montgomery v. English, 902 So. 2d 836 (Fla. Dist. Ct. App. 2005). 51

Morin Bldg. Products Co., Inc. v. Baystone Construction, Inc., 717 F.2d 413 (7th Cir. 1983). 191

Munchak Corp. v. Cunningham, 457 F.2d 721 (4th Cir. 1972). 200

New England Yacht Sales v. Commissioner of Revenue Serv., 504 A.2d 506 (Conn. 1986). 333

NLRB v. Bildisco & Bildisco, 465 U.S. 513 (1984). 444

Ocean Dunes of Hutchinson Island Dev. Corp. v. Colangelo, 463 So. 2d 437 (Fla. Dist. Ct. App. 1985). 88

Ohanian v. Avis Rent A Car Sys., Inc., 779 F.2d 101 (2d Cir. 1985). 170

Okun v. Morton, 203 Cal. App. 3e 805 (1988). 229

O'Neill v. DeLaney, 415 N.E.2d 1260 (Ill. App. Ct. 1980). 74

O'Neill v. Gallant Ins. Co., 769 N.E.2d 100 (Ill. App. Ct. 2002). 235

Outdoor Serv., Inc. v. Pabagold, Inc., 230 Cal. Rptr. 73 (Ct. App. 1986). 202

Pace Constr. Corp. v. OBS Co., 531 So. 2d 737 (Fla. Dist. Ct. App. 1988). 201

Pacific Gas & Elec. Co. v. Bear Stearns & Co., 791 P.2d 587 (Cal. 1990). 242

Parker v. Arthur Murray, Inc., 295 N.E.2d 487 (Ill. App. Ct. 1973). 192

Parker v. Twentieth Century-Fox Film Corp., 474 P.2d 689 (Cal. 1970). 214

Parma Tile, Mosaic & Marble Co. Inc. v. Estate of Short, 590 N.Y.S.2d 1019 (N.Y. Sup. Ct. 1992) 163

Penley v. Penley, 332 S.E.2d 51 (N.C. 1985). 85

Perdue Farms, Inc. v. Motts, Inc. of Miss., 459 F. Supp. 7 (N.D. Miss. 1978). 301

Performance Chevrolet, Inc. v. Mkt. Scan Info. Sys., Inc., No. CV-04-244-S-BLW, 2007 U.S. Dist. LEXIS 23257, at *1 (D. Idaho Mar. 29, 2007). 282

PGA Tour, Inc. v. Martin, 532 U.S. 661 (2001). 461, 463, 466

Philip Morris USA v. Williams, 549 U.S. 346 (2007). 413

Plumlee v. Paddock, 832 S.W.2d 757 (Tex. App. 1992). 124

Porsche Cars N. Am., Inc. v. Spencer, No. CIV. S-00-471 GEB PAN, 2000 U.S. Dist. LEXIS 7060, at *1 (E.D. Cal. May 18, 2000). 283

Portland Elec. and Plumbing Co. v. City of Vancouver, 627 P.2d 1350 (Wash. Ct. App. 1981). 201

Powell v. Thompson-Powell, No. 04-12-0027, 2006 Del. LEXIS 10, *1 (C.P. Kent Jan.18, 2006). 23

P.P. Inc. v. McGuire, 509 F. Supp. 1079 (D.N.J. 1981). 449

Prewitt v. Numismatic Funding Corp., 745 F.2d 1175 (8th Cir. 1984). 320

ProCD, Inc. v. Zeidenberg, 86 F.3d 1447 (7th Cir. 1996). 281

PSEG Power N.Y., Inc. v. Alberici Constructors, Inc., No. 1:05-CV-657 (DNH/RFT), 2007 U.S. Dist. LEXIS 66767 (N.D.N.Y. Sept. 7, 2007). 335

Raffles v. Wichelhaus, 159 Eng. Rep. 375 (Ex. 1864). 130

Rebstock v. Birthright Oil & Gas Co., 406 So. 2d 636 (La. App. 1981). 4

Reno v. American Civil Liberties Union, 521 U.S. 844 (1997). 248

Rich & Whillock, Inc. v. Ashton Dev., Inc., 204 Cal. Rptr. 86 (Ct. App. 1984). 143

Robert Chuckrow Constr. Co. v. Gough, 159 S.E.2d 469 (Ga. Ct. App. 1968). 86

Romasanta v. Mitton, 234 Cal. Rptr. 729 (Ct. App. 1987). 82

Rosenfeld v. Zerneck, 776 N.Y.S.2d 458 (App. Div. 2004). 167

Ryno v. Tyra, 752 S.W.2d 148 (Tex. App. 1988). 109

Schaneman v. Schaneman, 291 N.W.2d 412 (Neb. 1980). 146

Schluter v. United Farmers Elevator, 479 N.W.2d 82 (Minn, App. 1992). 327

Schultz v. County of Contra Costa, Cal., 203 Cal. Rptr. 760 (Ct. App. 1984). 146

Sebasty v. Perschke, 404 N.E.2d 1200 (Ind. Ct. App. 1980). 309

Sedmak v. Charlie's Chevrolet, Inc., 622 S.W.2d 694 (Mo. Ct. App. 1981). 360

Self v. General Motors Corp., 116 Cal. Rptr. 575 (Ct. App. 1974). 417

Shattuck v. Klotzbach, 14 Mass. L. Rep. 360 (Super. Ct. 2001). 157

Shepard v. Mozzetti, 545 A.2d 621 (Del. 1988). 172

Shoshone Coca-Cola Bottling Co. v. Dolinski, 420 P.2d 855 (Nev. 1966). 399

Silver v. Wycombe, Meyer & Co., 477 N.Y.S.2d 288 (N.Y. Civ. Ct. 1984). 334

Simpson v. Norwesco, Inc., 583 F.2d 1007 (8th Cir. 1978). 482

Smith v. General Motors Corp., 116 Cal. Rptr. 575 (Ct. App. 1974). 422

Smith v. Williamson, 429 So. 2d 598 (Ala. Civ. App. 1982). 104

Sofias v. Bank of America, 218 Cal. Rptr. 388 (Ct. App. 1985). 200

Soldau v. Organon, Inc., 860 F.2d 355 (9th Cir. 1988). 54

Sta-Rite Indus., Inc. v. Peterson, 837 So. 2d 988 (Fla. Dist. Ct. App. 2003). 405

St. Charles Cable TV v. Eagle Comtronics, Inc., 687 F. Supp. 820 (S.D.N.Y. 1988). 308

Steele v. Goettee, 542 A.2d 847 (Md. 1988). 146

Stirlen v. Supercuts, Inc., 60 Cal. Rptr. 2d 138 (Ct. App. 1997). 117

Sulzer Bingham Pumps, Inc. v. Lockheed Missiles & Space Co., 947 F.2d 1362 (9th Cir. 1991). 149

Super Valu Stores, Inc. v. Peterson, 506 So. 2d 317 (Ala. 1987). 216

Sutton v. Warner, 15 Cal. Rptr. 2d 632 (Ct. App. 1993). 156

Swan Island Sheet Metal Works, Inc. v. Troy's Custom Smoking Co., 619 P.2d 1326 (Or. Ct. App. 1980). 387

Texaco, Inc. v. Penzoil Co., 729 S.W.2d 768 (Tex. App. 1987). 233

Toys "R" Us, Inc. v. Abir, No. 97 Civ. 8673 (JGK), 1999 U.S. Dist. LEXIS 1275, at *1 (S.D.N.Y. Feb. 10, 1999). 476

Traco, Inc. v. Arrow Glass Co., 814 S.W.2d 186 (Tex. App. 1991). 468

Tri-State Petroleum Corp. v. Saber Energy, Inc., 845 F.2d 575 (5th Cir. 1988). 363

In re Unimet Corp., 842 F.2d 879 (6th Cir. 1988), cert. denied, 488 U.S. 828 (1989). 445

United States v. Michaels Jewelers, Inc., No. N 85-242 (JAC), 1985 U.S. Dist. LEXIS 15142, at *1 (D. Conn. Oct. 8, 1985). 333

United States v. Mitnick, No. 97-50365, 1998 U.S. App. LEXIS 10836, at *1 (9th Cir. May 20, 1998). 276

Uzan v. 845 UN Ltd. P'ship, 778 N.Y.S.2d 171 (App. Div. 2004). 218

Walgreen Co. v. Sara Creek Prop. Co., 966 F.2d 273 (7th Cir. 1992). 242

Wallace C. Drennen, Inc. v. Haeuser, 402 So. 2d 771 (La. App. 1981). 240

Wallach Marine Corp. v. Donzi Marine Corp., 675 F. Supp. 838 (S.D.N.Y. 1987). 309

Welch v. Metro-Goldwyn-Mayer Film Co., 254 Cal. Rptr. 645 (Ct. App. 1988). 241

Welles v. Academy of Motion Picture Arts & Sci., No. CV 03-05314 DDP (JTLx), 2004 U.S. Dist. LEXIS 5756, at *1 (C.D. Cal. Mar. 4, 2004). 13

Wells Fargo Credit Corp. v. Martin, 650 So. 2d 531 (Fla. Dist. Ct. App. 1992). 129

Whitman Heffernan Rhein & Co. v. Griffin Co., 557 N.Y.S.2d 342 (App. Div. 1990). 160

Whitmire v. Watkins, 267 S.E.2d 6 (Ga. 1980). 86

Wilson v. Kealakekua Ranch, Ltd., 551 P.2d 525 (Haw. 1976). 123

Wilson v. Western Nat'l Life Ins. Co., 1 Cal. Rptr. 2d (Ct. App. 1991). 138

Wilson v. World Omni Leasing, Inc., 540 So. 2d 713 (Ala. 1989). 307

Winkel v. Family Health Care, P.C., 668 P.2d 208 (Mont. 1983). 31

In re Wirth, 789 N.Y.S.2d 69 (App. Div. 2005). 77

Woodcock v. Chemical Bank, 144 F.3d 1340 (10th Cir. 1998). 450

Wrench LLC v. Taco Bell Corp., 256 F.3d 446 (6th Cir. 2001). 19

Yale Diagnostic Radiology v. Estate of Fountain, 838 A.2d 179 (Conn. 2004). 97

Ybarras v. Modern Trailer Sales, Inc., 609 P.2d 331 (N.M. 1980). 363

Yost v. Rieve Enter., Inc., 461 So. 2d 178 (Fla. Dist. Ct. App. 1984). 148

Zivich v. Mentor Soccer Club, Inc., 696 N.E.2d 201 (Ohio 1998). 113

CRITICAL LEGAL THINKING TECHNIQUES FOR CASE BRIEFING

Judges apply *legal reasoning* in reaching a decision in a case. That is, a judge must specify the issue presented by the case, identify the key facts in the case and the applicable law, and then apply the law to the facts to come to a conclusion that answers the issue presented. This process is called **critical legal thinking.** Skills of analysis and interpretation are important in deciding legal cases.

■ KEY TERMS

Before you embark on the study of law, you should know the following key legal terms:

- **Plaintiff.** The party who originally brought the lawsuit.
- **Defendant.** The party against whom the lawsuit has been brought.
- **Petitioner or appellant.** The party who has appealed the decision of the trial court or lower court. The petitioner may be either the plaintiff or the defendant, depending on who lost the case at the trial court or lower court level.
- **Respondent or appellee.** The party who must answer the petitioner's appeal. The respondent may be either the plaintiff or the defendant, depending on which party is the petitioner. In some cases, both the plaintiff *and* the defendant may disagree with the trial court's or lower court's decision, and both parties may appeal the decision.

■ BRIEFING A CASE

It is often helpful for a student to "brief" a case to clarify the legal issues involved and to gain a better understanding of the case.

The procedure for briefing a case is as follows. The student must summarize, or brief, the court's decision in no more than 400 words (some professors may shorten or lengthen this limit). The assignment's format is highly structured, consisting of five parts, each of which is numbered and labeled (see Exhibit A.1).

■ ELEMENTS OF A CASE BRIEF

Briefing a case consists of making a summary of each of the following items of the case:

1. *Case name, citation, and court*—The name of the case should be placed at the beginning of each briefed case. The case name usually contains the names of the parties to the lawsuit (for example, *PGA Tour, Inc. v. Martin*).

Exhibit A.1 Briefing a Case

PART	MAXIMUM WORDS
1. The case name, citation, and court	25
2. A summary of the key facts in the case	125
3. The *issue* presented by the case, stated as a one-sentence question answerable only by *yes* or *no*	25
4. The court's resolution of the issue (the "holding")	25
5. A summary of the court's reasoning justifying the holding	200
Total words	400

Where there are multiple plaintiffs or defendants, however, some of the names of the parties may be omitted from the case name. Abbreviations are often used in case names as well

The case citation, which consists of a number plus the year in which the case was decided, such as "532 U.S. 661, 121 S.Ct. 1879, 2001 U.S. Lexis 4115," is set forth below the case name. The case citation identifies the book in the law library or the Internet site where the case may be found. For example, the case in the citation just listed may be found in volume 532 of the *United States Reports*, page 661, in volume 121 of the *Supreme Court Reporter*, page 1879, and on the Lexis website at 2001 U.S. Lexis 4115. The name of the court that decided the case should be set forth below the case name for the case.

2. ***Summary of the key facts in the case***—The important facts of a case should be stated briefly. Extraneous facts and facts of minor importance should be omitted from the brief. The facts of the case can usually be found at the beginning of the case, but not necessarily. Important facts may be found throughout the case.

3. ***Issue presented by the case***—In the briefing of a case, it is crucial to identify the issue presented to the court to decide. The issue on appeal is most often a legal question, although questions of fact are sometimes the subject of an appeal. The issue presented in each case is usually quite specific and should be asked in a one-sentence question that is answerable only by *yes* or *no*. For example, the issue statement "Is the PGA Tour, Inc. liable?" is too broad. A more proper statement of the issue would be "Does the Americans with Disabilities Act require the PGA to accommodate Martin by permitting him to use a golf cart while playing in PGA tournaments?"

4. ***Holding***—The *holding* is the decision reached by the present court. It should be *yes* or *no*. The holding should also state which party won.

5. ***Summary of the court's reasoning***—When an appellate court or a supreme court issues a decision, which is often called an *opinion*, the court normally states the reasoning it used in reaching its decision. The rationale for the decision may be based on the specific facts of the case, public policy, prior law, or other matters. In stating the reasoning of the court, the student should reword the court's language into his or her own language. This summary of the court's reasoning should pick out the meat of the opinions and weed out the nonessentials.

■ CASE FOR BRIEFING

The following is an excerpted decision by the Supreme Court of the United States.
The case is presented in the language of the Supreme Court.

U.S. SUPREME COURT	**CASE A.1**

PGA TOUR, INC. v. MARTIN
532 U.S. 661, 121 S.Ct. 1879, 2001 U.S. Lexis 4115 Supreme Court of the United States

OPINION, STEVENS, JUSTICE   This case raises two questions concerning the application of the Americans with Disabilities Act of 1990 [42 U.S.C. § 12101 et seq.] to a gifted athlete: first, whether the Act protects access to professional golf tournaments by a qualified entrant with a disability, and second, whether a disabled contestant may be denied the use of a golf cart because it would "fundamentally alter the nature" of the tournaments to allow him to ride when all other contestants must walk.

    Petitioner PGA TOUR, Inc., a nonprofit entity formed in 1968, sponsors and cosponsors professional golf tournaments conducted on three annual tours. About 200 golfers participate in the PGA TOUR; about 170 in the NIKE TOUR; and about 100 in the SENIOR PGA TOUR. PGA TOUR and NIKE TOUR tournaments typically are four-day events, played on courses leased and operated by petitioner. The revenues generated by television, admissions, concessions, and contributions from cosponsors amount to about $300 million a year, much of which is distributed in prize money. The "Conditions of Competition and Local Rules," often described as the "hard card," apply specifically to petitioner's professional tours. The hard cards for the PGA TOUR and NIKE TOUR required players to walk the golf course during tournaments, but not during open qualifying rounds. On the SENIOR PGA TOUR, which is limited to golfers age 50 and older, the contestants may use golf carts. Most seniors, however, prefer to walk.

    Casey Martin is a talented golfer. As an amateur, he won 17 Oregon Golf Association junior events before he was 15, and he won the state championship as a high school senior. He played on the Stanford University golf team that won the 1994 National Collegiate Athletic Association (NCAA) championship. As a professional, Martin qualified for the NIKE TOUR in 1998 and 1999, and based on his 1999 performance, qualified for the PGA TOUR in 2000. In the 1999 season, be entered 24 events, made the cut 13 times, and had six top-10 finishes, coming in second twice and third once.

    Martin is also an individual with a disability, as defined in the Americans with Disabilities Act of 1990 (ADA or Act). Since birth he has been afflicted with Klippel-Trenaunay-Weber syndrome, a degenerative circulatory disorder that obstructs the flow of blood from his right leg back to his heart. The disease is progressive; it causes severe pain and has atrophied his right leg. During the latter part of his college career, because of the progress of the disease, Martin could no longer walk an 18-hole golf course. Walking not only caused him pain, fatigue, and anxiety, but also created a significant risk of hemorrhaging, developing blood clots, and fracturing his tibia so badly that an amputation might be required.

    When Martin turned pro and entered petitioner's Qualifying-School, the hard card permitted him to use a cart during his successful progress through the first two stages. He made a request, supported by detailed medical records, for permission to use a golf cart during the third stage. Petitioner refused to review those records or to waive its walking rule for the third stage. Martin therefore filed this action.

    At trial, petitioner PGA TOUR did not contest the conclusion that Martin has a disability covered by the ADA, or the fact that his disability prevents him from walking the course during a round of golf. Rather, petitioner asserted that the condition of walking is a substantive rule of competition and that waiving it as to any individual for any reason would fundamentally alter the nature of the competition. Petitioner's evidence included the testimony of a number of experts, among them some of the greatest golfers in history. Arnold Palmer, Jack Nicklaus, and Ken Venturi explained that

Margin notes (right column):

Case name, Citation, and Court

Opinion of the Court

Issue

Facts

Petitioner: PGA Tour Inc.

Respondent: Casey Martin

District Court's Decision, 994 F. Supp. 1242, 1998

U.S. Dist. Lexis 1980 [District: Oregon (1998)]

fatigue can be a critical factor in a tournament, particularly on the last day, when psychological pressure is at a maximum. Their testimony makes it clear that, in their view, permission to use a cart might well give some players a competitive advantage over other players who must walk.

The judge found that the purpose of the rule was to inject fatigue into the skill of shot-making, but that the fatigue injected "by walking the course cannot be deemed significant under normal circumstances." Furthermore, Martin presented evidence, and the judge found, that even with the use of a cart, Martin must walk over a mile during an 18-hole round, and that the fatigue he suffers from coping with his disability is "undeniably greater" than the fatigue his able-bodied competitors endure from walking the course. As a result, the judge concluded that it would "not fundamentally alter the nature of the PGA Tour's game to accommodate him with a cart." The judge accordingly entered a permanent injunction requiring petitioner to permit Martin to use a cart in tour and qualifying events.

Court of Appeals Decision, 204 F.3d 994, 2000 U.S. Appplexis 3376 [9th Circuit (2000)]

The Court of Appeals concluded that golf courses remain places of public accommodation during PGA tournaments. On the merits, because there was no serious dispute about the fact that permitting Martin to use a golf cart was both a reasonable and a necessary solution to the problem of providing him access to the tournaments, the Court of Appeals regarded the central dispute as whether such permission would "fundamentally alter" the nature of the PGA TOUR or NIKE TOUR. Like the District Court, the Court of Appeals viewed the issue not as "whether use of carts generally would fundamentally alter the competition, but whether the use of a cart by Martin would do so." That issue turned on "an intensively fact-based inquiry," and, the court concluded, had been correctly resolved by the trial judge. In its words, "all that the cart does is permit Martin access to a type of competition in which he otherwise could not engage because of his disability."

Federal Statute Being Interpreted

Congress enacted the ADA in 1990 to remedy widespread discrimination against disabled individuals. To effectuate its sweeping purpose, the ADA forbids discrimination against disabled individuals in major areas of public life, among them employment (Title I of the Act), public services (Title II), and public accommodations (Title III). At issue now is the applicability of Title III to petitioner's golf tours and qualifying rounds, in particular to petitioner's treatment of a qualified disabled golfer wishing to compete in those events.

U.S. Supreme Court's Reasoning

It seems apparent, from both the general rule and the comprehensive definition of "public accommodation," that petitioner's golf tours and their qualifying rounds fit comfortably within the coverage of Title III, and Martin within its protection. The events occur on "golf courses," a type of place specifically identified by the Act as a public accommodation [Section 12181(7)(L)]. In this case, the narrow dispute is whether allowing Martin to use a golf cart, despite the walking requirement that applies to the PGA TOUR, the NIKE TOUR, and the third stage of the Qualifying-School, is a modification that would "fundamentally alter the nature" of those events.

As an initial matter, we observe that the use of carts is not itself inconsistent with the fundamental character of the game of golf. From early on, the essence of the game has been shot-making—using clubs to cause a ball to progress from the teeing ground to a hole some distance away with as few strokes as possible. Golf carts started appearing with increasing regularity on American golf courses in the 1950s. Today they are everywhere. And they are encouraged. For one thing, they often speed up play, and for another, they are great revenue producers. There is nothing in the rules of golf that either forbids the use of carts or penalizes a player for using a cart.

Petitioner, however, distinguishes the game of golf as it is generally played from the game that it sponsors in the PGA TOUR, NIKE TOUR, and the last stage of the Qualifying-School—golf at the "highest level." According to petitioner, "the goal of the highest-level competitive athletics is to assess and compare the performance of different competitors, a task that is meaningful only if the competitors are subject to identical substantive rules." The waiver of any possibly "outcome-affecting" rule for a contestant would violate this principle and therefore, in petitioner's view, fundamentally alter the nature of the highest-level athletic event. The walking rule is one such rule, petitioner submits, because its purpose is "to inject the element of fatigue into the skill of shot-making," and thus its effect may be the critical loss of a stroke. As a consequence, the reasonable modification Martin seeks would fundamentally alter the nature of petitioner's highest-level tournaments.

The force of petitioner's argument is, first of all, mitigated by the fact that golf is a game in which it is impossible to guarantee that all competitors will play under exactly the same conditions or that an individual's ability will be the sole determinant of the outcome. For example, changes in the weather may produce harder greens and more head winds for the tournament leader than for his closest pursuers. A lucky bounce may save a shot or two. Whether such happenstance events are more or less probable than the likelihood that a golfer afflicted with Klippel-Trenaunay-Weber Syndrome would one day qualify for the NIKE TOUR and PGA TOUR, they at least demonstrate that pure chance may have a greater impact on the outcome of elite golf tournaments than the fatigue resulting from the enforcement of the walking rule.

Further, the factual basis of petitioner's argument is undermined by the District Court's finding that the fatigue from walking during one of petitioner's 4-day tournaments cannot be deemed significant. The District Court credited the testimony of a professor in physiology and expert on fatigue, who calculated the calories expended in walking a golf course (about five miles) to be approximately 500 calories—"nutritionally less than a Big Mac." What is more, that energy is expended over a 5-hour period, during which golfers have numerous intervals for rest and refreshment. In fact, the expert concluded, because golf is a low-intensity activity, fatigue from the game is primarily a psychological phenomenon in which stress and motivation are the key ingredients. And even under conditions of severe heat and humidity, the critical factor in fatigue is fluid loss rather than exercise from walking. Moreover, when given the option of using a cart, the majority of golfers in petitioner's tournaments have chosen to walk, often to relieve stress or for other strategic reasons. As NIKE TOUR member Eric Johnson testified, walking allows him to keep in rhythm, stay warmer when it is chilly, and develop a better sense of the elements and the course than riding a cart. As we have demonstrated, the walking rule is at best peripheral to the nature of petitioner's athletic events, and thus it might be waived in individual cases without working a fundamental alteration.

Under the ADA's basic requirement that the need of a disabled person be evaluated on an individual basis, we have no doubt that allowing Martin to use a golf cart would not fundamentally alter the nature of petitioner's tournaments. As we have discussed, the purpose of the walking rule is to subject players to fatigue, which in turn may influence the outcome of tournaments. Even if the rule does serve that purpose, it is an uncontested finding of the District Court that Martin "easily endures greater fatigue even with a cart than his able-bodied competitors do by walking." The purpose of the walking rule is therefore not compromised in the slightest by allowing Martin to use a cart. A modification that provides an exception to a peripheral tournament rule without impairing its purpose cannot be said to "fundamentally alter" the tournament. What it can be said to do, on the other band, is to allow Martin the chance to qualify for and compete in the athletic events petitioner offers to those members of the public who have the skill and desire to enter. That is exactly what the ADA requires. As a result, Martin's request for a waiver of the walking rule should have been granted.

The judgment of the Court of Appeals is affirmed. It is so ordered.

DISSENTING OPINION, SCALIA, JUSTICE In my view today's opinion exercises a benevolent compassion that the law does not place it within our power to impose. The judgment distorts the text of Title III, the structure of the ADA, and common sense. I respectfully dissent.

Agility, strength, speed, balance, quickness of mind, steadiness of nerves, intensity of concentration—these talents are not evenly distributed. No wild-eyed dreamer has ever suggested that the managing bodies of the competitive sports that test precisely these qualities should try to take account of the uneven distribution of God-given gifts when writing and enforcing the rules of competition. And I have no doubt Congress did not authorize misty-eyed judicial supervision of such a revolution.

Margin notes:

Holding and Remedy

Dissenting Opinion

■ BRIEF OF CASE A.1

The brief of Case A.1, *PGA Tour, Inc. v. Martin* appears in Exhibit A.2.

Exhibit A.2 Brief of Case: *PGA Tour, Inc. v. Martin*

1. **Case Name, Citation, and Court**
   PGA TOUR, Inc. v Martin
   532 U.S. 661, 121 S.Ct. 1879, 2001 Lexis 4115 (2001)
   U.S. Sup. Ct.
2. **Key Facts**
   A. PGA TOUR, Inc., is a nonprofit organization that sponsors professional golf tournaments.
   B. The PGA establishes rules for its golf tournaments. A PGA rule requires golfers to walk the golf course and not use golf carts.
   C. Casey Martin is a professional golfer who suffers from Klippel-Trenaunay-Weber Syndrome, a degenerative circulatory disorder that atrophied Martin's right leg and causes him pain, fatigue, and anxiety when walking.
   D. When Martin petitioned the PGA to use a golf cart during golf tournaments, the PGA refused.
   E. Martin sued the PGA, alleging discrimination against a disabled individual in violation of the Americans with Disabilities Act of 1990, a federal statute.
3. **Issue**
   Does the Americans with Disabilities Act require the PGA to accommodate Martin by permitting him to use a golf cart while playing in PGA tournaments?
4. **Holding**
   Yes. The Supreme Court held that the PGA must allow Martin to use a golf cart when competing in PGA golf tournaments. Affirmed.
5. **Court's Reasoning**
   The Supreme Court held that:
   A. Martin was disabled and covered by the act.
   B. Golf courses are "public accommodations" covered by the act.
   C. The use of golf carts is not a fundamental character of the game of golf.
   D. Other than the PGA rule, there is no rule of golf that forbids the use of golf carts.
   E. It is impossible to guarantee that all players in golf will play under exactly the same conditions, so allowing Martin to use a golf cart gives him no advantage over other golfers.
   F. Martin, because of his disease, will probably suffer more fatigue playing golf using a golf cart than other golfers will suffer without using a cart.
   G. The PGA's "walking rule" is only peripheral to the game of golf and not a fundamental part of golf.
   H. Allowing Martin to use a golf cart will not fundamentally alter the PGA's highest-level professional golf tournaments.

APPENDIX B

MARK REALTY, INC. v. ROGNESS, 418 SO. 2D 373 (FLA. DIST. CT. APP. 1982).

Tilman Rogness, owner, entered into four separate agreements with Mark Realty, Inc., a real estate broker. They were entitled "exclusive right of sale" and gave the broker, for a stated period of time, the exclusive right to sell the property for a certain stated price and on certain terms. The broker sued on the four agreements for brokerage commissions, alleging that during the time provided in the agreements the owner had conveyed the four properties. The owner's answer alleged affirmative defenses to the effect that the owner had "canceled, revoked and terminated" the brokerage agreements before the properties were sold and that the broker had never performed under the agreements.

The trial judge construed the brokerage agreements to constitute mere offers to enter into unilateral contracts under which the broker would be entitled to a commission only if he performed by "finding a purchaser of the above property." If the documents in question are merely offers limited to acceptance by performance only, the trial judge's analysis and conclusion would be correct.

We cannot agree that the documents were only offers for a unilateral contract. The documents illustrate what has been termed "the usual practice" in the making of bargains. One party indicates what he will do and what he requires in exchange and the other then agrees. These documents, when first executed by the owner and tendered to the broker, constituted offers which, when accepted by the broker by his execution, constituted contracts. The contract is bilateral because it contains mutual promises made in exchange for each other by each of the two contracting parties.

The most common recurring brokerage transaction is one in which the owner employs a broker to find a purchaser able and willing to buy, on terms stated in advance by the owner, and in which the owner promises to pay a specific commission for the service. Such a transaction as this is an offer by the owner of a unilateral contract, an offered promise to pay by the owner, creating in the broker a power of accepting the offer by actual rendition of the requested services. The only contemplated contract between the owner and broker is a unilateral contract—a promise to pay a commission for services rendered. Such an offer of a promise to pay a commission for services rendered is revocable by the owner by notice before the broker has rendered any part of the requested service. On the other hand, the transaction between the owner and the broker can be a bilateral contract. An owner who puts his land in the hands of a broker for sale usually clearly promises to pay a commission but the broker rarely promises in return that he will produce a purchaser, although he often promises, expressly or impliedly, that he will make certain efforts to do so. If the parties have thus made mutual promises, the transaction no longer has the status of an unaccepted offer—there is an existing bilateral contract and neither party has a power of revocation. During the term of such a contract the owner may withdraw any power the owner has given the broker to contract with a third party in the owner's name, but this is not a revocation of the contract between the owner and the broker and normally such action constitutes a breach of the brokerage contract.

In this case, the broker promised to inspect the property, to list the property with a multiple listing service, to advertise the property in the local newspaper or other media, to furnish information to inquiring cooperating brokers and prospective purchasers, to show the property, to make efforts to find a purchaser, to "make an earnest and continued effort to sell," and to direct the concentrated efforts of his organization in bringing about a sale.

In the instant case, the contract clearly provided that the brokerage commissions would be paid "whether the purchaser be secured by you or me, or by any other person." Thus the contract granted the broker an exclusive right of sale and the trial court erred in constructing the agreement as an offer of a unilateral contract revocable at will at any time prior to performance.

The final judgment is REVERSED.

CASE B.2

TRACO, INC. v. ARROW GLASS CO., 814 S.W.2D 186 (TEX. APP. 1991).

This is a construction dispute stemming from a quotation given by Traco, Inc., a Three Rivers Aluminum Company, a material supplier of preengineered aluminum and glass sliding doors and windows, to Arrow Glass Company, Inc., a subcontractor, in connection with the USAA Towers project in San Antonio, Texas. Arrow initially brought suit against Traco on the theories of promissory estoppel and negligence for Traco's failure to supply aluminum and glass sliding doors at the quoted price. After a bench trial, the trial court held for Arrow solely under the theory of promissory estoppel and awarded Arrow judgment against Traco for damages in the amount of $75,843.38, plus attorneys' fees and prejudgment interest.

The facts of this case reflect that on or about October 9, 1986, construction bids were due for the USAA Towers, a $49,000,000 retirement housing project located near Fort Sam Houston, Texas. There were numerous suppliers, subcontractors, and general contractors bidding to obtain work on this project including the appellant, Traco, and the appellee, Arrow.

On bid day, a representative for Arrow received a telephone call from Dale Ferrar of Traco. Mr. Ferrar told Bill Morris, the general manager of Arrow Glass, that Traco was a very large window and sliding glass and aluminum door manufacturer in Pennsylvania. Mr. Ferrar offered its A-2 aluminum and glass sliding doors, as an alternate product substitution, to Arrow, which was bidding that portion of the project. However, after some discussion of the required specifications, the parties realized that Traco's doors would have to be modified in order to comply with the project specifications. Arrow declined to use Traco's bid and, instead, submitted its original bid, using a different supplier of doors. At approximately noon on bid day, Mr. Ferrar phoned Mr. Morris, quoting a new price for the doors which included a modification of the frame depth which, supposedly, enabled the doors to comply with the specifications. At this time, Mr. Morris informed Mr. Ferrar that his bid was low and asked him to recheck his figures. Mr. Ferrar explained that because of Traco's size and the fact that it could manufacture its products under one roof, Traco could sell the project for that amount. Mr. Ferrar also indicated that Traco was seeking a high profile project to represent Traco in the San Antonia area.

After receiving these assurances, Mr. Morris told Mr. Ferrar that he was going to use Traco's bid. Mr. Morris then phoned the contractors to whom he had originally submitted his bid, and deducted $100,000 in reliance upon Traco's bid. Mr. Morris later told Mr. Ferrar that he had received favorable responses from three or four general contractors, and that it appeared Arrow would get the project. Mr. Morris advised Mr. Ferrar that if Arrow obtained the project, then Traco would be awarded the contract on the doors.

The oral quote by Traco was followed with a written bid confirmation on the next day, which reflected the product that would be supplied and the price agreed upon by the parties. The confirmation also included the 1-¼" frame extended at a cost of $27,860, which, allegedly, brought the doors into compliance with the project specifications.

Sometime in November, long after Mr. Morris had relied upon Mr. Ferrar's representations in submitting his bid, Mr. Morris began hearing rumors that there was a problem with the doors. Mr. Morris contacted Mr. Ferrar, who admitted that there was a problem with the doors meeting the architect's wind load deflection requirements in the specifications. Shortly after learning of this problem, Mr. Morris received a second quote from Traco, wherein Traco offered its A-3 doors, which were a more expensive, heavy grade commercial door that met the deflection requirement, for a price of $304,300. After receiving this bid, Morris objected to the price and demanded that Traco deliver doors meeting the project specifications at the original price quoted. Traco refused and when it became obvious that Arrow would not be able to use Traco's product, Mr. Morris contracted with another supplier who had bid on the project.

The record clearly reflects the following: that it was Traco that initially contracted Arrow and offered to do a certain specific act, i.e., supply the sliding doors required; that Mr. Ferrar phoned Mr. Morris on several occasions and discussed, among other things, the fact that the doors which Traco wished to bid would not comply with the specifications without some modification; and, that Mr. Ferrar assured Mr. Morris that the doors could be modified to comply with the specifications. Thus, under the present facts, Traco's bid gave Arrow "a right to expect or claim the performance of some particular thing"; specifically, Traco's bid constituted a promise to supply sliding doors meeting the project specifications at a specified price.

Appellant initially argues that the trial court erred in rendering judgment for Arrow because Traco's bid was revocable and properly withdrawn 30 days after it was made. Appellant primarily relies upon the argument that its sliding doors are goods as defined by the Texas Business and Commerce Code. Nevertheless, appellant's arguments ignore the appellee's basic contention and legal theory under which this suit was brought. Appellee sought relief under the equitable doctrine of promissory estoppel, on the premise that the appellant's promises, by way of its *oral* bid, caused appellee to substantially rely to its detriment. The appellee relied to its detriment when it reduced its bid based on a telephone conversation with the appellant, prior to the time appellant's confirmation letter was sent or received. We must now resolve whether the equitable theory of promissory estoppel applied to bid construction cases and, if so, whether this doctrine applies under the specific facts of this case. While no Texas case has previously applied the theory of promissory estoppel in a bid construction case, other jurisdictions have consistently applied this doctrine under similar facts, recognizing the necessity for equity in view of the lack of other remedies.

The Texas Supreme Court, in emphasizing that the underlying function of the theory of promissory estoppel is to promote equity, has stated that: "The Vital principal is that he who by his language or conduct leads another to do what he would not otherwise have done, shall not subject such person to loss or injury by disappointing the expectations, upon which he acted. This remedy is always so applied as to promote the ends of justice." Clearly promissory estoppel is "a rule of equity" applied to prevent injustice. As is true in most, if not all, bid construction cases, the present situation does not involve a contract. Therefore, were we to hold that promissory estoppel does not exist in bid construction cases, this would necessarily mean that, notwithstanding any language or conduct by the subcontractor which leads the general contractor to do that which he would not otherwise have done and, thereby, incur loss or injury, the general contractor would be denied all relief. This proposition is untenable and conflicts with the underlying premise of promissory estoppel.

Section 90 of the STATEMENT (SECOND) OF CONTRACTS (1981) states the principle of promissory estoppel as follows: "A promise which the promisor should reasonably expect to induce action or forbearance on the part of the promisee or a third person and which does induce such action or forbearance is binding if injustice can be avoided only by enforcement of the promise." Accordingly, the requirements of promissory estoppel are: "(1) a promise, (2) foreseeability of reliance thereon by the promisor, and (3) substantial reliance by the promisee to his detriment." In order to invoke the doctrine of estoppel, all the necessary elements of estoppel must be present and the failure to establish even one of these elements is fatal to the claimant's cause of action.

Appellant insists, however, that because Traco was not an approved manufacturer and bid its doors as an alternate, that by its nature, Traco's bid was conditional and, therefore, promissory estoppel cannot lie. We fail to see how a bid for a specific door at a specific price, which was submitted in response to solicitations that detailed project specifications, is contingent, or somehow not final, merely because the wrong door was bid upon. The appellant's failure to receive the architect's approval was not due to new specifications but was caused by the appellant's failure to regard those specifications originally required when the appellant offered its doors. Appellant's point is rejected.

Notwithstanding the existence of this promise, the appellant argues that the appellee could not have justifiably and reasonably relied upon appellant's bid because: Traco was not an approved manufacturer and bid its A-2 doors as an alternate and, further, Traco's bid was lower than the other suppliers who bid upon the contract.

Because of the withdrawal of Traco's bid, Arrow was compelled to seek another supplier of doors at a much greater cost; clearly, this constituted an injustice to the appellee. Additionally, appellee's reliance upon appellant's bid was reasonable in view of the appellant's attempts to modify its doors, and Mr. Ferrar's assurances that the doors, as modified, would meet the project specifications.

We hold that the controlling findings of fact support the promissory estoppel theory.

The judgment is AFFIRMED.

CASE B.3

CONGREGATION KADIMAH TORAS-MOSHE v. DELEO, 540 N.E.2D 691 (MASS. 1989).

Congregation Kadimah Toras-Moshe (Congregation), an Orthodox Jewish synagogue, commenced this action in the Superior Court to compel the administrator of an estate (estate) to fulfill the oral promise of the decedent to give the Congregation $25,000. The Superior Court transferred the case to the Boston Municipal Court, which rendered summary judgment for the estate. The case was then transferred back to the Superior Court, which also rendered summary judgment for the estate and dismissed the Congregation's complaint. We granted the Congregation's application for direct appellate review. We now affirm. The facts are not contested. The decedent suffered a prolonged illness, throughout which he was visited by the Congregation's spiritual leader, Rabbi Abraham Halbfinger. During four or five of these visits, and in the presence of witnesses, the decedent made an oral promise to give the Congregation $25,000. The Congregation planned to use the $25,000 to transform a storage room in the synagogue into a library named after the decedent. The decedent died intestate in September 1985. He had no children, but was survived by his wife. The Congregation asserts that the decedent's oral promise is an enforceable contract under our case law, because the promise is allegedly supported either by consideration and bargain, or by reliance. The Superior Court judge determined that "this was an oral gratuitous pledge, with no indication as to how the money should be used, or what [the Congregation] was required to do if anything in return for this promise." There was no legal benefit to the promisor nor detriment to the promisee, and thus no consideration. Moral obligation is not legal obligation. Furthermore, there is no evidence in the record that the Congregation's plans to name a library after the decedent induced him to make or renew his promise. As to the lack of reliance, the judge stated that the Congregation's "allocation of $25,000 in its budget, for the purpose of renovating a storage room, is insufficient to find reliance or an enforceable obligation." We agree. The inclusion of the promised $25,000 in the budget, by itself, merely reduced to writing the Congregation's expectation that it would have additional funds. A hope or expectation, even though well founded, is not equivalent to either legal detriment or reliance.

We are of the opinion that in this case there is no injustice in declining decedent's promise. The promise to the Congregation is entirely unsupported by consideration or reliance. To enforce such a promise would be against public policy.

Judgment AFFIRMED.

CARNIVAL LEISURE INDUS., LTD. v. AUBIN, 938 F.2D 624 (5TH CIR. 1991).

During a January 1987 visit to the Bahamas, George J. Aubin, a Texas resident, visited Cable Beach Hotel and Casino (the Casino), which was owned and operated by Carnival Leisure Industries, Ltd. (Carnival. Leisure). While gambling at the Casino, Aubin received markers or chips from the Casino and the Casino received drafts drawn on Aubin's bank accounts in Texas. Aubin spent all of the markers provided on gambling, although he could also have spent them on food, beverages, souvenirs, or lodging at the Casino. Aubin ultimately gambled and lost $25,000, having given the Casino the same amount in bank drafts.

Carnival Leisure was unable to cash the bank drafts because Aubin had subsequently directed his bank to stop payment. Carnival Leisure sued Aubin in the United States District Court for the Southern District of Texas to enforce the debt. The district court granted Carnival Leisure's motion for summary judgment against Aubin in the amount of $25,000 and attorney's fees and costs. Carnival Leisure claimed that the debt was enforceable under Texas law because public policy had changed and now favored enforcement of gambling debts. The district court agreed. Aubin raises on appeal only the issue of whether public policy in Texas continues to prevent the enforcement of gambling debts.

Carnival Leisure claims, however, that since 1973 the public policy of Texas toward gambling and the legality of gambling debts has changed. Although gambling is generally proscribed in Texas, there has been an exception for the "social" gambler since 1973. The Texas legislature enacted the Bingo Enabling Act in 1981, the Texas Racing Act in 1986, and the Charitable Raffle Enabling Act in 1989. Provisions were added to the Texas Penal Code excepting these three activities from its general proscription against gambling.

The enactment of statutes legalizing some forms of gambling admittedly evidences some dissipation or narrowing of public disapproval of gambling. However, such statutes hardly introduce a judicially cognizable change in public policy with respect to gambling generally. The social gambling permitted is confined to private places where no one receives any benefit other than his personal winnings and all participants are subject to the same risks, a categorically vastly different kind of activity from the sort involved here. The racing, bingo, and raffling exceptions are narrow, strictly regulated exceptions to a broad public policy in Texas against most forms of gambling. Further, the kind of gambling engaged in here is not of the sort permitted by any of these exceptions.

Even if gambling legislation in Texas were evidence sufficient to warrant judicial notice of a shift in public policy with respect to legalized gambling, such a shift would not be inconsistent with a continued public policy disfavoring gambling on credit. Although Aubin could have used the loaned markers for nongambling purposes at the Casino, it is undisputed that they were in fact used exclusively for gambling. Aubin's gambling debt therefore fits squarely within the terms of the public policy of Texas prohibiting enforcement of gambling debts owed to gambling participants incurred for the purpose of gambling.

We hold that the public policy in Texas against gambling on credit prevents enforcement of a debt incurred for the purpose of gambling and provided by a participant in the gambling activity. The district court's grant of summary judgment in favor of Carnival Leisure is accordingly REVERSED and this case is remanded to the district court for further proceedings consistent with this opinion.

CONTINENTAL AIRLINES, INC. v. McDONNELL DOUGLAS CORP., 264 CAL. RPTR. 779 (CT. APP. 1989).

This action was commenced by plaintiff and respondent Continental Airlines (Continental) in Los Angeles Superior Court on December 3, 1979, and alleged, against defendant and appellant McDonnell Douglas Corporation (Douglas), causes of action for deceit. In January 30, 1986, the jury returned verdicts in favor of Continental for $17 million on its claim for fraud by misrepresentation and fraud by nondisclosure of known facts. The judgment was granted. This appeal is from that judgment. We affirm the judgment as modified.

On March 1, 1978, a Continental DC-10 aircraft, which had been delivered to Continental by Douglas in 1972, was in its take-off roll at Los Angeles International Airport when two tires burst on the left landing gear. The captain elected to try to stop the plane, but it ran off the end of the runway at 8 miles per hour. The landing gear broke through the tarmac, burrowed into the ground, and was ripped from the wing, making a 3.7 hole which allowed fuel to pour from the wing fuel tanks. The plane was severely damaged by the resulting fire and rendered unrepairable.

Douglas had approached Continental in 1968 to sell Continental DC-10 aircraft. Douglas used a series of briefings and sales brochures in its sales campaign. The sales brochure given to Continental consisted of hundreds of pages of technical information drafted by Douglas's engineers, and reviewed by its top management, for the express purpose of explaining the DC-10 design and a "Detail Type Specification" to potential aircraft purchasers. That Specification, as its name implies, described the technical details of the DC-10. The Douglas briefings covered the landing gear and wing design, as did many of its brochures. Continental personnel used the brochures to write portions of Continental's "Tri-Jet Evaluation," a comparison between the DC-10 and Lockheed's L-1011, which became a basis for Continental's decision to purchase the DC-10. When Continental decided to purchase the DC-10 instead of the L-1011 aircraft, it finalized a Purchase Agreement with Douglas which incorporated by reference the Detail Specifications for the DC-10.

The brochures contained statements that "the fuel tank will not rupture under crash load conditions"; that the landing gear "are designed for wipe-off without rupturing the wing fuel tank"; that "the support structure is designed to a higher strength than the gear to prevent fuel tank rupture due to an accidental landing gear overload"; that the DC-10 "is designed and tested for crashworthiness"; that the "landing gear will be tested" to demonstrate the fail safe integrity and wipe-off characteristics of the gear design; and that "good reliability" for the DC-10 landing gear could be predicted with an "unusually high degree of confidence" because of its close similarity to the successful design on the DC-8 and DC-9 aircraft.

Douglas argues that "the Uniform Commercial Code and cases interpreting it have recognized that general promotional observations of this type are merely expressions of opinion that are not actionable as fraudulent statements. The alleged false representations in the subject brochures were not statements of "opinion or mere puffing." They were, in essence, representations that the DC-10 was a safe aircraft. Promises of safety are not statements of opinion—they are representations of fact.

Douglas contends in its opening brief that there was no substantial evidence that its precontract representations were *material* or that Continental reasonably *relied* on them in deciding to purchase the DC-10. The materiality of the representations can hardly be questioned. Any airline shopping for aircraft to service its customers naturally searches for planes that are safe. Where representations have been made in regard to material matter and action has been taken in the absence of evidence showing the contrary, reliance on the representations will be presumed. Here, both materiality and reliance are demonstrated by the fact that Continental evaluated the DC-10 breakaway design in its "Tri-Jet Evaluation," which compared the DC-10 with the L-1011 for the purpose of deciding which aircraft to purchase. Douglas was the only possible source for the information; there was no way Continental could independently investigate or analyze the adequacy of that design. The foregoing provides more than substantial evidence that Continental *relied* on Douglas's representations regarding landing gear breakaway in choosing to purchase the DC-10 and that those representations were *material.*

False representations made recklessly and without regard for their truth in order to induce action by another are equivalent of misrepresentations uttered. Therefore, there is substantial evidence of the requisite intent for intentional fraud. For the foregoing reasons we conclude the evidence supports the jury's findings of liability for fraud. The judgment is modified to reflect an award of prejudgment interest in the amount of $9,549,750. As so modified, the judgment is AFFIRMED.

CASE B.6

HAMPTON v. FEDERAL EXPRESS CORP., 917 F.2D 1119 (8TH CIR. 1990).

In March 1988, Carl Gerome Hampton, a 13-year-old cancer patient at Children's Memorial Hospital in Omaha, Nebraska, was awaiting a bone marrow transplant. A transplant operation was scheduled at the University of Iowa Hospital in Iowa City, Iowa, where five potential bone marrow donors had been found. On March 21, 1988, in order to match Carl with the most suitable donor, five samples of Carl's blood were sent by the shipper, the Children's Memorial Hospital in Omaha, to Dr. Nancy Goeken, at the Veterans Administration Medical Center in Iowa City. The shipper, the Children's Memorial Hospital, entered into a contract with the carrier, Federal Express, for the transport of the blood samples.

In a paragraph entitled "Damages or Loss," the contract of carriage, set forth in the airbill, stated: "We are liable for no more than $100 per package in the event of physical loss or damage, unless you fill in a higher Declared Value to the left and document higher actual loss in the event of a claim. We charge 30 cents for each additional $100 of declared value up to the maximum shown in our Service Guide." The reverse side of the airbill contains several paragraphs, entitled "Limitations On Our Liability," which state that: "Our liability for loss or damage to your package is limited to your actual damages or $100, whichever is less, unless you pay for and declare a higher authorized value." It is not disputed that the blood samples were never received by Dr. Goeken; that Carl Hampton, the infant cancer patient, never obtained a bone marrow transplant; and that he died on May 19, 1988. Alleging causes of action for personal injury, wrongful death, and loss of services, Carl Jerry Hampton, individually and on behalf of his deceased son, Carl Gerome Hampton, filed suit in the United States District Court for the Western District of Missouri, seeking $3,081,000 in damages. The district court granted Federal Express's motion for partial summary judgment, and entered judgment in favor of Hampton for $100. Hampton appeals from judgment of the district court.

We have held that, under federal common law, "a common carrier may not exempt itself from liability for its negligence; however, a carrier may limit its liability" [Hopper Furs, Inc. v Emery Air Freight Corp, 749 F.2d 1261, 1264 (8th Cir. 1984)].

In this case, that contract entered into by the shipper, the Children's Memorial Hospital, with the carrier of $100, and provided the shipper with an opportunity to declare a higher value. Furthermore, it is not disputed that the shipper never declared a higher value for the blood samples. Hence, the liability of the carrier would be limited to $100. Clearly, Federal Express had no knowledge of Hampton, and did not know that the package contained blood samples. It is equally clear that the shipper, Children's Memorial Hospital, did not declare a value higher than $100 for the package. Under the circumstances, Federal Express could not reasonably foresee any injury to Hampton, or the nature and extent of the injury.

Since, on the facts presented, the nature and extent of damages suffered by plaintiff Hampton was not reasonably foreseeable to the carrier, Federal Express, we AFFIRM the judgment of the district court granting Federal Express's motion for partial summary judgment.

CHASE PRECAST CORP. v. JOHN J. PAONESSA CO., 566 N.E.2D 603 (MASS. 1991).

This appeal raises the question whether the doctrine of frustration of purpose may be a defense in a breach of contract action in Massachusetts, and, if so, whether it excuses the defendant J. J. Paonessa Company, Inc. (Paonessa), from performance.

The claim of the plaintiff, Chase Precast Corporation (Chase), arises from the cancellation of its contracts with Paonessa to supply median barriers in a highway construction project of the Commonwealth. Chase brought an action to recover its anticipated profit on the amount of the media barriers called for by its supply contracts with Paonessa but was not produced. Paonessa brought a cross action against the Commonwealth for indemnification in the event it should be held liable to Chase. After a jury waived trail, a Superior Court judge ruled for Paonessa on the basis of impossibility of performance. Chase and Paonessa cross-appealed. The appeals court affirmed, noting that the doctrine of frustration of purpose more accurately described the basis of the trial judge's decision than the doctrine of impossibility. We agree. We allowed Chase's application for further appellate review and we now affirm.

The pertinent facts are as follows. In 1982, the Commonwealth, through the Department of Public Works (department), entered into two contracts with Paonessa for resurfacing and improvements to two stretches of Route 128. Part of each contract called for replacing a grass median strip between the north- and southbound lanes with concrete resurfacing and precast concrete median barriers. Paonessa entered into two contracts with Chase under which Chase was to supply, in the aggregate, 25,800 linear feet of concrete median barriers according to the specifications of the department for highway construction. The quantity and type of barriers to be supplied were specified in two purchase orders prepared by Chase.

The highway reconstruction began in the spring of 1983. By late May, the department was receiving protests from the angry residents who objected to use of concrete barriers and removal of the grass median strip. Paonessa and Chase became aware of the protest around June 1. On June 6, a group of about 100 citizens filed an action in the Superior Court to stop installation of the concrete barriers and other aspects of the work. On June 7, anticipating modification by the department, Paonessa notified Chase by letter to stop producing concrete barriers for the project. Chase did so upon receipt of letter the following day. On June 17, the department and the citizens group entered into a settlement which provided, in part, that no additional concrete median barriers would be installed. On June 23, the department deleted the permanent concrete median barriers item from its contract with Paonessa.

Before stopping production on June 8, Chase had produced approximately one-half of the concrete median barriers called for by its contracts with Paonessa, and had delivered most of them to the construction sites. Paonessa paid Chase for all that it had produced, at the contract price. Chase suffered no out-of-pocket expense as a result of cancellation of the remaining portion of barriers.

This court has long recognized and applied the doctrine of impossibility as a defense to an action of breach of contract. Under that doctrine, "where from the nature of the contract it appears that the parties must from the beginning have contemplated the continued existence of some particular specified thing as the foundation of what was to be done, then, in the absence of any warranty that the thing shall exist . . . the parties shall be excused . . . when[cb] performance becomes impossible from the accidental perishing of the thing without the fault of either party."

On the other hand, although we have referred to the doctrine of frustration of purpose in a few decisions, we have never clearly defined it. Other jurisdictions have explained the doctrine as follows: when an event neither anticipated nor caused by either party, the risk of which was not allocated by the contract, destroys the object or purpose of the contract, thus destroying the value of performance, the parties are excused from further performance.

In *Mishara Construction Co.,* we called frustration of purpose a "companion rule" to the doctrine of impossibility. Both doctrines concern the effect of supervening circumstances upon the rights and duties of the parties. The difference lies in the effect of the supervening event. Another definition of frustration of purpose is found in the *Restatement (Second) of Contracts* §265 (1981). "Where, after a contract is made, a party's principal purpose is substantially frustrated without his fault by the occurrence of an event the nonoccurrence of which was a basic assumption on which the contract was made, his remaining duties to render performance are discharged, unless the language or the circumstances indicate the contrary."

Paonessa bore no responsibility for the department's elimination of the median barriers from the projects. Therefore, whether it can rely on the defense of frustration turns on whether elimination of the barriers was a risk allocated by the contracts to Paonessa. The question is, given the commercial circumstances in which the parties dealt: "Was the contingency which developed one which the parties could reasonably be thought to have foreseen as a real possibility which could affect performance? Was it one of that variety of risks which the parties were tacitly assigning to the promisor by their failure to provide for it explicitly? If it was, performance will be required. If it could not be considered, performance is excused."

The record supports the conclusion that Chase was aware of the department's power to decrease quantities of contract items. The judge found that Chase had been the supplier of median barriers to the department in the past. The provisions giving the department the power to eliminate items or portions thereof was standard in its contracts. The judge's finding that all parties were well aware that lost profits were not an element of damage in either of the public works projects in issue further supports the conclusion that Chase was aware of the department's power to decrease quantities, since the term prohibiting claims for anticipated profit is part of the same sentence in the standard provision as that allowing the engineer to eliminate items or portions of work. In this case, even if the parties were aware generally of the department's power to eliminate contract items, the judge could reasonably have concluded that they did not contemplate the cancellation for a major portion of the project of such a widely used item as concrete median barriers, and did not allocate the risk of such cancellations.

Judgment AFFIRMED.

CASE B.8

E.B. HARVEY & CO. v. PROTECTIVE SYS., INC., NO. CA NO. 840, 1989 TENN. LEXIS 105, AT *1 (CT. APP. FEB. 19, 1989).

The plaintiff-appellant, E.B. Harvey Company, Inc. (Harvey), is engaged in the manufacture and wholesale of fine jewelry in Chattanooga. It has been engaged in this business for about 10 years. It maintains an inventory in excess of $1 million of gold, silver, precious stones, pearls, and other such materials related to the manufacture of jewelry. A considerable amount of its jewelry is on consignment and, by the very nature of its business, it requires a great deal of insurance. However, the insurance companies will not write the insurance unless it maintains an Underwriters Laboratories (U.L.)-approved AA burglary protection alarm system. The defendant-appellee, Protective Systems, Inc. (Protective), is one of two companies in Hamilton County which furnishes and maintains a U.L.-approved AA burglary protection system. In June 1981, Harvey entered into a three-year contract with Protective to install and maintain a burglary protection system. The contract provided:

It is agreed that Protective is not an insurer and that the payments hereinbefore named are based solely upon the value of the services herein described and it is not the intention of the parties that Protective assume responsibility for any losses occasioned by malfeasance or misfeasance in the performance of the services under this contract or for any loss or damage sustained through burglary, theft, robbery, fire, or other cause or any liability on the part of Protective by virtue of this Agreement or because of the relation hereby established.

If there shall at any time be or arise any liability on the part of Protective, by virtue of this Agreement or because of the relation hereby established, whether due to the negligence of Protective or otherwise, such liability is and shall be limited to a sum total in amount to the rental service charge hereunder for a period of service not to exceed six months, which sum shall be paid and received as liquidated damages.

The burglary and hold-up system provided to Harvey operated by means of Grade AA telephone lines between the central monitoring station of Protective and Harvey's premises. Said telephone lines were at all times owned and maintained by the South Central Bell Telephone Company. On July 22, 1984, at 11:14 P.M., an outage condition was indicated on the E.B. Harvey & Company account. For a period of two weeks prior to this date, Protective's computer had been registering an inordinate number of outage signals which had all been traced back to problems in telephone company equipment. For this reason, on July 22, 1984, Protective's president, Pendell Meyers, notified the telephone company of this condition and reported a potential problem to the police department but did not contact a representative of Harvey to notify them of the outage condition.

The phone company was unable to locate the exact nature of the problem despite several telephone conversations with Meyers. The Chattanooga Police Department patrolled the premises surrounding Harvey's place of business twice that evening but did not note any unusual activity. The following morning, when an employee of Harvey reported to work, it was discovered that a burglary had in fact taken place. Some $200,000 worth of jewelry and inventory was stolen. Harvey sued Protective for damages resulting from the burglary. It alleged that Protective was guilty of negligence for its failure to notify Harvey or its employees of the outage which appeared on the burglary monitoring equipment.

Protective, for answer, denied the allegations of Harvey's complaint, and as an affirmative defense, alleged the contract between the parties with its exculpatory and limitation of liability provisions was enforceable and binding upon Harvey. After hearing testimony, the trial court held the extent of Harvey's recovery against Protective would be 650 percent as liquidated damages. A final judgment was entered and Harvey has appealed.

There is nothing in public policy to render inoperative or nugatory the contractual limitations contained in the agreement. Limitations against liability for negligence or breach of contract have generally been upheld in this state in the absence of fraud or overreaching. Limitations such as those contained in the present contract have generally been deemed reasonable and have been sustained in actions against the providers of burglary and fire alarm systems. Such clauses do not ordinarily protect against liability for fraud or intentional misrepresentation.

We concur with the trial court. The issues are found in favor of the appellees. The judgment of the trial court is AFFIRMED. The cost of this appeal is taxed to the appellant and the case is remanded to the trial court for collection of cost.

CASE B.9

TOYS "R" US, INC. v. ABIR, NO. 97 CIV. 8673 (JGK), 1999 U.S. DIST. LEXIS 1275, AT *1 (S.D.N.Y. FEB. 10, 1999).

In 1997, plaintiff Toys "R" Us, Inc., filed an action alleging violations of federal law related to trademark dilution against the defendants, Eli Abir and Website Management, who had registered the name *Toysareus.com* as their Internet domain name. The plaintiffs alleged that this domain name diluted the plaintiff's mark TOYS "R" US. In November 1997, this court issued a temporary restraining order enjoining the defendants from 'using or inducing others to use the names or marks or any colorable imitation of Plaintiff's TOYS "R" US, BABIES "R" US and/or the family of "R" US marks' pending a decision on the plaintiff's motion for a preliminary injunction.

In December 1997, this court heard argument on the motion for preliminary injunction. At that time the plaintiffs alleged that the defendants had also registered the domain name *Kidsareus.com*. This court then issued a preliminary injunction enjoining the defendants from, among other things, using or inducing others to use any colorable imitation of the family of "R" US marks pending final judgment. On August 27, 1998, this court granted the plaintiff's motion for summary judgment on the trademark dilution claims. The following day, the court issued a separate Judgment and Order permanently enjoining the defendants from further infringement of the family of "R" US marks and ordering the transfer of the *Toysareus.com* and *Kidsareus.com* Internet domain names to the plaintiff.

In addition, this court held that because the defendants' conduct in this case was willful, intentional, deliberate, and in bad faith, the plaintiff is entitled to recover attorneys' fees and costs. In order to determine what constitutes "reasonable" attorneys' fees, the starting point is the "lodestar amount," which is the number of hours reasonably expended on the litigation multiplied by a reasonable hourly rate for attorneys and paralegals.

In determining a reasonable hourly rate, courts consider, inter alia, the size and experience of the firm. In this case, Darby & Darby is a well-known New York firm which specializes in intellectual property; the rates charged for its attorneys are comparable to other specialized intellectual property firms in the New York City legal market. The plaintiff's counsel swore in her declaration in support of this application that care was taken to enhance efficiency by assigning, at any one time, only one partner, one mid- to senior-level associate, one to two junior associates and one to two legal assistants to the prosecution of this case. Having carefully reviewed the itemized request for disbursements, the court finds them neither unnecessary nor excessive for a case of this duration and complexity. The plaintiff is also entitled to costs, as well as those reasonable out-of-pocket expenses incurred by the attorneys and which are normally charged fee-paying clients.

Defendant Eli Abir, who is the owner of defendant Website Management, does not argue that the award requested by the plaintiffs is excessive. Instead, he argues that due to his business and personal circumstances he has limited financial resources and would be unable to pay more than a "symbolic" amount in attorneys' fees. However, nothing in the record in this case justifies a financially based reduction in the award of attorneys' fees and costs. For the reasons stated above the plaintiff's motion for attorneys' fees and costs is granted in the amount of $55,162.76. SO ORDERED.

CASE B.10

CAFAZZO v. CENT. MED. HEALTH SERV., INC., 668 A.2D 521 (PA. 1995).

In 1986, appellant Albert Cafazzo underwent surgery for implantation of a mandibular prosthesis. In 1992, some time after it was discovered that this device was defective, a complaint was filed against Dr. Normal Stern, the physician who performed the surgery, and the hospital where the operation took place, claiming that "all defendants sell, provide, or use certain prosthetic devices," and that they should be held strictly liable as having "provided, sold, or otherwise placed in the stream of commerce products manufactured by Vitek, Inc., known as Proplast TMJ Implants." The complaint alleged that the prosthesis was defectively designed, unsafe for its intended use, and lacked any warning necessary in order to ensure safety.

Section 402A of the *Restatement (Second) of Torts*, provides in relevant part as follows:

(1) One who sells any product in a defective condition unreasonably dangerous to the user or consumer or to his property is subject to liability for physical harm thereby caused to the ultimate user or consumer, or to his property, if:

(a) the seller is engaged in the business of selling a product, and

(b) it is expected to and does reach the consumer without substantial change in the condition in which it is sold.

The thrust of the inquiry is not on whether a separate consideration is charged for the physical material used in the exercise of medical skill, but what service is performed to restore or maintain the patient's health. The determinative question becomes not what is being charged, but what is being done. The provision of medical services is regarded as qualitatively different from the sale of products.

This distinction is made clearer by the fact that case law also supports the application of 402A where what has been provided is not medical service or products connected with diagnosis and treatment, but rather materials related to mechanical or administrative functions. See *Thomas v. St. Joseph Hospital*, 618 S.W.2d 791 (Tex. Civ. App. 1981) (hospital held strictly liable where hospital gown ignited when lighted match fell on it).

It must be noted that the "seller" need not be engaged solely in the business of selling products such as the defective one to be held strictly liable. An example supporting this proposition appears in comment *f* of the *Restatement (Second) of Torts*, §402A and concerns the owner of a motion picture theater who offers edibles such as popcorn and candy for sale to movie patrons. The analogue to the instant case is valid in one respect only: both the candy and the TMJ implant are ancillary to the primary activity, viewing a film or undergoing surgery respectively. However, beyond that any comparison is specious. A movie audience is free to purchase or not any food items on offer, and regardless of which option is exercised the primary activity is unaffected. On the other hand, while the implant was incidental to the surgical procedure here, it was a necessary adjunct to the treatment administered, as were the scalpel used to make the incision, and any other material objects involved in performing the operation, all of which fulfill a particular role in provision of medical service, the primary activity.

When one enters the hospital as a patient, he goes there, not to buy medicines or pills, not to purchase bandages or iodine or serum or blood, but to obtain a course of treatment in the hope of being cured of what ails him. We find, consistent with the decisions cited above which distinguish medical services from merchandising, that appellees are not sellers, providers, suppliers or distributors of products such as to activate 402A.

CASE B.11

BURNETT v. PURTELL, NO. 91 L-094, 1992 OHIO LEXIS 3467, AT *1 (CT. APP. JUNE 30, 1992).

Appellees agreed to purchase a mobile home with shed from appellant. On Saturday, March 3, 1990, appellees paid appellant $6,500 and in return were given the certificate of title to the mobile home as well as a key to the mobile home, but no keys to the shed. At the same time the certificate of title was transferred, the following items remained in the mobile home: the washer and dryer, mattress and box springs, two chairs, items in the refrigerator, and the entire contents of the shed. These items were to be retained by the appellant and removed by appellant. To facilitate removal, the estate retained one key to the mobile home and the only keys to the shed.

On Sunday, March 4, 1990, the mobile home was destroyed by fire through the fault of neither party. At the time of the fire, appellant still had a key to the mobile home, as well as the keys to the shed, and she had not removed the contents of the mobile home nor the shed. The contents of the shed were not destroyed and have now been removed by appellant. The referee determined that the risk of loss remained with appellant because there was no tender of delivery. Appellant objected to the conclusion of law, but the trial court overruled the objection and entered judgment in favor of appellee. First, the appellant argues that because the certificate of title was transferred, appellees were given a key to the mobile home and the full purchase price was paid by appellees, that the risk of loss had shifted from appellant to appellees. The risk of loss passes to the buyer on his receipt of the goods if the seller is a merchant: otherwise the risk passes to the buyer on tender of delivery.

Analyzing the foregoing elements it is clear that, as the trial court stated, appellant did not tender delivery. The parties agreed that appellees would purchase the mobile home and shed from appellant. The contents of both the shed and the mobile home were to be retained by appellant and removed by appellant. At the time of the fire, appellant had not removed the items that she was required to remove from either the mobile home or the shed. Additionally, all keys to the mobile home were not surrendered and none of the keys to the shed were relinquished. Under this scenario, appellant did not tender conforming goods free of items belonging to her which remained in the trailer, nor did she put the mobile home at the appellee's disposition without being fettered with the items previously enumerated. Accordingly, the trial court was correct in determining that appellant did not tender delivery within the meaning of the statute, and consequently the risk of loss remained with her. The trial court was correct in determining that appellant did not tender delivery in a manner sufficient to shift the risk of loss to appellees. Therefore, when it ordered appellant to rerun appellee's purchase money, it effactually mandated that the contract was "avoided."

Based on the foregoing, the judgment of the trial court is AFFIRMED.

CASE B.12

LNS INV. CO. v. PHILLIPS 66 CO., 731 F. SUPP. 1484 (D. KAN. 1990).

Plaintiff is the successor to a company known as CompuBlend Corporation ("CBC"), which blended, labeled, and packaged quart plastic bottles of motor oil for, among others, defendant Phillips 66 Company. On July 29, 1986, W. Peter Buhlinger, defendant's manager of lubricants ("Buhlinger"), wrote a letter to Dan Tutcher, Plaintiff's vice-president of operations ("Tutcher"), which read as follows: This will confirm our verbal agreement wherein Phillips will purchase additional quantities of plastic bottles from CBC during 1986. CBC, in an effort to increase their packaging capacity, has committed to purchase several additional molds to blow the Phillips plastic one-quart container. In order to amortize the cost of the additional equipment, Phillips has agreed to take delivery of a maximum of 4,000,000 bottles to be made available by December 31, 1986. This agreement includes the production available now and to be supplemented by the additional equipment. Should CBC not be able to produce the full 4,000,000 quarts by December 31, 1986, this agreement shall be considered satisfied. Phillip's desire is to receive as many bottles packaged with Phillips motor oil in 1986 from CBC as possible.

Plaintiff experienced numerous problems in maintaining even its precontract capacity. Moreover, the quality of goods plaintiff was able to deliver was frequently unacceptable to defendant. Laughlin reiterated defendant's dissatisfaction with plaintiff's products by letter dated October 15, 1986. Discussing bottles tendered by plaintiff, Laughlin stated that "we definitely do not want bottles on the shelf of the quality submitted." On December 16, 1986, Buhlinger wrote that defendant would not renew any commitments to purchase goods from the plaintiff after March 31, 1987, due to plaintiff's poor performance under the July 29 agreement. Plaintiff filed this suit on March 12, 1987, alleging, inter alia, that defendant breached the July 29 agreement by failing to purchase plaintiff's full output of plastic bottles through December 31, 1986.

Plaintiff's failure to provide either the quantity or quality of goods contemplated by the July 29 agreement entitled defendant to suspend its performance. Section 84-2-609 of the Code states as follows: Right to adequate assurance of performance. (1) A contract for sale imposes an obligation on each party that the other's expectation of receiving due performance will not be impaired. When reasonable grounds for insecurity arise with respect to the performance of either party the other may in writing demand adequate assurance of due performance and until he receives such assurance may if commercially reasonable suspend any performance for which he has not already received the agreed return.

It was incumbent upon plaintiff to provide adequate assurance of its future performance to defendant. Plaintiff failed to provide defendant with adequate assurance of its future performance. Official UCC Comment 4 states that what constitutes "adequate" assurance of due performance is subject to the same test of factual conditions as what constitutes "reasonable grounds for insecurity." For example, where the buyer can make use of a defective delivery, a mere promise by a seller of good repute that he is giving the matter his attention and that the defect will not be repeated, is normally sufficient. Under the same circumstances, however, a similar statement by a known corner-cutter might well be considered insufficient without the posting of a guaranty or, if so demanded by the buyer, a speedy replacement of the delivery involved. By the same token where a delivery has defects, even though easily curable, which interfere with easy use by the buyer, no verbal assurance can be deemed adequate which is not accomplished by replacement, repair, money-allowance, or other commercially reasonable cure.

Plaintiff's continual excuses for failure to perform, unaccompanied by corresponding remedial action, cannot be deemed adequate assurance under the Code. Accordingly, defendant was entitled to suspend its own performance of the contract by refusing to place orders with plaintiff and/or canceling unfilled orders already placed, thirty days after either or both the September 18, 1986, and October 15, 1986, letters. In view of this conclusion, defendant did not breach the contract by suspending performance in December, 1986, and judgment will be entered in its favor.

Judgment for defendant.

CASE B.13

CATE v. DOVER CORP., 776 S.W.2D 680 (TEX. APP. 1989).

In September 1984, Edward Cate bought three Rotary brand vehicle lifts from Beech Tire Mart. Dover Corporation manufactured the lifts, which were designed to elevate vehicles for repair work underneath the vehicle. In his deposition, Cate stated that he received a five-year written warranty from Dover when he purchased the lifts. On at least three occasions, vehicles fell from the lifts. Although Beech and Dover made numerous inspections, Cate said that the lifts never functioned properly. The warranty expressly provided that Dover would replace all parts returned to the factory which proved to be defective. Cate did not return the lifts, but rather sued Dover for breach of the implied warranty of merchantability about two and one-half years after he bought the lifts.

The issue is whether a material issue of fact exists regarding the conspicuous nature of the disclaimer contained in the warranty. If the disclaimer is conspicuous, then Cate is limited to a cause of action based upon the express warranty that was created, and precluded from suing on the implied warranty of merchantability, since the express warranty disclaimed the implied warranty. An express warranty that specifically disclaims an implied warranty controls.

A warranty of merchantability is implied in a contract for the sale of goods by a merchant unless the warranty is excluded or modified in accordance with statutory requirements. An implied warranty of merchantability . . . may be disclaimed by the seller . . . so long as the disclaimer is conspicuous.

"Conspicuous" is defined as follows: A term or clause is conspicuous when it is so written that a reasonable person against whom it is to operate ought to have noticed it. A printed heading in capitals (as: NON-NEGOTIABLE BILL OF LADING) is conspicuous. Language in the body of a form is conspicuous if it is larger or of other contrasting type or color. But in a telegram, any stated term is conspicuous. Whether a term or clause is conspicuous or not is for decision by the court.

The trial court found that the disclaimer contained in Dover's warranty complied with Tex. Bus. & Com. Code Ann. Section 2.316, and accordingly granted Dover's motion for summary judgment. The warranty page itself is headed by the sentence, written in solid blue one-half inch block type,

"YOU CAN TAKE ROTARY'S NEW 5-YEAR WARRANTY AND TEAR IT APART." Then the warranty itself is set out below that, framed by double blue lines entitled "WARRANTY" in solid blue letters three-eighths inch high. The text of the warranty is in black type. The disclaimer portion, contained in a separate paragraph within the warranty, provides the following: "This warranty is exclusive and is in lieu of all other warranties expressed or implied including any implied warranty of merchantability or any implied warranty of fitness for a particular purpose, which implied warranties are hereby expressly excluded."

We affirm the trial court's judgment.

CASE B.14

HORN v. GEN. MOTORS CORP., 551 P.2D 398 (CAL. 1976).

In this action for damages for personal injuries, defendants General Motors Corporation and Fletcher Chevrolet, Inc., appeal from a judgment entered upon a jury verdict in favor of plaintiff.

About 9 P.M. on the evening of September 23, 1966, plaintiff Lillian Y. Horn was driving her 1965 Chevrolet station wagon down Laurel Canyon Boulevard, a curving Los Angeles street. She was accompanied by her two sons; her six-year-old son was in the front seat and her nine-year-old son in the rear. As she wound downhill, at approximately 25 miles per hour, a car rounding a curve suddenly swung into her lane, its headlights temporarily blinding her. She swerved to her right to avoid the car, bounced off the right curb across the street to the left and into a concrete reinforced abutment.

As she steered to the right, plaintiff brought her left hand across the horn cap in the center of the steering wheel; at the same time, with her right hand, she tried to hold her son on the front seat. She felt and saw something fly between herself and her son; it was later established that this was the horn cap. When the car hit the abutment, plaintiff felt a burning sensation as her face hit the "center part" of the steering wheel. The "center part," following removal of the horn cap, contained three sharp prongs that held the horn cap in place. Plaintiff sustained a laceration of the chin, a displaced fracture of her jaw, a fracture of her left ear canal, and the loss of two teeth.

Plaintiff brought this action against defendant General Motors Corporation, the manufacturer of the station wagon, and defendant Fletcher Chevrolet, Inc., the dealer from whom she purchased it. The case was tried on the single theory of strict liability in tort based on a defective product. In detail plaintiff's theory was that the automobile was defective in that the horn cap was easily removable in normal use of the vehicle thereby exposing three sharp prongs, and that, as a result, when plaintiff was involved in a collision not caused by defendants, she sustained injuries which were measurably aggravated because of this defect in design or manufacture. In short: the defective horn cap caused plaintiff injuries which were greater than the injuries she otherwise would have received as a result of the collision. The jury returned a verdict against both defendants for damages in the sum of $ 45,000.

Defendants contend that they are not liable as a matter of law because a collision is not a normal, proper or intended use of an automobile and therefore the manufacturer is under no duty to design an automobile so as to prevent any aggravation of injuries resulting from a collision which occurs for reasons wholly unconnected with the design and manufacture of the automobile. In *Cronin v. J.B.E. Olson Corp.* (1972) 8 Cal.3d 121, 126 [104 Cal.Rptr. 433, 501 P.2d 1153], this court acknowledged the existence of this line of authority but specifically rejected it: "Although a collision may not be the 'normal' or intended use of a motor vehicle, vehicle manufacturers must take accidents into consideration as reasonably foreseeable occurrences involving their products. The design and manufacture of products should not be carried out in an industrial vacuum but with recognition of the realities of their everyday use." In *Cronin* the driver of a bakery truck was injured when another vehicle forced the truck off the road and into a ditch. The impact broke an aluminum hasp holding the bread trays in place and the trays were driven forward against the driver, propelling him through the windshield. We upheld a verdict in favor of the plaintiff and against the manufacturer of the truck declaring that liability rested not on the basis that the hasp caused the collision "but only that its defectiveness was a substantial factor contributing to [the plaintiff's] injuries." (*Id.,* at p. 127.)

In the instant case the jury was properly instructed to the effect that if the station wagon was defectively designed or manufactured in such a manner that the horn assembly caused plaintiff to sustain greater injuries in the collision than she would have otherwise sustained absent the defect, then the manufacturer and distributor of the vehicle would be liable to the extent of such aggravation of her injuries. This instruction contained a principle of liability consistent with our ruling in *Cronin.*

The judgment is affirmed.

CASE B.15

SIMPSON v. NORWESCO, INC., 583 F.2D 1007 (8TH CIR. 1978).

When Simpson went to work for Nowesco, the parties signed an employment contract that provided he would be paid specified percentages on sales of certain items, as a commission. The contract was "terminable at the will of either party upon six months' written notice."

When difficulties arose in its business and it decided there was a need to reduce operating costs, Norwesco informed Simpson by letter that it was reducing his commission rate. Simpson sent a letter back which clearly stated that he planned "to continue with the same efforts in accordance with the terms of the original agreement." When Norwesco began sending monthly commission checks reflecting the change in commission rates, Simpson went ahead and cashed them. Later, a second similar cut in commission rate was made by Norwesco. Simpson maintained that he again refused to acquiesce.

Eventually, Norwesco sold the business to another corporation and Simpson received a letter giving him six months' notice that his employment was terminated. When he sued to recover the money he should have received had he been paid at the commission rates stipulated in his original contract, the jury awarded him $90,381.68.

A party to a contract cannot alter his obligation thereunder without the consent of the other party, and this principle extends to any labor or employment contract. Such a unilateral change is precisely what Norwesco attempted—twice. Simpson never acquiesced to a change in his commission rates. Indeed, he actively expressed his disapproval of such an attempt and declared his intention to continue work under the old contract terms. Whether or not his action of cashing the commission checks, which bore no written declaration that acceptance of them constitutes settlement in full, estopped him from making any further claims to commissions was a jury question and was properly decided by the jury.

The final judgment is AFFIRMED.

APPENDIX C

SAMPLE CONTRACTS

As you go through the sample contracts provided in this appendix, remember that these are *sample* contracts. They are provided to give you a sense of the many different forms a contract may take and the various ways a contract might look. These samples are from many different sources and states. So a particular type of contract might look different—and might not be valid—in your state.

Some of the sample contracts are simple and short (such as the Corporation Formation Agreement); some are detailed and lengthy (such as the Real Estate Property Sales Agreement). Some have blanks where you would insert information if you were drafting a contract; some have information within them so you can see how the specifics might be set forth.

Paralegals are often asked to draft contracts. But remember that ethically, a paralegal cannot draft the contract *directly for the client*. This would amount to the unauthorized practice of law. Terminology *is* important here; the paralegal is always drafting the contract for *the attorney's review*.

When drafting the contract for the attorney's review, always view the contract as a living, breathing document. *One size doesn't fit all.* In other words, just because a form is titled "Real Estate Purchase Agreement" doesn't necessarily mean that contract will specifically fit the real estate transaction at hand. For instance, maybe the form is for commercial real estate, but what if the actual contract needed is for *residential* real estate?

Once the contract is drafted—whether by you as the paralegal or by the other party to the real estate transaction—you may be asked to review the contract to make sure it serves the client's needs properly. What follows are some practice tips on how you should approach this contract review, whether or not you have the title "contract review paralegal."

■ HOW THE CONTRACT "ARRIVES"

For a contracts review paralegal, unless he or she specifically drafted the contract, many times a contract drafted by someone else lands on the paralegal's desk mysteriously. Sometimes someone leaves it in the paralegal's mailbox like a present. Or maybe someone e-mails the contract to the paralegal. Many times the contract is in a pdf format, which, of course, you can't alter. Maybe they are hoping the paralegal *won't* make changes. But the job of a contract review paralegal is to make changes where appropriate—or at least to suggest changes to the attorney—in an effort to serve the best interests of the client.

■ CONTRACT REVIEW IS NECESSARY

If you are drafting a contract, you must remember that ethically the contract should be reviewed by an attorney. Just as importantly, the client should review the contract to be sure he or she is capable of complying with the representations in the contract; in other words, not agreeing to something that he or she cannot do.

■ TIMING FOR CONTRACT COMPLETION

It is always interesting how many vendor contracts need to be done "right away" when it is getting toward the end of the month or quarter. Usually this occurs because the rate listed in the contract is good only through that particular time. But many times it really has to do with commissions and sales quotas. This doesn't mean a time deadline isn't important. It does mean you should ask the reason for the rush put on finalizing the contract in question.

■ CHECKLISTS FOR CONTRACT REVIEWS

A contract review paralegal finds it helpful to use a contract review sheet. Usually this is a form the person submitting the contract for review attaches to the contract he or she wants reviewed. The contract review sheet should always include the date you received the contract and the date by which the review must be completed. The contract review sheet should contain a checklist to make sure the contract is properly reviewed. That checklist should contain items such as the following:

1. Name and Address of the Parties

   Surprisingly, many times this information is missing from the contract given to the contract review paralegal. You need to obtain this information. Once you get the correct name, do a quick Google search on the party. This background check can be especially important relating to the value of the contract (see later) and the time given to review the contract. If the party is a company, find out how long the company has been in business and who owns the company.

2. Value of the Contract

   This is another important topic for review. If a party is a large company, you may need to have various personnel (e.g., the manager or the president) sign off on the contract depending on the dollar amount.

   Determine if the stated value is the actual value of the contract. For instance, you may be told the value of the contract is $10,000 per year. But, perhaps someone failed to mention this is a five-year contract. So, in this case, the actual value of the contract would be $50,000. Be aware there is sometimes a licensing fee for servicing the product. If so, that amount would need to be added into the contract as well. Be sure to ask questions regarding the value of the contract.

3. What Is the Contract For?

   Be diligent in questioning the staff on what the contract is for. They need to be able to describe what the product will do and how they plan to use it. You should not be left trying to figure out what the product or service is by a vague or abbreviated purchase order.

4. Loopholes

   Is there a way out of the contract? How can the contract be terminated? What if a better product comes out next year? Do you want a three- to five-year contract you cannot terminate? Some contracts provide for an automatic renewal unless the parties provide 30 to 60 days written notice. Consider marking the calendar for renewal of the contract, typically before the advance written notice is required. This calendar system also serves to make you look very organized and on top of matters!

5. Assignment Clauses

   Always look at the assignment clauses contained in a contract. There should always be a way to assign a contract if necessary. If one of the parties is a company—and if the company is sold or merged with another company—one very time-consuming part of due diligence will be the review of each contract for assignability. Determine if they can add an assignment clause, if permission is needed to assign the contract, or if there only needs to be providing of a notice to assign the contract. If key contracts cannot be assigned, the client may not have a deal. Also, there may be regulatory restrictions on assignment of a contract and a shareholder's vote may be needed before assignment can be completed. Some regulations consider a "change of control" to be an assignment even if it is to an affiliated company.

6. Outside Agreements

   Always remember this key point: *If it isn't in the writing, then it isn't part of the contract.*

7. Changing the Contract

   Do not be afraid to ask for changes to the contract, even when the other party tells you that "this is our standard agreement." Always keep the best interests of the client in mind. You might be surprised at what changes to that so-called standard agreement might be negotiated!

Sample Contracts

Agreement Among Devisees

Agreement for Common Driveway Easement

Attorney/Client Fee Agreement

Business Purchase Agreement

Corporate Formation Agreement

Credit Card Agreement (Selected Section)

Employment Agreement

Event Contract

Physician Employment Agreement

Real Estate Purchase Agreement

Stock Purchase Agreement

AGREEMENT AMONG DEVISEES

THIS AGREEMENT is made and entered into as of this _____ day of _____, 20___, by and between _____, a (married/single man/woman), dealing with his/her sole and separate property, (hereinafter "_____"), _____, a (married/single man/woman), dealing with his/her sole and separate property, (hereinafter "_____"), _____, a (married/single man/woman), dealing with his/her sole and separate property, (hereinafter "_____"), _____, a (married/single man/woman), dealing with his/her sole and separate property, (hereinafter "_____"), and _____, a (married/single man/woman), dealing with his/her sole and separate property (hereafter "_____").

Article I.

All the parties to this Agreement acknowledge and agree that they are all devisees named in the Last Will and Testament of _____, deceased, which said Last Will and Testament was filed in an informal probate proceeding in the District Court of the _____ Judicial District of the State of _____ in and for the County of _____, as Case No. _____.

Article II.

Each of the parties hereto acknowledges and agrees that the Last Will and Testament of _____, deceased, generally provides in Paragraph Seventh thereof for the creation of a Trust in which one of the parties hereto is a Beneficiary. Said Trust is identified in the Will as the _____ Trust (hereinafter "_____'s Trust"). A copy of the Last Will and Testament of _____ is attached hereto as Exhibit "A".

_____'s Trust generally provides that _____ will receive the net income from the Trust during his/her life and is also entitled to have the principal invaded for his/her care and support upon terms as specifically set forth in the Trust. _____'s Trust further provides that on _____'s death _____ will receive the income from the Trust for his/her life. _____'s Trust also makes provisions for _____ to receive principal from the Trust upon the conditions set forth therein. Upon the death of both _____ and _____, _____'s Trust provides that the Trust assets will be distributed equally to _____, _____ and _____.

Article III.

Each of the parties to this agreement hereby acknowledges that they are entering into this agreement as a private agreement among devisees of the decedent which shall be binding on the personal representative of the Estate of _____, deceased, pursuant to _____ Code Section.

Article IV.

Each of the parties to the Agreement acknowledges and agrees that _____ created _____'s Trust by the terms of his/her Last Will and Testament at _____'s request and as part of _____ and _____'s estate planning to keep the Trust assets from being taxable in _____ and _____'s estate. Since the time of execution of _____'s Last Will and Testament, the exemption amount for estate taxes has substantially increased and the estate planning need for holding assets in _____'s Trust no longer exists.

Article V.

Each of the parties hereto acknowledge and agree that the assets which are to pass to _____'s Trust under the terms of the Last Will and Testament of _____, deceased, shall not be placed in Trust, and shall be distributed to _____ outright and free of trust. Thus the parties hereto, being all the Beneficiaries of _____'s Trust agree that _____'s Trust shall not be created or funded and all the assets which otherwise would have passed to _____'s Trust under the terms of the Last Will and Testament of _____, deceased, will be distributed to _____.

Article VI.

The parties to this agreement hereby acknowledge and agree that the residual assets of the estate are more than sufficient to pay all debts, expenses of last illness, medical and funeral expenses, and administration expenses of the estate. The terms and provisions of this agreement to the extent that it alters the provisions of the decedent _____'s Last Will and Testament shall not be a detriment to any federal or state taxing authorities or to any creditors of the estate.

Article VII.

Each of the parties hereto acknowledge that good, valuable and adequate consideration exists for each of the parties entering into this agreement.

IN WITNESS WHEREOF, each of the parties hereto have executed this agreement as of the day and year hereinabove first written.

_____
******

_____
******

_____
******

_____
******

_____
******

NOTARY ACKNOWLEDGMENTS NEEDED

AGREEMENT FOR COMMON DRIVEWAY EASEMENT

THIS AGREEMENT made this _____ day of _____, 2008, by and between JOHN SMITH and JANE SMITH, husband and wife, hereinafter referred to as "first parties", and SCOUT JONES and SARA JONES, husband and wife, hereinafter as "second parties".

WITNESSETH:

WHEREAS, the first parties are the owners of that certain real property situated in the City of Lewiston, County of Nez Perce, State of Idaho, and more particularly described as follows, to-wit:

SEE EXHIBIT A

WHEREAS, the second parties are the owners of that certain real property situated in the City of Lewiston, County of Nez Perce, State of Idaho, and more particularly described as follows:

SEE EXHIBIT B

WHEREAS, there is currently in existence a paved driveway shared in common by said premises and the parties desire to create an easement, half of which is on each parcel, to assure that the parties and their successors, heirs, assigns, and devisees shall continue to have the use of said roadway.

NOW THEREFORE, the parties hereto do agree as follows:

1.   An easement for a common driveway in favor of Parcel 2 is created over six (6) feet of the twelve (12) feet of Parcel 1.

2.   An easement for a common driveway in favor of Parcel 1 is hereby created over six (6) feet of the twelve feet (12) of Parcel 2.

3.   The purpose of the easements described in parts 1 and 2 above is to preserve a common driveway one hundred forty-four (144) feet in width for the benefit of both lots.

4.   These easements so created are superior and paramount to the rights of any of the parties hereto in the respective servient estates so created and that they are covenants running with the land.

IN WITNESS WHEREOF, the parties have hereunto set their hands on the day and year first above indicated.

_____
JOHN SMITH, First Party

_____
JANE SMITH, First Party

_____
SCOUT JONES, Second Party

_____
SARA JONES, Second Party

ATTORNEY/CLIENT FEE AGREEMENT

_____, 2008

_____

_____

Toledo, Ohio

Re:

Dear _____:

It was a pleasure meeting with you and _____ on _____ in our offices. You have advised me that you would like our office to represent you in the _____. We are very pleased to be retained by you as counsel for this purpose. Unless a separate contract for legal services is negotiated, it is understood that the fees for services do not include representation concerning a different subject matter. This letter describes the basis on which our firm will provide legal services to you and how our services shall be billed.

Please be assured that we (sometimes referred to as "Attorney") will give our best efforts to serve you (sometimes referred to as "Client") effectively. Although we cannot guarantee or give assurances of the success of any given matter, we will strive to represent your interests professionally in a diligent and efficient manner. The Client further understands and agrees that the Attorney does not make, and will not make, any guarantee about the outcome of any proceedings, or negotiation in which the Client might be a party. The Attorney is not obligated to take any action that is repugnant to the Attorney's sense of honor and propriety. The Attorney's representation of the Client does not constitute an endorsement of the Client's political, economic, social, or moral views or activities.

With respect to conflict matters, we are performing or have performed a formal conflicts check within our office. As you understand, we represent many clients on a broad range of matters. Based upon our initial conversations, we have found no apparent conflicts relative to our representation of your interests. However, if we become aware of a conflict, we will discuss it with you. We specifically reserve the right to withdraw from representation if we feel that we cannot properly represent your interests.

Some aspects of legal representation will certainly require a higher expertise than other aspects. It is our policy to assign and delegate responsibilities based upon the degree of experience and expertise required. All legal work performed will, however, be monitored and approved by one of the partners of the firm, which under most circumstances will be me.

I will have primary responsibility for your representation. If, at any time, you have any questions, concerns, or criticisms, please contact me at once.

In addition to our responsibility, it shall be your responsibility to cooperate fully with us and to provide all information known by or available to you which may aid us in representing you. Further, it shall be your responsibility to promptly pay us for the performance of all legal services upon rendering of a statement and for all expenses incurred in connection therewith.

For our services, you shall pay us a sum for services rendered based on the hourly fees specified below for each hour devoted by each attorney, paralegal, or legal assistant to your case, as shown by our Attorney's records for this purpose. Hourly fees may change during the period that you retain us. If such a change occurs, we will notify you at least 30 days before the changes take effect.

Our schedule of hourly rates for attorneys and other members of the professional staff is based upon years of experience, specialization in training and practice, and level of professional attainment. My present hourly rate is $_____ per hour. You will be charged at the above hourly rate for consultations, correspondence, phone calls, office and research work, court time, filing, and hearings.

You agree that a retainer of $_____ shall serve as the minimum fee retainer for the express purpose of engaging our expertise and professional services for the above-referenced matters and that said retainer may be used from time to time for payment of fees incurred in representation pertaining to the above-referenced matters. You further agree that the retainer shall be paid on or before _____ _____. You consent to the deposit of trust funds into a common Attorney's Clients' Trust Account and to the payment of any interest on those deposits as provided by law into an Interest on Lawyer Trust Account (IOLTA). You agree that because of the commitment hereby made of the attorney's expertise, time, staff, resources, and calendar, to the exclusion of other employment, the full retainer is not refundable after the attorney accepts this employment. Any retainer fee will, at the end of each month, be credited first to your obligation for costs and expenses and then to any fees you owe to the Attorney under this agreement. As the retainer fee is reduced in this way, we may, from time to time, require you to pay an additional sum to return the amount of the retainer fee to the original amount specified in this paragraph.

In addition, we will bill and expect payment for out-of-pocket expenses, such as photocopies, long distance tolls, certified mail, filing fees with the Ohio Secretary of State, facsimile transmission, etc. Any extraordinary expenses, such as printing costs, will generally be billed directly to you. Regardless of any other provision of this agreement that permits deferred payment, expenses under this paragraph will be billed and shall be paid by you as they are actually incurred.

We take into account many factors in billing for services rendered, and I will review all statements before they are issued to ensure that the amount charged is appropriate. Although it is difficult to estimate the time that will be required to satisfactorily complete most legal matters, the principal factor employed in billing is our schedule of hourly rates. While the Ohio Code of Professional Responsibility allows for setting fees based upon other factors such as the result obtained, most statements for services rendered are simply the product of the hours worked including phone time multiplied by the hourly rates for the attorneys and legal assistants who performed the work. I will review all billings in order to make certain that they fairly reflect the value of our services to you. If we feel that too much time was expended for the nature of the matter, or the result obtained, we will reduce the fees accordingly.

Our statements generally will be prepared and mailed at least quarterly, but, depending upon the extent of services rendered, may be as frequent as monthly during the month following the billing period in which services are rendered and costs advanced. Our statements generally summarize the nature and extent of services performed for the period, for which detailed time charges will be available at your request. Payment is expected promptly, in accordance with customary vouchering and payment procedures.

We agree to notify you promptly of any significant developments and to consult with you on significant decisions involving your case. We agree to send you a copy of all pertinent written materials sent or received by the Attorney and pertaining to the case. You agree to reimburse our costs for reproducing those materials. You agree to keep us advised of changes in phone number and address and of any significant changes in your situation. You will share with us information that affects the case. You will answer requests for information promptly.

The work product produced in the course of our representation generally will remain as our property, although you shall always be given reasonable access to it. Files will be retained and maintained by us for a sufficient period of time following the conclusion of such matter and following termination of representation, so as to afford you continued reasonable access to files.

In the event of disputes, whether over fees or any other matter, we will promptly attend to effecting a reasonable resolution of same as soon as such is brought to our attention. Should any dispute not be satisfactorily resolved, the same shall be submitted to arbitration for prompt resolution, and both counsel and client agree to be bound by the results of such arbitration.

You will have the right to terminate our representation at any time. Notification of termination shall be made in writing to us and no further fees or expenses shall accrue after that point in time. You shall promptly pay us for all fees, charges, and expenses incurred on your behalf prior to notification of termination, and we shall refund any unearned portion of fees otherwise previously paid or advanced by you. We likewise reserve the right to discontinue legal services and to withdraw from representation if you fail to honor this Letter of Engagement, or for any just reason as permitted or required under the Ohio Code of Professional Responsibility, or as permitted by the rules of the courts of the State of Ohio. Notification of withdrawal shall be made in writing to you and, in the event of such withdrawal, you agree to promptly pay us for all fees, charges, and expenses incurred prior to the date of withdrawal, and we shall refund any unearned portion of fees otherwise previously paid or advanced by you.

You may terminate this agreement, with or without cause, on written notice to us. If you terminate this agreement, we shall return your file immediately after duplicating it. You agree to pay the cost incurred to duplicate the file. Termination shall not affect your responsibility to pay for the legal services rendered and the costs incurred up to the date of termination.

Please review the foregoing and, if it meets with your approval, sign a copy of the letter and return it to my attention in the enclosed, self addressed, stamped envelope.

If you have any questions, please feel free to call upon me at your convenience. In the meantime, we look forward to being of service to you and to both reflect and project on your behalf a high degree of professionalism and quality of service.

Very truly yours,

_____

Enclosures

AGREED AND ACCEPTED *this* _____ *day of* _____, *2008*

By: _____

BUSINESS PURCHASE AGREEMENT

THIS AGREEMENT made and entered into at _____, _____ County, Ohio this _____ day of _____, 2008 by and between _____, an Ohio corporation ("Seller") and _____, ("Buyer").

WITNESSETH:

WHEREAS, Seller owns the business, fixtures, furnishings and equipment (collectively, "the Business") known as _____ located at _____, _____, _____ County, Ohio and in connection therewith has a D_____ permit issued by the Ohio Department of Liquor Control being number _____, expiring _____.

WHEREAS, Seller is desirous of selling same and Buyer is desirous of purchasing said Business:

NOW, THEREFORE, IT IS AGREED AS FOLLOWS:

Purchase and Sale

1. Seller agrees to sell and deliver to Buyer who agrees to purchase the Business, including all its stock of goods, equipment, fixtures, and other assets described in the inventory attached to this Contract as Exhibit A.

Purchase Price

2. Seller agrees to accept and buyer agrees to pay for the Business (not including stock of goods provided for in Paragraph 4 of this contract) the total sum of _____ ($_____) dollars as follows:
    a. Furniture, fixtures and equipment.....................$ _____
    b. Liquor permit..$ _____
    c. Goodwill..$ _____

Payment Terms

3. The parties agree that payment of the total sum stated in Paragraph 2 shall be made in the following manner:
    (a) Buyer shall pay to Seller at the signing of this Contract the sum of _____ ($_____) dollars, to be held in the trust account of Jake M. Vogelsong as trustee, for Seller, for payment to Seller at Settlement. This amount is non-refundable.
    (b) Buyer shall execute a promissory note to Seller at Settlement in the amount of _____ ($_____) dollars to be amortized over _____ (_____) years at _____ (_____%) percent per annum, with a balloon payment after _____ (_____) years.
    (c) Buyer and Seller agree that in the event Buyer pays the purchase price in full at Settlement, the purchase price shall be discounted to _____ ($_____) dollars. Buyer and Seller agree that in the event Buyer pays the purchase price in full within (_____) year of Settlement, then the note shall be discounted by _____ ($_____) dollars.

Sale of Stock of Goods

4. In addition to the total sale price of $_____, the consideration shall be increased by the current wholesale value of food inventory, alcoholic beverages and merchandise in sealed containers at Settlement. This additional consideration shall be paid at Settlement.

Bill of Sale

5. Seller agrees to provide a Bill of Sale warranting that all of the goods and equipment are free and clear of any and all encumbrances, said original documents to be held in escrow pending the transfer of the permit and delivered to Buyer at the time of Settlement.

Settlement

6. Settlement shall take place within _____ (_____) days of the receipt of the approval of the transfer of the liquor permit to Buyer. At the time of Settlement, possession of the Business shall be given to Buyer. It is understood that time is of the essence and that this transaction shall be closed as soon as possible.

Payment of Taxes and Obligations

7. Seller warrants that all taxes, assessments, and unemployment compensation contributions due in connection with the operation of the Business to any city, county, state, or federal governmental agencies, shall be paid in full up to the date of Settlement and that all due returns, forms, and taxes required to be filed with those agencies will be properly filed and paid as of the Settlement date, or will be filed and paid in due course after that date.

Transfer of Liquor Permit

8. At the time of the signing of this Contract, Buyer and Seller shall execute all papers necessary for transfer of Liquor Permit number _____ to Buyer, and the papers shall be filed with the Department of Liquor Control within _____ (_____) days. Seller agrees to render any and all assistance reasonably required by Buyer in connection with the transfer. The liquor license renewal cost shall be prorated as of the date of Settlement.

Contract Contingent on Transfer of Liquor Permit

9. This Contract is contingent on and subject to obtaining a written approval of transfer of Liquor Permit number _____ from Seller to the Buyer by the Department of Liquor Control not later than ninety (90) days from the date of this Contract, unless the time is extended by mutual agreement of the parties in writing or if delay is due to processing delays by Department of Liquor Control. In the event that the Department of Liquor Control refuses to approve the transfer to Buyer on proper application, all monies held in escrow, except the portion which is non-refundable, shall be returned to Buyer without any deductions whatsoever. On return of the

monies, this Contract shall be null and void, and the parties shall have no liability one to the other.

Seller's Title to Property

10. Seller represents that Seller is the owner of and has good and marketable title to all equipment, fixtures, and other assets being sold under this Contract as set forth in the inventory attached hereto as Exhibit A; and that at the time of Settlement those assts shall be free and clear of all debts, encumbrances, liens, mortgages, or claims and demands whatsoever.

   Seller has purchase agreements for an ATM machine at the business premises and for security cameras and monitor at the business premises. Buyer agrees to assume Seller's liability, rights and responsibilities on each of these contracts. Buyer and Seller agree that each shall cooperate in executing any and all documents necessary to effectuate said assumption or assignment of these contracts.

Competition

11. Seller agrees that Seller shall not, either as an individual or a corporation, or in any other business form, directly or indirectly, enter into competition with Buyer or engage in the same or similar type of business, whether as principal, agent, employee, or straw party within a radius of 2 miles from the address of the business for a period of one (1) year from the date of this Contract.

Actions and Other Proceedings

12. Seller represents that:
    (a) Seller presently has, and at the time of Settlement will have, no judgments, liens, actions, or proceedings against it and no claims of any nature whatsoever for which Buyer or the assets being sold under this Contract might be subject to liability with the exception of a lawsuit pending against Seller in the Lucas County Common Pleas Court entitled _____ under case number _____ of which Buyer is aware.
    (b) There are no violations or actions pending or arising from noncompliance or wrongful compliance with any regulations or requirements of any governmental agencies, whether federal, state, or local. Seller will indemnify, defend and hold harmless Buyer from any undisclosed violations, or violations that may arise in the future that accrued prior to Settlement.
    (c) There are no actions presently pending before the Department of Liquor Control for citations against Seller; and that in the event that any actions or citations may arise, the obligation for payment of any fines or penalties imposed shall be that of Seller.
    (d) Seller has no knowledge of any notices of an governmental authority requiring alterations, corrections, additions, or improvements to the Business premises in order to continue the conduct of a _____ business in the premises.

Sale of Real Estate

13. Buyer shall have the right of first refusal to purchase the real estate located at _____, _____, _____ County, Ohio, in the event Seller decides to sell said real estate in the future.

Business Name

14. Seller grants to Buyer the right to the use in any manner the name _____. Seller also grants to Buyer exclusive use of any telephone numbers used in connection with the Business either at the time of signing of this Contract or at the time of the Settlement.

Destruction of Business

15. In the event that the Business, or any part of it, is destroyed by fire or other catastrophe prior to Settlement, this Contract, at the option of Seller, shall become null and void, all deposit monies shall be returned to Buyer without deduction, and there shall be no further liability under this Contract on the part of either party.

Service Contracts

16. Seller represents that Seller has no contracts in existence for any vending machines or other service contracts, but in the event that there are any such contracts in existence at the time of Settlement, it will be Seller's sole obligation to cancel or have the contracts transferred to Buyer at Buyer's option.

Entire Agreement

17. This Contract constitutes the sole and only agreement between Buyer and Seller respecting the Business or the sale and purchase of the Business. This Contract correctly sets forth the obligations of Buyer and Seller to each other as of its date. Any agreements or representations respecting the Business or its sale to Buyer not expressly set forth in this Contract are null and void.

Binding on Heirs

18. This Contract shall be binding on and shall inure to the benefit of the heirs, executors, administrators, successors, and assigns of the parties.

Executed at Toledo, Ohio, on the day and year first above written.

SELLER: BUYER:

_____, an Ohio corporation.   _____, an Ohio corporation

By:_____   By:_____

_____, (Title)   _____, (Title)

EQUIPMENT LIST

BILL OF SALE

_____ date, 2008

KNOW ALL MEN BY THESE PRESENTS that _____, an Ohio corporation, the Grantor, for full consideration paid by _____, an Ohio corporation, the Grantee, the receipt of which is hereby acknowledged, does hereby grant, bargain, sell, transfer, and deliver unto the Grantee, the following assets of the Grantor as of the above-noted date, all equipment and furniture, and fixtures presently used by the Grantor at the business known as _____ located at _____, _____, Ohio as described in Exhibit A, attached hereto and incorporated herein for all purposes.

TO HAVE AND TO HOLD the same unto Grantee and his successors and assigns forever.

Grantor hereby covenants to and with the Grantee that the Grantor is the lawful owner of the above-described goods and chattels; that the same are free and clear from all encumbrances whatsoever; that the Grantor has good right to sell the same as aforesaid; and that the Grantor will warrant and defend the same against all lawful claims and demands whatsoever.

IN WITNESS WHEREOF, _____ has hereunto set its hand, by and through its _____(President), _____, the day and year first hereinabove written.

Signed and delivered in the presence of:

_____, an Ohio corporation

_____

By: _____

_____, _____(President)
Grantor

_____

CORPORATE FORMATION AGREEMENT

- **First:** The name of the limited liability company is <u>Joe Smith LLC</u>

- **Second:** The address of its registered office in the State of Delaware is <u>2711</u> Centerville Road Suite 400 _____ in the City of Wilmington, DE 19808. The name of its Registered agent at such address is _____ Corporation Service Company

- **Third:** (Use this paragraph only if the company is to have a specific effective date of dissolution:) "The latest date on which the limited liability company is to dissolve is _____

- **Fourth:** (Insert any other matters the members determine to include herein.)

  _____

  _____

  _____

  _____

  _____

  _____

  _____

In Witness Whereof, the undersigned have executed this Certificate of Formation this 21st_____ day of ____January____ ___20___ 08

Is/ Joe C. Smith

By:

Authorized Person(s)

Name: Joe C. Smith _____

Typed or Printed

CREDIT CARD AGREEMENT[1]

(Selected Section)

Bank customers are given this Agreement when approved for an Account, or on request. By opening an Account and making Transactions (as defined below), you agree to use this Account only for personal, family or household purposes and to comply with, and be bound by, this entire Agreement.

Unless otherwise specified, "you," "your" and "yours" mean each person or persons who applied (by Internet, orally, or in writing) to the Bank for an Account, which application has been approved by the Bank, and each person(s) who uses the Account with your permission; the terms "we," "our," and "us" mean the Bank and its successors and assigns; and the term "Card" means each Gold, Platinum, Select, Secured/Good Neighbor and Secured MasterCard and VISA that we issue on your Account, unless the context indicates otherwise.

You should retain and carefully review this entire Agreement. You and we agree as follows:

1. **Accepting this Agreement.** This Agreement will be effective on the earlier of the date (a) you sign or otherwise submit an application for the Account that we approve; or (b) you use, or someone authorized by you uses, the Card or the Account. You acknowledge and agree that any use, signing of an Account application or other document, or other acceptance of the Account or the Card constitutes your acceptance of the terms and conditions of this Agreement.

2. **Promise to Pay.** By using your Card or your Account, you agree to pay us an amount equal to the sum of all Transactions made in connection with, and posted to, your Account plus any Finance Charges (as defined below), fees and other charges provided for in this Agreement, regardless of the medium by which the Transaction occurs. If your Account is established by two or more persons, each of you, together and individually, is responsible for all amounts owed, even if the Account is used by only one of you.

3. **Your Responsibility.** You are responsible for all Transactions and other transactions arising from the authorized use of your Account or Card by you by any means. If you have authorized another person to use your Account or Card in any manner, that authorization will be deemed to include the authorization to make Transactions of any kind using your Account or Card and to incur related fees and charges, and such authorization will be deemed to continue until you have taken all steps necessary to revoke it by preventing such use by that person. We are not responsible for controlling any person who you have asked us to add to your Account or someone

---

[1]Remember that some agreements - such as software agreements and credit card agreements - don't actually have to have signatures to be effective. Software agreements can take effect immediately upon installing the software. Credit card agreements can take effect upon application and/or issuance of the credit card.

you let use your Account or Card. If you let someone use your Account or Card, you are responsible for all Transactions made in connection with, and posted to, your Account plus all Finance Charges, fees and other charges. If you wish to remove such person's ability to use your Account or Card, you must notify us in writing. No such notice will be effective until we receive and have had a reasonable opportunity to act on it.

EMPLOYMENT AGREEMENT

This Agreement entered into this _____day of _____, 20____, between_____ , an Ohio corporation, of Toledo, Ohio, hereinafter referred to as "Employer," and _____ , of Toledo, Ohio, hereinafter referred to as "Employee."

WITNESSETH:

WHEREAS, Employee has recently been hired as _____of Employer in consideration of his agreeing to enter into this Employment Agreement with Employer, and

WHEREAS, Employee will of necessity during his employment, become well acquainted with Employer's customers, sources of supply, other employees, and all other facets of Employer's business.

NOW THEREFORE, in consideration of the mutual covenants hereinafter set forth, and particularly in consideration of Employer's employing Employee, and continuing to employ him in the same capacity, it is mutually covenanted and agreed between the parties as follows:

1. Employer employs Employee as _____ for a period of _____ years, commencing _____, and ending _____, unless his employment is sooner terminated pursuant to provisions hereof. Employee shall be elected an officer of Employer, and Employer shall use its best efforts to have him elected. If elected, Employee agrees to accept the office of _____and any other office to which he may be elected, and without additional compensation to perform the duties thereof.

2. Employee shall devote his entire business time, attention and skill, reasonable vacations and unforeseen illnesses excepted, to developing and increasing the business of Employer in the sale and leasing of its products and shall perform his duties to the best of his ability, and in a reasonably efficient and satisfactory manner. During the period of his employment, Employee will not make any other corporate affiliations without the approval of Employer's Board of Directors.

3. Employee for all services to be rendered to Employer, shall be paid so long as he shall be employed:

   a. A fixed salary of _____ per year, payable in equal consecutive semi-monthly installments. On the first anniversary date Employee's salary shall be increased to _____ per year, and on the second anniversary date to _____ per year, providing sufficient profits are being generated from which to pay the aforesaid increases. It is the intention of the parties that Employee's base salary will not be increased unless the Employer is financially capable of doing so without incurring a deficit; provided, however, that Employee's base salary shall never be reduced below _____ per year.

   b. Additional compensation payable on the first anniversary date hereof, equal to _____ % of the net income before provision for federal income taxes and bonuses, but after all officers' salaries are paid; _____ % on the second anniversary date and _____ % on the third anniversary date. The payment of a bonus hereunder shall be restricted exclusively to the total net income available to pay bonuses to all other employees of the Company with whom it has entered into a similar Employment Agreement. In the event that sufficient net earnings are not available on any one or more of the anniversary dates hereof with which to pay said bonuses to all employees in their entirety, then in such event, the bonuses to all employees with whom the Employer has an employment contract shall be pro rated. If pro-rata bonus payments are made on any anniversary date they shall be non-cumulative.

    c. Employer's net income before provision for Federal Income Taxes and bonuses, but after the payment of all officers' salaries, shall be determined in accordance with generally accepted accounting practices and shall be based upon the Profit and Loss Statement prepared by Employer's independent accounting firm within _____ days after each anniversary date. The computation by such firm of net income and of Employee's additional compensation made in the manner herein provided shall be final and binding upon Employer and Employee, and Employer shall pay such additional compensation to Employee within _____ days after each anniversary date.

4. Upon Employee's death, resignation, or discharge for cause, Employee's fixed compensation shall be paid to the last day of the calendar month in which such event occurs, and his additional compensation shall be computed pro rata and be paid in the manner provided in paragraphs 3 (b and c) above.

5. In the event of Employee's illness or other disability which prevents him from performing his duties for a period in excess of _____ days, this agreement may be terminated by serving written notice on employee fixing a date not less than _____ days after the occurrence of said event and this agreement shall terminate.

6. In the event of Employee's protracted illness or disability, resignation, discharge by Employer, or upon the expiration of this Agreement, it is expressly agreed that all of the provisions below shall remain in full force and effect for a period of _____ years.

7. Employee agrees that he will not during his employment or for a period of _____ years thereafter by Employer, for himself or in conjunction with any other person, persons, firm, company, partnership, association or corporation, engage either directly or indirectly in any business competitive with the Employer in the following geographic areas:

    a. in the City of _____

    b. in the County of _____

    c. in the State of _____

    d. within a radius of _____ (____) miles from the center of the above City, County, and State.

8. Employee agrees that he will not, during his employment and for a period of _____ years immediately following the termination thereof with Employer, whether such termination is voluntary or involuntary, either service or solicit, or both, customers of Employer which are located in the geographical area specified above.

9. Employee agrees that he will not during his employment and for _____ years immediately following the termination of his employment with Employer, for himself or in conjunction with any other person, persons, firm, company, partnership, association, or corporation, cause to be employed any person either now or hereafter employed by Employer.

10. Employee agrees that he will not, during the term of his employment, and for _____ years immediately following the termination thereof, communicate or divulge to any person or entity any of Employer's trade secrets, advertising techniques, practices, policies or customers' lists, or any other information which he might acquire from time to time pertaining to the business of Employer.

11. Employee agrees upon termination of employment by Employer to forthwith surrender all records and data of every nature, kind, and description in his possession, or under his control, prepared by Employer or him during the course of his employment.

12. The validity, construction and enforceability of this agreement shall be determined exclusively by the laws of the State of _____.

13. This agreement supersedes all prior oral and/or written agreements and understandings between the parties and constitutes the entire contract between them and may not be altered, amended, or revoked except by written instrument signed by both parties and executed in accordance herewith.

14. If any of the covenants or conditions of this agreement should be found to be unenforceable in a Court of law, then this agreement is severable and all remaining covenants and conditions shall be enforceable by said Court.

15. This Agreement shall inure to and be binding upon the parties hereto, their respective executors, administrators, heirs, successors and assigns.

IN WITNESS WHEREOF, the parties have hereunto executed this Agreement in duplicate, each of which shall be deemed to be an original on the day and year first above written.

Witnesses:

As to Employer:

_____   By_____
                                                      Employer

As to Employee:

_____   _____
                                                      Employee

_____

EVENT CONTRACT

This contract is between The University of Ohio, located at 2801 West Smith Street, Toledo, Ohio 43606 on behalf of the University's Undergraduate Legal Specialties Program ("the University"), and Judge Roy Bean ("the Speaker"), whose main office is located at 1234 Lady Justice Boulevard, Washington, DC 00386.

1. The parties wish to provide faculty, students, or guests of the University the following event:
   A 2-hour presentation titled "A Day in the Life of An Old West Justice Man" at the annual Paralegal Christmas Party on December 11, 2008, 7:30 P.M. until 9:30 P.M. This event will be held in the Student Union Auditorium of the Main Campus of the University.

2. Tickets will be available for sale in the amounts and for the prices as follows:
   Total number of tickets available: Not applicable
   University Student Price: Not applicable
   Non-Student Ticket Price: Not applicable

3. The University will pay $5,000 to Speaker for a 2-hour presentation of his topic beginning at 7:30 P.M. And, in addition, the University will pay for the specific travel and lodging expenses not to exceed $500, which specifically include reasonable air travel, accommodations, and ground transportation expenses that are approved in advance and meals.

4. Checks should be made payable to: Judge Roy Bean, who will provide the University with either his Social Security Number or Federal Tax ID Number.

5. Technical Requirements (insert N/A if none): Microphone, podium, computer with PowerPoint capabilities and a large screen.

6. Other requirements or special payment conditions: None known.

7. The University reserves the right to refuse and forbid the requested service or arrangements as being impermissible on the grounds of safety, security, or caution in the operation of the University.

8. If appropriate, University will obtain all necessary licenses and permits for the event. Speaker will pay all applicable taxes.

9. Speaker guarantees that the Event will start at the time listed above. The University will not pay Speaker until after the performance is complete, unless otherwise specified above.

10. In the event the University premises are rendered unsuitable for the Event by reason of Force Majeure, the University may terminate this Agreement and the University will not be responsible for any damages sustained by Speaker. "Force Majeure" will mean fire, earthquake, flood, act of God, adverse weather conditions, shortage of energy to the University, strikes, epidemic, work stoppages, or other labor disturbances, riots or civil commotions, litigation, war or other act of any foreign nation, power of government, or governmental agency or authority, or any other cause that is beyond the control or authority of the University.

11. Failure of the Speaker to appear, present, or perform does not relieve Speaker of the responsibility of paying the costs and expenses incurred by the University in preparation for the Event, unless such failure is caused by or due to the physical disability of the Speaker, or acts or regulations of public authorities, labor difficulties, civil tumult, strike, epidemic, acts of God, or other cause beyond the control of the Speaker or the University.

12. Speaker must obtain written approval from the University for any advertising in any medium before it is to appear.

13. Speaker will obtain and maintain public liability insurance against personal bodily injury in the overall amount of $1,000,000 and against property damage in the amount of $1,000,000 with bodily injury and property damage liability insurance in the amount of $1,000,000 for each person for bodily liability and $1,000,000 for each occurrence for property damage liability to cover such liability caused by, or arising out of, activities of Speaker, and their members, agents, or employees while engaged in preparing for, or presenting the Event hereunder, or such other insurance that is required by the University. Speaker agrees to furnish the University with a certificate of insurance evidencing this coverage at least 5 days prior to the Event and to have the University, its governing board, officers, and employees named as additional insureds.

14. Speaker will indemnify the University, its governing board, officers, employees, and agents, from all liability and claims arising in connection with such liability caused by, or arising out of death or injury to any person or damage to property, caused by or arising out of activities of Speaker, and their members, agents, or employees while engaged in preparing for or presenting the Event hereunder, except that the University retains the right to retain and select counsel to represent the University in any such claim. Speaker will indemnify the University for all liability and claims arising in connection with the actual presentation of the material contained in the Event, whether occurring due to defamation, copyright infringement or otherwise and the University reserves the right to retain and select counsel.

15. The failure or delay of either party to exercise its rights under this Agreement for a breach will not be deemed to be a waiver of such rights. And no waiver by either party, whether written or oral, express or implied, of any rights under or arising from this Agreement will be binding on any subsequent occasion; and no concession by either party will be treated as an implied modification of the Agreement unless specifically agreed in writing.

16. Any notice to either party hereunder must be in writing signed by the party giving it, and will be served either personally or by registered or certified mail to the party at the addresses listed above.

17. This Agreement (and its attachments, if any) contains all the terms between the parties and may be amended only in writing signed by an authorized representative of both parties. The parties may not assign this Agreement without the written consent of the other party, and it is legally binding upon the heirs, representatives, successors, and assigns of both parties.

18. The laws of the State of Ohio govern this Agreement and any conflict arising out of this Agreement.

Agreed to this _____ day of _____,
20_____, by each party's duly authorized representative.

THE UNIVERSITY OF OHIO   SPEAKER

By: _____   By: _____
      Par T. President   Judge Roy Bean
      Executive Vice President   SSN or Tax ID:
                                       _____

PHYSICIAN EMPLOYMENT AGREEMENT

THIS AGREEMENT ("Agreement") is between John Q. Public, M.D. ("Physician") and USA Hospital North, Inc. ("Employer"), a not-for-profit corporation. This Agreement shall continue for the initial term and any renewal terms, unless earlier terminated as provided herein.

RECITALS:

WHEREAS, in furtherance of its charitable, scientific, and educational purposes, Employer provides various healthcare and medical services, including emergency medical services, to residents of Any County, USA (the "Community"), initially at USA Hospital North.

WHEREAS, Employer provides the emergency medical services to residents of the Community specifically within the Emergency Department.

WHEREAS, there is presently an insufficient number of physicians to provide Emergency Department coverage and needed administrative direction of the Emergency Department, and Employer has determined that employment of Physician will enable it to better serve the residents of the Community and thereby further its charitable mission and purposes; and

WHEREAS, Employer desires to obtain the services of Physician as an employee, to render health care services to residents of the Community, in order to further its charitable mission and purposes.

NOW, THEREFORE, in consideration of this premises and the mutual covenants and agreements herein contained and for other good and valuable consideration, the receipt and adequacy of which are hereby acknowledged, the parties hereby agree as follows:

1. Definitions. Whenever used in this Agreement, the terms listed in Exhibit 1 have the meanings stated in such Exhibit unless the context should clearly require otherwise.

2. Employment. Employer hereby employs Physician, and Physician accepts employment with Employer, effective as of January 1, 2008, upon all of the terms and conditions set forth below.

3. Duties and Extent of Services. Physician shall render professional emergency medical services for patients of Employer, and Emergency Department administrative services for the hospital, as mutually determined from time to time by and between Employer and Physician, in the manner and extent permitted by the laws of the State of Anywhere and the canons of professional ethics. Physician agrees to devote his best abilities and full working time to the practice of medicine at the hospital for the Term of this Agreement. Physician shall use best efforts to provide Emergency Department coverage and Emergency Department Administrative services during at least, but not limited to, two (2) 24-hour shifts per week, a total of forty-eight (48) hours per week for forty-eight (48) weeks, or two thousand three hundred four hours (2,304) per year, the exact schedule for which to be determined by Hospital Administrator, or his or her designee. Physician also shall perform such other reasonable tasks and services, as mutually agreed upon by and between Physician and Employer, including other administrative tasks and duties as are consistent with the relationship described herein. Commencing with his employment by Employer, Physician also agrees as follows:

3.01 Practice Compliance.   Physician will use Physician's best efforts to comply with any Employer practice protocols and productivity standards as may be adopted by Employer from time to time and in a manner consistent with community norms for the same type of practice.

3.02 Program Participation.   Physician will participate in Employer's programs of professional education, quality and utilization management, marketing and practice administration.

3.03 License and Medical Staff Requirements.   Physician will maintain an unrestricted license to practice medicine in the State of Anywhere, as well as an unrestricted narcotics number. Physician shall be a medical staff member in good standing with appropriate clinical privileges at USA Hospital North, and such other facilities as designated and/or approved by Employer in writing.

3.04 Policies and Procedures.   Physician shall observe and comply with all written policies and procedures of Employer as adopted and amended from time to time with respect to Physician's obligations.

3.05 Competitive Activities.   Physician agrees not to engage directly or indirectly in any activity which is competitive with any business of Employer or its Affiliates as such businesses are being conducted during the Term of this Agreement, without the prior written consent of Employer.

3.06 Professional Liability Insurance.   Physician agrees to practice medicine in such a manner that professional liability insurance can be obtained and maintained at reasonable rates which are comparable to rates commonly available to physicians of comparable specialty to that of Physician in the Community.

3.07 Community Benefit.   Physician recognizes that Employer is a tax-exempt organization with charitable goals, interests and responsibilities, and agrees to support and to participate in the community benefit, charitable, and indigent care initiatives and programs of Employer. In connection with such participation, Physician agrees to provide services to patients whose healthcare services are reimbursed by the Medicare/Medicaid programs, and other programs as may be designated by Employer from time to time.

4. Covenants and Agreements of Employer.   Commencing with the employment of Physician, Employer agrees as follows:

4.01 Facilities.   Employer will make available to Physician reasonable facilities, equipment, services, and supplies necessary to engage in Physician's professional practice of medicine in the Community. Employer shall maintain such equipment in good order and repair, reasonable wear and tear excepted. Physician shall use such facilities, services, and supplies for purposes of providing the professional services described in Section 3, but shall not use the facilities, services, and supplies for other purposes. If Employer and Physician determine that the continuation of

Physician's practice at the initial location is unsatisfactory from a practice development standpoint, Employer, in consultation with Physician, shall reassign Physician to facilities of comparable quality to the initial location. Employer will be responsible for all non-physician personnel decisions at the Practice (including but not limited to hiring, termination, and compensation of such personnel). Hiring decisions shall be made in consultation with Physician.

4.02 Practice Compensation. Physician shall be compensated by Employer in the amount and manner set forth on Exhibit 4.02, attached hereto and incorporated herein by reference. All payments to Physician for which provisions are made in this Agreement shall be subject to appropriate state or federal tax and other withholding, as required by law.

4.03 Benefits. Physician shall be eligible for those benefits listed in Exhibit 4.03 attached hereto and incorporated herein by reference; provided, however, that Employer may unilaterally alter, from time to time, those benefits set forth in Exhibit 4.03 which are applicable to all employees of Employer, and Physician shall only be entitled to such benefits as are otherwise available to all such employees of Employer.

5. Billing and Fees. Employer shall bill and collect for all services provided by Physician under this Agreement on a monthly or more frequent basis, as Employer shall deem appropriate, and Employer shall retain all revenues received from such billings. Physician's charges for professional services rendered shall be established from time to time by Employer. Physician acknowledges that his employment does not confer upon him any ownership interest in or personal claim upon any fees charged or revenue received for his services, whether said fees are collected during the Term of this Agreement or after termination thereof. Further, Physician shall execute in a timely fashion such forms, including without limitation, assignments, as may be reasonable or necessary to facilitate billing and collection by Employer. Physician shall not directly or indirectly bill any party for any services provided pursuant to this Agreement including, without limitation, Medicare and Medicaid beneficiaries. Notwithstanding anything herein to the contrary, the parties agree that any fees for publications, honoraria for speeches, fees for directorship(s) with civic organizations, compensation from insurance board(s) or any payment received for a service contract that is not in conflict with this Agreement and has been agreed to by the parties hereto in writing, shall be the sole property of Physician.

6. Term of this Agreement. The term of this Agreement shall commence on January 1, 2008, and shall remain in effect through December 31, 2008, ("Initial Term"), subject to the termination provisions set forth below. Unless Employer gives to Physician, or Physician gives to Employer, written notice of nonrenewal at least ninety (90) days prior to the end of the Initial Term or of any renewal term, this Agreement shall be automatically renewed for additional periods of one (1) year each. The Initial Term and any renewal terms of this Agreement are referred to herein as Term of this Agreement.

6.01 Termination Without Cause. This Agreement may be terminated by either party, without cause, by providing the other party at least ninety (90) days prior written notice that such party wishes to terminate this Agreement. In the event Physician gives notice of termination in compliance with this Section, Employer shall have the right to terminate the continued provision by Physician of the services set forth in Section 3 prior to the termination date specified in the notice. If the Employer takes such action, Physician shall be entitled to continue to receive the compensation set forth in Section 3 up to the date of termination provided in the notice.

SIGNATURE PAGE

IN WITNESS WHEREOF, the parties have executed this Agreement effective as of the dates set forth below.

EMPLOYER:
USA Hospital North, Inc.

By:_____

Title: _____

Date: _____

PHYSICIAN:
John Q. Public, M.D.

By:_____

Social Security #: _____

Date: _____

EXHIBIT 1

DEFINITIONS

Affiliate. "Affiliate" means a person, corporation, partnership, or other form of entity that directly or indirectly controls, or is controlled by, or is under common control with another designated person, corporation, partnership, or other form of entity. For purposes of this definition, "control" (including, with correlative meanings, the terms "controlling," "controlled by" and "under common control with," as applied to any person or entity, means the power, directly or indirectly, to vote 50% or more if the securities having ordinary voting power for the election of directors or managers of such person, or to directly or cause the direction of the management and policies of that person, whether by voting power, contract or otherwise.

Disability. "Disability" shall mean Physician's inability to perform the essential functions of his job as required in this Employment Agreement, with a reasonable accommodation as required by the Americans with Disabilities act, because of a physical or mental impairment that substantially limits one or more of the major life activities of Physician.

Hospital Administrator. "Hospital Administrator" shall mean the Administrator of USA Hospital North, Inc., Anytown, Anywhere USA or his/her designee.

Managed Care Plans. "Managed Care Plans" shall mean plans through which health care services are reimbursed in a manner other than traditional indemnity reimbursement on a fee for service basis, and shall include but not be limited to health maintenance organizations, preferred provider organizations, competitive medical plans, managed care products offered by Blue Cross/Blue Shield or related entities and similar plans.

Practice. "Practice" means the medical practice established by Employer to which this Agreement relates and shall also include any other location to which the medical practice to which this Agreement relates is subsequently relocated.

EXHIBIT 4.02

PHYSICIAN'S COMPENSATION

Physician shall be compensated for all of his services as an employee of Employer during the Term of this Agreement as provided in this Exhibit 4.02. Fees attributable to Physician's professional services during the term of this Agreement shall belong to Employer.

As used in this Exhibit, the following words shall have the meaning specified in this section.

a. "Base Salary" shall mean the compensation set forth below, as adjusted by Employer annually in accordance with its compensation adjustment procedures.

b. "Period" shall mean January 1, 2008 to December 31, 2008, and each twelve (12) month period thereafter unless modified by Employer.

1. Physician shall receive Base salary in the amount of fifty Thousand and no/100 Dollars ($50,000.00) per month, payable with the regular pay periods of Employer, for Emergency Department medical services to patients of Employer.

2. Physician may receive a Bonus based upon improvement of certain "Benchmarks" of Emergency Room quality of service. The Benchmarks and the plan for measuring this quality of service will be mutually developed and approved by Physician and Employer.

3. Physician shall also receive Administrative Salary in the amount of Fifteen Thousand and 00/100 Dollars ($15, 000.00) annually for the provision of Emergency Department administrative services provided on behalf of Employer at the Practice. In the event Physician's employment commences or terminates during a month, Administrative Salary shall be prorated to reflect the portion of the month during which Physician was employed by Employer and shall be payable with the regular pay periods of Employer, unless earlier payment is required by law in the case of termination of employment.

EXHIBIT 4.03

EMPLOYEE BENEFITS

Physician will be entitled to participate in any benefit plans that Employer may offer to its employees, subject to eligibility requirements and waiting periods, if any. Presently, Employer offers its employees group health insurance, group dental insurance, and life insurance. Employer currently pays 100% of the monthly premium for an individual employee's health, dental, and life insurance coverage.

Employer also offers employees the opportunity to participate in a 401(k) retirement savings plan. The Company does not have an obligation to match an employee's contributions or contribute to an employee's account. In addition, Employer offers participation in sponsored flexible spending accounts for both health care and dependent care to all employees.

Physician will earn 24 days of Paid Time Off ("PTO") per year. PTO includes vacation time, sick days and personal time. PTO accrues at the rate of 7.38 hours per pay period.

Physician will receive more information about Employer's benefits upon execution of this Agreement.

REAL ESTATE PURCHASE AGREEMENT

THIS REAL ESTATE PURCHASE AGREEMENT (this "**Agreement**") is made this 20th day of January, 2008, by and between Land Company, an Idaho corporation ("**Seller**") and Real Estate Developers, LLC, an Idaho limited liability company ("**Buyer**").

RECITALS

A.   Seller owns that certain property located in the City of Star, County of Ada, State of Idaho, more particularly described in **Exhibit A**, attached hereto and made a part hereof.

B.   Seller desires to sell, transfer and convey such property and Buyer desires to purchase such property all according to the provisions hereinafter set forth.

AGREEMENT

NOW, THEREFORE, for good and valuable consideration, the receipt and sufficiency of which are hereby acknowledged and agreed, and in consideration of the recitals above, which are incorporated herein, and the premises and the mutual representations, covenants, undertakings and agreements hereinafter contained, Seller and Buyer represent, covenant, undertake, and agree as follows:

1. DESCRIPTION OF PROPERTY.

Seller agrees to sell, transfer, and convey and Buyer agrees to purchase and have transferred and conveyed, all for a purchase price and subject to and upon each of the terms and conditions hereinafter set forth, the following:

(a) <u>Property</u>.   The land legally described in **Exhibit A**, attached hereto and made a part hereof, together with all right, title, and interest of Seller in and to all easements, tenements, hereditaments, privileges, and appurtenances thereunto belonging (the "**Land**"), and improvements and structures located on the Land (collectively the "**Improvements**"). The Improvements and the Land are hereinafter collectively referred to as the "**Real Property.**"

(b) <u>Personalty</u>.   All personal property and other tangible property, if any, whether enumerated herein or not, in which Seller has an interest and which is not owned by any tenant, now or hereafter located on or in the Land or the Improvements, used in connection with the operation or maintenance thereof (the "**Personalty**").

(c) <u>Intangible Property</u>.   All intangible property, whether enumerated herein or not, in which Seller has an interest, now or hereafter used in connection with the operation or maintenance of the Improvements, the Land, or the Personalty, including, without limitation, all leases, licenses, and other agreements to occupy all or any part of the Real Property (all hereinafter collectively referred to as the "**Intangible Property**").

(d) <u>Appurtenant Rights</u>.   All right, title, and interest of Seller to land, if any, lying in the bed of any street, road, or avenue, open or proposed, at the foot of or adjoining the Land to the center line of such street, road, or avenue, and to the use of all easements, if any, whether of record or not, appurtenant to the Land and the use of all strips and rights-of-way, if any, abutting, adjacent, contiguous, or adjoining such Land, and to all water and water rights, ditch and ditch rights, water storage and water storage rights (all hereinafter collectively referred to as the "**Appurtenant Rights**").

The Real Property, Personalty, Intangible Property, and Appurtenant Rights are hereinafter sometimes collectively referred to as the "**Property**."

2. PURCHASE PRICE AND PAYMENT TERMS.

The purchase price to be paid by Buyer to Seller for the Property (the "**Purchase Price**") shall be Five Million and No/100 Dollars ($5,000,000.00). The Purchase Price shall be payable in the following manner:

(a) Earnest Money.   Within two (2) business days of the execution of this Agreement, Buyer shall deposit with First American Title Company, located at 123 Any Street, Boise, Idaho, as escrowee (the "**Escrowee**"), an amount equal to One Hundred Thousand and No/100 Dollars ($100,000.00) (the "**Earnest Money**"). The Earnest Money shall be held under the standard escrow instructions currently in use by the Escrowee. All Earnest Money and interest earned thereon, if any, shall be applied toward the Purchase Price at Closing, provided the transaction contemplated herein proceeds through Closing.

(b) Disbursement of Earnest Money.   The Earnest Money shall be returned to Buyer or delivered to Seller in accordance with the terms hereof. The parties hereto agree to promptly direct the Escrowee to deliver the Earnest Money in accordance with the terms hereof.

(c) Cash.   The balance of the Purchase Price, plus or minus prorations set forth herein, shall be paid by wire transfer or official bank check on the Closing Date, defined below.

3. TITLE MATTERS.

(a) Documents Evidencing Title.   Seller shall deliver or cause to be delivered to Buyer, not more than ten (10) days after the date hereof, a commitment for an owner's title insurance policy, dated after the date hereof issued by First American Title Insurance Company (the "**Title Insurer**") in the amount of the Purchase Price, with standard form coverage (the "**Title Commitment**") showing marketable and insurable title to the Property to be in the Seller subject only to: (i) title exceptions pertaining to liens or encumbrances of a definite or ascertainable amount which may be removed by the payment of money or otherwise on the Closing Date and which Seller shall so remove at that time; (ii) standard exceptions printed by the Title Insurer; and (iii) permitted exceptions as set forth in **Exhibit B**, attached hereto and made a part hereof (the "**Permitted Exceptions**").

(b) Title Defects.   Buyer shall have fifteen (15) business days after receipt of the Title Commitment within which to object in writing to any material exception shown thereon and if said exception cannot be removed by Seller on or before the Closing Date, Buyer shall have the right to terminate this Agreement, in which event the Earnest Money shall be returned to Buyer and all parties thereafter released and discharged from any further obligation under this Agreement. The failure of the Buyer to deliver written notice of an objection to a material exception shown on the Title Commitment within the time provided shall conclusively constitute the approval by Buyer of the exceptions shown in the Title Commitment.

4. INSPECTION.

(a) <u>Right to Inspect</u>.   For a period of sixty (60) days from the date hereof (sometimes hereinafter referred to as the "**Review Period**"), Buyer and its agents shall have the right, during reasonable hours, to inspect the Property, and to undertake, at Buyer's expense, such tests and surveys and other activities as it shall determine in connection therewith, including, without limitation, the right to make: (i) a complete physical inspection of the Property; (ii) investigations regarding zoning, subdivision, and code requirements; (iii) real estate tax analysis and investigation of available financing; (iv) investigation of all records and all other documents and matters, public or private, pertaining to Seller's ownership of the Property; and (v) to make application for and receive any and all permits, approvals, and written agreements satisfactory to Buyer (including, without limitation, site plan approvals, subdivision plat(s), building and use permits) required by the appropriate public or governmental authorities to permit the development of the Property in accordance with Buyer's intended use. The foregoing shall hereinafter sometimes be collectively referred to as the "**Inspection**." Seller shall give Buyer access to the Property for its Inspection. The Inspection to be conducted by Buyer shall not disturb the quiet enjoyment of Seller or be without prior notice to Seller.

Buyer agrees to indemnify and hold Seller harmless from any and all costs and expenses incurred or sustained by Seller as a result of such acts of Buyer, or Buyer's agents or independent contractors, pursuant to the right granted by this paragraph; provided Buyer's liability and indemnity shall not extend to any condition currently existing or discovered on the Property.

(b) <u>Approval Notice</u>.   In the event that Buyer, in its sole and exclusive discretion, is not satisfied for any reason with the results of the Inspection, Buyer may, by written notice (the "**Termination Notice**") delivered to Seller on or before the expiration of the Review Period (the "**Approval Date**"), terminate this Agreement, which thereafter shall be of no force and effect without further action by the parties hereto. Upon a termination as herein provided, the Earnest Money shall be returned to Buyer. It is understood and agreed that the failure of Buyer to deliver a Termination Notice for any reason, as a result of its Inspection, on or before the Approval Date shall constitute a waiver of Buyer's right to terminate this Agreement pursuant to the terms of this paragraph.

(c) <u>Continuing Right to Inspect</u>.   Notwithstanding the limitations of this paragraph, Buyer shall have the continuing right to continue the Inspection after the Review Period expires.

5. CONDITIONS PRECEDENT TO CLOSING.

(a) <u>Conditions Precedent</u>.   This Agreement, and Buyer's obligation to close the transaction contemplated herein, are subject to the following express conditions precedent. Notwithstanding anything to the contrary which may be contained herein, each of the conditions precedent may be waived in writing by Buyer, such conditions being for the exclusive protection and benefit of Buyer. Seller agrees to cooperate with Buyer and to execute any documents which may be necessary or convenient to the performance or satisfaction of these conditions by Buyer on or before closing:

(i) That at closing, the Property and the Buyer's intended use is (or will be) zoned and/or subdivided and all studies, reports, permits, approvals, and written agreements satisfactory to Buyer (including, without limitation, site plan approvals, subdivision plat(s), building and use permits, and environmental reports and permits) required by the appropriate public or governmental authorities to permit the development of the Property in accordance with Buyer's intended use have been finally adopted, all without conditions that, in Buyer's reasonable opinion, would cause construction of facilities and/or site work on the Property to be economically unfeasible.

(ii) Buyer has obtained, in Buyer's sole discretion and at Buyer's expense, a current certified boundary survey of the Property prepared by a licensed surveyor in accordance with Buyer's requirements (the "**Survey**") which shall show (1) the legal description of the Property (it is agreed that the legal description contained in the Survey shall be the legal description used in the Warranty Deed conveying the Property to Buyer); (2) that the Property extends to all adjacent streets, alleys and rights-of-way, which streets, alleys and rights-of-way have been dedicated to, and accepted for public use by, the appropriate governmental authority; (3) that utilities are available to the boundaries of the Property adequate to serve Buyer's proposed use; and (4) if the Property contains more than one parcel, then all of the parcels together form one parcel, and each parcel forming the larger parcel shares its interior boundary lines with the other parcel or parcels. The Survey shall be sufficient to cause the Title Insurer to delete the standard printed survey exception and to issue a title policy free from any survey-related objections or exceptions, whatsoever.

(iii) Title to the Property shall be good and marketable and shall be free and clear of all liens, encumbrances, easements, assessments, restrictions, tenancies (whether recorded or unrecorded), and other exceptions to title, except the lien of taxes not yet due and payable, and the Permitted Exceptions.

(b) <u>Failure of a Condition Precedent</u>.   In the event of a failure of any other condition precedent set forth herein, then Buyer may declare this Agreement null and void, in which event the refundable Earnest Money shall be returned to Buyer, and the parties shall have no further obligations or liabilities hereunder.

6. REPRESENTATIONS, WARRANTIES AND COVENANTS OF SELLER.

Seller hereby represents, warrants, and covenants to Buyer that as of the date hereof and as of the Closing Date:

(a) That Seller is and shall be the owner of marketable and insurable fee simple title to the Property, free and clear of all liens, encumbrances, covenants, conditions, restrictions, rights-of-way, easements, leases, tenancies, licenses, claims, options, options to purchase, and any other matters affecting title, except, as of the date hereof, for the exceptions shown on the Title Commitment, and those liens of a definite and ascertainable amount which shall be removed at closing. There shall be no change in the ownership, operation, or control of the Property from the date hereof to the Closing Date.

(b) To the actual knowledge of Seller that there are no condemnation or judicial proceedings, administrative actions or examinations, claims, or demands of any type which have been instituted or which are pending or threatened against Seller, the Property, or any part thereof. In the event Seller receives notice of any such proceeding, action, examination, or demand, Seller shall promptly deliver a copy of such notice to Buyer.

(c) That there is legal access to the Property from adjoining private or public streets, highways, roads, and ways and adequate access to all electric, telephone, drainage, and other utility equipment and services required by law or necessary for the operation of the Property. No fact or condition exists which would result in the termination or impairment of the furnishing of service to the Property of electric, telephone, drainage, or other such utility service.

(d) To the actual knowledge of Seller that Seller and the Property, and the use and operation thereof, are in compliance with all applicable municipal and governmental laws, ordinances, regulations, licenses, permits, and authorizations, and there are presently in effect all licenses, permits, and other authorizations necessary for the use, occupancy, and operation of the Property as it is presently being operated. That there exists no condition with respect to the operation, use, or occupancy of the Property which violates any environmental, zoning, building, health, fire, or similar law, ordinance, or regulation. There has been no notice of any violation of any environmental, zoning, building, health, fire, or similar law, ordinance, or regulation relative to the maintenance, operation, use, or occupancy of any building or other improvements constituting part of the Property which has not been fully complied with, nor has Seller received any notice, written or otherwise, from a government agency requiring the correction of any condition with respect to the Property which has not been fully complied with. Seller shall promptly comply with any notices received after the date hereof and shall promptly deliver to Buyer a copy of any such notice together with evidence of compliance therewith.

(e) That from and after the date hereof and until the Closing Date, Seller shall maintain, or cause to be maintained, the Property in good condition and repair, and shall continue to make or cause to be made ordinary repairs, replacements, and maintenance between the date hereof and the Closing Date with respect to the Property.

(f) To the actual knowledge of Seller that there are no material latent or patent defects in the Property.

(g) That there are and will be no unrecorded mechanic's or materialmen's liens or any claims for such liens affecting the Property, and as of the Closing Date, there will be no work or material performed or furnished for which payment will not have previously been made.

7. CLOSING AND RELATED MATTERS.

(a) <u>Closing Date</u>.   The closing shall take place on or before April 1, 2008, at the office of Escrowee at a time mutually agreed upon by the parties (the "**Closing Date**"). Provided, however, Buyer shall be obligated to close only if the conditions provided for in Section 5 have been satisfied and/or waived by Buyer.

(b) <u>Seller's Deposits</u>.   On the Closing Date, Seller shall deliver the following documents to Escrowee:

     (i) Warranty Deed executed by Seller conveying the Property to Buyer subject only to the Permitted Exceptions.

     (ii) Bill of Sale executed by Seller conveying the Personalty, if any, to Buyer.

     (iii) A Closing Statement.

     (iv) Such other documents as the Title Insurer, Buyer, or its attorneys may reasonably require in order to effectuate or further evidence the intent of any provision in this Agreement.

All of the documents and instruments to be delivered by Seller hereunder shall be in form and substance reasonably satisfactory to counsel for Buyer.

(c) <u>Buyer's Deposits</u>.   On the Closing Date, Buyer shall deliver the following documents to Escrowee:

     (i) A Closing Statement.

     (ii) Cash or certified funds in an amount sufficient to meet Buyer's obligations hereunder.

     (iii) Such other documents as the Title Insurer, Seller, or Seller's attorneys may reasonably require in order to effectuate or further evidence the intent of any provision in this Agreement.

All of the documents and instruments to be delivered by Buyer hereunder shall be in form and substance reasonably satisfactory to counsel for Seller.

(d) <u>Conditions to Closing</u>.   In all events, the obligations of Buyer to make payments and to close this transaction are contingent upon: (i) title to the Property being shown to be good and the Title Insurer committing to issue a title policy in the form as required by this Agreement; (ii) the Conditions Precedent to closing provided for in this Agreement being satisfied or waived by Buyer in writing; (iii) the representations, warranties, and covenants of Seller being true and accurate; and (iv) Seller otherwise having performed all of Seller's obligations hereunder. In the event that Seller fails to perform any of Seller's obligations hereunder, as set forth in the preceding sentence.

(e) <u>Escrow Closing</u>.   The closing of the transaction contemplated herein shall take place at the office of the Escrowee, using form escrow instructions then in use by the Escrowee, modified to reflect the terms and conditions of the transaction contemplated herein. The parties shall use their best efforts to have the Title Insurer commit to insure the title of Buyer upon receipt of all of Buyer's and Seller's deposits. The cost of the escrow relating to the transaction contemplated herein shall be equally divided between Seller and Buyer. This Agreement shall not be merged into any escrow agreement, and the escrow agreement shall always be deemed auxiliary to this

Agreement. The provisions of this Agreement shall always be deemed controlling as between Seller and Buyer. The respective attorneys for Seller and Buyer are hereby authorized to enter into and execute such escrow agreement and any amendments thereto.

(f) <u>Possession</u>.   Possession of the Property shall be delivered to Buyer on the Closing Date.

(g) <u>Tax-deferred Exchange</u>.   Notwithstanding any other provisions contained herein, Buyer may use the transaction contemplated herein to facilitate a tax-deferred exchange of property under such terms and conditions that qualify as a tax-deferred exchange under Section 1031 of the Internal Revenue Code of 1986, as amended, and Seller may use the transaction contemplated herein to facilitate such a tax-deferred exchange of property. The parties hereby agree to cooperate with each other fully in completing such tax-deferred exchange(s), provided, however, that such tax-deferred exchange(s) creates no additional liability to the party not effecting such tax deferred exchange, and that all costs of facilitating such tax-deferred exchange are paid by the party effecting the 1031 Exchange.

8. PRORATIONS AND ADJUSTMENTS.

The following items shall be prorated and adjusted as of the Closing Date:

(a) General real estate taxes and all other levies and charges against the Property for the year of closing that are accrued but not yet due and payable. Such taxes shall be prorated on the basis of the most recent ascertainable tax bills.

(b) If, on the Closing Date, the Property or any part thereof shall be or shall have been affected by an assessment or assessments which are or may become payable in annual installments, of which the first installment is then a charge or lien, or has been paid, then for the purposes of this Agreement all the unpaid installments of any such assessment, including those which are to become due and payable after the Closing Date, shall be deemed to be due and payable and to be liens upon the premises affected thereby and shall be paid and discharged by Seller on the Closing Date.

(c) All charges for utilities, including water charges, shall be paid by Seller to the Closing Date. Bills received after closing which relate to expenses incurred or services performed allocable to the period prior to the date of closing shall be paid by Seller post-closing as and when due.

(d) Title insurance and any other impositions on the conveyance shall be paid by Seller. Buyer shall not be liable for any state, county, federal income, excise, or sales tax liabilities of Seller. All recording fees in connection with the conveyance shall be paid by Buyer.

(e) All accounts payable and other obligations incurred by Seller in connection with the Property prior to the Closing Date shall be caused to be paid or performed by Seller on or before the Closing Date or as soon as practical thereafter, and Buyer assumes no obligation or responsibility for the payment or performance thereof.

(f) Such other items as are customarily prorated in transactions of the type contemplated in this Agreement.

9. DEFAULT AND REMEDIES.

(a) <u>Default by Buyer</u>. If Buyer should fail to consummate the transaction contemplated herein for any reason other than default by Seller, Seller may elect, without limitation, any one or more of the following remedies: (i) to enforce specific performance of this Agreement; (ii) to bring a suit for damages for breach of this Agreement; (iii) to terminate this Agreement whereupon Buyer will reimburse Seller for Seller's out-of-pocket expenses incurred with respect to this transaction, including reasonable attorneys' fees and inspection costs; or (iv) pursue any and all remedies at law or equity. No delay or omission in the exercise of any right or remedy accruing to Seller upon the breach by Buyer under this Agreement shall impair such right or remedy or be construed as a waiver of any such breach theretofore or thereafter occurring. The waiver by Seller of any condition or the breach of any term, covenant, or condition herein contained shall not be deemed to be a waiver of any other term, covenant, condition, or any subsequent breach of the same or any other term, covenant, or condition contained herein.

(b) <u>Default by Seller</u>. If Seller should fail to consummate the transaction contemplated herein for any reason other than default by Buyer, Buyer may elect, without limitation, any one or more of the following remedies: (i) to enforce specific performance of this Agreement; (ii) to bring a suit for damages for breach of this Agreement; (iii) to terminate this Agreement whereupon Seller will reimburse Buyer for Buyer's out-of-pocket expenses incurred with respect to this transaction, including reasonable attorneys' fees and inspection costs; or (iv) pursue any and all remedies at law or equity. No delay or omission in the exercise of any right or remedy accruing to Buyer upon the breach by Seller under this Agreement shall impair such right or remedy or be construed as a waiver of any such breach theretofore or thereafter occurring. The waiver by Buyer of any condition or the breach of any term, covenant, or condition herein contained shall not be deemed to be a waiver of any other term, covenant, condition, or any subsequent breach of the same or any other term, covenant, or condition contained herein.

10. INDEMNIFICATIONS AND DEFENSE OF CLAIMS.

(a) <u>Seller's Indemnity</u>. Seller will indemnify, defend, and hold Buyer harmless against and in respect of: (i) any damage or deficiency resulting from any breach of warranty or any non-fulfillment of any agreement on the part of Seller under this Agreement or from any misrepresentation in or omissions from any document or other instrument executed and delivered by Seller under this Agreement, unless waived in writing by Buyer; and/or (ii) all actions, suits, proceedings, demands, assessments, judgments, reasonable court costs and attorneys' fees, and expenses incident to or incurred by Buyer in connection with any of the foregoing.

(b) <u>Buyer's Indemnity</u>. Buyer shall indemnify, defend and hold Seller harmless against and in respect of: (i) any damage or deficiency resulting from any breach of warranty or any non-fulfillment of any agreement on the part of Buyer under this Agreement or from any misrepresentation in any document or other instrument executed and delivered by Buyer under this Agreement, unless waived in writing by Seller; and/or (ii) all actions, suits, proceedings, demands, assessments, judgments, reasonable court costs and attorneys' fees, and expenses incident to or incurred by Seller in connection with any of the foregoing.

11. BROKERAGE.

Each of the parties represents and warrants to the other that it has not incurred and will not incur any liability for finder's or brokerage fees or commissions in connection with this Agreement, other than John Smith of Real Estate Brokers, Inc., representing Buyer, and whose fees or commissions shall be paid by Buyer. It is agreed that if any claims for finder's or brokerage fees or commissions are ever made against Seller or Buyer in connection with this transaction, all such claims shall be handled and paid by the party (the "**Committing Party**") whose actions or alleged commitments form the basis of such claim. The Committing Party further agrees to indemnify and hold the other harmless from and against any and all claims or demands with respect to any finder's or brokerage fees or commissions or other compensation asserted by any person, firm, or corporation in connection with this Agreement or the transaction contemplated hereby. This representation shall survive closing indefinitely.

12. INTERVENING DAMAGE OR LOSS.

Seller shall deliver the Property to Buyer in substantially the same condition on the Closing Date as on the date hereof, excepting therefrom ordinary wear and tear. If, prior to the Closing Date, all or a substantial portion of the Property having a replacement value in excess of Ten Thousand and No/100 Dollars ($10,000.00) is destroyed by fire or other casualty or is taken or made subject to eminent domain proceedings, then Seller shall immediately notify Buyer. Thereupon Buyer shall, at its option, have the right to: (i) terminate this Agreement; or (ii) complete this transaction, in which event Seller shall: (x) deliver to Buyer a duly executed assignment of all insurance proceeds or condemnation awards payable as a result of such fire, casualty, or condemnation, in form and substance satisfactory to Buyer; and (y) pay the amount of any deductible thereunder (Seller represents and warrants that Seller shall maintain until the Closing Date full replacement cost insurance and the present amount of rent loss insurance for the Property).

13. NOTICES.

All notices, demands, requests, and other communications under this Agreement shall be in writing and shall be deemed properly served or delivered if delivered by hand to the party to whose attention it is directed, or when sent, three (3) days after deposit in the U.S. mail, postage prepaid, certified mail, return receipt requested, or one (1) day after deposit with a nationally recognized air carrier providing next day delivery, or if sent via facsimile transmission, when received, addressed as follows:

(a) If to Seller:

Land Company, Inc.
Attention: Joe Smith, President
987 Real Estate Lane
Boise, Idaho 83702
208/123-4567 (facsimile)

(b) If to Buyer:

> Real Estate Developers, LLC
> Attention: Jane Doe, Manager
> 1010 Big Money Lane
> Sun Valley, Idaho 83353
> 208/987-6543 (facsimile)

14. MISCELLANEOUS.

(a) As used herein, the term "**the date hereof**" shall mean the date first written above.

(b) This Agreement shall be binding upon and shall inure to the benefit of the parties hereto, and their respective heirs, personal representatives, successors, and assigns.

(c) Wherever under the terms and provisions of this Agreement the time for performance falls upon a Saturday, Sunday, or Legal Holiday, such time for performance shall be extended to the next business day.

(d) This Agreement may be executed in counterparts, each of which shall constitute an original, but all together shall constitute one and the same Agreement.

(e) The terms, provisions, and covenants (to the extent applicable) and indemnities shall survive the closing and delivery of the deed, and this Agreement shall not be merged therein, but shall remain binding upon and for the parties hereto until fully observed, kept or performed.

(f) This Agreement embodies the entire contract between the parties hereto with respect to the subject matter hereof. No extension, change, modification, or amendment to or of this Agreement of any kind whatsoever shall be made or claimed by Seller or Buyer, and no notice of any extension, change, modification, or amendment made or claimed by Seller or Buyer shall have any force or effect whatsoever unless the same shall be endorsed in writing and be signed by the party against which the enforcement of such extension, change, modification, or amendment is sought, and then only to the extent set forth in such instrument.

(g) All parties hereto have either: (i) been represented by separate legal counsel; or (ii) have had the opportunity to be so represented. Thus, in all cases, the language herein shall be construed simply and in accordance with its fair meaning and not strictly for or against a party, regardless of which party prepared or caused the preparation of this Agreement.

(h) The captions at the beginning of the several paragraphs, respectively, are for convenience in locating the context, but are not part of the text.

(i) In the event any term or provisions of this Agreement shall be held illegal, invalid, or unenforceable or inoperative as a matter of law, the remaining terms and provisions of this Agreement shall not be affected thereby, but each such term and provision shall be valid and shall remain in full force and effect.

(j) This Agreement shall be governed by the laws of the State of Idaho.

(k) If either party shall default in the full and timely performance of this Agreement and said default is cured with the assistance of an attorney for the other party and before the commencement of a suit thereon, as a part of curing said default, the reasonable attorneys' fees incurred by the other party shall be reimbursed to the other party upon demand.

In the event that either party to this Agreement shall file suit or action at law or equity to interpret or enforce this Agreement hereof, the unsuccessful party to such litigation agrees to pay to the prevailing party all costs and expenses, including reasonable attorneys' fees, incurred by the prevailing party, including the same with respect to an appeal.

(l) All times provided for in this Agreement or in any other instrument or document referred to herein or contemplated hereby for the performance of any act will be strictly construed, it being agreed that time is of the essence of this Agreement.

(m) The parties may at any time hereafter modify or amend this Agreement by a subsequent written agreement executed by all parties. This Agreement shall not, however, be changed orally, nor shall it be deemed modified in any way by the act of any of the parties hereto. Nothing herein is intended, nor shall it be construed, as obligating either party to agree to any modification to this Agreement.

IN WITNESS WHEREOF, the undersigned, being duly authorized, have executed this Agreement as of the date first written above.

SELLER:

LAND COMPANY, INC.,
an Idaho corporation

By:_____
   Joe Smith, President

BUYER:

REAL ESTATE DEVELOPERS, LLC,
an Idaho limited liability company

By:_____
   Jane Doe, Manager

EXHIBIT A

LEGAL DESCRIPTION

This parcel is all that of the Northeast quarter of the Southwest quarter and a portion of the Northwest quarter of the Southwest quarter of Section 1, Township 4 North, Range 2 West of the Boise Meridian and is more particularly described as follows:

BEGINNING at the Northwest corner of said Northwest quarter of the Southwest quarter; thence North 89°30'55" East along the North boundary of said Southwest quarter a distance of 2668.47 feet to the Northeast corner of said Southwest quarter; thence

South 0°28'38" West along the East boundary of said Northeast quarter of the Southwest quarter a distance of 1323.66 feet to the Southeast corner of said Northeast quarter of the Southwest quarter; thence

South 89°31'36" West along the South boundary of said Northeast quarter of the Southwest quarter a distance of 1337.39 feet to the Southwest corner of said Northeast quarter of the Southwest quarter; thence

South 89°35'18" West along the South boundary of said Northeast quarter of the Southwest quarter a distance of 1337.51 feet to the Southwest corner of said Northeast quarter of the Southwest quarter; thence

North 0°45'27" East along the West boundary of said Northwest quarter of the Southwest quarter a distance of 60.00 feet; thence

North 89°35'18" East parallel with the South boundary of said Northwest quarter of the Southwest quarter a distance of 1248.03 feet; thence

North 0°19'12" West a distance of 534.10 feet to a point on the centerline of a canal as it now exists; thence traversing said centerline as follows:

South 89°47'21" West a distance of 451.20 feet;
South 88°36'48" West a distance of 165.45 feet;
North 88°48'06" West a distance of 103.44 feet;
North 87°30'18" West a distance of 137.96 feet;
North 87°02'06" West a distance of 119.63 feet;
North 83°34'46" West a distance of 101.01 feet;
North 73°14'49" West a distance of 47.95 feet;
North 57°31'01" West a distance of 46.05 feet;
North 45°52'21" West a distance of 102.64 feet to a point on the West boundary of said Northwest quarter of the Southwest quarter; thence leaving said centerline and bearing North 0°45'27" East along said West boundary a distance of 588.71 feet to the POINT OF BEGINNING.

Also shown as Parcels 3 and 5 on Record of Survey recorded December 13, 2001 as Instrument No. 20011234567.

EXHIBIT B

PERMITTED EXCEPTIONS

1. Taxes, including any assessments collected therewith, for the year 2008 which are a lien not yet due and payable.

2. Levies and assessments of the Star Irrigation District and the rights, powers, and easements of said district as provided by law.

3. Levies and assessments of the Hilltop Ditch Company and the rights, powers, and easements of said district as provided by law.

4. Levies and assessments of the Drainage District No. 25 and the rights, powers, and easements of said district as provided by law.

5. Ditch, road, and public utility easements as the same may exist over said premises.

6. An easement for the purpose shown below and rights incidental thereto as set forth in a document.
Granted to: Idaho Power Company
Purpose: Public Utilities
Recorded: October 14, 1970
Instrument No.: 255889701

7. All matters, and any rights, easements, interests, or claims as disclosed by Record of Survey recorded December 13, 2001 as Instrument No. 20011234567.

8. An easement for the purpose shown below and rights incidental thereto as set forth in a document.
Granted to: Idaho Power Company
Purpose: Public Utilities
Recorded: July 18, 2003
Instrument No.: 20039876543

9. An easement for the purpose shown below and rights incidental thereto as set forth in a document.
Granted to: Idaho Power Company
Purpose: Public Utilities
Recorded: July 18, 2003
Instrument No.: 200300112233

10. Terms, provisions, conditions, and restrictions contained in Crossing Agreement by and between Star Ditch Company; Star Irrigation Association, Inc., an Idaho corporation; Water Lateral and XYZ Lateral and Intermountain Gas Company.
Recorded: January 10, 2005
Instrument No: 200509080706

STOCK PURCHASE AGREEMENT

THIS AGREEMENT is made and entered into this _____ day of _____, 20_____, by and between _____, (hereinafter referred to as "Seller") and _____, (hereinafter referred to as "Purchaser");

WITNESSETH:

WHEREAS, the Seller is the record owner and holder of the issued and outstanding shares of the capital stock of _____, (hereinafter referred to as the "Corporation"), a _____ corporation, which Corporation has issued capital stock of _____ shares of $_____ par value common stock, and

WHEREAS, the Purchaser desires to purchase said stock and the Seller desires to sell said stock, upon the terms and subject to the conditions hereinafter set forth;

NOW, THEREFORE, in consideration of the mutual covenants and agreements contained in this Agreement, and in order to consummate the purchase and the sale of the Corporation's Stock aforementioned, it is hereby agreed as follows:

1. PURCHASE AND SALE:

Subject to the terms and conditions hereinafter set forth, at the closing of the transaction contemplated hereby, the Seller shall sell, convey, transfer, and deliver to the Purchaser certificates representing such stock, and the Purchaser shall purchase from the Seller the Corporation's Stock in consideration of the purchase price set forth in this Agreement. The certificates representing the Corporation's Stock shall be duly endorsed for transfer or accompanied by appropriate stock transfer powers duly executed in blank, in either case with signatures guaranteed in the customary fashion, and shall have all the necessary documentary transfer tax stamps affixed thereto at the expense of the Seller.

The closing of the transactions contemplated by this Agreement (the "Closing"), shall be held at _____, on _____, at _____, or such other place, date, and time as the parties hereto may otherwise agree.

2. AMOUNT AND PAYMENT OF PURCHASE PRICE.

The total consideration and method of payment thereof are fully set out in Exhibit "A" attached hereto and made a part hereof.

3. REPRESENTATIONS AND WARRANTIES OF SELLER.

Seller hereby warrants and represents:

(a) Organization and Standing.

Corporation is a corporation duly organized, validly existing and in good standing under the laws of the State of _____ and has the corporate power and authority to carry on its business as it is now being conducted.

(b) Restrictions on Stock.

i. The Seller is not a party to any agreement, written or oral, creating rights in respect to the Corporation's Stock in any third person or relating to the voting of the Corporation's Stock.

ii. Seller is the lawful owner of the Stock, free and clear of all security interests, liens, encumbrances, equities, and other charges.

iii. There are no existing warrants, options, stock purchase agreements, redemption agreements, restrictions of any nature, calls, or rights to subscribe of any character relating to the stock, nor are there any securities convertible into such stock.

4. REPRESENTATIONS AND WARRANTIES OF SELLER AND PURCHASER.

Seller and Purchaser hereby represent and warrant that there has been no act or omission by Seller, Purchaser, or the Corporation which would give rise to any valid claim against any of the parties hereto for a brokerage commission, finder's fee, or other like payment in connection with the transactions contemplated hereby.

5. GENERAL PROVISIONS

(a) Entire Agreement.

This Agreement (including the exhibits hereto and any written amendments hereof executed by the parties) constitutes the entire Agreement and supersedes all prior agreements and understandings, oral and written, between the parties hereto with respect to the subject matter hereof.

(b) Sections and Other Headings.

The section and other headings contained in this Agreement are for reference purposes only and shall not affect the meaning or interpretation of this Agreement.

(c) Governing Law.

This agreement, and all transactions contemplated hereby, shall be governed by, construed, and enforced in accordance with the laws of the State of _____. The parties herein waive trial by jury and agree to submit to the personal jurisdiction and venue of a court of subject matter jurisdiction located in _____ County, State of _____. In the event that litigation results from or arises out of this Agreement or the performance thereof, the parties agree to reimburse the prevailing party's reasonable attorney's fees, court costs, and all other expenses, whether or not taxable by the court as costs, in addition to any other relief to which the prevailing party may be entitled.

IN WITNESS WHEREOF, this Agreement has been executed by each of the individual parties hereto on the date first above written.

_____

_____

Signed, sealed and delivered in the presence of:

_____

_____

EXHIBIT "A"

AMOUNT AND PAYMENT OF PURCHASE PRICE

(a) Consideration.

As total consideration for the purchase and sale of the Corporation's Stock, pursuant to this Agreement, the Purchaser shall pay to the Seller the sum of _____(20)_____ Dollars ($_____), such total consideration to be referred to in this Agreement as the "Purchase Price".

(b) Payment.

The Purchase Price shall be paid as follows:

i. The sum of _____(21)_____ Dollars ($_____) to be delivered to Seller upon the execution of this Agreement.

ii. The sum of _____(22)_____ Dollars ($_____) to be delivered to Seller at Closing.

APPENDIX D

UNIFORM COMMERCIAL CODE (UCC)

Articles of the Uniform Commercial Code (UCC)

- Article 1: General Provisions
- Article 2: Sales*
- Article 2A: Leases*
- Article 3: Commercial Paper
- Article 4: Bank Deposits and Collections
- Article 4A: Funds Transfers
- Article 5: Letters of Credit
- Article 6: Bulk Transfers
- Article 7: Warehouse Receipts, Bills of Lading and Other Documents of Title
- Article 8: Investment Securities
- Article 9: Secured Transactions; Sales of Accounts and Chattel Paper

■ UNIFORM COMMERCIAL CODE (UCC) LOCATOR

Go to: www.law.cornell.edu/uniform/ucc.html

This locator links to state statutes that correspond to Articles of the Uniform Commercial Code.

---

*The articles of the UCC that most relate to Contract Law are Article 2: Sales and Article 2A: Leases.

Sales

UCC Article 2

Uniform Law Commissioners drafts bearing on past and future revisions

• Alabama • Alaska • Arizona - §§ 47-2101 to 47-2725 • Arkansas • California - §§ 2101 to 2801 • Colorado - §§ 4-2-101 to 4-2-725 • Connecticut - §§ 42a-2-101 to 42a-2-725 • Delaware • District of Columbia • Florida • Georgia - § 11-2-101 • Hawaii • Idaho • Illinois • Indiana • Iowa • Kansas - § 84-2-101 (Chapt. 84): Fee based service • Kentucky (PDF) • Louisiana - did not adopt this article • Maine	• Maryland - article = "Commercial Law" §§ 2-101 to 2-725 • Massachusetts • Michigan • Minnesota §§ 336.2-101 to 336.2-725. • Mississippi - § 75-2-101 • Missouri • Montana • Nebraska - § U2-101 • Nevada • New Hampshire - §§ 382-A:1-101 to 382-A:1-208. • New Jersey -§§ 12A: 2-101 to 12A: 2-725 • New Mexico - §§ 55-2-101 through 55-2-725. • New York • North Carolina - §§ 25-2-101 to 25-2-725 • North Dakota (PDF) • Ohio (Title 1302) • Oklahoma -12A §§ 2-101 • Oregon	• Pennsylvania • Rhode Island • South Carolina • South Dakota • Tennessee • Texas • Utah • Vermont • Virgin Islands • Virginia • Washington • West Virginia Chapter 46-2-101 to 46-1-725 • Wisconsin • Wyoming

Leases

UCC Article 2A

Uniform Law Commissioners drafts bearing on past and future revisions

• Alabama • Alaska • Arizona - §§ 47-2A101 to 47-2A532 • Arkansas • California - §§ 10101 to 10600 • Colorado - §§ 4-2.5-101 to 4-2.5-533 • Connecticut - not adopted • Delaware • District of Columbia • Florida • Georgia • Hawaii • Idaho • Illinois • Indiana • Iowa • Kansas - § 84-2a-101 (Chapt. 84): Fee based service • Kentucky (PDF) • Louisiana - did not adopt this article • Maine	• Maryland - article = "Commercial Law" §§ 2A-101 to 2A-532. • Massachusetts • Michigan • Minnesota - §§ 336.2A-101 to 336.2A-531. • Mississippi - § 75-2a-101 • Missouri • Montana • Nebraska - § U2A-101 • Nevada • New Hampshire - §§ 382-A: 2A-101 to 382-A:2A-532. • New Jersey - §§ 12A: 2A-101 to 12A: 2A-532 • New Mexico - §§ 55-2A-101 through 55-2A-532. • New York • North Carolina - §§ 25-2A-101 to 25-2A-532 • North Dakota (PDF) • Ohio (Title 1310) • Oklahoma - 12A §§ 2A-101	• Oregon • Pennsylvania - article not online • Rhode Island • South Carolina • South Dakota • Tennessee • Texas • Utah • Vermont • Virgin Islands • Virginia • Washington • West Virginia Chapter 46-2A-101 to 46-2A-532 • Wisconsin • Wyoming

GLOSSARY

abnormal misuse Considerably irregular or an atypical level of usage.

acceptance Acquiescence (acceptance of guilt).

acceptance-upon-dispatch rule A rule that states that an acceptance is effective when it is dispatched, even if it is lost in transmission.

acceptor Someone who becomes liable on a draft by his or her acceptance of it.

access contract Where a software licensor grants the licensee the right to access information in the possession of the licensor for an agreed-upon time or for a number of uses.

accommodation A shipment that is offered to the buyer as a replacement for the original shipment when the original shipment cannot be filled.

accord An agreement whereby the parties agree to accept something different in satisfaction of the original contract.

accord and satisfaction The settlement of a contract dispute.

account party The buyer in regard to a letter of credit.

adequate assurance When a party has reasonable grounds to believe the other party will not perform his or her contractual obligations they may demand a writing assuring them that performance will occur.

adequate consideration A value of the bargain that is equal to or reasonably proportioned to the value of that for which it is given.

adjudged insane A person who has been adjudged insane by a proper court or administrative agency. A contract entered into by such a person is void.

admissions in pleadings or court When a party admits in pleadings, testimony, or otherwise in court that a contract for the sale or lease of goods was made, the oral contract is enforceable against that party.

advertisement A general advertisement is an invitation to make an offer. A specific advertisement is an offer.

AFL-CIO The 1955 combination of the AFL and the CIO.

agency The principal-agent relationship: the fiduciary relationship "which results from the manifestation of consent by one person to another that the other shall act in his behalf and subject to his control, and consent by the other so to act."

agency law The large body of common law that governs agency; a mixture of contract law and tort law.

agent A person who has been authorized to sign a negotiable instrument on behalf of another person. The party who agrees to act on behalf of another.

agreement The manifestation by two or more persons of the substance of a contract.

alternative dispute resolution (ADR) Methods of resolving disputes other than litigation.

American Federation of Labor (AFL) One of the first federations of labor unions in the United States.

anti-assignment clause A clause that prohibits the assignment of rights under the contract.

anti-delegation clause A clause that prohibits the delegation of duties under the contract.

anticipatory breach A breach that occurs when one contracting party informs the other that he or she will not perform his or her contractual duties when due.

anticipatory repudiation The repudiation of a sales or lease contract by one of the parties prior to the date set for performance.

Anticybersquatting Consumer Protection Act A law specifically aimed at "cybersquatters"—persons who register Internet domain names of famous companies and people and hold them hostage by demanding ransom payments from the famous companies or people.

approval clause A clause that permits the assignment of the contract only upon receipt of an obligor's approval.

arbitration A form of ADR in which the parties choose an impartial third party to hear and decide the dispute. A nonjudicial method of dispute resolution whereby a neutral third party decides the case.

Article 2 (Sales) The second article of the Uniform Commercial Code which prescribes the rules for the creation and enforcement of contracts for the sale of goods.

Article 2A (Leases) Article of the UCC that governs lease of goods.

Article 5 (Letters of Credit) A section of the UCC that governs letters of credit unless otherwise agreed to by the parties.

Article 6 (Bulk Sales) The section of the UCC that governs when an owner transfers a major part of a business's material, merchandise, inventory, or equipment not in the ordinary course of business.

assignee The party to whom the right has been transferred. The transferee in an assignment situation. The party to whom rights have been transferred.

assignment and delegation Transfer of both rights and duties under the contract.

assignment of future rights A currently nonexistent right that a party expects to have sometime in the future.

assignment of rights The transfer by the parties of their contractual rights.

assignor The party who transfers the rights. The transferor in an assignment situation. The obligee who transfers the right.

assumption of duties When a delegation of duties contains the term *assumption, I assume the duties,* or other similar language; the delegatee is legally liable to the obligee for nonperformance.

assumption of the risk A defense a defendant can use against a plaintiff who knowingly and voluntarily enters into or participates in a risky activity that results in injury. A defense in which the defendant must prove that (1) the plaintiff knew and appreciated the risk and (2) the plaintiff voluntarily assumed the risk.

assurance of performance Where each party expects that the other party will perform his or her contractual obligations.

attribution procedure A procedure using codes, algorithms, identifying words or numbers, encryption, callback, or other acknowledgment to verify an authentication of a record.

auction with reserve Unless expressly stated otherwise, an auction is an auction with reserve; that is, the seller retains the right to refuse the highest bid and withdraw the goods from sale.

auction without reserve An auction in which the seller expressly gives up his or her right to withdraw the goods from sale and must accept the highest bid.

authenticate Signing the contract or executing an electronic symbol, sound, or message attached to, included in, or linked with the record.

bail bond A three-party contract that involves the state, the accused, and a surety under which the surety guarantees the state that the accused will appear in court as the case proceeds.

bailee A holder of goods who is not a seller or a buyer (e.g., a warehouse or common carrier).

bargained-for exchange Exchange that parties engage in that leads to an enforceable contract.

basis of the bargain All statements by the seller or lessor prior to or at the time of contracting.

battle of the forms Where the parties to a contract go back and forth with each other trying to get the other to agree to their standard contract form.

beneficiary A person or organization designated in the will that receives all or a portion of the testator's property at the time of the testator's death. The person who is to receive the life insurance proceeds when the insured dies. Person for whose benefit a trust is created.

best-efforts contract A contract clause that requires one or both of the parties to use their best efforts to achieve the objective of the contract.

bilateral contract A contract entered into by way of exchange of promises of the parties; a "promise for a promise."

bill of lading A document of title that is issued by a carrier when goods are received for transportation.

breach of contract If a contracting party fails to perform an absolute duty owed under a contract.

bulk transfer When an owner transfers a major part of a business's material, merchandise, inventory, or equipment not in the ordinary course of business.

buyer in the ordinary course of business A person who in good faith and without knowledge of another's ownership or security interest in goods buys the goods in the ordinary course of business from a person in the business of selling goods of that kind [UCC 1-201(9)].

C & F Cost and freight. Pricing terms indicating the cost for which the seller is responsible.

cancellation The termination of a contract by a contracting party upon the material breach of the contract by the other party. A buyer or lessee may cancel a sales or lease contract if the seller or lessor fails to deliver conforming goods or repudiates the contract or if the

buyer or lessee rightfully rejects the goods or justifiably revokes acceptance of the goods.

capture The process by which a buyer or lessee can recover goods when seller or lessor becomes insolvent within 10 days of receiving the buyer's or lessee's first payment.

certificate of deposit (CD) A two-party negotiable instrument that is a special form of note created when a depositor deposits money at a financial institution in exchange for the institution's promise to pay back the amount of the deposit plus an agreed-upon rate of interest upon the expiration of a set time period agreed upon by the parties.

chain of distribution All manufacturers, distributors, wholesalers, retailers, lessors, and subcomponent manufacturers involved in a transaction.

check An order by the drawer to the drawee bank to pay a specified sum of money from the drawer's checking account to the named payee (or holder). A distinct form of draft drawn on a financial institution and payable on demand.

CIF Cost, insurance, and freight. Pricing terms indicating the cost for which the seller is responsible.

classical law of contracts Objective rules of forming contracts which give certainty and predictability in their enforcement.

COD (cash on delivery) Buyers must pay for the goods upon delivery without the right to inspect them first.

collateral Security against repayment of the note that lenders sometimes require; can be a car, a house, or other property. The property that is subject to the security interest.

collateral note Notes secured by personal property.

collective bargaining The act of negotiating contract terms between an employer and the members of a union.

collective bargaining agreement The resulting contract from a collective bargaining procedure.

commercial impracticability Nonperformance that is excused if an extreme or unexpected development or expense makes it impractical for the promisor to perform.

common law Developed by judges who issued their opinions when deciding a case. The principles announced in these cases became precedent for later judges deciding similar cases.

common law of contracts Contract law developed primarily by state courts.

comparative fault The measurement of damages by percentage. The victim's damages are reduced proportionate to the amount of negligence attributable to the victim.

compensatory damages An award of money intended to compensate a non-breaching party for the loss of the bargain; they place the nonbreaching party in the same position as if the contract had been fully performed by restoring the "benefit of the bargain." Damages that are generally equal to the difference between the value of the goods as warranted and the actual value of the goods accepted at the time and place of acceptance.

complete integration Where the written contract is a complete and final statement of the parties' agreement.

complete performance Occurs when a party to a contract renders performance exactly as required by the contract; discharges that party's obligations under the contract.

computer information transactions Under UCITA Section 102(a)(II), a computer information transaction "is an agreement to create, transfer, or license computer information or informational rights."

concurrent condition A condition that exists when the parties to a contract must render performance simultaneously; each party's absolute duty to perform is conditioned on the other party's absolute duty to perform.

condition A qualification of a promise that becomes a covenant if it is met. There are three types of conditions: conditions precedent, conditions subsequent, and concurrent conditions.

condition precedent A condition that must happen or be performed before some right dependent thereon accrues or some act dependent thereon is performed.

condition precedent based on satisfaction Clause in a contract that reserves the right to a party to pay for the items or services contracted for only if they meet his or her satisfaction.

condition subsequent A condition, if it occurs or doesn't occur, that automatically excuses the performance of an existing contractual duty to perform.

Congress of Industrial Organizations (CIO) A federation of unions that organized workers in industrial unions in the United States and Canada from 1935 to 1955. The CIO was more aggressive and militant than the American Federation of Labor (AFL). The CIO merged with the AFL in 1955.

consequential (special) damages Foreseeable damages that arise from circumstances outside the contract. To be liable for these damages, the breaching party must know or have reason to know that the breach will cause special damages to the other party.

consideration Something of legal value given in exchange for a promise.

consignee The person to whom the bailed goods are to be delivered.

consignment An arrangement where a seller (the consignor) delivers goods to a buyer (the consignee) for sale.

consignor The person shipping the goods. The bailor.

conspicuous A requirement that warranty disclaimers be noticeable to the average person.

consumer expectation test A test to determine merchantability based on what the average consumer would expect to find in food products.

contracts contrary to public policy Contracts that have a negative impact on society or that interfere with the public's safety and welfare.

contracts in restraint of trade An economic policy of competition in the U.S.; contracts restraining trade are illegal.

contractual capacity The legal qualification or competency to understand the nature and effects of one's acts so as to enter into a contract.

contributory negligence An unreasonable act or omission by the victim

(plaintiff) which, along with the defendant's negligence, is the proximate cause of the injury.

convenant of good faith and fair dealing Under this implied covenant, the parties to a contract not only are held to the express terms of the contract but are also required to act in "good faith" and deal fairly in all respects in obtaining the objective of the contact.

correspondent A securities firm, bank, or other financial organization that regularly performs services for another in a place or market to which the other does not have direct access (a correspondent on an exchange; correspondent bank).

Counterfeit Access Device and Computer Fraud and Abuse Act of 1984 A federal law that makes it a crime to access restricted government and other information by computer for unauthorized purposes.

counteroffer A response by an offeree that contains terms and conditions different from or in addition to those of the offer. A counteroffer terminates an offer.

course of dealing A sequence of previous acts and conduct between the parties to a particular transaction, which fairly establishes a common basis of understanding for interpreting their communications and other conduct.

course of performance The history of previous conduct of the parties regarding the contract in question.

covenant An unconditional promise to perform.

covenant not to compete An agreement where a party agrees not to engage in a similar business or occupation within a specified geographic area for a specified period of time following a sale.

cover Right of a buyer or lessee to purchase or lease substitute goods if a seller or lessor fails to make delivery of the goods or repudiates the contract or if the buyer or lessee rightfully rejects the goods or justifiably revokes their acceptance. The licensee's right to engage in a commercially reasonable substitute transaction after the licensor has breached the contract.

crashworthiness doctrine A doctrine that says automobile manufacturers are under a duty to design automobiles so they take into account the possibility of harm from a person's body striking something inside the automobile in the case of a car accident.

creditor beneficiary   Original creditor who becomes a beneficiary under the debtor's new contract with another party.

creditor beneficiary contract   A contract that arises in the following situation: (1) a debtor borrows money, (2) the debtor signs an agreement to pay back the money plus interest, (3) the debtor sells the item to a third party before the loan is paid off, and (4) the third party promises the debtor that he or she will pay the remainder of the loan to the creditor.

cure   An opportunity to repair or replace defective or nonconforming goods.

damages for accepted nonconforming goods   A buyer or lessee may accept nonconforming goods and recover the damages caused by the breach from the seller or lessor or deduct the damages from any part of the purchase price or rent still due under the contract.

declaration of duties   If the delegatee has not assumed the duties under a contract, the delegatee is not legally liable to the obligee for nonperformance.

deed of trust   An instrument that gives the creditor a security interest in the debtor's property that is pledged as collateral.

defect in design   A defect that occurs when a product is improperly designed.

defect in manufacture   A defect that occurs when the manufacturer fails to (1) properly assemble a product, (2) properly test a product, or (3) adequately check the quality of the product.

defect in packaging   A defect that occurs when a product has been placed in packaging that is insufficiently tamperproof.

delegatee   The party to whom the duty has been transferred.

delegation of duties   A transfer of contractual duties by the obligor to another party for performance.

delegator   The obligor who transferred his or her duty.

demand draft   An order to pay a certain sum of money that expressly states it is payable on demand, on presentation, or on sight.

demand note   A note payable on demand.

destination contract   A sales contract that requires the seller to deliver conforming goods to a specific destination. The seller bears the risk of loss during transportation. A contract that requires the seller to deliver the goods either to the buyer's place of business or to another destination specified in the sales contract.

disaffirmance   The act of a minor to rescind a contract under the infancy doctrine. Disaffirmance may be done orally, in writing, or by the minor's conduct.

discharge   Actions or events that relieve certain parties from liability on negotiable instruments. There are three methods of discharge: (1) payment of the instrument; (2) cancellation; and (3) impairment of the right of recourse. The termination of the legal duty of a debtor to pay debts that remain unpaid upon the completion of a bankruptcy proceeding. Creditors' claims that are not included in a Chapter 11 reorganization are discharged. A discharge is granted to a debtor in a Chapter 13 consumer debt adjustment bankruptcy only after all the payments under the plan are completed by the debtor.

disposition of goods   A seller or lessor who is in possession of goods at the time the buyer or lessee breaches or repudiates the contract may in good faith resell, release, or otherwise dispose of the goods in a commercially reasonable manner and recover damages, including incidental damages, from the buyer or lessee.

doctrine of strict liability in tort   A tort doctrine that makes manufacturers, distributors, wholesalers, retailers, and others in the chain of distribution of a defective product liable for the damages caused by the defect irrespective of fault.

doctrine of unconscionability   Where an otherwise lawful contract will not be enforced because it is so oppressive or manifestly unfair that it is unjust.

document of title   An actual piece of paper, such as warehouse receipt or bill of lading, that is required in some transactions of pick up and delivery. A negotiable instrument developed to represent the interests of the different parties in a transaction that uses storage or transportation between the parties.

domain name   A unique name that identifies an individual's or company's website.

donee beneficiary   The third party on whom the benefit is to be conferred.

donee beneficiary contract   A contract entered into with the intent to confer a benefit or gift on an intended third party.

draft   A three-party instrument that is an unconditional written order by one party that orders the second party to pay money to a third party.

drawee of a check   The bank where the drawer has his or her account.

drawee of a draft   The party who must pay the money stated in the draft. Also called the acceptor of a draft.

drawer of a check   The checking account holder and writer of the check.

drawer of a draft   The party who writes the order for a draft.

duress   Occurs where one party threatens to do a wrongful act unless the other party enters into a contract.

duty of restitution   Where, upon disaffirmance, the competent party returns the consideration of the contract back to the minor.

duty of restoration   Where, upon disaffirmance, the minor returns the goods or property back to the competent party.

e-commerce   The sale of goods and services by computer over the Internet.

easement   A right to use someone else's land without owning or leasing it. A given or required right to make limited use of someone else's land without owning or leasing it.

economic duress   Occurs when one party to a contract refuses to perform his or her contractual duties unless the other party pays an increased price, enters into a second contract with the threatening party, or undertakes a similar action.

Electronic Communications Privacy Act (ECPA)   A federal law that, with some exceptions, makes it a crime to intercept an electronic communication.

Electronic Funds Transfer Act A law regulating the payment and deposit of funds by electronic transfer.

electronic mail (e-mail) Electronic written communication between individuals using computers connected to the Internet.

Electronic Signature in Global and National Commerce Act (SIGN Act) A federal statute designed to recognize electronic contracts as meeting the writing requirement of the Statute of Frauds for most contracts.

emancipation When a minor voluntarily leaves home and lives apart from his or her parents.

employer-employee relationship A relationship that results when an employer hires an employee to perform some form of physical service.

entrustment rule A UCC section allowing certain merchants to transfer all rights in goods, including title.

equal dignity rule A rule that says that agents' contracts to sell property covered by the Statute of Frauds must be in writing to be enforceable.

equitable relief The kind of relief sought in a court with equity powers (e.g., injunction, specific performance of a contract).

equitable remedies Remedies based on settled rules of fairness, justice, and honesty, such as specific performance, reformation, and injunction.

equity A doctrine that permits judges to make decisions based on fairness, equality, moral rights, and natural law.

ex-ship (from the carrying vessel) The seller bears the expense and risk of loss until the goods are unloaded.

exclusive license A license that grants the licensee exclusive rights to use informational rights for a specified duration.

exculpatory clause A contractual provision that relieves one (or both) of the parties to the contract from tort liability for ordinary negligence.

executed contract A contract that has been fully performed on both sides; a completed contract.

executory contract A contract that has not yet been fully completed or performed. With Court approval, executory contracts may be rejected by a debtor in bankruptcy.

express authorization A stipulation in the offer that says the acceptance must be by a specified means of communication.

express contract An agreement that is expressed in written or oral words.

express warranty Any affirmation of fact or promise by the licensor about the quality of its software or information. A warranty that is created when a seller or lessor makes an affirmation that the goods he or she is selling or leasing meet certain standards of quality, description, performance, or condition.

failure to provide adequate instructions A defect that occurs when a manufacturer does not provide detailed directions for safe assembly and use of a product.

failure to warn A defect that occurs when a manufacturer does not place a warning on the packaging of products that could cause injury if the danger is unknown.

FAS Free alongside. The seller bears the expense and risk of loss until the goods are alongside a named vessel or the dock designated.

Federal Trade Commission (FTC) Federal government agency empowered to enforce federal franchising rules. Federal administrative agency empowered to enforce the Federal Trade Commission Act and other federal consumer protection statutes.

finance lease A three-party transaction consisting of the lessor, the lessee, and the supplier.

firm offer rule Under the UCC, a merchant who offers to buy, sell, or lease goods and who gives a written and signed assurance that the offer will be held open cannot revoke the offer for the time stated or a reasonable time.

FOB Free on board. The seller must bear the expense and risk of loss until the goods are put in carrier's possession.

FOB place of destination The seller bears the expense and risk of loss until the goods are tendered to the buyer.

force majeure clauses Certain events, such as floods, earthquakes, or tornadoes, that will excuse nonperformance of a contract.

foreign substance test A test to determine merchantability based on foreign objects that are found in food.

formal contract A contract that requires a special form or method of creation.

fraud by concealment Occurs when one party takes specific action to conceal a material fact from another party.

fraud in the inception Occurs if a person is deceived as to the nature of his or her act and does not know what he or she is signing. A real defense against the enforcement of a negotiable instrument; a person has been deceived into signing a negotiable instrument thinking that it is something else.

fraud in the inducement Occurs when the party knows what he or she is signing, but has been fraudulently induced to enter into the contract. A personal defense against the enforcement of a negotiable instrument; a wrongdoer makes a false statement to another person to lead that person to enter into a contract with the wrongdoer.

fraudulent misrepresentation (fraud) Where one person to a contract intentionally induces (or causes) another person to rely and act on an assertion not in accord with the facts.

fully disclosed agency Where the fact that the agent is acting on behalf of an agency is fully revealed and free from secrecy.

fungible Goods consisting of identical and interchangeable particles or components.

future goods Goods not yet in existence (ungrown crops, unborn stock animals).

gambling statutes Statutes that make certain forms of gambling illegal.

gap-filling rule A rule that says an open term can be "read into" a contract.

generally known dangers A defense that acknowledges that certain products are inherently dangerous and are known to the general population to be so.

genuine assent Where agreement (or assent) to the contract by both parties is genuine and real.

genuineness of assent The requirement that a party's assent to a contract be genuine.

gift promise An unenforceable promise because it lacks consideration.

glossary A detailed definition section in a written contract.

good faith purchaser for value A person to whom good title can be transferred from a person with voidable title. The real owner cannot reclaim goods from a good faith purchaser for value.

good faith subsequent lessee A person to whom a lease interest can be transferred from a person with voidable title. The real owner cannot reclaim the goods from the subsequent lessee until the lease expires.

goods Tangible things that are movable at the time of their identification to the contract.

government contractor defense A defense that says a contractor who was provided specifications by the government is not liable for any defect in the product that occurs as a result of those specifications.

guarantor The person who agrees to pay the debt if the primary debtor does not. The third person who agrees to be liable in a guaranty arrangement.

guaranty contract The contract between the guarantor and the original creditor.

identification of goods Distinguishing the goods named in the contract from the seller's or lessor's other goods.

Identity Theft and Assumption Deterrence Act of 1998 A federal law making it a federal felony to commit identity fraud or theft.

illegal consideration A promise to refrain from doing an illegal act. Such a promise will not support a contract.

illegal contract A contract to perform an illegal act.

illusory promise A contract into which both parties enter, but one or both of the parties can choose not to perform their contractual obligations. Thus the contract lacks consideration.

immoral contract A contract whose objective is the commission of an act that is considered immoral by society.

implied authorization Mode of acceptance that is implied from what is customary in similar transactions, usage of trade, or prior dealings between the parties.

implied term A term in a contract that can reasonably be supplied by the courts.

implied warranty of authority An agent who enters into a contract on behalf of another party impliedly warrants that he or she has the authority to do so.

implied warranty of fitness for a particular purpose An implied warranty that information is fit for the licensee's purpose that applies if the licensor (1) knows of any particular purpose for which the computer information is required and (2) knows that the licensee is relying on the licensor's skill or judgment to select or furnish suitable information.

implied warranty of fitness for human consumption A warranty that applies to food or drink consumed on or off the premises of restaurants, grocery stores, fast-food outlets, and vending machines.

implied warranty of informational content An implied warranty that there is no inaccuracy in the informational content caused by the merchant-licensor's failure to perform with reasonable care.

implied warranty of merchantability Unless properly disclosed, a warranty that is implied that sold or leased goods are fit for the ordinary purpose for which they are sold or leased, and other assurances.

implied warranty of merchantability of the computer program An implied warranty that the copies of the computer program are within the parameters permitted by the licensing agreement, that the computer program has been adequately packaged and labeled, and that the program conforms to any promises or affirmations of fact on the container or label.

implied-in-fact condition A condition that can be implied from the circumstances surrounding a contract and the parties' conduct.

implied-in-fact contract A contract where agreement between parties has been inferred because of their conduct.

impossibility of performance (objective impossibility) Nonperformance that is excused if the contract becomes impossible to perform; must be objective impossibility, not subjective.

in pari delicto In equal fault; equally culpable or criminal.

incidental beneficiary A party who is unintentionally benefited by other people's contracts.

incidental damages When goods are resold or released, incidental damages are reasonable expenses incurred in stopping delivery, transportation charges, storage charges, sales commissions, and so on.

incorporation by reference When integration is made by express reference in one document that refers to and incorporates another document within it.

independent contractor A person who contracts with another to do something for him who is not controlled by the other nor subject to the other's right to control with respect to his physical conduct in the performance of the undertaking. [*Restatement (Second) of Agency*].

infancy doctrine A doctrine that allows minors to disaffirm (cancel) most contracts they have entered into with adults.

inferior performance Occurs when a party fails to perform express or implied contractual obligations that impair or destroy the essence of the contract.

informal contract A contract that is not formal. Valid informal contracts are fully enforceable and may be sued upon if breached.

Information Infrastructure Protection Act (IIP Act) A federal law making it a federal crime to access and acquire information from a protected computer without authorization.

injunction A court order that prohibits a person from doing a certain act.

innocent misrepresentation Occurs when a person makes a statement of fact that he or she honestly and reasonably believes to be true, even though it is not. Occurs when an agent makes an untrue statement that he or she honestly and reasonably believes to be true.

insane but not adjudged insane A person who is insane but has not been adjudged insane by a court or administrative agency. A contract entered into by such person is generally voidable. Some states hold that such a contract is void.

installment contract A contract that requires or authorizes the goods to be delivered and accepted in separate lots.

installment note An agreement to pay a portion of a debt at successive periods until paid in full.

intangible property Rights that cannot be reduced to physical form such as stock certificates, certificates of deposit, bonds, and copyrights.

integration of several writings Where several different writings or documents are considered to form one enforceable contract.

intentional interference with contractual relations A tort that arises when a third party induces a contracting party to breach the contract with another party.

intentional misrepresentation Intentionally defrauding another person out of money, property, or something else of value. When a seller or lessor fraudulently misrepresents the quality of a product and a buyer is injured thereby. Occurs when one person consciously decides to induce another person to rely and act on a misrepresentation. Also called fraud. Occurs when an agent makes an untrue statement that he or she knows is not true.

Internet A collection of millions of computers that provide a network of electronic connections between computers.

Internet service providers (ISPs) An operator maintaining a server upon which individuals and businesses can have their own websites.

intoxicated person A person who is under contractual incapacity because of ingestion of alcohol or drugs to the point of incompetence.

issuing bank The institution that issues the letter of credit.

jumbo CD A certificate of deposit in a very large denomination, usually at a minimum of $100,000. Also called negotiable certificates of deposit, these large investments are usually considered low-risk, stable investments for large investors.

labor contract Also called a collective bargaining agreement that applies to the employees a union represents. The collective bargaining agreement defines the terms and conditions of employment for represented employees.

lapse of time An offer terminates when a stated time period expires. If no time is stated, an offer terminates after a reasonable time.

lawful contracts To be an enforceable contract, the object of the contract must be lawful.

lawful object Where the focus or purpose of the contract is legal.

lease A contract for the exclusive possession of lands or tenements for a determinate period; a contract by which the lessor grants the lessee the exclusive right to possess and use personal property of the lessor for a specified period.

lease contracts Contracts for the exclusive possession of real or personal property for a specified period.

legal insanity A state of contractual incapacity as determined by law.

legal value Where the promisee suffers a legal detriment or the promisor receives a legal benefit.

legally enforceable contract If one party fails to perform as promised, the other party can use the court system to enforce the contract and recover damages or other remedy.

lessee The person who acquires the right to possession and use of goods under a lease.

lessor The person who transfers the right of possession and use of goods under the lease.

letter of credit A written instrument addressed by one person to another requesting the latter to give credit to the person in whose favor it is drawn.

license A contract that transfers limited rights in intellectual property and

informational rights. Grants a person the right to enter upon another's property for a specified and usually short period of time.

licensee The party who is granted limited rights in or access to intellectual property or informational rights owned by the licensor.

licensee's damages The amount of monetary compensation the licensee can recover when the licensor breaches a contract.

licensing agreement Detailed and comprehensive written agreement between the licensor and licensee that sets forth the express terms of their agreement.

licensing statute Statute that requires a person or business to obtain a license from the government prior to engaging in a specified occupation or activity.

licensor The owner of intellectual property or informational rights who transfers rights in the property or information to the licensee.

licensor's damages If a licensee breaches a contract, the licensor may sue and recover monetary damages from the licensee caused by the breach.

life estate An interest in the land for a person's lifetime; upon that person's death, the interest will be transferred to another party.

limited warranty A product guarantee that is limited or restricted in some way.

liquidated damages Damages to which parties to a contract agree in advance if the contract is breached. Damages that are specified in the contract rather than determined by the court. Damages that will be paid upon a breach of contract and that are established in advance.

Magnuson-Moss Warranty Act A United States federal law (15 U.S.C. § 2301 et seq.). Enacted in 1975, it is the federal statute that governs warranties on consumer products.

main purpose or leading object exception If the main purpose of a transaction and an oral collateral contract is to provide pecuniary benefit to the guarantor, the collateral contract does not have to be in writing to be enforced.

maker of a CD The bank (borrower).

maker of a note The party who makes the promise to pay (borrower).

material breach   A breach that occurs when a party renders inferior performance of his or her contractual duties.

merchant   A person who (1) deals in the goods of the kind involved in the transaction or (2) by his or her occupation holds himself or herself out as having knowledge or skill peculiar to the goods involved in the transaction.

merger   Occurs when one corporation is absorbed into another corporation and ceases to exist.

minor   A person who has not reached the age of majority.

minor breach   A breach that occurs when a party renders substantial performance of his or her contractual duties.

mirror image rule   States that for an acceptance to exist, the offeree must accept the terms as stated in the offer.

misrepresentation   An assertion that is made that is not in accord with the facts.

misrepresentation of law   When a party to a contract misstates the law related to that contract—whether innocently or intentionally.

mistake   An unintentional act, omission, or error arising from ignorance, surprise, imposition, or misplaced confidence (mutual mistake).

misuse   A defense that relieves a seller of product liability if the user abnormally misused the product. Products must be designed to protect against foreseeable misuse.

mitigation of damages   When a contract has been breached, the law places a duty on the innocent non-breaching party to avoid and reduce the resulting damages.

mixed sale   A sale that involves the provision of a service and a good in the same transaction.

model act   A statute proposed to legislatures for adoption (e.g., the Model Probate Code proposed by the National Conference of Commissioners of Uniform Laws).

modification   An alteration that does not change the general purpose and effect of that which is modified (modification of the agreement).

monetary damages   An award of money.

moral obligation   A duty that rests on moral considerations alone and is not imposed or enforced by positive law; a duty binding in conscience but not in law.

mortgage   An interest in real property given to a lender as security for the repayment of a loan.

mortgage note   A promise to pay that secures the debt obligation.

mutual mistake   A mistake common to both contracting parties, where each is laboring under the same misconception as to a past or existing material fact.

mutual rescission   Where the parties enter into a second agreement that expressly terminates the first one.

National Labor Relations Board (NLRB)   A federal administrative agency that oversees union elections, prevents employers and unions from engaging in illegal and unfair labor practices, and enforces and interprets certain federal labor laws.

necessaries of life   A minor must pay the reasonable value of food, clothing, shelter, medical care, and other items considered necessary to the maintenance of life.

negligence   A tort related to defective products where the defendant has breached a duty of due care and caused harm to the plaintiff. Failure of a corporate director or officer to exercise the duty of care while conducting the corporation's business.

negotiable instrument   Commercial paper that must meet these requirements: (1) be in writing, (2) be signed by the maker or drawer, (3) be an unconditional promise or order to pay, (4) state a fixed amount of money, (5) not require any undertaking in addition to the payment of money, (6) be payable on demand or at a definite time, and (7) be payable to order or to bearer. A special form of contract that satisfies the requirement established by Article 3 of the UCC. Also called commercial paper.

no-arrival, no-sale contract   The seller bears the expense and risk of loss during transportation only.

nominal damages   Damages awarded when the nonbreaching party sues the breaching party even though no financial loss has resulted from the breach; usually consists of $1 or some other small amount.

nondisclosure agreement   A contract not to reveal any facts or information on a particular matter.

novation   An agreement that substitutes a new party for one of the original contracting parties and relieves the exiting party of liability on the contract.

objective theory of contracts   A theory that says that the intent to contract is judged by the reasonable person standard and not by the subjective intent of the parties.

obligation   An action a party to a sales or lease contract is required by law to carry out.

offer   The manifestation of willingness to enter into a bargain, so made as to justify another person in understanding that his assent to that bargain is invited and will conclude it. [Section 24 of *Restatement (Second) of Contracts*]

offeree   The party to whom an offer to enter into a contract is made. The party to whom an offer has been made.

offeror   The party who makes an offer to enter into a contract. The party who makes an offer.

one-year rule   An executory contract that cannot be performed by its own terms within one year of its formation must be in writing.

open price term   Where a sales contract does not contain a specific price: a "reasonable price" is implied at the time of delivery.

open term   A section of a sales or lease contract on which the parties are allowed to "read into" the meaning of that section.

original (primary) contract   In a guaranty situation, this is the first contract between the debtor and the creditor.

output contract   A contract in which one party agrees to sell his or her entire output and the other agrees to buy it.

parol evidence   Any oral or written words outside the four corners of the written contract.

parol evidence rule A rule that says if a written contract is a complete and final statement of the parties' agreement, any prior or contemporaneous oral or written statements that alter, contradict, or are in addition to the terms of the written contract are inadmissible in court regarding a dispute over the contract. There are several exceptions to this rule.

part acceptance When a sales or lease contract is oral but should have been in writing, the contract is enforceable only to the extent to which the goods have been received and accepted by the buyer or lessee.

part performance An equitable doctrine that allows the court to order an oral contract for the sale of land or transfer of another interest in real property to be specifically performed if it has been partially performed and performance is necessary to avoid injustice.

partially disclosed agency Where the agency is partially disclosed, both the Agent and the Principal are bound.

past consideration A prior act or performance. Past consideration (e.g., prior acts) will not support a new contract. New consideration must be given.

payee of a CD The depositor (lender).

payee of a check The party to whom the check is written.

payee of a draft The party who receives the money from a draft.

payee of a note The party to whom the promise to pay is made (lender).

penalty Punishment imposed by law (the penalty of imprisonment).

perfect tender rule A rule that says if the goods or tender of a delivery fail in any respect to conform to the contract, the buyer may opt either (1) to reject the whole shipment, (2) to accept the whole shipment, or (3) to reject part and accept part of the shipment.

personal satisfaction test Subjective test that applies to contracts involving personal taste and comfort.

personal service contracts Contracts for providing personal services such as for an artist painting someone's portrait.

preexisting duty A promise lacks consideration if a person promises to perform an act or do something he or she is already under an obligation to do.

prenuptial agreement A contract entered into by parties prior to their marriage that defines their ownership rights in each other's property; it must be in writing.

principal A person who authorizes an agent to sign a negotiable instrument on his or her behalf. The party who employs another person to act on his or her behalf.

principal–agent relationship An employer hires an employee and gives that employee authority to act and enter into contracts on his or her behalf.

privity of contract The state of two specified parties being in a contract.

pro bono For the good; work or services performed free of charge.

product defects In a strict liability lawsuit, the injured party must show that the product that caused the injury was defective.

products liability The liability of manufacturers, sellers, and others for the injuries caused by defective products.

promisee One to whom promise has been made.

promisor One who makes a promise.

promissory estoppel (equitable estoppel) An equitable doctrine that prevents the withdrawal of a promise by a promisor if it will adversely affect a promisee who has adjusted his or her position in justifiable reliance on the promise. An equitable doctrine that permits enforcement of oral contracts that should have been in writing. It is applied to avoid injustice.

promissory note A two-party negotiable instrument that is an unconditional written promise by one party to pay money to another party.

proper dispatch The acceptance must be sent in a way that is properly addressed, packaged, and postage applied.

proposed additions If one or both parties to the contract are nonmerchants, any additional terms do not constitute a counteroffer or extinguish the original offer. If the offeree's proposed conditions are accepted by the original offeror, they become part of the contract. If they are not accepted, the sales contract is formed on the basis of the original offer.

puffing A seller's opinion on the quality of goods; usually overpraise, exaggeration, or hype.

punitive damages Damages that are awarded to punish the defendant, to deter the defendant from similar conduct in the future, and to set an example for others.

quasi-contract An obligation created by the law to avoid unjust enrichment in the absence of an agreement between the parties.

ratification The act of a minor after the minor has reached the age of majority by which he or she accepts a contract entered into when he or she was a minor. When a principal accepts an agent's unauthorized contract. The acceptance by a corporation of an unauthorized act of a corporate officer or agent.

real property The land itself as well as buildings, trees, soil, minerals, timber, plants, crops, and other things permanently affixed to the land.

reasonable person standard The standard by which the court decides if the parties intended to create a contract. A "reasonable person" is a fictitious person of ordinary prudence.

reasonable person test Objective test that applies to commercial contracts and contracts involving mechanical fitness.

reclamation The right of a seller or lessor to demand the return of goods from the buyer or lessee under specified situations.

recovery of damages A seller or lessor may recover damages measured as the difference between the contract price (or rent) and the market price (or rent) at the time and place the goods were to be delivered, plus incidental damages, from a buyer or lessee who repudiates the contract or wrongfully rejects tendered goods.

recovery of lost profits   When the buyer breaches performance of the contract and the seller seeks damages for profits he or she would have received from the full performance of the contract.

recovery of the purchase price or rent   A seller or lessor may recover the contracted-for purchase price or rent from the buyer or lessee if the buyer or lessee (1) fails to pay for accepted goods, (2) breaches the contract and the seller or lessor cannot dispose of the goods, or if (3) the goods are damaged or lost after the risk of loss passes to the buyer or lessee.

reformation   An equitable doctrine that permits the court to rewrite a contract to express the parties' true intentions.

regulatory statute   A licensing statute enacted to protect the public.

rejection   Nonacceptance or withdrawal of the offer prior to its acceptance.

remedies at law   Economic compensation in the form of real property, personal property, and money.

replevin   An action by a buyer or lessor to recover scarce goods wrongfully withheld by a seller or lessor.

requirement contract   A contract in which the purchaser agrees to buy all of its needs of specified material from a particular supplier, and the latter agrees to fill all of the purchaser's needs during the period of the contract.

rescission   An action to rescind (undo) the contract. Rescission is available if there has been a material breach of contract, fraud, duress, undue influence, or mistake.

Restatement of the Law of Contracts   A compilation of model contract law principles drafted by legal scholars. The *Restatement* is not law.

restitution   Returning of goods or property received from the other party to rescind a contract; if the actual goods or property is not available, a cash equivalent must be made.

revenue-raising statute   A licensing statute with the primary purpose of raising revenue for the government.

Revised Article 2   A recent revision of Article 2 to the Uniform Commercial Code that deals with the sale of goods.

revocation of acceptance   Where the buyer or lessee who has accepted goods subsequently withdraws that acceptance.

reward   To collect a reward, the offeree must (1) have knowledge of the reward offer prior to completing the requested act and (2) perform the requested act.

right to cover   When a buyer or lessee purchases or rents substitute goods.

right to cure   A licensor has the right to cure a contract under certain conditions.

Sabbath law   A law that prohibits or limits the carrying on of certain secular activities on Sundays.

sale   The passing of title from a seller to a buyer for a price. Also called a conveyance.

sale on approval   A type of sale in which there is no actual sale unless and until the buyer accepts the goods.

sale or return contract   A contract that says that the seller delivers goods to a buyer with the understanding that the buyer may return them if they are not used or resold within a stated or reasonable period of time.

sales contracts   Refers to the sale of goods under Article 2 of the UCC.

satisfaction   The performance of an accord.

scienter   Guilty knowledge; intent to deceive or manipulate.

Section 5   Prohibits unfair and deceptive practices.

Section 201 of the Uniform Commercial Code (UCC)   A rule sometimes referred to as "the Statute of Frauds"; requiring that contracts for the sale of goods costing $500 or more be in writing.

shipment contract   A contract that requires the seller to ship the goods to the buyer via a common carrier. The buyer bears the risk of loss during transportation. A sales contract that requires the seller to send the goods to the buyer, but not a specifically named destination.

sight draft   A draft payable on sight. Also called a demand draft.

signature requirement   A negotiable instrument must be signed by the drawer or maker. Any symbol executed or adopted by a party with a present intent to authenticate a writing qualifies as his or her signature.

small CD   A certificate of deposit under $100,000.

specially manufactured goods   Goods manufactured specifically for the buyer.

specific performance   A remedy that orders the breaching party to perform the acts promised in the contract; usually awarded in cases where the subject matter is unique, such as in contracts involving land, heirlooms, and paintings. Judgment of the court that orders a seller or lessor to perform his or her obligations under the contract.

standards of interpretation   If the parties have not defined the words and terms of a contract, the courts apply those words and terms in the manner they normally are defined.

Statute of Frauds   State statute that requires certain types of contracts to be in writing.

statute of limitations   Statute that establishes the time period during which a lawsuit must be brought; if the lawsuit is not brought within this period, the injured party loses the right to sue.

statute of repose   A statute that limits the seller's liability to a certain number of years from the date when the product was first sold.

stop delivery of the goods   When a seller or lessor, upon learning of a buyer's or lessee's insolvency, stops goods from being delivered while they are in transit.

strict liability   Liability without fault.

subsequent assignee (subassignee)   When an assignee transfers the rights under the contract to yet another person.

substantial performance   Performance by a contracting party that deviates only slightly from complete performance.

substituted contract   A new contract that revokes and discharges a prior contract.

supervening event An alteration or modification of a product by a party in the chain of distribution that absolves all prior sellers from strict liability.

supervening illegality The enactment of a statute, regulation, or court decision that makes the object of an offer illegal. This action terminates the offer.

supplier One engaged in the business of making products available to consumers; all persons in the chain of production and distribution of a consumer product.

tender of delivery The obligation of the seller to transfer and deliver goods to the buyer in accordance with the sales contract.

tender of performance Tender is an unconditional and absolute offer by a contracting party to perform his or her obligations under the contract. Occurs when a party who has the ability and willingness to perform offers to complete the performance of his or her duties under the contract.

third-party beneficiary A third person that the contracting parties intended should receive a benefit from the contract.

time draft A draft payable at a designated future date.

time note A note payable at a specific time.

title Legal, tangible evidence of ownership of goods.

tort A wrong. There are three categories: (1) intentional torts, (2) unintentional torts (negligence), and (3) strict liability.

tort of bad faith A breach of the requirement that the parties act and deal fairly in all respects in obtaining the objective of the contract.

UCC Statute of Frauds A rule that requires all contracts for the sale of goods costing $500 or more and lease contracts involving payments of $1,000 or more to be in writing.

unconscionability Where there is unequal bargaining power between the parties such that it would be manifestly unfair to enforce the contract.

unconscionable contracts A contract so oppressive or unfair that it would be unjust for the court to enforce it.

undisclosed agency Where the agency is undisclosed, both the Agent and the Principal are bound.

undue influence Taking advantage of a person's weakness, infirmity, age, or distress in order to change that person's actions or decisions.

unenforceable contract A contract where the essential elements to create a valid contract are met, but there is some legal defense to the enforcement of the contract.

unequivocal acceptance Where acceptance of the contract is definite and absolute.

Unified Contract Law (UCL) A new business and commercial contract law enacted by China.

Uniform Commercial Code (UCC) Comprehensive statutory scheme that includes laws that cover aspects of commercial transactions.

Uniform Commercial Code—Leases Article 2A of the UCC directly addresses personal property leases including the formation, performance, and default of leases in goods.

Uniform Computer Information Transactions Act (UCITA) A model act that provides uniform and comprehensive rules for contracts involving computer information transactions and software and information licenses.

Uniform Customs and Practices for Documentary Credits (UCP) Rules created by the International Chamber of Commerce which govern the formation and performance of letters of credit.

Uniform Electronic Transactions Act (UETA) A model act that—along with the UCITA—provides uniform and comprehensive rules for contracts involving computer information transactions and software and information licenses.

Uniform Sales Act A law governing sales of goods that was adopted by most states. It was later subsumed within Article 2 of the Uniform Commercial Code.

unilateral contract A contract in which the offeror's offer can be accepted only by the performance of an act by the offeree; a "promise for an act."

unilateral mistake When only one party is mistaken about a material fact regarding the subject matter of the contract.

United Nations Convention on Contracts for the International Sale of Goods (CISG) Seventy countries and several international organizations created this law which governs contracts for the international sale of goods.

usage of trade A regularly observed or adhered to practice or method of dealing in a particular trade or industry.

usury law A law that sets an upper limit on the interest rate that can be charged on certain types of loans.

valid contract A contract that meets all of the essential elements to establish a contract; a contract that is enforceable by at least one of the parties.

void contract A contract that has no legal effect; a nullity.

void title A thief acquires no title to the goods he or she steals.

voidable contract A contract where one or both parties have the option to avoid their contractual obligations. If a contract is avoided, both parties are released from their contractual obligations.

voidable title Title that a purchase has if the goods were obtained by (1) fraud, (2) a check that is later dishonored, or (3) impersonating another person.

warranty A buyer's or lessee's assurance that the goods meet certain standards. A representation of the insured that is expressly incorporated in the insurance contract.

warranty against infringements A seller or lessor who is a merchant who regularly deals in goods of the kind sold or leased automatically warrants that the goods are delivered free of any third-party patent, trademark, or copyright claim.

warranty disclaimer Statements that negate express and implied warranties.

warranty of good title Sellers warrant that they have valid title to the goods they are selling and that the transfer of title is rightful.

warranty of no infringement An implied promise that there are no interferences or interventions that will affect the contract.

warranty of no interference An implied promise that there are no conflicts that will encroach upon a contract.

warranty of no security interests Sellers of goods warrant that the goods they sell are delivered free from any third-party security interests, liens, or encumbrances that are unknown to the buyer.

World Intellectual Property Organization (WIPO) An international arbitration and mediation center where domain owners can bring actions to recover a domain name.

World Wide Web An electronic connection of millions of computers that support a standard set of rules for the exchange of information.

writ of attachment A document that orders a sheriff or other government officer to seize the breaching party's property, and to sell the property at auction to satisfy a judgment.

writ of garnishment A document that orders the breaching party's wages, bank accounts, or other property held by a third party be paid over to the nonbreaching party to satisfy a judgment.

writing and form Certain contracts must be in writing or in a particular form in order to be enforceable.

INDEX

A

Abnormal misuse. *See also*
    Unforeseeable misuse, 416, 421
Acceptance, 33, 51, 53, 62, 344, 345,
    357, 360
  in contracts,
    revocation of, 345
    rules of, 62
    silence as, 53
    time and mode of, 54, 55
    unequivocal, 51
  methods of, 54, 55
  unequivocal, 51
Acceptance-upon-dispatch
  rule, 54, 56, 62
Acceptor, 428, 448
Access contract, 261, 278
Accommodation, 296
Accommodation shipment, 296, 306
Accord, 81, 85, 192, 198
Accord and satisfaction, 81, 85, 192, 198
Account party, 303, 306
Adequate consideration, 74, 85
Adequate assurance of performance,
  353, 360
Adjudged insane, 100, 119, 121
Admissions in pleadings or
  court, 299, 306
Advertisements, 33, 40, 41, 42, 43, 61,
  62
  exception, 40, 61
  general rule, 61
Age
  of majority, 92, 93, 94, 95, 96, 99,
    118, 119, 122
  misrepresentation of, 94
Agency, 434, 447, 448
Agency contract, 446
  agency law, 446
  principal, 446
  agent, 447
  agency, 447
  principal-agency relationship, 447
  employer-employee relationship, 447

independent contractor, 447
power of attorney, 447
Agency formation, 434
  agent, 434, 435, 436, 437, 438, 440,
    441, 447, 449
  principal, 430, 434, 435, 436, 437,
    438, 439, 440, 441, 446, 447, 449
Agency law, 434, 446, 448
Agency termination, 440
  lapse of time, 440
  mutual agreement, 440
  occurrence of a specified event, 440
  purpose achieved, 440
Agent, 434, 447, 448
  contracts of, 427, 439
  formation, 434
  fully disclosed agency, 436, 437,
    438, 448
  implied warranty of authority, 437,
    438, 448
  partially disclosed agency, 436,
    437, 448
  undisclosed agency, 437, 449
Agreement, 5, 33, 34, 35, 36, 37, 38, 39,
    40, 43, 46, 48, 50, 52, 53, 56, 57,
    58, 59, 60, 61, 62, 63, 65, 329,
    331, 354, 355, 356
  affecting remedies, 354
  of the parties, 356
Alteration of contract, 194, 198
Alternative dispute resolution (ADR), 7
American Federation of Labor
    (AFL), 442, 448
  AFL-CIO, 442, 448
  Congress of Industrial Organizations
    (CIO), 442
American rule, 196
Anti-assignment clauses, 179, 196, 198
Anticipatory breach, 208, 239
Anticipatory repudiation, 237, 354,
  359, 360
Anticybersquatting Consumer
    Protection Act (1999), 251,
    277, 278
Anti-delegation clause, 183, 197, 198

Appropriate bargaining union, 447
Approval clauses, 180, 196, 199
Arbitration, 7
Article 2 (Sales), 9, 288, 304, 306
  Article 2 revised, 288
Article 2A (Leases), 9, 288, 304, 306
Article 3 of the UCC, 530
Article 5 (Letters of Credit), 304, 306
Article 6 (Bulk Sales), 328, 331
Assent, 127, 129, 132, 142, 144, 145
  genuineness of, 127, 144, 145
  mutual, 127, 128, 130, 138, 144, 146
Assignee, 176, 177, 178, 179, 181, 196,
  199, 201
  subsequent, 175, 176, 181, 190, 191,
    198, 199, 200
Assignment, 175, 176
  alteration of risk and, 194, 198
  form of, 176, 189, 196
  of future rights, 177
  notice of, 177, 179, 196
  of rights, 176, 178, 179, 196
  success, of same right, 181, 196, 200
Assignment and delegation, 183,
  196, 199
Assignor, 176, 177, 178, 179, 181,
  196, 199
Assumption of duties, 182, 197, 199
Assumption of the risk, 415, 420, 421
Assurance of performance, 353,
  359, 360
Attribution procedure, 263, 278
Auctions, 44, 61
  with reserve, 44, 45, 46, 61, 62
  without reserve, 44, 45, 46, 61, 62
Authenticate, 263, 278
Authorization
  express, 18
  implied, 18

B

Bad faith, tort of, 233, 235, 236, 237,
  239, 240, 243
Bail bond, 25

Bailee, 317, 331
  goods in possession of, 317
Bankruptcy, 194, 198
Bankruptcy Code, 445
Bargain, basis of the, 69
Bargained-for exchange, 69, 84, 85
Basis of the bargain, 369, 384
Battle of the forms, 298, 306
Beneficiary, 303, 306
Beneficiaries, 176, 183, 184, 186, 187,
    197, 200
  creditor, 177, 184, 185, 186, 187,
    194, 197, 199
  donee, 184, 185, 187, 197, 199
  incidental, 183, 186, 187, 197,
    199
  intended third-party, 176, 183, 184
  third-party, 175, 176, 177, 180, 183,
    184, 186, 192, 196, 197, 198,
    199, 200
Best-efforts contracts, 80, 84, 85
Bilateral contracts, 16, 29
Bill of lading, 303, 306
Both parties are merchant, 305
Breach, 112, 117, 213, 206, 331
  anticipatory, 237
  of contract, 203, 206, 239, 331
  of implied covenant of good faith
    and fair dealing, 233, 235, 239
  of licensing agreement, 261, 264,
    265, 266, 268, 270, 278, 279, 281,
    282
  material, 205, 206, 207, 208, 212,
    213, 224, 231, 237, 238,
    239, 241
  minor, 206, 207, 208, 212,
    237, 239
  performance and, 205, 206, 207, 228,
    229, 237
  of sales contract, 213, 225
  of warranty, damages recoverable
    for, 213
Brougham, Henry Peter, 286
Bulk transfer, 328, 331
Business duress, 143, 145
Business ethics, 217
  entrustment rule and, 237, 324,
    331, 332, 333
  equity, 67, 68, 81, 82, 83, 84, 85
  good faith and reasonableness
    in governing performance of
      sales, 237
    and lease contracts, 285, 287,
      288, 289, 291, 293, 294, 295,
      296, 297, 298, 299, 300, 301,
      303, 305, 306, 307, 309
  licensing statutes, 258

oral contract, 154, 155, 156, 157,
    159, 160, 161, 162, 167, 168, 170,
    171, 172
  return of engagement ring and, 227
  unconscionable contracts, 355, 359
Buyer
  in breach, 322, 330
  in ordinary course of business,
    324, 331
  remedies of, 205

C

Cancellation, 268, 278, 348, 358, 360
  of contract, 348, 358, 360
  of sale or lease contract, 268
Capture, 350, 360
Cardozo, C. J., 66
Career Front (feature):
  Alternative Dispute Resolution
    (ADR) Paralegal, 8
  Bankruptcy Paralegal, 12
  Business Formation Paralegal, 211
  Business Franchise Paralegal, 69, 255
  Construction Law Paralegal, 165
  Contract Administration Paralegal, 92
  Collections Paralegal, 39
  Corporate Contracts Paralegal, 400
  Criminal Law Paralegal, 300
  Employee Benefits Paralegal, 371
  Labor/Employment Paralegal, 323
  Municipal Paralegal, 439
  Personal Injury/Medical
    Malpractice/Product Liability
    Paralegal, 180
  Securities/Municipal Bonds
    Paralegal, 137
  Trust Paralegal, 353
Carrier cases, 339
Carriers, substitution of, 340, 346, 356
Carroll, Lewis, 32
Certificate of Deposit (CD), 430, 448
  jumbo CDs, 431
  small CDs, 431
C & F (cost and freight), 316, 331
Chain of distribution, 395, 421
Chambre, Judge, 426
Check, 429, 448
  three party instrument, 428, 429,
    446
Chinese *chops*, as signatures, 166
CIF (cost, insurance, and freight), 316,
    330, 331
Claims, 80
  settlement of, 80
Classical law of contracts, 6
Classifications of contracts, 16

Clause(s), 91, 110, 112, 115, 117, 120,
    176, 177, 179, 180, 183, 188,
    189, 190, 191, 194, 196, 197,
    198, 199, 201
  anti-assignment, 179, 196, 198, 201
  anti-delegation, 183, 197, 198
  approval, 177, 179, 180, 196, 199,
    200, 202
  exculpatory, 91, 96, 110, 112, 113,
    114, 120, 121, 123
  force majeure, 194, 198, 199
  merger, 181
C.O.D. (cash on delivery) shipment,
    344, 360
Collateral, 430, 448
Collateral notes, 430, 448
  mortgage notes, 430
Collective bargaining, 444, 447, 448
  compulsory subjects, 444, 447
  illegal subjects, 444, 448
  permissive subjects, 444, 448
Collective bargaining agreement, 444,
    447, 448
  balance of equities, 445
Commercial impracticability, 194,
    198, 199
  commercial paper, 427
Commercial reasonableness, 356
Common law, 6
Common law of contracts, 6, 8
Communication, 61
Comparative fault, 418, 421
Comparative negligence, 420
Compensatory damages, 212, 238,
    239, 371, 384
Competent party's duty of
    restitution, 93, 119
Complete integration, 166, 169
Complete performance, 207, 239
Compulsory subjects, 444, 447
Computer information
    transactions, 246, 278
Concealment, 134, 136, 138,
    139, 140, 145
  fraud by, 134, 136, 138, 140, 145
Concurrent conditions, 190,
    198, 199
Conditional sales, 319, 321, 330
Condition precedent, 188, 199
Conditions, 188, 197, 199
  concurrent, 175, 188, 190,
    191, 198, 199
  implied-in-fact, 198
  of performance, 197
  precedent, 188, 190, 198, 199
  precedent based on satisfaction,
    189, 199

Condition subsequent, 190, 198, 199
Congress of Industrial Organizations
    (CIO), 442, 448
Consequential damages, 216,
    238, 239
Consideration, 5, 28, 67, 68, 69, 70, 71,
    73, 74, 75, 76, 77, 78, 79, 80, 81,
    82, 83, 84, 85, 86
    adequacy of, 74, 85
    bargained-for exchange, 69, 70, 84, 85
    contracts lacking, 75, 84
    defined, 67, 68, 76
    gift promises and, 70, 84, 85
    illegal, 75, 79, 84, 85
    inadequate, 74
    legal value, 67, 68, 69, 70, 84, 85
    past, 67, 77, 79, 84, 85, 86
    promissory estoppel, 67, 82, 85, 86,
        87, 89
Consignee, 319, 332
Consignment, 319, 330, 332
Consignor, 319, 332
Conspicuous, 379, 383, 384
Construction contracts, 213
Consumer expectation test, 375, 384
Contract(s). See also Acceptance;
    Consideration; E-contracts; Sales
    and lease contract, acceptance of
    access, 261
    adhesion, 115
    agency, 427, 434, 435, 436, 437, 438,
        440, 441, 442, 444, 445, 446, 447,
        448, 449, 451
    formation, 434
    agents', 434, 435, 438
    agreement in, 427, 430, 432, 434,
        435, 437, 439, 440, 441, 444, 445,
        447, 448, 449, 451, 452
    bilateral, 16, 26, 29
    breach of sales, 315, 321, 329, 330
    cancellation of, 268, 278
    classical law of, 6, 28
    collateral, 167
    to commit crimes, 106
    common law of, 6, 8
    construction, 213
    contrary to public policy, 106,
        120, 121
    contrary to statutes, 105
    creditor beneficiary, 184, 185,
        186, 187, 197, 199
    defenses to enforcement of, 6, 28
    defined, 4
    destination, 313, 315, 316,
        329, 330, 332
    donee beneficiary, 184, 185,
        187, 197, 199
    e-commerce and, 15, 205, 211
    elements of, 5, 28

employment, 213
executed, 26, 27, 207
executory, 26, 27
express, 18, 26, 29
form, 7
formal, 24, 26, 29
guaranty, 158, 159, 167, 169,
    170, 171
illegal, 435, 441, 442, 444, 448
illusory, 76, 85
immoral contract, 106, 120
implied-in-fact, 3, 10, 18, 19, 20,
    21, 22, 26, 29, 30
implied-in-law, 21, 22, 23, 26, 30
informal, 24, 25, 26
installment, 342, 356, 360
Internet law and, 9
labor, 441
lacking consideration, 75, 84
lease contract, 9
legally enforceable, 4
modern law of, 28
objective theory of, 10
offer, 5, 7, 10, 13, 16, 17, 18, 21,
    22, 24, 28, 30, 31
    communication in, 34, 39
    counteroffer by the offeree in, 47
    definiteness of terms in, 36
    lapse of time in, 49
    objective intent in, 35
    special situations in, 40
    termination of, 46, 50
one-year rule for, 158, 169
option, 50
oral, 153, 154, 156, 157, 158, 159,
    160, 161, 162, 166, 167, 168, 169,
    170, 171, 172
parties to, 5, 28
prenuptial agreements, 160, 169
quasi-, 22, 26, 29
ratification, 95, 119, 121, 122
requirements, 68, 69, 75, 76, 79,
    80, 84, 85
in restraint of trade, 110, 120, 121
right to recover the damages
    for breach of contract,
    347, 358
sales contract, 9
shipment, 339, 340, 341, 344, 346,
    349, 356, 357, 360, 362
simple contracts, 25
sources of law of, 8, 28
special business, 80
special types of minor, 99
substituted, 191
torts associated with, 205, 232,
    233, 239
transfer of interests in real
    property, 167

unconscionable, 120
under seal, 25
unenforceable, 26, 27
unilateral, 16, 26, 29
valid, 26, 27
void, 26, 27
voidable, 26, 27
writing requirements for, 6
Contract overview, 4
Contractual capacity, 5, 91, 121, 434, 448
Contributory negligence, 418, 420, 421
Correction of a defect, 420
Correspondent (confirming bank),
    303, 306
Counterfeit Access Device and
    Computer Fraud and Abuse Act
    of 1984, 273, 278
Counteroffers, 33, 45, 47, 48, 49, 52, 56,
    57, 58, 59, 61, 62, 64, 66
    electronic agents and, 261, 262, 263,
        268, 280, 281
    by the offeree, 47
Course of dealing, 301, 306
Course of performance, 300, 306
Court admissions, 299, 306, 308
Covenants, 115, 120, 187, 197, 199,
    235, 239
    implied, of good faith and fair
        dealing, 235, 239
    not to compete, 115, 120, 121
Covenants and conditions, 187, 197
Cover, 270, 278, 350, 358
    right to, 350, 358
Crashworthiness doctrine, 404, 421
Credit, 289, 290, 301, 303, 304, 305,
    306, 307
    letters of, 289, 303, 304, 306
Creditor beneficiary, 185, 197, 199
Creditor beneficiary contracts, 184,
    199
Criminal statutes, 120
Cure, 340, 356, 360
Cybersquatters, 251

D

Damages, 212, 347, 351, 358, 360
    compensatory, 212, 238
    consequential, 212, 238
    incidental, 347
    liquidated, 212, 217, 238
    mitigation of, 214, 238
    monetary, 212
    nominal, 212, 222, 238
    punitive, 392, 397, 402, 406, 411,
        412, 413, 414, 417, 418, 421
    recoverable for breach of contract,
        347, 358
    recoverable for breach of warranty, 371

right to recover for accepted nonconforming goods, 352, 360
for non-delivery or repudiation, 351
right to recover, for breach of contract, 358
unpaid purchase price or rent, 359
Death, 49, 50, 52
of offeror or offeree, 49
Death or incompetency, 62
Deceit, 136
fraud, 127, 128, 132, 133, 134, 137, 138, 139, 140, 144, 145, 147, 149
misrepresentation, 127, 132, 133, 134, 135, 136, 137, 138, 139, 140, 144, 145, 146, 148
Decision, 11
Declaration, of duties, 182, 197, 199
Deed of trust, 155, 169
Defect in design, 401, 420, 421
Defect in manufacture, 398, 420, 421
Defect in packaging, 410, 411, 420, 421
Defenses to the enforcement of a contract, 6
Genuineness of assent, 6
Writing and form, 6
Definite terms, 61
Delagatee, 181, 197, 199
Delegation, 181, 197
of duties, 181, 197, 199
Delegator, 181, 197, 199
Delivery, 345, 346, 357
right to stop, of goods in transit, 346, 357, 360
right to withhold, 345, 357
Demand note, 430, 448
Destination contracts, 315, 316, 329, 332, 339, 356, 360
Destruction, 342, 356
of goods, 342, 356
of subject matter, 49, 61
Detrimental reliance, 82, 85
Disaffirmance, 93, 119, 121
Discharge, 194, 199
by agreement, 190, 198
by impossibility, 192, 198
by operation of law, 194, 198
of performance, 198
Disclaimer(s), 383
conspicuous display of, 349, 380, 383, 384
warranty, 383
in software licenses, 379
Disposition of goods, 346, 357, 360
Doctrine of strict liability in tort, 394, 421
Doctrine of unconscionabilty, 115, 121
Document of title, 315, 332

Domain names, 245, 277, 278
extensions for, 250, 251
registration of, 277
Donee beneficiaries, 184, 197, 199
Donee beneficiary contracts, 184, 199
Draft, 428, 448
demand draft, 428, 448
sight of draft, 428
time of draft, 428
Drawee of a check, 429, 448
Drawee of a draft, 428, 448
Drawer of a check, 429, 448
Drawer of a draft, 428, 448
Duress, 142, 143, 145
business, 143
defined, 142
economic, 143
extortion, 145
physical duress, 145
Duties, 175, 177, 181, 182, 183, 185, 190, 191, 192, 194, 197, 198, 199, 201
assumption of, 182, 197, 199
declaration of, 182, 197, 199
delegation of, 181, 182, 183, 197, 199, 201
to notify, 179, 196
of restoration and restitution, 93, 119, 121
Duty to pay, 357

E

Easements, 155, 169
E-commerce, 15, 245, 278, 302
Anticybersquatting Consumer Protection Act, 245, 251, 252, 253, 277, 278
contracts and, 245, 246, 247, 255, 256, 257, 258, 260, 261, 262, 263, 267, 269, 270, 277, 279
cybersquatters, 251
domain names, 245
electronic errors and, 267
electronic self-help, 269
ineffectiveness of counteroffers in, 261, 262
licensing and, 245, 246, 257, 258, 259, 261, 262, 264, 265, 266, 268, 270, 278, 279, 281, 282, 283
nondisclosure agreements, 63
signatures and, 245, 256, 257, 258, 260, 277
warranty disclaimers in software licenses, 367, 379
Economic coercion, 143
Economic duress, 143, 145
E-contracts. *See also* Contract(s), 205, 256

Effect of illegality, 108
Electronic agents, counteroffers and, 261, 262
Electronic commerce (e-commerce), 15
Electronic Communications Privacy Act (ECPA), 272, 278, 279
Electronic Funds Transfer Act, 274, 279
Electronic mail, 249, 277
Electronic self-help, 269
Electronic Signature in Global and National Commerce Act (SIGN Act) of 2000, 256, 277, 279
E-licensing, 257, 278
Elements of a contract, 5
Elements of undue influence, 145
E-mail, 249, 277
Emancipation, 97, 119, 121
Employer-employee relationship, 435, 447, 448
Employment, 434, 435, 438, 441, 442, 444, 445, 447
English rule, 196
Entrepreneur, 115
insuring against loss, 322
noncompete clause and, 115, 120, 121
successive assignments of same right, 181, 196
Entrustment rule, 324, 331, 332
Equal dignity rule, 160, 169
Equitable relief, 82, 85
Equitable remedies, 68, 83, 84, 85, 206, 227, 231, 238, 239
types of, 231
Equity, 67, 68, 81, 82, 83, 84, 85
E-signatures, 256, 257, 277
Exclusive license, 259, 279
Exculpatory clauses, 112, 120, 121
Executed contract, 26, 207, 239
Executory contracts, 26, 318, 332
Express authorization, 55, 62
Express contracts, 18, 79
Express warranties, 265, 279, 368, 384
Ex-ship (from carrying vessel), 316, 330, 332

F

Fact, 127, 128, 129, 130, 132, 133, 134, 135, 137, 138, 139, 142, 143, 144, 145, 146, 147, 149, 150
material misrepresentation of, 133, 138, 139
mutual mistake of, 127, 128, 130, 138, 144, 146
Failure to give notice, 196
Failure to provide adequate instructions, 413, 420, 421
Failure to warn, 405, 420, 421

FAS (free alongside) port of shipment, 316, 330
FAS (vessel) port of shipment, 316, 332
Federal Labor Statutes
    Labor-Management Relations Act, 447
    Labor-Management Reporting and Disclosure Act, 447
    National Labor Relations Act (NLRA), 447
    Norris-LaGuardia Act, 447
    Railway Labor Act, 447
Federal Trade Commission (FTC), 302, 306
    Section 5, 302
Finance leases, 293, 305, 306, 331
Firm offer rule, 295, 305, 306
Fitness for human consumption, implied warranty of, 374, 383, 384, 385
FOB (free on board) point of shipment, 316, 330, 332
FOB place of destination, 316, 330, 332
Force majeure clauses, 194, 198, 199
Foreign substance test, 375, 384
Foreseeable misuse, 416, 420
Form contracts, 7
Formal contracts, 24, 29
Formality of writing, 162
Francis, Justice, 366
Fraud, 132, 134, 394
    by concealment, 134, 145
    elements of, 144
    in the inception, 132, 144, 145
    in the inducement, 132, 145
    intentional misrepresentation, 394
Fraudulent misrepresentation, 132, 144, 145
Fully disclosed agency, 436, 448
Fungible, 373, 384
Future goods, 314, 332
Future rights, assignment on, 177

G

Gambling statutes, 108, 120
Gap-filling rule, 294, 305, 306
General rule, 120
Generally known dangers, 415, 420, 421
Genuine assent, 127, 145
Genuineness of assent, 6, 127, 145
Gift promises, 70, 84, 85
    gratuitous promises, 70, 71, 84, 85
Glossary, 164, 169
Goldwyn, Samuel, 152
Good faith, 356
Good faith purchaser for value, 324, 332
Good faith subsequent lessee, 324, 332
Goods, 290, 304, 306, 342, 346
    destruction of, 342

disposition, 346
identification of, 314, 332
insurable interest in, 313, 322, 334
right to dispose of, 346, 357
right to reclaim, 346, 357, 362
right to recover, from insolvent seller or lessor, 350
right to recover damages for accepted nonconforming, 352, 360
right to reject nonconforming, 349
right to replevy, 351
right to stop delivery of, in transit, 346, 357
specially manufactured, 290, 298, 306, 307
stolen, 313, 317, 322, 323, 326, 331, 333, 334, 335
that do not move, 329
unfinished, 347
Good title, 367, 380, 381, 384
    warranty of, 367, 380, 381, 384
Government contractor defense, 415, 420, 421
Gratuitous promises, 70, 71, 84, 85
Guarantor, 158, 169
Guaranty contracts, 158, 169

H

Holmes, Oliver Wendell, Jr., 126
Human consumption, implied warranty of fitness for, 374, 383, 384, 385

I

Identity Theft and Assumption Deterrence Act of 1998, 274, 279
Identification of goods, 314, 332
Illegal consideration, 75, 79, 84, 85
Illegal contract, 91, 107, 121
Illegal subjects, 444, 448
Illegality, 49, 50, 62, 63
    contracts contrary to public policy, 106, 120, 121
    contracts contrary to statutes, 105, 120
    supervening effect of, 49, 50, 62, 63
Illusory promises, 76, 85
Immoral contracts, 106, 121
Implied authorization, 56, 62
Implied-in-fact conditions, 190, 198, 199
Implied-in-fact contracts, 18, 29
Implied-in-law contracts, 22, 231
Implied terms, 36, 62
Implied warranties, 372
Implied warranty of authority, 437, 448
Implied warranty of fitness for human consumption, 374, 383, 384

Implied warranty of fitness for a particular purpose, 266, 279, 375, 383, 384
Implied warranty of informational content, 266, 279
Implied warranty of merchantability, 372, 383, 384
Implied warranty of merchantability of the computer program, 265, 279
Impossibility of performance, 192, 198, 199
Impracticability, commercial, 175, 194, 195, 198, 199
Inadequate consideration, 74
Inception, fraud in the, 132, 140, 144, 145
Incidental beneficiary, 186, 197, 199
Incidental damages, 347, 360
Incorporation by reference, 163, 169
Independent contractor, 438, 447, 448
Inducement, fraud in the, 132, 133, 140, 145
Infancy doctrine, 93, 118, 121
Inferior performance, 207, 239
Influence, undue, 127, 128, 140, 141, 142, 145, 146
Informal contracts (simple contract), 25
Information, 245, 246, 247, 250, 255, 257, 258, 259, 260, 261, 262, 263, 264, 265, 266, 267, 268, 269, 270, 273, 274, 275, 276, 277, 278, 279, 280, 281, 282
    licensing of, 246, 257, 258, 259, 262, 266
Information Infrastructure Protection Act (IIP Act), 275, 279
Injunction, 68, 82, 83, 84, 85, 231, 238, 239
Injury, 133, 134
    to innocent party, 133
Innocent misrepresentation, 138, 145
In pari delicto, 109, 121
Insane, but not adjudged insane, 101, 119, 121
Inspection, right of, 343, 344, 349, 356
Installment contracts, 342, 356, 360
Installment notes, 430, 448
Instrument, 427, 428, 429, 430, 431, 432, 433, 434, 438, 445, 446, 448, 449, 450
Intangible property, 288, 306, 427, 428, 430, 431, 432, 433, 434, 445, 446, 448, 449
Integration, 153, 163, 164, 165, 166, 168, 169
    complete, 166
    implied, 33, 34, 36, 56, 61, 62, 63
    of several writings, 163, 168, 169
Intended beneficiaries, 183, 197

Intentional interference with contractual relations, 232, 233, 239
International law. *See also* Law, 166
 letters of credit, 289, 303, 304, 306
Intentional misrepresentation, 394, 421, 438, 448
International trade, letters of credit in, 303
Internet, 246, 247, 277, 279
Internet law, 245, 246, 249
 contracts and, 245, 257, 258
 cybersquatters, 251
 domain names, 245, 246, 250, 251, 252, 253, 254, 255, 277, 279, 282, 283
 electronic errors and, 267
 electronic self-help, 269
 warranty disclaimers in software licenses, 379
Internet service providers (ISP), 247, 279
Intoxicated persons, 103, 119, 121
Issuing bank, 303, 306

J–K

Jumbo CD, 431, 448

L

Labor contracts, 441, 444, 447, 448
Labor and Employment Law, 445
Labor law, 442
Labor-Management Relations Act, 447
Labor-Management Reporting and Disclosure Act, 447
Land, 128, 140, 147
Landmark law, 289, 380, 442
Lapse of time, 49, 50, 62
Law. *See also* Antitrust laws; International law; Internet law, 166
 discharge by operation of, 194, 198
 termination of an offer by operation of, 49, 50, 61
Lawful contracts, 105, 121
Lawful object, 5
Leading object exception, 158
Lease contract, 9
Lease contracts, risk of loss in, 313, 322, 329, 331
Lease, 9, 155, 169, 292, 293, 304, 306
Legal insanity, 100, 121
Legally enforceable contract, 4
Legal value, 67, 68, 69, 70, 84, 85
 of consideration, 67, 68, 69, 70, 74, 75, 77, 78, 79, 83, 84, 85
Legality, 105, 120

Lessee, 293, 304, 305, 306
Lessor, 293, 304, 305, 306
 recovery of goods from insolvent, 350, 352, 357, 359
Letters of credit, 25, 303, 306
Liability. *See also* Criminal liability, 96, 97, 112, 113, 114, 120, 123, 391, 392, 393, 394, 395, 396, 397, 398, 399, 400, 401, 402, 403, 404, 405, 406, 407, 408, 409, 411, 412, 413, 415, 416, 417, 418, 419, 420, 421, 422, 423
 for children's contracts, 97
Liability without fault, 395
License, 259, 278, 279
 exclusive, 259
Licensee, 259, 269, 278, 279
 damages, 269, 279
Licensing, 245, 246, 257, 258, 259, 261, 262, 264, 265, 266, 268, 270, 278, 279, 281, 282, 283
 electronic, 245, 246, 247, 248, 249, 256, 257, 258, 261, 262, 263, 264, 267, 268, 269, 272, 273, 274, 276, 277, 278, 279, 280, 281, 282
 of information rights, 259, 262
 of intellectual property, 259, 278
Licensing agreements, 261, 278, 279
Licensing statutes, 110, 120, 121
Licensor, 259, 268, 278, 279
 damages of, 268, 279
 right to cure, 269, 279
Life estates, 155, 169
Limited warranty, 380, 384
Limitations, 359
 of remedies, 359
Liquidated damages, 212, 217, 238, 239, 270, 279, 354, 360

M

Magnuson-Moss Warranty Act (1975), 380, 384
Mailbox Rule, 54, 56
Main purpose exception, 158, 169
Maine, Sir Henry, 2
Majority, age of, 92, 93, 94, 95, 96, 99, 118, 119, 122, 123
Maker of a CD, 446, 448
Maker of a note, 430, 448
Marketplace (feature):
 Business Law Paralegal Job Announcement, 349
 Civil Rights Paralegal Job Announcement, 100
 Commercial Litigation Paralegal Job Announcement, 318
 Construction Litigation Paralegal Job Announcement, 412

 Contract Specialist Paralegal Job Announcement, 17
 Corporate Paralegal Job Announcement, 232
 Corporate Real Estate Paralegal Job Announcement, 46
 Corporate Securities Paralegal Job Announcement, 260
 Labor Litigation Paralegal Job Announcement, 295
 Lease Administration Paralegal Job Announcement, 157
 Litigation Paralegal Job Announcement, 378
 Medical Malpractice Paralegal Job Announcement, 185
 Securities Litigation Paralegal Job Announcement, 131
 Transactional Paralegal Job Announcement, 79
 Vendor Contracts Paralegal Job Announcement, 434
Material breach, 207, 239
Mentally incompetent persons, 100, 119
Merchant, defined, 292, 307
Merchantability, implied warranty of, 265, 266, 279
Merchant-seller, 317, 330
Merger, 165, 169
Minor, necessaries of life and, 93, 97, 101, 106, 119, 121
Minor breach, 207, 239
Minority, 93, 95, 119
 period of, 93, 95, 115, 119, 123
Minors, 92, 119, 121
 duty of restitution, 93, 119, 121
 duty of restoration, 93, 119, 121
 duty upon disaffirmance, 119
 infancy doctrine, 91, 93, 99, 118, 121
 ratification, 95, 119, 121, 122
Mirror image rule, 51, 52, 62, 297, 307
Misrepresentation, 48, 137, 138, 145, 146, 394, 419, 421
 of age, 93
 fraudulent, 127, 132, 133, 135, 136, 144, 145
 innocent, 138, 145
 intentional, 394
 of law, 137, 145, 146
Mistakes, 128, 130, 144
 mutual, 127, 128, 130, 138, 144, 146
 mistake of value, 130, 131, 144
 unilateral, 128, 129, 130, 144, 146
 exceptions, 144
 general rule, 144
Misuse of the product, 416, 420, 421
Mitigation, 214, 215, 216, 238, 239

Mitigation of damages, 214, 238, 239
Mixed sale, 290, 307
Mode of acceptance, 62
Model act, 289, 307
Modification, 159, 169
Monetary damages, 206, 212, 238, 239
Moral obligations, 51, 76, 79, 84, 85
Mortgage, 155, 169
Mortgage notes, 430, 448
Mutual assent, 35, 57, 58
Mutual mistakes, of fact, 144
Mutual rescission, 190, 191, 198, 199

N

National Labor Relations Act
    (NLRA), 447
National Labor Relations Board
    (NLRB), 442, 447, 448
Necessaries of life, 97, 119, 121
Negligence, 392, 419, 421
Negotiable instruments, 24, 427, 448
No agreement, 329, 331, 355
No-arrival, no-sale contract, 316, 330, 332
Nominal damages, 212, 222, 238, 239
Non-carrier cases, 317, 330
Noncompete clause, 115, 120, 121
Nonconforming goods, rejection of, 349
Non-delivery, right to recover
    damages for, 351
Non-disclosure agreements (NDA), 18
Non-employee union, 443
Nonmerchant-seller, 317, 330
Non-negotiable instruments, 427
Non-union, 444
    retired employees, 444
Norris-LaGuardia Act, 447
Notice, 177, 179, 181, 196
    of assignment, 176, 179, 183, 196
Novation, 192, 198, 199

O

Objective impossibility, 192, 199
Objective intent, 35, 61
Objective theory of contract(s), 10, 13, 35
Obligations, 337, 360
    seller's and lessor's, 338, 345, 348,
        355, 357
Offer, 33, 34, 35, 36, 39, 40, 41, 42, 43,
        44, 45, 46, 47, 48, 49, 50, 51, 52,
        53, 53, 54, 55, 56, 57, 58, 59, 61,
        62, 63, 64, 65
    definiteness of terms in, 36
    expression of an opinion, 35
    lapse of time in, 49, 50, 62
    objective intent in, 35, 61
    made in jest, anger, or undue
        excitement, 35

    special situations in, 40
    termination of, 61
Offeree, 28, 34, 61
    rejection of offer by, 59
Offeror, 28, 34, 61
One or both parties are
    nonmerchants, 305
One-year rule, 158, 169
Open assortment term, 295, 305
Open delivery term, 294, 305
Open payment term, 294, 305, 307
Open price term, 294, 305
Open term, 294, 305, 307
Open time term, 294
Opinion, 369, 370, 384, 387
    statements of, 369
Option contract, 52, 62
Ordinary lease, 331
Ordinary words, 168
Organizing a union, 443, 447
    Section 7 of the NLRA, 447
Original contracts, 158, 169
Output contracts, 80, 84, 85

P

Paralegal Perspective (feature):
    Alger, Allison, 34
    Bartel, Susan, 73
    Billieu, Karen, 206
    Bromark, Raeann, 246
    Burnett, Fern, 292
    Cain, Rebecca, 68
    Canny, Cathy D., 288
    Davis, Cathy Lynn, 338
    Dickens, Robert Lee, 75
    Dietzel, Angel, 92
    Evard, Amy, 4
    Fauber, Heather, 181
    Gabbard, Amy, 222
    Gambill, Stephannie Keefe, 368
    Gray, Rhonda, 10
    Hall, Sara, 50
    Holman, Natalie, 43
    Kechter, Patty, 132
    Laquinta, Cynthia A., 257
    Ledford, Linda, 24
    Leeb, Kristen A., 439
    Mers, Toni, 103
    Powell, Andrea, 321
    Rickard, Lori, 314
    Runion, Stephanie, 164
    Schmidt, Denise, 140
    Spitzmiller, Kim A., 161
    Spurgin, Brandy, 99
    Taylor, Ron J., 398
    Turner, Teresa J., 128
    Wallace, Della, 176

    Wallace, Jennifer, 392
    Williams, Tracey A., 433
    Wasil, Karen, 351
    Zwegat, Andrea A., 378
Parents' liability for their children's
    contracts, 97
Parol evidence, 165, 166, 168, 169
Parol evidence rule, 165, 166, 168,
    169, 300, 307
    exceptions to, 168
Part acceptance, 299, 306, 307
Part performance, 156, 169
Partially disclosed agency, 436, 448
Parties, 34, 35, 36, 38, 48, 49, 52, 54,
    55, 56, 57, 58, 60, 61, 65
    termination of offers by actions, 46
Parties to a contract, 5
Parties to a lease, 304
Passage of title, 329
    in lease contracts, 329
    where there is no agreement, 329
Past consideration, 67, 77, 79, 84,
    85, 86
Payee of a CD, 446, 448
Payee of a check, 446, 448
Payee of a draft, 446, 448
Payee of a note, 446, 449
Payment, 344, 357
Perfect tender rule, 339, 340,
    356, 360
    exceptions to, 340
Penalty, 218, 239
Performance, 206
    adequate assurance of, 267
    breach and, 206, 237
    complete, 207, 237
    conditions of, 212
    inferior, 206, 207, 208, 215,
        237, 239
    non-carrier cases, 317, 330
    risk of loss, 313, 314, 315, 316, 317,
        318, 319, 320, 321, 322, 328, 329,
        330, 331, 334, 335
        breach of sales contract, 315, 321,
            329, 330
        conditional sales, 319, 321, 330
        lease contracts, 313, 315, 317,
            319, 321, 322, 323, 325, 327,
            329, 331, 333, 335
        no breach of sales contract,
            315, 329
    of sales and lease contracts, 313, 317,
        319, 321, 323, 325, 327, 329, 331,
        333, 335
    specific, 314, 315, 316, 319, 320,
        326, 327, 329, 333
    substantial, 207, 237
    tender of, 317, 322, 330, 331, 335

Period of minority, 93, 95, 119
Permissive subjects, 444, 448
Personal satisfaction test, 189, 199
Personal service contracts, 177, 199
Place of delivery, in sales and lease
  contracts, 338
Pleadings, 299, 306
  admissions in, 299, 306
Power of attorney, 447
Precedents
  conditions, 175, 176, 187, 188, 190,
    191, 197, 198, 201
Preexisting duty, 67, 76, 79, 84,
  85, 86
Preliminary negotiations, 35
Prenuptial agreements, 160, 169
Presumption, 145
Principal, 434, 446, 449
Principal-agent relationship, 435,
  447, 449
Privity of contract, 175, 199
Pro bono, 134, 146
Product defects, 398, 421
Products liability, 391, 421
Promisee, 184, 199
Promises, 67, 70, 71, 76, 77, 79, 84, 85
  gift, 70, 71, 72, 73, 78, 84, 85
  illusory, 76, 79, 84, 85, 88
Promisor, 184, 199
Promissory estoppel, 67, 82, 85, 86, 87,
  89, 161, 169
Promissory note, 169, 173, 430, 449
  maker (i.e., borrower), 155
Proper dispatch rule, 62
Properly dispatched, 55, 62
Proposed additions, 297, 307
Puffing, 369
Punitive damages, 233, 239, 397, 413,
  421
Purchase price, right to recover, 347,
  357, 362

Q

Quantum meruit, 231
Quasi-contracts, 21, 22, 231, 239
Quasi-contract (implied-in-law
  contract), 29, 231
Quixote, Don, 174

R

Railway Labor Act, 447
Ratification, 95, 119, 121
Real property, 154, 169
Reasonableness, 356
Reasonable person standard, 10
Reasonable person test, 189, 199

Reclamation, 346, 360
Recognizances, 25
Recovery, 347, 360
  for breach of contract, 347
  for breach of warranty, 371
  of damages, 347, 360
  of goods from insolvent seller or
    lessor, 350, 359
  of purchase price or rent, 347, 360
  lost profits, 349, 360
Reformation, 231, 238, 239
Regulatory statutes, 111, 121
Rejection of an offer by the
  offeree, 47, 49
Rejection, 49, 61, 349, 358
  of nonconforming goods, 349, 358
Remedies, 68, 83, 84, 85
  at law, 83, 84, 85
  enforcement of, 82, 222, 228
  equitable, 68, 81, 82, 83, 84, 85, 88,
    89, 227, 238
  for unconscionability, 121
  limitations of, 87
Rent, 342, 347, 349, 350, 351, 352, 354,
  357, 358, 359, 360, 362, 363
  right to cover, 350, 355, 360, 363
Replevin, 351, 360
Replevy the goods, 359
Repudiation, 351, 354, 359, 360
  anticipatory, 354, 359, 360
  right to recover damages for, 351
Required signature, 168
Requirements contracts, 80, 84, 85
Rescission, 68, 83, 85, 128, 146,
  224, 238, 239
Restatement of the Law of Contracts, 9
Restitution, 83, 85, 119, 224, 238, 239
  competent party's duty of, 93, 119
  duties of, 119
Restoration, duties of, 93, 121
Restraint of trade, 110, 120, 121
  contracts in, 110, 120
Revenue-raising statutes, 111, 121
Revised Article 2, 289, 307
Revocation, 46, 49, 61, 345, 358, 360
  of acceptance, 345, 358, 360
  of offer by the offeror, 46, 48
Rewards, 43, 45, 61
Rights, 175, 176, 177, 178, 179, 181,
  183, 185, 186, 187, 189, 191, 193,
  195, 196, 197, 199, 269, 279, 343,
  345, 346, 347, 349, 350, 357, 360
  assignment of, 175, 176, 177, 178,
    179, 180, 196, 199
  of inspection, 343, 356
  successive assignment of
    same, 181, 196

that can and cannot be assigned,
  177, 182
  to cancel contract, 351, 358
  to cover, 350, 360
  to cure, 269, 279
  to dispose of goods, 357
  to obtain specific performance, 350
  to reclaim goods, 346, 357
  to recover damages for accepted
    nonconforming goods, 352
  to recover damages for nondelivery
    or repudiation, 351
  to recover the purchase price
    or rent, 347, 357
  repudiation, 208, 237, 239, 240
  to recover damages for breach of
    contract, 347, 358
  to recover goods from insolvent
    seller or lessor, 350
  to reject non-conforming
    goods, 349
  to replevy goods, 351
  to stop delivery of goods in transit,
    346, 357
  to withhold delivery, 345, 357
Risk, 177, 181, 189
  alteration of, assignment
    and, 194, 198
Risk of loss, 313, 314, 315, 316, 317,
  318, 319, 320, 321, 322, 328, 329,
  330, 331, 334, 335
  breach of sales contract, 315, 321,
    329, 330
  conditional sales, 319, 321, 330
  lease contracts, 313, 322, 329, 331
  in lease contracts, 329

S

Sabbath laws, 106, 120, 121
Sale, 213, 289, 307, 319, 330, 332
  on approval, 319, 330, 332
  of goods, 213
Sale or return, 319, 330, 332
Sales contract, 9
Sales and lease contracts, 337, 338,
  343, 356, 359
  acceptance, 344, 345, 348, 350, 351,
    352, 357, 358, 360, 361, 363
  offer, 341, 342, 363
  good faith and reasonableness in
    governing performance of, 343,
    355
  non-carrier cases, 339, 355
  performance of, 337, 338, 340, 343,
    347, 348, 350, 352, 353, 354, 355,
    356, 359, 360, 361
  remedies for breach of, 337

risk of loss, 313, 314, 315, 316, 317, 318, 319, 320, 321, 322, 328, 329, 330, 331, 334, 335
  breach of sales contract, 315, 321, 329, 330
  conditional sales, 319, 321, 330
  in lease contracts, 329
  sales by non-owners, 323, 331
Sales contract, breach of, 315, 321, 329, 330, 331, 335
Satisfaction, 81, 85, 87, 192, 198, 199
  accord and, 192
  conditions precedent based on, 198
Scienter, 133, 146
Scope of Article 2, 304
Scope of Authority, 437
Scott, Sir Walter, 312
Section 5 (FTC), 302, 307
Section 7 of the NLRA, 447
Section 201 of the Uniform Commercial Code (UCC), 159, 169
Sellers, 345, 346
  in breach, 321, 330
  obligations of, in breach of sales and lease contracts, 313
  recovery of goods from insolvent, 350, 352, 359
  remedies of, 337, 338, 340, 345, 348, 349, 350, 351, 352, 354, 355, 357, 358, 359
Service, 177, 178, 182, 183, 189, 192, 193, 199, 201, 202
Shipment contracts, 315, 316, 329, 332, 339, 356, 360
Shipping terms, 316, 330
"Shocks the conscience of the court" standard of consideration, 74
Sight draft, 428, 449
Signatures, 446, 449
  Chinese *chops* as, 166
  e-commerce and, 245, 246, 247, 250, 257, 258, 260, 261, 278
  Japanese *hankos*, 166
  required, 446, 449
Silence, 33, 53, 54
  as acceptance, 53
  as misrepresentation, 145
Small CD, 431, 449
Software licenses, 272
Sources of contract law, 8
Special damages, 216, 223, 238, 239
Special contracts, 119
Special performance, 83
Specially manufactured goods, 298, 306, 307

Specific performance, 68, 82, 83, 84, 85, 86, 88, 227, 238, 239, 270, 279, 350, 359, 360
  right to obtain, 350
Specific terms, 168
Standards of interpretation, 164, 169
Statements of opinion (puffing), 369, 384
Statute of Frauds, 154, 159
  exceptions to, 298, 300, 306
    written confirmation rule, 287, 299, 301, 306
Statute of limitations, 194, 198, 199, 345, 354, 359, 360, 418, 420, 421
Statutes, 91, 93, 94, 99, 105, 108, 110, 111, 117, 118, 119, 120
  contracts contrary to, 105, 106, 120, 121
  gambling, 108, 109, 110, 120
  licensing, 110, 111, 120
  regulatory, 111, 120, 121
  revenue-raising, 111, 120, 121
Statute of repose, 418, 420, 421
Stevens, Justice, 244
Stolen goods, 323, 331, 333, 334
Stop delivery of the goods, 346, 360
Stowell, Lord, 204
Strict liability, 394, 419, 421
Subassignee, 176, 199
Subsequent assignee, 176, 199
Substantial performance, 207, 239
Substituted contract, 191, 198, 199
Substitution of carriers, 356
Sue for damages, 358
Supervening illegality, 49, 51, 62
Supervening event, 416, 420, 421
Supplier, 293, 305, 307

T

Technical words, 168
Tender, 207, 239, 264, 279, 338, 355, 360
  of delivery, 338, 355, 360
  of performance, 207, 240, 264, 279
Termination, 46, 49, 50, 61, 440
  of offers, 46, 49, 50, 61
    death, insanity, bankruptcy, impossibility, changed circumstances, war, 440
Terms, 33
  definiteness of, 36
  implied, 33, 34, 36, 56, 61, 62, 63
Third-party beneficiaries, 183, 186, 197, 199

Thoreau, Henry D., 336
Time of acceptance, 54
Time draft, 428, 449
Time note, 430, 449
Title, 315, 332
  document of, 315, 318, 329, 332
  passage of, 313, 314, 315, 327, 329, 333
  void, 323, 324, 325, 327, 331, 332
  voidable, 324, 325, 327
Tort, 232, 239, 240
  associated with contracts, 232, 239
  of bad faith, 235, 240
Trade, contract in restraint of, 121
Typed words, 168

U

Unconscionability, 121, 355, 360
  doctrine of, 355
  elements of, 121
Unconscionable contracts, 91, 115, 120, 121
Unconscionable limitations, 359
Unconscionable sales and lease contracts, 359
Undisclosed agency, 437, 449
Undue influence, 140, 141, 145, 146
Unenforceable contract, 26, 27
Unequivocal acceptance, 51, 53
Unexpired lease, 318
Unfinished goods, 347
Unforeseeable misuse. *See also* Abnormal misuse, 416, 421
Unforeseen difficulties, 76
Unified contract law (UCL), 60
Uniform Commercial Code (UCC), 8, 288, 304, 307
  Article 2 (Sales), 288, 304
  Article 2 revised, 289
  Article 2A (Leases), 288, 292, 307
  Article 3 (Negotiable Instruments), 427, 428, 432, 433, 446
  Article 4A (Funds Transfers), 274, 278, 279
  Article 5 (Letters of Credit), 304
UCC Statute of Frauds, 159, 169
  statute of limitations of, 354, 359, 360
Uniform Computer Information Transactions Act (UCITA), 9, 246, 279
  breach of license agreements and, 266
  electronic errors and, 267
  remedies, 266, 267, 268, 269, 270, 271, 272

Uniform Customs and Practices for
  Documentary Credits (UCP),
  304, 307
Uniform Electronic Transactions Act
  (UETA), 246, 279
Uniform Sales Act, 287, 307
Unilateral contracts, 16
Unilateral mistakes, 128, 144, 146
Union, 441, 442, 443, 444, 445, 447
  appropriate bargaining union, 447
  non-employee, 443
United Nations Convention on
  Contracts for the International
  Sale of Goods (CISG), 27
Usage of trade, 301, 307
Usury laws, 106, 120, 121

V

Valid contract, 26
Value, 67, 68, 69, 70, 72, 74, 75, 81, 83,
  84, 85, 88
  mutual mistake of, 127, 128, 130,
  144, 146
Void contract, 26

Voidable contract, 26
Void title, 323, 327, 331, 332
Voidable title, 324, 331, 332

W–Z

Warranty, 367, 368, 380, 381, 383, 384
  damages recoverable for breach of, 371
  express, 368, 382, 383
  full, 383
  implied, 372, 383
  of good title, 381, 384
  of fitness for human consumption,
  374, 383
  of fitness for particular purpose, 266,
  279, 375, 383
  of merchantability, 367, 372, 373,
  374, 375, 377, 378, 379, 380, 383,
  384, 385, 386
  against interference, 382
  against infringements, 381, 384
  of no infringements, 381, 384
  of no interference, 382, 384
  of no security interests, 381, 384
  of quiet possession, 382

limited, 380, 383
limitation on disclaiming implied
  warranties, 384
Warranty disclaimers, 378, 383, 384
  conspicuous display of, 379, 380,
  383, 384
  in software license, 379
World Intellectual Property
  Organization (WIPO),
  254, 279
World Wide Web (WWW). *See also*
  Internet, 247, 277, 279
Writing, 153, 154, 155, 156, 157, 158,
  159, 160, 161, 162, 163, 165, 167,
  168, 169, 171, 172
  for e-contracts, 153
  formality of, 153, 162, 168, 173,
  integration of several, 153, 163,
  164, 165, 166, 168, 169
Writing and form, 6
Writ of attachment, 222, 240
Writ of garnishment, 224, 240
Written confirmation rule, 306
Written modification in sales and lease
  contracts, 299